The Making of Urban America

The Making of Urban America

Third Edition

Edited by
Raymond A. Mohl and Roger Biles

ROWMAN & LITTLEFIELD PUBLISHERS, INC.
Lanham • Boulder • New York • Toronto • Plymouth, UK

Published by Rowman & Littlefield Publishers, Inc.
A wholly owned subsidiary of The Rowman & Littlefield Publishing Group, Inc.
4501 Forbes Boulevard, Suite 200, Lanham, Maryland 20706
http://www.rowmanlittlefield.com

Estover Road, Plymouth PL6 7PY, United Kingdom

British Library Cataloguing in Publication Information Available

Library of Congress Cataloging-in-Publication Data
The making of urban America / edited by Raymond A. Mohl and Roger Biles. — 3rd ed.
    p.   cm.
    Includes bibliographical references and index.
    ISBN 978-0-7425-5234-0 (cloth : alk. paper) — ISBN 978-0-7425-5235-7 (pbk. : alk. paper)
    1. Cities and towns—United States—History. 2. Urbanization—United States—History. I.
Mohl, Raymond A. II. Biles, Roger, 1950–
    HT123.M286 2012
    307.760973—dc23
                                                                                    2011036160

∞™ The paper used in this publication meets the minimum requirements of American National
Standard for Information Sciences—Permanence of Paper for Printed Library Materials, ANSI/
NISO Z39.48-1992.

Printed in the United States of America

Contents

Preface

Urban history has come a long way since the 1960s, when scholars first began the systematic exploration of the American urban experience. Influenced by the emerging new social history and by contemporary concerns about the "urban crisis," as it was then called, younger historians began delving into the history of the American city, broadly considered. Over time, the subjects of urban history inquiry, the research strategies, the methodologies, and the interpretations have changed. In the 1960s, few urban historians had pushed their research and writing beyond the Progressive Era. Now, in the second decade of the twenty-first century, a much larger number of American urban historians have probed deeply into the post–World War II period, sought to understand the complexities of the 1960s, pushed out into suburbia and metropolitan regions, traced more recent urban powerful political and policy moves, and explored shifting patterns of race, residence, and culture. In the decades after the 1960s, historians of the city have expanded their range of vision and fully incorporated race, ethnicity, gender, and class into their conceptual frameworks and interpretations. In the early stages of the field's development, urban politics, reform movements, and urban growth and economic development attracted the attention of urbanists. Today, the subjects of urban historical research range from technology, environment, planning, housing, and suburbanization to consumption, sexuality, crime, sports and leisure, and the significance of space and place. From the perspective of half a century, the results of this academic excursion into urban history have been impressive. We now have a much richer and fuller understanding of the American historical experience as a consequence of the research carried out by at least three generations of urban historians. In one sense, given that more than 83 percent of Americans now reside in urban and suburban places, urban history is American history.

This third edition of *The Making of Urban America*, like its predecessors, is designed to introduce students of urban history to important interpretive literature in the field. Its goal is to provide a coherent framework for understanding the pattern of American urbanization in all its complexity, while at the same time offering specific examples of the work of historians in the field. The essays presented in this book il lustrate many of the important questions, issues, and interpretive ideas that American urban historians have been pursuing over the past few decades. They deal in various ways with race, ethnicity, class, women, politics, policy, housing, suburbs, environment, leisure, violence, and popular culture. Taken together, they reflect the many currents of contemporary research in American urban history. Eight of the essays are carried over from the previous edition, and most of the seven new pieces have been published within the past decade. All make important interpretive contributions.

As in the previous editions, the scholarly essays are presented within a three-part chronological framework, covering the preindustrial city, the industrial city, and the modern metropolis. Each of the three sections begins with an analytical introduction, laying out the patterns of urban development and change for that particular period. These introductions have been extensively revised and expanded from the second edition of the book. They have also been updated with new demographic data when appropriate, and the population tables in part III have been updated to include data on cities and metropolitan areas reported in the censuses of 2000 and 2010. The historiographical essay in part IV has more than doubled in size, as we sought to incorporate the flood of new research in some seventeen separate subfields of American urban history.

We would also like to take this opportunity to express our appreciation to several individuals who provided important assistance as this book began to take shape. Rebecca Dobrinski, a graduate student in history at the University of Alabama at Birmingham (UAB), contributed enormously in the preparation of the manuscript for this book. Her computer skills quickly became essential in converting printed journal articles and book chapters into Word documents through Adobe Acrobat's OCR (optical character recognition) program. She proofed the entire manuscript and assembled it all in a single folder for transmission to Rowman & Littlefield. Also at UAB, graduate students Jordan Bauer and Cheyenne Haney helped with tasks ranging from copying and scanning to typing population tables. Many urban historians who have used earlier editions of this book in their classes have provided thoughtful suggestions that helped shape the material included in this third edition. We thank them all for their assistance.

Raymond A. Mohl
Roger Biles

Part I

THE PREINDUSTRIAL CITY

Introduction

Twenty-first-century Americans live in an overwhelmingly urban age. The process by which a group of tiny colonial settlements in an untamed wilderness grew into a populous nation of great cities is one of the central themes of American history. Over a period of four hundred years, as the United States moved from the colonial period to the contemporary age, Americans passed from a society characterized by small farms and villages to one dominated by huge central cities and massive sprawling suburbs. An understanding of the dynamic forces and values that nurtured, stimulated, and shaped American urban and metropolitan development is essential in comprehending the contours and the complexities of contemporary America.

Town, village, and urban life emerged quite early during the American colonial period. British and European settlers congregated in seaport towns and villages from the very beginning of the colonization effort. Many of the first colonists had been town or city dwellers in England or Europe, and they brought to the American wilderness urban values, attitudes, and aspirations. Although the populations of most colonial communities remained small through most of the prerevolutionary period, each colonial settlement, village, or town to some degree served traditional urban functions—that is, they became centers for the exchange of goods, services, and ideas. By the end of the seventeenth century, colonial Americans had created a fairly dynamic urban society. In 1700, the larger seaport cities of Boston, Philadelphia, New York, Charleston, and Newport which had populations ranging from about 2,000 to 7,000—exercised an influence throughout the colonies far out of proportion to their relatively small populations.

THE GROWTH OF SEAPORT CITIES

Several forces promoted colonial urban growth. In the early stages of settlement and on the colonial frontier, newcomers gathered together for security and mutual defense. At the beginning, a wooden stockade or wall often surrounded such primitive colonial

3

outposts, as in Plymouth, Jamestown, and Savannah, while settlers in other communities clustered around a fortress, as in New York, Charleston, St. Augustine, and Mobile. Most of these early defensive communities rapidly became agrarian towns. This pattern prevailed especially in New England, where a community-centered society required towns to effectively regulate social and religious life. Town building was also promoted by English or European merchant companies. Jamestown, Plymouth, New York, New Haven, and other colonial towns had such origins. English entrepreneurs and investors viewed towns as necessary for successfully tapping the raw materials and resources of the New World. Thus, they not only sponsored much of the early colonization effort, but they provided the capital and manpower required to sustain new overseas outposts during the difficult early years of community building.

Many of the largest colonial seaport towns grew because of their political and administrative functions. British mercantilist policies required a close supervision and regulation of colonial trade, providing an impetus for town and city growth. Moreover, each colony had its governing center—the residence of the colonial governor, the location of the administrative offices of government, and the meeting place of the colonial assembly. The imperatives of mercantilism and colonial government encouraged urban development, even in the southern colonies where geography and emerging agricultural and land distribution patterns militated against town life. As historical geographer Carville V. Earle has suggested, "the English regarded towns as indispensable frontier-cultural institutions, and colonization was unthinkable without them."[1]

Above all, commercial activity in the colonies stimulated urbanization. During the seventeenth century, port towns such as Boston and Philadelphia grew rapidly as a consequence of the economic demands generated by new immigrant arrivals. By the end of the seventeenth century, colonial merchants and entrepreneurs had developed profitable trading networks based on staple products derived from the New World environment. The market-oriented production of colonial farmers, especially those with good transportation to nearby cities, stimulated the urban economy as well. They produced not only foodstuffs for urban markets but also grain, rice, and tobacco for export. Built primarily on the products of an extractive economy—fish and furs, tobacco and rice, wheat and indigo, lumber and livestock, naval stores and minerals—colonial trade with Britain, Europe, Africa, and the West Indies expanded and prospered. Returning ships carried new immigrants, slaves, sugar, manufactured goods, and products unobtainable in the New World. Intensive economic exchange, then, stimulated market functions, strengthened economic links between city and farm, and promoted the growth of seaport towns and cities up and down the Atlantic coastline.[2]

Ultimately, these urban places became market cities, where goods changed hands. As some urban geographers have noted, the colonial seaport cities served as an economic "hinge," as central points for the collection of staple agricultural products for export and for the distribution of imported goods throughout the surrounding hinterland. In addition, the export-import function spawned numerous supplementary industries in the towns. Most ports became centers for flour milling, ship building, the processing of naval stores, and other simple manufacturing. Numbers of small shops produced rope, sails, barrels, ship fittings, and other products geared to a waterfront economy. The maritime economy also required an extensive labor force of seamen, as well as dock workers to load and unload sailing ships engaged in overseas or intracoastal trade. Meanwhile, a growing class of urban craftsmen serviced expanding town and city populations by building houses and producing consumer goods. As a result of these advances in craft and commerce, the colonial economy prospered at times. The gradual expansion of the domestic consumer market strengthened the cities' economic role, thus further intensifying the urbanizing trend.

The economically developing colonial seaport cities experienced social and class distinctions at a very early date. Racial, ethnic, and religious diversity prevailed. New York City and Charleston had large black populations, mostly slaves and some free blacks in New York. Some 50,000 German immigrants arrived in Philadelphia between 1730 and 1760, with many staying in and around the city. The continuous influx of new immigrants tended to keep wages down and economic opportunity circumscribed in all the seaports. Although geographical mobility was always high, upward social and economic mobility was more limited in the cities than in other segments of colonial society. More so than in agricultural and frontier regions, the colonial cities experienced a growing gap between the rich and the poor. In Boston, for instance, the class of propertyless laborers was increasing twice as rapidly as the population as a whole by the time of the American Revolution. In Philadelphia, the richest 5 percent of the population controlled as much wealth as the rest of the population combined. Thus, class lines were hardening by the mid-eighteenth century. At the same time, the colonial dependence on commerce meant that the New World settlements had become part of an intricate web of world trade, subject to economic fluctuations due to war, depression, inflation, currency declines, and rising or falling crop prices. As a result, most of the colonial urban economies suffered periodic economic stagnation and often severe problems of unemployment, poverty, and poor relief.

CITIES IN THE REVOLUTIONARY ERA

The primacy of the colonial cities' economic functions contained the seeds of future social and political change. As historian Gary Nash noted in his important book *The Urban Crucible* (1979), colonial society from the beginning had been strongly deferential in nature—that is, it was a society in which people knew their place and accepted it, in which the middle and lower classes generally yielded decision-making authority to the local political and economic elites. However, people at every level of society shared certain basic assumptions about the mutual obligations of classes and the need for social harmony, good government, and personal liberty. When the urban elites challenged or undermined or violated these assumptions, the middle and lower classes often abandoned deferential attitudes and asserted their collective power in the streets in the form of the communal mob or riot to protect traditional values and restore the old order. Until the 1740s, these colonial crowd actions were goal-oriented and not particularly violent, and they often achieved their limited objectives. Moreover, the growth of the market economy by the mid-eighteenth century, with the new emphasis on individual profit and the new reality of periodic depression, stimulated lower-class discontent, weakened deference, and undergirded the rise of a popular and participatory politics in the seaport cities. As the artisans and the urban working classes developed an increasingly radical political consciousness, they began to take charge of their lives in new and dramatic ways. Initiated in the colonial towns and cities, this sort of political mobilization unleashed forces that hastened the coming of the American Revolution.[3]

The exchange function of the seaport cities produced other consequences as well. By the middle of the eighteenth century, British manufactured products—ceramics, glassware, cutlery, metal tools, cloth, clothing, carpets, furniture, paper—began to inundate the colonial consumer market. In his recent book *The Marketplace of Revolution* (2004), historian T. H. Breen argues that the "consumer revolution" of the eighteenth century transformed the daily lives of American colonists, especially in the towns and cities. Wealthy elites and ordinary people alike shared the experience of consumption—"a common framework of experience," Breen contends—which in turn helped stimulate a nascent national self-consciousness. However, new British taxation in the 1760s and 1770s had the effect of politicizing consumption, leading to colonial boycotts of imported products. Colonial resistance to British taxation in the form of boycotts culminated in the Boston Tea Party, in which nonconsumption became linked to constitutional rights and a radicalized political ideology. The emergence of a consumer society and the subsequent self-denial of British products during the boycotts contributed in important ways to the urban political mobilization that triggered the decision for independence.[4]

Indeed, the impact of the seaport cities on the coming of the Revolution cannot be overestimated. As urban historian Stanley K. Schultz contended, "without urban grievances, the American Revolution never would have occurred."[5] During the revolutionary crisis, the colonial cities emerged as important centers of radical activity and propaganda. Based in the seaport cities, many colonial merchants saw urban prosperity and their own profits threatened by new British taxes and economic policies. The boycotts organized by the urban merchants and implemented in the port towns helped strike down the hated Stamp Act and the Townshend duties. The dissatisfaction and radicalism of urban workers, artisans, and sailors, stimulated by unemployment and the economic pressures of the 1760s, found frequent outlet in anti-British rioting; the Sons of Liberty was primarily an urban group. For many patriots, mob actions against the British and those who supported the colonial establishment seemed a legitimate expression of popular sentiment. These mob actions tended to be more violent than those of earlier decades. Pivotal events such as the Boston Massacre originated in the conflict between colonial urbanites and British troops stationed in the cities, while the Boston Tea Party reflected urban concerns about consumption and Parliamentary control of the economy. Radical urban organizations, such as the Boston Committee of Correspondence and its counterparts in other cities and towns, conveyed revolutionary propaganda to the countryside. The emergence in the cities by the mid-eighteenth century of a popular tavern culture provided a public arena for discussion, debate, and revolutionary propaganda. By the 1750s, most cities had a weekly newspaper—some had two or three—that reported news from the surrounding area, other colonies, and England. Because these weeklies were read aloud at taverns and coffeehouses, newspaper debates over independence reached a wide audience. And as historian Arthur M.

Schlesinger suggested many years ago, the patterns of community life over the course of the colonial period provided a sort of "training in collective action" upon which patriot leaders drew during the intensifying revolutionary crisis.[6]

The urban dimension of American life during the colonial period, then, was significant and influential in several respects. The colonial towns and cities became the economic, political, and cultural centers of an extensive but sparsely populated agricultural hinterland. They provided the arena for the emerging market-oriented commercial economy, which in turn pulled the American colonies into the wider, more interdependent network of world trade—both more lucrative and more risky. Social and economic stratification intensified as the urban populations grew, stimulating discontent, some class conflict, and a new emphasis on democratic and participatory urban politics. As deference declined in the cities, simultaneous movements began seeking both independence from Great Britain and social and democratic change in America. By the end of the Revolutionary era, about 5 percent of the American population— some 200,000 people—lived in twenty-four urban places of 2,500 or more residents. The proportion of urbanites was relatively small, but the growing cities dominated their surrounding regions and set the pace for social, economic, and political change.

CITIES, TRANSPORTATION, AND THE MARKET REVOLUTION

The pace of urbanization picked up substantially in the decades following the American Revolution. In fact, urban growth accelerated at a more rapid rate between 1820 and 1860 than at any other time in U.S. history. In the years between the Revolution and the Civil War, a capitalist revolution also transformed the United States. A national economic market emerged, involving the cotton kingdom in the South, an agrarian empire in the West, and the beginnings of industrialization in the Northeast. The dramatic rise of an urban marketplace became indispensable to the progress of the national economy. New York City emerged as a sort of "primate" city, a national metropolis dominating the economy of the entire country. A city of about 33,000 in 1790, New York increased in population by more than 50 percent each decade until 1860 (with the exception of the 1810–1820 period). By 1860, more than 813,000 people crowded the island of Manhattan. The other eastern seaports also grew into large commercial metropolises. Philadelphia's 28,000 people of 1790 had multiplied to more than 565,000 by the time of the Civil War. Brooklyn, a village of less than 5,000 in 1790, and perhaps the nation's first true suburb, had become the nation's third-largest city by 1860, with a population of more than 265,000. Boston and Baltimore also increased their populations at substantial rates during the early nineteenth century. The east coast seaports comprised a regional system of cities. These marketplace cities each depended on overseas commerce and a rising manufacturing sector, while continuing to serve as regional marketing and distribution centers for expanding agricultural hinterlands.

Urbanization also spread into the interior of the continent during these preindustrial years. The city, it seemed, preceded the westward movement of people into frontier areas. In the trans-Appalachian region, according to historian Richard C. Wade, two new systems of cities "spearheaded" the westward movement and the settlement of the frontier.[7] One group of cities sprouted along the Ohio and Mississippi rivers. Experiencing similar patterns of development, the cities of Pittsburgh, Louisville, Cincinnati, Saint Louis, and New Orleans emerged as regional marketing and early manufacturing or processing centers. Spurred by transportation innovations, notably steam navigation and canal building, a second system of cities grew up along the shores of the Great Lakes—Buffalo, Cleveland, Detroit, Chicago, and Milwaukee. Although Cincinnati was being promoted as the Queen City of the West and had become the nation's third-largest manufacturing center by the Civil War, it was clear that Chicago was rising quickly as the dominant western metropolis. These ten interior cities, which by 1860 ranged in population from about 45,000 to nearly 170,000, gave an urban aspect to the westward movement and to American society generally.

The transportation revolution of the early nineteenth century provided the catalyst for western urbanization. New York merchants and promoters, as well as New York's state government, actively supported or invested in new transportation innovations, which in large measure accounted for the great success of the eastern metropolis. Perhaps more than any other single accomplishment, the opening of the Erie Canal in 1825 assured the commercial primacy of New York City. The completion of the Erie route set off a wave of canal building and then railroad construction, as other eastern cities sought to compete with New York for the trade and produce of the Ohio Valley. This so-called urban imperialism not only hastened the completion of new transportation arteries but also fostered urbanization in the western regions and along the routes of the new canals and railroads. A whole string of cities grew up along the Erie Canal route between Albany and Buffalo, and the presence of an uninterrupted water route to the interior via the Great Lakes ensured Chicago's rise as the major metropolis of the Midwest. The opening of the Illinois and Michigan Canal in 1848 provided the necessary link to the Illinois River and then the Mississippi River, which allowed boats to travel all the way from New York City to New Orleans. Railroads followed the canals, underscoring Chicago's prominence as the major hub of the east-west national transportation network and tying countless other cities into the nascent mercantile system developing in the region. State and federal subsidies and land grants, as well as private investor capital, underwrote the transportation revolution of the early nineteenth century.[8]

The growth of early-nineteenth-century American cities accompanied the rise of a capitalist economy. Commerce, shipping, urban construction, and a host of supplementary trades and businesses combined to stimulate city economies during this period. New invention and technology, as reflected in the steam engine, the telegraph, the sewing machine, textile machinery, and the creation of the canal and railroad network, also facilitated the growth of a capitalist economy. Historian Ross Thomson, in a recent book on technological innovation in the early nineteenth century, argues the primacy of early machinists with scientific and mathematical knowledge—men who invented and perfected new tools, machines, and factory technology. Essential to economic development, as well, was the growth of consumer demand in the domestic market. In a significant book, *The Roots of American Industrialization* (2003), historical geographer David R. Meyer argues that prosperity among farmers in rural

America, where more than 80 percent of Americans resided before 1860, created sufficient consumer demand to trigger rising industrial production.[9]

The growth of the domestic market in the decades before the Civil War turned cities increasingly toward production for internal consumption. However, the process of industrial development came slowly at first. New tools and methods of production undermined older artisanal workshop methods, deskilling the workforce over time. In many places, merchant capitalists shifted from small artisanal shops to a rural "putting-out" system in which manual workers, often women, took work home. Before 1820, Boston capitalists built the first large cotton mills in Lowell, Massachusetts, relying on water-powered looms. As technology advanced, other entrepreneurs initiated factory production of woolen goods, finished clothing, boots and shoes, leather items, iron products such as tools and farm implements, firearms, paper, and furniture and household goods. Western cities, drawing on local resources and agricultural production, turned to flour milling, brewing, meatpacking, mining, and lumbering. In New England, the textile and footwear industries fostered the development of a number of smaller factory towns such as Lawrence, Lowell, Lynn, Haverhill, Fall River, New Bedford, and Manchester. A similar shift toward manufacturing was evident elsewhere, too, as cities ranging from Richmond and Lexington in the South to Newark, Paterson, Providence, Albany, and Troy in the North turned to factory production. By the 1850s, the factory had become a recognizable feature of city and small-town landscapes and provided substantial employment for workers, many migrating from rural areas to the rising urban places. In some of the New England textile-factory towns, such as Lowell and Lawrence, young women from rural areas provided much of the labor, while residing in dormitory-style housing and sending earnings home to families.[10]

The emerging manufacturing sector of the early national period anticipated the industrial revolution of the late nineteenth century, but the commercial role of the large eastern cities persisted until the post–Civil War era. By 1850, less than 15 percent of the nation's workforce labored in any form of manufacturing. As late as 1860, according to economic historian Eric Lampard, of the nation's fifteen largest cities, only five had more than 10 percent of their workforce engaged in manufacturing. Thus, although the market revolution had transformed the United States in fundamental ways, the industrial takeoff had not yet fully begun.[11]

THE URBAN SOCIAL ORDER

Like the growing factories, the social and political conditions of the preindustrial cities provided some hints about the shape of the urban future. European immigration, for instance, had begun to have a significant impact on the urban population. The immigrant tide began slowly at first, in the early decades of the nineteenth century. During the 1830s, however, more than 490,000 newcomers arrived on American shores. During the following decade, European immigration to the United States surged to more than 1.4 million, and during the 1850s the seaborne influx almost doubled to more than 2.6 million. Mostly Irish, English, and German, these newcomers received their first introduction to American life in the immigrant arrival ports of New York, Boston, Philadelphia, Baltimore, San Francisco, and New Orleans. Large numbers of the newcomers moved on to interior towns or settled in the midwestern farm belt. But many remained in the cities, where their influence was increasingly felt in politics, culture, and the workplace. By 1860, immigrants made up more than 50 percent of the populations of St. Louis, Chicago, Milwaukee, and San Francisco. Close behind were New York, Buffalo, Cincinnati, Cleveland, and Detroit, where the proportion of foreign-born ranged from 45 to 48 percent of the total city population.[12]

Internal migration and geographical mobility also affected the growing cities. While newcomers from abroad flooded into urban America in unprecedented numbers, native-born migrants from the farm and from rural towns boosted city populations as well, especially at first in the Northeast and then in the Midwest. This pattern continued into the late nineteenth century, as new agricultural technology began to displace the rural peasantry of farm workers and hired hands. In addition, a substantial degree of population turnover within the cities contributed to the pace of urbanization and social change. Many early-nineteenth-century observers noted the transiency and the migratory habits of the lower stratum of urban society. The working classes and the poor were often described as a "floating" population or as being "constantly on the wing." Immigrants and natives alike passed in and out of the cities in search of jobs, better housing, or more opportunity. According to a study by urban historian Peter R. Knights, population turnover in Boston amounted to about 30 percent per year in the 1830s and 1840s and 40 percent per year in the 1850s. This sort of intensive internal migration and mobility reflected the dynamic character of the urbanization process in the United States, even in the preindustrial period.[13]

While immigration and internal migration altered the composition and character of the American urban population, preindustrial cities changed in other ways as well. The larger cities, for instance, had begun to experience to a limited degree some of the problems that later plagued city people and municipal governments. Pre–Civil War urban growth was disorderly and unplanned, as the older cities outgrew the human-scale streetscapes of the colonial era. Heavy population increases imposed pressure on limited housing resources; immigrants, workers, and the urban poor crowded into densely packed apartments, tenements, cellars, and shacks. Public health measures remained primitive, and most cities experienced periodic epidemics of typhoid, yellow fever, and cholera, often with devastating consequences. Poverty, unemployment, crime, and violence became common. A rage of urban riots afflicted most large cities in the 1830s and 1840s, reflecting social, economic, religious, racial, and ethnic tensions.[14]

As these and other problems developed, city governments seemed weak and ineffective. American cities first established professional, uniformed police forces only in the 1840s, after the riots and social conflicts of previous decades. Professional fire departments replaced volunteer fire companies only after devastating fires burned large sections of Boston, New York, Pittsburgh, and other cities in the 1830s and 1840s. Municipal governments were slow in providing services to the citizenry, and they generally had difficulty managing the bigger, more populous, more heterogeneous, and more socially unstable cities of the mid-nineteenth century. In the absence of effective municipal government, private religious, philanthropic, and civic organizations assumed some responsibility for providing some services, such as schooling, assistance to the poor, and maintaining moral order.[15]

By the 1850s, the transition from the preindustrial to the modern industrial city was nearly complete. The transitional process actually had been under way for some time. The colonial city was truly preindustrial in the sense described by sociologist Gideon Sjoberg in his classic study *The Preindustrial City* (1960). For Sjoberg, the marketplace function and handicraft or artisanal manufacturing characterized the preindustrial city. The system of production required animate sources of power—that is, human or animal power. Preindustrial urban workers labored in small shops with a few other craftsmen and apprentices. There was little specialization of work or division of labor. Using hand tools and individual skills, urban artisans created finished products from raw materials. Skill remained important and was transferred through the apprenticeship process.[16]

A relatively high degree of order and stability prevailed in the early preindustrial city; urban residents generally shared a sense of community. The walking cities of the colonial era had densely settled populations, and rich and poor lived close together, although they were not necessarily neighborly. Land uses were unspecialized, and very often living and working quarters were one and the same. Business and the household were intimately connected. Ethnic and religious homogeneity generally prevailed in early settlement years, but social diversity was on the rise well before the Revolutionary period. A literate elite dominated the social and political structure. In this hierarchical and deferential society, upward economic and social mobility remained limited. Kinship ties were important, the extended family was more typical than not, and communication and personal contact typically were of the face-to-face variety. A sense of localism predominated, and change and innovation came slowly, if at all. All of these social and economic patterns prevailed in American colonial towns and cities until about the mid-eighteenth century. By the Revolutionary era, social conflict and political mobilization began to challenge the existing social order.

In contrast with pre-Revolutionary colonial social patterns, the first half of the nineteenth century experienced substantial change. For example, the system of production began to undergo changes. The small-shop pattern of the colonial years increasingly gave way to larger workplaces and factories by the 1830s and 1840s. New technology brought new machinery, especially in textiles, supplanting the hand tools of the urban craftsman. The factory system with its division of labor revolutionized the social organization of work. Skill became less important, since machines rather than laborers did the work. The specialization of tasks rationalized the production process, but the constant repetition of a single task meant a daily grind of mindless monotony for such workers. New sources of inanimate power—first the harnessing of water power to drive gears, shifts, and pulleys, and later the application of the steam engine to operate factory machinery—replaced the human and horse power of earlier years. Defying time and distance, the railroad and the telegraph speeded transportation and communication, thus contributing to a breakdown of localism and personalized human contacts.

Similarly, the social order experienced big changes during the early nineteenth century. By the 1830s, increasingly heavy immigration and a substantial degree of rural-to-urban internal migration further undermined social, ethnic, and religious homogeneity. The shared sense of community of the early colonial town disappeared, along with deferential attitudes and adherence to generally accepted behavioral norms. A new working-class political culture emerged by the 1820s and 1830s, accompanied by an engaged rhetoric of "republicanism" and worker solidarity, as craftsmen responded to the reorganization of work patterns and the beginnings of industrialization. Mobility, at least of the geographical or residential sort, intensified—a development reflecting a loosening of the ties binding the individual to kin and community. Chances for upward economic mobility do not seem to have been improved by the breakdown of traditional society, for the loss of skill and the rise of the factory and commercial capitalism meant that individuals had less control over their economic destiny. In the modernizing city itself, various spatial changes began to reshape the physical environment. Land uses became more specialized and functional, as sections of the growing cities were given over to residential, retail, and productive purposes. A more sharply defined class structure accompanied the mid-nineteenth-century transformation of urban America. Social segregation increased, as immigrants, workers, and the poor crowded older housing in city centers, while the urban political and economic elites, as well as the rising middle class, moved from the center toward the periphery. Above all, change and innovation became commonplace. The fixed and timeless character of the preindustrial society began to break down, as the American Revolution unleashed new political forces and as the capitalist revolution transformed the national economy.[17] The emerging patterns of the transitional city also set the stage for the tremendous surge of urbanization and industrialization during the second half of the nineteenth century.

The essays in part I demonstrate some of the interpretive concerns of recent historians about the early American town and city. Gary B. Nash's essay, "The Social Evolution of Preindustrial American Cities, 1700–1820," offers an alternative interpretive model for understanding the dynamics of urban social development in eighteenth-century America. The colonial cities, Nash notes, were located at the cutting edge of economic, social, and political change. His essay portrays urban change as an evolutionary process that reshaped community patterns, social networks, and group experience in the preindustrial city. Drawing on the exciting research of a new generation of urban and social historians, Nash reveals the growing ethnic, religious, and racial diversity of the early American city, a social pluralism that challenged and reshaped established ideas about community, conformity, and deference. New social realities were imposed on the cities by the growing numbers of free urban blacks and by the widening gap between rich and poor. The social geography of urban places also began to change, and physical growth was accompanied by spatial separation and segregation of social and economic groups. Nash emphasizes the resilience of the human spirit—the ability of urban people to cope and adapt, individually and collectively, to the changing urban environment. In particular, the rise of a popular and participatory politics, along with the emergence of voluntary associations, reflected the active role of city people in adjusting and adapting to change. The social forces underlying the American Revolution carried into the early nineteenth century and formed the basis for new conceptions of community, social institutions, and political participation.

Leslie M. Harris's essay, "Slavery, Emancipation, and Class Formation in Colonial and Early National New York City," challenges established ways of thinking about the social history of early American cities. Harris reconstructs racial patterns in early New York City, compelling readers to shed preconceived notions about the history of slavery in America. African slaves dominated the labor force in southern colonies and states, but they also became an essential element in New York City's economy as early as the mid-seventeenth century. For almost two hundred years, New York City had the largest black population—slave and free—of any city in the North, but few historians wrote about black workers or the evolution of the city's black community. Harris's study is notable for its attention to the occupational roles of black women in the city's labor market, especially as domestic servants. The racial ideologies of the time dictated that black lives were shaped by racism and inequality throughout the colonial period and after; slavery persisted in the state of New York into the early nineteenth century, with full emancipation finally achieved only in 1827. After 1800, European immigrants, especially the Irish, altered local labor markets, as employers favored white workers for even the lowest-paid jobs. Emancipation freed bonded labor by the 1820s, but blacks in New York continued to be denied voting rights; by the time of the Civil War, when New York City's black population surpassed 15,000, only a few hundred blacks were eligible to vote. However, despite the severe constraints on freedom imposed on blacks during and after slavery, Harris argues that blacks in New York City found ways to resist repression and develop a strong sense of community. Black community institutions, such as "African Free schools," religious organizations, and the New York Manumission Society provided important support and nurtured a sense of black identity. The essay also finds evidence of divisions within New York's black community. Intraclass relations became a divisive issue, as tensions emerged after emancipation between the large black working class and a much smaller black middle class—tensions often based on cultural differences and efforts by middle-class community leaders to control working-class behavior. On virtually all of these points of interpretation, Harris's essay helps illuminate a long-hidden aspect of early American social history.

In his essay on the impact of European immigrants in pre–Civil War southern cities, Randall M. Miller provides abundant evidence to contradict some well-established historical conceptions about the American South. Generally, the South has been portrayed as rural and agrarian, with little social or cultural distinction between countryside and city. More particularly, the argument runs, European immigrants were attracted to northern cities and repelled by the idea of competing with slave labor, leaving the white populations of southern cities ethnically and culturally homogeneous. By contrast, and surprisingly, Miller's essay demonstrates not only rapid urban growth in the South between 1820 and 1860 but also high proportions of immigrants attracted to economic opportunities in southern port and river cities. By the time of the Civil War, most southern cities had developed a substantial white, ethnic working class that shared few of the cultural values of the Old South. These immigrant workers caused a restructuring of urban labor markets, disrupted established patterns of race relations, and altered the physical landscapes of southern cities. Assimilating slowly, if at all, these pre–Civil War immigrants to the urban

South challenged mainstream regional cultural values, and they posed problems of social order and social control. Eventually, they asserted political influence through the vote and through control of some types of city jobs; the Irish, for example, came to dominate the police forces of New Orleans, Memphis, Charleston, and Savannah. Immigrant influences on southern cities diminished greatly after the Civil War, but Miller's essay provides a persuasive antidote to established interpretations of antebellum urban life in the South.

These three essays only begin to suggest the diversity and richness of historical reinterpretations on the preindustrial American city. They do, however, serve to introduce the reader to the historical imagination at work.

NOTES

1. Carville V. Earle, *Geographical Inquiry and American Historical Problems* (Stanford, CA: Stanford University Press, 1992), 84.

2. Michael Merrill, "Cash Is Good to Eat: Self-Sufficiency and Exchange in the Rural Economy of the United States," *Radical History Review* 4 (Fall 1976): 42–71.

3. Gary B. Nash, *The Urban Crucible: Social Change, Political Consciousness, and the Origins of the American Revolution* (Cambridge, MA: Harvard University Press, 1979); Nash, "Artisans and Politics in Eighteenth-Century Philadelphia," in *The Origins of Anglo-American Radicalism*, ed. Margaret C. Jacob and James R. Jacob (London: Allen & Unwin, 1991), 258–78.

4. T. H. Breen, *The Marketplace of Revolution: How Consumers Shaped the American Revolution* (New York: Oxford University Press, 2004); Breen, "'Baubles of Britain': The American and Consumer Revolutions of the Eighteenth Century," *Past and Present* 119 (May 1988): 73–103, quotation on p. 76.

5. Stanley K. Schultz, "The Growth of Urban America in War and Peace, 1740–1810," in *The American Revolution: Changing Perspectives*, ed. William M. Fowler, Jr., and Wallace Coyle (Boston: Northeastern University Press, 1981), 127.

6. Thomas P. Slaughter, "Crowds in Eighteenth-Century America: Reflections and New Directions," *Pennsylvania Magazine of History and Biography* 115 (January 1991): 3–34; Benjamin L. Carp, *Rebels Rising: Cities and the American Revolution* (New York: Oxford University Press, 2007), 62–98; Arthur M. Schlesinger, "The City in American History," *Mississippi Valley Historical Review* 27 (June 1940): 46.

7. Richard C. Wade, *The Urban Frontier: The Rise of Western Cities, 1790–1830* (Cambridge, MA: Harvard University Press, 1959); Wade, "Urban Life in Western America, 1790–1830," *American Historical Review* 64 (October 1958): 14–30; Carl Abbott, *Boosters and Businessmen: Popular Economic Thought and Urban Growth in the Antebellum Middle West* (Westport, CT: Greenwood Press, 1981).

8. George Rogers Taylor, *The Transportation Revolution, 1815–1860* (New York: Rinehart, 1951); John Lauritz Larson, *Internal Improvements: National Public Works and the Promise of Popular Government in the Early United States* (Chapel Hill: University of North Carolina Press, 2001). On the Erie and other canals, see Ronald E. Shaw, *Canals for a Nation: The Canal Era in the United States, 1790–1860* (Lexington: University Press of Kentucky, 1993); Carol Sheriff, *The Artificial River: The Erie Canal and the Paradox of Progress, 1817–1862* (New York: Hill & Wang, 1996); Peter L. Bernstein, *Wedding of the Waters: The Erie Canal and the Making of a Great Nation* (New York: Norton, 2005).

9. Ross Thomson, *Structures of Change in the Mechanical Age: Technological Innovation in the United States, 1790–1865* (Baltimore: Johns Hopkins University Press, 2009); David R. Meyer, *The Roots of American Industrialization* (Baltimore: Johns Hopkins University Press, 2003), 15–54.

10. Charles Sellers, *The Market Revolution: Jacksonian America, 1815–1846* (New York: Oxford University Press, 1991); John Lauritz Larson, *The Market Revolution in America: Liberty, Ambition, and the Eclipse of the Common Good* (Cambridge, UK: Cambridge University Press, 2010); Thomas C. Cochran, *Frontiers of Change: Early Industrialization in America* (New York: Oxford University Press, 1981); Bruce Laurie, *Artisans into Workers: Labor in Nineteenth-Century America* (Urbana: University of Illinois Press, 1997), 15–46; Alan Dawley, *Class and Community: The Industrial Revolution in Lynn* (Cambridge, MA: Harvard University Press, 1976); Thomas L. Dublin, *Women at Work: The Transformation of Work and Community in Lowell, Massachusetts, 1826–1860* (New York: Columbia University Press, 1979).

11. Sean Wilentz, "Society, Politics, and the Market Revolution, 1815–1848," in *The New American History*, ed. Eric Foner (rev. ed.; Philadelphia: Temple University Press, 1997), 61–84, quotation on p. 63; Eric Lampard, "The History of Cities in the Economically Advanced Areas," *Economic Development and Cultural Change* 3 (January 1955): 126.

12. Raymond A. Mohl, *The New City: Urban America in the Industrial Age, 1860–1920* (Arlington Heights, IL: Harlan Davidson, 1985), 7–26, especially tables 3 and 4.

13. Peter R. Knights, *The Plain People of Boston, 1830–1860: A Study in City Growth* (New York: Oxford University Press, 1971), 58; Stephan Thernstrom and Peter R. Knights, "Men in Motion: Some Data and Speculations about Urban Population Mobility in Nineteenth-Century America," *Journal of Interdisciplinary History* 1 (1970): 7–35.

14. Charles E. Rosenberg, *The Cholera Years: The United States in 1832, 1849, and 1866* (Chicago: University of Chicago Press, 1962); Michael Feldberg, *The Turbulent Era: Riot and Disorder in Jacksonian America* (New York: Oxford University Press, 1980); Carl E. Prince, "The Great 'Riot Year': Jacksonian Democracy and Patterns of Violence in 1834," *Journal of the Early Republic* 5 (Spring 1985): 1–19.

15. Alan I. Marcus, *Plague of Strangers: Social Groups and the Origins of City Services in Cincinnati* (Columbus: Ohio State University Press, 1991); Carroll Smith-Rosenberg, *Religion and the Rise of the American City: The New York City Mission Movement, 1812–1870* (Ithaca, NY: Cornell University Press, 1971); Paul Boyer, *Urban Masses and Moral Order in America, 1820–1920* (Cambridge, MA: Harvard University Press, 1978).

16. Gideon Sjoberg, *The Preindustrial City: Past and Present* (New York: Free Press, 1960).

17. On these various points, see Sean Wilentz, *Chants Democratic: New York City and the Rise of the American Working Class* (New York: Oxford University Press, 1984); Daniel Walker Howe, *What Hath God Wrought: The Transformation of America, 1815–1848* (New York: Oxford University Press, 2007), 532–46.

Chapter 1

The Social Evolution of Preindustrial American Cities, 1700–1820

Gary B. Nash

As the eighteenth century began, the population of Boston, the largest city in the English overseas world, stood at 7,000. New York City bustled with 5,000 inhabitants, while the villages of Philadelphia and Charleston, with only a few score buildings that had progressed beyond frame to brick structures, had about 2,000 people each. Four generations later, as the century ended, Boston had grown to 25,000, New York to 60,000, Philadelphia to 62,000, Charleston to 13,000, and Baltimore, a newcomer on the urban scene, to 27,000. Twenty-eight other towns exceeded 2,500 inhabitants, and just over 6 percent of the American population lived in urban centers of more than 2,500. Much greater growth lay just ahead, with Philadelphia and New York burgeoning to 118,000 and 131,000, respectively, by 1820. But even as Thomas Jefferson assumed the presidency, population increase and commercial development had reconfigured what had been an almost cityless landscape at the beginning of the century into one studded with urban places. Relative to England, probably the most urbanized country in the world in 1800, the United States lagged behind by half a century. Occupied after the Revolution in the business of expanding across the continent, land-hungry Americans remained largely a rural people for more than a century. Hence, not until 1840 would the United States be able to match the 15 cities over 20,000 in population that England boasted in 1800, and not until the 1880s would 30 percent of the population live in towns of 2,500 or more, as did this percentage of the English population in 1800.[1] Nor would the kind of industrial cities that grew so rapidly in the second half of the eighteenth century in England—cities such as Manchester, Liverpool, and Birmingham—be found in America at this time (table 1.1). Yet like all modern nations, the United States was launched on the historic course that would make it a nation of urban rather than rural people.

What did it mean for an urban center to increase from 5,000 to 60,000 over four generations? How did social relations, political life, and patterns of association change in

Reprinted from *Journal of Urban History* 13 (February 1987): 115–45. Reprinted with the permission of Sage Publications.

Table 1.1. Population of English and American Cities, 1700–1800

1700	1750	1800
Norwich (30,000)	Norwich (36,000)	Manchester (90,000)
Bristol (20,000)	Bristol (25,000)	Liverpool (88,000)
Manchester (10,000)	Birmingham (24,000)	Birmingham (74,000)
Boston (7,000)	Liverpool (22,000)	Bristol (64,000)
Leeds (6,000)	Manchester (19,000)	Philadelphia (62,000)
Birmingham (6,000)	Boston (16,000)	New York (61,000)
New York (5,000)	New York (13,000)	Leeds (53,000)
Liverpool (5,000)	Philadelphia (13,000)	Norwich (37,000)
Portsmouth (5,000)	Sheffield (11,000)	Bath (34,000)
	Portsmouth (10,000)	Portsmouth (33,000)
	Leeds (10,000)	Sheffield (31,000)
		Baltimore (27,000)
		Boston (25,000)

Sources: C. W. Chalkin, *The Provincial Towns of Georgian England* (London, 1974); B. R. Mitchell, *European Historical Statistics, 1750–1820* (2nd ed.; New York, 1980); Gary B. Nash, *The Urban Crucible: Social Change, Political Consciousness, and the Origins of the American Revolution* (Cambridge, MA, 1979); U.S. Bureau of the Census, *Return of the Whole Number of Persons within the Several Districts of the United States [1800]* (Washington City, 1802).

the course of such development? Elsewhere I have argued that the seaboard cities were at the cutting edge of change in early America. It was here that almost all the alterations associated with the advent of modern capitalist society first occurred, and then slowly radiated outward to the small farming communities of the hinterland. In the colonial cities, people first made the transition from an oral to a literate culture, from a moral to a market economy, from an ascriptive to a competitive social order, from a communal to an individualistic orientation, from a hierarchical and deferential policy to a participatory and contentious civic life. In the cities factory production first began to replace small-scale artisanal production, and the first steps were taken to organize work by clock time rather than by sidereal cycles. These were, in fact, among the critical changes that Ferdinand Tönnies identified as constituting the transition from *gemeinschaft* to *gesellschaft*—a historic process that he identified as quintessentially an urban phenomenon.[2]

How, amid such changes, did urban people experience life differently and, most important, how did they confront these changes? Following Thomas Bender's seminal suggestion, I propose that we reconsider the *gemeinschaft* to *gesellschaft* formulation of change in which the vocabulary of analysis is composed of words like decay, decline, dissolution, and disintegration of community. This analytic model is not without its uses for urban historians. However, enough has been discovered about the dynamics of urban social development in eighteenth-century towns to keep us mindful that communities change at different rates of speed, sometimes in different directions, not always in unilinear fashion, and rarely with all members of the community cleaving to the same values and responding identically to the same stimuli. Moreover, the organizing notion of decline and decay implicitly, if unintentionally, consigns to a passive role the city dwellers themselves, and especially those who were most adversely affected by change.[3]

The tendency has been almost irresistible to interpret the rise of materialistic, self-interested, contentious, class-oriented urban polity as a sign of social declension and shattered harmony. As in most things, we look backward to what we imagine were better days—a simpler time when mutuality, order, and a universal regard for the commonweal prevailed. Social cohesion and harmony, alas, were never so prevalent in the prerevolutionary cities as sometimes imagined, even if the richest and poorest inhabitants lived next door to each other, even if the poor were succored with familial forms of relief, even if journeymen lived with masters and worked with them under one roof. Moreover, the emerging urban social order of the late eighteenth century, while at many times difficult and hardly bearable, brought compensating advantages that offset some of the strains. Free black Americans, for example, were usually denied respect and equal access to jobs, education, and political rights when they migrated into these cities; but none of them would have traded their lot for their prior status as slaves, for freedom in the postrevolutionary cities, with all its disadvantages, was preferable to slavery, even in its mildest forms. Struggling shoemakers in the age of Jefferson no longer lived across the street from the mayor or worshiped in the same church as lofty merchants; but such socially integrating mechanisms had never guaranteed them employment in "the old days." Moreover, in their emerging working-class neighborhoods, where they frequented their own taverns, churches, and craft organizations, they found the opportunity to create a stronger culture of their own than had proven possible in the more class-mixed and socially mobile cities of the eighteenth century. Journeymen no longer lived with the master and ate at his table, but when it came time to vote, they were more likely to be found at the polls and went there more autonomously than before. *Gesellschaft,* in some of its forms, was in fact more likely to occur in cities where growing social stratification and social zoning occurred than in the less stratified and more socially integrated cities of the past.

Bender aptly asks: "Why cannot *gemeinschaft* and *gesellschaft* simultaneously shape social life," for both are "forms of human interaction that can act reciprocally on each other?"[4] Extending this, it may be asked whether homogeneity and smallness are the indispensable elements of community and viable social relations. In seeking to substitute new paradigms of social change for the overused *gemeinschaft* to *gesellschaft* model, it may be best to begin by observing life as close to the street level and the kitchen hearth as possible, searching for signs of how urban people struggled to create, adapt to, oppose, defend, or legitimize new circumstances. Rather than nostalgically tracing the *eclipse* of community, we need to trace the continuously evolving *process* of community. We need to look for the *different* meanings (rather than the *less satisfactory* ones) that urban life took and the various strategies of living that people devised as their cities grew in size and complexity. In important ways, this article argues, the kinds of structural changes occurring in the cities created conditions that encouraged—even necessitated—the fabrication of communities within communities by energized and mobilized groups that had previously often been politically and socially quiescent and detached from group activity, except in churches.

Even in their earliest years, the capitals of Massachusetts, Pennsylvania, New York, and South Carolina were not so ethnically and religiously homogeneous as is sometimes supposed. But they were relatively unified by their settlers' common religious orientations and social backgrounds, with East Anglican Puritans, Dutch Calvinists, English Quakers, and West Indian Anglicans shaping the early social contours of the four provincial capitals respectively. This religious homogeneity broke down rapidly in Manhattan in the late seventeenth century and in Philadelphia and Boston in the eighteenth, despite efforts to maintain it in Boston and because no one attempted to maintain it in Philadelphia. After the Peace of Utrecht in 1713, Philadelphia became the port of entry for thousands of immigrants from Ulster, the Rhine, the West Indies, and other points of the compass. In Boston, although as late as 1718 five boatloads of Ulster immigrants would be hustled out of town and directed to the New Hampshire frontier, the process eventually was much the same. Street signs would never be rendered both in German and English in John Winthrop's Boston, as in William Penn's Philadelphia, but the immigrants came, particularly after the Revolution, when the volume of immigration was heavier than previously believed, according to recent estimates, to complete the process that the early town fathers had so much feared—the diversifying of a community formerly composed of supposedly like-minded souls.[5]

Urban historians still know very little about the exact patterns of migration—from the rural hinterland, from other mainland colonies, and from overseas—that spurred growth and turned American towns into ethnic and religious bouillabaisses that in England had a counterpart perhaps only in Liverpool and London. But while the timing and dynamics of this rapid diversifying of the urban populaces is murky, the overall effects would have been obvious to any visitor strolling the streets of the major seaport cities on a Sunday morning in 1800. In Philadelphia, for example, such a visitor would have witnessed people crowding into thirty-five churches representing fourteen denominations and eight ethnic groups, whereas a century before worshipers had attended only the churches of four English denominations and one Swedish chapel. Even in Boston, less than half the size of Philadelphia, nineteen churches of eight denominations existed at the end of the eighteenth century.[6]

Amid this growing cosmopolitanism, religious persecution, if not religious prejudice, faded. In the process, the early Boston meaning of "community"—a collection of like-minded believers who extended to "strangers" only the freedom "to be gone as fast as they can, the sooner the better"—was eclipsed by the Philadelphia meaning of "community"—a collection of believers, disbelievers, mystics, agnostics, and nihilists who learned to see themselves linked to those around them by material rewards and social necessities rather than by heavenly quests. In this growing acceptance of the idea that diversity could be the cement rather than the dissolvent of unity lay the roots of the pluralism that was to become a mainstay of American society. That it set American cities off from their English counterparts, London excepted, seems apparent from the comments of English visitors, who often remarked on the multichromatic and multilingual mélanges in the American cities.

One immigrant group of a special character, largely absent in every English town except London, figured importantly in the urban landscape. At the beginning of the century the cities contained only small numbers of America's involuntary immigrants—the sons and daughters of Africa. But their proportion of the population grew rapidly between 1720 and 1760, spurred by the demand for labor in the growing towns and, during the Seven Years' War, by the nearly complete stoppage of the indentured servant trade. Boston's slave population grew from about 300 to 1,544 between 1710 and 1752; slaves in New York City increased so rapidly in the same era that by 1746 half the white households held slaves. In Philadelphia, where those investing in bound labor had chosen Irish and German indentured servants more often than African slaves in the first half of the century, merchants and artisans alike purchased record numbers of Africans during the Seven Years' War, multiplying the black population to above 1,400 by war's end. In Charleston, capital of the colony with the highest proportion of slaves in British North America, 54 percent of the city's 11,000 residents were slaves by 1770.[7]

In the last third of the century, however, this rapid growth of black laborers underwent two enormous changes. First, slave imports to the growing cities came to an abrupt halt except in Charleston. The depression that followed the Seven Years' War convinced many urban capitalists of the advantages of free laborers, whom they could hire and fire as economic cycles dictated. The growth of abolitionism in the cities and their occupation by the British during the Revolution put the finishing touches on slave imports. All over the northeastern seaboard the black slave populations in the cities plummeted in the revolutionary era, as dying slaves went unreplaced by new recruits from Africa and as younger slaves fled to the British when they occupied the towns.

The second change was the dramatic rise of the free black populations in the postrevolutionary cities, including those in the South such as Norfolk, Baltimore, Savannah, and Charleston. In the northern cities, just as quickly as the black slave population had diminished between 1765 and 1780, the free black population rose from 1780 to 1800. Philadelphia, the southernmost of the northern cities, was especially notable. Its free black population of perhaps 250 on the eve of independence approached 10,000 by 1810. Almost every northern seaport exerted a powerful magnetic force upon freed blacks, for the city represented a place to make a living (which was very difficult in the countryside for those lacking capital to invest in land and equipment), a place to find marriage partners and compatriots, a place, in short, to start a community within a community.[8] In the southern cities, the free black population also grew rapidly, far outstripping increases in the white and slave populations. In Baltimore, where only a handful of free blacks resided at the end of the Revolution, nearly 6,000 free blacks congregated by 1810. Richmond and Petersburg, Virginia, and Charleston, South Carolina, all had free black communities exceeding 1,000 by 1810 (table 1.2).[9]

America's northern city dwellers, in an average person's lifetime, witnessed the rapid growth of slavery, a sudden black depopulation during the war, the dismantling of urban slavery, and then a swift repopulation of the cities by free blacks, many of them streaming in from the hinterland and the upper South. New York lingered half a generation behind in this manumission process, and the southern cities represented a different case altogether, but in all the cities the urban character of modern Afro-American life was taking shape. When Cato, Cudgo, and Betty, who had formerly lived *in* the houses of merchants and artisans as lifelong servants, became Cato Freeman, William Thomas, and Elizabeth Anderson, who lived *down the street* as free persons who controlled their own destinies, white and black urbanites both had to make

Table 1.2.   Urban Free Black Population, 1790–1810

	Free Black Population		Percent Change, 1790–1810		
	1790	*1810*	*Free Blacks*	*Whites*	*Slaves*
Boston	761	1,484	+95	+90	NA
Providence	427	865	+103	+56	−88
New York	1,101	8,173	+639	+192	−29
Philadelphia	2,078	9,653	+365	+17	−99
Baltimore	323	5,671	+1,656	+204	+272
Richmond	265	1,189	+349	+138	+153
Petersburg	310	1,089	+251	+92	+72
Charleston	951	1,412	+55	+31	+29

Sources: U.S. Bureau of the Census, *Heads of Families at the First Census of the United States Taken in the Year 1790: Pennsylvania* (Washington, D.C., 1908); *Aggregate Number of Persons within the United States in the Year 1810* (Washington, D.C., 1811).

psychological adjustments. Some could not, and consequently the black emancipation process was fraught with difficulties. Nonetheless, growing black populations smithied out the elements of modern Afro-American life and culture on the anvil of urban coexistence with those who had formerly been their masters. In the southern cities (and in New York City until about 1820), free blacks lived precariously among blacks still enslaved. They too, albeit under more difficult circumstances, formed neighborhoods, established families, and organized churches, schools, and benevolent societies.[10] One important urban group had made the transition from individuals whose collective action was strictly prohibited to persons who eagerly formed religious and social groups and acted collectively in a number of other ways.

Blacks emerging from the house of bondage in the late-eighteenth-century cities sought opportunity as other poor immigrants had done for decades. The parallel was closest with those who had arrived as indentured servants and worked off their labor contract. However, manumitted blacks at the end of the eighteenth century (along with newly arriving immigrants) were entering an economy that differed markedly from that which humble aspirants had found before the Revolution. The early-eighteenth-century towns were filled with men who had risen to modest wealth from artisan backgrounds, mostly through the mechanism of urban land speculation or military subcontracting in time of war. Still young and fluid, the cities were arenas of opportunity for the industrious and bold. Benjamin Franklin was everyone's model of the plucky, shrewd, and frugal leather-apron man who might advance rapidly from apprentice to journeyman to master. Many, like Franklin, watched their wives replace the pewter spoon and earthen porringer at the breakfast table with a silver spoon and china bowl, symbolizing the ascent beyond a "decent competency" that was the artisan's self-proclaimed goal in the preindustrial city. Of course, only a handful rose so rapidly and stylishly as Poor Richard in the early years; yet few ever imagined that their families would go hungry or that they might awaken one morning inside an almshouse. More and more that fate awaited those who entered urban life at the bottom of the social ladder in the last third of the century.

Even those who faithfully followed Poor Richard's precepts of industry and frugality sometimes fell into poverty in the prerevolutionary generation. Boston suffered earlier and more intensively than other towns, its economy racked after the 1720s by war-induced inflation and heavy taxes and its coffers strained from supporting hundreds of war widows and their fatherless children. By midcentury, New England's commercial center was the widow capital of the Western world, with one of every three married women heading a husbandless household. By the early 1750s Boston officialdom was describing the abodes of the poor where "scenes of Distress we do often behold! Numbers of Wretches hungry and naked shivering with Cold, and, perhaps, languishing with Disease."[11] Although it has been axiomatic among historians that poverty corroded the lives of ordinary people to a far greater extent in English than in American towns, the selectmen, in this same year, ventured to claim that poverty was so widespread that they were obliged to expend relief monies double those of any town of equal size "upon the face of the whole Earth."[12]

In all the cities poverty spread during the deep recession following the Seven Years' War. Nobody in the cities of Cotton Mather, Robert Hunter, and James Logan could have imagined a report such as came from the Philadelphia almshouse managers, who wrote, as the Continental Congress was conducting its epic debate over independence a few blocks away, that "of the 147 Men, 178 Women, and 85 Children [admitted to the almshouse during the previous year] most of them [are] naked, helpless and emaciated with Poverty and Disease to such a Degree, that some have died in a few Days after their Admission."[13] To control the strolling poor, whose support drove up poor taxes and whose very appearance threatened social disorder, town leaders tightened residency requirements, systematically examined and expelled non-residents, and built workhouses and almshouses with harsh daily regimens to control those who qualified for relief.[14]

Research conducted by a second wave of those who have followed in the wake of the pioneering work done on tax lists a generation ago by Robert E. Brown and Jackson T. Main has led to the discovery that urban poverty on the eve of the Revolution was far more extensive than ever imagined. We now know that the tax lists that once were regarded as snapshots of the entire community do not include a very large group of urban adult males. In Providence and Newport, Rhode Island, for example, about 30 and 45 percent of all adult males were too poor to be included on the assessors' lists on the eve of the Revolution.[15] In Philadelphia, at least one fifth of the population, mostly people who lived as roomers in boardinghouses or rented back buildings, sheds, and crude apartments in alleys, courtyards, and side streets, is missing from the assessors' rolls.[16] This large floating population, associated conceptually with a society in which opportunities are restricted and in which geographical rather than social mobility gives rise to the term "strolling poor," lends an entirely new look to the contours of urban society on the eve of the Revolution. It was into this altered urban scene that newly emancipated blacks would stride during and after the war.

The postwar reconstruction of the American cities, most of which were physically ravished during the British occupation, by no means eliminated urban poverty. In fact, it grew as the cities suffered through several severe trade depressions in the decade after the Peace of Paris. Struggling to absorb new waves of immigrants, particularly poor Irish sojourners who often could not find work, urban people were also scourged repeatedly by yellow fever at the end of the century. In the worst microbic attack ever to afflict American cities, the fever struck unremittingly from New York to New Orleans in the 1790s, especially striking down laboring families who could not afford to flee to the countryside, as did their social superiors. In several cities yellow fever claimed nearly 10 percent of the population in a single year (which amounts to something like 15 percent of the working classes) and strained poor relief resources in every municipality.[17]

The urban centers of the new American republic, while busy centers of growing overseas trade and early manufacturing, also became the centers of the highest mortality, criminality, and poverty rates ever known on the eastern seaboard. What a visiting committee of the Methodist Hospitable Society found in Philadelphia in 1803 was by no means unusual. Prowling the back alleys and the laboring-class neighborhoods on the edge of the city, the Methodists described scores of families living "in rooms with shattered furniture, in tenements almost in ruins, [some] laying on straw with a few rags to cover them."[18] This kind of urban immiseration, primarily associated by historians with European cities or with the industrializing, immigrant-filled American cities of the mid-nineteenth century, was, in fact, much in evidence by the time of Jefferson's presidency.

Alongside urban poverty rose urban elegance, architecturally visible in the handsome Georgian mansions that rose in the cities in the last third of the century; and evident in the cobbled streets—twisted in Boston, curved in New York, and straight in Philadelphia—as a growing battalion of four-wheeled carriages rolled by. One of the by-products of this new urban wealth, which also produced a broader middle class than existed earlier, was the growth of a consumer ethos. The sheer range of articles available for purchase in the cities grew enormously in the eighteenth century, as can be traced in newspaper advertisements, in urban occupational specialization, and in inventories of wealth in the probate records.[19]

A revolution fought for liberty and equality, but also for property and the right to acquire it as plentifully and competitively as people knew how, did nothing to retard the polarization of wealth and the growing material appetites of middle- and upper-class urbanites. The Revolution, in fact, removed several obstacles to the quest for wealth. Among the casualties of the victory over England was the concept of the commonweal and of a corporate economy in which the guarantee of the right to eat outweighed private pursuit of gain. Such a traditional ideology, with roots deep in the medieval past, had been losing ground steadily in the eighteenth century, even among master craftsmen. However, it had a revival amid the millennial fervor of the early years of revolution, when many men hoped the conflict would achieve a double victory: independence from corrupt and oppressive England and self-purification through a restoration of civic virtue, Spartan living, and disdain for worldly things. The yearning of an urbanite like Samuel Adams for a return to ancestral virtue and communal attachment quickly dissipated, however, even before the war's end. The *novus ordo seclorum* that large numbers of city dwellers sought was not Adams's "Christian Sparta" but an unfettered stage on which a drama composed by Adam Smith could be played out by actors who spoke not of the fair wage and the just price but of the laws

of supply and demand and the greater benefits to the community of unbridled competition and consumer choice freed from the restraining hand of government.

The changes wrought in the second half of the eighteenth century, during a protracted
period of war, economic volatility, and commercial expansion, were systematically
recorded in the tax lists and the probate records of the period. These records, although
understating the case because they do not include large numbers of the poorest city
dwellers, confirm what was evident architecturally in the cities—that a substantial
redistribution of wealth occurred, particularly, it appears, in the period from 1740 to
1765 when a number of large fortunes, based on overseas trade and urban land speculation, created America's first truly wealthy urban elite (table 1.3). More important
than the shifting proportion of wealth held by each stratum of urban society was the
fact that the concentration of the community's resources in the hands of the elite was
accompanied by a hefty increase in the proportion of propertyless and indigent urban
dwellers. This growing economic inequality might have continued for some time
without objections if middle- and lower-class city dwellers had not seen the amassing
of great fortunes as one of the main causes of the growing poverty and indigence that
afflicted every city in the second half of the eighteenth century.[20] From the revolutionary era to the early nineteenth century, the distribution of urban wealth seems to
have changed less rapidly. Then, during a period of early industrialization from about
1820 to 1850, a second major period of wealth redistribution further widened the gap
between the top and bottom of urban society and left in the purses of the bottom half
of society little more than 10 percent of the community's assets—about half as much
as they had possessed a century before.[21]

It has been suggested that these changes in the division of economic resources
stemmed primarily from the increasing youthfulness of eighteenth-century American
society and that propertylessness was primarily a function of "social age." The propertyless, according to this argument, were mostly younger sons waiting for their landed
inheritance. Because they were increasing as a proportion of the population, it appears
that wealth became less equally divided when, in reality, it was age inequality that had
spread.[22] This argument may hold for rural communities where ownership of land was

Table 1.3. Wealth Held by Richest Ten Percent of Urban Population

	Late 17th Century	*Mid-18th Century*	*Late 18th Century*
Boston (t)	46	64	65
Boston (i)	41	60	56
New York (t)	45	46	61
Philadelphia (t)	45	66	61
Philadelphia (i)	36	60	72

Sources: Nash, *Urban Crucible,* 395–98, Tables 3, 5; Allen Kulikoff, "The Growth of Inequality in Postrevolutionary
Boston," *William and Mary Quarterly,* 28 (1971), 381; Billy G. Smith, "Inequality in Late Colonial Philadelphia: A
Note on Its Nature and Growth," Ibid., 41 (1984), 629–45; Gloria Main, "Inequality in Early America: The Evidence
from Probate Records of Massachusetts and Maryland," *Journal of Interdisciplinary History,* 7 (1977), 559–81; Bruce
Martin Wilkenfeld, *The Social and Economic Structure of New York City, 1695–1796* (New York, 1978), 161–62.
Note: t = based on tax assessment; i = based on probated inventories of wealth.

the rule and sons waited far beyond the taxable age of eighteen to acquire their fathers' estates. However, in the cities, where propertylessness was becoming the rule at the lower ranks of society, changes in the age structure of the population, according to the one empirical study available, do not account for the widening disparity between rich and poor.[23]

In urban centers, enhanced opportunities for amassing great wealth among those positioned advantageously increased the relative wealth of those at the top of the social pyramid. Meanwhile, depressed real wages (partly caused after the Revolution by the increase in immigrant labor available in the cities), cyclical economic buffetings that struck hardest at those with the thinnest margin of security, and the vengeful yellow fever of the 1790s, which was America's first class disease, appear to have been the main factors bearing on the deepening social inequalities. Benjamin Franklin Bache, a Philadelphia newspaper editor, understood the growing disparity of wealth in much this way. "Is it not heart rending," he wrote in 1797, "that the laboring poor should almost exclusively be the victims of the disease introduced by that commerce, which, in prosperous times, is a source of misery to them, by the inequality of wealth which it produces?"[24]

Although comparable data for provincial towns in England are not available, it seems possible, because the old English provincial towns were exporting their dispossessed while American seaboard towns were absorbing them, that by the end of the eighteenth century the American cities harbored as many or possibly more transient poor than their English counterparts. By 1790, if one can generalize from one case study of Philadelphia, more than a third of the population was too poor to pay even the most modest tax—and this ratio would increase to more than half by 1830.[25] The smokestack towns that were already growing rapidly in Manchester, Liverpool, and Birmingham were still a generation away in America as the eighteenth century closed, so the proper comparison is between the American cities and the older provincial towns such as Norwich, Bath, and Bristol. The unflattering comments of almost all Americans who traveled in England notwithstanding, American towns may have differed in their social structure from their English counterparts primarily in that the English urban poor were indigenous and white (and therefore noticed) whereas in America the poor were immigrant and black (and therefore overlooked).

While a century of urban growth increased the gap between gentry and common folk, it also transformed the spatial patterns of working and living, and, perforce, social relations. Much of the changing social geography stemmed from the rapid rise of urban land values in the old cores of the seaport towns. Before the Revolution, except in the stagnant town of Boston, land values multiplied many times, making real estate investment a greater source of wealth than trade. After the Revolution, land values again soared. In Manhattan, they climbed 750 percent between 1785 and 1815 alone, and a similar trend prevailed in other cities.[26] In Philadelphia, "A Friend to Equal Justice" complained bitterly in 1793 that rents (which reflected the market value of land) had doubled, trebled, and even quadrupled after Congress moved to Philadelphia from New York in 1789.[27]

The century-long rise of land values and rents, because it far outstripped advances in the wages of artisans and laborers, led to two historic changes in the social geography of the cities. First, property ownership became more concentrated in the hands of merchants, professionals, shopkeepers, and speculative builders. As the price of urban land spiraled upward, leather-apron men found that a building lot cost four or five years' wages, rather than the four or five months' pay it had cost their grandfathers earlier in the century. Hence, tenancy rates climbed from about 30 percent of all heads of household at the beginning of the eighteenth century to about 80 percent one hundred years later.[28] In Baltimore, a young town where the entire process of social formation lagged several generations behind that of the older cities, the proportion of lower artisans without real property increased from about 48 percent to 69 percent in a single decade after 1804.[29]

Second, facing the urban real estate market with wages that increased only slowly in the second half of the eighteenth century, working people were obliged to seek cheaper land and rental housing on the periphery of the city. This, in turn, led to another change—the separation of the place of residence from the place of production. Thus emerged the pattern of concentric residential zones that became common to all growing urban centers of the Atlantic basin. Towns whose neighborhoods had previously been integrated by occupation and class now began to develop a core dominated by the wealthy, a surrounding belt containing primarily the middle class, and a periphery populated by the laboring poor. This "social zoning," as Peter Clark has termed it, has been traced in several cities where inspection of the tax lists revealed median assessments in the core from four to ten times as great as on the outlying edges.[30]

Overlapping this increasing class segregation, which was still in the early stages at the beginning of the nineteenth century, was a growing racial clustering that occurred when free blacks establishing their own residences replaced slaves living with masters throughout the cities. The modern term "segregation," connoting a racial separation imposed by the dominant group, is not entirely appropriate in the early-nineteenth-century American context because the concentration of black families in certain neighborhoods, as they worked their way free of the residual effects of bondage after the Revolution in the northern cities, or made their way thence from the upper South, was partly the result of their own desire to live near the independent black churches they built, near the schools associated with these churches, and near relatives, friends, and associates.[31] Nonetheless, the physical separation of blacks and whites, if we can generalize from the Philadelphia example, increased rapidly, with the index of dissimilarity growing from .149 in 1790 to .514 in 1820.[32]

As well as reflecting rising land values and rents, the social geography of the cities changed with the reorganization of work. Early in the century, apprentices and journeymen, working within a household mode of production, had usually lived with the master artisan in a familial setting in which residence and work location were merged. By the end of the century, a larger scale production led many masters to relocate their shops away from their place of residence, journeymen usually lived independently of the master, typically in rented rooms or in that new urban phenomenon of the late eighteenth century—the boardinghouse. Moreover, journeymen increasingly found themselves in an antagonistic relationship with their masters, for by the early nineteenth century the traditional pathway that led from apprentice to master craftsman was becoming severely clogged.[33] In Boston, for example, where as late as 1790 a majority of journeymen carpenters could expect to become masters, only one in five achieved that goal in the decades after 1810.[34] By the early nineteenth century, artisans who formerly would have expected to achieve the status of master were increasingly obliged to depend on others for wage work. "The time before long will come," decried one craftsman, "when we shall tread in the steps of Old England."[35] The term "walking cities" still applied at the end of the eighteenth century because urban geographical spread was still not very great, and people of many stations lived within hailing distance of each other. But while the geographical proximity of urban social classes remained relatively close, the social distance grew between employers and employees, rich and poor, black and white.

For urban women somewhat different changes in the social environment of work were taking place, particularly in the late eighteenth and early nineteenth centuries. First, the gradual transfer of male productive labor from the household to a commercial place of business "reduced the transmission of business and craft knowledge within the family" and thus decreased the likelihood that widows would continue their husbands' enterprises after their death.[36] A trend away from female proprietorships, noted in the case of Boston many years ago by Elisabeth Dexter on the basis of newspaper advertisements, has been statistically demonstrated for Philadelphia in a study of women's occupations listed in city directories. As late as the 1790s the probability remained high that widows would manage their deceased husbands' businesses—including the widows of ironmongers, pewterers, printers, coopers, turners, and tallow chandlers. However, by the antebellum era, the likelihood of this had been much reduced, and midwifery, although for different reasons, was also being taken out of women's hands.[37] In these areas of work, women of middling rank were pushed out of the public realm and into the private sphere.

At the same time the middle-class female proprietorships were decreasing, lower-class female household production in one important area—textiles—grew rapidly after the middle of the eighteenth century. The first attempts to utilize the labor of poor urban women—and increasingly their children—came in Boston, the capital of impoverished widowhood in America. But women balked at the separation of domestic responsibilities and income-producing work, and this resistance played a large part in the failure of the linen manufactory that merchants opened in 1750. However, women adapted readily to the putting-out system under which they spun thread in their homes while simultaneously discharging familial responsibilities.[38] In most of the cities after the Revolution, merchant-entrepreneurs established large putting-out networks for the domestic spinning of cotton yarn. Where immigrant labor was available, as in Philadelphia, the system soaked up the labor of poor urban women until as late as the 1830s, thus maintaining the home as a workplace.[39] In other cities, such as Boston and Pawtucket, the mechanization of cotton spinning drew large numbers of women and children out of their homes and into textile factories as early as the 1790s, in imitation of the much more developed practice in English industrial towns.[40] Thus began a long history of urban women and children of the lower orders in textile work—a chapter of urban history that would take another turn in the antebellum years with the movement of poor women and their children into the needle trades.[41]

In the last generation, historians have discovered much more about structural changes in eighteenth-century urban society than they have about how people responded to these alterations. The utilization of quantifiable sources, such as deeds, tax and probate documents, and poor relief records, has advanced our knowledge of what Tönnies called "gemeinschaft of locality"—the physical life of the community—more than our comprehension of what he termed "gemeinschaft of mind"—the mental life of the community. Hence, any agenda of research in eighteenth- and early-nineteenth-century urban history ought to be headed by topics relating to the individual and collective strategies of urban people as they sought to cope with their changing environment.

Insofar as they have inquired into the mental and behavioral responses of urban people to the passage of their locales from seaport villages to commercial and proto-industrial cities between 1690 and 1820, historians have looked primarily to the realm of politics. Some of them have argued that while the chasm between rich and poor grew and movement between the tiers of society decreased, conditions associated with the transition from *gemeinschaft* to *gesellschaft,* the reverse was happening in the political arena. The urban upper class in the American cities, as in England, had long believed in a system of political relations defined by gentle domination from above and willing subordination from below—a contractual arrangement that historians call deference politics. However, deference eroded markedly in the eighteenth-century cities, especially during critical periods when unemployment and declining real wages impoverished many working people and threatened the security of many more, thus sharpening their consciousness of inequalities of wealth and status. When artisans (and even laborers and mariners) mobilized politically, no longer believing that the elite managed affairs in the interest of the whole community, then the traditional rules of genteel politics began to change.

Long before the Revolution the instrumentalities of popular politics appeared in the cities—outdoor political rallies, vitriolic campaign literature, petition drives, club and caucus activity, and attacks on the wealthy as subverters rather than protectors of the community's welfare. During the Revolution this transformation of mechanic consciousness ushered in a new era of politics in which laboring people began to think of themselves as a distinct political entity. This led in turn to campaigns for transforming the political process through annual elections, secret balloting, universal male suffrage, rotation of office holding, inclusion of artisans as candidates for municipal offices, formation of extralegal committees for enforcing trade restrictions, self-convened outdoor political assemblages, and the opening of legislative debates to the public.[42] In the drawing rooms of polite society, men sputtered that "the Mechanics have no Right to *Speak* or *Think* for themselves," and should not presume to "intermeddle in state affairs."[43] The genie was out of the bottle, however, and would never be imprisoned again.

The political self-empowerment that was occurring in the revolutionary cities is often seen as a breakdown of an older social system in which interclass relations were marked by harmony, trust, mutual respect, and a sense of partnership within hierarchy. To some extent this notion of a prior social equilibrium is a convenient fiction created by historians who wish to chart change from a golden age. But the *relative* social equilibrium that had prevailed in the cities before the 1760s *was* in disarray because the conditions necessary for its survival were crumbling—an economy in which labor-ing people could fulfill their goals of earning a "decent competency," achieving an independent status, and obtaining respect in their communities.

Yet the overturning of the old system of political management partially mitigated the social disequilibrium because it offered the possibility that through a democratic political system each interest group in the urban polity could contend equally for its particular advantages. In time, the new system would be celebrated as uniquely Amer-ican, although many urban nabobs could never accept the active participation in the political process of the "mere mechanics," the "rabble," the "unthinking multitude." This popularization of politics continued after the Revolution, despite a conservative reaction in the last decade of the century. While economic development, population growth, and the differential effects of war on urban society had led to a widening chasm between the top and bottom of urban society, in politics the increasingly dis-tinct social ranks were forced into a common political process in which it was entirely legitimate for the lower orders to raise their voices, take to the streets, and formulate demands arising from their understanding of how the social system was changing. For those panjandrums who sat at the pinnacle of the more sharply defined social pyramid, popular politics carried the horrifying ring of anarchy, especially after the outbreak of the French Revolution. Beneficiaries of the advancing social exclusiveness, they were obliged to tolerate a growing political inclusiveness. Their discomfort was made all the more acute by the popular attacks mounted against them in the postrevolution-ary era—fusillades that increased in intensity by the end of the century and escalated further as merchant capitalists organized banks, built factories, and penetrated such crafts as shoemaking and house building.[44]

Eventually finding a home in the Democratic-Republican party that formed in the 1790s, urban workingmen, often led by small merchants, professionals, and master artisans turned manufacturers, pressed hard for a more democratic system of politics and for specific changes in the way power was distributed in such varied aspects of urban life as the availability of credit, schooling, taxation, militia duty, and indebted-ness laws. Strains of the old corporatist ethic remained alive in artisan republican-ism, although the upward movement of many master craftsmen into the ranks of manufacturers carried them into a realm where Madisonian political economy was particularly congenial.[45]

Meanwhile, within the lower orders the egalitarian ideology enunciated during the Revolution was refurbished from about 1790 to 1830 and adapted to the new conditions of labor taking hold in the first third of the nineteenth century. Running deeply through this thought of the radical urban democracy was a deep suspicion of wealth and of the concentrated power that lower-class and many middle-class city residents believed was its handmaiden. The belief grew that republican "simplicity and equality of manners essential to equal rights" was being undermined by a para-sitic class of merchant capitalists—nonproducers whose unrestrained acquisitive-ness and lack of concern for the community led, eventually, to the degradation of productive labor. As William Duane, the fiery immigrant editor of the Philadelphia *Aurora* expressed it in 1806 (in the context of the conviction of striking journeymen shoemakers for conspiring to restrain trade), "the doors of industry are to be closed so that a breed of *white slaves* may be nursed up in poverty to take the place of the *blacks* upon their emancipation."[46]

This is not to argue that the lower orders were able to use their newly gained political voice to transform the conditions under which they lived and worked in urban society. Far from it. There emerged in the postrevolutionary era no crystallization of artisan consciousness or all-craft solidarity, and short-term working-class victories were outweighed by long-range defeats. Despite structural changes in shoemaking, tailoring, printing, and other trades that were separating journeymen from masters, it proved difficult for working people to unite in a society in which the ideology of laissez-faire had penetrated deeply. In New York, it took until 1804 for those who did not own property—a growing proportion of the laboring population—even to obtain the vote in municipal elections, and thereafter they were able to accomplish much less than they hoped for at the ballot box. In Philadelphia, prosperous mechanics, allied with professionals and some merchants, even formed their own wing of the Jeffersonian party in the early nineteenth century, adopting positions on economic and fiscal issues that made them hardly distinguishable from the Federalists. Such men did not share the radical social perspective that inspired the periodic insurgency of the lower artisans, mariners, and laborers, who imbibed a small producers' ideology stressing egalitarianism and communitarianism—and who were less than a generation away from embracing socialism and from founding workingmen's parties in all the major cities.[47]

In spite of the effects of westward movement and political cooptation in dissipating political radicalism in the seaboard cities, the revolutionary and postrevolutionary experience heightened artisan consciousness and brought working people into the political arena as never before. Once in that arena, they did not unify completely or act collectively at all moments. But the realization spread that the changes overcoming urban society could not be addressed by autonomous individuals who singly exercised their political rights but only by collective actions and intertrade alliances. The advent of a "gemeinschaft of mind" was hastened, moreover, by the residential class clustering that was emerging. For the first time in the history of American cities, political alignments became closely connected with neighborhoods and wards and were reflected not simply in national and state political parties but also in the subcommunities that gathered themselves in trade associations, militia companies, and mutual aid societies.[48]

Much remains to be done on urban politics, especially in the neglected period between the end of the Revolution and the beginning of the Jacksonian era. Preoccupation with the emerging national party system has obscured the dynamics of local politics, which seem, to judge by a few recent studies, to have been far more clamorous and less cleansed of mob activity than is usually supposed (although there is no gainsaying the fact that public authorities became less tolerant of mob activity and moved ruthlessly to suppress it after the Revolution). There may be much more continuity between the revolutionary period and the 1820s than meets the eye. By the latter decade, the democratic strivings inherited from the revolutionary era were bursting through the boundaries of conventional Jacksonian party politics in most of the cities. An extraordinary set of characters—Paineite free thinkers, Jacobin

feminists, Owenite visionaries, radical political economists, and early socialists—
were mobilizing the lower orders and sometimes middle-class people with their
various formulas for reforming a republic that they believed had turned its back on
the revolutionary promise of freedom, equality, and the elimination of corruption
and exploitation. The work of Sean Wilentz and Paul Gilje on New York's plebian
politics after the 1780s and Susan Davis's fruitful explorations of the rise of the folk
street drama "as a mode of political communication" in early-nineteenth-century
Philadelphia are just three of the new pioneering works that are illuminating the neglected period in the history of the early republic in ways that suggest the responses
outside the formal realm of politics devised by urban people who saw themselves
contending with threatening new situations.[49]

A brief look at voluntary organizations in the postrevolutionary cities provides evidence of one important way in which urban people knit themselves together in subcommunities in order to cope with the forces of social change that were rending the
larger community. Three decades into the nineteenth century, Alexis de Tocqueville
would marvel at the fervor of Americans to join local voluntary groups. "Americans
of all ages, all conditions, and all dispositions," he wrote, "constantly form associations. They have not only commercial and manufacturing companies . . . but associations of a thousand other kinds, religious, moral, serious, futile, general or restricted,
enormous or diminutive."[50] What the French observer described had its roots, in fact,
in the postrevolutionary seaboard cities where a phenomenal growth of voluntary associations occurred.

For Tönnies, voluntary associations were characteristic of a system of *gesellschaft*
because they were special interest groups directed at particular, not universal, ends
and were based on contractual agreements among their members, whose principal
aim was to advance their own wealth. In a *gesellschaftlich* society, "which presup-
poses every individual person with separate spheres of rational will," Tönnies argued,
these associations provided "the only possible type of interrelationship." Yet, after
witnessing the rise of producer and consumer cooperatives among the laboring poor
of Germany in the early twentieth century, Tönnies discerned in these associations the
revival of "a principle of gemeinschaft economy" that might lead to the resuscitation
of "other forms of gemeinschaft."[51]

The potential of voluntary associations in the postrevolutionary era to act as an-
tipodal centers of urban group activity deserves much more attention from historians.
Voluntary societies were not new to the postrevolutionary cities, of course. Charitable societies and fire companies had existed since the early eighteenth century, and
journeymen's societies were not far behind. The latter, established to buffer aspiring
craftsmen against the economic cycles that could undermine the security of those
living close to the margin, served first as mutual aid associations but almost as importantly as nodal points of social and political organization.

After 1760, urban voluntary associations multiplied rapidly, if we are to judge
by the cases of New York and Boston, the two cities that have been most closely
examined in this regard.[52] Volunteer fire companies, reform-minded benevolent organizations, volunteer militia companies, and literary, artistic, and scientific groups

mushroomed, attracting thousands of city dwellers to endeavors that provided them with the satisfactions of sociability as well as service. Composed only of men before the Revolution, such associations began forming among urban women as well by the late 1780s, bringing into collective activity the social group that had been tradition-ally most restricted to functioning within the family and whose options in the eco-nomic sphere were beginning to narrow at this time. By 1800, at least seventy-eight voluntary organizations were meeting in Boston, whereas only fifteen had existed in 1760.[53] Parallel growth, as yet charted only imperfectly, seems to have occurred in other cities as well. Among urban women, the 1790s and the first decade of the nineteenth century witnessed a spectacular growth of such groups, which far more than their male counterparts were devoted to religion, reform, and supporting the marginal people of the growing cities—the poor and sick, the orphaned and insane, and criminals and prostitutes.[54]

Why did this movement that made America a nation of joiners blossom in the late-eighteenth-century cities? To some extent the new concept of citizenship ushered in by the Revolution, which enjoined the active involvement of citizens, nourished the desire to enlist in order to improve and perfect the new republic. Apathy, the revolutionary generation learned, was the enemy of a virtuous, improving people. A number of voluntary associations in the cities, founded out of educational, artistic, and reformist motives, fit this explanation. But a larger number of voluntary groups seem to have originated as mechanisms for buffering people against the forces of change or as a means of promoting or resisting change. Some organizations were explicitly meant to advance or defend the interest of a group, such as the journeymen's societ-ies that grew rapidly between 1780 and 1820. Others were purposefully exclusionary, offering members a "surrogate community of harmony" in a world that had thrown off the patriarchal ideal and, in its political ideology, had abandoned hierarchy.[55] The best example here is the Masonic lodges, which grew at a dizzy pace in the late-eighteenth-century cities. Modeling their organization to recapture the world as they thought it used to be, the Masons instituted an elaborate hierarchy, maintained strict deference between ranks, and prized harmony and stability.[56] Their fraternity was, in fact, a surrogate family, although by drawing heavily on the leisure time and emotional resources of their male members, they may have simultaneously weakened traditional family life.

More research is needed on urban voluntary associations to determine the com-position and motives of their members and their meaning to those who joined. Tentatively, it appears that they were of many kinds and purposes; but all of them served particular segments of much enlarged and diversified urban populations by creating communities within communities. Facilitating interpersonal contact, providing small-scale arenas for self-improvement and mutual reinforcement, and training ordinary people in organizational skills, they helped to stitch together urban centers that sometimes seem, in historical perspective, to have been coming apart at the seams. Often engaging in highly ritualized public display, such associations sharpened their members' group consciousness and impressed upon their fellow urbanites the extent to which various groups regarded themselves as distinct. Yet the marching of Masons through the streets, or the procession of artisans under emblems of their trade, also made visible how extensively urban life involved group as against individual activity.[57]

The eighteenth-century cities, in sum, while places of rapid change, were also places of continuous readjustment. Urban people had to be resilient, for they were regularly buffeted by serious blows from economic and natural sources. Bostonians, for example, suffered major fires on ten occasions between 1653 and 1760 that wiped out as much as a tenth of the town's buildings with each conflagration. They withstood eight raging smallpox epidemics between 1640 and 1730, sustained military casualties proportionate to World War II death tolls four times from 1690 to 1780, and twice between 1740 and 1780 experienced hyperinflation that nearly wiped out the value of currency. Nevertheless, Boston, like other cities, survived, recovered, and grew. To a considerable extent this was possible because city people became adept at creating viable subcommunities, ranging from neighborhoods to voluntary associations, and they learned to use them to defend their interests, perpetuate sociability, and cope with (and sometimes counteract) structural changes affecting urban life.

NOTES

1. P. J. Corfield, *The Impact of English Towns, 1700–1800* (Oxford, 1982), 7–8; the population data for American towns are drawn from the published decade censuses.

2. Gary B. Nash, *The Urban Crucible: Social Change, Political Consciousness, and the Origins of the American Revolution* (Cambridge, 1979), passim; Ferdinand Tönnies, *Community and Society,* translated and ed. by Charles P. Loomis (East Lansing, MI, 1957).

3. Thomas Bender, *Community and Social Change in America* (New Brunswick, NJ, 1978), ch. 1–2.

4. Ibid., 31, 33. In attenuated form this had been Tönnies's original formulation. See *Community and Society,* 227.

5. Henry A. Gemery, "European Emigration to North America, 1700–1820: Numbers and Quasi-Numbers," *Perspectives in American History,* New Series, 1 (1984). 283–342.

6. The churches are listed in the Boston and Philadelphia city directories for 1800.

7. Statistics on urban slave populations are taken from Nash, *Urban Crucible,* passim, and, for Charleston, from Evarts B. Greene and Virginia S. Harrington, *American Population Before the Census of 1790* (New York, 1932), 178. On the absence of blacks in all English towns except London, see James Walvin, *Black and White: The Negro and English Society, 1555–1945* (London, 1973), ch. 4.

8. Gary B. Nash, "Forging Freedom: The Emancipation Experience in the Northern Seaport Towns, 1775–1820," in Ira Berlin and Ronald Hoffman, eds., *Slavery and Freedom in the Age of the American Revolution* (Charlottesville, VA, 1983), 3–48.

9. Ira Berlin, *Slaves Without Masters: The Free Negro in the Antebellum South* (New York, 1974), ch. 2.

10. Among the new community studies of free blacks are Jay Coughtry, *Creative Survival: The Providence Black Community in the 19th Century* (Providence, RI, 1982); Robert J. Cottrol, *The Afro-Yankees: Providence's Black Community in the Antebellum Era* (Westport, CT, 1982); Leroy Graham, *Baltimore: The Nineteenth Century Black Capital* (Washington, DC, 1982); Susanne Lebsock, *The Free Women of Petersburg: Status and Culture in a Southern Town, 1784–1860* (New York, 1984).

11. *Industry and Frugality Proposed as the Surest Means to Make Us a Rich and Flourishing People* . . . (Boston, 1753), 8–10.

12. *Reports of the Record Commissioners of the City of Boston* (39 vols., Boston, 1876–1908), XIV, 222, 240.

13. "Report of the Contributors to the Relief and Employment of the Poor," in *Pennsylvania Gazette,* May 29, 1776.

14. John Alexander, *Render Them Submissive: Responses to Poverty in Philadelphia, 1760–1800* (Amherst, MA, 1980); Raymond A. Mohl, *Poverty in New York, 1783–1825* (New York, 1971); Douglas Jones, "The Transformation of the Law of Poverty in Eighteenth Century Massachusetts," *Publications of the Colonial Society of Massachusetts,* 62 (1984), 153–190; Lynn Withey, *Urban Growth in Colonial Rhode Island: Newport and Providence in the Eighteenth Century* (Albany, 1984), ch. 4.

15. Withey, *Urban Growth in Colonial Rhode Island,* 123.

16. Sharon V. Salinger and Charles Wetherell, "A Note on the Population of Prerevolutionary Philadelphia," *Pennsylvania Magazine of History and Biography,* 109 (1985), 369–386.

17. J. H. Powell, *Bring Out Your Dead: The Great Plague of Yellow Fever in Philadelphia in 1793* (Philadelphia. 1949); John Duffy, *A History of Public Health in New York City, 1625–1866* (New York, 1968).

18. *The Nature and Design of the Hospitable Society* (Philadelphia, 1803), quoted in Ronald Douglas Schultz, "Thoughts Among the People: Popular Thought, Radical Politics, and the Making of Philadelphia's Working Class" (Ph.D. diss., University of California, Los Angeles, 1985), 322.

19. Among the occupations listed on the 1789 Philadelphia tax assessor's list that indicate the specialization occurring within the luxury trades were bucklemaker, combmaker, muffmaker, looking glass maker, fan maker, and piano maker. On the rise of a consumer ethos, see Carole Shammas, *The Pre-industrial Consumer in England and America* (Oxford, Eng., 1990).

20. The causal connection that many urban commentators perceived between the simultaneous rise of great wealth and dire poverty was expressed repeatedly from the 1760s onward. See Nash, *The Urban Crucible,* passim.

21. Peter H. Lindert and Jeffrey Williamson, *Inequality in America: A Macroeconomic History* (New York, 1980); James A. Henretta, "Wealth and Social Structure," in Jack P. Greene and J. R. Pole, eds., *Colonial British America: Essays in the New History of the Early Modern Era* (Baltimore, 1984), 276.

22. John J. Waters, "Patrimony, Succession, and Social Stability: Guilford, Connecticut in the Eighteenth Century," *Perspectives in American History,* 10 (1976), 156; Jackson Turner Main, "The Distribution of Property in Colonial Connecticut," in James Kirby Martin, ed., *The Human Dimensions of Nation Making: Essays on Colonial and Revolutionary America* (Madison, WI, 1976); and James A. Henretta, "Families and Farms: *Mentalité* in Pre-Industrial America," *William and Mary Quarterly,* 35 (1978), 6–8.

23. Billy G. Smith, "Inequality in Late Eighteenth-Century Philadelphia: A Note on Its Nature and Growth," *William and Mary Quarterly,* 41 (1984), 629–645.

24. Quoted in James Douglas Tagg, "Benjamin Franklin Bache and the Philadelphia 'Aurora'" (Ph.D. diss., Wayne State University, 1973), 155.

25. Tom W. Smith, "The Dawn of the Urban-Industrial Age: The Social Structure of Philadelphia, 1790–1830" (Ph.D. diss., University of Chicago, 1980), 151. The exclusion of a large percentage of free black householders from the assessment lists is not usually noted by historians; when this omission is corrected, the percentage of unassessed in the urban population by the early nineteenth century grows to about 50–60 percent.

26. Betsy Blackmar. "Rewalking the 'Walking City': Housing and Property Relations in New York City, 1780–1840," *Radical History Review,* no. 21 (1980), 131–148; Arthur L. Jensen, *The Maritime Commerce of Colonial Philadelphia* (Madison, WI, 1963), 126–27.

27. *Federal Gazette,* April 27, 1793.

28. Blackmar, "Walking City," 132–139; Smith, "Dawn of the Urban-Industrial Age," 151, table 60; Sharon V. Salinger and Charles Wetherell, "Wealth and Renting in Prerevolutionary Philadelphia," *Journal of American History,* 71 (1985), 829.

29. Charles G. Steffen, *The Mechanics of Baltimore: Workers and Politics in the Age of Revolution, 1763–1812* (Urbana, IL, 1984), 40; Smith, "Inequality in Late Colonial Philadelphia," 633, table 1.

30. Peter Clark, ed., *The Transformation of English Provincial Towns, 1600–1800* (London, 1984); Allan Kulikoff, "The Progress of Inequality in Revolutionary Boston," *William and Mary Quarterly,* 28 (1971), 375–412; Smith, "Dawn of the Urban-Industrial Age," 278–279; Carl Abbott, "The Neighborhoods of New York, 1760–1775," *New York History,* 55 (1974), 35–54.

31. Nash, "Forging Freedom," 40–43; Leonard P. Curry, *The Free Black in Urban America, 1800–1850: The Shadow of the Dream* (Chicago, 1981), ch. 4.

32. Smith, "Dawn of the Urban-Industrial Age," 278, table 89.

33. Steffen, *Mechanics of Baltimore,* ch. 2, 5; Sean Wilentz, *Chants Democratic: New York City and the Rise of the American Working Class, 1788–1850* (New York, 1984), ch. 1–2, passim; Bruce Laurie, *Working People of Philadelphia, 1800–1850* (Philadelphia, 1980), ch. 1–2, passim.

34. Lisa Lubow, "Journeymen and Masters: The Changing Relations of Artisan Labor [in Boston]" (dissertation in progress, University of California, Los Angeles).

35. *1820 Census of Manufactures, National Archives, Return of Robert Wellford [Philadelphia],* quoted in Schultz, "Thoughts Among the People," 320.

36. Claudia Golden, "The Changing Status of Women in the Economy of the Early Republic: Quantitative Evidence" (paper delivered at the Social Science History Association Conference on Quantitative Methods in History, California Institute of Technology, March, 1983), 13.

37. Ibid., 13–18. Golden's findings largely confirm what Mary Beard argued four decades ago in *Women as Force in History: A Study in Traditions and Realities* (New York, 1946).

38. Gary B. Nash, "The Failure of Female Factory Labor in Colonial Boston," *Labor History,* 20 (1979), 165–188.

39. Cynthia Shelton, "The Role of Labor in Early Industrialization: Philadelphia, 1787–1837," *Journal of the Early Republic,* 4 (1984), 365–394.

40. Kulikoff, "Progress of Inequality," 379; Gary Kulik, "Pawtucket Village and the Strike of 1824: The Origins of Class Conflict in Rhode Island," *Radical History Review,* 17 (1978), 5–37; Barbara M. Tucker, *Samuel Slater and the Origins of the American Textile Industry, 1790–1860* (Ithaca, NY, 1984).

41. Christine Stansell, "The Origins of the Sweatshop: Women and Early Industrialization in New York City," in Michael H. Frisch and Daniel J. Walkowitz, eds., *Working-Class America: Essays on Labor, Community, and American Society* (Urbana, IL, 1983), 78–103.

42. Edward Countryman, *A People in Revolution: The American Revolution and Political Society in New York, 1760–1790* (Baltimore, 1981); Gary B. Nash, "Artisans and Politics in Eighteenth-Century Philadelphia," in Margaret Jacob and James Jacob, eds., *The Origins of Anglo-American Radicalism* (London, 1984), 162–182; Steven Rosswurm, "'As a Lyen out of His Den': Philadelphia's Popular Movement, 1776–1780," in ibid., 300–323; Richard Walsh, *Charleston's Sons of Liberty: A Study of the Artisans, 1763–1789* (Columbia, SC, 1959). For a contrasting view of prerevolutionary urban politics and the tension between capitalist develop-

ment and the structure of urban values, see Christine Leigh Heyrman, *Commerce and Culture: The Maritime Communities of Colonial Massachusetts, 1690–1750* (New York, 1984). Heyrman's study stops on the eve of the Seven Years' War and therefore is not altogether comparable to the studies cited above.

43. *Pennsylvania Gazette,* September 27, 1770.

44. Alfred F. Young, *The Democratic-Republicans of New York: The Origins, 1763–1797* (Chapel Hill, NC, 1967), passim; William Bruce Wheeler, "Polities in Nature's Republic: The Development of Political Parties in the Seaport Cities in the Federalist Era" (Ph.D. diss., University of Virginia, 1967); Schultz, "Thoughts Among the People," ch. 4–5; Steffen, *Mechanics of Baltimore;* Howard B. Rock, *Artisans of the New Republic: The Tradesmen of New York City in the Age of Jefferson* (New York, 1979).

45. Drew R. McCoy, *The Elusive Republic: Political Economy in Jeffersonian America* (Chapel Hill, NC, 1980); Schultz, "Thoughts Among the People"; Wilentz, *Chants Democratic;* Rock, *Artisans of the New Republic;* Steffen, *Mechanics of Baltimore.*

46. Philadelphia *Aurora,* January 14, 1807; November 28, 1805, quoted in Schultz, "Thoughts Among the People," 296, 303.

47. Schultz, "Thoughts Among the People," and Wheeler, "Politics in Nature's Republic" are the two best studies to consult.

48. Rock, *Artisans of the New Republic*; Steffen, *Mechanics of Baltimore*; Schultz, "Thoughts Among the People."

49. Wilentz, *Chants Democratic;* Thomas Slaughter, "Mobs and Crowds, Riots and Brawls: The History of Early American Political Violence" (unpublished), 18–22, 47; Paul A. Gilje, "Mobocracy: Popular Disturbances in Post-Revolutionary New York City, 1783–1829" (Ph.D. diss., Brown University, 1980); Susan G. Davis, *Parades and Power: Street Theatre in Nineteenth-Century Philadelphia* (Philadelphia, 1986); Amy Bridges, *A City in the Republic: Antebellum New York and the Origin of Machine Politics* (Cambridge, 1984).

50. Alexis de Tocqueville, *Democracy in America,* quoted in Richard D. Brown, "The Emergence of Voluntary Associations in Massachusetts, 1760–1830," *Journal of Voluntary Action Research,* 2 (1973), 64.

51. Tönnies, *Community and Society.*

52. Brown, "Voluntary Associations in Massachusetts," 64–73; Jacquetta Mae Haely, "Voluntary Organizations in Pre-Revolutionary New York City, 1750–1776" (Ph.D. diss., SUNY, Binghamton, 1976); Anne M. Boylan, "Women in Groups: An Analysis of Women's Benevolent Organizations in New York and Boston, 1797–1840," *Journal of American History,* 71 (1984), 497–523.

53. Brown, "Voluntary Associations in Massachusetts."

54. Boylan, "Women in Groups," passim.

55. Brown, "Voluntary Associations in Massachusetts," 71.

56. Dorothy Ann Lipson, *Freemasonry in Federalist Connecticut* (Princeton, NJ, 1977), ch. 2.

57. Davis, *Parades and Power,* passim.

Chapter 2

Slavery, Emancipation, and Class Formation in Colonial and Early National New York City

Leslie M. Harris

In 1626, the first African slaves arrived on Manhattan Island. As in the South, black slave labor was central to the day-to-day survival and the economic life of Europeans in the colonial North, and no part of the colonial North relied more heavily on slavery than Manhattan. Slave labor enabled the survival of the first European settlers in Dutch-governed New Amsterdam in the seventeenth century. In the eighteenth century, the British sought to heighten white New Yorkers' reliance on slave labor and the slave trade to make Manhattan the chief North American slave port and economic center. Under both the Dutch and the British, slaves performed vital agricultural tasks in the rural areas surrounding New York City. As New York became known as a center of slave labor, few European laborers, free or indentured, chose to emigrate there. By the end of the seventeenth century, New York City had a larger black population than any other North American city. The ratio of slaves to whites in the total population was comparable to that in Maryland and Virginia at the time. In the eighteenth century, New York City was second only to Charleston and New Orleans in the number of slaves it held. Until 1827, when New York State emancipated its remaining slaves, New York City contained the largest urban slave population outside of the South. New York State was second only to New Jersey in holding the greatest number of slaves in the northern states.[1]

In colonial New York, Europeans created a predominantly black and enslaved working class. Racial slavery became the foundation of New Yorkers' definitions of race, class, and freedom far into the nineteenth century. This essay, rooted in the growing secondary literatures on blacks in New York City, North American colonial slavery, and pre–Civil War labor history, demonstrates the centrality of slavery, emancipation, and race to class formation in colonial and early national New York City. Labor historians studying the roots of the American working class in the antebellum period have only begun to explore the role that racial identity plays in defining class identity

Reprinted from *Journal of Urban History* 30 (March 2004): 339 59. Reprinted with the permission of Sage Publications for blacks, whites, and other racial and ethnic groups in America.[2] The latest works in pre–Civil War labor history build on the model of class formation and identity in the United States formulated by historian Herbert Gutman, who drew on the work of British labor historian E. P. Thompson to examine the existence of class identity and ideology not only on the job but in the social and cultural expressions of U.S. workers and in their lived experiences.[3] But these works neglect the unique role that slavery and racism played for both whites and blacks in the development of definitions of the American working class in the North as well as in the South.[4] Sean Wilentz's *Chants Democratic: New York City and the Rise of the American Working Class, 1789–1850* and Christine Stansell's *City of Women: Sex and Class in New York, 1789–1860* are, deservedly, among the most acclaimed studies on the roots of the American working class, and on New York City in particular. But slavery and emancipation in New York have no bearing on the class developments they describe. Black New Yorkers barely exist in these books. Both authors create a white hegemony more powerful than that which actually existed in the eighteenth and nineteenth centuries.[5]

African slavery and emancipation were central to the creation of New York's (and the nation's) working class. As Ira Berlin, Barbara Fields, and others have argued, the initial purpose of slavery in the Americas was to secure a labor force—to make class. But as they created class with African slavery, white New Yorkers and others also developed the racial justifications for the enslavement of Africans above all other groups of workers. Haltingly under the Dutch, and more consistently under the British, Europeans in colonial New York defined blacks as the only group fit to be slaves, amid a society with numerous racial and religious groups. The use of racial ideologies that defined blacks as inferior to other racial groups and thus enslaveable condemned blacks to unequal status into the nineteenth century. Europeans did not always define the terms of racial inferiority consistently, but their creation of race meant that when blacks celebrated freedom in 1827, their struggle for equality in New York City had just begun.[6]

In 1626, the Dutch West India Company imported the first eleven African slaves to New Amsterdam at the southern tip of Manhattan Island, the major settlement in New Netherland. Throughout the Dutch period, the colony attracted few European indentured servants, especially relative to other North American colonies. African slaves became the most stable element of the New Netherland working class. The Dutch West India Company's importation and employment of most of the colony's slave labor enabled the survival of the Europeans at Manhattan and what limited economic success the colony experienced. Company slaves provided labor for the building and upkeep of the colony. The company also employed its slaves in agricultural labor. In 1625, the company, in an attempt to diversify the colony's economy, established six "bouwerys," or farms, along the eastern and western shores of Manhattan Island, just north of the settlement. By 1626, company slaves worked these farms, and the produce grown fed the colony's inhabitants.[7]

Throughout the North American colonies, the status of slaves fluctuated during the seventeenth century, and the Dutch colony of New Netherland was no exception to this. No European governments passed laws regulating slavery before the 1660s in the North American colonies; Virginia established the first comprehensive slave codes between 1660 and 1682. In addition, the Dutch did not establish separate slave or black codes rooted in racial difference—slavery was not explicitly limited to Africans, and indeed, the colony contained Native American slaves. In New Netherland, African slaves could testify in court and bring suit against whites; had the same trial rights as whites; could own property, excepting real estate or other slaves; and could work for wages. In 1644, the establishment of half-freedom gave landownership and some autonomy to the first eleven slaves as a reward for their role in defending the colony during Kieft's War. Although this status originally could not be passed down to the children of the half-free, many of these black landowners managed to negotiate similar conditions of autonomy for their wives, children, and other relatives. Slaves, white and black indentured servants, and free black and white workers held more rights and experiences in common in New Amsterdam (and indeed in North America) than would be true in the eighteenth and nineteenth centuries.[8]

But during the seventeenth century, African ancestry became increasingly important in defining the bound segment of the working class. Practically from the arrival of the first slaves, European indentured servants and free laborers sought to distinguish themselves from African slaves because of competition with them in a tight labor market; one slave could be purchased for the same amount as a free laborer's annual wages. In 1628, white workers requested that the Dutch West India Company not train slaves for skilled labor as it did in other American colonies. In appeasing white laborers by agreeing to exclude slaves from skilled occupations such as bricklayer and carpenter, the Dutch West India Company unwittingly encouraged settlers to use racial differences to determine who was suitable for certain occupations. By the 1650s, European settlers had begun to declare publicly that Africans were not as competent skilled laborers as Europeans. When the officers of the Dutch West India Company tried to encourage the New Netherland settlers to train slaves as skilled workers, Director General Stuyvesant replied that there were "no able negroes fit to learn a trade."[9] The Dutch were only the first group of Europeans to racialize jobs and skills in Manhattan, leading to the exclusion of blacks, slave and free, from lucrative occupations. Despite these attempts at exclusion, by 1660 New Amsterdam, through increasingly regular shipments of slaves from the Dutch West India Company, was the most important slave port in North America, and enslaved blacks were at work in many parts of the colony's economy.[10]

By the end of Dutch rule in New Netherland in 1664, Europeans in the colony had established beliefs and practices that reinforced concepts of racial inferiority and thus justified the enslavement of Africans. The British takeover of New Netherland in 1664 led to the legal codification of African slavery in the colony. The British government awarded the colony to the Duke of York, who renamed both New Netherland and New Amsterdam as New York. With British rule, slavery in New York gained a new stringency. Partly this was due to the Duke of York's interest in making Manhattan a major North American slave port, and the New York colony a major market for slaves. The colony continued to rely on African slave labor as the foundation of its working class. The British colonial administration expended little effort in attracting European free workers or indentured servants to the colony. As a result, few Europeans entered the New York labor market; rather, many attempted to establish independent farms or businesses. More Europeans went to Pennsylvania, which they perceived as having a better market for indentured servants and free laborers and better opportunities to own land. Between 1698 and 1738, the slave population increased at a faster rate than did the white population in the colony of New York.[11]

New York's creation of its slave code, beginning in 1665, was part of a trend in all North American colonies, led by Virginia, to solidify the right of Europeans to own slaves. These laws linked slavery to Africans alone, completely separating slavery from its previous religious foundation in which, at least theoretically, only non-Christians could be enslaved. New York's first laws stated that no Christians could be enslaved unless they had willingly sold themselves into slavery or been captured in war. Initially, Christian Native Americans and Africans were treated equally under this law. But increasingly the British placed Africans, Christian and non-Christian, in a class by themselves. By 1679, the provincial assembly, fearing retribution from the Native American tribes that lived in the colony, stated that no "native inhabitants" of the colony could be enslaved. And in 1706, a British law stated explicitly that "Negroes only shall be slaves" and that "baptism shall not alter the condition of servitude of the Negro slave." This legally sundered the already tenuous connection between Christianity and freedom for African slaves. In the same law, the British ensured the hereditary nature of slavery by having children inherit the mother's condition of slavery or freedom.[12]

Thus, by the first decade of the eighteenth century, the British had affirmed hereditary African slavery in the New York colony in law. But the economic role of slaves in the colony before midcentury was less clear. New York's economy grew slowly at the beginning of the eighteenth century, and settlers had no need for large numbers of unskilled laborers, slave or otherwise. Those colonists who did purchase slaves preferred small numbers of acculturated or skilled slaves, whom they could train for various businesses such as tailoring, carpentry, and sail making. Estate owners in rural areas of the colony who also might have bought unskilled slaves did not improve their acreage for agriculture on a large scale until later in the century. Adolph Philipse, one of the largest slave owners in the colony, had eleven hundred European tenants on his ninety thousand acres of Hudson Valley land but only 23 slaves. The Royal African Company's attempts to sell large cargoes of slaves at fixed prices, as it did in plantation areas, initially failed. By 1720, the New York colony contained only 5,740 slaves, compared to 12,499 in Maryland and 26,550 in Virginia. Still, New York held the largest number of slaves in the North—its closest northern rival was New Jersey, with 2,385 slaves in 1720.[13]

After 1737, the Manhattan port experienced a large increase in trade, generating a need for unskilled labor. At the same time, wars in Europe hampered the flow of European immigrants. The importation of slaves escalated to meet the city's demand for unskilled labor. In the thirty-four-year period between 1737 and 1771, the Royal African Company imported 4,394 slaves into Manhattan—more than double the number of slaves imported during the previous seventy-three years. The number of slaves in the colony—just more than 19,000—still lagged far behind the more than 250,000 slaves in the Chesapeake region. But New York had far and away the most slaves of the northern colonies—New Jersey's population was only 8,220, while Pennsylvania and Connecticut had 5,561 and 5,698, respectively. And the New York colony held more slaves at this time than either Georgia or Louisiana. By the mid-eighteenth century, New York held the largest number of slaves of any colony north of Maryland, and Manhattan held the third largest concentration of slaves in a North American city, after Charleston and New Orleans.[14]

Ownership of slaves in British New York spread widely among the white population. From the merchant elite to small businessmen, owning slaves was seen as a profitable enterprise. Overall in Manhattan, 40 percent of European households contained slaves, averaging 2.4 slaves per household. Because of the wide distribution of slaves in Manhattan, slaves performed every type of labor that free whites did. Particularly before midcentury, Europeans employed slave men in skilled occupations such as carpentry, tailoring, blacksmithing, shoemaking, baking, and butchering. As the need for laborers to service ships and warehouses increased after midcentury, larger numbers of male slaves were employed on the docks. Slave women, usually no more than one per household, aided free and indentured white women in cooking, cleaning, and child care. In artisan households, slave women, like the white women of artisan families, also assisted the men in their skilled tasks as necessary. In the rural hinterlands of the city, slave men and women performed agricultural labor on farms. But slaves on farms also learned skilled jobs. As self-contained units, farms depended on their male laborers to be able to construct or repair buildings, shoe horses, and perform other kinds of skilled labor necessary to operating an agricultural enterprise. Women might make clothing and even weave fabric. Thus, both rural and urban slaves had exposure to a variety of skilled and unskilled occupations.[15]

As had been true under Dutch rule, white workers continued to worry about the effects of competition with slave labor. In 1686, the licensed porters of New York City complained that the employment of slaves in the markets cut into their laboring opportunities. Although New York City's local governing body, the Common Council, banned the use of slaves as porters for imported or exported goods, apparently few slave owners paid attention to the law. In 1691, the porters again complained that they were "so impoverished . . . they could not by their labours get a competency for the maintenance of themselves and families." Skilled workers too feared competition from slaves. In 1737 and again in 1743, New York's coopers complained to the colonial government that "the pernicious custom of breeding slaves to trade" reduced "the honest and industrious tradesmen . . . to poverty for want of employ." They complained that New York City merchants used their slaves to build barrels for themselves, and sometimes even competed with the coopers by selling the barrels to others. Although the lieutenant governor agreed with the skilled workers, they were unable to convince New York's Colonial Assembly to pass protective legislation favoring white workers over slave owners. Only cart men successfully excluded blacks, slave and free, from their trade.[16]

The increased use of slave labor in the New York colony benefited slave owners at the expense of free white workers. The widespread use of slave labor was part of the reason that relatively few indentured servants chose Manhattan as a destination. Although exact numbers are unavailable for much of the colonial period, passenger lists of Europeans traveling from Europe and the Caribbean to the Americas reveal that few indentured servants listed Manhattan as their destination. Even the convict trade in servants appears to have favored the Chesapeake over the colony. New Yorkers at the time believed that the low numbers of indentured servants relative to other colonies were due to the presence of large numbers of slaves. New York's colonial governor William Cosby said in 1734, "I see with concern that whilst the neighboring Provinces are filled with honest, useful and labourious white people, the truest riches and surest strength of a country, this Province seems regardless of . . . the disadvantages that attend the too great importation of negroes and convicts." The classing of blacks with convicts despite the fact that the colony held few, if any, convict laborers reveals the low repute in which Europeans held slaves morally and as laborers. In 1757, Lieutenant-Governor James De Lancey urged the colonial legislature to place a poll tax on slaves to discourage their purchase. Declining numbers of slaves would "naturally tend to introduce white servants, which will augment the strength of the country."[17] However, the colony never enacted restrictions on the importation of slaves.

The fact that only small numbers of European indentured servants traveled to eighteenth-century New York exaggerated the distinction between enslaved blacks and white laborers. Unlike Pennsylvania or Massachusetts, where large numbers of indentured servants composed a vital part of the working class, few European immigrants to New York experienced bondage, and thus were less likely to identify with slaves. In this way, the labor system in New York City was similar to that of the southern colonies, which also experienced the arrival of a large number of slaves at the expense of European immigration.[18]

In addition, distinctions between the few bonded Europeans in New York and slaves increased in the eighteenth century. As Europeans survived their indentures in larger numbers, the similarities between their temporary status as white indentured servants and that of permanently enslaved blacks diminished. Colonial laws passed following the 1712 slave revolt exacerbated these distinctions by discouraging masters from freeing slaves and prohibiting blacks freed after 1712 from acquiring land. Such distinctions rooted the primary difference between black and white workers even more strongly in terms of slave or free status and then distinguished among free people according to racial difference, ultimately limiting free blacks to landless poverty. For blacks, the New York colony legally could not be a place of opportunity or upward mobility. Slave masters saw these racial and status distinctions rooted in free and slave labor as a means to keep control over their slaves and thus encouraged the growing division between white and black workers. White workers saw such differences as preserving their own access to wage work and to land, at the expense of slaves and free blacks.[19]

In New York City, however, distinctions between enslaved black and free white workers sometimes blurred. Slaves worked alongside and spent their leisure time with white workers. Together, slaves, indentured servants, and sailors frequented black- and white-run taverns as well as "tippling houses," private homes where individuals sold alcohol without licenses. As Thomas J. Davis has stated, though, the mixture of whites and blacks did not involve only entertainment. Rather, "sailors and other 'disorderly elements' exchanged views of the world with slaves. They brought news of wars, insurrections, protests, and defeats. They showed slaves a different philosophy and conception of life." Enslaved people, too, exchanged worldviews with white workers, providing local knowledge to sailors from distant ports, discussing the political economy of the city, and participating in the fencing operations that provided extra income to both blacks and whites. Many urban slave owners tolerated the relationships that evolved between blacks and whites of similar status as part of a parcel of privileges through which they hoped to keep the enslaved content.[20]

In small and large ways, enslaved black and free white workers joined together to protest their conditions and class-based grievances. The most dramatic instance of the interaction between these two groups within New York City's colonial working class was the so-called Negro Plot, a conspiracy among a group of blacks and whites to burn New York and seize the city for themselves. The 1741 conspiracy demonstrated that enslaved, free black, and white workers shared political and economic interests. Although the extent of the conspiracy remains unclear, a series of fires set between March 18 and April 6, 1741, led to a four-month investigation that revealed an extensive network of interracial relationships and crime among the lower classes.[21]

The ensuing trials revealed smoldering resentments among slaves and lower class whites toward the colony's elites. A difficult winter on top of a five-year economic depression had created resentment among suffering lower class whites against wealthier whites. Some lower class whites had moved to New York from rural areas, attracted by the excitement of the city and hoping to make their fortunes. Instead, they found themselves forced to resort to fencing stolen goods to survive. Irish soldiers and descendants of the original Dutch settlers who joined the plot felt like outsiders in New York's increasingly Anglicized society. For the majority of slave rebels, the specific grievance was enslavement: the conspirators hoped to become free by their actions. Slaves also resented masters who took away privileges from them, such as visiting family members or friends.[22]

Some white elites saw the 1741 plot as a way to prove to New Yorkers the need to rid the colony of blacks, enslaved and free. As one person stated, New York needed to be "replenished with white people," particularly laborers. But in general, New York's slave owners relied too heavily on slave labor to begin to end the system. Some tradesmen may have preferred to own slaves rather than to hold indentured servants or apprentices who would become rivals for them in business. Although white workers may have feared competition with slave labor, it was easier for them to travel to another colony for work than try to overthrow the slave system in New York. Those who remained in New York to seek their fortunes may have seen ownership of slaves as a sign of prestige to which they aspired.[23]

By the time of the Revolutionary War, black bondage was firmly entrenched in the city. Between 1703 and 1771, the slave population had doubled in New York. Masters had freed few slaves, and whites had driven free black people from the city. However, the influence of the Great Awakening also led New York City slaves, and a few whites, to believe more strongly in blacks' rights to freedom. The American Revolution would provide the next great opportunity for large numbers of slaves to pursue liberty.

In the decades between 1741 and the Revolutionary War, some whites slowly and haltingly began to question the role of slavery in society. Partially in response to the

Great Awakening, Quakers and Methodists began to reexamine the religious basis for
the enslavement of Africans. By the early 1770s, New York's Methodists and Quakers
had begun to fight against slavery by excluding slaveholders from their congregations.
Such actions encouraged enslaved blacks to continue to agitate for their freedom. But
the attempts by religious congregations and by blacks to call attention to the wrongs
of slavery had little impact in New York before the Revolutionary War.[24]

The ideology of the Revolution, with its emphasis on the unfairness of slavery,
provided a secular, political language with which to critique the holding of blacks as
slaves, one that New Yorkers embraced across differing religious affiliations. In addition, the practical effects of the war gave large numbers of blacks themselves an opportunity to seize their freedom. Both the British and American armies made limited
offers of freedom to those who would fight for them. And the disorder of the war itself
gave blacks the opportunity to flee their masters.[25]

Ultimately, however, the Revolution did not provoke the end of slavery in New
York. There were strong economic reasons for retaining slaves in New York City and
the Hudson Valley immediately after the Revolutionary War. Slaves continued to be
an important labor source for urban and rural New York until European immigration
increased in the 1790s. There were also ideological and political reasons for continuing to enslave blacks. The ideology of republicanism that emerged from the Revolutionary War depicted a society whose success depended on a virtuous, self-sufficient,
independent citizenry. This citizenry should not be beholden to any social group or
individual. Slaves, as the property of masters, were symbolically and literally the in-
verse of the ideal republican citizen. Furthermore, although whites resisting "slavery"
to England had been transformed into revolutionaries, whites interpreted black resistance to their enslavement negatively. This was particularly true in New York City,
where many blacks had sided with the occupying British during the war in return for
their freedom. Patriot whites saw such blacks as traitors. But whites viewed even those
slaves and free blacks who had assisted the colonists during the Revolutionary War
as unable to throw off the degradation of their own enslavement. White New Yorkers
only reluctantly granted freedom to those enslaved blacks who had fought on behalf
of the new nation.[26]

With the failure of the Revolutionary War to provide freedom for all blacks, a
group of men who became New York City's first antislavery activists, as well as
slaves themselves, began a new struggle to end slavery. The founding of the New
York Manumission Society in 1785 by a group of influential white New York City
residents was an important milestone in the process of convincing white New Yorkers that blacks were worthy of freedom. Soon after the founding of the society, a
prolonged state legislative debate on black freedom failed to produce an emancipation law. In response, the society established itself as the guardian of the rights of
New York State's slaves and free blacks. In 1787 in New York City, it founded the
first of several "African free schools" for free and enslaved black children. The society also provided legal assistance to those slaves sold South illegally and to those
blacks illegally held in bondage. In addition, the society's members began producing literature that they hoped would convince New Yorkers and others in the new
nation of the evils of slavery, and of the importance of freeing their slaves. Through

these activities, the society hoped to create, locally and nationally, an atmosphere increasingly unfriendly to slavery.[27]

But not until two decades after the Revolutionary War did the New York State legislature pass a law ending slavery. New York's first emancipation law, passed in 1799, freed no slaves and granted only partial freedom to the children of slaves: those born to slave mothers served lengthy indentures to their mothers' masters, until age twenty-three if female and twenty-eight if male. Finally, in 1817, Governor Daniel Tompkins convinced the New York State legislature to end slavery completely, and even then, the legislature took the longest time suggested by Tompkins—a decade.[28]

The gradual end of slavery and an influx of European immigrants into New York City in the 1790s led to a devaluation of black men and women as laborers. Increasingly, white employers hired European immigrants in positions in which they might have previously used slave labor. Partly, the new wage laborers were cheaper than owning and housing slaves. But whites were also increasingly uncomfortable with free black labor. This discomfort grew out of the ways in which republican ideology implicitly and explicitly defined blacks as unequal. Republican ideology defined the best citizens as men whose public, political virtue was based on their economic independence from others. Such independence would allow these virtuous men to exercise the duties of citizenship for the public good. The initial formulations of republicanism rooted economic independence in ownership of land. In the late eighteenth and early nineteenth century, white urban workers began redefining the ideal republican citizens as craftsmen who performed "honest" work with their hands. These workers partially defined their virtue in opposition to elite men whom they termed nonproducers, such as bankers and Federalists. These men, white workers claimed, gained their wealth by exploiting others.[29]

Republicanism also influenced ideologies about women. Middle-class and elite white women were able to carve out a space for themselves as "republican mothers" and wives, who prepared their children in the ways of virtuous citizenship and kept a moral domestic space for their husbands. Working-class white women, on the other hand, found it more difficult to achieve the moral status and political influence implied by republican motherhood, if indeed they desired this status. The fact that most needed to work for wages to help support their families, and that many rejected evolving middle-class norms of behavior for women, excluded them from virtuousness as defined by the middle class; their working-class fathers and husbands often did not respect them much more. Theoretically, though, working-class white women could remake themselves as virtuous, if limited, republicans, and middle-class reformers offered to show working-class white women the way to achieve such a transformation.[30]

In contrast, blacks' historical and continuing association with enslavement devalued them in the eyes of whites. There were no virtuous roles possible for "slaves" in republican ideology. Slaves were the main symbol of dependency and lack of virtue in the new nation, particularly after the Revolutionary War's emphasis on freedom from "slavery" to England. In addition, the unskilled, low-status, low-wage jobs at which most free blacks worked devalued them as much in the eyes of whites as did the legacy of slavery. Whites believed that blacks who had been enslaved and in freedom held jobs as servants were the most degraded of workers, and farthest removed from the ideal republican citizen. In addition, whites often conflated the status of free blacks and slaves, conferring the alleged negative attributes of slavery—dependency, immorality—onto free blacks as well. In New York City, of those black domestics who lived in, one-third were employed by households that also owned slaves. Thus, in the minds of their employers and many other whites, the lines between slavery and freedom for these blacks during the emancipation period blurred. The intimate role that domestic servants played in the households of their employers supposedly rendered servants dependent on their employers not only for jobs but for political guidance. In a sense, domestic servants, male or female, were like wives and children, dependent on the master of the house for political protection and unable to vote. Domestic servants were not candidates for full republican citizenship.[31]

The employment of black domestics by Federalists and other elites impugned the political virtue of all blacks in the eyes of whites. But black men's and women's roles as domestics affected whites' views of blacks differently. Whites excluded black women from the best of women's roles in the new republic, as republican wives and mothers, because of their history of slavery and their continued servitude to others, rather than to their own families. In addition, for women working in the households of others, away from the watchful eyes of their families, such servitude could also imply a lack of sexual virtue. But even if freed from association with domestic servitude, black women would not attain the status of full citizens or represent the virtue of all blacks because they were women.

The position of black male domestic servants affected the definition of the black community more directly. The responsibility for control of women and for political representation in the early republic fell most fully on men. But whites believed that black male domestic servants' labor made them dependent and feminized, and thus incapable of being true republican citizens. Black men's roles as domestics devalued claims of independent black political activism, particularly when those men were domestics in the homes of Federalists. Newspaper editor Manuel Mordecai Noah caricatured a group of black servants discussing their participation in a recent election in 1821. "Harry," asks one male servant, "who did you vote for at de election?" Harry replies, "De federalists to be sure; I never votes for de mob." According to Harry, "Our gentlemen"— meaning his employers—"brought home tickets, and after dinner, ve all vent and voted." In the eyes of whites, the black population as a whole was feminized, politically dependent, and thus unfit for citizenship, first because of the fact that there were more women than men in New York City and, second, because black men held a disproportionate number of jobs as domestics.[32]

White workers also saw blacks as symbolic of changes in their own status that they feared in the newly industrializing nation. Increasingly in the early 1800s, new work processes limited white workers to unskilled, low-paying jobs. Master mechanics began to abandon the apprentice and journeyman systems and hired unskilled laborers to perform piecework to produce goods. Unskilled men but especially women and children put together shoes, clothing, and other articles in large supervised workshops (soon known as sweatshops) or at home. Employers paid these workers cheaply for their labor so that they could compete nationally and internationally and gain greater profits. These practices led to deskilling among white men formerly trained to become masters themselves. Masters increasingly used as cheap, unskilled labor the young white male apprentices and journeymen they had previously trained to own independent shops. These young men increasingly worked under masters long past the age at which they would have opened their own shops, for their wages no longer enabled them to save enough money to do so. The embargo of 1807 further clouded their chances for advancement and independence. When merchants were forbidden from trading with Britain, the major market for American goods, workers lost jobs. In New York by 1809, more than a thousand men were imprisoned for debt; half of these owed only a week's wages.[33]

Although free blacks were not heavily involved in the new putting-out system, their history of enslavement and their occupation in freedom of low-status jobs such as domestic work, chimney sweeping, sailing, and waitering represented symbolically and literally the worst fates that could befall white workers. Blacks themselves symbolized enslavement. Chimney sweeps' sooty appearance and resulting depiction as "black" in British and American accounts no doubt kept whites away from the occupation. Sailing, another occupation that employed large numbers of blacks, was seen as resembling slavery. Sailors since the eighteenth century had been referred to as children and as slaves, and they carried reputations of dependency and immorality. The discipline aboard ship could be interpreted by those on land as depriving sailors of independent political thought.[34]

In menial jobs that both blacks and whites held, workers occasionally organized across racial lines. In 1802, black and white New York sailors struck for a raise from ten dollars to fourteen dollars a month. And in 1853, black and white waiters together formed a waiters' union and struck for higher wages. But in general, New York City's white workers excluded blacks from most jobs in which unions formed and excluded both skilled and unskilled blacks from their organizing activities. Thus, whites excluded blacks from the evolving definition of working-class republicanism and white working-class organizing.[35]

Black workers did not simply acquiesce to whites' understanding of their occupational roles. Rather, they claimed varying levels of autonomy in the jobs to which they were limited, negotiating with their employers for their own or their families' needs. The struggle for autonomy was most difficult for live-in domestic workers, the vast majority of whom were women. Everyday tensions between domestics and employers sometimes erupted dramatically into arson during the emancipation years. But most domestics mediated in less dramatic ways between their desire for autonomy and stability for themselves and their families and the labor needs of the households they served. Some live-in domestics managed to convince their employers to help them pay to board their young children with neighbors. Others convinced employers to hire additional family members. More commonly, domestic laborers were able to take home cast-off clothing and extra food as well as their wages to their families.[36]

Black men and women also actively sought jobs that provided greater autonomy than domestic service. Washerwomen collected laundry at various households but washed the clothes in their own homes. Some washerwomen supplemented their income by taking in the children of domestic workers and other parents who worked outside the home. Male and female fruit peddlers, ragpickers, cart men, and day laborers also retained a relatively independent existence. The price of such independence, however, could be unreliable income that threatened economic stability.[37] Other occupations, such as bootblacking, chimney sweeping, and sailing, although viewed negatively in the eyes of whites, could provide the basis for community and economic stability for blacks. Although sailors' lives could result in long separations from families, black male sailors attained a greater degree of equality and freedom at sea than on land. This sense of equality combined with relatively high and stable earnings to enable black sailors to provide well for their families when in port. Seneca Village, the area of the city with the highest degree of black landownership in the antebellum era, was founded by a black bootblack, Andrew Williams, and the majority of black landowners there worked in service trades or were unskilled laborers.[38]

Manumission Society members also tried to elevate black labor in the eyes of white New Yorkers. Beginning in the 1790s, the society encouraged apprenticeship programs with skilled master craftsmen for black boys. In 1793, the society placed an article in the New York newspaper *The Argus*, encouraging whites and the small group of free black skilled workers to take in free black children as apprentices. In doing so, skilled workers would "raise the *African* character more" by "rescuing blacks from the state of servitude, to which they are now universally condemned."[39] Manumission Society members also encouraged equal value to the different types of work blacks and whites did. In 1808 and again in 1814, Samuel Wood published a picture book for children titled *The Cries of New-York*, which depicted a variety of jobs performed by blacks and whites throughout the city. At the heart of the book was an attempt to prevent both the poor and the wealthy, black and white, from disparaging honest labor. Wood stated that "we are formed for labour; and it is not only an injunction laid upon, but an honour to us, to be found earning our bread by the sweat of our brows."[40]

But the Manumission Society's support of blacks further distanced black workers from heavily Democratic-Republican white workers. Although New York's white artisans had supported the Federalists and George Washington in the 1780s, by the early 1800s many had begun to turn away from the Federalists to ally with the Jeffersonian Democratic-Republicans. The elitism of Federalist Party leaders, who wished to control the lower classes more than give them a free voice in politics, was a major factor in the defection of white workers from the party. Alexander Hamilton's belief that "Mechanics and Manufacturers will always be inclined with a few exceptions to give their voices to merchants in preference to persons of their own professions" encapsulated the hopes of the majority of Federalists for elite rule. In addition, the Federalists reneged on promises to control international trade through a tariff that would have favored New York's manufacturers. By 1794, a group of New York artisans had formed a Democratic Society, which criticized nonproducers such as bankers, merchants, and speculators as antirepublican and elevated small independent producers as the basic building blocks of a virtuous society.[41]

Although a number of blacks were artisans before the War of 1812, white Democratic-Republicans made no attempt to appeal to them politically. Because of the role of the Federalist Party in securing emancipation for New York's slaves, and Democratic-Republican ties to the slave South, New York's blacks largely supported the Federalists. The Republican Party in New York City exacerbated this antagonism by focusing on blacks as a key voting bloc that could prevent a Republican ascendancy in local and state politics. Republican inspectors at polling booths attempted to dissuade blacks from voting by harassing them for proof of their freedom. In 1811, the Republican-dominated New York State legislature made such harassment legal by passing "an Act to prevent frauds at election and slaves from voting." Blacks who wished to vote first had to obtain proof of their freedom from the mayor, recorder, or register; pay that person to draw up the necessary certificate; and then bring this proof of their freedom to the polls to vote. When a close assembly election in 1813, in the midst of war, was declared in favor of the Federalists, Republicans blamed the victory on the three hundred black New York City voters.[42]

Economic difficulties in the wake of the War of 1812 led to greater poverty for both blacks and whites, and white workers feared competition with blacks even more. After the War of 1812, white criticism of black public life grew sharper and more explicitly linked to issues of equal citizenship for blacks. The decision by the state legislature to free all slaves as of July 4, 1827, raised fears among whites that New York City's black population would continue to grow and potentially influence politics there.[43] Some white critics of black public life disparaged blacks' activities as weak attempts to behave as equal citizens. The rise of the colonization movement, which claimed that free blacks could not survive in the United States and should be "returned" to Africa, heralded a period of increased racism. Crime pamphlets more pointedly depicted the alleged dangers to the city of grog shops, dance halls, and oyster bars that catered to working-class blacks. Middle- and working-class whites excluded blacks from mainstream civic celebrations and threatened blacks' parades with jeers, mockery, and violence. Central to this time of disappointment for blacks was the disfranchisement of the majority of the state's black men in the new 1821 constitution, even as white men gained universal suffrage. State legislators focused on the alleged immoral and dependent behavior of New York City blacks to demonstrate that blacks should have to prove their political equality before gaining the right to vote.

Some legislators compared New York City to London, which was known for its "rotten boroughs," electoral districts in which aristocrats bought the votes of the poor. On this basis, New York legislators opposed universal suffrage for working-class whites as well as blacks, claiming that all poor people might have their votes bought by the wealthy.[44] But others argued that blacks in particular were more likely to sell their votes.[45] General Erastus Root of Delaware County stated that if blacks were given the vote, "this species of population" would follow "the train of those . . . whose shoes and boots they had so often blacked," rather than vote independently.[46] Such remarks characterized blacks as dependents who would become subject to the "aristocracy" that had freed them and now employed them. This characterization placed free black workers on a lower level than white workers, one of dependence, degradation, and mistrust. Black men were not comparable to women, another large class of dependents, for women were "the better part of creation." Legislators' praise of women was directed at white women; they did not discuss black women during this debate at all. Several conventioneers put blacks on the mental and political level of children, who "are deemed incapable of exercising [the suffrage] discreetly, and therefore not safely, for the good of the whole community."[47]

Those in favor of black suffrage tried to refute such arguments. Peter Jay of West-chester County, and son of John Jay, stated that blacks were not "naturally inferior." Furthermore, blacks' degradation due to slavery was "fast passing away" through the advent of schools and other programs enacted by reformers for their uplift.[48] Rob-ert Clarke of Delaware County stated that blacks had proven themselves worthy of citizenship through service in the Revolutionary War and the War of 1812. Further-more, blacks were not the only group potentially subject to becoming followers of the aristocracy. Clarke claimed that there were "many thousands of white ambitious fawning, cringing sycophants, who look up to their more wealthy and more ambitious neighbours for direction at the polls, as they look to them for bread."[49] Thus, Clarke equated blacks' and whites' potential for civic virtue.

Such arguments were not strong enough to prove blacks equal to whites in the eyes of the legislature, which voted to raise the property requirement for black men to $250. White men who served in the militia or paid taxes could vote without a property require-ment. By 1826, the legislature removed both the militia and tax requirements for white men, who could now vote based on age, citizenship, and residence.[50] While preventing blacks' complete disfranchisement, the property requirement raised to the level of law the idea that blacks needed to erase the degradation of slavery and earn their place in society. Chancellor Kent of Albany said that the law "would not cut [blacks] off from all hope" of full citizenship. Rather, it would improve them by making them "industri-ous and frugal, with the prospect of participating in the right of suffrage." The law's tendency to encourage moral reform among blacks also "might in some degree alleviate the wrongs we had done them"—the wrongs of slavery and thus moral degradation.[51]

Thus, according to whites, the law would provide additional impetus for blacks to improve themselves. The law essentially required blacks to serve an apprenticeship to political equality. Blacks, to prove their worth as citizens, could not simply be born in New York, or simply be industrious workers. Rather, through acquisition of property, blacks had to achieve middle-class status to vote. Those blacks who did achieve this status allegedly proved beyond a shadow of doubt their independence. At the same time, however, such proof reinforced the idea that "unimproved" blacks were inferior to any whites. Through this law, the legislature drew an indelible line between blacks and whites of all classes. The law devalued blacks in comparison to whites, for white men gained the vote despite their occupations and wealth or lack of it. The law also continued the belief that black workers, like slaves in republican ideology, could not think for themselves but were under the influence of whites.

By 1826, only sixteen blacks in New York County were eligible to vote; by the Civil War, that number had grown only to an estimated three hundred, out of a popu-lation of more than fifteen thousand.[52] Some of those blacks eligible to vote in the antebellum period were residents of Seneca Village. Although depicted at the time and remembered later as a community of dissolute persons, Seneca Village gave a group of black workers the opportunity to achieve some of the goals of citizenship required by the 1821 suffrage law, and esteemed by the wider community: property ownership and residential stability, which allegedly gave blacks political independence.[53] The ex-istence of Seneca Village, however, could not erase the negative stereotypes of blacks in the minds of New Yorkers.

By July 4 and 5, 1827, the days on which New York State's blacks celebrated the end of slavery, whites had defined free blacks as unequal citizens in multiple ways. For New York's whites, the "badge of servitude" of dependency and immorality that marked blacks under slavery did not completely disappear on freedom. Thus, full freedom for New York's blacks did not result in equality. Hampered by the continuation of indentures and job discrimination and its resultant poverty, blacks lived on the margins of the growing New York City economy. But despite these hardships, New York City, with large numbers of blacks in close proximity, provided unparalleled opportunities for community, freedom, and political activism for blacks. Throughout the antebellum period, New York City's blacks would be leaders in efforts to end southern slavery and attain racial equality throughout the nation.

NOTES

1. On comparisons between New York and southern slavery, see Ira Berlin, *Many Thousands Gone: The First Two Centuries of Slavery in North America* (Cambridge, MA: Harvard University Press, 1998), 50-1. For explicit arguments on the reliance of southern colonists on slave labor and on African knowledge, see Edmund S. Morgan, "Idle Indian and Lazy Englishman," in *American Slavery, American Freedom: The Ordeal of Colonial Virginia* (New York: Norton, 1975); Peter Wood, "Black Labor—White Race," and "Black Pioneers," in *Black Majority: Negroes in Colonial South Carolina from 1670 through the Stono Rebellion* (1974; New York: Norton, 1975). See also Berlin, *Many Thousands Gone*, throughout. For the reliance of New England on the slave trade, see David Richardson, "Slavery, Trade, and Economic Growth in Eighteenth-Century New England," in Barbara Solow, ed., *Slavery and the Rise of the Atlantic System* (Cambridge: Cambridge University Press, 1991), 237–64.

2. New works focusing on the interaction between race and class include David Roediger, *The Wages of Whiteness: Race and the Making of the American Working Class* (London: Verso, 1991); Alexander Saxton, *The Rise and Fall of the White Republic: Class Politics and Mass Culture in Nineteenth-Century America* (London: Verso, 1990); and Eric Lott, *Love and Theft: Blackface Minstrelsy and the American Working Class* (New York: Oxford University Press, 1993). These works, however, examine whites' definitions of class and race in the nineteenth century.

3. See Herbert Gutman, "Work, Culture and Society in Industrializing America, 1815–1919," in *Work, Culture and Society in Industrializing America* (New York: Knopf, 1977), 3–78.

4. In his seminal essay, Gutman states that "bound workers [and] nonwhite free laborers, mostly blacks and Asian immigrants and their descendants . . . were affected by the tensions" that he describes as central to working-class formation in the United States, "a fact that emphasizes the central place they deserve in any comprehensive study of American work habits and changing American working-class behavior." Ibid., 12–3. Despite his own extensive research in the history of slavery, Gutman omitted these workers from his analysis. Unfortunately, many subsequent labor historians (excepting those historians committed to excavating the history of racial minorities in the United States, such as those cited in note 2 above), have followed his practice rather than his theory. For an assessment of Gutman's research into black workers, race, and class in the twentieth century, see Herbert Hill, "Myth-Making as Labor History: Herbert Gutman and the United Mine Workers of America," *International Journal of Politics, Culture and Society* 2 (1988): 132–200, and roundtable responses, *International Journal of Politics, Culture and Society* 2 (1988): 361–595.

5. Sean Wilentz, *Chants Democratic: New York City and the Rise of the American Working Class, 1789–1850* (New York: Oxford University Press, 1984; rpt. ed., Oxford, 1986), and Christine Stansell, *City of Women: Sex and Class in New York, 1789–1860* (New York: Knopf, 1986; rpt. ed., Urbana: University of Illinois, 1987), are not alone in their omissions. The literature on New York's working class is voluminous, and in it very little attention is paid to black workers. Works that begin to address these issues in New York are Shane White, *Somewhat More Independent: The End of Slavery in New York City, 1770–1810* (Athens: University of Georgia Press, 1991), and Roediger, *Wages of Whiteness*.

6. On class, race, and slavery, see Berlin, "Making Slavery, Making Race," prologue to *Many Thousands Gone*, 1–14; Barbara J. Fields, "Slavery, Race and Ideology in the United States of America," *New Left Review* 181 (1990): 95–118. On class divisions in colonial America, see Stephen Innes, *Labor in a New Land: Economy and Society in Seventeenth-Century Springfield* (Princeton, NJ: Princeton University Press, 1983); Ronald Schultz, "A Class Society? The Nature of Inequality in Early America," in Carla Gardina Pestana and Sharon V. Salinger, eds., *Inequality in Early America* (Hanover, NH: University Press of New England, 1999), 203–21.

7. Oliver Rink, *Holland on the Hudson: An Economic and Social History of Dutch New York* (Ithaca, NY: Cornell University Press, 1986), 85–6; Joyce Goodfriend, "Burghers and Blacks: The Evolution of a Slave Society at New Amsterdam," *New York History* 59 (1978): 129–30; Henri and Barbara Van der Zee, *A Sweet and Alien Land: The Story of Dutch New York* (New York: Viking, 1978), 13; Thelma Wills Foote, "Black Life in Colonial Manhattan, 1664–1786" (Ph.D. dissertation, Harvard University, 1991), 9–10.

8. On the growth of laws regulating slavery in the colonial period, see A. Leon Higginbotham Jr., *In the Matter of Color: Race and the American Legal Process: The Colonial Period* (New York: Oxford University Press, 1978), esp. 19–20. Details of the legal rights of New Netherland's slaves in Peter Christoph, "The Freedmen of New Amsterdam," in Nancy Anne McClure Zeller, ed., *A Beautiful and Fruitful Place: Selected Rensellaerswijck Seminar Papers* (Albany, NY: New Netherland, 1991), 157; Graham Hodges, *Root and Branch: African Americans in New York and East Jersey, 1613–1863* (Chapel Hill: University of North Carolina Press, 1999), 10–2. On half-freedom, see Edgar McManus, *A History of Negro Slavery in New York* (Syracuse, NY: Syracuse University Press, 1966, 1970), 13–5; Christoph, "Freedmen of New Amsterdam," 158–9; Thomas Davis, "Slavery in Colonial New York City" (Ph.D. dissertation, Columbia University, 1975), 54–6; Berlin, *Many Thousands Gone*, 52–3; Foote, "Black Life," 12–3; Joyce Goodfriend, *Before the Melting Pot: Society and Culture in Colonial New York City, 1664–1730* (Princeton, NJ: Princeton University Press, 1992), 116; and Hodges, *Root and Branch*, 12–3.

9. McManus, *Negro Slavery in New York*, 10. On the limited opportunities available to free white workers, see Edwin Burrows and Mike Wallace, *Gotham: A History of New York City to 1898* (New York: Oxford University Press, 1999), 31. On the 1628 agreement, see Foote, "Black Life," 9. On the 1657 agreement, see Goodfriend, "Burghers and Blacks," 131.

10. McManus, *Negro Slavery in New York*, 5–8. On the importance of New Amsterdam as a slave port, see Hodges, *Root and Branch*, 29; Burrows and Wallace, *Gotham*, 48–9.

11. Michael Kammen, *Colonial New York: A History* (New York: Oxford University Press, 1975), 179; McManus, *Negro Slavery in New York*, 41–3.

12. Foote, "Black Life," 128–31; Davis, "Slavery in Colonial New York City," 72–80; Hodges, *Root and Branch*, 36–38. On parallel trends in other colonies, see Higginbotham, *In the Matter of Color*.

13. Foote, "Black Life," 28–9, 25–6; McManus, *Negro Slavery in New York*, 25–7. On Adolph Philipse and the responsibilities of tenants, see Kammen, *Colonial New York*, 174, 301–2. For slave population, see Berlin, *Many Thousands Gone*, Table 1, 369–70.

14. Berlin, *Many Thousands Gone*, Table 1, 369–70, 183, 54; Foote, "Black Life," 54–8.

15. McManus, *Negro Slavery in New York*, 47; Goodfriend, *Before the Melting Pot*, 118–21; White, *Somewhat More Independent*, 10–3, 36–7. On women's work in artisan households, Jeanne Boydston, *Home and Work: Housework, Wages, and the Ideology of Labor in the Early Republic* (New York: Oxford University Press, 1990), 14–5, 37–8. For listings of the various skilled jobs held by whites between 1694 and 1706, see Davis, "Slavery in Colonial New York City," 64–6. On slaves' work on farms, see Hodges, *Root and Branch*, 82–3.

16. Details of porters' and coopers' petitions and quotations in McManus, *Negro Slavery in New York*, 48–9; Hodges, *Root and Branch*, 108. On cart men, Hodges, *Root and Branch*, 43.

17. Samuel McKee, *Labor in Colonial New York, 1626–1664* (New York: Columbia University Press, 1935), 90–5, quotations on 91 n., 94; Goodfriend, *Beyond the Melting Pot*, 55, 118, 134–5.

18. For the increased reliance on slave labor at the expense of European servants in North America, see Berlin, *Many Thousands Gone*, 82, 109, 110, 113–4, 181–2, 184; Morgan, "Towards Slavery," in *American Slavery, American Freedom*, esp. 299–300. The exception that proves the rule in the southern colonies is Georgia, which limited slave importations almost until the Revolutionary War in favor of European immigrants.

19. On 1712 laws, see Hodges, *Root and Branch*, 67–8. On the changing status of slaves and free blacks, see Foote, "Black Life," 231; Davis, "Slavery in Colonial New York City," 112–3; David Cohen, *The Ramapo Mountain People* (New Brunswick, NJ: Rutgers University Press, 1974), 31–4; Foote, "Crossroads or Settlement? The Black Freedmen's Community in Historic Greenwich Village, 1644–1855," in Rick Beard and Leslie Cohen Berlowitz, eds., *Greenwich Village: Culture and Counterculture* (New Brunswick, NJ: Rutgers University Press, 1993), 123.

20. Davis, "Slavery in Colonial New York City," 85. Other works on relationships between enslaved black and free white workers include Peter Linebaugh and Marcus Rediker's chapter on the 1741 New York Conspiracy, "The Outcasts of the Nations of the Earth," chapter 6 of *The Many-Headed Hydra: Sailors, Slaves, Commoners, and the Hidden History of the Revolutionary Atlantic* (Boston: Beacon, 2000); Foote, "Black Life," 229–31.

21. Since the time of the conspiracy, there have been debates as to whether a conspiracy actually existed. Doubtless, slaves and some whites talked of burning the city and taking it over for their own benefit, and some slaves burned the city's main fort, Fort George, and several other buildings over the course of three weeks. The primary source from which all accounts of the plot are based is Daniel Horsmanden, *Journal of the Proceedings in the Detection of the Conspiracy Formed by Some White People in Conjunction with Negro and Other Slaves for Burning the City of New-York in America and Murdering the Inhabitants* (New York: James Parker, 1744). The standard secondary account of the plot is Thomas J. Davis, *A Rumor of Revolt: The "Great Negro Plot" in Colonial New York* (New York: Free Press, 1985). The most recent account, which emphasizes the class-based grievances the rebels shared across status lines, is Linebaugh and Rediker, chapter 6 of *The Many-Headed Hydra*. See Foote, "Black Life," 274–340, for an account that focuses on the ways in which whites shaped the meaning of the arson attacks by slaves into a wide-ranging international plot. Other accounts include Hodges, *Root and Branch*, 88–99; McManus, *Negro Slavery in New York*, 124–39.

22. On the motives of the rebels, see Davis, *Rumor of Revolt*, 89–91, 96–7, 131–7, 225; Linebaugh and Rediker, chapter 6 of *The Many-Headed Hydra*.

23. Quotation from Davis, *Rumor of Revolt*, 37; support for ending slavery, 44, 31–2. For slaves as status symbols, see McManus, *Negro Slavery in New York*, 46–7. For slaves as status symbols in the late eighteenth century, see White, *Somewhat More Independent*, 44.

24. On Quakers, see Jean Soderlund, *Quakers and Slavery: A Divided Spirit* (Princeton, NJ: Princeton University Press, 1985). For an overview of the impact of the Great Awakening and

the efforts of religious denominations to fight slavery, see Leslie M. Harris, *In the Shadow of Slavery: African Americans in New York City, 1626–1863* (Chicago, 2003), 46–52. The best discussion of the Great Awakening and other changes in religion after 1741 is Hodges, *Root and Branch*, 119–28.

25. On the language of slavery during the American Revolution, see Bernard Bailyn, *The Ideological Origins of the American Revolution* (Cambridge, MA: Harvard University Press, 1967), 232–46; David Gellman, "Inescapable Discourse: The Rhetoric of Slavery and the Politics of Abolition in Early National New York" (Ph.D. dissertation, Northwestern University, 1997), 50–4. Major works on black opportunities for freedom during the war include Benjamin Quarles, *The Negro in the American Revolution* (Chapel Hill: University of North Carolina Press, 1961); Graham Hodges, "Black Revolt in New York City and the Neutral Zone, 1775–1783," in *Slavery, Freedom and Culture among Early American Workers* (Armonk, NY: M. E. Sharpe, 1998), 65–86; Ira Berlin, "The Revolution in Black Life," in Alfred Young, ed., *The American Revolution: Explorations in the History of American Radicalism* (DeKalb: Northern Illinois University Press, 1976), 349–82.

26. The literature on republicanism is voluminous. For useful overviews, see Robert Shallhope, "Toward a Republican Synthesis: The Emergence of an Understanding of Republicanism in American Historiography," *William and Mary Quarterly* 39 (1982): 334–56; Idem., "Republicanism and Early American Historiography," *William and Mary Quarterly* 29 (1972): 49–80. On revolutionary republicanism, see Gordon Wood, *The Creation of the American Republic, 1776–1787* (Chapel Hill: University of North Carolina Press, 1969). On working-class republicanism, see Wilentz, *Chants Democratic*. On the interaction between republicanism and antislavery, see David Brion Davis, *The Problem of Slavery in the Age of Revolution, 1770–1823* (Ithaca, NY: Cornell University Press, 1975).

27. On the failure of the 1785 emancipation bill and the founding of the New York Manumission Society, see Harris, *In the Shadow of Slavery*, 56–65. The most complete account of the history of the Manumission Society is Thomas Moseley, "A History of the New-York Manumission Society, 1785–1849" (Ph.D. dissertation, New York University, 1963). See also White, *Somewhat More Independent*, 83–4; Davis, *The Problem of Slavery in the Age of Revolution*, 239–42.

28. On the passage of the 1799 and 1817 emancipation laws, see Harris, *In the Shadow of Slavery*, 11, 70–1, 94–5; Arthur Zilversmit, *The First Emancipation: The Abolition of Slavery in the North* (Chicago: University of Chicago Press, 1967; rpt. ed., Phoenix Books, 1970), 181–4.

29. On Revolutionary republicanism, see Wood, *Creation of the American Republic*; Bailyn, *Ideological Origins of the American Revolution*. On working-class republicanism, see Wilentz, *Chants Democratic*, esp. 4–5, 23, 61–103. See also Ruth Bloch, "The Gendered Meanings of Virtue in Revolutionary America," *Signs* 13 (1987): 37–58.

30. On republican motherhood, see Linda Kerber, *Women of the Republic: Intellect and Ideology in Revolutionary America* (1980; New York: Norton, 1986), 11–2, 283–6; Bloch, "Gendered Meanings of Virtue," 46–7. On women in republican ideology and class distinctions, see Stansell, *City of Women*, 19–37.

31. On black domestic servants in white households, see White, *Somewhat More Independent*, 43–5; Stansell, *City of Women*, 13. On the conflation of free blacks and slaves, see White, *Somewhat More Independent*, 47; for a similar conflation of free blacks and slaves in New England, see Joanne Pope Melish, *Disowning Slavery: Gradual Emancipation and "Race" in New England, 1780–1860* (Ithaca, NY: Cornell University Press, 1998), 95–118. On slavery, servants, and republicanism, see Roediger, *Wages of Whiteness*, 43–64, esp. 47–50.

32. On the devaluation of domestic labor, see Boydston, *Home and Work*, 35–74. Manuel Mordecai Noah, "Africans," *National Advocate*, August 3, 1821, reprinted in Marvin McAl-

lister, "'White People Do Not Know How to Behave at Entertainments Designated for Ladies and Gentlemen of Colour': A History of New York's African Grove/African Theatre" (Ph.D. dissertation, Northwestern University, 1997), 153–4.

33. On the changes in skilled labor during this time, see Wilentz, *Chants Democratic*, 24–60; Charles Sellers, *The Market Revolution: Jacksonian America, 1815–1846* (New York: Oxford University Press, 1991), 21–7. On the embargo and debt imprisonment, see Sellers, *Market Revolution,* 25.

34. William Jeffrey Bolster, *Black Jacks: African-American Seamen in the Age of Sail* (Cambridge, MA: Harvard University Press, 1997), 69–75; Roediger, *Wages of Whiteness*, 45.

35. Sailors' strike in Paul Gilje, *The Road to Mobocracy: Popular Disorder in New York City, 1763–1834* (Chapel Hill: University of North Carolina Press, 1987), 181. Waiters' strike in Philip Foner and Ronald Lewis, eds., *The Black Worker: A Documentary History from Colonial Times to the Present* (Philadelphia: Temple University Press, 1978), vol. 1, 191–5. On white workers' exclusion of blacks, see Roediger, *Wages of Whiteness*, 43–60, esp. 44–6. Implicitly, Sean Wilentz places unskilled jobs, in which the vast majority of black workers and at least half of all other workers participated, outside of his schema of working-class development and consciousness. He focuses on a class of skilled artisans and tradesmen who, by his own accounting, make up for only two-fifths to one-half of all employed males in New York City. Wilentz, *Chants Democratic*, p. 27 n. These figures also exclude the numbers of working-class women who held jobs outside of the workshops. See Stansell, *City of Women.* For a work that gives attention to nonartisan workers in New York, see Richard Stott, *Workers in the Metropolis: Class, Ethnicity and Youth in Antebellum New York City* (Ithaca, NY: Cornell University Press, 1990).

36. Harris, *In the Shadow of Slavery*, 80–1.

37. Stansell, *City of Women*, 13–4. For a comparison with black women's work in the late-nineteenth century South, see Tera Hunter, *To 'Joy My Freedom: Black Women's Lives and Labors after the Civil War* (Cambridge, MA: Harvard University Press, 1997); Carter G. Woodson, "The Negro Washerwoman, a Vanishing Figure," *Journal of Negro History* 15 (1930): 269–77.

38. Harris, *In the Shadow of Slavery*, 74–5, 81–2; on Seneca Village, see Elizabeth Blackmar and Roy Rosenzweig, *The Park and the People: A History of Central Park* (Ithaca, NY: Cornell University Press, 1992), 64–73. For the lives of black maritime workers, see Bolster, *Black Jacks.*

39. Quotations from *American Minerva*, August 22, 1793.

40. Samuel Wood, *The Cries of New-York* (1808; rpt. ed., New York: Harbour, 1931), 15–6.

41. Wilentz, *Chants Democratic*, 66–77; Hamilton quoted on 67.

42. Dixon Ryan Fox, "The Negro Vote in Old New York," *Political Science Quarterly* 32 (1917): 256–7.

43. According to Leonard Curry's calculations, between 1810 and 1820, the city's free black population gained 2,231 people, while the slave population declined by 1,168. The entire black population, slave and free, increased by 1,063. Leonard Curry, *The Free Black in Urban America, 1800–1850: The Shadow of the Dream* (Chicago: University of Chicago Press, 1981; rpt. ed., 1986), Tables A-1, A-4, A-7, 244–5, 247, 250.

44. Nathaniel Carter and William Stone, eds., *Reports of the Proceedings and Debates of the Convention of 1821, Assembled for the Purpose of Amending the Constitution of the State of New-York: Containing All the Official Documents Relating to the Subject, and Other Valuable Matter* (Albany, NY: Hosford, 1821), 195–6.

45. Ibid., 189–90.

46. Ibid., 195–6, 189–90, 185–6.

47. Ibid., 180–3.

48. Ibid., 183–5.

49. Ibid., 186–8.

50. Chilton Williamson, *American Suffrage from Property to Democracy, 1760–1860* (Princeton, NJ: Princeton University Press, 1986), 202–6.

51. Carter and Stone, *Reports of the Proceedings*, 364.

52. Numbers of eligible voters in Rhoda Golden Freeman, *The Free Negro in New York City in the Era before the Civil War* (New York: Garland, 1994), 92–3.

53. Blackmar and Rosenzweig, *Park and the People*, 67.

Chapter 3

The Enemy Within: Some Effects of Foreign Immigrants on Antebellum Southern Cities

Randall M. Miller

Among American historical perennials, few have persisted so long as the concept of Southern distinctiveness. However much historians differ on the exact configuration, they do agree that the Old South was unique. Historians trace the roots of Southern distinctiveness to the pervasive influences of evangelical Protestantism, plantation agriculture, and black slavery, all of which nourished a common folk culture among whites regardless of class or condition. In such a Southern gemeinschaft society, cities appear largely as extensions of the countryside, performing commercial and financial functions to sustain an agricultural economy and remaining subservient to the values of a planter-dominated world. The rootless, impersonal, diverse cities of modern society have no place in this portrait of Southern distinctiveness.[1]

Antebellum Southern society was never so tidy. In the late antebellum period Southern cities tugged in two directions—toward continued support of the traditional, rural interests that service to the region's plantation economy demanded and toward increasing commercialization and social diversity that urban growth encouraged. Neither force was quite yet capable of overcoming the other, but the tensions the contrary pulls created threatened to reshape Southern urban society in several ways. Cities played vital social and political roles in Southern life, in addition to their economic functions. They also diverged in important ways from prevailing Southern social and political norms as the Old South veered toward secession. From the 1830s through the 1850s the expansion of urban economies and the attendant growth of urban populations fundamentally altered the urban landscape. New city dwellers, a majority of whom were foreign-born, created new social conditions to accommodate their needs, as they also fostered values at war with the countryside. By recasting the conceptual framework of Southern life to include immigrant and working-class culture in cities, it is possible to see the extent of urban-rural divergence in the late antebellum era. It is also possible to get new angles from which to view Southern society generally.

Reprinted from *Southern Studies: An Interdisciplinary Journal of the South* 24 (Spring 1985): 30–53. Reprinted with the permission of *Southern Studies*.

In the rural world the slaveholders made, social order hinged on the informal bonds of family and race. Proslavery apologists, among others, preached the social unity of a Herrenvolk democracy, a concept of white supremacy that obscured any class or cultural differences among whites, and they reminded white Southerners of all classes that as white men stood together to protect slavery, they also preserved order. In defending the region's peculiar institution, and thereby Southern culture itself, Southerners developed a philosophy of social stasis that derived from the strong sense of cultural and social unity in the Old South. Slavery and the Southern brand of evangelical Protestantism, which infused so much of the region's life, bred among white Southerners a conservative social temperament distrustful of government and fatalistic toward human suffering. Then, too, the region had enjoyed a remarkably high level of ethnic homogeneity, having a significantly smaller proportion of new immigrants in its total population than did the North. The cultural and racial consensus among whites allowed political participation to expand in the 1840s and 1850s without the dissensions and disruptions that marked Northern political life.[2]

The philosophy of social stasis praised agrarianism and traditionalism while it simultaneously, if sometimes only implicitly, fostered mistrust of modern cities where poverty, class tension, and ethnic division brought on social disorder. Southerners increasingly drew invidious distinctions between their ruralism and Northern urbanism during the late antebellum era. In doing so, they fastened on the instability and social turmoil they saw in Northern cities as evidence of the dangers of modernism. It was highly significant for them that so many immigrants in the 1840s and 1850s congregated in the North, as it was equally significant that so many fewer immigrants went South. More than anything else, the growing number of poor, unassimilated, working-class urban dwellers and the crime and violence in Northern cities provided grist for the Southern proslavery mill.

Although Southern diatribes against Northern ills contributed to the defense of slavery, they also falsely reassured Southerners that diversity and disorder were not great problems for their section. By exaggerating the contrast between urban North and pastoral South, Southerners were able to submerge their own fears about potential trouble at home. It was, however, a case of denying painful reality, for even as the South basked in its self-proclaimed rural superiority, its cities were becoming seedbeds of modern social and economic change, and it was surely a portent of danger that Southern cities too were filling up with poor, unassimilated, working-class immigrants.[3]

Southern cities grew at a rapid rate between 1830 and 1860. The vast majority of newcomers to Southern cities were foreigners, some traveling southward from New York or Philadelphia and others entering Southern ports directly, particularly through New Orleans. Southern urban populations doubled and even tripled in some instances in the thirty years before the Civil War as a result of the large immigrant influx and, to a lesser extent, the movement of Northern-born migrants and Southern-born blacks and whites. However transient their intentions, many immigrants remained long enough in Southern cities to burden charities, transform labor relations, and create a new social order.[4]

The heavy immigration of the 1840s and 1850s made its chief impact on the size, composition, and character of the working classes of the urban South. By 1860 foreign-born workers comprised the principal source of free labor in all important Southern river and port cities. Indeed, the proportion of foreign-born persons in the whole adult male population of the South's ten largest cities was higher than in almost every Northern city. Because immigrants to Southern cities were disproportionately male, they comprised a higher percentage of the urban workforce, which tended to be male-oriented in its job categories, than their numbers in the whole urban population might suggest. Adding the Northern-born migrants to the foreign-born population reveals even more clearly the non-Southern character of the late antebellum Southern urban working class. In Savannah, a representative case, the arrival of immigrants and Northern-born workers accounted for over 60 percent of the increase in the whole free population during the 1850s, a decade when the city's population tripled. According to the 1860 federal census, approximately 70 percent of Mobile's free adult males came from outside the South.[5]

During the 1850s Southern cities developed a large white working class in which the typical worker likely shared few values of the Old South. The growth of this labor force in no way represented an extension of the countryside into the city, for very few nonslaveholding whites left the rural South for work or residence in Southern cities. In the 1850s, in many Southern cities, European immigrants, Northern-born migrants, and blacks made up more than 90 percent of the entire working class, and most of that working class was free and foreign-born. The immigrant infusion whitened up the Southern work force generally and even restored white numerical majorities in Charleston and New Orleans.

The arrival of Irish and German workers in large numbers in the 1840s and 1850s injected a new and somewhat dangerous dynamic into the urban workplace. The new workers displaced local white and black labor in several occupations—a process already under way in the Lower South by the 1840s where significant immigration had occurred in the 1830s, but only beginning in the late 1840s in the Upper South, which received its foreign immigration later than did most Southern seaboard cities. Probably the most affected by the significant immigrant competition were Southern-born white workers who all but vanished from the urban workplace. They survived only in such select trades as printing and building, where their native origins might have given them some advantage, and where their self-imposed insulation from the bulk of the working classes by means of closed shops, unions, and clubs allowed them to avoid debasement by association with blacks and immigrants. Virtually everywhere in the urban South by the 1850s immigrants had come to dominate most artisan work, except in Charleston where free black and slave artisans thrived through the Civil War. In the unskilled occupations Southern-born whites hardly existed by the 1850s. Immigrants and blacks alone competed for manual labor and unskilled positions—work that white Southerners increasingly deemed unworthy and degrading.[6]

Across the urban South immigrant workers elbowed free black competitors aside in skilled and unskilled occupations and eroded the already precarious economic and social conditions of many free blacks. Using numerical strength and incipient organizations, throughout the 1850s immigrant workers forced municipal authorities to acknowledge the old, but often unenforced, legal restrictions on black employment in many different trades. Even small cities did not escape such pressures. In 1858 in

Little Rock, Arkansas, for example, a German blacksmith led a protest meeting to remove free blacks, as well as slaves and convicts, from the crafts.[7]

Licensing fees and other legal impediments, pressure on white employers, and violence were the "public" means of proscription, but, more than anything else, it was the immigrants' initial willingness to underbid local labor for any and all work that drove free blacks into despair and poverty. Immigrants ignored local taboos about "nigger work" and crashed into free black monopolies everywhere, from drayage to barbering. Immigrant women also participated in this process, entering into domestic service, particularly in the Upper South where they were often preferred to blacks, and competing with free black women as washerwomen, seamstresses, and prostitutes.[8]

The history of immigrant versus black competition in Norfolk, Virginia, illustrates the changing dynamics in Southern cities. Until the 1850s blacks dominated the wharves and shipping-related occupations as common laborers or mechanics—carpenters, cordwainers, plasterers, caulkers, coopers, riggers, blacksmiths, stonecutters, pilots. They also controlled domestic service. Widespread hiring of free black domestics contributed to the stability of free black households by providing women with incomes to supplement or, in some instances, to sustain their men's contributions. Because so many blacks relied on those occupations, any competition threatened their survival and autonomy as a community. Black females were especially vulnerable because they had only domestic service or prostitution available as important sources of employment.[9]

By 1860 immigrant Irish girls had begun to displace black women in domestic service. Black males also suffered from new competition. The number of black carpenters, shoemakers, shopkeepers, among several occupations, declined in the face of immigrant rivals. Even drayage, which contemporaries commonly assumed was impervious to white encroachment, attracted immigrants in the 1850s. By 1860 the skilled trades in Norfolk had passed from black to white hands. The increasing number of immigrants entering Norfolk and becoming naturalized citizens there—that is, committing themselves to settlement—largely accounted for the shift. A carpenter from Spain, a shoemaker from Germany, a tailor from England, a stonecutter from England, a weaver from Ireland, a baker from Germany, and so on, were among the 648 naturalized citizens in Norfolk in 1860 who found urban employment in trades once ruled by free blacks.

Increased competition between white and black workers led the former to try to circumscribe black workers altogether. Angry white laborers and artisans demanded that employers justify any hiring of blacks. Although protests often proved unsuccessful, immigrant opposition to black hiring apparently discouraged some preference for blacks and introduced a new voice into Norfolk's labor and social relations.

The fluctuations of urban market economies in the 1840s and 1850s, however, interrupted or slowed the decline of the free blacks' position, as a free market in labor operated everywhere but in the realm of municipal employment, where whites held political advantage. In New Orleans yellow fever and cholera epidemics combined with spasmodic economic growth to create periodic shortages of skilled and unskilled labor and to raise wage rates considerably. When the epidemics ended or the economy flagged, black and white job competition intensified in the city, but during periods of economic prosperity the seeming need for an enlarged labor pool convinced many white employers and local authorities to ignore restrictions on free black employment, and slave hiring too for that matter, thereby preserving black places in the economy. Irish and German immigrants had pushed blacks out of drayage, taxi service, and hotel employment in the 1850s, but dockwork and the river trades remained open to blacks. The militancy of dissident Irish workers who demanded improved wages and working conditions on the docks and riverboats, once they became firmly established there, induced several white employers to support a free black labor reserve. Also, some employers recruited blacks in efforts to drive down wage rates in unskilled occupations and to disrupt any sense of class commonality among working people generally.[10]

In Charleston free blacks staved off complete displacement by immigrants. Charleston's employers simply preferred free blacks in several skilled trades, thereby undermining the immigrants' efforts to penetrate all areas of employment. The seasonal nature of much of the Irish immigration before the 1850s also favored the native Charleston working population in moving into and controlling skilled trades. Failing to get state legislative support in their campaigns to restrict black employment in skilled occupations, the immigrants turned to city government for relief. Only a few upwardly mobile immigrants, particularly Germans, won places in skilled trades, but many did receive municipal employment. The Irish especially benefited from government largess.[11]

The truculence and unpredictability of foreign workers dissatisfied employers and helped to keep slaves and free blacks employed. The Irish, once they had gained their bearings in the new land, seemed to be particularly intractable. Disgruntled workers abandoned employers at a moment's notice, refused to work beyond their contractual times, and spoke out against abuses—actions few slaves or free blacks could safely take. Irish laborers at Fort Jackson, outside New Orleans, rebelled in 1849 when their employer tried to keep them at work amid rumors of a cholera outbreak. The laborers ceased work and threatened to tar and feather their work boss. In 1856 the Irish longshoremen in Savannah, who had a history of work stoppages, exasperated local merchants by calling a strike. The merchants pledged to "dispense altogether" with immigrant labor and to employ black labor instead. Complaints about the lack of deference, sloppy work, and excessive demands by Irish workers echoed throughout the urban South.[12]

The erratic work performances of immigrants, the preference of some whites to be served by blacks, and the movement of free blacks and runaway slaves into the interstices of urban economies allowed "free" blacks to survive in the late antebellum period, but the immigrant advance into the workplace was inexorable. Most white employers were indifferent to the fate of free blacks. Others no doubt thought that the destruction of free black autonomy was a good thing in a slave society. Besides, newly arrived immigrants often came cheap.

The immigrants' relationship with urban slave labor was more complex and somewhat contradictory. The size of the urban slave population fluctuated in response to several factors, including the price of slaves, the character and vigor of the local economy, the labor demands of the surrounding countryside, and the rate of foreign immigration. Slavery declined in some cities while it grew, even prospered, in others amid the floodtide of immigration in the 1850s. Between 1820 and 1860 the slave population's share of the total population fell in the ten largest cities, but it rose in the ten second largest cities. Numbers, however, do not reveal the social dynamics at work. As an institution, slavery resisted immigrant competition, but slaveholders, and surely slaves too, recognized changes in the assumptions about slavery's place in a changing city once immigrants arrived to build a working-class world of their own.[13]

Slaves continued to work in virtually every field of manual labor throughout the 1850s, and in some cities, especially Charleston, they clung tenaciously to several artisanal occupations. But the presence of immigrant workers, when combined with the transfer of many slave artisans into the agricultural sector in the 1850s, severely limited slave participation in the crafts and the petit bourgeois urban economy, and so crippled slave leadership in the cities. Urban slaves became increasingly concentrated in a few trades, such as carpentry, or they moved into such industries as tobacco and iron manufactures. Many slaves remained as domestics or day laborers. Meanwhile, German immigrants gravitated toward the mechanical arts and retailing, while, by 1860, Irish immigrants predominated in the semi- and unskilled occupations.

Immigrants wanted jobs and resented hired slaves jostling them for places. Unskilled workers relied on their strong backs to drive slaves from the labor market. Failing that, they used their fists. Skilled workers sought legislative remedies for their problems, but they enjoyed only minor successes. Planter-dominated legislatures balked at any attempt to deny slaves access to the urban economy. Urban slave ownership and the need to hire slaves remained sufficiently widespread in the 1840s and 1850s to insure that city councils would respect slavery's interest in urban employment, although city authorities found it increasingly difficult to ignore demands for stricter enforcement of slave codes limiting slave hiring. The elasticity of labor demand in Southern cities relieved some of the pressures, for as rural demand for slave labor in the 1850s siphoned off slaves from cities, immigrants moved in to fill the gaps. The rising costs of hiring slaves in the cities—due to high demands for labor generally, high slave prices, and the slaves' greater control over their arrangements through the regularization of bonus payments and other accommodations hirers had to make to attract slaves—also enhanced immigrants' employability by making the actual cost of hiring a slave more than the cost of hiring a white person in many instances. Still, an inherent conflict between immigrant workers and slavery remained built into the Southern urban economy, and slaveholders knew it. When attempts to reserve places for slaves broke down because immigrants demanded not only the most menial jobs, but also the most lucrative ones, slaveholders became assertive everywhere in holding on to their slave-hiring prerogatives.[14]

Immigrants' willingness to engage in work that Southern whites considered fit only for slaves blurred distinctions between white and black, free and slave. Economic necessity and cultural preference led Irish girls to ignore the strong Southern prejudice against domestic service, which whites identified with blacks. Gangs of immigrant Irish and German men dug ditches, repaired levees, built roads, and loaded and unloaded cargoes, just as blacks did. The immigrant workers' mean diet, wretched shelter, onerous labor, and poor health degraded them in Southern eyes. Indeed, the parallels between black slavery and the gang labor of the ditchers and others did not escape contemporaries, who thought that such immigrants reeked of servitude.[15]

If the immigrants' work debased them, it also threatened to elevate the blacks. The *Richmond Enquirer* spoke for many Southerners in 1857 when it warned against blacks and whites competing in any menial occupation, for "slaves or negroes may be inclined to consider themselves on a par of equality with white servants." Some pro-slavery apologists insisted that slaves should do all work and that all workers should be slaves, but slaveholders' rhapsodies about white solidarity made little sense to immigrant workers pitted against blacks in the labor market.[16]

Skilled mechanics complained about the degradation they felt because of competition with slaves. By permitting slaves to compete with whites, slaveholders dragged the whites down to the level of the blacks, thereby breeding "discontent and hatred" against slavery. Rather, as one master mechanic in Charleston wrote in 1860, slaveholders should relegate blacks to their "true position" of subordination "under a master workman" to effect "a closer bond of union" among the white classes of the city. Of course, enlarging opportunities in skilled trades for whites meant increasing competition among blacks and whites in the unskilled ones.[17]

Satisfying the demands of all white workingmen required the removal of slaves from the urban economy, something slaveholders were not willing or able to do even to achieve white unity. Thus, on the eve of secession, white workers and slaveholders did not necessarily stand together. As long as white immigrants performed tasks identified with bondage and competed for work with slaves, the natural affinity of race and property that bound slaveholder and nonslaveholder together in the countryside suffered strains in the city.

The economic growth of Southern cities, which brought immigrants into competition with slavery, also altered the physical environment of the city, making Southern cities similar to Northern ones in many ways and, also, transforming the social dynamics governing black and white, foreign-born and native-born, worker and employer, poor and rich. Warehouses, manufacturing establishments, and tenements consumed open spaces, foliage, and grass, particularly along the waterfront and on the peripheries of cities. The older, rural features of urban life—parks, trees, gardens, and yards—survived almost solely in areas occupied by the upper classes. The appearance of distinct areas within cities, differentiated by physical landscape, revealed the breakdown of urban community into subdivisions based on economic function, class, and culture. The proliferation of city directories in the 1850s, which has allowed us to map the physical and social terrain of urban change, further attested to the shift from an organic, small-town, even rural, sense of community as a direct and personal experience to one that was increasingly impersonal, abstract, fragmented, and formal.

Such unsettling effects were new to Southern experience. During the 1830s Irish and German immigrants in Southern cities had generally dispersed within each city, although they occupied places around or close to the central business area. Before efficient local transportation or the centralization of urban employment, workers sought residences within short walks to work to compensate for the long hours on the job.

Unskilled occupations offered irregular and short-term employment at best so that laborers needed easy access to the main wharves, warehouses, and business district where employment was available and daily hiring took place. As long as the labor pool remained small or grew moderately, the walking cities accommodated newcomers without undue stress on housing or dramatic changes in the cityscape. The physical proximity and integration of all classes facilitated communication and interaction, retarding class or cultural exclusiveness and preserving the rhythms of small-town life.[18]

The dispersal of small immigrant populations in geographically confined cities made possible their incorporation into traditional Southern social and political communities. In Charleston, gentlemen of property and standing early became acutely self-conscious about their racial and social vulnerability in a city where blacks outnumbered whites and where wealth was concentrated in few hands. Consequently, they fostered a familial, paternalistic urban ethos and appealed to immigrants and native-born white workers on the basis of common racial interest. Any ethnic division among whites threatened white solidarity. In Northern cities associational life increasingly reflected neighborhood, ethnic, or class exclusiveness, but Charleston's clubs and social organizations were "broadly inclusive" and assimilative in practice, open to whites regardless of national background or religion. In turn, by the 1830s all the important ethnic societies, such as the Hibernian Society and the German Friendly Society, had adopted the Charleston way, ending membership restrictions based on ethnic identity. In the 1840s such organizations were electing to office persons who had no ethnic ties to the original membership, and throughout the 1850s they were honoring Southern statesmen and supporting Southern rights. By that time the organizations had little connection with the new Irish and German immigrants who were streaming into Charleston.[19]

The process of assimilating outsiders into Southern interests remained incomplete even in the 1830s. New, poor Irish arrivals did not participate in Charleston's older associations, although the Hibernian Society did provide relief to the very needy among them. Irish Catholics preferred their own organizations or none at all, cutting them off from the Protestant-dominated Hibernian Society. The party preferences of association members reveal other fissures within ethnic groups. The leaders of the Hibernian Society supported the Nullifiers in the 1830s, but the rank and file remained heavily Unionist in sentiment. Insomuch as leaders of ethnic organizations function as connectors, binding disparate elements within the group together through newspapers, petitions, and public service in dealing with the host society, the Charleston "leaders" were sending false signals to the larger Southern community. They did not speak for their groups, which were changing rapidly anyway. Neither cohesion nor consensus fully occurred in the 1830s and 1840s, before the great crunch of new immigrants in the 1850s shattered any illusions of unity.[20]

During the 1850s the sheer volume of immigrants coming into Southern cities combined with the economic expansion of those same cities to prevent older assumptions about social community from operating. Between 1850 and 1860 residential patterns revealed that urban dwellers were dividing along lines of class, race, culture, and wealth. Free blacks and Irish immigrants tended to be the most residentially segregated in virtually every city in which they lived in significant numbers. Their poverty condemned them to the least desirable locations. Even Germans, who had a wider range of skills and wealth and religious divisions among Protestant, Catholic, and Jew, clustered together into definite "German blocks" within neighborhoods. The rise of a commercial middle class of clerks, professionals, and managers—drawn largely from Northern-born or second-generation immigrants and native Southerners—further bifurcated the cities. Separate associations sprang up around each clustering of function, class, residence, race, or whatever, thereby solidifying separate identities.[21]

In Charleston, Irish immigrants crowded into the low, dirty streets along the Cooper River, north and east of the city's warehouses and wharves. Frederick Law Olmsted thought the "packing filth, and squalor" there equal to the worst he had seen in any comparable Northern town. Savannah's working-class immigrants, who were largely Irish, jockeyed with blacks for space in the "low, dingy, squalid, cheerless negro huts" along the city's fringes, wherever rents were cheapest. Even small inland cities like Augusta had ethnic/working-class neighborhoods. In Augusta the Irish employees of the Georgia Railroad shared "Dublin" with a small black community.[22]

Richmond's topography of hills and waterways created natural enclosures that allowed different classes and groups to isolate themselves from one another. Isolation bred strong neighborhood identities. So, too, did the segregation of economic functions into distinct areas. The working classes composed of blacks, Irish, and Germans massed along Shockoe Creek and the James River, near the factories and wharves; as that area filled up, they settled on the outskirts of the city.[23]

Immigrants spread throughout New Orleans, but they concentrated in the lower and upper reaches of the waterfront, close to their work. In the Third Municipality, where most immigrants entered the city, numerous immigrant shanties cropped up. Other immigrants swarmed into the Second Municipality and, by the 1850s, also controlled the suburbs of Lafayette and Carrollton. Neighborhoods with such names as "Little Saxony" and the "Irish Channel" staked off ethnic and class boundaries within the city. They also corresponded with the poorest and least healthy sections, which, as one observer remarked in 1853, had "as many destitute poor crowded together" as any city in Europe. Contemporaries measured the class, and by implication the ethnic, differences in New Orleans according to the "declivity of the soil." Anyone living below the water line belonged to the lower class. Grog shops, groceries, and brothels flourished in the poor districts, giving an unsavory, sordid reputation to the neighborhoods—and their denizens.[24]

Crammed into low-lying areas along waterways, debilitated by travel and work, and undernourished, poor immigrants became easy prey for diseases, but their suffering evoked more contempt than compassion from native-born Southerners in the 1850s. The high mortality among immigrants during the epidemics became a source of animus toward them. That immigrants burdened hospitals and poor houses was problem enough in a society that regarded poverty as a personal failing. That they shared those facilities with blacks was cause for further disgust. That the unacclimated immigrants proved unusually susceptible to the regional plagues of cholera and yellow fever convinced many Southerners that immigrants would never fit into Southern society and that they posed an immediate danger to it.

In the antebellum period most Americans equated disease with moral failure. Disease and social disorder both emanated from violations of natural law. To prevent or cure such ills, society had to inculcate proper values in its members, and individuals had to practice good hygiene. Although some Southern medical doctors urged sewer-age and drainage improvements in cities to stave off epidemics, most educated persons continued to believe that "disease was a judgment." Dr. E. H. Barton of the New Orleans Board of Health confessed as much in 1849, when he blamed the victims of cholera for their affliction: "The liability being individual, the municipal power can only aid by cleanliness and ventilation." The presence of immigrants, others added, actually imperiled Southern cities because their vicious habits and improvidence invited disease, and the epidemics they "caused" discouraged more responsible persons, capital, and trade from entering Southern cities. The immigrants were pariahs.[25]

In surveying the ethnic/working-class districts, too many Southerners missed the internal diversity among the lower classes and saw only disease and disorder. They lumped the lower classes into one alien mass, irrespective of differences in color, caste, or condition. Southerners regarded the lower classes collectively as "the worst elements" and treated them accordingly. In Savannah, in 1855, the police chief believed the worlds of the "quieter" people and lower-class "disturbers of the peace" were so incompatible in values and interest that he urged the city to build two police stations as a barrier to safeguard life and property in the respectable sections from the disruptive elements surrounding them. Southerners expected the working-class immigrants to cause trouble.

When a series of fires broke out in Mobile during a yellow fever epidemic, Mobile authorities initially charged that "the low Irish populations about the harbor" committed the arson to plunder a prostrate city. Only the confessions of several runaway slaves shifted blame away from the immigrants.[26]

City authorities across the South sought control over an alien population of immigrants and blacks. Police practice seemed to operate on the assumption that immigrants, especially the "fighting Irish," and blacks made up a criminal class needful of close, constant supervision. Municipal arrest and court records reveal that the Irish and blacks comprised the overwhelming majority of persons charged with criminal or antisocial behavior, including vagrancy, disorderly conduct, drunkenness, petit larceny, and brawling. In New Orleans immigrants were uniquely prone to arrest for being "dangerous and suspicious characters," even when they had broken no law. Throughout the arrest proceedings the city authorities identified the immigrant by his foreignness. He was Irish, "a stranger," or whatever. Like blacks, the new immigrants did not quite belong among the respectable classes and bore watching. The disproportionately high percentage of foreign-born in Southern prisons further confirmed the Southern "guardians" worst suspicions about the aliens among them, and about the social disorder in their own changing cities. Where once, in the 1830s, Charleston authorities assigning work and charity for poor people on relief refused "to break down any of the distinctions" between black and white poor "by subjecting them to a common mode of punishment" or work, by the 1850s the immigrant poor came in for rougher handling. All the residents of the poor districts required discipline.[27]

By the 1850s the immigrant workers represented more than just potential criminal types: they were social disruption personified. Southerners feared workers who spent much time in grog shops, groceries, saloons—all those places and activities where the host society's control was weakest, and where, too, slaves mingled easily with free blacks and lower-class whites. Thrown together in the workplace and lower-class neighborhoods, and often practicing the same trades, immigrants and blacks did not just fight one another. Immigrant tradesmen kept up an illegal traffic with country slaves bringing produce into the city, dispensed liquor to blacks with complete disregard for city ordinances and social custom, and, on occasion, assisted slave runaways. Immigrants violated the etiquette of race relations and disgusted Southerners by living, trading, drinking, and even sleeping with blacks, slave and free. More than anything else, slaveholders feared a world in which blacks were elevated above whites. In the poor districts white prostitutes took money from black men for sexual services, and white workers sometimes worked for black employers. Blacks in cities had the experience of seeing whites under them in several ways.[28]

Antebellum Southern cities, unlike their Northern counterparts, lacked many formal means of imposing order. The factory system did not exist to regiment life, nor did most people toil in large-scale workplaces where they came under a common discipline. Southern cities failed to establish enough public schools capable of inculcating a shared set of values in children of all classes. German-born Christopher G. Memminger, among others, argued that Charleston could reverse economic stagnation and alleviate class tensions by building a common school system. Its principal purpose, he contended, would be to battle the disaffection and lack of "public spirit" among lower-class whites, especially immigrants, and so achieve the unity of purpose and white solidarity necessary to preserve Southern institutions. In 1849 the commissioners of the free schools of St. Philip's and St. Michael's warned that, unless immigrants were brought into common schools, they would "always be an easy prey to political seduction, and trouble, under the excitement of general elections or the promptings of an unprincipled leader, to break out into excesses," and to defy the law. In cities, they continued, the "ignorant and uneducated" poor were the first to engage "in outrage and violence" and to oppose Southern institutions. During the 1850s, New Orleans followed Charleston in building a public school system to provide a common language and experience in an otherwise culturally and socially divided city. But the Charleston and New Orleans cases were exceptional, and even in those cities most lower-class whites did not attend schools regularly or for very long, if at all.[29]

Religion, a powerful matrix of Southern civilization, also failed to generate much centripetal force in Southern cities. Most of the new immigrants were Catholics for whom the dominant evangelical Protestantism of the region meant little, except perhaps as a source of oppression, and Protestant churches made few efforts to bring immigrants under the Southern religious canopy. Methodists did, for example, support a mission among Germans in Mobile in the 1840s, and various ministers attempted to effect death-bed conversions of individual immigrants in hospitals, but too many evangelicals recognized the immigrants only to condemn them. Even the Catholic church, whose leaders shared Southern values regarding slavery and a conservative social order, failed to provide unity among the newer immigrants. As in the North, ethnic divisions within the church, grafted onto longstanding disputes between the laity and the hierarchy over church finances and control of pastors, wracked the universal church and kept it weak and defensive.[30]

Responding to public fears about a breakdown of law and order amid increasing population density and diversity, city authorities, like their Northern counterparts, established uniformed police forces. Along with the creation or extension of poor houses, sewer systems, waterworks, health boards, and the like, the introduction of a professional police force promised to restore discipline and harmony by enforcing common standards of morality and private behavior. But immigrants intruded in the process by making police work their own. While native-born Southerners and second-generation immigrants commanded the better paying positions of constables, marshals, detectives, and captains and lieutenants, immigrant Irish and German laborers filled the ranks of the police on the beats or in patrols. The Irish were especially over-represented in the New Orleans, Memphis, Charleston, and Savannah police forces, although a reform administration in Charleston and Know Nothing administrations in Memphis and New Orleans in the late 1850s reduced the size of the Irish presence in their police departments. Without marketable skills, lower-class immigrants found police work attractive. Despite low pay and unpleasant duties, it afforded them regular work or, frequently, a second income and the possibility of upward mobility in municipal employment. Poor pay and their affinity to the lower-class persons they were supposed to control led to graft, abuses, and countless infractions of police regulations. The police were not fit or able to impose Southern order on the cities. Control of police departments also became a major political issue in local elections, and it encouraged increased immigrant involvement in urban politics.[31]

The entrance of immigrants into city politics further threatened social control. As long as "respectable" people served as policemen, magistrates, and jurors, Southerners thought they could maintain discipline over the lower classes. By the 1850s the native-born Southerners' political hegemony in several cities had been so eroded that they had to resort to ethnic politics just to stay in power. Charleston patricians symbolically conceded as much when they added Irish and German candidates (acceptable to them) to their tickets in municipal elections. In Savannah the issues of police harassment of immigrant shopkeepers specifically and police department reform generally (which meant closer surveillance of and interference in lower-class activities) defined political categories from 1854 to the Civil War. Democrats there appealed openly for immigrant support, declaiming on the party's love of laborers and, more importantly, providing patronage jobs in city government or on public projects and winking at immigrants who violated laws regarding the sale of liquor to blacks.[32]

Democrats, who tended to align with immigrant voting blocs, were themselves never wholly comfortable with the new politics. Political leaders still tried to preserve some of the older political style, based on assumptions of an organic and natural relation among all whites, by using race as a weapon, but immigrant workers' insistence on issues related to their interest made such appeals increasingly anachronistic in a divided metropolis. The experience of Thomas Avery, running for Congress in 1848, illustrates the uneasy adjustment of the Democrats to their own politics. Avery ventured into "Pinch," the rough Irish working-class neighborhood of north Memphis, to attend a social gathering put on by an Irish workingmen's union. Avery brought his three young sisters to the affair, and the boys of Pinch danced all night with the Southern belles. After the meeting Avery thanked his sister Elizabeth for her sacrifice on his behalf: "You have done splendidly. I know how you feel, but luckily I don't think those fellows know. You made them think you were having the time of your life. It will make them feel kindly toward me." A natural affinity among whites of all classes was nowhere apparent in Avery's confession. Going among the immigrants was strictly business, or politics.[33]

Immigrants flexed their political muscles to win places in city governments, which, in turn, made those governments less an instrument of social control. Native-born Southerners joined businessmen, many of whom were Northern-born or second-generation immigrants, in crusades to clean out the vice and corruption of the poor districts. Out-of-power, such persons formed vigilante groups to drive out the ruffians and evildoers in their midst. Whitecaps in Atlanta in 1851 and vigilantes in New Orleans in 1859 bracketed a decade of extra-legal "justice." Nativism also functioned as a weapon of control. Election day riots by the Irish in several Southern cities in the 1850s inflamed public opinion against immigrants, while businessmen and slaveholders fanned the controversies by reminding Southerners about the immigrant working classes' contributions to disorder. Know Nothing leaders in New Orleans ran on promises to crack down on corruption and vice, especially prostitution, in the poor districts. The South's most cosmopolitan city escaped a class war only because the Know Nothings failed to deliver on their pledges once in power, becoming preoccupied with building railroads and improving the city's business climate.[34]

The anti-immigrant, antiworking-class movement reached its apogee in the late 1850s when planters enlisted businessmen and manufacturers in the campaign to re-open the African slave trade. As Governor James Adams of South Carolina explained, the South demanded a subordinate, unenfranchised labor force, for the influx of unassimilated but enfranchised immigrant workers into Southern cities invited conflicts between capital and labor. The South, Adams concluded, needed more slaves and fewer white workers if it was going to retain its liberty. During the secession proceedings in Virginia, Alexander Stuart, among other conservative businessmen, urged his state to use the opportunity of secession to reassert control over the immigrants and working classes already in the South. He suggested that Virginians revise the state constitution so that propertyless whites would lose the suffrage. Other Southern statesmen shared Stuart's concern about the loyalties of the urban working class and expressed their dire forebodings about internal chaos erupting at home during the secession crisis, unless slaveholders acted to curb the working-classes' political power.[35]

The fears were real, and in some ways justified, but the Civil War did not bring civil war to Southern cities. Many working-class immigrants fled the cities to escape Confederate service; others signed oaths swearing that they never intended to become citizens, thereby making them ineligible for the draft; and some openly taunted the Confederacy by falling in with federal forces or rallying with Southern unionists. For reasons of pride, profit, or personality, however, enough immigrants joined the Confederate armies to dispel fears of white chaos from within the South. After the war the dangers from immigrant workers seemed to fade. Foreign immigration to Southern cities virtually ended, and blacks, newly freed from bondage and poor, now flooded Southern cities. Many immigrants and their children who survived the war edged up the economic and social order in Southern cities. Where great gaps of wealth and culture had separated the upper class from the working class in Charleston in the 1850s, and elsewhere to a lesser extent, race now became the index of class. The poor were black. They did the "nigger work" and left the "respectable" trades, management, and property to whites of all national backgrounds. Although ethnic and class differences did not disappear completely from politics and social relations, these differences receded in the face of the new racial demographics of Southern cities. Southerners lapsed back into their philosophy of social stasis as whites. In the countryside and city alike they united to resist Reconstruction. The end of significant urban immigration from abroad and the rise of a black unskilled working class in Southern cities reversed the divergence between countryside and city. Ruralism, racism, and regionalism again governed the whole South.[36]

On the eve of secession, immigration, cultural diversity, urban disorder, and class conflict all posed real threats to the slaveholding way of life, but the Southern philosophy of stasis denied their very existence. Ironically, when external forces besieged the Old South, it was that philosophy's mythical homogeneity that somehow prevailed. Created to describe a present that did not actually exist, the myth became instead a self-fulfilling prophecy that shaped the South's postwar future. Thanks in part to its belated accuracy, it has also informed historical treatments of the antebellum past, obscuring the impact of immigration on mid-nineteenth-century Southern society.

NOTES

1. The literature on Southern character and distinctiveness is enormous and still growing. A good recent statement, which includes references to other important works, is James M. McPherson, "Antebellum Southern Exceptionalism: A New Look at an Old Question," *Civil War History:* 29 (September 1983): 230–44. But see also Bertram Wyatt-Brown, *Southern Honor: Ethics and Behavior in the Old South* (New York, 1982); Carl Degler, *Place Over Time: The Continuity of Southern Distinctiveness* (Baton Rouge, 1977); and David Potter, *The South and the Sectional Conflict* (Baton Rouge, 1968). A recent attempt to deny Southern distinctiveness is Edward Pessen, "How Different from Each Other Were the Antebellum North and South?" *American Historical Review* 85 (December 1980): 1119–49, which also has many useful references; but see also the reactions to Pessen's arguments by Thomas Alexander, Stanley L. Engerman, and Forrest McDonald and Grady McWhiney, and Pessen's reply, in "*AHR* Forum—Antebellum North and South in Comparative Perspective: A Discussion," ibid., 1150–66.

2. On Herrenvolk democracy, see especially George M. Fredrickson, *The Black Image in the White Mind: The Debate on Afro-American Character and Destiny, 1817–1914* (New York, 1971), 61ff. On the unity imposed by religion, see Samuel S. Hill, Jr., *The South and the North in American Religion* (Athens, Ga., 1981), 46–89; Anne C. Loveland, *Southern Evangelicals and the Social Order, 1800–1860* (Baton Rouge, 1980); and Donald G. Mathews, *Religion in the Old South* (Chicago, 1977), chapters 3 and 4. On the increased political participation among all classes of white Southerners, see especially William J. Cooper, Jr., *Liberty and Slavery: Southern Politics to 1860* (New York, 1983), 184–87 and passim. Cooper focuses almost exclusively on the rural South.

3. The most recent, and best, overview of the proslavery argument is Drew Gilpin Faust's excellent introduction in Faust, ed., *The Ideology of Slavery: Proslavery Thought in the An-*

tebellum South, 1830–1860 (Baton Rouge, 1981), 1–20. See also William S. Jenkins, *Pro-Slavery Thought in the Old South* (Chapel Hill, 1935), 285–308; and Eugene Genovese, *The Political Economy of Slavery: Studies in the Economy and Society of the Slave South* (New York, 1965), 28–36.

4. An excellent discussion of the changing urban workplace in the Old South is Ira Berlin and Herbert Gutman, "Natives and Immigrants, Free Men and Slaves: Urban Workingmen in the Antebellum American South," *American Historical Review* 88 (December 1983): 1175–1200. No full survey of foreign immigration in the South exists. Several useful overviews are Ella Lonn, *Foreigners in the Confederacy* (Chapel Hill, 1940), 1–32; Randall M. Miller, "Immigrants in the Old South," *Immigration History Newsletter* 10 (November 1978): 8–14; and Herbert Weaver, "Foreigners in Ante-Bellum Towns of the Lower South," *Journal of Southern History* 13 (1947): 62–73. The best studies of immigrants in particular cities are Edward L. Ayers, *Vengeance and Justice: Crime and Punishment in the Nineteenth-Century South* (New York, 1984), chapter 3 (on Savannah principally); Kathleen C. Berkeley, "'Like a Plague of Locusts': Immigration and Social Change in Memphis, Tennessee, 1850–1880" (Ph.D. diss., University of California, Los Angeles, 1980); Christopher Silver, "A New Look at Old South Urbanization: The Irish Worker in Charleston, South Carolina, 1840–1860," in Samuel M. Hines and George W. Hopkins, eds., *South Atlantic Urban Studies* (Columbia, S.C., 1979), 141–72; and Fredrick M. Spletstoser, "Back Door to the Land of Plenty: New Orleans as an Immigrant Port, 1820–1860," 2 vols. (Ph.D. diss., Louisiana State University, 1978). On Southern cities, with some discussion of foreign-born immigration, see Clement Eaton, *The Growth of Southern Civilization* (New York, 1961), chapter 11; and especially David R. Goldfield, *Cotton Fields and Skyscrapers: Southern City and Region, 1607–1980* (Baton Rouge, 1982), chapter 2, who makes a strong case for continuity between countryside and city throughout Southern history.

5. Based on the Seventh Census of the United States, 1850, Population and Industrial Schedules; and Eighth Census of the United States, 1860, Population and Industrial Schedules (National Archives) for the various cities under review: Augusta, Atlanta, Charleston, Louisville, Memphis, Mobile, Nashville, New Orleans, Norfolk, Richmond, Savannah. For aggregate data, see U.S. Bureau of Census, *The Seventh Census of the United States, 1850* (Washington, 1853); J. D. B. DeBow, *Statistical View of the United States* (Washington, 1854); and U.S. Bureau of Census, *Population of the United States in 1860* (Washington, 1864). Some of this data is conveniently tabulated by Berlin and Gutman, "Natives and Immigrants," 1176–84; Dennis Rousey, "Town Versus Country in the Antebellum South: Presidential Balloting, 1836–1860" (paper read at the Southern Historical Association meeting, November 1983); Lonn, *Foreigners,* 2–9, 29–32; and Weaver, "Foreigners," 66–67. Some representative figures are: In New Orleans between 1850 and 1860 foreign-born males (eighteen years or older) constituted 70 percent of the entire white, adult male population of the city. In Charleston they numbered between 45 percent (1850) and 49 percent (1860); in Savannah their share rose from 37 percent (1850) to 51 percent (1860); and in Memphis it grew from 35 percent (1850) to 49 percent (1860). Except for Atlanta, Georgia, and Montgomery, Alabama, all sizable inland cities also experienced a significant increase in the percentage of foreign-born persons in the white, adult male population. The proportion of foreign-born in Augusta's white, adult male population went from roughly 21 percent in 1850 to 35 percent in 1860; Nashville's from 22 to 38 percent; and Richmond's from 25 to 34 percent, to cite three examples. Immigrant populations in Southern cities were probably higher, but their transiency no doubt caused census takers to miss many of them in their canvasses.

6. On the effects of immigrant competition, see Berlin and Gutman, "Natives and Immigrants," 1175–1200, for a convenient summary of the data

7. On immigrant competition with free blacks, see Ira Berlin, *Slaves Without Masters: The Free Negro in the Antebellum South* (New York, 1974), 230–33; and Leonard P. Curry, *The Free Black in Urban America, 1800–1850* (Chicago, 1981), 29. Curry underestimates the influence of immigrants in the South largely because he ends his discussion with 1850. On the Arkansas example, see Orville Taylor, *Negro Slavery in Arkansas* (Durham, N.C., 1958), 111–12.

8. See, for example, Spletstoser, "Back Door to the Land of Poverty," 383–85; Joseph Holt Ingraham, *The Sunny South; or, The Southerner at Home, Embracing Five Years' Experience of a Northern Governess in the Land of the Sugar and the Cotton* (Philadelphia, 1860), 504; Amelia Murray, *Letters from the United States, Cuba and Canada* (New York, 1856), 212; Narrative of Tom Eikel, "Irish Channel Narratives—Unpublished" (1941), Louisiana Federal Writers' Project Narratives (Northwestern State University of Louisiana, Natchitoches); Commissioners' Minutes, 7 January 1836. Charleston Orphan House Records (South Carolina Historical Society); Berlin, *Slaves Without Masters,* 231–32. For an early example, see Martha Richardson to James P. Screven, 25 February 1821, Arnold-Screven Papers (Southern Historical Collection, University of North Carolina at Chapel Hill). See also the federal census schedules for 1850 and 1860 to identify immigrant employment in Southern cities.

9. The paragraphs on Norfolk are based on the Eighth Census of the United States, 1860, Population Schedule, Norfolk, Virginia (National Archives); and Tommy L. Bogger, "The Slave and Free Black Community in Norfolk, 1775–1865" (Ph.D. diss., University of Virginia, 1976), 163–67, 174–79.

10. In New Orleans many workers in the 1850s earned two dollars per day for manual labor: Spletstoser, "Back Door to the Land of Poverty," 377–79. On employment patterns in New Orleans, see Richard R. Tansey, "Economic Expansion and Urban Disorder in Antebellum New Orleans" (Ph.D. diss., University of Texas at Austin, 1981), 94–97, 103; H. A. Murray, *Lands of the Slave and the Free, or Cuba, the United States, and Canada,* 2 vols. (London, 1855), II: 25; Frederick Law Olmsted, *A Journey in the Seaboard Slave States* (New York, 1856), 589; John S. C. Abbott, *South and North: or Impressions Received During a Trip to Cuba and the South* (New York, 1860), 112–13. New Orleans' laws discouraged boat captains from hiring blacks so that blacks did not necessarily benefit from employers' dissatisfaction with white workers or upswings in the local economy. In Mobile police protected black stevedores and dockworkers when they were attacked by tough "Dagoes" in 1852, and at least one newspaper supported the move because blacks were law-abiding and spent their money in the city: Mobile *Advertiser,* 23 December 1852.

11. Silver, "A New Look at Old South Urbanization," 157–59; Eighth Census of the United States, 1860, Population Schedule, Charleston, South Carolina (National Archives).

12. Octavia Smith to Richard Smith, 29 June 1839, Richard Smith Correspondence (Louisiana State University); Walter H. Stevens to W.S. Rosecrans, 2 January 1849, William S. Rosecrans Papers (University of California, Los Angeles); *New Orleans Picayune,* 11 December 1856; Sara Lawton to Mrs. A.L. Alexander, 6 March 1847, Alexander-Hillhouse Papers (Southern Historical Collection, University of North Carolina at Chapel Hill). For an example of the bounding from job to job by an Irish immigrant, follow the course of John Abbott, who worked on board a brig sailing between Charleston and Havana, as a servant in the Mills House in Charleston, and as a policeman, among other jobs, within a span of less than three years; *Report of the Committee on Health and Drainage, on the Origin and Diffusion of Yellow Fever in Charleston in the Autumn of* 1856 ([Charleston], n.d.), 3, 14; and *Report on Yellow Fever* (n.p., n.d.), 6–7, 9.

13. The viability of slave labor in cities has occasioned a hot debate among historians. The debate is framed by Richard Wade, *Slavery in the Cities: The South, 1820–1860* (New York, 1964), who argues that the social arrangements of urban life, combined with economic factors,

threatened slavery's existence; and by Claudia Goldin, *Urban Slavery in the American South, 1820–1860: A Quantitative History* (Chicago, 1976), who argues that increasing rural demand for slaves, rather than any imminent decline in the institution's economic health in cities, drew off slaves. Only Goldin addresses the place of immigrants in this process; she suggests that immigrant labor in cities contributed to the elasticity of the Southern labor system.

14. Goldin, *Urban Slavery,* 28–33; Wade, *Slavery in the Cities,* 50–51; Ronald T. Takaki, *Iron Cages: Race and Culture in Nineteenth-Century America* (Seattle, 1982 ed.), 123.

15. Roger W. Shugg, *Origins of Class Struggle in Louisiana: A Social History of White Farmers and Laborers During Slavery and After, 1840–1875* (Baton Rouge, 1972 ed.), 93–94; *Harper's Magazine* 7 (1853): 755; Frederick Law Olmsted, *The Cotton Kingdom,* Arthur M. Schlesinger, ed. (New York, 1953), 70. On Irish girls' preference for domestic service, see Hasia R. Diner, *Erin's Daughters in America: Irish Immigrant Women in the Nineteenth Century* (Baltimore, 1983), 74–84.

16. *Richmond Enquirer,* 27 August 1857. The previous year the *Enquirer* had welcomed the arrival of immigrant workers: ibid., 17 October 1856.

17. Charleston *Courier,* 7 December 1860. The connection between wage slavery and chattel slavery was well developed in the British Isles and may have been known by Irish immigrants. Irish abolitionists tried to mobilize the working classes against slavery on that basis. On these points, see Marcus Cunliffe, *Chattel Slavery and Wage Slavery: The Anglo-American Context, 1830–1860* (Athens, Ga., 1979), chapters 1 and 2, for the general view; and Douglas Riach, "Blacks and Blackface on the Irish Stage, 1830–60," *Journal of American Studies* 7 (1973): 241.

18. On urban residence patterns generally, see David Ward, *Cities and Immigrants: A Geography of Change in Nineteenth-Century America* (New York, 1971), 105–7.

19. Jane H. Pease and William H. Pease, "Social Structure and the Potential for Urban Change: Boston and Charleston in the 1830s," *Journal of Urban History* 8 (1982): 173–75, 177–79; Frederic Cople Jaher, *The Urban Establishment: Upper Strata in Boston, New York, Charleston, Chicago, and Los Angeles* (Urbana, 1982), 332–34, 375, 393–95; Hibernian Society, *Constitution and Rules . . . revised . . . 1838* (Charleston, 1838), 21–30; George J. Gongaware, *The History of the German Friendly Society of Charleston, South Carolina, 1766–1916* (Richmond, Va., 1935), 206–17; German Friendly Society, Charleston, Minutes VIII (12 February 1840), IX (24 April 1850), IX (30 April 1851), German Friendly Society Papers (South Carolinian Library, University of South Carolina).

20. Jane H. Pease and William H. Pease, "The Economics and Politics of Charleston's Nullification Crisis," *Journal of Southern History* 47 (1981): 346–47. On the function of ethnic leaders, see John Higham, ed., *Ethnic Leadership in America* (Baltimore, 1978), 8 and passim.

21. My conclusions are based on my mapping of the various groups, compiled from city directories and the federal census for 1850 and 1860 in Charleston, Memphis, Mobile, New Orleans, Richmond, and Savannah. Good summaries of ethnic concentrations include Berkeley, "'Like a Plague of Locusts,'" 29–30, 39–57; Victor Hugh Treat, "Migration into Louisiana, 1834–1880" (Ph.D. diss., University of Texas at Austin, 1967), 260–77, 288–98; Alan S. Thompson, "Mobile, Alabama, 1850–1861: Economic, Political, Physical, and Population Characteristics" (Ph.D. diss., University of Alabama, 1979), 200–13. On the relationship between geographical proximity and intensity of ethnic identity and associational life, see, especially Kathleen Neils Conzen, "Immigrants, Immigrant Neighborhoods, and Ethnic Identity: Historical Issues," *Journal of American History* 66 (1979): 603–15. The rise of modern retailing and the general expansion of financial and commercial activity also broke down older conceptions of ties between the artisan and shopkeeper. A new "middle class" of salaried workers emerged in the 1840s and 1850s with few ties to the craftsmen. This class also tended to live apart from the artisans. For the process of change in Charleston, see Stuart Blumin,

"Black Coats to White Collars: Economic Change, Nonmanual Work, and the Social Structure of Industrializing America," in Stuart Bruchey, ed., *Small Business in American Life* (New York, 1980), 105–06 and passim. For the emerging pattern wherever large amounts of goods had to be moved and sold, see also Grigsby H. Wooton, Jr., "New City of the South: Atlanta, 1843–1873" (Ph.D. diss., Johns Hopkins University, 1973), 52–55; Thompson, "Mobile, Alabama," 250, 255, 279–80; Richard H. Haunton, "Savannah in the 1850s" (Ph.D. diss., Emory University; 1968), 50–51; Robert C. Reinders, "A Social History of New Orleans, 1850–1860" (Ph.D. diss., University of Texas at Austin, 1957), part I, 159–63. That some of this class were foreign-born, and many second-generation immigrants, suggests that upward mobility was occurring in Southern cities.

22. Olmsted, *Journey in the Seaboard Slave States,* 404; Charles G. Parsons, *Inside View of Slavery: or a Tour Among the Planters* (Boston, 1855), 23; *Savannah Daily Journal and Courier,* 23 March 1855; *Savannah Evening Journal,* 22 March 1853; *Directory for the City of Augusta and Business Advertiser for 1859* (Augusta, Ga., 1859).

23. Michael B. Chesson, *Richmond After the War: 1865–1890* (Richmond, Va., 1981), 121–23.

24. Treat, "Migration into Louisiana," 260–77; Spletstoser, "Back Door to the Land of Plenty," 366–69; J. Henna Deiler, *Geshichte der New Orleanser Deutschen Presse* (New Orleans, 1901), 9–11; John F. Nau, *The German People of New Orleans, 1850–1900* (Leiden, 1958), 17; Shugg, *Origins, of Class Struggle,* 40; [Edward Henry Durell], *New Orleans As I Found It* (New York, 1845), 17–18; Samuel Cartwright, "On the Prevention of Yellow Fever," *New Orleans Medical and Surgical Journal* 10 (1853–54): 315 (quote); and New Orleans *Daily Picayune,* 19 May 1849 (quote). Earl F. Niehaus, *The Irish in New Orleans, 1800–1860* (Baton Rouge, 1965), 28–34, argues that the Irish were not concentrated in any one district; rather, he places them throughout the city. My research in the federal census, local business directories, and hospital and poor house records leads me to think otherwise. Although the Irish dispersed, newer and poor immigrants in the 1840s and 1850s settled in identifiable "Irish districts." Most contemporaries thought so.

25. On attitudes toward health generally, see William B. Walker, "The Health Reform Movement in the United States, 1830–1870" (Ph.D. diss., Johns Hopkins University, 1955); John B. Blake, "Health Reform," in Edwin Gaustad, ed., *The Rise of Adventism: Religion and Society in Mid-Nineteenth Century America* (New York, 1974), 30–49; Charles S. Rosenberg, *The Cholera Years: The United States in 1832, 1849, and 1866* (Chicago, 1962), 142–50. For Southern examples, see Shugg, *Origins of Class Struggle,* 53–55, who describes the "medical Know Nothingism" of the day; John Duffy, *Sword of Pestilence: The New Orleans Yellow Fever Epidemic of 1853* (Baton Rouge, 1966); New Orleans *Daily Delta,* 31 July, 31 August 1853; Cartwright, "On the Prevention of Yellow Fever," 305–6, 312–16; I. H. Charles to John Liddell, 18 November 1847, Isaac H. Charles Letters (Louisiana State University); E. H. Barton, "Annual Report of the New Orleans Board of Health," *Southern Medical Reports* 1 (1849): 83 (quote). For an opposing view, see J. C, Simonds, "On the Sanitary Condition of New Orleans, as Illustrated by Its Mortality Statistics," ibid., 2 (850): 207. The disease environment of Southern cities, which discouraged many immigrants from settling there, raises the counterfactual question of how Southern cities might have developed if they had compared more favorably with Northern cities.

26. *Savannah Republican,* 24 March 1855; *Savannah Daily Journal and Courier,* 25 March 1855; George Lewis, *Impressions of America and American Churches* (Edinburgh, Scotland, 1845), 173.

27. Herbert Weaver, "Foreigners in Ante-Bellum Savannah," *Georgia Historical Quarterly* 37 (1953): 8; Ayers, *Vengeance and Justice,* 72–106, 319–20; Chatham County Superior Court

Minutes, 1850–1861 (Georgia Department of Archives and History); Record Book of Arrests Charges, Penalties, Charleston Police Records, 1855–1856 (Charleston Library Society); Charleston Police Morning Reports, Lower Wards, 1861–1863 (Charleston Library Society); Vagrant Record Books (1859–61, 1861–62), Recorder's Office, Third District, New Orleans (City Archives, New Orleans Public Library); Reports of Arrests (1852–61), Department of Police, Recorder's Court Records, Third District, New Orleans (City Archives, New Orleans Public Library); "Station House Register, 1858–1860," Memphis Police Department Records (Memphis and Shelby County Archives, Old Cossitt Library, Memphis Public Library); Reinders, "A Social History of New Orleans," part I, 219–31; *Report of the Board of Control of the Louisiana Penitentiary . . . 1859* (Baton Rouge, 1859), 45–57; Charleston Alms House Records, vol. 1834–40, p. 298 (South Carolina Historical Society); Board of Commissioners of Charleston Poor House Minutes, Record Book 1852–58, 54–56, and Record Book 1858–66, 38–39 (City Archives, Charleston); Minute Book, Board of Managers, Savannah Poor House and Hospital, 1836–76, 16, 17 September 1839, 6 February 1844, Savannah Hospital Papers (Georgia Historical Society); Roper Hospital Case Book, number 2, 1859–62 (Waring Historical Library, Medical University of South Carolina).

28. Weaver, "Foreigners in Ante-Bellum Savannah," 7; Haunton, "Savannah in the 1850s," 18; Richard H. Shryock, ed., *Letters of Richard D. Arnold, M.D., 1808–1876* (Durham, N.C., 1929), 39, 44; Wade, *Slavery in the Cities,* 149–60, for a general view; J. Milton Mackie, *From Cape Cod to Dixie and the Tropics* (New York, 1864), 162; Olmsted, *Journey in the Seaboard Slave States,* 589; David Kaser, "Nashville's Women of Pleasure in 1860," *Tennessee Historical Quarterly* 23 (1964): 379–82; William Still, *The Underground Railroad, . . .* (Chicago, rpt. 1970), 251; Grand Jury Presentment, May 1851, Grand Jury Presentments, Charleston District, 1790–1865 (South Carolina Department of Archives, Columbia).

29. Memminger quoted in Laylon Wayne Jordan, "Education for Community: C. G. Memminger and the Origination of Common Schools in Antebellum Charleston," *South Carolina Historical Magazine* 83 (1982): 110; Memminger to J. H. Hammond, 28 April 1849, James H. Hammond Papers (Library of Congress); Minutes of Commissioners of Free Schools St. Philip's and St. Michael's [Charleston], January 1844–January 1855 [1858], 11 November 1846, 34–35, 20 November 1854, p. 121 (quote) (City Archives, Charleston). See also Jaher, *Urban Establishment,* 380–82. On New Orleans, see *Annual Report of the Superintendent of Public Schools, Fourth District, New Orleans,* May 12, 1855 (New Orleans, 1855), 7–8. More typical was the divided nature of "public" education in Mobile in which the Catholics created their own system because they were excluded from public support. No sense of the organic whole operated there to bring Catholic children, many of them immigrants, and Protestant children together. See Thompson, "Mobile, Alabama," 164–66.

30. On the German mission, see *Mobile Register,* 24 January 1844. On the failure of the Catholic church to impose cultural unity, see Randall M. Miller, "A Church in Cultural Captivity: Some Speculations on Catholic Identity in the Old South," in Randall M. Miller and Jon L. Wakelyn, eds., *Catholics in the Old South; Essays on Church and Culture* (Macon, Ga., 1983), especially 20–37.

31. Laylon Wayne Jordan, "Police Power and Public Safety in Antebellum Charleston: The Emergence of a New Police, 1800–1860," in Hines and Hopkins, eds., *South Atlantic Urban Studies,* 122–40; Dennis C. Rousey, "'Hibernian Leatherheads': Irish Cops in New Orleans, 1830–1880," *Journal of Urban History* 10 (November 1983): 61–84; Ayers, *Vengeance and Justice,* 82–91. For a study of the cries for public order and the ineffectiveness of the new police even to impose order on its immigrant recruits in one city, see *Charleston Courier,* 6 February, 1 May 1854, 25 October 1855, 15 January 1856; *Charleston Mercury,* 2 September 1835 (for early criticisms of foreigners on the city guard), 7 January 1856, *Statement of Receipts and*

Expenditures of the City Council of Charleston, 1849–1850 (Charleston, 1850); *Mayor's Report on City Affairs* . . . 1857 (Charleston, 1857), 17–18; Records of Arrests, Charges, Penalties . . . Charleston Police Records, 1855–1856 (on officers' neglect of duty and other infractions). In New Orleans the police department became a patronage nest, ruining its credibility and effectiveness. See Reinders, "Social History of New Orleans," part I, 216–218; Board of Police Minutes, 1854–56 (City Archives, New Orleans Public Library); Record of Police Oaths, New Orleans, 1856–61 (City Archives, New Orleans Public Library); and Mayor's Office, Personnel Records of the Police Department, 1852–1868 (City Archives, New Orleans Public Library). The Southern ethic of honor, with its attendant distrust of government, relied on private justice to control society. In the countryside where an organic relationship among whites operated, communal pressures worked well enough, but in the diverse and commercially-oriented cities citizens turned to formal means of control, which demanded deference to law as an abstract principle. For some good insights into the process whereby a society moves away from organic or formal conceptions of law, see David T. Konig, *Law and Society in Puritan Massachusetts: Essex County, 1629–1692* (Chapel Hill, 1979). On Southern honor and communal control, see Wyatt-Brown, *Southern Honor,* 71–72, 365–66; Michael Hindus, *Prison and Plantation: Crime, Justice, and Authority in Massachusetts and South Carolina, 1767–1878* (Chapel Hill, 1980); Dickson Bruce, *Violence and Culture in the Antebellum South* (Austin, Texas, 1979). For some perceptive observations on the differences between city and countryside, see Ayers, *Vengeance and Justice,* chapters 3 and 4.

32. Robert N. Olsberg, "A Government of Class and Race: William Henry Trescot and the South Carolina Chivalry, 1860–1865" (Ph.D. diss., University of South Carolina, 1972), 81–84; Shryock, ed., *Letters of Richard D. Arnold,* 39, 44–46, 47, 55; *Savannah Republican,* 20 November 1852, 26 July 1854, 1 December 1855; Weaver, "Foreigners in Ante-Bellum Savannah," 8–11.

33. Elizabeth Avery Meriwether, *Recollections of Ninety-Two Years, 1824–1916* (Nashville, 1958), 40–41. The organization of workingmen's clubs and unions, like the one that hosted Avery, became common in the 1850s. Many such associations were exclusive, allowing only members of a particular ethnic, social, or occupational group to join. See, for example, Nau, *German People of New Orleans,* 57; J. Henno Deiler, *Geschichte der Deutschen Gesellschaft von New Orleans mit einer Einlectung* . . . (New Orleans, 1897), 54–84; Shugg, *Origins of Class Struggle,* 114–15; Spletstoser, "Back Door to the Land of Plenty," 380–81; Proceedings of the Charleston Typographical Union, number 43, September 1859 (South Caroliniana Library, University of South Carolina). Indicative of the ethnic links to workingmen's groups, Gerald Stith, organizer of the heavily native-born Southerner New Orleans Typographical Society, used his Southern working-class ties to combat both immigrants and blacks in mayoral campaigns of the 1850s: Leon Soule, *The Know-Nothing Party in New Orleans: A Reappraisal* (Baton Rouge, 1961), 94. The old-style personal politics generally made little sense in the 1850s, not only because of ethnic and party differences, but also because differences based on occupation became more pronounced. See n. 21 above. More importantly, great gaps in wealth increasingly separated the white classes. By 1860 in Charleston "most whites had in common with blacks a very low level of wealth," Michael P. Johnson, "Wealth and Class in Charleston in 1860," in Walter J. Fraser, Jr., and Winfred B. Moore, Jr., eds., *From the Old South to the New: Essays on the Transitional South* (Westport, Conn., 1981), 71.

34. For examples of ruffianism, crowd activity, and immigrant and native-born clashes, see C. E. Taylor to father, 11 September 1854, C. E. Taylor Letters (Tulane University); Gustave A. Breaux Diaries, 2, 16 September, 11 October 1859 (Tulane University); George D. Armstrong, *The Summer of Pestilence: A History of the Yellow Fever in Norfolk, Virginia, A.D., 1855* (Philadelphia, 1856), 45–47; and W. Darrell Overdyke, *The Know-Nothing Party in the*

South (Baton Rouge, 1950), 240–60, for a general treatment. On the New Orleans law-and-order appeals of the Know Nothing party, see Tansey, "Economic Expansion," chapter 2.

35. Theodore Jervey, *The Slave Trade* (Columbia, S.C., 1925), 114. For Stuart and a perceptive analysis of developments elsewhere, see Fred Siegel, "Artisans and Immigrants in the Politics of Late Antebellum Georgia," *Civil War History* 27 (1981): 221–30. See also Michael P. Johnson, *Toward a Patriarchal Republic: The Secession of Georgia* (Baton Rouge, 1977), 100–1. The threatened clash between native-born and foreign-born whites compelled some city leaders to oppose nativism, reminding their fellow Southerners of the need to maintain a white consensus above all else. See Samuel Mordecai, *Richmond in By-Gone Days* (Richmond, Va., 1856), 246.

36. Berlin and Gutman, "Natives and Immigrants," 1199–1200; Peter Jay Rachleff, "Black, White, and Gray: Working-Class Activism in Richmond, Virginia, 1865–1890" (Ph.D. diss., University of Pittsburgh, 1981), 5, 14–16, and passim; Shugg, *Origins of Class Struggle,* 54–55, 107–12; Berkeley, "'Like a Plague of Locusts,'" chapter 6. On the postbellum developments, see especially Howard N. Rabinowitz, *Race Relations in the Urban South, 1865–1890* (New York, 1978); and Goldfield, *Cotton Fields and Skyscrapers,* chapter 3.

Part II

THE INDUSTRIAL CITY

Introduction

By the time of the Civil War, the United States was poised on the threshold of the industrial era. In the years between 1860 and 1920, the face of urban America was reshaped and restructured by demographic shifts, technology and invention, transportation innovations, entrepreneurialism, and the rise of corporations and industrial capitalism. Powerful and dynamic forces such as urbanization, immigration, capitalism, technology, and consumerism triggered economic and social changes. Driven by the profit motive, the process of modernizing change did not always have pleasant results. The large American industrial city—for the most part congested, noisy, smelly, smoky, unhealthy, and ill-governed—emerged during this period. At the same time, city people tried to understand, manage, and overcome the dynamic forces changing and reorganizing cities and urban life. Politicians, reformers, businessmen, engineers, educators, and experts of various sorts sought to shape, manage, govern, and reform the industrial city. Heterogeneous groups of immigrants and rural migrants, unaccustomed to urban life and work, struggled to adjust to new conditions. As the cities grew to enormous size, they also became more divided, segmented, and disorderly.

DEMOGRAPHIC CHANGE

One of the most noticeable differences between the industrial city of the late nineteenth century and the commercial metropolis of the pre–Civil War period was population size. New York, with less than one million people in 1860, exceeded five and one-half million by 1920. Chicago, with little over 100,000 in 1860, neared the three million mark in 1920. Most of the older eastern and midwestern cities grew at a startling pace. In addition, explosive urban growth occurred in a number of smaller cities in the South, the trans-Mississippi West, and the Pacific Coast region, as evidenced by the rise of Omaha, Kansas City, Minneapolis, Denver, Seattle, Portland, San Francisco, Oakland, Los Angeles, and Atlanta. Amazingly, the Lake Superior city of Duluth, Minnesota, grew tenfold in the 1880s, from 3,300 to more than 33,000; even more amazing was that Duluth's annual shipping tonnage exceeded that of New York City, mostly because of the enormous bulk of grain, timber, and iron ore shipped out on lake freighters to supply food producers, house construction, and the growing iron and steel industry. In the South, Birmingham, Alabama, grew from 3,000 to more than 26,000 in the 1880s, the result of new railroads and coal and iron ore mining that nurtured a rising iron and steel industry during the decade. By 1920 the U.S. Census revealed that more than 50 percent of all Americans lived in urban places, a vast jump from the less than 20 percent who lived in cities in 1860. "We cannot all live in cities," New York editor Horace Greeley wrote in 1867, "yet nearly all seem determined to do so." Greeley's analysis was not far off the mark, for the nation had become truly "citified" by the early twentieth century.[1]

The rapid urban population growth of the industrial era stemmed from a great release of rural population, both in the United States and in Europe. A rising birthrate, a falling death rate, and annexation by cities of surrounding areas accounted for some of the urban population increase, but most of the new urbanites came from rural America and peasant villages in Europe. Taken together, large families and agricultural mechanization created a population surplus in rural America, pushing out millions of young farm workers and hired hands who hoped for a better life in the cities. Periodic economic depressions, lower crop prices, and the hardships of farm life also encouraged farmers and their families to join the urban migration for new economic opportunities. The city had a special allure for young men and women who sought a more active social, cultural, and recreational life than that available in isolated rural places.

Rural population was on the move not only in New England and the Midwest, but also in the American South. In the immediate post–Civil War era, southern rural blacks began migrating to urban areas, primarily in the South at first. By 1890, according to historian Howard Rabinowitz, author of *Race Relations in the Urban South, 1865–1890* (1978), blacks comprised between 39 percent and 59 percent of the populations of Nashville, Atlanta, Richmond, Montgomery, and Raleigh. Atlanta, mostly destroyed during the Civil War, attracted rural freedmen, who found new opportunities in the rebuilt city. Despite continuing patterns of discrimination and racial violence, they established new communities based on churches, schools, colleges, fraternal organizations, and businesses. Atlanta's black population reached 35,000 by 1900, or about 40 percent of the city's total population. By the early twentieth century, southern black migrants headed in greater numbers to northern cities—initially Washington, D.C., Philadelphia, and New York, but later to industrial cities such as Detroit, Chicago, and Cleveland, and still later to west coast cities, especially Los Angeles. Over the entire period from 1870 to 1920, about 1.1 million southern blacks became northern urban dwellers. Huge black communities grew in the nation's largest cities, even as early as 1920. The black exodus continued for a century after the Civil War, eventually reshaping the racial demography of urban America in the process.[2]

Coinciding with the migration patterns of black and white rural Americans, millions of European peasant farmers and villagers cast their lot with the cities in migrating to the "land of opportunity." During the century after 1820, about 34 million immigrants arrived in the United States. The first wave consisted primarily of Irish, German, British, and Scandinavian newcomers. By the 1880s, southern and eastern Europeans also began arriving at immigrant ports. In the early twentieth century, the European influx to the cities was swelled by the migration of rural southern blacks to cities in the North, West, and South. Substantial numbers of West Indian immigrants contributed to early-twentieth-century urban diversity, primarily Jamaicans in New York City and Bahamians in Miami. And by the 1920s, migrants from rural Mexico had joined the migration to the American city, not just in California and the Southwest, but as far away as Chicago, Minneapolis, and Detroit.[3]

These demographic shifts contributed to the social reorganization of the modern American city. The presence of such large numbers of rural newcomers, unaccustomed to city ways and industrial labor, drastically altered the fabric of urban life. Ethnic, religious, and racial diversity became common in almost every city. The foreign-born presence was especially pervasive. By 1910, more than 70 percent of the populations of New York, Chicago, Boston, Cleveland, Detroit, Buffalo, and Milwaukee was composed of immigrants and their American-born children. The percentage of foreign stock ranged between 50 percent and 70 percent in such other major cities as Saint Louis, Philadelphia, Cincinnati, Pittsburgh, Newark, and San Francisco. Even as late as 1920, the foreign-born proportion of big city populations remained enormous (see table P2.1). Swelling the inner districts of the cities where housing was cheap and jobs were available, the immigrants made the city look, sound, and feel different.

Strangers in new surroundings, immigrants sought identity in common with their fellow countrymen. They could not completely re-create the village society of peasant Europe in the American industrial city, but old institutions such as family and church remained strong. Moreover, they established new community institutions and agencies such as newspapers, benevolent societies, unions, groceries, even saloons, that helped maintain their group culture and identity. Catholic parochial schools enrolled large numbers of Irish children in New York, Chicago, Philadelphia, and Boston. Language maintenance remained a key issue for many groups, and in cities where German immigrants dominated, some public schools taught in German by community demand. Politically, demography alone made the Irish a significant voting bloc in Boston, New York, and Philadelphia, while Germans had similar power at the polls in Cincinnati, Milwaukee, and Saint Louis. Despite the pressures for adaptation and conformity to American and urban ways, newcomers from rural areas and from across the seas often maintained their sense of group identity and their old life patterns to a remarkable degree.[4]

However, over time and across generations, through the public schools, the political system, the workplace, and community agencies, the adjustment and assimilation process for newcomers began. A second social process occurred simultaneously, as upward economic and occupational mobility took place across generations. Americanization and upward mobility occurred faster for some ethnic groups than others. Over several decades, immigrants became ethnic Americans, although they often retained key elements of their native cultures. Children of unskilled immigrant laborers often moved up the occupational ladder. Farmers and peasant folk

Table P2.1.   Population and Composition of the Twenty-five Largest Cities, 1860–1920

Rank	City	Population	Percent Black	Percent Foreign Born
1860				
1	New York	813,669	1.5	47.6
2	Philadelphia	565,529	3.9	28.9
3	Brooklyn	266,661	1.6	39.2
4	Baltimore	212,418	13.1	24.7
5	Boston	177,840	1.3	35.9
6	New Orleans	168,675	14.3	38.3
7	Cincinnati	161,044	2.3	45.7
8	Saint Louis	160,773	2.1	59.8
9	Chicago	109,260	0.9	50.0
10	Buffalo	81,129	1.0	46.4
11	Newark	71,941	1.8	37.0
12	Louisville	68,033	10.0	33.7
13	Albany	62,367	1.0	34.7
14	Washington	61,122	18.0	17.6
15	San Francisco	56,802	2.1	50.1
16	Providence	50,666	3.0	24.8
17	Pittsburgh	49,221	2.3	36.7
18	Rochester	48,204	0.9	39.2
19	Detroit	45,619	3.1	46.8
20	Milwaukee	45,246	0.2	50.5
21	Cleveland	43,417	1.8	44.8
22	Charleston	40,522	42.3	15.6
23	New Haven	39,267	3.8	27.1
24	Troy	39,235	1.6	34.3
25	Richmond	37,910	37.7	13.1
1920				
1	New York	5,620,048	2.7	36.1
2	Chicago	2,701,705	4.1	29.9
3	Philadelphia	1,823,779	7.4	22.0
4	Detroit	993,678	4.1	29.3
5	Cleveland	796,841	4.3	30.1
6	Saint Louis	772,897	9.0	13.4
7	Boston	748,060	2.2	32.4
8	Baltimore	733,826	14.8	11.6
9	Pittsburgh	588,343	6.4	20.5
10	Los Angeles	576,673	2.7	21.2
11	Buffalo	506,775	0.9	24.0
12	San Francisco	506,676	0.6	29.4
13	Milwaukee	457,147	1.3	24.1
14	Washington	437,571	25.1	6.7
15	Newark	414,524	4.1	28.4

16	Cincinnati	401,247	7.5	10.7
17	New Orleans	387,219	26.1	7.1
18	Minneapolis	380,582	0.9	23.2
19	Kansas City	324,410	9.5	8.5
20	Seattle	315,312	0.9	25.7
21	Indianapolis	314,194	11.0	5.4
22	Jersey City	298,103	2.7	25.6
23	Rochester	295,750	0.8	24.1
24	Portland	258,288	0.5	19.3
25	Denver	256,491	2.5	14.9

Sources: U.S. Census, 1860 and 1920.

became city people, shepherds and fruit growers became factory workers, Sicilians and Calabrians became Italians, and foreigners became Americans. Throughout the industrial era, high levels of residential or geographic mobility resulted in urban neighborhoods that lacked continuity and permanence. All of these changes were occurring simultaneously at different levels and at different rates, and faster in some towns and cities than others. Changes of this sort became a constant feature of life in the city, because new immigrants continued to arrive until the restrictive immigration legislation of the 1920s. If anything, the industrial city was a place of continual social interaction and cultural change.[5]

URBAN TRANSPORTATION

If population changes dramatically affected urban life during this period, so also did new transportation technology that did away with the "walking city." Beginning with the horse-drawn omnibus in the 1830s, a series of transportation innovations revolutionized life in the city by the late nineteenth century. These innovations—the commuter railroad, the horsecar, the electric trolley, the cable car, and finally the subway and the elevated railroad—brought structural and spatial change to growing cities. A key innovation, the electric streetcar, completely replaced horse-drawn passenger vehicles by 1900, eliminating more than a million horses from city streets and dramatically improving the urban environment. New forms of urban transit opened up distant, peripheral areas to development and permitted the physical expansion of the city. New housing sprouted along streetcar, trolley, and subway lines. Wealthy and middle-class residents moved from the central districts to the outer fringes and suburbs, as city workers and immigrants began occupying older housing vacated in the center.[6]

The streetcar transportation lines focused on the city center, driving up land prices, creating downtown shopping districts, and bringing shoppers and workers to centrally located businesses and factories. Land uses became much more differentiated and specialized. Functionally, urban regions split between the center (comprising older, low-income housing and industrial, commercial, and business establishments) and the outlying ring of expanding suburbs; often separating the two was a "zone of emergence," working-class sections on the inner edges of the central district. By the end of this period, the motor truck and the automobile had begun to have an impact as well, intensifying some of the earlier patterns of physical development but creating new ones as well.[7]

New methods of urban transit had other long-range results. Physical growth of the city promoted social fragmentation, as community life tended to segregate by class, ethnicity, and race. Impersonal human relationships increasingly replaced the personal and face-to-face contacts that had characterized the walking city. The sense of community among urban residents, already weakening in the early nineteenth century, eroded still further in the industrial city. The common value structure of a prior era had little impact on a heterogeneous population composed of numerous ethnic, religious, and racial subcultures, of immigrants speaking many different languages, and of rural migrants unfamiliar with urban ways. Similar patterns prevailed in the streetcar suburbs, which most new residents conceived of only as an escape from the city and where, according to some interpretations, community life seemed to be less centered than in the older urban neighborhoods.

Transportation innovations between cities also had a powerful effect on urban life and economic development. Railroad mileage increased from 30,000 miles in 1860 to 190,000 miles in 1900, reflecting the completion of an integrated national railroad network by the end of the nineteenth century. During these years, smaller rail lines were consolidated into large railroad empires, while the transcontinental railroads pushed out across the Great Plains and the Rocky Mountains to Pacific Coast cities. These developments linked far-flung cities to one another, connected urban centers with rural hinterlands, and fostered the growth of new urban places, some of which became great regional cities. The rail network also brought a national market within reach of manufacturers and businessmen and helped make an industrial revolution possible after the Civil War.[8]

ECONOMIC DEVELOPMENT

By the late nineteenth century, the stage was set for the rise of the large, sprawling industrial city. Population growth had created an enormous internal market, and transportation innovations offered a means of gathering raw materials and distributing finished products and consumer goods. The rural migrants and new immigrants pouring into the cities provided a ready pool of cheap labor. Invention and new technology supplied the machinery and equipment needed for industrial output and mass production, and new sources of energy such as steam, oil, and electricity provided the necessary power. The emergence of finance capitalism, as opposed to the older and more localized merchant capitalism, made investment funds readily available for new industrial endeavors. New and consolidated forms of business organization, especially the corporation, tended to cut competition, facilitate economies in production, and spur large-scale economic activity. A managerial revolution resulted in a surge of business consolidation and the centralization of office functions of large national corporations. In the cities, the signature downtown skyscraper office buildings, such as the Woolworth Building in New York City, completed in 1913, symbolized the power of corporate America. All of these developments helped spur an industrial takeoff in the last decades of the nineteenth century.[9]

One final ingredient contributed immeasurably to the surge of industrialization: The federal government promoted economic growth as an end in itself. Challenging earlier interpretations of a weak administrative state during the industrial era, historian Brian Balogh's recent book, *A Government Out of Sight* (2009), contends that the federal government played an active role as an enabler of economic expansion. Supreme Court decisions, for instance, protected American corporations from state regulation and labor union actions. Congress established a national monetary policy based on the gold standard, deemed essential to a stable financial system in which credit and capital provided the necessary underpinnings for economic growth, a policy more fully formalized with the creation of the Federal Reserve Bank in 1913. Other scholars have pointed to the importance of federal subsidies of various kinds, such as immense land grants to support construction of the transcontinental railroads, thus extending essential support for key infrastructure. The U.S. Postal Service played a significant role in the nation's emerging communications network, protective tariffs shielded domestic industries from foreign competition, and federal funding of urban harbor and river improvements contributed to the still-important commercial shipping sector. State and local governments also provided subsidies, tax incentives, and direct investment in canal and railroad companies. Thus, government at every level nurtured the expansion of American industry in the late nineteenth century.[10]

As a result of government action and other important stimulating forces, American cities became massive centers for manufacturing and related economic enterprise. The cities of the period differed markedly from the mercantile and commercial cities of the pre–Civil War years. The largest urban centers in the Northeast and the Midwest all developed highly diversified economies, while smaller ones often gained reputations for specialized manufacturing. Most big cities also served regional financial and marketing functions, as subsidiary industries and businesses emerged.

Late-nineteenth-century Chicago provides a perfect example of the links between economic development and urbanization. Historian William Cronon's book, *Nature's Metropolis: Chicago and the Great West* (1991), documented the city's place at the center of a vast economic network and ecosystem that stretched from the Ohio Valley to the Pacific Coast. The Midwest metropolis, Cronon contended, owed its rapid growth and development not only to individual entrepreneurs but to the functioning of powerful economic forces, especially the enormous flows of raw materials and commodities such as meat, timber, and grain. The city became a major processing center, with great grain elevators, immense stockyards for cattle and hogs, and numerous timber yards, sawmills, and furniture factories. New technology and machinery, as well as the establishment of a commodities futures market, made Chicago's rural-based industries possible and profitable. The commodities flow, for instance, was facilitated by a complex railroad transportation system that linked the city and a rapidly widening hinterland. The relationship between city and region was a symbiotic one. As commodities flowed into Chicago, outward-bound trains carried farm machinery, processed meat, and mail-order catalog items like clothing, kitchenware, and furniture. The great West had been pulled into the orbit of the world capitalist system.[11]

The growth of the urban market encouraged a consumer revolution. The new downtown shopping districts boasted newly popular department stores and chain stores, all stocking standardized products, while promotional advertising helped create a mass consumer market. The new mail-order houses of Sears, Roebuck, and Montgomery Ward, centered in Chicago and relying on widely distributed catalogs, typified the businessman's new approach to capturing the consumer dollar. Even in the midst of the industrial era, the growth of a mass consumer society was causing a shift of the workforce toward a variety of service occupations. The giant corporations, for example, developed huge bureaucracies of managers, clerks, secretaries, messengers, and telephone operators, and mass marketing required tens of thousands of service workers to move products from the assembly line to consumers.[12]

Department stores changed the faces of downtowns and performed a number of important functions in the developing mass urban culture. Macy's in New York City, Filene's in Boston, Wanamaker's in Philadelphia, Marshall Field's in Chicago, Hudson's in Detroit, and dozens of others acted as "palaces of consumption," prominently displaying the nation's mass-produced goods to potential buyers. Whereas central business districts had once been the exclusive domain of men—teamsters, dry goods clerks, bankers, attorneys, saloon keepers, and other businessmen—women began riding streetcars downtown to purchase items at department stores. Catering to the desires of female shoppers, merchants displayed their wares in large plate-glass windows, swept sidewalks, and otherwise improved the downtown environment. At the same time, as men gravitated toward the better-paying jobs in the expanding industrial economy, women increasingly worked as salesclerks in retail outlets. Eager for regular employment in clean, comfortable surroundings rather than in dingy, unsafe sweatshops, women gladly took their places behind department store counters to serve predominantly female clients. Women found new freedom in industrial cities, simultaneously acting as wage earners and shoppers, clerks and consumers.[13]

While serving as the city's principal shopping district, the downtown also became the entertainment center. The growing number of women and men who found white-collar employment in the industrial city enjoyed more leisure time and disposable income to spend on commercial amusements. Dance halls, ballrooms, vaudeville palaces, cabarets, and early motion picture theaters attracted individuals and families seeking outlets for respectable entertainment. The advent of electric lighting gave a huge boost to the city's nightlife, reducing fears of crime and adding an element of glamour and adventure to an evening on the town. Streetcar lines also provided cheap transportation to locations on the urban periphery, where amusement parks such as New York City's Coney Island and Chicago's Riverview Park attracted huge and enthusiastic crowds.[14]

Technology, entrepreneurialism, and the widespread American faith in competition, consumerism, and economic growth rapidly propelled the United States into the industrial era. By the end of the nineteenth century, the value of American industrial output surpassed the combined totals for Britain, France, and Germany, the world's industrial leaders in 1860. Emerging in the late nineteenth century, the American industrial city became an economic dynamo with wide-reaching functions. It was a center for manufacturing, wholesaling, and retailing; it was the point of concentration for financial and corporate decision-making; and it was the place of work for millions of new urbanites. Clearly, the changes introduced by transportation, economic growth, and industrialization had important and long-lasting impacts on life in the American city.

URBAN POLITICS AND GOVERNMENT

Changes of this kind can be perceived in urban political developments during the industrial era. City politics provided an arena for interaction among conflicting interest groups. Not surprisingly, municipal politics reflected the emerging residential pattern that ordered urban neighborhoods and communities according to class, ethnicity, and race. Representatives of these groups vied for city council positions, school board seats, municipal patronage, and a share of power in the allocation of funds for urban physical development. As individuals sought economic advancement in the competitive society, so also did local interest groups compete for city jobs for relatives and friends; better parks, schools, and streets in their neighborhoods; or governmental favoritism of one kind or another.

Holding these fragmented political communities together in the big cities was the political machine and the city boss. Numerous recent studies have demonstrated that the urban bosses did more than simply rob the public treasuries. As sociologist Robert K. Merton has noted, the machine had a number of "latent functions"—services beyond those provided by the official government. Such services could take the form of a municipal job, a Christmas turkey, winter fuel for the poor, a utility or transit franchise for the businessman, or lax law enforcement for gamblers, saloon keepers, and prostitutes. The machine, however, exacted something in return, such as votes, graft, kickbacks, and protection money. The link between machine politicians and such popular sports as baseball, boxing, and horse racing also suggests the complex ways in which the bosses played to a varied urban constituency.[15]

It also appears now that most of the classic urban bosses—Tweed in New York, Shepherd in Washington, D.C., Cox in Cincinnati, the Pendergasts in Kansas City, and many others—supported and promoted urban physical development. They lavishly spent municipal funds for new streets and docks, public buildings, schools, parks, transit facilities, public utilities, and other services. Important sectors of the business community such as real estate interests, banking, building and construction concerns, and transit and power companies often found an ally in the boss, who provided cheap municipal land, bank deposits of municipal funds, construction contracts, tax exemptions, franchises, and other payoffs. The costs were high and the political corruption reprehensible, but according to recent interpretations, the bosses often mastered the fragmented metropolises, brought order out of chaos, and provided a kind of positive government. At the same time, the boss was something of a philanthropist and social reformer, promoting the interests and serving the needs of a large immigrant and working-class constituency. As Cincinnati boss George B. Cox famously noted in 1893, the boss was "not necessarily a public enemy."[16]

In addition to the contributions of the urban bosses, American industrial cities benefited from the expertise of a number of professional technicians and administrators who staffed local bureaucracies. Free from the constraints of electoral politics, civil engineers, landscape architects, park superintendents, public health officials, educators, public librarians, and other professionals utilized their expertise and new technology to improve the delivery of city services. As a consequence, observed historian Jon C. Teaford in his aptly titled book *The Unheralded Triumph* (1984), by the late nineteenth century the residents of American cities enjoyed the healthiest drinking water, brightest street lights, best parks, largest public libraries, and most efficient mass transportation systems in the world. Despite the substantial cost of service provision and the graft, embezzlement, and political patronage that continued to plague municipal governments, American cities met the challenges of rapid growth and social upheaval remarkably well.[17]

The many successes of local governments notwithstanding, municipal reformers pushed hard to make industrial cities more livable places for the expanding urban populations. As recent historians have suggested, these middle-class, good-government advocates were often "structural" reformers who promoted changes in the constitutional structure of city government. They sought city charter changes granting home rule, creating stronger mayors and smaller councils, consolidating school boards, and in general centralizing authority. They advocated a streamlined government administered by experts, an objective thought achievable through the city manager or commission form of municipal government. They promoted civil service reform to eliminate patronage jobs favored by political machines. Reform goals included greater efficiency, more honest government, less extravagance, and lower taxes. Thus, these structural reformers usually took an anti-development stance, and they opposed the huge expenditures and growing indebtedness required to support urban physical development.[18]

Drawn from the professions and the bureaucracy of the new corporate structure and often residents of the periphery and the suburbs, middle-class reformers fought bosses and machines for control of urban government. In one sense, as historian Bruce M. Stave has suggested, it was a struggle "between the center-as-residence (for the bosses and their immigrant following) and the center-as-place-of-business (for the reformers)." The reformers represented the forces of centralization, while the machines sought to preserve the decentralized structure held together by the ward heeler, the precinct captain, and the boss. When elected, the reformers found it difficult to retain the support of the voters, who wanted services and patronage, and the business groups that profited from urban development. Thus, although reformers were periodically swept into office on a wave of revulsion against corruption and the machine, the bosses were just as regularly put back into power by a constituency fed up with efficiency experts, moral preaching, the merit system, reduced social programs, and rigorous law enforcement in immigrant and working-class neighborhoods. In short, over the long span of American urban history, machine politics demonstrated a surprising strength and resiliency. It was a political system that fit remarkably well with the business values of the industrial era.[19]

PROGRESSIVISM AND PLANNING

The structural reformers who fought the political machines represented only one dimension of the diverse Progressive Movement from about 1890 to 1920. Equally important were the many strands of progressive social reform that targeted the excesses and abuses of the industrial era. Progressives sought to improve working-class housing, end child labor abuses, protect women workers, and regulate utilities in the public interest. They fought for mothers' pensions, unemployment insurance, urban parks and playgrounds, neighborhood health clinics, factory safety standards, improved municipal sanitation, and consumer safety legislation. Middle-class women in many cities, drawing on their experience as homemakers, organized women's clubs that took on the role of municipal housekeepers. As historian Maureen Flanagan has noted, the club women "applied their experience of how the home worked to what a city government should try to do." Other dedicated college-educated women, and some men, participated in the social settlement movement typified by Hull House in Chicago, founded by the legendary Jane Addams, or the Henry Street Settlement in New York City, founded by social worker Florence Kelley. Community service centers in working-class, mostly immigrant neighborhoods, the settlements provided health clinics, public baths, and gymnasiums; boarding houses for young, single women; and educational programs for mothers and children. In pursuing their reform goals, settlement workers variously worked with machine politicians, state government agencies that inspected factories or regulated charities, some new federal agencies (such as the Women's Bureau and the Children's Bureau), and national voluntary service organizations (such as the National Consumers' League and the Women's Trade Union League). Daphne Spain's recent book *How Women Saved the City* (2001) contends that urban women working in voluntary organizations and social settlements "saved" the city from the social consequences of industrial abuse.[20]

Progressive reformers worked mostly on social issues, but early city planners sought to remake, modernize, and beautify American cities physically and spatially. Urban land in the United States traditionally had been conceived of as a private resource; city landowners sought to use their land in the most profitable ways, without much regard for public convenience or human welfare or physical consequences. The resulting mixed patterns of land use left much to be desired. Valuable business property in downtown areas was gobbled up for port facilities, factories, railroad yards, and office and storage buildings. Entire neighborhoods were uprooted in the interests of business and industrial groups, and the impact upon the urban environment was ignored. The widespread adoption of the rectangular, gridiron street pattern brought a monotonous sameness to American cities, but it was the most efficient and profitable method of dividing up urban land for business purposes and for speculation. When zoning ordinances and city planning commissions were introduced in the early twentieth century, these tools mostly served the interests of the business leaders and affluent property owners who controlled the urban economy. In southern cities, zoning was used to impose rigorous patterns of racial segregation, as well.[21]

The city planning profession that emerged in the industrial era both reinforced and challenged such patterns. Urban planners usually worked for real estate developers or for municipal governments dominated by business interests, so that wealth, power, and political influence generally determined the planning and physical development of the industrial city.

At the same time, however, some planners sought to improve the quality of urban life through the application of principles commonly used by landscape architects, engineers, and other experts. The efforts to create large landscaped parks within cities, beginning with Frederick Law Olmsted's creation of New York City's Central Park, affirmed the need to provide the residents of densely crowded cities with bucolic retreats for rest and repose. In 1893, planners, architects, and landscape architects under the direction of Daniel Burnham created the World's Columbian Exposition in Chicago and launched the City Beautiful Movement, which prescribed wholesale changes for disorderly and unattractive industrial cities. Calling for the construction of wide boulevards, downtown civic centers, and great public buildings, the City Beautiful Movement emphasized the need for rational planning and redevelopment of central business districts on a massive scale. In the early twentieth century, Burnham, Charles M. Robinson, Harland Bartholomew, and others drafted comprehensive city plans to remake the urban environment as a whole. Constrained by financial limitations, prevailing entrepreneurial values, and public wariness of centralized decision-making, communities across the nation most often opted for piecemeal improvements rather than the sweeping changes touted by urban planners.[22]

Entrepreneurial values affected many other aspects of American urban life in the industrial era. In the competitive society, the business ethic prevailed; economic success and individual achievement were valued over human welfare and the idea of community. In a large range of areas—housing, sanitation, public health, education, working conditions, wages—the bulk of urban residents and workers fared poorly. The overcrowded tenement house came to typify living conditions in large metropolises like New York City, while unsightly two- and three-family structures characterized Boston, Chicago, and Saint Louis, and dingy bungalows prevailed in working-class districts in smaller industrial cities like Detroit, Buffalo, and Milwaukee. By the twentieth century, new technology had only begun to bring improvements in municipal sewage systems, sanitation, and public health. Public schooling for most city children encompassed only the elementary years, and thousands of teenagers were annually thrown onto the labor market and forced into dead-end jobs. Factory, mine, and mill jobs were dangerous and industrial accidents common. Social services for sick, injured, unemployed, or otherwise dependent persons were inadequate. Incredibly, during the long depressions from the 1870s to the 1980s, public relief was abolished in many big cities.[23]

For those who could not compete, there were few rewards. But even for many who did compete by selling their labor for wages, the rewards were differential—that is, they were distributed in inequitable ways. The periodic depressions of the industrial era buffeted industrial laborers. Unprotected by unions, they worked long hours at subsistence or even below subsistence wages. Women and children slaved away in garment "sweatshops" or in the factories, mines, and mills of America. As historian Jackson Lears notes in his book *Rebirth of a Nation* (2009), the economic ideology of the industrial age "left unprotected labor at the mercy of unregulated capital."[24]

Conditions were even worse for black Americans in the industrial cities. Rural southern blacks envisioned northern cities as a kind of "promised land." They found economic opportunity, but white workers faced with competition for work and housing responded with discrimination and racism and violence. Tension often resulted in bitter racial conflicts by the end of the period. The race riots in East Saint Louis in 1917 and in Chicago in 1919 exemplified these patterns of response and reaction. The racial ghettoes so common in mid-twentieth-century America were first created during the industrial era.[25]

The urban society that emerged during the industrial era, then, contained the seeds of the contemporary American city. Population changes, transportation and other technological innovations, and economic advances all combined to thrust the city into the industrial revolution. The competitive drive for entrepreneurial success, a phenomenon most apparent in the cities, moved the United States into the front ranks of modern industrial nations. But the same kinds of values—individualism, consumerism, competition, and economic achievement—made acceptable the appalling kinds of social and working conditions that prevailed in the city. Neighborhoods and communities often were divided by class, race, and ethnicity. Cities were fragmented functionally and politically. Bosses and businessmen, both driven by the dollar, controlled urban destinies. Economic growth and urban expansion was unplanned and unregulated. Most Americans conceived of such growth in positive ways, but social and environmental costs were ignored in the process. In many of its physical aspects, the city represented the triumph of expedience and profits over aesthetic and environmental considerations.

The city had its problems, to be sure. But there was a positive side to the urban pattern, especially as reflected in the ways in which the human spirit not only survived but thrived in the urban centers. Indeed, it was argued at the time that man's best achievements had been encouraged by urban life, particularly in the cultural, artistic, and intellectual sense. Planners, civil engineers, and progressive reformers made their mark on the city, but the problems were overwhelming and remained for future remedies, both public and private.

The essays that follow illustrate some of the significant patterns of urban life and change in the industrializing city to about 1920. Traditional interpretations of urban politics in the industrial era have emphasized the conflicts between the political bosses and the municipal reformers. Daniel Czitrom takes a new look at this subject in his essay on "Big Tim" Sullivan, an important cog in New York City's notorious Tammany Hall political machine. What he found suggests the complexity of the subject. A state assemblyman representing a densely populated Irish immigrant slum neighborhood, and later a state senator and U.S. congressman, Sullivan mastered not only traditional forms of patronage and constituent service but also new methods of appealing to urban voters with massive summer outings and extensive programs for providing food and clothing to needy New Yorkers. Opponents charged that "Big Tim" lived off the profits of commercialized vice, but in reality the Tammany leader was in the forefront of efforts to bring organized modern leisure and entertainment to the city. Along with political and business partners, Sullivan helped legalize boxing and horse racing, built burlesque and vaudeville theaters in New York, developed a national chain of vaudeville theaters, and later brought the nascent movie industry to New York City. By the early years of the twentieth century, Sullivan also helped steer Tammany toward support of a variety of social reforms, especially at the state level. These reforms included protections for women workers, factory safety legislation, women's suffrage, even gun control. The many sides of "Big Tim" Sullivan's career—as a powerful Tammany boss, as a social reformer, and as a businessman facilitating New Yorkers' access to new forms of mass culture and entertainment—all suggest the inadequacy of the boss-reformer dichotomy.

Few working-class and immigrant neighborhoods in the industrializing city were without their saloons. In her article "The 'Poor Man's Friend,'" Madelon Powers elaborates on the significant role of the saloon and the saloon keeper in the urban community and in working-class culture. According to Powers's analysis, a popular code of reciprocity characterized late-nineteenth-century drinking culture—a code that had many varied implications. On one level, the reciprocal code seemed simple enough, as saloon customers treated one another and the barkeeper to drinks and expected to be treated in return. But there were deeper dimensions to the symbolic code of reciprocity. As an important operative in the urban political machine, the saloon keeper treated customers to food and drink—but was expected to deliver the "saloon vote" on election day. Bar drinkers voted for machine candidates not only because it was expected according to the unwritten reciprocal code, but also because they derived practical benefits from doing so. Similarly, saloons provided free lunches, cashed workers' paychecks, and provided rooms for club and union meetings, but a lot of beer was sold at lunch, on paydays, and during meetings. The social functions of the saloons, with their mutually beneficial practices, extended throughout the urban neighborhood over many decades during the industrial era. However, several important forces for change after 1900 gradually undermined the role of the saloon as the "poor man's club." First, the increasing control of the saloons by the large breweries diminished the force of the reciprocal code in favor of greater profits. Second, the rise of other forms of mass entertainment and culture such as movie theaters and spectator sports provided alternative leisure time activities for the working class. Finally, the now more powerful anti-saloon forces, with help from some in the labor movement, successfully pushed for temperance and then prohibition, which was achieved by passage of the Eighteenth Amendment to the U.S. Constitution in 1919. Nevertheless, few social institutions in the industrializing city played such an important role in working-class life as the saloon.

The corner saloon rarely opened its doors to women, but working-class girls and women were developing their own leisure-time culture in the city. In her essay "Leisure and Labor," about working-class women in turn-of-the-century New York City, Kathy Peiss illustrates the social impact of changing work patterns in the industrializing city. As late as 1880, most working women in the city labored in domestic service or other home-based occupations. A dramatic transformation in the social organization of work by 1900 created new opportunities for working-class women. Increasingly, by the twentieth century women worked in a factory setting, especially in the garment trades. The centralization of retailing and corporate activities in the city also opened up jobs for women as salesclerks in department stores and as secretaries, typists, and telephone operators in business offices. For a variety of reasons, the workday was shortened as well, leaving more time for female recreation and leisure. Peiss contends that a distinctive women's work culture developed during this era, one through which women collectively gained some degree of control over the workplace and over their pleasure-oriented, leisure-time activities. Peiss's essay represents a neat blending of new urban approaches to labor history, women's history, and cultural history.

Dominic Pacyga's essay on the Chicago race riot of 1919 provides a powerful example of how social tension and violence stemmed from new configurations of race and ethnicity, and of class and neighborhood, in the industrial city. As blacks moved out of the South during the World War I years, they encountered new social realities in big immigrant cities such as Chicago, where they competed with other groups for jobs, housing, schooling, and recreational space. A violent confrontation at a Lake Michigan beach provided the spark for Chicago's 1919 racial conflagration, but underlying the triggering incident were several layers of ethnic, racial, and class conflict. Pacyga places the 1919 riot in the context of Chicago's South Side neighborhoods, whose settlers were mostly Irish, Polish, and African American. His analysis provides a startling degree of specificity by demonstrating why the upwardly mobile, more Americanized, lower-middle-class Irish, whose Catholic neighborhoods were physically adjacent to the expanding black community, actively participated in the prolonged race riot. The role of the Irish athletic clubs and youth gangs in pursuing organized violence was especially important. By contrast, the Polish community was more distant from black neighborhoods, had not yet fully accommodated to the racism of American society, seemed more sensitive to the plight of Chicago's newly arrived black migrants (the Poles were relatively recent arrivals, as well), and actually sought to build alliances with black workers in the packinghouse union. Pacyga provides considerable evidence to support his analysis of the riot—both the underlying conditions and the actual instigation. Unfortunately, the outcome of the 1919 race riot was to intensify racial barriers on Chicago's South Side, as the Poles and other East European immigrants discovered race to be a more important self-identifier than class in the process of Americanization.

The essay by Timothy M. Collins, Edward K. Muller, and Joel A. Tarr on the changing relationship between Pittsburgh and its three principal waterways—the Allegheny, Monongahela, and Ohio rivers—reflects the increased attention urban historians have given to environmental factors affecting the growth of cities. These historians have noted both the ways in which the environment has shaped urban development and the critical impact that cities have had on their natural surroundings. The authors posit that Pittsburgh's relationship with its three rivers changed as the city proceeded through three distinct periods of economic life. During the lengthy preindustrial era, when Pittsburgh existed largely as a gateway for trade with the developing midwestern frontier, the city's residents seldom attempted any physical improvements to the rivers. When industrialism transformed Pittsburgh into a leading center of iron and steel production in the nineteenth century, the rivers provided vital transportation links between the region's coalfields and the sprawling steel mills built on the river floodplains. As a critical component of the urban industrial infrastructure, the three rivers carried the municipal sewage, industrial wastewater, and mine acid runoff that Progressive Era reformers and conservationists cited as serious health hazards to the growing city population. When Pittsburgh's industrial base withered away in the last decades of the twentieth century, civic leaders, developers, and environmentalists saw an opportunity to convert abandoned factories and warehouses into waterfront parks, retail shops, and office buildings following a pattern established in Baltimore, Portland, and other U.S. cities. Along with riverfront commercial development, these civic activists also sought an ecological restoration for the three rivers that had for decades been suffused with industrial waste and pollution. The attempt to erase the negative effects of large-scale manufacturing—in effect, to restore the rivers to their original pristine state—is a reminder of industrialism's undeniable impact on the environment and the urban landscape.

These essays suggest some of the exciting and innovative research pursued by urban historians. Each offers important interpretive perspective on urban America during the industrial era.

NOTES

1. Quoted in Charles N. Glaab and A. Theodore Brown, *A History of Urban America* (New York: Macmillan, 1967), 136. On the meteoric rise of Duluth as a shipping port, see Ryck Lydecker and Lawrence J. Sommer, eds., *Duluth: Sketches of the Past* (Duluth, MN: Duluth Bicentennial Commission, 1976), 143–79; Nancy Eubank, *The Zenith City of the Unsalted Sea* (Duluth, MN: Duluth Heritage Preservation Commission, 1991), 17–23. On the rise of Birmingham as an iron and steel center, see W. David Lewis, *Sloss Furnaces and the Rise of the Birmingham District: An Industrial Epic* (Tuscaloosa: University of Alabama Press, 1994).

2. Howard N. Rabinowitz, *Race Relations in the Urban South, 1865–1899* (New York: Oxford University Press, 1978); Allison Dorsey, *To Build Our Lives Together: Community Formation in Black Atlanta, 1875–1906* (Athens: University of Georgia Press, 2004); James N. Gregory, *The Southern Diaspora: How the Great Migration of Black and White Southerners Transformed America* (Chapel Hill: University of North Carolina Press, 2005).

3. John Bodnar, *The Transplanted: A History of Immigrants in Urban America* (Bloomington: Indiana University Press, 1985); Irma Watkins-Owens, *Blood Relations: Caribbean Immigrants and the Harlem Community, 1900–1930* (Bloomington: Indiana University Press, 1996); Mark Reisler, *By the Sweat of Their Brow: Mexican Immigrant Labor in the United States, 1900–1940* (Westport, CT: Greenwood Press, 1976).

4. For a sampling of works on the persistence of immigrant culture, see Josef J. Barton, *Peasants and Strangers: Italians, Rumanians, and Slovaks in an American City, 1890–1950* (Cambridge, MA: Harvard University Press, 1975); Virginia Yans-McLaughlin, *Family and Community: Italian Immigrants in Buffalo, 1880–1930* (Ithaca, NY: Cornell University Press, 1977); William M. DeMarco, *Ethnics and Immigrants: Boston's Italian North End* (Ann Arbor, MI: UMI Research Press, 1981); Stanley Nadel, *Little Germany: Ethnicity, Religion, and Class in New York City, 1845–80* (Urbana: University of Illinois Press, 1990). On Catholic parochial schools, see James W. Sanders, *The Education of an Urban Minority: Catholics in Chicago, 1833–1965* (New York: Oxford University Press, 1977). On immigrants and politics, see Edward R. Kantowicz, *Polish-American Politics in Chicago, 1888–1940* (Chicago: University of

Chicago Press, 1975); Steven Erie, *Rainbow's End: Irish Americans and the Dilemma of Urban Machine Politics, 1840–1985* (Berkeley: University of California Press, 1988).

5. Bodnar, *The Transplanted*, 117–43, 169–216; Stephan Thernstrom, *Poverty and Progress: Social Mobility in a Nineteenth-Century City* (Cambridge, MA: Harvard University Press, 1964); Humbert Nelli, *Italians in Chicago, 1880–1930: A Study in Ethnic Mobility* (New York: Oxford University Press, 1970); Dean R. Esslinger, *Immigrants and the City: Ethnicity and Mobility in a Nineteenth-Century Midwestern Community* (Port Washington, NY: Kennikat Press, 1975); Thomas Kessner, *The Golden Door: Italian and Jewish Immigrant Mobility in New York City, 1880–1915* (New York: Oxford University Press, 1977).

6. Sam Bass Warner Jr., *Streetcar Suburbs: The Process of Growth in Boston, 1870–1900* (Cambridge, MA: Harvard University Press, 1962); Joel A. Tarr, *Transportation Innovation and Changing Spatial Patterns in Pittsburgh, 1850–1934* (Chicago: Public Works Historical Society, 1978); Charles W. Cheape, *Moving the Masses: Urban Public Transit in New York, Boston, and Philadelphia, 1880–1912* (Cambridge, MA: Harvard University Press, 1980).

7. Robert A. Woods and Albert J. Kennedy, *The Zone of Emergence: Observations of the Lower Middle and Upper Working Class Communities of Boston, 1905–1914* (Cambridge, MA: MIT Press, 1962); Kenneth T. Jackson, *Crabgrass Frontier: The Suburbanization of the United States* (New York: Oxford University Press, 1985).

8. Maury Klein, *The Genesis of Industrial America, 1870–1920* (Cambridge, UK: Cambridge University Press, 2007); Walter Licht, *Industrializing America: The Nineteenth Century* (Baltimore: Johns Hopkins University Press, 1995), 79–101; George Rogers Taylor and Irene D. Neu, *The American Railroad Network, 1861–1890* (Urbana: University of Illinois Press, 2003).

9. Alfred D. Chandler, *The Visible Hand: The Managerial Revolution in American Business* (Cambridge, MA: Harvard University Press, 1977).

10. Brian Balogh, *A Government Out of Sight: The Mystery of National Authority in Nineteenth-Century America* (Cambridge, UK: Cambridge University Press, 2009).

11. William Cronon, *Nature's Metropolis: Chicago and the Great West* (New York: Norton, 1991).

12. Glenn Porter and Harold C. Livesay, *Merchants and Manufacturers: Studies in the Changing Structure of Nineteenth-Century Marketing* (Chicago: Ivan R. Dee, 1989).

13. William Leach, *Land of Desire: Merchants, Power, and the Rise of a New American Culture* (New York: Pantheon, 1993); Susan Porter Benson, *Counter Cultures: Saleswomen, Managers, and Customers in American Department Stores, 1890–1940* (Urbana: University of Illinois Press, 1986).

14. John F. Kasson, *Amusing the Million: Coney Island at the Turn of the Century* (New York: Hill & Wang, 1978); Kathy Peiss, *Cheap Amusements: Working Women and Leisure in Turn-of-the-Century New York* (Philadelphia: Temple University Press, 1986); David Nasaw, *Going Out: The Rise and Fall of Public Amusements* (New York: Basic Books, 1993).

15. Robert K. Merton, *Social Theory and Social Structure* (rev. ed., Glencoe, IL: Free Press, 1957), 71–82.

16. On reinterpretations of boss and machine politics, see Seymour J. Mandelbaum, *Boss Tweed's New York* (New York: Wiley, 1965); Zane L. Miller, *Boss Cox's Cincinnati: Urban Politics in the Progressive Era* (New York: Oxford University Press, 1968), quotation on p. 240; Lyle W. Dorsett, *The Pendergast Machine* (New York: Oxford University Press, 1968); William M. Maury, *Alexander "Boss" Shepherd and the Board of Public Works* (Washington, DC: George Washington University, 1975); John M. Allswang, *Bosses, Machines, and Urban Voters: An American Symbiosis* (Port Washington, NY: Kennikat Press, 1977); Raymond A.

Mohl, *The New City: Urban America in the Industrial Age, 1860–1920* (Arlington Heights, IL: Harlan Davidson, 1985), 83–107.

17. Jon C. Teaford: *The Unheralded Triumph: City Government in America, 1870–1900* (Baltimore: Johns Hopkins University Press, 1984).

18. See, for example, Melvin G. Holli, *Reform in Detroit: Hazen S. Pingree and Urban Politics* (New York: Oxford University Press, 1969); Kenneth Fox, *Better City Government: Innovation in American Urban Politics, 1850–1937* (Philadelphia: Temple University Press, 1977); Martin J. Schiesl, *The Politics of Efficiency: Municipal Administration and Reform in America, 1880–1920* (Berkeley: University of California Press, 1977); Bradley R. Rice, *Progressive Cities: The Commission Government Movement in America, 1901–1920* (Austin: University of Texas Press, 1977).

19. Bruce M. Stave, "Urban Bosses and Reform," in *The Urban Experience: Themes in American History*, ed. Raymond A. Mohl and James F. Richardson (Belmont, CA: Wadsworth, 1973), 188.

20. Allen F. Davis, *Spearheads for Reform: The Social Settlements and the Progressive Movement, 1890–1914* (New York: Oxford University Press, 1967); Maureen A. Flanagan, *Seeing with Their Hearts: Chicago Women and the Vision of the Good City, 1871–1913* (Princeton, NJ: Princeton University Press, 2002); Daphne Spain, *How Women Saved the City* (Minneapolis: University of Minnesota Press, 2001).

21. Sam Bass Warner Jr., *The Urban Wilderness: A History of the American City* (New York: Harper & Row, 1972), 15–37; Seymour I. Toll, *Zoned American* (New York: Grossman, 1969); Robert M. Fogelson, *Downtown: Its Rise and Fall, 1880–1950* (New Haven, CT: Yale University Press, 2001), 160–72.

22. Witold Rybczynski, *A Clearing in the Distance: Frederick Law Olmsted and America in the Nineteenth Century* (New York: Scribners, 1999); William H. Wilson, *The City Beautiful Movement* (Baltimore: Johns Hopkins University Press, 1989); Jon A. Peterson, *The Birth of City Planning in the United States, 1840–1917* (Baltimore: Johns Hopkins University Press, 2003).

23. Robert H. Bremner, *From the Depths: The Discovery of Poverty in the United States* (New York: New York University Press, 1956); Roy Lubove, *The Progressives and the Slums: Tenement House Reform in New York City, 1880–1917* (Pittsburgh, PA: University of Pittsburgh Press, 1962); Thomas L. Philpott, *The Slum and the Ghetto: Neighborhood Deterioration and Middle-Class Reform in Chicago, 1880–1930* (New York: Oxford University Press, 1978); Raymond A. Mohl, "The Abolition of Public Outdoor Relief, 1870–1900: A Critique of the Piven and Cloward Thesis," in *Social Welfare or Social Control? Some Historical Reflections on Regulating the Poor*, ed. Walter I. Trattner (Knoxville: University of Tennessee Press, 1983), 35–50.

24. Jackson Lears, *Rebirth of a Nation: The Making of Modern America, 1877–1920* (New York: Harper, 2009), 81.

25. Elliott Rudwick, *Race Riot at East St. Louis, July 2, 1917* (Carbondale: Southern Illinois University Press, 1964); William H. Tuttle, *Race Riot: Chicago in the Red Summer of 1919* (New York: Atheneum, 1970); Gilbert Osofsky, *Harlem: The Making of a Ghetto: Negro New York, 1890–1930* (New York: Harper, 1966).

Chapter 4

Underworlds and Underdogs: Big Tim Sullivan and Metropolitan Politics in New York, 1889–1913

Daniel Czitrom

I believe in liberality. I am a thorough New Yorker and have no narrow prejudices. I never ask a hungry man about his past; I feed him, not because he is good, but because he needs food. Help your neighbor, but keep your nose out of his affairs. . . . I never sued a man in my life and no man was ever arrested on my complaint. I am square with my friends, and all I ask in a square deal in return. But even if I don't get that, I am still with my friends.

—Timothy D. ("Big Tim") Sullivan, 1907

On April 17, 1889, members of the New York State Assembly crowded around an obscure young colleague as he angrily and tearfully defended himself against charges that he was the boon companion of thieves, burglars, and murderers. Timothy D. Sullivan had first been elected to represent the Five Points slum district of New York City in 1886, at the age of twenty-three. His accuser was the formidable Thomas F. Byrnes, chief inspector of the New York police department, hero of a popular series of mystery novels, and the most famous detective in the nation. Sullivan had angered the inspector by opposing a bill that would have given city police the power to jail on sight any person who had ever been arrested. After learning that his two saloons had been suddenly "pulled" for excise law violations and after reading Byrnes's denunciations of him in the New York press, Sullivan disregarded the advice of friends, rose on the assembly floor, and made what everyone agreed was an extraordinary response. "The speech," reported the *New York Herald,* "was given in the peculiar tone and language of a genuine Fourth Warder, and while it was interesting in that respect to the country-men, its tone was so manly that Tim gained much sympathy. If the Inspector's bill had come up today it would have been beaten out of sight."[1]

Sullivan's defense consisted of an autobiographical sketch stressing his impoverished and fatherless childhood, the saintly influence of his mother, the necessity that

Reprinted from *Journal of American History* 78 (September 1991): 536–58. Reprinted with the permission of the Organization of American Historians.

he go to work at age seven, and his steady progress from bootblack and newsboy to wholesale news dealer. He had known some thieves in school and on the street, as there were a good many in his district. But Sullivan, in rejecting Byrnes's guilt-by-association charge, proudly detailed his own commitment to honest work "and outlined such a busy, struggling life that, when, at the conclusion, he asked if he had any time or money to spend with thieves, there was a 'No' on nearly every member's lips."[2]

This story already contained the key elements of the "honest Bowery boy" narrative at the core of Tim Sullivan's enormous personal popularity and political power in New York. For the next twenty-five years, Sullivan effectively cultivated a public persona, the character of Big Tim, on the way to creating a new metropolitan political style. That style was rooted in a deep knowledge of city street life, particularly as experienced by the city's immigrant and tenement populations. It ingeniously fused traditional machine politics, the techniques (and profits) of commercialized entertainment, and influence within New York's underworld. Sullivan and his circle used it to accumulate enormous political and cultural power. Significantly, Sullivan consistently celebrated the strong guiding hand of women in his own personal development. That celebration translated into a social feminism combining support for woman suffrage and protective welfare legislation with the promotion of a heterosocial popular culture.

Hotly contested by politicos, journalists, business partners, and constituents, the public character of Big Tim had many sides. Sullivan himself left no private papers or diaries and only a few brief letters. Historians attempting to reconstruct the life and thought of the private man are utterly dependent on journalistic accounts, what others said about him, and attention to Sullivan's own construction of a persona. The battles over Big Tim's true meaning and significance illuminate the complex connections among machine politics, the urban underworld, commercial entertainment, and the emerging welfare state. As a Tammany boss, Sullivan ruled the political districts below Fourteenth Street when that area had the highest population density and percentage of immigrants in the city. As an entrepreneur of vaudeville, amusement parks, and motion pictures, Sullivan amassed a personal fortune by consciously pleasing his public in entertainment as well as in politics. As a political protector of certain figures in the city's flourishing vice economy, he left himself open to charges from middle-class reformers that he was "King of the Underworld."

Over the years Sullivan countered those charges with an ethnic- and class-inflected rhetoric and restatements of his own personal honesty and probity. At the same time, he effectively socialized portions of the vice economy, particularly gambling and the alcohol trade, to support welfare activities in his district. Sullivan understood that the term *underworld,* popularized in the 1890s, was ambiguous, evincing contradictory meanings in the cosmopolis.[3] The underworld was simultaneously a zone of pleasure for visiting businessmen, tourists, and slummers; raw material for journalists and guidebook writers; a potent political weapon for upstate politicians; an economic and organizational resource for Tammany Hall and the police department; and a space associated with the commercial amusements of the city. Sullivan understood, too, that enormous political and economic power could be created by exploiting the structural fact of transience so central to metropolitan life.

Sullivan was born on July 23, 1863, at 125 Greenwich Street, in a neighborhood and city still smoldering from the most violent and destructive civil rebellion in the nation's history. The racial, class, and political hatreds that had exploded in the draft riots only a week before, between Irish immigrants and blacks, tenement house dwellers and the uptown elite, and working poor and the Metropolitan police, would haunt the city's collective memory for decades to come. Sullivan's parents, Daniel O. and Catherine Connelly Sullivan, had been part of the great Irish migration into the city during the 1840s. Like many New York families of their class and background, the Sullivans moved frequently from tenement to tenement within the neighborhood near the lower Hudson River docks. For them, as for the vast majority of the half-million people packed into the roughly two-square-mile area south of Fourteenth Street, housing and health conditions were abominable.[4]

Daniel Sullivan died around 1867, leaving his twenty-six-year-old widow, Catherine, with four small children. She remarried soon after and moved, with her new husband, Lawrence Mulligan, an Irish immigrant laborer three years younger than herself, to the Five Points district in lower Manhattan. As the geographical center of the city's burgeoning Irish community, the Points had been notorious for decades as the worst slum in the nation. It was very likely the most thoroughly chronicled neighborhood in the United States, a favorite subject for city journalists, foreign visitors like Charles Dickens, and popular novelists. The 1870 manuscript census shows the Mulligan/Sullivan household of ten, including five children and three boarders, living in a packed wooden tenement at 25 Baxter Street. Dysentery, consumption, and heart disease had killed 3 of the building's 51 residents in the previous year alone. In the surrounding election district, 99 people had died out of a total population of 3,680, for an annual death rate of about 1 in 37.[5]

If the less empathic sanitary inspectors of the day routinely labeled portions of the downtown population as ignorant and depraved, some also tried to distinguish the "very poor, yet respectable, hard-working persons," or "the laboring classes," from the "vicious, intemperate, and degraded." Such distinctions must have been especially important within a family not only struggling to get a living but also warring against itself. Tim Sullivan's stepfather, Lawrence Mulligan, was a violent alcoholic who beat his wife and children. His behavior led to Tim's early decision never to drink alcohol. In reminiscences about his life, Sullivan carefully excluded any mention of Mulligan's role or presence, an act of willful amnesia. The public construction of his childhood, so important to his political identity, would always emphasize the powerful presence of his mother, who took in neighborhood laundry to make ends meet, and his older sister, who went to work in a garment sweatshop when she was fourteen.[6]

At age seven Sullivan started working on Manhattan's Newspaper Row, bundling papers for delivery at $1.50 per week. He also worked as a bootblack in the Fourth Precinct police station house on Oak Street. He completed his course at the Elm Street grammar school at age eleven and was eligible to attend the free high school on Twenty-third Street, but as he later recalled, "as free as it was, it was not free enough for me to go there." Sullivan gained his real education as he progressed to wholesale news dealer. He won a local reputation as a leader and patron of poor newsboys. "He not only furnished my working capital," recalled the Bowery writer Owen Kildare, "but also taught me a few tricks of the trade and advised me to invest my five pennies in just one, the best selling paper of the period." By age eighteen he was working for five different papers, establishing connections with news dealers all over the city, and serving as manager for a large circulation agency. His job took him as far north as Fifty-ninth Street and gave him an intimate knowledge of the city's geography in a time when most Fourth Warders might spend their entire lives without ever venturing above Fourteenth Street.[7]

Sullivan, grown to over six feet tall and weighing two hundred pounds, with a round handsome face, bright smile, and piercing blue eyes, had an imposing physical presence that was an important asset in a day when local political careers frequently began as extensions of masculine prowess or athletic skill. The widely repeated story of how he won the Second District Democratic nomination for the state assembly in 1886, at age twenty-three, may well be apocryphal, but its persistent retelling reinforces this point. Sullivan, so the tale went, encountered a local prizefighter beating up a woman in front of the Tombs, the city prison on Centre Street. He intervened, conquered the rough in a fair fight, and thereby won a great reputation among the male youth of the district.[8]

Sullivan's 1889 fight with Inspector Byrnes attracted publicity from the city press and the attention of the Tammany leadership. It gave him a double-edged celebrity that would define the basic tension in his political persona; in future campaigns he would proudly recall how Byrnes's attacks "made a man of me." The *New York Times*, for example, supported Byrnes and attacked Sullivan for "attracting attention to himself and the criminal resorts which he keeps." A reporter assigned to visit Sullivan's small saloon on Doyers Street, right off the Bowery, cast himself as an explorer in a dangerous foreign land: "It is safe to say that there are not a hundred people in this city who live above Canal street who know where Doyers street is, and if they did they would shun it as the plague. . . . It is narrow and dirty, and in the day time is repulsive enough to keep anybody from trying to penetrate its mysteries, but at night, in addition to its ugliness, it looks dangerous."[9]

Such newspaper attacks served only to increase Sullivan's standing with downtown voters and Richard Croker, the shrewd, taciturn, and menacing leader of Tammany Hall. After the electoral triumph of 1892, in which Tammany swept city offices and helped return Grover Cleveland to the White House, Croker made Sullivan the leader for the new Third Assembly District, a populous, polyglot area bisected by the Bowery, and not previously a Tammany stronghold. Sullivan sold off his saloons, won election to the state senate in 1893, and concentrated on creating the powerful fiefdom that would dominate the political life of lower Manhattan. A tightly knit group of literal and figurative kin ran this machine within the machine: first cousin Timothy P. ("Little Tim") Sullivan, a canny lawyer and political power in his own right; half brother Lawrence ("Larry") Mulligan; and three other Sullivan "cousins," the brothers Florence, Christopher, and Dennis Sullivan. By 1895, the *Tammany Times* hailed Big Tim as "the political ruler of down-town New York" and "the most popular man on the East Side." Tammany's enemies grudgingly acknowledged his district to be "the most perfectly organized and the strongest in New York."[10]

Big Tim's election to the state senate in 1893 solidified the Sullivan machine's control of the Bowery district. This was a sprawling, multiethnic area of some three hundred thousand people, crowded into the tenement-lined streets surrounding Manhattan's busiest boulevard. The mile-long Bowery was the shopping and commercial center for a vast, largely foreign-born, and poor population. Workers with irregular hours (railroad men, streetcar drivers, printers, and restaurant employees), as well as transients and the unemployed, found shelter in Bowery lodging houses. These were jammed alongside theaters, concert saloons, lager beer gardens, dime museums, restaurants, oyster bars, pawnshops, clothing stores, and jewelry shops. At night the Bowery was "probably the most brilliantly lighted thoroughfare on this planet," a magnet for tourists, sailors, slummers, and others in search of a good time or a cheap place to spend the night. Late-nineteenth-century observers had long noted the distinctly German flavor of Bowery life, but other languages, increasingly heard in the theaters, tenements, and shops, reflected the new immigration to Manhattan's Lower East Side: Yiddish, Italian, Chinese, Greek. Tammany Hall as an institution remained, of course, distinctly Irish, as reflected in the overwhelming number of Irish district leaders and patronage appointees. How to organize new immigrant voters and to make them regular Democrats in the face of strong Republican and Socialist appeals was the central political task facing the Sullivan machine.[11]

Operating out of his modest three-story clubhouse, Sullivan hitched electoral politics to the commercial flash of the Bowery. Huge, carnivalesque summer chowders gave tenement dwellers a much appreciated escape to the country. Although these summer excursions were by no means invented by Sullivan, he developed them into a new sort of extravaganza, remembered by Al Smith and others as always the biggest Tammany affairs of the year. As many as ten thousand five-dollar tickets might be sold; but the great majority of those who came did not pay, obtaining their tickets from saloonkeepers, businessmen, and others who bought them in large bunches as campaign contributions.

The chowder began with Tim himself leading a street parade to an East River dock where steamboats ferried the eager picnickers up to Harlem River Park or out to College Point, Long Island. The all-day celebration typically included a clam fritter breakfast, amateur track and field competition, fish and chicken dinner, beer, band music and dancing, and a late night return with torchlight parade and fireworks. Side-show entertainments ran the gamut from impromptu prize fights to pickup baseball games to pie-eating contests to the awarding of a barrel of flour to the couple with the largest family. Gambling was ubiquitous, with stakes ranging from pennies to thousands of dollars. The assortment of games reflected the ethnic mixture of the crowds who eagerly played Italian *saginetto*, Jewish *stuss*, and Chinese *fan-tan*, alongside the less exotic poker, craps, and monte. Speechmaking was held to a minimum, but scores of politicians from all over the city paid their respects and mingled.[12]

Sullivan's friendship with two older, Tammany-connected New York theatrical producers helps explain the enormous success of his chowders. Henry C. Miner, prosperous owner of five vaudeville theaters, preceded Sullivan as district leader in the Third and donated the clubhouse at 207 Bowery, next door to his thriving People's Theatre. After relinquishing the post to devote more time to his business and to run for Congress, Miner took the much younger Sullivan under his wing, introducing him to theatrical society in New York and Saratoga. An even closer ally was George J.

Kraus, proprietor of two Bowery and Tenderloin concert saloons. Kraus's experience as a musician, caterer, bookkeeper, law clerk, and theater manager made him the perfect producer for these events. Sullivan and Kraus formed a partnership in 1896 that eventually managed several burlesque houses and music halls.[13]

With his own origins in the crowded, life-threatening tenements of the Five Points, Sullivan understood the deep significance of democratizing public and commercial recreational space in the city. Tenement dwellers especially appreciated greater opportunities to get out of the house and enjoy themselves. As a state senator in the 1890s, Sullivan first grasped the possibilities for using state power to improve the living conditions of his constituents through his intimate involvement with the creation, sale, and regulation of commercial leisure. Sullivan championed a liberal policy of state licensing for leisure activities associated with the bachelor male subculture of the city, such as boxing and horse racing. In Albany, he led the movement to legalize and regulate professional boxing, and he had a commercial interest in several city athletic clubs that sponsored matches. After the turn of the century, he became more identified with protecting (and investing in) heterosocial popular amusements such as vaudeville, motion pictures, and Coney Island's Dreamland.[14]

In the depression winter of 1894, Sullivan also started the tradition of feeding thousands of poor people a free Christmas dinner. Under the direction of Kraus, the suppers were served in relays to all comers by election district captains and other local politicians at Sullivan's Bowery headquarters, which could seat about 250 at a time. Enough turkey, ham, stuffing, potatoes, bread, beer, pie, and coffee were provided for as many as five thousand hungry diners, most of them single men from the neighborhood lodging houses. Local vaudeville singers and musicians entertained at these feasts, once described by the senator as "the best Christmas meal ever gotten up with the object of making people forget they are poor."[15]

In 1903 Sullivan began giving away shoes and wool socks every February to as many as six thousand people who lined up for blocks around the Bowery clubhouse. The inspiration for this practice was a kindly female schoolteacher who had arranged to get the impoverished young Tim a free pair of shoes during one of the brutal winters of his childhood. Sullivan's charity was not, of course, the only brand available on the Bowery. But it was famous for its total lack of conditions—no distinctions made between the deserving and the undeserving, no home investigations, no questions asked. "Help your neighbor, but keep your nose out of his affairs," Sullivan said in 1907, explaining his creed. "I stand with the poet of my people, John Boyle O'Reilly, against the charity that only helps when you surrender the pride of self-respect: 'Organized charity, scrimped and iced,/In the name of a cautious, statistical Christ.'" The innovative food and clothing giveaways and the popular summer chowders were widely covered in the press. They became simultaneously the most tangible and the most symbolic expressions of the Sullivan base of support among lower Manhattan's tenement and floating population—those New Yorkers most vulnerable to the worst economic and social insecurities of metropolitan life.[16]

The Sullivan machine was not all bread and circuses. It carefully organized the Bowery neighborhood using scores of loyal election district captains, each of whom might be responsible for an area containing several thousand people. A large number of the captains were Germans, Jews, and Italians; many were attorneys, liquor dealers, merchants, or other community influentials. Big Tim himself often led groups of workers in early morning treks to uptown public works, making sure the men got the employment he had promised them. He also regularly visited the city prison and local police courts, offering bail money, the promise of a job, or simple encouragement to petty thieves, vagrants, and others down on their luck.[17]

In an era when the New York State vote frequently determined the outcome of presidential elections, Sullivan's controversial efforts to mobilize the Bowery's large, semitransient population had national implications. He employed street-level, physical intimidation at the ballot box both to control and to expand the suffrage. It was the latter that most troubled Sullivan's critics, as in 1893 when, during his state senate campaign, the *New York Herald* routinely stigmatized Sullivan's supporters as "bullet headed, short haired, small eyed, smooth shaven, and crafty looking, with heavy, vicious features, which speak of dissipation and brutality, ready to fight at a moment's notice." The *New York Tribune* appeared most disturbed by Sullivan's success with the lodging house men, as an editorial noted uneasily that district registration exceeded that for 1892, a presidential election year. During an 1894 state senate investigation into police corruption and election fraud, Big Tim and Florence Sullivan were among those prominently accused of interfering with patrolmen assigned to maintain order at polling places and of physically beating Republican poll watchers who challenged voters' credentials. But none of the Sullivans were called to testify, perhaps because the Republican-dominated committee recognized that both parties were deeply implicated in the practices of machine politics.[18]

Court records show that Big Tim himself personally bailed out men arrested on election law violations, putting up thousands of dollars in cash or pledging his own property as security. He also arranged for legal counsel from the pool of politically ambitious lawyers at the machine's disposal. The defendants were mostly Italians and Jews, often ex-cons, petty criminals, or aggressive district captains, eager to please their leaders by stretching the ambiguous registration and naturalization laws as far as possible. The Sullivan machine occasionally employed rival gangs for strong-arm support at election time, especially during the rare but bruising intra-Tammany primary fights. The largest and most notorious of these were the Jewish Monk Eastman gang and the Italian Paul Kelly Association, whose bitter feuding sometimes exploded into gunfire on Lower East Side streets.[19]

The Sullivan machine's self-conception of its strength rested on a political version of the American work ethic and a notion of service that ironically inverted the ideals of genteel reformers. The Sullivans were nothing if not dedicated businessmen, political entrepreneurs as fiercely proud of their enterprise and as eager to chalk up success to individual initiative as any captain of industry. "All this talk about psychological power and personal magnetism over man is fine business for pretty writing," Big Tim observed in 1909, "but when you get down to brass tacks it's the work that does the business. . . . It's just plenty of work, keep your temper or throw it away, be on the level, and don't put on any airs, because God and the people hate a chesty man." The Tammany leader was successful precisely because he was working at his business on the Fourth of July and Christmas, tending all year round to the personal obligations that translated into votes on election day.[20]

Charges that the "King of the Bowery" was in reality "King of the Underworld" rang loudest at the turn of the century when Tim Sullivan emerged as the preeminent symbol of Tammany's connections with the carnal pleasures of gambling, drinking, prostitution, and commercial entertainments. With the creation of Greater New York, a vast metropolis of three hundred square miles and over three million people, the political stakes had never been higher. Charges that the city ran "wide open" became a regular, election-time rallying cry for Tammany's opponents. A crucial tactic for Sullivan's enemies was the elision of any differences between his interest in burlesque houses and his alleged profits from prostitution and "white slavery," or between his support for Sunday drinking and Sunday vaudeville and his supposed role as head of a secret "vice commission" that controlled all of New York's gambling.[21]

For example, Sullivan and his partner George Kraus remodeled the Yolks Garden Music Hall on East Fourteenth Street, previously a church, and reopened it in September 1898 as the fourteen-hundred-seat Dewey Theatre, named for the hero of Manila. Sullivan's political clout ensured lenient treatment from municipal departments responsible for fire safety and building permits and the continuation of a concert saloon license. The Dewey, with a novel policy of changing its program every week and presenting matinee and evening performances each day, quickly became one of the most popular theaters in the Union Square district. A typical program might include turns by singers, dialect comedians, performing monkeys, Irish clog dancers, chorus girls, acrobats, and pantomimists. Shows usually concluded with one-act musical burlesques with titles such as "King of the Hobo Ring," "A Wild Night in Washington," and "The Divorce Court." The black minstrel team of Bert Williams and George Walker appeared there regularly. Profits from the Dewey alone netted Sullivan around $25,000 a year, enabling him to purchase title to the property that first year for a reported $167,000 mortgage.[22]

Sullivan's new burlesque and vaudeville house became an issue in the very close 1898 gubernatorial campaign in which Theodore Roosevelt narrowly defeated Tammany's Augustus Van Wyck, brother of Robert Van Wyck, mayor of New York City. To Frank Moss, prominent Republican attorney, counsel for the Society for the Prevention of Crime, and former city police commissioner, Sullivan's theatrical venture epitomized the wide-open city. "What shall we say today," he asked a Cooper Union election rally, "about the Dewey Theatre, openly run with a city license, under police surveillance, patronized by men, women, and children, upon whose stage have been given those shows which have kindled unquenchable flames of passion in the breasts of hundreds of its patrons—a theatre boasting the Tammany cause, displaying the Tammany emblems, right opposite Tammany Hall." It was like all those "horrible concert halls and gardens besprinkling the Bowery and other streets in the city, running under license, which, while being by law under constant police observation, are patronized by men, women, and children, who see dances so immoral that the imported oriental dance of 'Little Egypt' would be a Sunday school lesson to their participants."[23]

In fact, the accusations that echoed throughout the city press had all been aired the previous year in the course of the state assembly's Mazet committee investigation into city corruption under Tammany rule. Moss had served as the chief counsel for that strictly partisan, highly selective inquiry, an effort by the state Republican machine to embarrass Tammany. But the Mazet hearings resulted in no indictments or resignations and produced no political earthquake. The notion of a secret, highly centralized, perfectly controlled "Gambling Commission," attractive as it was to Tammany's opponents and the newspapers, was nonetheless impossible to prove. It was all untrue, claimed Sullivan. "I was here during the whole session of the Mazet committee. Why didn't they subpoena me? They know they have nothing against me. They make a lot of talk, but they haven't a particle of proof."[24]

The most explosive and potentially damaging charge against Sullivan alleged that he directly profited from the growing prostitution trade on the Lower East Side. In the fall of 1900, an Episcopal bishop, Henry C. Potter, began to speak out publicly on the issue in response to complaints of open soliciting by prostitutes, pimps, and their runners on the streets and in the tenements. This was a sensitive point, too, for members of the expanding Jewish community, disturbed to see so many of their daughters and sisters forced by poverty into at least casual prostitution. An angry Richard Croker warned that any Tammany leader accepting vice tribute must resign, and he heatedly denied any personal involvement, declaring to his district chiefs, "Some people think that you leaders walk down to me every little while with handfuls of money collected from these people. I am not talking for political effect." Sullivan and his close ally, East Side district leader Martin Engel, had difficult private meetings with Croker, who announced creation of Tammany's own antivice committee for the purpose of investigating the moral conditions of the city. Skeptical reporters wondered out loud "how Martin Engel and Tim Sullivan make a living."[25]

Sullivan became a special target of the fusion campaign that ousted Tammany in the vitriolic elections of 1901. William Travers Jerome styled his candidacy for district attorney "a movement against the protection of vice and crime," a strategy that helped sway many East Side Jewish voters from the Democrats. Jerome repeatedly attacked Sullivan, reviving and embellishing the old charges made by Inspector Byrnes in 1889. On his home turf, at Miner's Bowery Theatre, Sullivan dismissed Jerome as "a liar, a four carat lawyer, a collegiate." He ridiculed Jerome's threat to invade the East Side with outside poll watchers: "If Jerome brings down a lot of football playing, hair-mattressed college athletes to run the polls by force, I will say now that there won't be enough ambulances in New York to carry them away."[26]

Did Sullivan and Engel, in fact, control and grow rich from the mushrooming East Side underworld, its prostitution, gambling, and related criminal activity? That is a difficult question to answer. Engel, one of the first Jews to achieve power within Tammany, no doubt had enormous authority within the increasingly Jewish red-light district centered on Allen Street. His brother Max owned 102 Allen, one of the most notorious fifty-cent houses in the neighborhood. But he manifested his real influence as a bail bondsman and fixer in the crowded halls of the nearby Essex Market Courthouse, the local police court. After making a fortune in the wholesale poultry business, Engel had begun to make himself useful to Tammany by regularly putting up various properties, worth around two hundred thousand dollars, as surety for accused criminals. By the mid-1890s Engel had come to dominate the day-to-day business of the Essex Market court, which, as the place where accused criminals directly confronted the police power of the state, was a critical site of political pull on the Lower East Side.[27]

Some of Sullivan's loyal lieutenants on the Lower East Side undoubtedly had a direct involvement with prostitution, and they enjoyed some political and legal protection in exchange for financial contributions. For his part, Tim Sullivan always vehemently denied any personal connection to the prostitution flourishing below Fourteenth Street. "Nobody who knows me well," he declared in 1901, "will believe that I would take a penny from any woman, much less from the poor creatures who are more to be pitied than any other human beings on earth. I'd be afraid to take a cent from a poor woman of the streets for fear my own mother would see it. I'd a good deal rather break into a bank and rob the safe. That would be a more manly and decent way of getting money." No solid evidence ever emerged linking him to prostitution or white slavery. Nonetheless, shortly after the 1901 election, partly in response to all the unfavorable publicity, both Sullivan and Engel resigned their district leaderships. Their replacements were Little Tim Sullivan and Florence Sullivan. The latter quickly acted to deflect the vice charges against the Sullivan clan by personally leading invasions of East Side brothels, throwing furniture out on the street and roughing up neighborhood pimps.[28]

Sullivan's main connection with the city's vice economy was gambling, not prostitution. He was himself a chronic, flamboyant, and, by all accounts, poor gambler, losing heavily at horse racing and cards all his life. He always tried to turn his habit to economic and political advantage by investing in gambling enterprises and insisting on a democratic approach to betting. Sullivan helped organize the Metropolitan Jockey Club and became a principal investor in its Jamaica racetrack. He offered protection to the scores of small pool rooms, policy joints, and *stuss* houses that dotted the East Side in exchange for using them as all-purpose hiring halls. Gamblers were expected to make five-dollar-per-day payments known as "CODs" to Big Tim's friends and supporters, usually for doing nothing. Private social clubs throughout the East Side brought professional gamblers and professional politicians together across ethnic lines. The Hesper Club on Second Avenue, founded around 1900 and dominated by the Sullivan clan, was the most prestigious of these, a place where Irish and Jewish Democrats came together for fund raisers, poker parties, annual balls, and outings.[29]

The 1901 election of Seth Low as mayor and the overall fusion sweep portended drastic changes for both Sullivan and Tammany as a whole. In 1902, after sixteen years as Tammany's leader, Croker, now a multimillionaire largely through real estate investments, finally retired to breed racehorses at his English estate. Sullivan himself could have replaced Croker, but he preferred to maintain his semi-independent power base and, instead, threw his considerable influence behind Charles F. Murphy, who ruled Tammany until his death in 1924. With Murphy's ascendancy, Sullivan began to withdraw from direct involvement in city politics, preferring to stay in the background and concentrate on expanding his business interests.[30]

He was elected to Congress in 1902 and 1904, but the House, dominated by Republicans, bored him. He missed the Bowery and declared that in Washington "they don't think any more of a Congressman than they would of a wooden Indian in front of a cigar store. Why, they hitch horses to Congressmen whenever they want to use them."

His stay in Washington, however brief, made him less of a provincial Tammany figure and opened his eyes to the commercial potential of national theatrical circuits. In 1904 he put up $5,000 to help John W. Considine, an ambitious theater manager in Seattle, purchase four small-time vaudeville houses in the Pacific Northwest. Considine had begun his career in the dance halls and honky-tonks of the Alaska gold rush, and with further financial assistance from Sullivan, he began mining the more lucrative Klondike of nationally organized vaudeville.[31]

By 1907 the Sullivan-Considine firm controlled or owned about forty midsized theaters, mostly west of Chicago, as well as a very profitable booking agency. Some of the biggest names in early-twentieth-century show business, including Charlie Chaplin and Will Rogers, got their start touring the circuit's popularly priced "ten-twent-thirt" houses, run by Considine with industrial precision. Sullivan's half interest in the company brought him as much as $20,000 a month, or around $200,000 each year. When the company sold its assets in 1914 to Loew Theatrical Enterprises (which added feature motion pictures to the live acts), the Sullivan estate's share of the stock was estimated to be worth at least $750,000.[32]

Sullivan's involvement with the early New York movie industry brought a steady stream of income from another popular yet somewhat disreputable form of leisure. By 1908, Manhattan alone had some two hundred vaudeville houses, storefront nickelodeons, and penny arcades projecting motion pictures to audiences. Nearly one-third of these were concentrated on the Lower East Side, and although no official records of Sullivan's interest in this trade survive, both he and cousin Little Tim evidently received several thousand dollars each month from direct nickelodeon investments and the granting of informal licenses to operate in their territory.[33]

As movies became a booming feature of the commercial amusement scene, the Sullivans made a political and business alliance with William Fox, the archetypal Jewish immigrant movie mogul. Fox pioneered the so-called small-time vaudeville that combined the cheap admission and movie program of the nickelodeon with live performances and a more "high-class" environment. In 1908 Fox paid $100,000 for a one-year lease on two Sullivan vaudeville theaters in prime locations, the Dewey on Fourteenth Street and the Gotham on One Hundred and Twenty-fifth Street. The trade press soon called the Dewey "the best run and most profitable" movie house in New York. Fox's relatively clean, comfortable theaters mixed seven or eight vaudeville acts with movies, attracting a more middle-class patronage, and anticipated the gaudy movie palaces of the teens.[34]

Fox became a leader, too, in organizing New York City motion picture exhibitors in response to continual wrangling over city licenses and suits brought for violations of the Sunday blue laws. The key spokesman for Fox's interests and ultimately the Moving Picture Exhibitors Association was Gustavus A. Rogers, a Jewish attorney from the Lower East Side and longtime lieutenant for Florence Sullivan. Simultaneously, as Tammany leader on the Board of Aldermen, Little Tim Sullivan led the fight for city ordinances allowing Sunday vaudeville and movies. Big Tim claimed in 1907 that "the best way to ruin a large cosmopolitan city like ours, which virtually lives off our visiting strangers, is to enforce or keep on the statute books such blue laws which don't belong to our age."[35]

Sullivan had become a wealthy man and generosity with money was an important part of the mystique. His geniality about it perhaps reflected a keen personal satisfaction at having traveled so far from the desperate insecurity of his childhood. But the political charity may have also substituted for the home life Sullivan lacked as an adult. He married Nellie Fitzgerald in 1886, but they became estranged and had no children. An illegitimate daughter, born in 1896, surfaced publicly only after his death, during the fight over his estate. He had no real home, dividing his time between an apartment in the Bowery's Occidental Hotel, a house on East Fourth Street, Albany hotels, and long vacations to Europe and Hot Springs, Arkansas. Sullivan could have retired comfortably, but in 1908 he decided to return to the New York State Senate. Sullivan refocused his political attention on legislative work in Albany as he withdrew from city politics and the internal affairs of Tammany Hall.[36]

In the final stage of his life Sullivan embodied and contributed to an important shift in Tammany and the Democratic Party—an expansion from a personal, service-based politics to one more centered on legislative achievements in social welfare. In the 1890s, as Robert F. Wesser has argued, Democrats stood basically for "personal liberty, negative government, and local autonomy." By the end of World War I, they had become identified with an economic and social liberalism stressing "labor and social reform as well as a broad advocacy and defense of the interests and values of immigrant groups and ethnic minorities." Sullivan's last years in Albany both exemplified and furthered this change.[37]

Sullivan had always publicly identified himself with the city's working class. Over the years he had quietly and effectively intervened in labor disputes and had persuaded large caterers and music hall proprietors to employ unionized waiters, bartenders, and musicians exclusively. While running for Congress in 1902 he had told supporters, "I never sat a day in the Senate without bein' glad as I wasn't on the front end of a motor car or on the rear, as a conductor." But in his final years in Albany he began translating his longtime rhetorical identification with working-class voters into important legislative achievements. A key collaborator in this last phase of his life was the young Frances Perkins.[38]

In 1911, in response to massive, socialist-led organizing drives in New York City's garment district and in the aftermath of the disastrous Triangle Shirtwaist fire, Democrats in Albany set up the Factory Investigating Commission (FIC) to survey working conditions throughout the state. For nearly four years, under the leadership of Senator Robert F. Wagner and Assemblyman Al Smith, the FIC conducted an unprecedented series of public hearings and on-site inspections that ultimately produced laws that dramatically improved state industrial conditions. Both Wagner and Smith were deeply affected by what they saw in the canneries, textile shops, and candy factories they visited. They were also changed by their collaboration with social Progressives such as Frances Perkins. Eventually appointed the first secretary of labor under Franklin D. Roosevelt, at the time Perkins was a lobbyist for the National Consumers' League and already an expert on comparative wage and hour rates around the state. Her first real political triumph, and the fight that brought her to public attention, was the passage in the final moments of the 1912 legislative session of the fifty-four-hour law limiting the hours of labor for about four hundred thousand women in New York factories.[39]

In both published and private versions of that battle, Perkins portrayed Tim Sullivan as her first political mentor. Unlike Wagner, Smith, Charles F. Murphy, or the haughty young state senator Franklin Roosevelt, Sullivan impressed her as the only politician who accepted the principle of the bill and was willing to guide it through the rough shoals of the legislature. As Perkins recalled in interviews with an oral historian: "'Well,' he said, 'me sister was a poor girl and she went out to work when she was young. I feel kinda sorry for them poor girls that work the way you say they work. I'd like to do them a good turn. I'd like to do you a good turn. You don't know much about this parliamentary stuff, do you?'" With Sullivan's aid in the senate, she outwitted opposition to the measure by accepting an amended assembly version that exempted about ten thousand cannery workers—a compromise that neither manufacturers nor reluctant Democrats believed she would accept.[40]

After a tumultuous, last-minute vote in which two waverers switched and voted no, the bill's supporters called for a reconsideration. Perkins frantically telephoned the boat dock where Big Tim and his cousin, Sen. Christy Sullivan, were just about to leave Albany for New York City, believing the bill had safely passed. They rushed back to the capitol, running up the steep hill, "one red-faced and puffing, one white-faced and gasping," and dramatically burst into the senate chamber. Their hands were upraised, and they were yelling to be recorded in the affirmative. The bill passed, and as Perkins recalled the scene, "The Senate and galleries broke into roars of applause. . . . The Sullivans were heroes. I got some of it."[41]

Sullivan tied his views on labor to an outspoken support for woman suffrage. "Years ago," he noted in a 1910 campaign speech, "if you stood on a corner most anywhere down here early in the morning you would see twenty men to one woman going to work. But it's different now. Now, there's about as many women going past the corner to work every morning as there are men. They break about even. If women are going to be the toilers I'm going to give them all the protection I can." As one of the first prominent Tammany men to support the vote for women, Sullivan became a close ally of Harriot Stanton Blatch, leader of the Equality League of Self-Supporting Women. The two shared a basic understanding of the connections between women's economic status and their political rights. Blatch, daughter of Elizabeth Cady Stanton, was part of a new generation of women leaders making a labor-based appeal for suffrage. "It is with woman as a worker that the suffrage has to do," she argued. "It is because she is the worker the state should have the value of her thought." Blatch combined militant street demonstrations with backroom political lobbying. She and Sullivan struck up a friendship during her regular trips to Albany to testify before legislative committees and press for suffrage bills. He told her that workingmen who came to Albany were listened to far more respectfully than working women. "And," Blatch wrote in 1912, "he has declared again and again that he wants to give women the same advantage as men enjoy in dealing with the legislators who incline a listening ear to the voters of their district." Sullivan made his argument repeatedly before the senate and also became a popular speaker before women's groups around the state.[42]

Sullivan's views dovetailed with his defense of the broadest possible franchise, a politics of inclusion when it came to voting. Always sensitive about defending the voting rights of recent immigrants, casual laborers, the very poor, and transients in his district, he made an explicit analogy between women and blacks. Independent of the question of women's economic status, he told the senate in 1911, they deserved the suffrage. "Just recollect that less than fifty years ago you would not let a man vote on account of his color; because his color was not right he could not vote. . . . It's going to come and you can't stop it." But opposition and fence straddling by Tammany powers like Murphy and Smith continued to help defeat woman suffrage measures in New York until 1917 when, four years after Sullivan's death, the urban immigrant vote provided the margin of victory in a statewide referendum.[43]

Big Tim's political career came full circle with passage of the so-called Sullivan Law. The politician whose public identity had for years been routinely associated with the city's underworld authored the state's first gun control legislation, making it a felony to carry a concealed weapon and requiring the licensing and registration of small firearms. Sullivan introduced the measure partly in response to a marked increase in highly publicized violent street crime below Fourteenth Street. "The gun toter and the tough man—I don't want his vote," he insisted in his 1910 election campaign. "There are a lot of good, law-abiding people in the lower east side. They do not like to have the red badge of shame waved over that part of the city. They have no sympathy with the tough men, the men who tote guns and use them far too frequently."[44]

Yet Sullivan remained a favorite target for sensational and nativist exposés. Writing in *McClure's* in 1909, George Kibbe Turner dredged up the twenty-year-old charges of Inspector Byrnes, portrayed Sullivan as a white slaver, and held him responsible for positioning Tammany to control the city primarily through its alliance with professional criminals. In an emotional campaign speech, made to a packed house at Miner's Bowery Theatre, Sullivan responded by denying any involvement with prostitution and noting that he had made money from his theatrical interests. He paid special tribute to his mother and then moved the crowd with the melodramatic story of how a kindly female schoolteacher had arranged for him to get a free pair of shoes during a hard winter, thus inspiring his own brand of charity.[45]

Sullivan's end was both bizarre and pathetic. He had decided to return to Congress in 1912, anticipating a national Democratic victory that could give him the influence in Washington previously denied him under Republican rule. He never took his seat. In July 1912 he began to suffer from severe mental disorders that included bouts of manic depression, delusions of food poisoning, violent hallucinations, and threats of suicide. In September 1912, after the funeral of his wife, from whom he had been separated for many years, Sullivan had a complete nervous breakdown. Desperate family members had him committed to a private sanitarium in Yonkers. In January 1913, a sheriff's jury declared him "a lunatic and incapable of managing himself or his affairs" and implied that his illness was caused by tertiary syphilis—although this point did not make it into most press accounts. One doctor described Sullivan as "absolutely dominated by delusions of terrifying apprehension, fear, conspiracy, plot, attempts of poisoning, and efforts to do him bodily harm in every conceivable direction. . . . He had an expression which was consistent with his mental trait. It was one of terror and depression, and it was impossible to divert his attention or to engage him in conversation in any subject whatever apart from the terrifying delusions and hallucinations." A court-appointed committee of family and close friends took charge of his business and personal affairs and shuttled Sullivan between sanitariums, trips to mineral baths in Germany, and private home care.[46]

He lived out his last few months in the seclusion of his brother Patrick's country house in Eastchester, in the Bronx. He had virtually no contact with the press or his friends; the few who saw him found a haggard, thin, and melancholy man who occasionally brightened when talk turned to old Bowery days. Publicly, the family held out hope for recovery. He ran away a few times to the city by catching rides on freight trains, but he would inevitably call to be picked up. On August 31, 1913, during an all-night card game that had put his male nurses to sleep, Tim disappeared for the last time. For two weeks the city's press was filled with conflicting rumors and stories about his whereabouts. Old cronies swore to reporters that they had seen and talked with him on the Bowery, or Fourteenth Street, or Fifth Avenue. Others feared suicide. Finally, on September 13, a patrolman assigned to the Bellevue Morgue recognized an unmarked, mangled body as that of Big Tim, just before it was to be shipped off for a pauper's burial in Potter's Field. Sullivan, it turned out, had been run over by a train on the night he slipped away, perhaps as he tried to hop a freight. The body of one of New York's best-known citizens had lain unidentified in the Fordham and Bellevue morgues for thirteen days before being sent downtown for final disposal.[47]

As many as seventy-five thousand people lined the Bowery for a funeral procession described as one of the largest in New York history and remarkable for its class and ethnic diversity. "There were statesmen and prizefighters," the *New York Sun* reported, "judges, actors, men of affairs, police officials, women splendidly gowned and scrubwomen, panhandlers and philanthropists—never was there a more strangely heterogeneous gathering." Even his oldest enemies now recognized that he could not be dismissed as merely the chum of criminals. As the *New York World* put it, "he welcomed the title of 'King of the Underworld' in the sense that he had won his kingship through his friendship for the underdog."[48]

His career and fortune were rooted in the merger of politics and show business. Sullivan thus helped shape a key feature of modern American life. His power had rested upon an uncanny and shrewd melding of job patronage and legal services, charity and poor relief, urban carnival, protection of gambling and the saloon trade, and tolerance for a broad range of commercial entertainments. He supported the vote for women and their full inclusion in the newly emerging world of mass culture. Sullivan's sensitivity to women's issues no doubt reflected his own female-centered upbringing. But in a deeper sense, the evolution of Sullivan's metropolitan style suggests that an explicit ideology of gender informed the political and legislative agenda of the emerging welfare state.[49] Above all, as a pure product of life among the city's poorest tenement Irish, Big Tim saw as no one else before him the political and cultural power latent in an urban underclass too easily dismissed as inherently criminal, depraved, and vicious.

NOTES

1. *New York Herald,* April 18, 1889, p. 7. No verbatim account of Timothy D. Sullivan's speech appeared in contemporary press accounts, but for the most complete coverage, see *New*

York Sun, April 18, 1889, p. 5. Thomas F. Byrnes had recently gained national prominence as the author of a book on criminals and as the hero of a series of five popular detective novels based on his diaries, ghostwritten by Julian Hawthorne, son of Nathaniel, and published in 1887 and 1888. Thomas F. Byrnes, *Professional Criminals of America* (New York, 1886).

2. *New York Herald,* April 18, 1889, p. 7.

3. The term *underworld* was first popularized by Josiah Flynt, who made a journalistic career writing first-person accounts of his experiences with tramps and professional criminals. See Josiah Flynt and Francis Walton, *Powers That Prey* (New York, 1900); and Josiah Flynt, *The World of Graft* (New York, 1901). Both of these books were originally published in serial form in *McClure's Magazine.*

4. There are no official birth records for Sullivan in Municipal Archives and Record Center, New York, N.Y. I have based the birth information on an account he gave during his 1902 congressional campaign. See *New York Times,* Oct. 16, 1902, p. 3; and *New York Herald,* Oct. 16, 1902, p. 5. Adrian Cook, *The Armies of the Streets: The New York City Draft Riots of 1863* (Lexington, Ky., 1974), 2–17; Iver Bernstein, *The New York City Draft Riots: Their Significance for American Society and Politics in the Age of the Civil War* (New York, 1990).

5. Schedule I, "Inhabitants in 6th District, 6th Ward, in the County of New York," p. 11, "Census, New York City, 1870, 6th Ward" (New York County Clerk's Office, Surrogate Court Building, New York City); Schedule 2, "Persons who Died during the Year ending 1st June, 1870 in Sixth Elect. Dist., 6th Ward," pp. 1–3, *ibid.* My thanks to Joseph Van Nostrand for making these records available to me. "Riots and Their Prevention," *American Medical Times,* July 25,1863, pp. 41–42; Albon P. Man, Jr., "The Irish in New York in the Early 1860s," *Irish Historical Studies,* 7 (Sept. 1950), 81–108.

6. Citizens Association of New York, *Report of the Council of Hygiene and Public Health Upon the Sanitary Condition of the City* (New York, 1865), 77. For information on Lawrence Mulligan, I am grateful to Patricia Sullivan, granddaughter of Sullivan's brother Patrick. The baptismal records of the Transfiguration Church, 29 Mott Street, show that Catherine Connelly bore at least four more children to Mulligan between 1870 and 1881.

7. *New York Times,* Oct. 16, 1902, p. 3; Owen Kildare, *My Mamie Rose: The Story of My Regeneration* (New York, 1903), 51. See also James L. Ford, *Forty Odd Years in the Literary Shop* (New York, 1921), 169–70.

8. *New York Herald,* May 19, 1907, magazine section, pt. 1, p. 2.

9. *New York Times,* April 17, 1889, p. 4; *ibid.,* April 22, 1889, p. 5. See also *New York Sun,* April 16, 1889, p. 1; *ibid.,* April 17, 1889, p. 1; *New York World,* April 17, 1889, p. 3; and *ibid.,* April 18, 1889, p. 3. Byrnes had given a statement to reporters in which he named nine notorious criminals as Sullivan's companions or patrons. Part of the controversy involved the arrest of two of Sullivan's bartenders for excise law violations, allegedly in retaliation for his opposition to Byrnes's bill in Albany.

10. On Richard Croker and his leadership of Tammany, see Martin Shefter, "The Emergence of the Political Machine: An Alternative View," in *Theoretical Perspectives on Urban Politics,* ed. Willis D. Hawley et al. (Englewood Cliffs, 1976), 14–44; and David C. Hammack, *Power and Society: Greater New York at the Turn of the Century* (New York, 1982), 158–81. *Tammany Times,* Nov. 4, 1895, p. 3; Hartley Davis, "Tammany Hall, The Most Perfect Political Organization in the World," *Munsey's,* 24 (Oct. 1900), 67. For a recent, comparative study that stresses Irish ethnicity as the key factor in the construction, maintenance, and limits of political machines, see Stephen P. Eric, *Rainbow's End: Irish-Americans and the Dilemmas of Urban Machine Politics, 1840–1985* (Berkeley, 1988). See also Thomas Henderson, *Tammany Hall and the New Immigrants: The Progressive Years* (New York, 1976), 1–15.

11. Julian Ralph, "The Bowery," *Century,* 43 (Dec. 1891), 234. For other contemporary descriptions of the Bowery, see H. C. Bunner, "The Bowery and Bohemia," *Scribner's,* 15 (April 1894), 452–60; Arthur Montefiore, "New York and New Yorkers," *Temple Bar,* 84 (Nov. 1888), 343–57; and Helen Campbell et al., *Darkness and Daylight; or, Lights and Shadows of New York Life* (Hartford, 1897), 459–75. On the early development of the Bowery as a distinctive cultural milieu, see Christine Stansell, *City of Women: Sex and Class in New York, 1789–1860* (New York, 1986), 89–101; and Peter G. Buckley, "Culture, Class, and Place in Antebellum New York," in *Power, Culture, and Place: Essays on New York City,* ed. John Hull Mollenkopf (New York, 1988), 25–52.

12. On the chowders, which seem to have begun in 1892, see *Tammany Times,* Aug. 6, 1893, p. 5; *ibid.,* Aug. 4, 1894, p. 4; *ibid.,* Sept. 19, 1898, p. 5; *ibid.,* Sept. 13, 1902, p. 11; *New York Times,* Aug. 2, 1892, p. 2; *ibid.,* Aug. 2,1893, p. 5; *ibid.,* Sept. 14, 1897, p. 4; *ibid.,* Sept. 13, 1898, p. 7; *ibid.,* Sept. 11, 1900, p. 14; *ibid.,* Sept. 15, 1903, p. 2; *New York Tribune,* Aug. 2, 1893, p. 5; and Al Smith, *Up to Now: An Autobiography* (New York, 1929), 31–32. In the early years, press accounts included detailed results of the amateur track and field events.

13. On Henry C. Miner, see *Tammany Times,* Aug. 4, 1894, p. 4; *ibid.,* Nov. 3, 1894, p. 4; *New York Times,* Feb. 23, 1900, p. 1; Henry C. Miner Clipping File (Theatre Collection, Performing Arts Research Center, New York Public Library, Lincoln Center, New York, N.Y.); and *Harry Miner's American Dramatic Directory* (New York, 1884). On George J. Kraus, see *Tammany Times,* Aug. 20, 1893, p. 11; *ibid.,* Oct. 28, 1893, p. 7; *New York Times,* June 3, 1914, p. 13; *ibid.,* June 16, 1914, p. 10.

14. Steven A. Riess, "In the Ring and Out: Professional Boxing in New York, 1896–1920," in *Sport in America: New Historical Perspectives,* ed. Donald Spivey (Westport, 1985), 95–128; Steven A. Riess, "Sports and Machine Politics in New York City, 1870–1920," in *The Making of Urban America,* ed. Raymond A. Mohl (Wilmington, 1988), 99–121. On the shift from homosocial to heterosocial popular culture, see Kathy Peiss, *Cheap Amusements: Working Women and Leisure in Turn of the Century New York* (Philadelphia, 1986), 6–33.

15. *New York Times,* Dec. 24, 1897, p. 7. See also *ibid.,* Dec. 25, 1897, p. 2; *ibid.,* Dec. 26, 1898, p. 3; *ibid.,* Dec. 26, 1899, p. 12; and *Tammany Times,* Dec. 25, 1899, p. 7.

16. *New York Herald,* May 19, 1907, magazine section, pt. 1, p. 2. For descriptions of the shoe giveaways, see the interviews conducted in 1955 by Dean Albertson, *The Reminiscences of Frances Perkins,* Columbia University Oral History Collection, pt. 3, no. 182 (microfiche, Glen Rock, N.J., 1977), transcript, 225–26, *New York Tribune,* Feb. 7, 1905, p. 8; *ibid.,* Feb. 7, 1908, p. 4; *New York Times,* Feb. 7, 1909, p. 8. For a competing notion of scientific charity, see, for example, Mrs. C. R. Lowell, "The Unemployed in New York City, 1893–94," *Journal of Social Science,* 32 (Nov. 1894), 19–23.

17. *New York Herald,* Oct. 22, 1893, sec. 3, pp. 2–3; Davis, "Tammany Hall," 66–67; Henderson, *Tammany Hall and the New Immigrants,* 135–36.

18. *New York Herald,* Oct. 22, 1893, sec. 3, p. 2; *New York Tribune,* Oct. 24, 1893, p. 6; New York, State Senate, *Report and Proceedings of the Senate Committee Appointed to Investigate the Police Department of the City of New York* (5 vols., Albany, 1895), III, 191–253. The best discussion of the city's election process in these years is still William Mills Ivins, *Machine Politics and Money in Elections in New York City* (New York, 1887). See also C. K. Yearley, *The Money Machines: The Breakdown and Reform of Governmental and Party Finance in the North, 1860–1920* (Albany, 1970), 97–118. For a persuasive overview showing how election fraud was endemic to the political system of the day, see Peter H. Argersinger, "New Perspectives on Election Fraud in the Gilded Age," *Political Science Quarterly,* 100 (Winter 1985–1986), 669–87.

19. Lower court justices friendly to Tammany dismissed nearly all of these cases due to "insufficient evidence." District Attorney's Book of Cases, 1900–1902 (Municipal Archives and Record Center, New York, N.Y.). See, for example, *People v. Charles Kramer* (1900), Court of General Sessions of the County of New York, *ibid.;* and *People v. Sonny Smith* (1900–1902), *ibid.* See also *New York Times,* Nov. 11, 1898, p. 1; *ibid.,* Oct. 17, 1902, p. 1; and *ibid.,* Nov. 5, 1902, p. 3. On Monk Eastman, a very shadowy historical figure, see *People v. William Delaney* (1904), Court of General Sessions of the County of New York. Paul Kelly was born Paolo Vaccarelli and later became vice-president of the International Longshoreman's Association. On street violence between the Eastman and Kelly gangs, see *New York Times,* Sept. 17, 1903, p. 8; and *ibid.,* Sept. 20, 1903, p. 1. On the Kelly and Eastman gangs as training grounds for a later generation of crime figures, including Al Capone and Charles ("Lucky") Luciano, see Humbert S. Nelli, *The Business of Crime: Italian and Syndicate Crime in the United States* (New York, 1976), 101–40.

20. "Big Tim Sullivan, the Rain Maker," *Current Literature,* 47 (Dec. 1909), 623–24.

21. See, for example, "Editorial," *Harper's Weekly*, Oct. 30, 1897, p. 1030; and Franklin Matthews, "Wide Open New York," *ibid.,* Oct. 22, 1898, p. 1046.

22. On the Dewey Theatre, see *Tammany Times,* Oct. 24, 1898, p. 12; *ibid.,* Oct. 31, 1898, p. 20; *New York Tribune,* Oct. 4, 1898, p. 2; and New York, State Assembly, *Report of the Special Committee of the Assembly Appointed to Investigate the Public Offices of the City of New York* (5 vols., Albany, 1900), II, 1364–69. For a review of a typical Dewey show, see *Tenderloin,* Nov. 12, 1898, p. 8.

23. *New York Herald,* Nov. 1, 1898, p. 7. Examples of extremely nativist views abound in Frank Moss, *The American Metropolis* (3 vols., New York, 1897), II, 399–410, III, 28–55. For continued attacks on the Dewey and unsuccessful attempts by the New York Sabbath Committee to get its license revoked for violation of the Sunday laws, see *New York Tribune,* June 7, 1899, pt. 2, p. 2; *New York Times,* April 28, 1900, p. 2; *ibid.,* May 2, 1900, p. 9; and *ibid.,* Jan. 27, 1901, p. 8.

24. *New York World,* March 10, 1900, p. 2. See also *New York Times,* March 9, 1900, p. 1; and *New York Herald,* March 10, 1900, p. 4.

25. *New York Times,* Nov. 16, 1900, p. 2; *New York Tribune,* Nov. 17, 1900, p. 2. For Henry C. Potter's open letter to the mayor, see *New York Times,* Nov. 17, 1900, p. 1. On the report of the Tammany antivice committee, see *ibid.,* March 12, 1901, p. 1.

26. *New York Times,* Oct. 25, 1901, p. 2; *ibid.,* Nov. 4,1901, p. 2; *New York Tribune,* Oct. 25, 1901, p. 2. For William Travers Jerome's revival of Byrnes's old charges and Sullivan's reply, see *New York Times,* Oct. 29,1901, p. 2; and *ibid.,* Oct. 30, 1901, p. 2.

27. On Engel, see *Tammany Times,* Sept. 7, 1895, p. 9; *New York Times,* May 4, 1901, p. 16; and Edward J. Bristow, *Prostitution and Prejudice: The Jewish Fight against White Slavery, 1870–1939* (New York, 1982), 146–68. On the Essex Market gang, see New York, State Senate, *Report and Proceedings of the Senate Committee Appointed to Investigate the Police Department of the City of New York,* III, 2975–3021, IV, 4719–4905.

28. *Tammany Times,* Jan. 21, 1901, p. 5. On Little Tim and Florence Sullivan as district leaders, see *ibid.,* Feb. 3, 1902, p. 13; and *ibid.,* April 18, 1903, p. 10. For confirmation of Florence's reputation for breaking up brothels, see Jonah J. Goldstein interview by Arthur A. Goren, Oct. 24, 1965, transcript, p. 32 (American Jewish Committee Archives, New York, N.Y.).

29. *Tammany Times,* Dec. 23, 1901, p. 9. On Sullivan's relations with East Side gamblers, see the confidential reports made by Abe Shoenfeld for the New York *Kehillah* in 1912 and 1913, "Case histories of criminals," stories 1–53, SP1126, reel 2434, Correspondence and Reports, New York, N.Y. 1912–1919, Judah L. Magnes Papers (American Jewish Archives,

Cincinnati, Ohio). The original papers are housed in the Central Archives for the History of the Jewish People, Jerusalem, Israel.

30. On Sullivan's role in Charles F. Murphy's succession, see *New York Times,* Sept. 20, 1902, p. 1; *Tammany Times,* Sept. 27, 1902, p. 1; and Alfred Connable and Edward Silberfarb, *Tigers of Tammany: Nine Men Who Ran New York* (New York, 1967), 238–40. On Murphy, see Nancy Joan Weiss, *Charles Francis Murphy, 1858–1924: Respectability and Responsibility in Tammany Politics* (Northampton, 1968).

31. *New York Times,* March 21, 1905, p. 1. On the origins and growth of the Sullivan-Considine circuit, see *Variety,* Dec. 14, 1907, p. 10. Sullivan endorsed notes for up to $30,000 after the initial $5,000 investment. *Ibid.,* Sept. 19, 1913, p. 7.

32. After Sullivan's death the circuit was bought out by Marcus Loew and his associates for an estimated $1.5 million. See *Variety,* March 13, 1914, p. 5; *ibid.,* March 27, 1914, p. 5; and *ibid.,* April 3, 1914, p. 1; *New York Times,* Feb. 13, 1943, p. 11; David Robinson, *Chaplin: His Life and Art* (New York, 1985), 92–98; Groucho Marx, *Groucho and Me* (New York, 1959), 133–35.

33. For the high concentration of movie shows on the Lower East Side, see Joseph McCoy, "Moving Picture-House Census," July 28, 1908, Motion Picture Patents Company Papers (Edison National Historic Site, West Orange, N.J.). See also Robert C. Allen, "Motion Picture Exhibition in Manhattan, 1906–1912," *Cinema Journal,* 18 (Spring 1979), 2–15.

34. On the relationship between small-time vaudeville and the evolution of the movie business, see Robert C. Allen, *Vaudeville and Film, 1895–1915: A Study in Media Interaction* (New York, 1980), 218–44, 310–34. On William Fox and the Sullivans, see *Variety,* July 4, 1908, p. 7; *Moving Picture World,* Dec. 28, 1907, pp. 699–700; Glendon Allvine, *The Greatest Fox of Them All* (New York, 1969), 37–53; and the William Fox Clipping File and City Theatre Clipping File (Theatre Collection, Performing Arts Research Center).

35. On Gustavus A. Rogers, see *Tammany Times,* Dec. 26, 1903, p. 8; *Moving Picture World,* Jan. 4, 1908, p. 7; and *New York Times,* March 20, 1944, p. 19. On Little Tim and Sunday blue laws, see *Moving Picture World,* Dec. 21, 1907, p. 684; *New York Times,* Dec. 11, 1907, p. 1; and *ibid.,* Dec. 18, 1907, p. 1 *New York World,* Dec. 9, 1907, p. 2.

36. On Sullivan's free spending and political charity, see accounts collected in Newspaper Clippings, vol. 1, Sept. 1911–March 1913, Edwin P. Kilroe Papers (Rare Book and Manuscript Library, Butler Library, Columbia University, New York, N.Y.); "The Reminiscences of John T. Hettrick: Interview Conducted by Dean Albertson," 1949, pp. 48, 191 (Oral History Research Office, Butler Library); Roy Crandall, "Tim Sullivan's Power," *Harper's Weekly,* Oct. 18, 1913, 14–15; and Oliver Simmons, "Passing of the Sullivan Dynasty," *Munsey's,* 50 (Dec. 1913), 407–16. Sullivan's illegitimate daughter, Margaret Catherine, was born in 1896 to Margaret A. Holland. She was granted a fifty-thousand-dollar life insurance policy from his estate. See *New York World,* Dec. 10, 1913, p. 1; and *New York Tribune,* Dec. 10, 1913, p. 5.

37. Robert F. Wesser, *A Response to Progressivism: The Democratic Party and New York Politics, 1902–1918* (New York, 1986), 218–19. See also J. Joseph Huthmacher, "Urban Liberalism and the Age of Reform," *Mississippi Valley Historical Review,* 49 (Sept. 1962), 231–41; and John D. Buenker, *Urban Liberalism and Progressive Reform* (New York, 1973). The journalistic tradition in historical writing thoroughly ignored this side of Sullivan's career. See, for example, Alvin F. Harlow, *Old Bowery Days: The Chronicles of a Famous Street* (New York, 1931), 487–528; M. R. Werner, *Tammany Hall* (Garden City, 1928), 497–510.

38. *New York Tribune,* Nov. 3, 1902, p. 2. On Sullivan's interventions in labor disputes at Donnelly's Grove on College Point, Long Island, site of the annual summer chowders, and at Schley's Music Hall on West Thirty-fourth Street, see *Tammany Times,* April 9, 1900, p. 6.

39. Frances Perkins, *The Roosevelt I Knew* (New York, 1946), 12–14. For a contemporary account, see Leroy Scott, "Behind the Rail: Being the Story of a Woman Lobbyist," *Metropolitan Magazine,* 36 (July 1912), 19–20, 52. George Martin, *Madame Secretary: Frances Perkins* (Boston, 1976), 90–100; Wesser, *Response to Progressivism,* 70–75.

40. *Reminiscences of Frances Perkins,* 110.

41. *Ibid.,* 114.

42. *New York Times,* Nov, 7, 1910, p. 4; Nancy F. Cott, *The Grounding of Modern Feminism* (New Haven, 1987), 24; *New York Times,* March 25, 1912, p. 10, Harriot Stanton Blatch recounted Sullivan's support for suffrage legislation in Harriot Stanton Blatch and Alma Lutz, *Challenging Years: The Memoirs of Harriot Stanton Blatch* (New York, 1940), 151–70. On Blatch's contribution to the cause, see Ellen Carol DuBois, "Working Women, Class Relations, and Suffrage Militance: Harriot Stanton Blatch and the New York Woman Suffrage Movement, 1894–1909," *Journal of American History,* 74 (June 1987), 34–58.

43. Blatch and Lutz, *Challenging Years,* 152; Doris Daniels, "Building a Winning Coalition: The Suffrage Fight in New York State," *New York History,* 60 (Jan. 1979), 59–80; John D. Buenker, "The Urban Political Machine and Woman Suffrage," *Historian,* 33 (Feb. 1971), 264–79.

44. *New York Times,* Nov. 7, 1910, p. 4; *ibid.,* Dec. 4, 1910, pt. 5, p. 3. For the debate over the Sullivan Law, which had a diverse coalition behind it, see *ibid.,* May 11, 1911, p. 3; *ibid.,* May 30, 1911, p. 1; and *ibid.,* Sept. 7, 1911, p. 5. On Sullivan's other legislative activity, see *New York Legislative Index, 1909–1912* (New York State Library, Albany).

45. *New York World,* Nov. 1, 1909, p. 4; *New York Times,* Nov. 1, 1909, p. 3; *New York Tribune,* Nov. 1, 1909, p. 4; George Kibbe Turner, "Tammany's Control of New York by Professional Criminals," *McClure's,* 33 (June 1909), 117–34; George Kibbe Turner, "The Daughters of the Poor," *ibid.,* 34 (Nov. 1909), 45–61.

46. New York Supreme Court, County of New York, "In the Matter of the Application for the Appointment of a Committee of the Person and Property of Timothy D. Sullivan," Jan. 24, 1913 (in Timothy P. Sullivan's possession); Dr. William B. Pritchard, Stenographer's Minutes, Sheriff's Jury, Jan. 22, 1913, *ibid.,* Timothy P. Sullivan is the grandson of Little Tim Sullivan and currently deputy clerk of New York County. See also Newspaper Clippings, vol. 2, 1913–1914, Kilroe Papers.

47. *New York Times,* Sept. 10, 1913, p. 1; *ibid.,* Sept. 11, 1913, p. 4; *ibid.,* Sept. 14, 1913, p. 1; *New York World,* Sept. 10, 1913, p. 3; *ibid.,* Sept. 11, 1913, p. 2; *ibid.,* Sept. 14, 1913, p. 1. Despite rumors of foul play, even murder, a coroner's jury ruled Sullivan's death an accident. *New York Times,* Sept. 30, 1913, p. 2.

48. *New York Sun,* Sept. 16,1913, p. 4; *New York World,* Sept. 14, 1913, p. 2.

49. See Seth Koven and Sonya Michel, "Womanly Duties: Maternalist Politics and the Origins of Welfare States in France, Germany, Great Britain, and the United States, 1880–1920," *American Historical Review,* 95 (Oct. 1990), 1076–1108; and Linda Gordon, "The New Feminist Scholarship on the Welfare State," in *Women, the State, and Welfare,* ed. Linda Gordon (Madison, 1990), 9–35.

Chapter 5

The "Poor Man's Friend": Saloonkeepers, Workers, and the Code of Reciprocity in U.S. Barrooms, 1870–1920

Madelon Powers

Saloonkeepers are notoriously good fellows. On an average they perform vastly greater generosities than do business men. When I simply had to have ten dollars, desperate, with no place to turn, I went to Johnny Heinhold. . . . And yet —and here is the point, the custom, and the code—in the days of my prosperity . . . I have gone out of my way by many a long block to spend across Johnny Heinhold's bar. . . . Not that [he] asked me to do it or expected me to do it. I did it, as I have said, in obedience to the code.

—Jack London[1]

The unwritten barroom "code" of which Jack London wrote in 1913 was the code of reciprocity, a centuries-old feature of tavern society that took on an extraordinary new significance in the hands of U.S. saloonkeepers during the turbulent industrializing years between 1870 and 1920. According to this code, men who did each other the honor of drinking together also were expected to celebrate and reinforce their special bond through the swapping of drinks, favors, small loans, and other gestures of mutual assistance and friendship. The saloonkeeper, too, was expected to participate in these rites of reciprocity, treating his regular customers to free drinks and offering other tokens of goodwill, just as tavern proprietors had been doing since colonial times.

Yet, the U.S. saloonkeeper after 1870 had one great advantage over his predecessors: The pivotal position he occupied between vote-seeking machine politicians and their liquor-industry allies on the one hand, and the nascent working class with its need for municipal services and assistance on the other. By brokering the interests of these groups in his own little corner of the urban scene, the proprietor of a local saloon could become a key figure in the social, political, and economic affairs of his community. Saloonkeepers, of course, were a varied lot. Some preferred to keep their operations small, informal, and neighborly; others turned their establishments into veritable

Reprinted from *International Labor and Working-Class History* 45 (Spring 1994): 1–15. Reprinted with the permission of *International Labor and Working-Class History*.

"reciprocity machines" in which drinks, favors, jobs, and votes were routinely and openly swapped. It was this latter group that particularly outraged the Anti-Saloon League and other temperance advocates, whose campaign against the liquor trade ultimately resulted in the implementation of nationwide prohibition in 1920. In their view, such favor-swapping saloonkeepers were not only peddling the poison of drink, but also perverting the political process and thereby imperiling the very survival of the republic. To workers in great need of small favors, however, the reciprocal arrangement between themselves and their bartenders—rooted in longstanding and venerable barroom tradition—seemed both legitimate and indispensable.[2]

A major reason for the strength of the reciprocal code between saloonkeepers and their customers was their similarity in occupational status, ethnic heritage, and gender identification. As the alcohol industry grew and consolidated in the late 1800s and early 1900s, the majority of urban saloonkeepers changed from being independent proprietors to dependent employees of one of the major breweries such as Pabst, Schlitz, Anheuser-Busch, and Miller. Through what was called the "tied-house" arrangement, the brewery industry gradually gained control of most saloons either through outright ownership or exclusive distributorship rights. Thus, many urban barkeepers by the early 1900s were essentially hired hands, as subject to the directives of their brewery bosses as their wage-earning customers were to their employers. It is true that, once hired, an ambitious barkeeper might cultivate political allies and parlay his plebian post into a position of considerable community influence. In class origin, income, and occupational status, however, most saloonkeepers were not far removed from the circumstances of their customers.[3]

Saloonkeepers often shared the ethnic background of their patrons as well. European immigrants who arrived by the millions in this era usually sought out barrooms run and patronized by their fellow countrymen. The man behind the bar who shared the ethnic heritage of his immigrant clientele was able to inspire considerable customer loyalty. Recognizing this fact, both breweries and independent bar owners who did not share the ethnic backgrounds of their clienteles often hired bartenders who did. Settlement worker Robert Woods observed, for example, that while several saloons in Boston's North End were owned by Jews, "Irish and Scandinavian bartenders are employed in them to draw in the trade of the Irish and Scandinavians." Similarly, native-born whites and blacks, especially those migrating from rural areas to northern industrial cities, were drawn to establishments where the clientele, bartender, and social atmosphere were familiar and supportive. This was particularly true of African Americans, who faced severe discrimination from whites in this period. The black saloonkeeper often had influential business and political contacts in the black community, so regular customers in search of advice or favors could turn to him just as immigrants turned to their saloonkeepers in times of need.[4]

A third reason for the affinity between saloonkeepers and their customers was that most were males participating in the predominantly masculine drinking culture of the saloon. The copious drinking, raucous talk, and sometimes obstreperous behavior of male customers, combined with the presence of nude female portraits on the walls, spittoons, mustache towels, and other indelicate bar accessories, meant that the barroom proper was anything but a proper social venue for most respectable working-class women. There were some family-style saloons, though most of these had moved to the suburban districts by the 1890s. In urban areas, some women did enter by the side or "ladies" entrance to proceed to the saloon's back room, where they could consume the "free lunch" (a hearty meal available for the price of a five-cent drink) or accompany their dates to the parties and modest vaudeville shows that were occasionally held there. Others used this same inconspicuous entrance to purchase carry-out beer by the pailful. Sometimes prostitutes might even ply their trade in the back room, though their haunts were usually the low saloons and dives of the worst slum districts.[5]

With these few exceptions, however, the world of the urban working-class saloon was primarily a masculine domain. It was a place where the workingman spent his time "in purely masculine ways . . . untroubled by skirts or domesticity" and received "a hearty recognition of his merits as a man," according to journalists Hutchins Hapgood and George Ade. Furthermore, the saloonkeeper was careful to supply his customers with the amenities of a men's social club. As settlement worker E. C. Moore observed,

> It is the workingman's club. . . . In it he finds more of the things which approximate to luxury than he finds at home, almost more than he finds in any other place in the ward. In winter the saloon is warm, in summer it is cool, at night it is brightly lighted . . More than that there are chairs and tables and papers and cards and lunch, and in many cases pool and billiards. . . . What more does the workingman want for his club?[6]

Female saloonkeepers were also a rarity, particularly by the 1890s when commercial, brewery-backed saloons and tougher licensing policies had all but crowded out the informal, unlicensed "kitchen saloons" which immigrant women (often widows) had formerly run in their tenement flats. Nevertheless, there were some women in the late nineteenth and early twentieth centuries who ran barrooms, either by themselves or as part of a mom-and-pop family business. Those in business for themselves often seem to have been very colorful characters indeed, running places with such unforgettable names as "Peckerhead Kate's" in South Chicago, "Indian Sadie's" in Green Bay, and "Big Tit Irene's" in Ashtabula. More commonly, though, saloonkeeping was a male occupation, and both bartenders and bar-goers appear to have zealously supported male-only exclusivity of the barroom proper.[7] Thus, identifying with one another in terms of gender, ethnicity, and economic background, barkeepers and their regulars developed a sense of commonality and fellowship that formed the foundation for the reciprocal code of the barroom.

To understand how the code of reciprocity among barkeepers and customers operated, it is useful to begin with the custom of the treat, one of the oldest and most widespread features of American drinking lore.[8] Jack London described how his mastery of treating won him acceptance and cooperation in dozens of workingmen's saloons in the 1890s and early 1900s. Upon entering a saloon for the first time, London would approach the bar counter—the center of barroom conviviality—and immediately treat himself to a drink, thereby establishing himself as a paying customer who understood the drink-buying imperative in every bar. He then made the strategic move of offering to treat the bartender, an overture that not only cultivated a valuable ally but also encouraged the keeper to warm to his time-honored role as public-house host. Next,

London made what he called his "opening query," often a request for travel information, though the subject of inquiry could have been almost anything. Since colonial times, taverns had traditionally served as clearinghouses for all kinds of information, be it local lore and gossip, political news, job opportunities, sporting-event updates, or any other topic of current interest. Counting on this as well as the barkeeper's treat-induced goodwill, London posed his question and waited. Then, as the motivated bartender fielded the question among regulars in the know, London knew his chance was at hand to gain full welcome to the club. He offered to treat those who offered to help him. And, unless they were hopeless barroom boors, he knew that they would feel inclined—indeed, obligated—to return the favor through the friendly exchange of more information and reciprocal treating. In this way, London was able to employ the treating ritual as a social catalyst that seldom failed him. In his words, "I was no longer a stranger in any town the moment I had entered a saloon."[9]

As London's example indicates, the first rule of barroom treating was that the recipient was expected to reciprocate, in drinks or favors or some other mutually acceptable manner. The term "treat" is somewhat misleading in this regard, for it tends to imply a one-way favor, and language purists might wish that saloon-goers had used the more precise term "reciprocal treat." But bar folk well knew the point of honor involved in accepting a treat, according to London. As he remarked of another drinking episode involving a friend and some regulars in the National Saloon in Oakland, California, "They treated, and we drank. Then, according to the code of drinking, we had to treat."[10]

Treating the bartender at first glance might appear a peculiar custom, since he had easy access to the bar stock and could presumably help himself to free drinks whenever he chose. For many barkeepers, however, their "first rule of conduct was not to do any nipping while 'on watch,'" according to George Ade. This claim was corroborated by George Washington Plunkitt, a powerful Tammany machine politician in New York who often dealt with bar owners in organizing the saloon vote. In Plunkitt's words, "The most successful saloonkeepers don't drink themselves and they understand that my temperance is a business proposition, just like their own." Furthermore, many bar owners strictly forbade their employees to imbibe on the job, under threat of immediate dismissal.[11] Oddly enough, then, the bartender, who was seemingly in the best position to drink freely and for free, was oftentimes the one person not drinking at all—not unless, that is, he was offered a treat.

For the bartender, just as for any other barroom denizen, a treat was an offer he could not refuse. This lesson was learned the hard way by Romanian immigrant M. E. Ravage when he began tending bar for one Mr. Weiss in New York in the early 1900s. "From him I first learned . . . that bar-men never drink," Ravage stated, "except at a customers' invitation, which is another story and is governed by a special ethical rule." Yet, though the young bartender had been told to accept customers' treats, he was reluctant to comply. He disliked beer and detested whiskey, the two drinks most commonly consumed in saloons and most often involved in treating. To resolve his dilemma, he suggested to one of his customers that the man simply give him the money for the treat instead. In terms of drinking tradition, however, Ravage had refused a treat, a grave personal affront to the customer. In addition, he had had the audacity to suggest money in place of drink, an action that struck both his customer and his boss as a baldly mercenary, unsociable solicitation for personal gain. Moreover, because the treat was supposed to be rung up on the cash register like any other sale, he had in effect proposed robbing the proprietor of his drink-selling revenue. Ravage might have lost his job over this egregious violation of the "special ethnical rule" that governed bartenders and treating, except that Mrs. Weiss intervened on his behalf. Thereafter, however, "My employer constantly impressed it upon me that it was my duty to his firm to accept every treat that was offered me," Ravage reported. "It pleased the customer, he explained, and it increased the sales."[12] Thus, the bartender, who often was forbidden to drink on his own during business hours, could accept a drink—indeed, was obligated to accept—when a customer invoked the ritual of the treat.

Had Ravage but known, there were some diplomatic dodges that the saloonkeeper could employ to give the appearance of accepting a treat without actually imbibing large quantities of alcohol. He might take a cigar instead, which was acceptable because it cost the same as beer (generally five cents), and because treating with tobacco was regarded as a sociable and roughly comparable gesture to treating with alcohol. Otherwise, if a customer insisted the bartender drink with him, he might use a special glass called a "snit," which according to Ade was "about the size of an eyecup and the supposed drink was all foam." Snits and cigars enabled the bartender to fulfill the requirements of treating tradition without incapacitating himself or insulting his customer. Such ruses point up the highly symbolic nature of barroom treating. The customer could make the offer, the bartender could pretend to accept, and both were satisfied as long as the spirit, if not actually the letter, of treating law was observed.[13]

It also was customary for the bartender to treat big spenders and particularly his regulars from time to time, to cultivate goodwill and to reciprocate treats offered him. "Once in so often, if a group of enthusiastic buyers had been pushing important money across the moist mahogany," observed Ade, the barkeeper "was expected to announce, smilingly and suavely, 'Gents, this one is on the house,' thereby establishing himself as one of nature's noblemen." A bartender might also treat his customers on special occasions, such as St. Patrick's Day. As Arizona saloonkeeper George Hand remarked in his diary entry for March 17, 1875, "Treated all the boys. Everyone drunk. . . . Got tight myself." Another Arizona bartender, M. E. Joyce of the Oriental Saloon in Tombstone, made a daily ritual of treating and storytelling. First he treated his morning customers to a round and a joke; after that, he reciprocated each customer's offer to treat with another anecdote, and so on all day until well past midnight.[14]

Temperance advocates complained that such treating by bartenders was simply a ploy to entice and obligate customers to spend extravagantly, particularly when business was bad. As reformer Robert Bagnell asserted, "often when the sales lag the saloon keeper himself treats to start business going again."[15] In some cases the saloonkeeper's treating may have been done for the sole purpose of promoting sales, but the congenial relationship that usually obtained between him and his regulars makes the bald profit motive an unlikely sole explanation. Rather, such treating was just as often motivated by the same code of reciprocity that obtained among the regulars.

In addition to social and economic motives, the saloonkeeper often had strong political motives for treating his clientele to drinks and other favors. In New York,

Chicago, San Francisco, and many other urban areas, saloonkeepers depended on the goodwill of voters to elect sympathetic machine politicians, who in turn would fight temperance advocates attempting to restrict or shut down saloonkeepers. Politicians, once in office, depended on saloonkeepers (and the powerful liquor industry behind them) to contribute to their campaign coffers and to help deliver the saloon vote at election time. Saloon-going voters, meanwhile, depended on ward politicians to secure them jobs and licenses, to bail them out of jail when necessary, and to perform various other favors, as well as to keep saloonkeepers in business by blocking passage and enforcement of temperance legislation.[16]

Saloons and politics were so thoroughly intertwined that many saloonkeepers themselves became machine politicians, such as Michael "Hinky Dink" Kenna, who ran a Chicago barroom significantly called the "Workingmen's Exchange" and, with his partner, "Bathhouse John" Coughlin, ran much of Chicago as well from the 1890s to the late 1930s.[17] Many other political machines utilized saloons as their headquarters, including the Tammany organization in New York and Christopher "The Blind Boss" Buckley of San Francisco, whose Alhambra Saloon back room was dubbed "Buckley's City Hall." In cities nationwide, then, the saloon was a principal arena of local politics, with the saloonkeeper serving as liaison and power broker between the machine politicians and the barroom voters. As Raymond Calkins observed, "By his position he is a leader. He is the man to whom the politicians must go before the realization of his schemes. If there is any bribery, it concerns the saloonkeeper, who is asked to treat 'the boys' in return. Such are the varied functions of the barkeeper; such is his social position; such is his influence."[18]

Reformers charged that the politically motivated treat was a bribe and that workers were being tricked and manipulated in a gross perversion of the American political process. In the context of drinking tradition and symbolism, however, the barkeeper's treat was more accurately a bid for fellowship and favor swapping, something that bargoers did among themselves all the time. Workers did not regard this use of treating as dishonorable or perverse, nor did it seem that they were being defrauded or duped. On the contrary, the treat sealed a pact between political leader and constituent that each would contribute and derive something of value from the arrangement. It was not subversion or trickery at all, but rather a very practical and mutually beneficial implementation of the barroom ideal of reciprocity.[19]

The unwritten code of reciprocity also governed workers' use of the saloonkeepers' celebrated free lunch. While the notion of serving food in drinking establishments was by no means new in the saloon period, the idea of serving it on a massive scale using the latest marketing and distribution techniques was most definitely an innovation of late-nineteenth-century industrial capitalism. In what amounted to one of the most successful public relations schemes of the era, the powerful liquor industry used its resources and connections to supply barkeepers with vast quantities of food at extremely low prices. As a result, in barrooms from San Francisco to New York, any poor man who bought at least one five-cent beer could then help himself to whatever "free" edibles the proprietor had to offer. By deftly combining age-old tavern tradition with modern marketing techniques, the saloon trade was able to provide an almost gratis repast that swiftly became the chief daytime food source for much of working-class America.[20]

Though the liquor trade performed an essential role in procuring cheap, plentiful foodstuffs, the resounding success of the free-lunch idea ultimately depended on the workingman's voluntary cooperation and sense of fair play. In fact, most bar-going folk appear to have observed an unwritten code of honor when it came to buying the requisite drink and monitoring how much food they consumed for their nickel. The saloonkeeper trusted his regulars not to take unfair advantage, in return for which they expected him to let them eat in peace. So pervasive was this atmosphere of mutual trust that even gourmands were usually persuaded to exercise some restraint. "It is only the man who comes seldom or evidently comes for the lunch alone who need fear the eye of the bartender," as Raymond Calkins explained. "However, there is a kind of etiquette about the use of the free lunch which acts as a corrective to the greed of some patrons."[21]

Temperance advocates, who in the 1880s had themselves demanded that barrooms offer food to counteract the intoxicating effects of alcohol, understandably were bewildered and appalled when the liquor industry responded by creating the tremendously popular free lunch. Some tried to discredit the custom by pointing out the mercenary motives of saloonkeepers who required the poor and hungry to buy drinks for the privilege of eating. Ironically, however, this policy of offering the free lunch primarily as a business proposition was probably one of its most appealing features to working people too proud to countenance outright charity. They knew a nickel was obviously just a token amount to pay for such bounty, and yet because it did cost them something, the deadly stigma of the handout was avoided. As Royal Melendy remarked of the saloon free lunch, "The general appearance of abundance, so lacking in their homes or in the cheap restaurants, and the absence of any sense of charity, so distasteful to the self-respecting man, add to the attractiveness of the place."[22]

To promote the loyalty of local residents toward his barroom, the saloonkeeper often extended special financial privileges to the steadiest members of his neighborhood clientele. A great many workingmen relied on saloonkeepers to cash their paychecks, with the understanding that they would purchase a drink or two to repay the favor. For example, a manufacturer in Joliet, Illinois, stated in 1908 that of the 3,600 paychecks his firm issued on one payday, 3,599 came back with a saloonkeeper's endorsement (the last one having been cashed in a grocery store selling liquor). It is probably true that this check-cashing custom was the cause of much unconscionable extravagance in saloons on payday. Yet, it is also important to note that banks were usually located miles from the factory districts and that many workers, especially first-generation immigrants, found the stiff institutionalism of banks confusing and intimidating. As Peter Roberts noted in his 1904 study of coal-mining communities in Pennsylvania, the company "pays the laborer and the saloon serves a useful purpose by accommodating these men with change." Thus, the saloon acted as the poor man's bank. Moreover, some workers exercised greater restraint than temperance advocates often gave them credit for. From reports on workers' household budgets in South Chicago, New York City, and Homestead, Pennsylvania, for example, it appears that a customary practice among many married men was to cash their paychecks in the saloon, go home and turn over the majority to their wives, and then return to the saloon with a moderate drinking allowance.[23]

Saloonkeepers also frequently permitted regulars to establish a credit account or "tick" (short for "ticket"), an account which they were honor bound to pay down as soon as they were able. In one Pennsylvania coal-mining town, for instance, Roberts asked a local proprietor what he did to encourage steady patronage. "His answer was, 'I keep good stuff, give good measure, keep a clean place and sell on tick.'" In saloon parlance, the privilege of drinking on credit was known as "getting trusted," a significant thing in the lives of the working poor. Furthermore, a man temporarily short of cash could always treat his neighbors to a friendly round and thereby maintain his status in the community. In the eyes of many reformers, this credit arrangement constituted an insidious trap to encourage extravagance and indebtedness, but to the bar-going worker, the fact that "the saloonkeeper trusts him for drinks" represented both a privilege and "a debt of honor," as E. C. Moore observed.[24]

Not only credit accounts, but small loans were a method by which the saloonkeeper courted and rewarded the loyalty of his neighborhood customers. For example, when Jack London was flat broke, he often turned to Johnny Heinhold, the proprietor of the Last Chance Saloon in Oakland, California, for loans "without interest, without security, without buying a drink." This was in sharp contrast to the only other place London knew to borrow money, his neighborhood barber shop, where he was charged five percent interest every month until the loan was repaid. Royal Melendy noted a similar philosophy underlying the loans extended to neighborhood customers in Chicago saloons in 1900. "No questions are asked about the 'deserving poor'; no 'work test is applied; and again and again relief is given in the shape of money, 'loaned expecting no return.'" But, of course, there was a return: the future patronage of a grateful customer.[25]

Saloonkeepers, particularly those with political ambitions, sometimes extended outright charity to needy families in the neighborhood even if the recipients were not regular patrons of their saloons. In 1897, for example, Moody Morton, a printer by trade, learned that the family of an ailing workman in his neighborhood was in desperate need of assistance, and so Morton suggested to his wife and a family friend that they solicit help from the Associated Charities. The friend contended, however, that from the charity organizations they would receive "nothing but red tape and blanks and tracts and references," and instead said, "I'd rather call on a few saloon keepers. They'll do more and do it quick." Deciding to try both avenues, Mrs. Morton and her friend went to the Associated Charities while Mr. Morton approached several local merchants, including saloonkeepers. "So we separate, and the ladies have just the experience predicted," reported Morton, "while I secure . . . a sack of flour from one grocer, bacon and coffee from another, and money from several liquor dealers." This duty of saloonkeepers to act as the "poor man's friend" in their districts was confirmed by a New York proprietor in 1909. "Whenever a case of distress became known in my neighborhood, it was to my place that the first appeal was made." Through such charitable gestures, the barkeeper earned the goodwill of his community and increased the loyalty of his regular customers.[26]

In addition to performing favors for individuals and families, saloonkeepers assisted workers' organizations through the offer of their back rooms as meeting space. Many places had at least one such room, and a few featured several that might also be located behind, beside, above, or in the basement below the barroom. Sometimes customers used the back room for gathering informally in order to chat, play games, consume the free lunch, or attend parties or shows. More often, however, this space was utilized by more formally organized groups that required a gathering space with more privacy than was possible in the barroom. As Raymond Calkins observed,

> A serious difficulty which confronts all the clubs of the working people is the lack of suitable club-rooms. . . . It is just here that the saloon makes its appeal. . . . Here groups are naturally formed from among those habitually meeting in the same place. Hither groups already formed come to meet because they have no other shelter. The saloon has been quick to see its advantage and to make the most of it. The process by which its hold is increased through the club instinct which it fosters and satisfies is an interesting study.[27]

With few other affordable facilities available to them, working-class groups of all varieties and persuasions depended on the saloon premises to accommodate them. According to Melendy, the back rooms of thousands of Chicago saloons hosted such groups as trade unions, fraternal organizations, political clubs, and even wedding parties. "It is, in very truth, a part of the life of the people of this district," he concluded. Similarly, Calkins noted that the Casino Saloon in New York City hosted twenty-eight groups each week in its back room, supplying mailboxes for their correspondence and encouraging them to display members' photographs on the walls. Thomas I. Kidd, secretary of the Amalgamated Wood Workers in 1900, summed up the place of saloons in workers' lives as follows:

> This institution is looked upon by the vast majority of workingmen as their club. When out of employment the workingman can get a free lunch and meet a congenial soul to cheer him in the saloon when there is nothing but discouragement for him elsewhere. Probably seventy-five per cent of our unions meet in halls in the rear or over saloons.[28]

Still, the saloonkeeper was a businessman, and his back room, a valuable commodity, was not to be had for free. According to an unwritten but widely honored rule, each member of a workers' group was duty-bound to contribute a minimum of five cents—though more commonly ten to twenty cents—toward the purchase of alcohol, usually beer, for consumption during the meeting. By this scheme, the saloonkeeper was assured of compensation by his profit on beer sales, while the workers were assured of meeting space. "For example," noted Melendy in Chicago in 1900, "a certain German musical society, occupying one of these rooms, fully compensates the saloonkeeper with the money that passes over the bar as the members go in and out of the club-room." Calkins reported in 1901 that the secretary of a 250-member trade union estimated "that probably on an average the members would drink two glasses of beer per meeting," amounting to sales of about twenty-five dollars per week for the saloonkeeper. Even more lucrative were the revenues from clubs associated with the socialist labor movement. "They gather each evening and on Sunday by the hundred," reported Calkins. "Their meeting-place, like that of all the other clubs of which we have spoken, is often in or over the saloon, where they are expected to 'drop' fifteen or twenty cents a night per member." Sometimes the proprietor also charged a small rental fee for the room, but the custom of club members "dropping" some change in the saloon that hosted them was always the centerpiece of the arrangement.[29]

How powerful the pressure was on club members to uphold their share of the group's drink-buying obligation was illustrated by the remarks of a Chicago labor leader, himself an abstainer, interviewed by Melendy in 1901:

> Mr. Thomas J. Morgan, speaking of the early days of the Socialist Labor Party, said that for years they met in the back room of a saloon, the churches and schoolhouses being closed against them, and that he felt a sensation akin to shame coming over him as night after night he passed the bar without paying his 5 cents for a drink.[30]

And shame he should have felt, for in the context of barroom society, he was a freeloader and a welsher on a deal. The saloon clubroom was "free" only in the sense that the free lunch was free: A customer who honored the barroom imperative of drink buying was welcome to enjoy the facilities. The same rule applied to organized groups, and each member knew that it was a matter of honor to uphold the code of reciprocity by paying his share to his brothers' keeper.

Though the relationship between saloonkeepers and their working-class customers was mutually beneficial in many respects, it was not without problems. Some of the difficulties were related to changes in the saloon trade at the turn of the twentieth century. As the breweries continued to seize control of saloons, they hired a legion of inexperienced bartenders who often had neither respect nor flair for the art of saloonkeeping. Meanwhile, the higher licensing fees and taxes demanded by antisaloon groups had the result of pushing many older, more respectable proprietors to the brink of desperation and bankruptcy. "We rented the rooms up-stairs to women, and have gambling wheels, and sell all the liquor we can to anybody who wants it, just to keep from going broke," one harried saloonkeeper admitted. "Don't think we're doing all those things because we like it. I wish to God we didn't have to do them."[31] As competition rose and competence and respectability fell, both the role and character of the typical saloonkeeper began to deteriorate.

Equally important was the growing self-sufficiency of the working-class itself in the early 1900s. As marriage rates rose, housing improved, and new entertainments like movie theaters and ballparks proliferated, workers were less dependent on the saloon as a refuge from the raw urban-industrial environment. An increasing number of lodges and social clubs offered an alternative source of financial help in the form of insurance and mutual aid benefits.[32] Perhaps most important, the labor movement was beginning to distance itself from the saloon, the saloonkeeper, and his political cronies. The barman who used his political and business contacts to provide jobs and other favors to customers had performed a valuable service when workers were disorganized and desperate. As the union movement grew, however, workers became better able to deal directly and collectively with employers, thereby lessening the need for a bartending middleman whose powerful friends might not always have labor's best interests at heart. Indeed, as more labor candidates ran for municipal office, they began criticizing entrenched machine politicians for caring more for corrupt business schemes than for the welfare of workers. As the twentieth century began, the graft, fraud, and bribery trials of such saloon-connected politicians as Boss Abraham Ruef of the Union Labor party in San Francisco tended to bear out the labor candidates' accusations.[33]

After 1900, an increasing number of labor leaders, such as Samuel Gompers of the American Federation of Labor, supported the idea of worker temperance (though not necessarily abstinence or prohibition) and believed that organized laborers needed more clear heads, steady hands, and sober surroundings to achieve their goals. Many workers apparently agreed, for a growing number of unions began establishing their own independent headquarters, a trend also observable among some fraternal organizations and other workers' groups.[34] For the saloonkeeper, the loss of liquor sales was problematic, but even more serious was the loss of influence and prestige when he could no longer depend on playing host to the workingman's club life. He might still have his loyal circle of customers, but his formerly powerful role in the working-class community was diminishing.

Before nationwide prohibition took effect in 1920, however, the barkeeper had managed to uphold the code of reciprocity and serve the many needs of his working-class constituency remarkably well. "He has often been called the 'poor man's friend,' and his place the 'poor man's club,' and I must say there is a kernel of truth in this," as one proprietor remarked in 1909.[35] It is important to keep in mind that the barman was first and foremost a businessman selling liquor for profit. That he also provided a wide array of comforts and services that for decades were not readily available to workers elsewhere is a revealing commentary on the condition of American society in its industrializing phase. To be sure, many criticisms could be made of the saloonkeeper's makeshift efforts to provide a workingman's employment bureau, union headquarters, political action center, immigrant way station, banking and credit agency, and neighborhood charity dispensary. Imperfect as his efforts were, though, the "poor man's friend" filled a void in workers' lives until better solutions could be devised.

NOTES

1. Jack London, *John Barleycorn: Alcoholic Memoirs* (1913; reprint, Santa Cruz, Calif., 1981).

2. Scholarly studies of the workingmen's saloon in the late nineteenth and early twentieth centuries include Madelon Powers, *Faces Along the Bar: Lore and Order in the Workingman's Saloon, 1870–1920* (Chicago, 1998); Perry R. Duis, *The Saloon: Public Drinking in Chicago and Boston, 1880–1920* (Urbana, 1983); Roy Rosenzweig, *Eight Hours for What We Will: Workers and Leisure in an Industrial City, 1870–1920* (New York, 1983); Thomas J. Noel, *The City and the Saloon: Denver, 1858–1916* (Lincoln, Nebr., 1982); and Elliott West, *The Saloon on the Rocky Mountain Mining Frontier* (Lincoln, Nebr., 1979). Detailed accounts of saloons by men who witnessed them firsthand include George Ade, *The Old-Time Saloon: Not Wet-Not Dry, Just History* (New York, 1931); Raymond Calkins, ed., *Substitutes for the Saloon* (Boston, 1901); and London, *John Barleycorn*. Regarding the temperance movement during the saloon period, some of the most useful studies include Jack S. Blocker, Jr., *American Temperance Movements: Cycles of Reform* (Boston, 1989); Harry Gene Levine, "The Discovery of Addiction: Changing Conceptions of Habitual Drunkenness in America," *Journal of Studies on Alcohol* 39 (January 1978): 143–74; Norman H. Clark, *Deliver Us from Evil: An*

Interpretation of American Prohibition (New York, 1976); James H. Timberlake, *Prohibition and the Progressive Movement, 1900–1920* (New York, 1970); Joseph R. Gusfield, *Symbolic Crusade: Status Politics and the American Temperance Movement* (Urbana, 1963); and Peter H. Odegard, *Pressure Politics: The Story of the Anti-Saloon League* (New York, 1928).

3. By 1909, the major brewing companies owned or controlled approximately 70 percent of the saloons nationwide, according to Timberlake, *Prohibition and the Progressive Movement,* 104–6. The impact of the tied-house system on the occupation of saloonkeeping is analyzed in Duis, *The Saloon,* 15–45. The working-class origin and orientation of most barkeepers are discussed in Rosenzweig, *Eight Hours for What We Will,* 52–53.

4. Robert A. Woods, *Americans in Process: A Settlement Study* (Boston, 1902), 201. For more discussion of immigrants and urban saloons, see Duis, *The Saloon,* 143–57, 160–71; Rosenzweig, *Eight Hours for What We Will,* 49–53, 55; Noel, *The City and the Saloon,* 9, 19–21; and William Kornblum, *Blue Collar Community* (Chicago, 1974), 77–79. The relationship between African Americans and their urban saloons is discussed in Duis, 157–60.

5. Royal L. Melendy, "The Saloon in Chicago: Part I," *American Journal of Sociology* 6 (November 1900): 298, 299, 303–4; Dorothy Richardson, "The Long Day: The Story of a New York Working Girl (1905)," in *Women at Work,* ed. William L. O'Neill (Chicago, 1972), 257–59, 287; Kathy Peiss, *Cheap Amusements: Working Women and Leisure in Turn-of-the-Century New York* (Philadelphia, 1986), 90–93; "The Experience and Observations of a New York Saloon-Keeper as Told by Himself," *McClure's Magazine* 32 (January 1909): 311; Calkins, *Substitutes for the Saloon,* 15. For my assessment of the few scattered references I have found regarding women in saloons, see Madelon Powers, "Rooftop Parties and Backroom Trysts: Women, Public Drinking, and Working-Class Saloons, 1890–1920" (unpublished paper, 1993).

6. Hutchins Hapgood, "McSorley's Saloon," *Harper's Weekly* (October 25, 1913): 15; Ade, *Old-Time Saloon,* 101; E. C. Moore, "The Social Value of the Saloon," *American Journal of Sociology* 3 (July 1897): 4–5.

7. Rosenzweig, *Eight Hours for What We Will,* 40–45; Kornblum, *Blue Collar Community,* 76.

8. "The roots of the [treating] custom can be traced as far back as the wassail bowl and loving cup of the fifth-century Saxons, and beyond them to practices of the Egyptians and Assyrians," according to West, *Saloon on the Rocky Mountain Mining Frontier,* 93–94. See also Frederick W. Hackwood, *Inns, Ales, and Drinking Customs of Old England* (New York, 1909), 141–52. For a comprehensive account of taverns and drinking customs in cultures worldwide over the centuries, see Robert E. Popham, "The Social History of the Tavern," in *Research Advances in Alcohol and Drug Problems,* vol. 4, ed. Yedy Israel et al. (New York, 1978), 225–302.

9. London, *John Barleycorn,* 122–23. For a discussion of the tavernkeeper's traditional role as a hospitable and knowledgeable host, see Popham, "Social History of the Tavern," 261–63, 271–74, 284–86.

10. London, *John Barleycorn,* 184.

11. Ade, *Old-Time Saloon,* 96–97; George Washington Plunkitt, quoted in William L. Riordon, *Plunkitt of Tammany Hall* (1905; reprint, New York, 1963), 77–78; "Experience and Observations of a New York Saloon-Keeper," 304.

12. M. E. Ravage, *An American in the Making: The Life Story of an Immigrant* (New York, 1917), 125–27.

13. Ade, *Old-Time Saloon,* 95. Frontier bartenders who appeared to keep up with their customers drink for drink "perhaps were employing a familiar deception by drawing upon a bottle of colored water," according to West, *Saloon on the Rocky Mountain Mining Frontier,* 61.

14. Ade, *Old Time Saloon*, 96; George Hand and M. E. Joyce, quoted in West, *Saloon on the Rocky Mountain Mining Frontier*, 60–61.

15. Robert Bagnell, *Economic and Moral Aspects of the Liquor Business* (New York, 1911), 22.

16. For an analysis of machine politicians' methods, see Harold Zink, *City Bosses in the United States: A Study of Twenty Municipal Bosses* (Durham, N.C., 1930), 194–201. Also informative is William L. Riordon, "When Tammany Was Supreme," introduction to Riordon, *Plunkitt of Tammany Hall*, vii–xxii.

17. Lloyd Wendt and Herman Kogan, *Bosses of Lusty Chicago: The Story of Bathhouse John and Hinky Dink* (Bloomington, 1967), v–xiv. This work was originally published in 1943 as *Lords of the Levee*. Michael Kenna acquired the nickname "Hinky Dink" because of his diminutive size; John Joseph Coughlin was known as "Bathhouse John" because he started out as a Chicago bathhouse "rubber" and later acquired a string of his own establishments. For a photograph of Kenna's saloon, the Workingmen's Exchange, see George Kibbe Turner, "The City of Chicago: A Study of the Great Immoralities," *McClure's Magazine* 28 (April 1907): 577. For statistics on the deep involvement of saloonkeepers and saloons in urban politics, see Odegard, *Pressure Politics*, 248.

18. William A. Bullough, *The Blind Boss and His City: Christopher Augustine Buckley and Nineteenth-Century San Francisco* (Berkeley, 1979), 139–40; Calkins, *Substitutes for the Saloon*, 11, 371–72.

19. "To the slum dweller and especially to the recent immigrant, machine politicians often seemed the only persons in the community who took a positive interest in their plight. . . . Perhaps most important of all, they gave the slum dweller a certain sense of power, the dignity of knowing that he counted, that at least his vote was worth something." John A. Garraty, *The New Commonwealth, 1877–1890* (New York, 1968), 218.

20. For more information on the free lunch, see Calkins, *Substitutes for the Saloon*, 15–19; Duis, *The Saloon*, 52–56; Richardson, "The Long Day," 257–59; Ade, *Old-Time Saloon*, 34–38.

21. Calkins, *Substitutes for the Saloon*, 16–17; Ade, *Old-Time Saloon*, 36–37.

22. Melendy, "Saloon in Chicago," 297. For more on the reaction of reformers to the free lunch and their efforts (mostly failures) to establish "tea saloons" to replace the food-dispensing role of barrooms, see Calkins, *Substitutes for the Saloon*, 15, 221–24.

23. Odegard, *Pressure Politics*, 45; Garraty, *New Commonwealth*, 202; Peter Roberts, *Anthracite Coal Communities* (New York, 1904), 236; Kornblum, *Blue Collar Community*, 75; Peiss, *Cheap Amusements*, 23; Margaret F. Byington, *Homestead: The Households of a Mill Town* (1910; reprint, Pittsburgh, 1974), 154–55.

24. Roberts, *Anthracite Coal Communities*, 236; Calkins, *Substitutes for the Saloon*, 11; Moore, "Social Value of the Saloon," 8.

25. London, *John Barleycorn*, 206–17; Melendy, "Saloon in Chicago," 297.

26. Moody Morton, "Man's Inhumanity to Man Makes Countless Thousands Mourn," *The Trestle Board* 11 (April 1897): 180; "Experience and Observations of a New York Saloon-Keeper," 310.

27. Calkins, *Substitutes for the Saloon*, 46–47.

28. Melendy, "Saloon in Chicago," 295; Calkins, *Substitutes for the Saloon*, 62; Thomas I. Kidd, quoted in Edward W. Bemis, "Attitude of the Trade Unions Toward the Saloon," in Calkins, Appendix 1, 312.

29. Melendy, "Saloon in Chicago," 295; Calkins, *Substitutes for the Saloon*, 55–56, 62.

30. Thomas J. Morgan, quoted in Royal L. Melendy, "The Saloon in Chicago: Part II," *American Journal of Sociology* 6 (January 1901): 438.

31. Duis, *The Saloon*, 73–76; "Jerry," a New York bartender, quoted in Frederick C. Howe, *The Confessions of a Reformer* (1925; reprint, New York, 1974), 51–52.

32. The percentage of single men fifteen years of age and older decreased from 40.2 percent in 1900 to 38.7 percent in 1910 and then to 35.1 percent in 1920. U.S. Bureau of the Census, *Population, 1920*, vol. 2 (Washington, D.C., 1922), 387. For a discussion of improvements in tenement housing, public parks, and other urban facilities, see Paul Boyer, *Urban Masses and Moral Order in America, 1820–1920* (Cambridge, Mass., 1978), 233–51. Regarding the competition that saloons faced from movies, see Robert Sklar, *Movie-Made America: A Social History of American Movies* (New York, 1975), 3–17; from stadiums and playgrounds, see Gunther Barth, *City People: The Rise of Modern City Culture in Nineteenth-Century America* (New York, 1980), 148–91. The growth of lodges and social clubs offering financial assistance to members is discussed in Mark C. Carnes, *Secret Ritual and Manhood in Victorian America* (New Haven, 1989), 8–9.

33. The prosecution of Boss Abraham Ruef and revelations about his betrayal of laborers' interests are detailed in Walton Bean, *Boss Ruef's San Francisco: The Story of the Union Labor Party, Big Business, and the Graft Prosecution* (Berkeley, 1952), 256–60. For more discussion of organized labor's problems with saloons and saloonkeepers, see David Brundage, "The Producing Classes and the Saloon: Denver in the 1880s," *Labor History* 26 (Winter 1985): 44–47; Timberlake, *Prohibition and the Progressive Movement*, 83–84; Calkins, *Substitutes for the Saloon*, 56–63.

34. For an analysis of the labor movement's support for temperance, though not necessarily abstinence or prohibition, see Ronald Morris Benson, "American Workers and Temperance Reform, 1866–1933" (Ph.D. diss., University of Notre Dame, 1974). Regarding the trend toward establishing independent union halls, see Bemis, "Attitude of the Trade Unions Toward the Saloon," 303–13.

35. "Experience and Observations of a New York Saloon-Keeper," 310.

Chapter 6

Leisure and Labor

Kathy Peiss

After ten or twelve hours a day bending over a sewing machine, standing at a sales counter, or waiting on tables, what energy could a turn-of-the-century working woman muster to attend a dance hall or amusement park? Quite a lot, according to the testimony of employers, journalists, and the wage-earners themselves. "Blue Monday" plagued employers. The head of a dressmaking shop, for example, observed that her employees "all took Sunday for a gala day and not as a day of rest. They worked so hard having a good time all day, and late into the evening, that they were 'worn to a frazzle' when Monday morning came." On week nights, working women hurriedly changed from work clothes to evening finery. Said one saleswoman, "You see some of those who have complained about standing spend most of the evening in dancing." The training supervisor at Macy's agreed, noting in exasperation, "We see that all the time in New York—many of the employees having recreation at night that unfits them for work the next day."[1]

Young, unmarried working-class women, foreign-born or daughters of immigrant parents, dominated the female labor force in the period from 1880 to 1920. In 1900, four-fifths of the 343,000 wage-earning women in New York were single, and almost one-third were aged sixteen to twenty. Whether supporting themselves or, more usually, contributing to the family economy, most girls expected to work at some time in their teens. Nearly 60 percent of all women in New York aged sixteen to twenty worked in the early 1900s. For many young women, wage earning became an integral part of the transition from school to marriage.[2]

Women labored for wages throughout the nineteenth century, but by the 1890s, the context in which they worked differed from that of the Victorian era. New jobs in department stores, large factories, and offices provided alternatives to domestic service, household production, and sweated labor in small shops, which had dominated women's work earlier. These employment opportunities, the changing organization

Reprinted from Kathy Peiss, *Cheap Amusements: Working Women and Leisure in Turn-of-the-Century New York* (Temple University Press, 1986) 34–55. Reprinted with the permission of Temple University Press.

of work, and the declining hours of labor altered the relationship between work and leisure, shaping the way in which leisure time was structured and experienced. The perception of leisure as a separate sphere of independence, youthful pleasure, and mixed-sex fun, in opposition to the world of obligation and toil, was supported by women's experience in the workplace. Far from inculcating good business habits, discipline, and a desire for quiet evenings at home, the workplace reinforced the wage-earner's interest in having a good time. Earning a living, an economic necessity for most young working-class women, was also a cultural experience organizing and defining their leisure activities.

WOMEN'S WORK IN THE VICTORIAN CITY

In the late nineteenth century, New York's economic landscape was crowded with flourishing commercial enterprises, a thriving port, manufacturing lofts, and work-shops. New York achieved prominence early in the century as the leading mercantile city in the United States, ensuring its primacy in commerce, shipping, and finance by dominating the Atlantic trade and developing transportation links to the hinterlands. By the Civil War, New York led the country in manufacturing, its strength lying in the garment trades, tobacco-processing and cigar-making, printing and publishing, metal-working, and furniture- and piano-making. Manufacturing was spurred by commercial trade, with merchant capitalists developing products such as ready-made clothing for the national market. Other types of business were developed to answer the clamor for goods and services arising from the city's burgeoning population. Unlike many American cities, where the age of industry was characterized by huge, mechanized factories, the city's high rental costs, cheap immigrant labor supply, and lack of a good energy source led to a myriad of small, highly specialized shops.[3]

This expanding mercantile and manufacturing economy brought many young women into the labor force after 1840, but not primarily as "mill girls" or factory hands, as was the case in cities where capital-intensive industries flourished. The majority of women workers in Victorian New York labored as domestic servants, needlewomen, laundresses, and in other employments seemingly marginal to an in-dustrial economy.[4] As late as 1880, 40 percent of all New York working women were in domestic service, an experience particularly common among adolescent Irish and German girls. Home-based occupations and street trades, such as keeping boarders, washing laundry, cleaning, ragpicking, and peddling, provided necessary income for poor working-class wives and widows. In manufacturing, New York women were concentrated in the needle trades, with over one-fifth working as dressmakers, tailors, and milliners in 1880. In these years, garments were produced in small workshops or in the home. Even after the introduction of the sewing machine, much of the cloth-ing trade was contracted to tenement sweatshops, often conducted as a family-based enterprise. A similar scale of production characterized cigar-making, a common em-ployment among women.[5] Relatively few women, married or single, were engaged in the type of large-scale, mechanized factory production considered the vanguard of an industrial society.

Much of women's wage work was centered in the home and followed household routines, or fitted into them without serious difficulty. This was especially true for married women, whose productive labor was often ignored by census enumerators. Keeping boarders, for example, a common occupation of working-class wives, involved the same tasks of cooking, washing, and cleaning that women performed for their families. Sewing and other forms of industrial homework, which endured among southern and eastern European immigrants well into the twentieth century, filled the days of mothers already occupied with child care and housework. As the daughter of an Italian homeworker observed in 1913, "My mother works all the time—all day, Sundays and holidays, except when she is cooking or washing. She never has time to go out or she would get behind in her work."[6] The task-oriented rhythms of such work, its lack of clear-cut boundaries, and the sheer burden of the "double day" left little time for leisure.

With greater job opportunities and limited household concerns, single women had fewer restrictions on their time than did working mothers. Indeed, by the mid-nineteenth century, some young working girls achieved notoriety in the city as pleasure seekers. While their mothers turned increasingly toward domestic pursuits, young factory hands, domestic servants, and prostitutes sought a life of finery, frolics, and entertainment. Industrial workers in particular found possibilities for leisure, sociability, and fun affirmed in the workplace. These Victorian "rowdy girls"—controversial figures within working-class communities—prefigure the broader trend toward a pleasure-oriented culture that swept working women's lives at the turn of the century.[7]

At the same time, women's access to a world of leisure at midcentury was limited by their work situations, as well as by poverty and social disapprobation. Single women who labored as domestic servants found that middle-class mistresses encroached upon their opportunities for leisure. Servants' desire to wear fine clothes and attend entertainments collided with employers' edicts limiting their time off. Maids were often on call twelve or thirteen hours a day and generally had only one afternoon and evening a week free.[8] Similarly, the exploitative conditions in the dominant manufacturing industries often permitted little free time. Grueling hours of labor for small wages in sweatshops and tenements characterized the work of seamstresses and needlewomen, cigar-makers, and others. Many of them labored fifteen to eighteen hours daily, working by gaslight late into the evening to earn enough for food and rent. Fatigue and poor health were more often their lot than finery and entertainment.[9]

Periods of sociability and amusement were often snatched within the rhythms of work. Domestic servants, for example, would meet together in the street or park to gossip and socialize while tending their mistresses' children. Yet for many, the relatively isolated nature of their labor, its long hours, and task-oriented rhythms did not reinforce a concept of leisure as a separate sphere of social life. One important exception to this pattern lay in the experience of female factory workers, whose work involved the segmentation of time and sociability among peers. By the end of the century, the distinction between household-based work and new forms of labor located in centralized production widened. While married women continued to do home-based work, single women increasingly entered an array of jobs not only in factories but in department stores, restaurants, and offices.

CHANGES IN WOMEN'S LABOR

By 1900, important changes in the social organization of labor and expanding job opportunities in New York created new work experiences for women. Small shops, lofts, and trading companies still crowded lower Manhattan, but the city's economic landscape was rapidly changing. The wards at the southern tip of Manhattan were increasingly given over to corporate headquarters, banking and investment firms, and specialized business offices. Towering skyscrapers and the canyons of Wall Street symbolized New York's transformation from a mercantile city to the nation's center for corporate industry. This expanding office complex created a demand for workers increasingly filled by female clerks, "typewriters," secretaries, and telephone operators. The explosive growth of the white-collar sector in the twentieth century, and women's participation in it, was anticipated in New York a decade before it affected the rest of the country. A negligible number of New York's clerks, typists, and book-keepers were female in 1880; in 1900, 7 percent of all New York working women were filling such positions; and by 1920, this number had increased to 22 percent. These were native-born women who had received a public school education, primarily daughters of American, German, and Irish parents.[10]

Women's opportunities for jobs in trade and services expanded as consumers, travelers, and businesses demanded a range of urban amenities. Retail trade grew substantially, symbolized by the emergence of such large department stores as Macy's, Bloomingdale's, and Lord and Taylor's. The center for retail business moved upward, near Fifth Avenue, Broadway, and Thirty-fourth Street, close to an emerging commercial center, railroad connections, and middle-class residents. This expansion coincided with a shift in the sex-typing of store work. Retail sales had been a predominantly male occupation as late as the 1880s, when only 12 percent of clerks and salespersons in New York stores were women. By 1900, the saleslady had become a fixture of the retail emporium, a much coveted position for young working women. Working as a saleswoman or store clerk was the second most common occupation of native-born single wage-earners, whether "American girls" or daughters of immigrants.[11] Other businesses catered to the work routines and pleasures of a mobile, hectic population. Restaurants and lunchrooms, laundries, hotels, beauty parlors, drugstores, and theaters offered young women desirable alternatives to domestic service.

Although small workshops and households continued to play an important role in manufacturing, the production process increasingly turned toward larger factories. In the complex world of garment-making, conditions varied in the different branches of the industry. Generally, however, production shifted from isolated homework toward small sweatshops housed in tenements by the 1880s; by 1910, as the demand for ready-made clothing grew and further mechanization of the industry occurred, it was increasingly based in large-scale factories. John Commons estimated that while 90 percent of ready-made garments had been produced in sweatshops in 1890, 75 percent were made in factories after 1900. While the clothing trades dominated New York industry, women also found work in a variety of light assembling and operative jobs producing consumer goods. Artificial flower-making, box-making, confectionery dipping, jewelry work, and bookbinding were typical female occupations.[12]

These new patterns of labor fostered differing work expectations across genera-tions, expectations that particularly affected the American-born daughters of immi-grant parents. Although domestic service remained the foremost occupation of single women, the daughters of immigrants increasingly refused to don the maid's uniform. In her 1914 study of 370 working mothers, Katharine Anthony found that almost half had been employed in domestic service and one-third in manufacturing before marriage; as working mothers, 70 percent of them labored in domestic and personal service. In contrast, most of their daughters worked in stores, offices, and factories, with only a small fraction going into service. "The German-American child wants a position in an office," noted anthropologist Elsa Herzfeld. "The daughter refuses to go into domestic service although her mother had formerly taken a 'position.'"[13] New immigrant groups from southern and eastern Europe repeated this pattern. As Thomas Kessner has shown for the years between 1880 and 1905, Italian and Jewish wives rarely worked outside the home, but depended on homework to supplement the fam-ily income. Their daughters' work patterns changed significantly in the twenty-five-year period. Italian girls' occupations shifted from unskilled labor and street trades to factory work. Jewish girls throughout the period worked in the small shops of the garment industry, but by 1905 were also finding positions in schools, offices, and department stores.[14]

Women flocked to these jobs in part because they allowed more free time and autonomy, splitting the realms of work and leisure more clearly than household-based labor. A bitter complaint about domestic service was its lack of leisure time. One woman, for example, who had turned to service after working in manu-facturing asserted, "as long as I had a trade I was certain of my evenings an' my Sundays. Now I'm never certain of anything." An investigation into the "servant question" agreed with this assessment: "Especially is objection made to the fact that her evenings are not her own, so that she may go out at will with her friends or may attend places of amusement."[15]

Among working women, leisure came to be seen as a separate sphere of life to be consciously protected. Whether their employer was exploitative or well-intentioned, women resented interference with their "own" time. Nonunionized bindery work-ers, for example, tried to protest overtime work that kept them on the job through Christmas Eve. Shopgirls, too, who had been urged at a public hearing to state their grievances over working conditions, complained chiefly about not getting out of work on time. "Make them close at 6 o'clock," one exclaimed, testifying that her employer rang the closing bell late, causing store workers to labor an extra fifteen to thirty min-utes: "Q. And that really has the result of depriving you of your evenings—of getting to places of entertainment in time, does it not? A. Yes, sir; that is right." Another store clerk observed that all the workers took turns closing up the department, so that each night one could leave early at 5:45 p.m.[16]

Those who could—predominantly the young, unmarried, and American-born—re-jected the household-based, task-oriented employments that had traditionally been women's work. They preferred to labor in stores and factories, where they sold their labor and submitted to employers' work discipline for a specified portion of time. The remainder of the day, while often limited by exhaustion and household obligations, they could call their own. This distinctive sphere of leisure, demarcated in new forms of wage-earning, grew as the hours of labor decreased from 1880 to 1920.

THE DECLINING HOURS OF LABOR

The actual time working women had for relaxation and amusement is difficult to assess, since women's occupations rarely conformed to a single standard. Variations in the size and scale of industries, the seasonable nature of many jobs, differences between piecework and hourly wages, and low levels of unionization contributed to the nonuniformity of women's workdays. The New York State Bureau of Labor Statistics in 1885, for example, in cataloguing hundreds of industrial concerns, found that women's working days ranged from eight to seventeen hours. Even within a single industry, vast differences among workers are apparent. In the cigar industry, for example, some cigar-makers, presumably unionized, worked only eight hours, while bunch-makers regularly worked fifteen to seventeen hours daily. Moreover, women doing piecework often felt compelled to labor extra hours in the factory or at home in the evening.[17]

For many, the seasonal demand for consumer goods and services created an alternating pattern of intense labor and slack work. Garment manufacturers made heavy demands on employees in the fall and spring, but laid off workers in the dull seasons after Christmas and in the summer. The work history of one milliner typifies the casual employment many women faced: from February to May she had steady work; she was then laid off and hunted for a job in June and July; from August to December, she worked a total of fourteen weeks at four different establishments. During intermittent layoffs and the monthlong slack period after Christmas, she sold candy. Cigarette-makers, carpet weavers, candy-makers, and bookbinders all experienced the seasonal rush to produce goods, and department store clerks put in ten- to sixteen-hour stints during the Christmas and Easter holidays. While posted hours in New York City factories were usually less than those upstate, many women regularly worked overtime as many as three or four nights a week during the busy season.[18] These spells allowed little time for leisure, while the slack season left women with time on their hands. Many looked for employment and filled in at other jobs, but others "took it easy" during the layoffs and, like Maria Cichetti, spent their hard-earned money going to vaudeville shows and movies.[19]

The contracting of jobs in some trades created a peculiar weekly rhythm of heavy labor and slack work. In many small task shops, garment-makers worked a fourteen-hour stretch for three days and then were idle the rest of the week. Similarly, laundries often had little work on Saturdays and Mondays, but might keep their employees at labor sixteen or seventeen hours on other days. In some jobs, labor intensity varied widely during the day. Waitresses, for example, often worked "split tricks"—on duty during the busy hours of lunch and dinner, relieved in the afternoon, hardly the best time for social engagements.[20]

Despite the irregularity of women's labor, the general trend of the period from 1880 to 1920 was toward shorter working days for female wage-earners in factories and stores. In 1885, women's workday ranged from ten to seventeen hours, but by the 1910s the long stints were much less common. Millinery workers, for example, who typically worked fourteen hours in 1885, put in only nine to ten hours in 1914. Similarly, a 1911 study of workers in lower Manhattan found that almost two-thirds of the female wage-earners worked less than ten hours daily. In addition, growing numbers of businesses closed early on Saturdays, particularly in the slow summer months, to give their workers a half-holiday.[21] The movement for protective legislation, greater union activity among working women, the increased rationalization of production, and changing attitudes toward workers' leisure contributed to this overall decline.

Protective legislation to lower women's work hours was pushed by middle-class reformers seeking to safeguard women's health and reproductive capacities, and by craft unions anxious about women's growing role in the workforce. Under pressure from these groups, New York's state legislature enacted a series of laws limiting the hours of labor, beginning in 1886 with the restriction of minors and women under twenty-one from working in manufacturing more than ten hours a day or sixty hours a week. This ceiling was extended to all female factory workers in 1899. In 1912, a revised statute curtailed the working day for women in manufacturing to nine hours, and two years later, this limit covered women's work in the city's mercantile stores. The nine-hour day and fifty-four-hour week continued to be the legal standard in New York well into the 1920s.[22]

Generous loopholes and ineffective enforcement limited the efficacy of these laws, however. The legislation failed to cover women who did not work in factories and stores. It also permitted mercantile and industrial employers to demand irregular hours and overtime on a daily basis, as long as they obeyed the weekly limit. Enforcement was hampered by the hostility of employers, the limited number of factory inspectors, and the perfunctory penalties for violations. Mary Van Kleeck echoed the criticism of many reformers in observing that "the limit of the law is exceeded in numerous instances and in many trades—so that it is by no means uncommon to find young girls in the factories of New York working twelve, thirteen, even fourteen hours in a day." Despite these limitations, protective legislation contributed to the gradual decline in hours by setting legal limits and popularizing the notion of the "right to leisure." Major employers of women, including large clothing manufacturers and department stores, generally adhered to the labor laws.[23]

For some women, the labor movement's demand for the eight-hour day held the most promise of greater leisure. Although the vast majority of working women were not organized in this period, the union movement made important inroads after 1905 in industries with high female employment, such as garment-making and bookbinding. Bookbinders successfully struck for the eight-hour day in 1907, while waistmakers and other clothing workers achieved shorter hours in the settlements following the famous garment strikes of the 1910s.[24] Workers in unionized shops experienced a dramatic increase in their leisure time, as this young woman attested:

> The shorter work day brought me my first idea of there being such a thing as pleasure. It was quite wonderful to get home before it was pitch dark at night, and a real joy to ride on the cars and look out the windows and see something. Before this time it was just sleep

and eat and hurry off to work. . . . I was twenty-one before I went to a theater and then I went with a crowd of union girls to a Saturday matinee performance. I was twenty-three before I saw a dance and that was a union dance too.[25]

Changes in the scale and organization of industry also hastened the decline in hours. As they achieved greater worker productivity through scientific management and mechanization, many major employers yielded to the shorter workday. Thus the trend in New York City toward larger mercantile establishments and factories had a salutary effect on lowering working hours. The reorganization of the garment trades, for example, sharply reduced hours. When the industry was dominated by home-sewing, there were no limits placed on the hours women might work. Workers in small task shops continued to be plagued with irregular employment and fourteen-hour workdays, while large clothing factories offered more steady work and a ten- to eleven-hour day. These establishments stopped work at 6:00 p.m., giving workers their evenings for rest and recreation. Similarly, the large department stores required only nine hours of labor except in the pre-Christmas season, in contrast to smaller neighborhood stores, which kept late hours to serve the working-class trade.[26]

Finally, liberalized attitudes toward workers' leisure began to take hold by the 1910s. The philanthropic bent of some large industrialists and retail merchants, joined with their desire to forestall unionization drives, led to welfare programs and practices designed to improve workers' health and well-being, in part by reducing hours. Josephine Goldmark's influential study of workers and efficiency, Louis Brandeis's brief on the hazards of long hours and night work for women, and the publicity campaigns of the Consumers' League contributed to the growing cultural legitimacy of the short day for women.[27]

By 1920, the hours of labor had declined sharply for many urban working women. In 1923, three-quarters of the women surveyed by the New York State Department of Labor worked only forty-eight hours or less in New York City, in contrast to their up-state sisters, of whom fewer than one-third worked such a short week. The memories of Nathan Cohen and Ruth Kaminsky, brother and sister, suggest the dimensions of change in the hours of labor. Nathan, a Russian immigrant who arrived in the United States in 1912, remembers doing little at night other than working, but his sister Ruth, who came to this country in 1921, had time to go to night school: "When I came over, they didn't work ten, twelve hours a day anymore. Tops was eight, nine, unless it was a small business, or some factories." Although she worked nine hours daily with a Saturday half-holiday in the 1910s, observed another immigrant woman, "at that time, we didn't consider it long."[28]

WORK CULTURES AND WOMEN'S LEISURE

While the shortened workday allowed more leisure time, women's experiences in the workplace reinforced the appeal of pleasure-oriented recreation in the public sphere. On one level, the desire for frivolous amusement was a reaction against the discipline, drudgery, and exploitative conditions of labor. A woman could forget rattling machinery or irritating customers in the nervous energy and freedom of the grizzly bear and turkey trot, or escape the rigors of the workplace altogether by finding a husband in the city's night spots. "You never rest until you die," observed one young box-maker, "but I will get out by marrying somebody." Indeed, factory investigators recorded the "widespread belief of the girls that marriage is relief from the trouble and toil of wage labor."[29]

At the same time, women's notions of leisure were reaffirmed through their positive social interactions within the workplace. In factories, stores, and offices, women socialized with other women and informally cooperated to affect working conditions. Their experience of work in a group context differed sharply from the home-bound, task-oriented, and isolated situation of domestic servants, outworkers, and housewives. There developed in this setting a shared and public culture, which legitimized the desires and behaviors expressed in young women's leisure.

Like other work groups, women workers developed degrees of autonomy and control in their relationship to managers and the work process by enforcing informal work rules and production quotas, socializing new employees into these patterns of behavior, and protecting their job skills from the bosses' encroachment. Given their status as low-skilled and easily replaced workers, wage-earning women rarely commanded the control over the work process that men in the skilled trades could exert, but neither were they merely victims of capitalist discipline.[30] Department store saleswomen, for example, used their selling skills to manipulate managers, supervisors, and customers, enforcing work rules among the women to sell only so many goods each day and employing code words to warn coworkers of recalcitrant customers. Bookbinders too employed the notion of a "fair day's work," controlling the output during each stint, while other factory hands orchestrated work stoppages and job actions over such issues as sexual harassment and pay cuts. Even waitresses worked out their resentment toward employers by pilfering pins and small objects, supplying themselves liberally with ice water and towels, and eating desserts ordered for imaginary customers.[31]

In mediating the relationship between the wage-earner and the labor process, work cultures involved not only informal efforts to control work but also the daily interactions that helped pass the long hours. While women characterized the workplace as tedious and demanding, a necessity to be endured, most tried to create places of sociability and support on the shop floor. Women sang songs, recited the plots of novels, argued politics, and gossiped about social life to counteract the monotony and routine of the workday. One feather-maker, for example, described her coworkers' conversations: "We have such a good time. We talk about books that we read, . . . the theatres, and newspapers, and the things that go on about town." Pieceworkers, who had more control over their time than hourly hands, could follow their own rhythms of intense work mixed with periods of sociability. "When I was a pieceworker," recalled one garment worker, "I would sing, I would fool around, say jokes, talk with the girls."[32] Singing helped pace the work, as in one box-maker's shop where songs would rise and fall while the workers sped through their tasks:

> Three o'clock, a quarter after, half-past! The terrific tension had all but reached the breaking point. Then there rose a trembling, palpitating sigh that seemed to come from a

hundred throats, and blended in a universal expression of relief. In her clear, high treble Angelina began the everlasting "Fatal Wedding." That piece of false sentiment had now a new significance. It became a song of deliverance, and as the workers swelled the chorus, one by one, it meant that the end of the day's toil was in sight.[33]

Even in factories with loud machinery, women would try to converse above the noise, while lunch hours and the after-work walk home also afforded time to socialize with workmates. At Macy's, employees were "fond of sitting down in a corner and eating a pickle and pastry and a cup of tea; they can do that very quickly and can then visit; for quite a long time during the rest of the noon hour."[34]

Women's work cultures varied according to type of employment, ethnic and religious affiliation, and larger cultural traditions. American-born union women, believing in self-education and uplift, often mirrored their male counterparts' behavior in the shop. In one New York cigar factory, for example, female trade unionists would pay one of their members to read aloud while they worked: "First the newspaper is read, then some literary work, such as for instance Morley's 'Life of Gladstone.'"[35] Even among nonunionized workers, the rituals, rules, and interactions governing work in stores and restaurants, where interpersonal skills were utilized, differed from semiskilled production, where machinery dominated the shop floor. The women themselves had a firm understanding of the occupational hierarchy indicated by language, mores, and "tone." The saleslady's patina of style and refinement differentiated her from the rougher manner of many tobacco or garment workers. Within a single industry, ethnic patterns also shaped different work cultures; cultural and political traditions, for example, contributed to the Jewish waist-makers' readiness to organize and strike, unlike their more hesitant Italian workmates.[36] Despite these distinctive differences, we can discern important commonalities in the work cultures of women that shaped and defined their attitudes toward leisure.

In the workplace, young women marked out a cultural terrain distinct from familial traditions and the customary practices of their ethnic groups, signifying a new identity as wage-earners, through language, clothing, and social rituals. "Learners" might adopt new names from storybook romances when they entered a workplace for the first time, and greenhorns shed their Old World names for Anglicized ones. Fads, modish attire, and a distinctive personal style were also encouraged, as wage-earners discussed the latest fashions, learned new hairstyles, and tried out cosmetics and cigarettes. Indeed, employers often found it necessary to proscribe the unseemly behavior of working women: "At Koch's there is a splendid system of rules prohibiting the chewing of gum, rougeing and excessively using face powder."[37]

For factory hands, talking and socializing forged links between the world of labor and the pleasures of leisure. Some working girls, noted Lillian Betts, "dance[d] on the street at lunch-time, in front of their factory, singing their own dance music."[38] Part of the enjoyment inherent in the evening's entertainment lay in recounting the triumphs of the ball or party to one's workmates. Moreover, co-workers became a circle of friends apart from neighborhood or ethnic group ties. One Jewish garment worker observed, for example, that "while working, [I] used to have friends—Gentile girls. Sometimes we used to go out, we used to attend weddings, [I] was in their homes a few times."[39] Others formed social clubs comprised of coworkers and school friends.

Department store workers also were irrepressible in integrating work and social life through their use of language, special events, and organizations. When extra employees were laid off at the end of the holiday season, for example, they referred to the mass exodus as the "cakewalk," after the popular Afro-American dance and strut. Holidays and engagements were constant excuses for parties, suppers, and celebrations. A popular ritual involved cutting a Halloween cake, wherein one lucky saleswoman found a ring, forecasting marriage, while an unfortunate coworker discovered a button or thimble, threatening spinsterhood. Numerous social clubs formalized the relationship between work and leisure. At the Siegel-Cooper department store, the workers banded together by department, forming, for example, the Foot Mould Social Club, comprised of women in the shoe department, and the Bachelor Girls Social Club, organized by the mail order clerks. These associations of women workers typically sponsored dances, entertainments, and excursions to Coney Island.[40]

In the workplace, women's conversations, stories, and songs often gravitated to the subject of dating and romantic entanglements with men, a discourse that accentuated the mixed-sex character of their leisure. During free moments, waitresses relished gossip about "the ubiquitous 'gentleman friend,' the only topic of conversation outside of the dining room interests." Women's socialization into a new workplace might involve a ritualistic exchange over "gentlemen friends." In one steam laundry, for example, an investigator repeatedly heard this conversation:

"Say, you got a feller?"
"Sure. Ain't you got one?"
"Sure."[41]

One Jewish garment worker recalled daydreaming about love and marriage in the shops: "We used to even sing the songs . . . Yiddish naturally, singing the dream songs, the love songs, and this is how we dreamed away our youth and go out gay and happy."[42]

In department stores, the mixed-sex workplace became a setting for romance, trysts, and discussion of male-female relations. *Thought and Work*, the in-house magazine of the Siegel-Cooper department store, which was written by workers, evinced little interest in selling skills and business news, but resonated with gossip about eligible bachelors, intrastore courtships, wedding notices, and entertainments about town. Personal popularity, beauty, hair styles, clothing, and dancing ability were newsworthy items. Cultural practices among department store workers emerge from the breathless commentary of the newsletter: the saleslady who changes her hair color because, the gossip speculates, she "wants a man"; the competition between departments for the most engagements and marriages; the delivery of roses and mash notes to young women; the debates among idle saleswomen on such topics as kissing mustachioed men. Some department managers were portrayed more as popular matchmakers than enforcers of work discipline. "Mr. Eckle is a past master at securing husbands for the young ladies in his department," noted *Thought and Work*. "He'd rather do that than sign time cards."[43] While doubtlessly the magazine embellished the business of romance at the store, management eventually reined in its editors, ordering less copy on personal life and more articles on the business of selling.[44]

Bound to the language of romance was the frank discussion of sexuality among laboring women, a practice in the workplace that mirrored that of popular amusements. Risqué jokes, swearing, and sexual advice were a common part of the work environment in restaurants, laundries, factories, and department stores. Waitresses bandied obscenities and engaged in explicit discussion of lovers and husbands before work and during breaks. As one surprised middle-class observer described the scene in a restaurant: "They were putting on their aprons, combing their hair, powdering their noses, . . . all the while tossing back and forth to each other, apparently in a spirit of good-natured comradeship, the most vile epithets that I had ever heard emerge from the lips of a human being."[45] Despite their image of gentility and upward mobility, department store workers relished a similar freedom in language and behavior. At Macy's, a store that sought to maintain strict standards of employee respectability, investigators found "salacious cards, poems, etc., copied with avidity and passed from one to another, not only between girls and girls, but from girls to men." While many workers remained aloof from such vulgarities, there was "more smutty talk in one particular department than in a dance hall."[46]

Sexual knowledge was communicated between married and single women, between the experienced and the naive. A YWCA study of the woman worker observed that "the 'older hands' initiate her early through the unwholesome story or innuendo. She is forced to think of sex matters in relation to herself by the suggestions made to her of what she may expect from suitors or find in marriage." Examples of such initiation abound in the reports of middle-class investigators and reformers. In one department at Macy's dominated by married women, for example, "there was enough indecent talk to ruin any girl in her teens who might be put at work on that floor."[47] Stripped of their moralistic overtones, such observations reveal the workplace as an arena in which women wage-earners articulated their sexual feelings and shared their acquired wisdom about negotiating the attentions of men, both on the job and in their leisure time.

It was also an arena in which they experienced sexual vulnerability, a world of harassment as well as the give-and-take of humor and conversation. Then as now, sexual harassment limited women's position in the workforce and maintained male privilege and control. Wage-earning women were perceived by bosses and male workers alike to be outside the realm of parental or community protection. As one cigar-maker observed, behavior that in another context would not be tolerated was given free rein on the shop floor:

> Many men who are respected—when I say respected and respectable, I mean who walk the streets and are respected as working men, and who would not, under any circumstances, offer the slightest insult or disrespectful remark or glance to a female in the streets, . . . in the shops, will whoop and give expressions to "cat calls" and a peculiar noise made with their lips, which is supposed to be an endearing salutation.[48]

Women learned to tread a fine line between participating in acceptable workplace practices and guarding their integrity and respectability. Macy's clerks, who could trade obscenities and *double entendres* with the salesmen, knew "just how to be very friendly, without permitting the least familiarity," when conversing with male customers. As one factory investigator observed, "such Women learn to defend themselves and to take care of themselves."[49] This sexual knowledge gained in the workplace informed women's relations with men in the world of leisure.

WOMEN'S WAGES AND TREATING

The work culture of women encouraged an ideology of romance that resonated with explicit heterosexual pleasures and perils at the same time that it affirmed the value of leisure. Still, working women's lack of financial resources posed a problem to their participation in an active social life, particularly in the world of commercial amusements. On the surface, low wages and little spending money would seem to have limited women's access to leisure, thus undercutting the heterosocial, pleasure-oriented culture of the workplace. Paradoxically, the material conditions of their lives at work and at home served instead to strengthen that culture.

Working women in New York typically earned below the "living wage," estimated by economists to be nine or ten dollars a week in 1910. Employers and workingmen alike justified women's low wages and their exclusion from higher-paying skilled trades by claiming that women were temporary wage-earners who worked only until marriage. Occupational segregation of the labor market was deeply entrenched, and women were concentrated in semiskilled, seasonal employment. As cashgirls and salesclerks, assemblers and machine-tenders, waitresses and servants, their average earnings were one-half of those received by men in their employments. In New York factories in the early 1910s, 56 percent of the female labor force earned under $8.00 a week. Despite their higher social status, the majority of women in retail stores earned under $7.50, although the large emporia offered higher wages than neighborhood stores and five-and-tens. Deductions for tardiness, poor workmanship, and other violations further depleted wage-earners' already meager earnings.[50]

Relatively few women were able to live alone in comfort. Among the large industrial cities of the United States, New York had one of the highest percentages of wage-earning women residing with parents or relatives, from 80 to 90 percent. Self-supporting workers lodging in boardinghouses or renting rooms tended to be older, native-born women who earned higher wages than those living at home.[51] Most found, nevertheless, that their earnings were consumed by the cost of room, board, and clothing, leaving little for recreation. To make ends meet, self-supporting women would scrimp on essential items in their weekly budgets. Going without meals was a common strategy, as was sleeping three to a bed to reduce the rent. "Some never boarded a street car for an evening's ride without planning days ahead how they could spare the nickel from their lunch or clothes money," noted reformer Esther Packard, describing women who lived on six dollars a week.[52] After work, the self-supporting woman sewed and washed her own clothing, cooked meals, and prepared for the next workday. Such scheduling and scrimping often left little time or money for evening amusements: "When the women or girls were visited at night, they were more likely to be found at home busy at the wash tub or ironing board than out at a dance or the theater." A movie and occasional ball were their only forms of leisure.[53]

By scrimping and making do, young women could provide some recreation for themselves. Yeddie Bruker, a factory worker earning seven dollars a week, spent almost two dollars of that on clothing and four dollars on room and board. A union member, she spent sixteen cents weekly for union dues and a benefit association, while for recreation she allocated ten cents a week for theatre tickets. Katia Markelov, a corset maker earning ten dollars, saved thirty dollars yearly for outings, while Rita Karpovna's low wages, six to seven dollars weekly, forced her to sacrifice essential items for union dues and the "Woman's Self-Education Society": "The Union and this club meant more to Rita than the breakfasts and luncheons she dispensed with, and more, apparently, than dress, for which she spent only $20 in a year and a half."[54]

For women living at home, recreation was limited not so much by the size of their income as by access to it. In exchange for their wages, most parents gave their daughters small sums of spending money, averaging twenty-five to fifty cents each week, in addition to lunch money and carfare. Like self-supporting women, those who lived at home necessarily scrimped and depended on others for recreation. They commonly saved their allowances for lunch by eating the free food served in saloons or skipping the meal altogether. Many, like Maria Cichetti, saved carfare by walking to or from work. Maria received ten cents for the roundtrip trolley ride to her shop; by walking home with friends at night, she could save a nickel for the movies. As one investigator of West Side girls observed, "A carfare saved by walking to work is a carfare earned for a trip to a dance hall 'away out in the Bronx.'"[55]

Women also relied on coworkers and female friends to help them out with food, clothing, and recreation. The low-wage cashgirl or salesclerk was "helped by those about her in the store with gifts of clothing or even with money," observed one sales-girl. In factories, older wage-earners would aid the youngest by paying her a dime to fetch tea or lunch. A tradition of mutual aid and support can be seen in the frequency of raffles and events to raise money for less fortunate workmates.[56]

Typically, however, young women looked to men for financial assistance and gifts. "If they didn't take me, how could I ever go out?" observed a young department store worker. Treating was a widely accepted practice, especially if the woman had a fiancé, or "steady," from whom she could accept food, clothing, and recreation without compromising her reputation. One woman, for example, counted on her steady for Sunday meals, exclaiming, "Why, if I had to buy all of my meals I'd never get along." Unable to save a penny of her seven-dollar weekly wage, Clara X. depended on her beau, who earned more than twice her income, to occasionally purchase her clothes and take her on vacation.[57] Rose Pasternak paid for an overcoat on installments until she was "keeping company": "I paid and paid and paid, till I got with the company with my fella. He paid eight dollars. After I was a long time married, he used to throw it in my face, 'you made so much money that I had to pay for the plush coat.'"[58] Other self-supporting women had no qualms about accepting treats from unknown men or chance acquaintances. As one observer concluded, "the acceptance on the part of the girl of almost any invitation needs little explanation when one realizes that she often goes pleasureless unless she does accept 'free treats.'"[59]

The culture of treating was reinforced in the workplace through women's interactions with employers, male workmates, and customers, particularly in service and sales jobs. In department stores, managers were said to advise shopgirls to find gentleman friends who could buy them the clothing and trinkets that their salaries could not cover. At a government hearing, one saleswoman testified: "One of the employers has told me, on a $6.50 wage, he don't care where I get my clothes from as long as I have them, to be dressed to suit him."[60] Some investigators denied the accuracy of these reports, but their widespread currency among saleswomen suggests the tacit legitimacy of treating as a means of gaining access to the world of amusements. Waitresses knew that suggestive familiarity with male customers often brought good tips, and some used their skills and opportunities to engage in an active social life with chance acquaintances. "Most of the girls quite frankly admit making 'dates' with strange men," observed a Consumers' League study. "These 'dates' are made with no thought on the part of the girl beyond getting the good time which she cannot afford herself."[61] These working women sought a way to negotiate dependency and claim some choice, autonomy, and pleasure in otherwise dreary lives. They understood, albeit hazily, that leisure was the realm in which that quest could most easily be achieved.

NOTES

1. [Siegel-Cooper Department Store], *Thought and Work,* Dec. 1904, p. 15; "A Salesgirl's Story," *Independent* 54 (31 July 1902): 1821; Harry B. Taplin, "Training for Store Efficiency," 17 March 1915, p. 2, Box 118, Welfare Department Subject File, National Civic Federation Papers, Rare Books and Manuscripts Division, New York Public Library, Astor, Lenox and Tilden Foundation.

2. U.S. Bureau of the Census, *Statistics of Women at Work* (Washington, D.C., 1907), pp. 270–271, 148–151; New York State Factory Investigating Commission, *Fourth Report Transmitted to Legislature*, Feb. 15, 1915 (S. Doc. no. 43; Albany, N.Y., 1915), vol. 1, p. 37, and vol. 4, p. 1478–1489. See also U.S. Bureau of the Census, *Women in Gainful Occupations, 1870–1920*, by Joseph A. Hill (Washington, D.C., 1929). Women's role in the labor force is surveyed in Leslie Woodcock Tentler, *Wage-Earning Women: Industrial Work and Family Life in the United States, 1900–1930* (New York, 1979); Alice Kessler-Harris, *Out to Work* (New York, 1982); Susan Estabrook Kennedy, *If All We Did Was to Weep at Home: A History of White Working-Class Women in America* (Bloomington, Ind., 1979); Miriam Cohen, "Italian American Women in New York City, 1900–1950: Work and School," in *Class, Sex, and the Woman Worker,* ed. Milton Cantor and Bruce Laurie (Westport, Conn., 1977), pp. 120–143.

3. David C. Hammack, *Power and Society: Greater New York at the Turn of the Century* (New York, 1982), pp. 31–58; Sean Wilentz, *Chants Democratic: New York City and the Rise of the American Working Class, 1788–1850* (New York, 1984), especially pp. 107–142; Bayrd Still, *Mirror for Gotham* (New York, 1956).

4. Mary Christine Stansell, "Women of the Laboring Poor in New York City, 1820–1860" (Ph.D. diss., Yale University, 1979); Amy Srebnick, "True Womanhood and Hard Times: Women and Early New York Industrialization, 1840–1860" (Ph.D. diss., State University of New York at Stony Brook, 1979); Carol Groneman, "'She Earns as a Child, She Pays as a Man': Women Workers in a Mid-Nineteenth-Century New York City Community," in *Class, Sex, and the Woman Worker,* ed. Cantor and Laurie, pp. 83–100; U.S. Senate, *Report on the*

Condition of Woman and Child Wage-Earners in the United States, Vol. 9: *History of Women in Industry in the United States* (S. 645, 61st Cong., 2d sess.; Washington, D.C., 1910), pp. 115–155.

5. U.S. Bureau of the Census, *Statistics of the Population at the Tenth Census, 1880,* vol. 1 (Washington, D.C., 1883), p. 892; U.S. Bureau of the Census, *Social Statistics of Cities, 1880* (Washington, D.C., 1883), pp. 594–596; Christine Stansell, "The Origins of the Sweatshop: Women and Early Industrialization in New York City," in *Working-Class America,* ed. Michael H. Frisch and Daniel J. Walkowitz (Urbana, Ill., 1983), pp. 78–103.

6. Mary Van Kleeck, *Artificial Flower-Makers* (New York, 1913), p. 235. On the prevalence of homework in New York, see Thomas Kessner, *The Golden Door: Italian and Jewish Immigrant Mobility in New York City, 1880–1915* (New York, 1977), pp. 72–77; Mabel Hurd Willett, *The Employment of Women in the Clothing Trades* (Studies in History, Economics and Public Law, vol. 16, no. 2; New York, 1902), pp. 102, 108; New York State Legislature, Special Committee of the Assembly Appointed to Investigate the Conditions of Female Labor in the City of New York, *Report and Testimony* (Albany, N.Y., 1896), vol. 1, pp. 17–19, and vol. 2, pp. 1024–1025. See also John Modell and Tamara K. Hareven, "Urbanization and the Malleable Household: An Examination of Boarding and Lodging in American Families," *Journal of Marriage and the Family* 35 (Aug. 1973): 467–479; Joan M. Jensen, "Cloth, Butter and Boarders: Women's Household Production for the Market," *Review of Radical Political Economics* 12, no. 2 (Summer 1980): 14–24; Margaret F. Byington, *Homestead: The Households of a Mill Town* (1910; rpt. Pittsburgh, 1974), pp. 138–157.

7. Stansell, "Women of the Laboring Poor," pp. 105–108, 204.

8. *Ibid.,* pp. 139–159; David M. Katzman, *Seven Days a Week: Women and Domestic Service in Industrializing America* (Urbana, Ill, 1981).

9. Stansell, "Women of the Laboring Poor," p. 73; James McCabe, *Lights and Shadows of New York Life* (Philadelphia, 1872), p. 822.

10. Percentage changes in women's employment are derived from U.S. Bureau of the Census, *Tenth Census, 1880,* vol. 1, p. 892; U.S. Bureau of the Census, *Statistics of Women at Work,* pp. 270–271; U.S. Bureau of the Census, *Women in Gainful Occupations,* pp. 204, 206. The demand for women clerical workers is discussed in Margery Davies, *Woman's Place Is at the Typewriter: Office Work and Office Workers, 1870–1930* (Philadelphia, 1982). New York's economy in the early twentieth century is discussed in Hammack, *Power and Society,* pp. 39–51.

11. See note 10, and Susan Porter Benson, "'The Customers Ain't God': The Work Culture of Department-Store Saleswomen, 1890–1940," in *Working-Class America,* ed. Frisch and Walkowitz, pp. 185–211.

12. John Commons quoted in U.S. Senate, *Woman and Child Wage Earners,* vol. 9, p. 143; see also Willett, *Women in the Clothing Trades.* Women's industrial jobs underwent extensive examination by New York reformers and social workers; see especially Annie M. MacLean, *Wage-Earning Women* (New York, 1910); Louise C. Odencrantz, *Italian Women in Industry: A Study of Conditions in New York City* (New York, 1919); Mary Van Kleeck, *Artificial Flower-Makers;* Mary Van Kleeck, *A Seasonal Industry: A Study of the Millinery Trade in New York* (New York, 1917); idem, *Women in the Bookbinding Trade* (New York, 1913).

13. Elsa G. Herzfeld, *Family Monographs: The History of Twenty-four Families Living in the Middle West Side of New York City* (New York, 1905), p. 12; Katharine Anthony, *Mothers Who Must Earn* (New York, 1914), pp. 49, 59, 62.

14. Kessner, *Golden Door,* pp. 71–99.

15. Helen S. Campbell, *Prisoners of Poverty; Women Wage-Earners, Their Trades and Their Lives* (1887; rpt. Westport, Conn., 1970), p. 148; Gail Laughlin, "Domestic Service,"

in U.S. Industrial Commission, *Report of the Industrial Commission on the Relations and Conditions of Capital and Labor Employed in Manufacturing and General Business,* vol. 14 (Washington, D.C., 1901), pp. 758, 756–757. See also Katzman, *Seven Days a Week,* pp. 236–243.

16. Special Committee to Investigate Female Labor, *Report and Testimony,* vol. 2, pp. 989–990, 994, 1083; Van Kleeck, *Women in the Bookbinding Trade,* p. 173.

17. New York State Bureau of Labor Statistics, *Third Annual Report* (Albany, N.Y., 1885), pp. 32–59, 169, and *Fourteenth Annual Report* (Albany, N.Y., 1896), pp. 918–919.

18. Alice P. Barrows, "The Training of Millinery Workers," in *Proceedings of the Academy of Political Science in the City of New York,* vol. 1 (Oct. 1910): 43–44. Testimony on irregular working hours by reformers and working women is extensive; see in particular New York Bureau of Labor Statistics, "Unorganized Workingwomen," *Fourteenth Annual Report* (1896); New York State Factory Investigating Commission, *Preliminary Report Transmitted to Legislature, March 1, 1912* (Albany, N.Y., 1912), vol. 1, p. 296, and *Fourth Report,* vol. 2, pp. 252, 516–517,592–595; and studies cited in note 12.

19. Tapes I-116 (side A) and II-30 (side B), New York City Immigrant Labor History Collection of the City College Oral History Project, Robert F. Wagner Archives, Tamiment Institute Library, New York University.

20. Consumers' League of New York City, *Behind the Scenes in a Restaurant: A Study of 1017 Women Restaurant Employees* (n.p., 1916), p. 15; Willett, *Women in the Clothing Trades,* p. 74; Sue Ainslie Clark and Edith Wyatt, *Making Both Ends Meet. The Income and Outlay of New York Working Girls* (New York, 1911), p. 190.

21. Cf. New York Bureau of Labor Statistics, *Third Annual Report* (1885), pp. 32–59, and New York Factory Investigating Commission, *Fourth Report,* vol. 2, pp. 424–425, 209–210, 320; Edward Ewing Pratt, *Industrial Causes of Congestion of Population in New York City* (Studies in History, Economics and Public Law, vol. 43, no. 1; New York, 1911), p. 124. The growing acceptance of the half-holiday may be followed in New York State Bureau of Labor Statistics, *Fifth Annual Report* (Albany, N.Y., 1887), p. 555; New York State Bureau of Labor Statistics, *Eighth Annual Report* (Albany, N.Y., 1890), pt. 1, p. 448; New York Bureau of Labor Statistics, *Fourteenth Annual Report* (1896), p. 935; New York Factory Investigating Commission, *Fourth Report,* vol. 2, p. 88.

22. Elizabeth Faulkner Baker, *Protective Labor Legislation* (Studies in History, Economics and Public Law, vol. 116, no. 2; New York, 1925), pp. 113–114, 133–138.

23. Mary Van Kleeck, "Working Hours of Women in Factories," *Charities and the Commons* 17 (6 Oct. 1906): 13; Baker, *Protective Labor Legislation,* pp. 151, 309–313. For an example of employers' maneuvers around the law, see Van Kleeck, *Women in the Bookbinding Trade,* pp. 134, 144–145. Oral testimony of working women confirms large employers' observance of the law, particularly with respect to minors; see, for example, tape II-30 (side A), Immigrant Labor History Collection.

24. Van Kleeck, *Women in the Bookbinding Trade,* pp. 177–181. On unionization in the garment industry, see Nancy Schrom Dye, *As Equals and as Sisters: Feminism, the Labor Movement and the Women's Trade Union League of New York* (Columbia, Mo. and London, 1980); Meredith Tax, *The Rising of the Women* (New York 1980), pp. 205–240.

25. "Making Ends Meet on the Minimum Wage," *Life and Labor* 3 (Oct. 1913): 302. See also tape I-105, Immigrant Labor History Collection.

26. Kessler-Harris, *Out to Work,* pp. 180–202; Baker, *Protective Labor Legislation,* p. 331; New York Factory Investigating Commission, *Fourth Report,* vol. 2, pp. 123; New York State Department of Labor, *Hours and Earnings of Women in Five Industries* (Special Bulletin no. 121, Albany, N.Y., Nov. 1923), p. 13; Willett, *Women in Clothing Trades,* p. 74; New York

Bureau of Labor Statistics, *Third Annual Report* (1885), p. 169; New York Special Committee to Investigate Female Labor, *Report and Testimony,* vol. 1, pp. 60, 86–87; Irving Howe, *World of Our Fathers* (New York, 1976), p. 82.

27. Daniel T. Rodgers, *The Work Ethic in Industrial America, 1850–1920* (Chicago and London, 1974); Alice Kessler-Harris, *Out to Work,* pp. 200–201; Florence Kelley, "Right to Leisure," *Charities* 14 (2 Sept. 1905): 1055–1062.

28. Tapes I-51 (side B) and I-21 (transcript), Immigrant Labor History Collection; New York Department of Labor, *Women in Five Industries,* p. 13.

29. New York Factory Investigating Commission, *Fourth Report,* vol. 4, pp. 1577–1578; Frances R. Donovan, *The Woman Who Waits* (1920; rpt. New York, 1974), p. 50. For an elaboration of this argument, see Tentler, *Wage-Earning Women.*

30. Pathbreaking studies of work cultures include David Montgomery, *Workers' Control in America* (Cambridge, Eng., 1979); Susan Porter Benson, "The Customers Ain't God"; Barbara Melosh, *'The Physicians' Hand': Work Culture and Conflict in American Nursing* (Philadelphia, 1982). See also Karen Brodkin Sacks and Dorothy Remy, eds., *My Troubles Are Going to Have Trouble with Me* (New Brunswick, N.J., 1984), pp. 193–263.

31. Benson, "The Customers Ain't God"; Mary Bularzik, "Sexual Harassment at the Workplace, Historical Notes," in *Workers' Struggles, Past and Present,* ed. James Green (Philadelphia, 1983), pp. 117–135; Amy E. Tanner, "Glimpses at the Mind of a Waitress," *American Journal of Sociology* 13 (July 1907): 50; Van Kleeck, *Women in the Bookbinding Trade,* p. 83.

32. Mary Gay Humphreys, "The New York Working Girl," *Scribner's* 20 (Oct. 1896): 505; tape II-30, Immigrant Labor History Collection.

33. Dorothy Richardson, *The Long Day: The Story of a New York Working Girl* (1905) in *Women at Work,* ed. William L. O'Neill (New York, 1972), pp. 105–106. Although colored by middle-class moralisms, Dorothy Richardson's autobiographical novel gives a particularly rich portrait of young, unskilled female wage-earners' interactions in the workplace.

34. Taplin, "Training for Store Efficiency," p. 2; MacLean, *Wage-Earning Women,* p. 35; Bessie and Marie Van Vorst, *The Woman Who Toils* (New York, 1903), p. 25.

35. Conference on Welfare Work at Chicago Commons, Minutes of Seventh Meeting, 15 May 1906, p. 3, Box 121, Welfare Conferences, National Civic Federation Papers.

36. New York Factory Investigating Commission, *Fourth Report,* vol. 4, p. 1588; Anthony, *Mothers Who Must Earn,* p. 51.

37. Department Store Study, *Civic Federation Review,* galley 20B, box 116, Department Store Subject File, National Civic Federation Papers; Clark and Wyatt, *Making Both Ends Meet,* p. 184; Richardson, *Long Day,* pp. 96–97.

38. Lillian W. Betts, "Tenement-House Life and Recreation," *Outlook* 61 (11 Feb. 1899): 365.

39. Tapes I-51 (side B) and I-132 (side A), Immigrant Labor History Collection.

40. *Thought and Work,* Dec. 1903, p. 9; Jan. 1904, pp. 10, 15; and Jan. 1905, pp. 1, 3; Department Store Study, draft typescript, p. 38, box 116, Department Store Subject File, National Civic Federation Papers.

41. Tanner, "Glimpses," p. 52; Clark and Wyatt, *Making Both Ends Meet,* pp. 187–188; See also Richardson, *Long Day,* pp. 94–95.

42. Tape I-59 (side A), Immigrant Labor History Collection.

43. *Thought and Work,* June 1903, p. 7; Sept. 1904, p. 5; Jan. 1904, pp. 10, 15; 15 April 1904, p. 6; Nov. 1904, p. 5; April 1905, p. 11; and Jan. 1905, p. 11.

44. *Thought and Work,* Feb. 1905, p. 1.

45. Donovan, *Woman Who Waits,* pp. 20, 26, 80–81; Clark and Wyatt, *Making Both Ends Meet,* p. 188.

46. Committee of Fourteen in New York City, *Department Store Investigation: Report of the Sub-committee* (New York, 1915), p. 10. See also Committee of Fourteen in New York City. *Annual Report* (New York, 1914), p. 40.

47. "Report of the Commission on Social Morality from the Christian Standpoint, Made to the Fourth Biennial Convention of the Young Women's Christian Associations of the U.S.A., 1913," Pamphlets on Marriage and Family Relations, Archives of the National Board of the Young Women's Christian Association of the U.S.A., New York City; Committee of Fourteen, *Department Store Investigation,* p. 10. Cf. Sharon Hartman Strom, "Italian American Women and Their Daughters in Rhode Island: The Adolescence of Two Generations, 1900–1950," in *The Italian Immigrant Woman in North America,* ed. Betty Boyd Caroli et al. (Toronto, 1978), p. 194, in which one informant explained: "You found out about sex through the shop where you worked. The mother don't tell you nothing. The married women would put us wise."

48. New York State Bureau of Labor Statistics, *Second Annual Report* (Albany, N.Y., 1884), pp. 153, 158. Examples of sexual harassment abound; see, New York Bureau of Labor Statistics, *Third Annual Report* (1885), pp. 150–151; Clara E. Laughlin, *The Work-a-Day Girl: A Study of Some Present-day Conditions* (New York, 1913), p. 112; Richardson, *Long Day,* p. 260; U.S. Industrial Commission, *Report of the Industrial Commission on the Relations and Conditions of Capital and Labor Employed in Manufacturing and General Business,* vol. 7 (Washington, D.C., 1901), pp. 389–390. See also Bularzik, "Sexual Harassment."

49. Committee of Fourteen in New York City, *Department Store Investigation,* p. 10; U.S. Industrial Commission, *Report,* vol. 7, p. 59.

50. Wage differentials in New York City according to sex may be seen in U.S. Bureau of the Census, *Report on Manufacturing Industries in the U.S. at the Eleventh Census* (Washington, D.C., 1895), pp. 390–407, 708–710; New York Factory Investigating Commission, *Fourth Report,* vol. 4, pp. 1507–1511, 1081, and vol. 1, pp. 35–36. Estimates for the living wage of self-supporting girls varied; see, for example, Clark and Wyatt, *Making Both Ends Meet,* p. 8.

51. The exact percentage of women living alone varies in different reports. U.S. Senate, *Report on the Condition of Woman and Child Wage-Earners in the United States,* Vol. 5: *Wage-Earning Women in Stores and Factories* (S. 645, 61st Cong., 2d sess.; Washington, D.C., 1910), p. 15, indicates that 87 percent of factory workers and 92 percent of retail clerks lived at home. Cf. New York Factory Investigating Commission, *Fourth Report,* vol. 5, p. 2561, which stated that 85 percent of women wage-earners lived with families, friends, or relatives. For testimony on women's inability to live alone on low wages, see New York Bureau of Labor Statistics, *Fourteenth Annual Report* (1896), p. 913–945. For a fictional account of the controversy surrounding a young woman who chooses to live alone, see Anzia Yezierska, *Bread Givers* (1925; rpt. New York, 1975).

52. New York Factory Investigating Commission, *Fourth Report,* vol. 4, p. 1685. For an excellent discussion of the survival strategies of self-supporting women, see Joanne J. Meyerowitz, "Holding Their Own: Working Women Apart from Family in Chicago, 1880–1930" (Ph.D. diss., Stanford University, 1983).

53. Odencrantz, *Italian Women in Industry,* p. 235; Lillian D. Wald, *The House on Henry Street* (1915; rpt. New York, 1971), p. 211; New York Factory Investigating Commission, *Fourth Report,* vol. 4, pp. 1675–1692; Clark and Wyatt, *Making Both Ends Meet,* p. 10.

54. Clark and Wyatt, *Making Both Ends Meet,* pp. 97, 103–104, 108.

55. Ruth S. True, *The Neglected Girl* (New York, 1914), p. 59; New York Factory Investigating Commission, *Fourth Report,* vol. 4, pp. 1512–1513; tape II-30 (side A), Immigrant Labor History Collection.

56. "Salesgirl's Story," p. 1818; New York Factory Investigating Commission, *Fourth Report,* vol. 4, p. 1576, 1585; Clark and Wyatt, *Making Both Ends Meet,* p. 189.

57. New York Factory Investigating Commission, *Fourth Report,* vol. 4, pp. 1698, 1678 (quotations), 1577, 1675–1678, 1695–1714.

58. Tape I-132, Immigrant Labor History Collection.

59. New York Factory Investigating Commission, *Fourth Report,* vol. 4, pp. 1685–1686.

60. New York Factory Investigating Commission, *Fourth Report,* vol. 5, p. 2809; U.S. Industrial Commission *Report,* vol. 7, p. 59; Laughlin, *Work-a-Day Girl,* p. 60–61; "Salesgirl's Story," p. 1821; Clark and Wyatt, *Making Both Ends Meet,* p. 28.

61. Consumers' League, *Behind the Scenes,* p. 24; Donovan, *Woman Who Waits,* p. 42.

Chapter 7

Chicago's 1919 Race Riot:
Ethnicity, Class, and Urban Violence

Dominic A. Pacyga

In 1919, Chicago was a city long shaped by mass migrations. Just nine years earlier immigrants and their children made up nearly 80 percent of its population. It was a city of vast ethnic differences. In addition, the period from 1915 to 1920 witnessed the Great Migration. Some 50,000 southern African Americans made their way to Chicago, doubling the city's black population. Not only the huge wartime industries but also the promises of freedom and individual mobility that the North seemed to offer attracted these long-exploited southerners. They joined immense numbers of white ethnic Chicagoans who already inhabited the grimy industrial neighborhoods of the city's South and West sides.[1]

Immigration, migration, and residential mobility were then already major forces in the history of Chicago. So, too, was the tradition of ethnic conflict, whether at the ballot box, in the church, or on the neighborhood street. Conflicts between white ethnic groups were frequent and legendary. The Irish and Germans of Bridgeport battled violently early in that neighborhood's history. Germans and Poles clashed on the North Side. Anti-Catholicism and anti-Semitism often raised their ugly heads in the city. First Catholic Germans and later Poles struggled against Irish-American domination of the Roman Catholic Church. The nature of Chicago's politics promoted ethnic and racial divisions. Divisiveness seemed to power the very engine that made Chicago grow as an industrial capitalist city.[2]

The particulars of the riot that broke out on that hot Sunday of July 27, 1919, are well known. The riot began after the killing of Eugene Williams, a young black boy, in Lake Michigan off the "white" beach at 29th Street. This event unlocked the racial rage and conflict that had been pent up for most of World War I. The riot resulted from the competition between whites and blacks over housing and jobs in the city. Both of these commodities seemed scarce in the aftermath of the war. The emergence of organized labor also presented a point of conflict. There is a good deal of evidence that the management of various enterprises, in particular the meatpackers, manipulated

Original essay published by permission of Dominic A. Pacyga

ethnic and racial differences between workers in order to destroy the labor movement emerging in Chicago's mass production industries.

The Chicago Commission on Race Relations published a long and detailed account of the riot in the early 1920s. In 1972, William M. Tuttle Jr. gave a detailed account of the riot and its causes.[3] Various studies that deal with related subjects have also explored the racial clash. All of these have pointed the finger of blame for the active rioting—though not for the causes—at the immigrant neighborhoods west of Wentworth Avenue. The historical literature often refers to these areas as Irish and Polish or simply as "white working class" in nature. To an extent, the investigators simply accepted the stereotype that everyone west of the racial dividing line belonged to a mostly homogeneous group. In fact, in making that judgment the various investigators ignored their own evidence.[4]

The European ethnic mix west of Wentworth Avenue was great and confusing. None of the white areas in Back of the Yards, Canaryville, Bridgeport, McKinley Park, or Englewood was totally occupied by any one ethnic group. It was far easier to call everyone west of Wentworth Avenue white. The reality, however, was that the white ethnic neighborhoods to the west of the Black Belt, and indeed to the south and east of the ghetto, were very mixed—and that not all groups shared in all of the institutions.[5]

There are various conflicting claims as to the ethnicity of the white rioters. The investigators simply called them white or hostile Polish and Irish Stock Yard District residents. At least one on-the-scene observer, however, Mary McDowell of the University of Chicago Settlement House, called them Americans and not immigrants. This was an interesting statement considering the large immigrant populations of the neighborhoods surrounding the stockyards.[6]

The question of exactly who the rioters were is a complex one. Of course, the members of a mob rarely leave memoirs or sign petitions. The anonymity of the urban crowd presents a difficult problem for both contemporary investigators as well as historians. The key to understanding who did and who did not participate in the riot, however, lies within the social and economic map of the city at the time. Geography, ethnicity, and class played equal roles in creating the white rioters in Chicago in July and early August 1919.

The human geography of the South Side is crucial for understanding the city's history. In a city that by World War I was predominantly Roman Catholic, parish boundaries also proved crucial for understanding urban society. Add to this a web of ethnicity and class, and Chicago's human geography seemed formidable to the outsider. To the Chicago native, however, ethnicity was easily discernible along the streets and alleys of a familiar world. Map 7.1 places the Irish and Polish Catholic parishes of the city's South Side in their relationship to each other, the Black Belt, and the Union Stock Yards. The map covers the area south of 26th Street to 79th Street from Lake Michigan to California Avenue. It therefore includes the major area of rioting in 1919 and the area where, up to 1930, racial clashes most often occurred.

Six Polish Roman Catholic parishes stood in this district. They are marked on the map by the letters A through F. Together they form a crescent-shaped area in which the majority of Polish South Siders lived in 1919. This Polish crescent stretched from an area to the north of the stockyards to one just to the south along the industry's western flank. No Polish churches existed east of Halsted Street, although without a doubt some Poles lived east of that major Chicago artery.

The Irish parish system that emerges by tracing the English-speaking territorial parishes is much more complex but nevertheless readily discernible. These parishes are marked by numbers on the map. Seven Irish ones circled the stockyards. An eighth, St. John the Baptist (5), while serving French Canadians, was nevertheless heavily attended by Irish-American families. This Irish "wheel" overlapped the Polish crescent in various spots. By 1919, however, these Irish parishes were, with the exception of those to the south and east of the yards, already in decline as Poles and other "new" immigrants occupied the neighborhoods to the north and southwest of the stockyards.

Another group of Irish parishes stood farther south, southwest, and to the east of the packing plants. These Catholic parishes reflected upward mobility for the South Side Irish. They ranged from Holy Angels (10) and St. Elizabeth's (11) on the east to St. Theodore's (19) and St. Justin Martyr (18) to the southwest. The core of Englewood and Washington Park parishes was extremely important for this grouping. Several parishes such as Visitation and St. Basil's seem to have played an intermediary role in providing a socioeconomic link from the stockyards to the more prosperous sections of Englewood and Washington Park. This Irish middle-class crescent touched, and in some cases crossed, the emerging Black Belt in 1919. Several of these parishes witnessed racial change during and after World War I.

The events of July and August 1919 occurred in various sections of the city. They centered, however, on the South Side, home to Chicago's largest African-American population and to vast European ethnic enclaves as well as to large lakefront white middle-class neighborhoods. Seventy-five percent of the more than five hundred Chicagoans hurt were injured in the area covered by map 7.1. Thirty-eight male Chicagoans died during the racial fighting. Twenty-three of these were black and fifteen white. While rioters injured ten women in the fighting, none died according to the official count. Thirty-three of the thirty-eight deaths, or 89 percent, occurred in the area covered by the map.[7] Since it would be impossible to detail the ethnicity and place of injury of all those hurt in the riot, this paper will focus on the fatalities.

Map 7.2 plots out the thirty-three deaths that took place on the South Side during the riot. These are placed in relation to the Irish and Polish neighborhoods in that section of the city. A casual look at the map suggests that riot-related deaths occurred primarily to the east of the Union Stock Yards. This fact is not surprising because of the geographic location of the Black Belt to the east of Wentworth Avenue.

Table 7.1 gives the breakdown of deaths by race in relationship to the ethnic parish locations. Of the nineteen South Side black deaths, none occurred north or west of the stockyards or in that part of the Polish crescent south of the packinghouses. Two killings took place in these areas, and they were both white males. These two deaths occurred near the Irish parishes of St. Rose of Lima and Our Lady of Good Counsel in that part of the Stock Yard District where the Irish working-class circle and the Polish crescent intersected. Meanwhile, of the twenty-three African-American deaths citywide, five occurred in the working-class neighborhoods between Halsted and Wentworth avenues in Irish-dominated Canaryville and Fuller Park. One African-

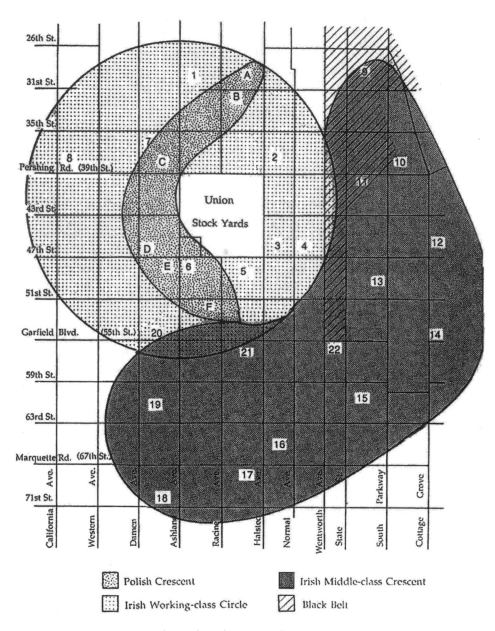

Map 7.1. Parish/Residential Areas in Chicago's South Side, 1919

Polish Crescent: Polish Roman Catholic South Side Parishes, 1919*

A. St. Barbara, 2859 S. Throop St. (Bridgeport)
B. St. Mary of Perpetual Help, 1039 W. 32d St. (Bridgeport)
C. SS. Peter and Paul, 3745 S. Paulina St. (McKinley Park)
D. Sacred Heart, 4602 S. Honore St. (Back of the Yards)
E. St. Joseph, 4821 S. Hermitage St. (Back of the Yards)
F. St. John of God, 1234 W. 52d St. (Back of the Yards)

Irish Working-Class Circle: English-Speaking (Irish) Roman Catholic South Side Parishes, 1919*

1. St. Bridget, 2928 S. Archer Ave. (Bridgeport)
2. Nativity of Our Lord, 653 W. 37th St. (Bridgeport)
3. St. Gabriel, 4522 S. Wallace Ave. (Canaryville)
4. St. Cecilia, 4515 S. Wells St. (Fuller Park)
5. St. John the Baptist, 911 W. 50th Pl. (Back of the Yards)**
6. St. Rose of Lima, 4747 S. Ashland Ave. (Back of the Yards)
7. Our Lady of Good Counsel, 3528 S. Hermitage St. (McKinley Park)
8. St. Agnes, 2648 W. Pershing Road (Brighton Park)
9. St. James, 2942 S. Wabash Ave. (Near South Side)
10. Holy Angels, 607 Oakwood Blvd. (Oakland)
11. St. Elizabeth, 4049 S. Wabash Ave. (Grand Boulevard)
12. St. Ambrose, 1012 E. 47th St. (Kenwood)
13. Corpus Christi, 4920 South Parkway (Grand Boulevard)
14. St. Thomas the Apostle, 5472 S. Kimbark Ave. (Hyde Park)
15. St. Anselm, 6045 S. Michigan Ave. (Washington Park)
16. St. Bernard, 340 W. 66th St. (Englewood)
17. St. Brendan, 6714 S. Racine Ave. (Englewood)
18. St. Justin Martyr, 1818 W. 71st St. (West Englewood)
19. St. Theodore, 1650 W. 62d St. (West Englewood)
20. St. Basil, 1850 W. Garfield Blvd. (Back of the Yards/Englewood)
21. Visitation, 843 W. Garfield Blvd. (Back of the Yards/Englewood)
22. St. Anne, 153 W. Garfield Blvd. (Washington Park/Englewood)

Other South Side Irish parishes were located farther south, southwest, and southeast.

Source: The map and list are based on the Rev. John McMahon, S.T.D., *City of Chicago Catholic Map Directory* (Chicago, 1954).
*The address listed is that of the parish rectory.
**A French-Canadian parish, it had a large Irish-American population.

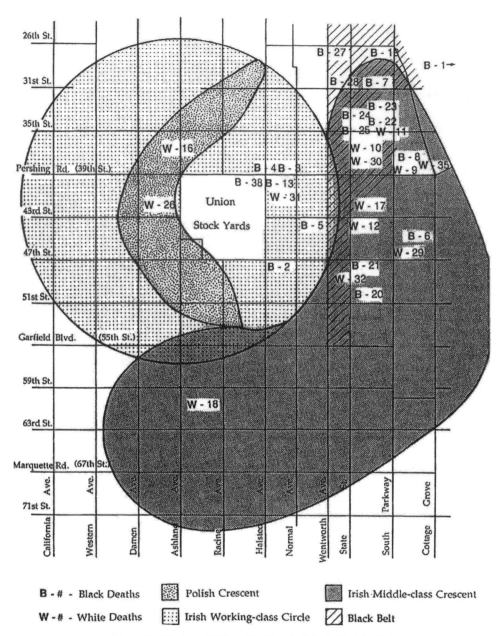

Map 7.2. Black and White Riot Deaths/Ethnic Residential Areas in Chicago's South Side, 1919 (Name/Race/Date/Location)

1. Eugene Williams B 7/27 Lake Michigan at 29th St.
2. John Mills B 7/28 Normal Avenue, 150 ft. south of 47th St.
3. Oscar Dozier B 7/28 39th St. and Wallace Ave.
4. Henry Goodman B 7/28 39th and Union Ave.
5. Louis Taylor B 7/28 Root St. and Wentworth Ave.
6. B. F. Hardy B 7/28 46th and Cottage Grove Ave.
7. John Simpson B 7/28 31st St. between Wabash Ave. and the El
8. Henry Baker B 7/28 544 E. 37th St.
9. David Marcus W 7/28 511 E. 37th St.
10. Eugene Temple W 7/28 3642 S. State St.
11. William J. Otterson W 7/28 35th and Wabash Ave.
12. Stefan Horvath W 7/28 Root and State St.
13. Edward W. Jackson B 7/29 40th and Halsted
14. Samuel Bass B 7/29 22d and Halsted or Union Ave.*
15. Joseph Lovings B 7/29 839 Lytle St.*
16. Nicholas Kleinmark W 7/28 38th and Ashland Ave.
17. Clarence Metz W 7/28 43d St. between Forrestville and Vincennes Ave.
18. Berger Odman W 7/29 60th and Ada St.
19. James Crawford B 7/27 29th and Cottage Grove Ave.
20. Thomas Joshua B 7/29 51st and Wabash Ave.
21. Ira Henry B 7/30 4957 S. State St.
22. Joseph Sanford B 7/28 35th and Wabash Ave.
23. Hymes Taylor B 7/28 35th and Wabash Ave.
24. John Walter Humphrey B 7/28 35th between Wabash and the El
25. Edward Lee B 7/28 35th and State St.
26. Joseph Schoff W 7/30 4228 S. Ashland Ave.
27. Samuel Banks B 7/30 2729 Dearborn St.
28. Theodore Copling B 7/30 2934 S. State
29. George Flemming W 8/5 549 E. 47th St.
30. Casmere Lazzeroni W 7/28 3618 S. State
31. Joseph Powers W 7/29 Root and Emerald Streets
32. Walter Parejko W 7/29 51st near Dearborn St.
33. Morris I. Perel W 7/29 51st and Dearborn St.
34. Harold Brignadello W 7/29 1021 S. State St.*
35. George L. Wilkins W 7/30 3825 S. Rhodes St.
36. Paul Hardwick B 7/29 Wabash Ave. and Adams St.*
37. Robert Williams B 7/29 State and Van Buren St.*
38. William Dozier B 7/31 Union Stock Yards, Sheep Pens, Exchange Avenue near Cook Street

Source: The map and list are based on the Chicago Commission on Race Relations, *The Negro in Chicago: A Study of Race Relations and a Race Riot* (Chicago: University of Chicago Press, 1922).
*Not marked on map.

Table 7.1.   Distribution of South Side Race Riot–Related Deaths, 1919

	Polish Crescent Deaths	Irish Working-Class Circle Deaths	Irish Middle-Class Crescent Deaths	Black Belt Deaths	Other	South Side Total	City Total
Black deaths	0	5	4	8	2	19	23
White deaths	2*	3*	8	3	0	14	15

Source: Chicago Commission on Race Relations, *The Negro in Chicago: A Study of Race Relations and a Race Riot* (Chicago: University of Chicago Press, 1922).
*Two deaths counted in Polish Crescent also counted in Irish Working-Class Circle.

American victim also died in the stockyards, which the map treats as neutral territory. Four more blacks and seven whites died in the middle-class Irish crescent farther to the south and east of the stockyards. These died at least a mile from any Polish Catholic parish, but all were within close proximity of an Irish church. Thus, twenty deaths occurred within the Irish working-class and middle-class zones pictured on the maps. This accounts for more than 50 percent of the riot-related deaths. Eleven additional deaths took place within the Black Belt or in areas adjacent to it. Eugene Williams died in Lake Michigan, which the map also treats as neutral territory.

A closer look at both maps reveals an interesting relationship between the Irish middle-class crescent and the Black Belt. A cluster of four black and one of the white deaths occurred at the intersection of 35th Street and Wabash Avenue in the Irish parish of St. James. The Catholic boys' high school, De La Salle, was also located at this intersection across the street from the Angelus House, the site of a major confrontation between Chicago police and a mob of blacks. The Angelus House was basically an Irish boardinghouse left over from the era when the Irish dominated the neighborhood. De La Salle, sometimes referred to as the "poor boy's college," served both the Irish working-class and middle-class neighborhoods of the South Side.[8] Two other whites died just south of 35th Street on State Street, one an Italian peddler, the other a white laundry owner of unknown ethnicity. Farther south another cluster of deaths took place in the Washington Park neighborhood near 51st and Wabash. This area lay within the boundaries of Corpus Christi Parish, yet another Irish middle-class parish threatened by racial change. A group of deaths also centered on Holy Angels Church just south of 39th Street. Here, too, African Americans were moving into still another Irish middle-class neighborhood. The linkage of thirty-one riot deaths to the Irish districts or to areas of the city once part of it, and by 1919 in the Black Belt, points to the ethnic and socioeconomic focus of the riot. This relationship may even point to the very nature of the riot itself.

A look at the backgrounds of those whites who died in the fighting is of some help in tracing the socioeconomic basis of the riots. Some of the whites were innocent victims killed during the most violent phases of the riots. Several of these were middle-class South Side residents. Morris I. Perel, a Jewish small businessman who lived on the 5200 block of South Indiana, died not far from his home. A mob murdered David Marcus, a sixty-year-old Jewish shoemaker, next door to his place of business on East 37th Street. Eugene Temple, a thirty-five-year-old white laundry owner of unknown ethnicity, and Casmere Lazzeroni, a sixty-year-old Italian peddler, both died on the 3600 block of South State Street on the second day of the rioting. George L. Wilkins, a Metropolitan Life Insurance agent, died while visiting black customers at 3825 South Rhodes. Wilkins lived at 5010 South Calumet Avenue. Among white working-class victims, Stefan Horvath and Walter Parejko both died while working in the Black Belt. William J. Otterson, a plasterer, died while driving past the corner of 35th and Wabash, the site of the Angelus House riot. These eight casualties do not seem to have been actively involved in the rioting. That leaves seven other white fatalities.[9]

The striking characteristics of those active participants who died, and for whom information can be found, are their age, socioeconomic background, and mixed ethnicity. The rioters were a group of young men from lower-middle-class backgrounds and old immigrant stock. Twenty-year-old Nicholas Kleinmark, who died in a streetcar attack and lived at 3449 South Ashland Avenue in the McKinley Park neighborhood, appears to have been the lone working-class fatality. The two Kleinmarks listed in the prewar Chicago directories at that address both had working-class jobs. The McKinley Park area contained large Irish and German populations as well as many Poles. Kleinmark's wake was held at Hickey's Funeral Parlor in the neighborhood.

Berger Odman, an Englewood resident probably of Swedish descent, died while participating in an attack on African-American homes in Englewood. The twenty-one-year-old Odman lived at 5737 South Morgan and worked for the telephone company, a job considered lower middle class in 1919. The three Odmans listed in the 1917 directories at the Morgan Street address worked in white-collar positions. The directory listed Gustave Odman as an inspector, Arthur Odman as a clerk at Swift & Company, and Ethel Odman as a clerk at a business on 59th and Halsted.

Joseph Powers was the oldest of this group of riot victims. The twenty-nine-year-old streetcar conductor died in an attack on a black man in the Canaryville neighborhood. The newspapers listed Powers's address both as 525 West 42d Street and 3571 South Archer Avenue. In either case, Powers's position as a streetcar conductor shows that he was not a stockyard worker, thereby adding to the evidence that lower-middle-class Chicagoans were very active in the riot.

Clarence Metz, a seventeen-year-old youth, also died in the fighting. Metz lived at 5201 South Ingleside in the middle-class Washington Park neighborhood. His wake was held at Sullivan's Funeral Parlor at 425 East 61st Street. A thirty-five-year-old Rock Island, Illinois, resident, Harry Brignadello, died in the South Loop north of the South Side. Nothing could be found on Joseph Schoff, while George Flemming died in a conflict with the militia. The backgrounds of Metz, Odman, and Powers combined with the sites of the killings point to the lower middle class and northwestern European ethnic nature—that is, "old immigrants"—of the riot.[10]

Contemporaries blamed the white gangs of the Stock Yard District for much of the trouble. Emily Frankenstein, the daughter of a South Side doctor, remarked in her diary that "it was mostly the unruly element of the employees of the stockyards; the colored people who had been brought up north recently, and overstepped their freedom and privileges and rights, and thought they were better than white folkse [*sic*]. And some of the rowdy whites, etc. took it upon themselves to seek vengeance on the innocent of the colored."[11] While there is no doubt that the gangs played a central role in the fighting, the social, ethnic, and geographic definition of these gangs must be looked into more closely. They do not seem to be simply stockyard workers.

Sterling Morton, who served in the Illinois Reserve Militia during 1919, remarked years later that African Americans only acted in self-defense. Morton also pointed to "young toughs who would dash about in cars shooting and sometimes pillaging." He further discussed the presence of the athletic clubs and the fact that they were sponsored and protected by local politicians. He mentioned in particular Ragen's Colts, the Hamburgs, and the Lorraine Club. All of these had their headquarters in the Irish sections of the South Side.[12]

Gang activity during the riot seemed to center in the Irish-dominated districts of the South Side. Wentworth Avenue in 1919 passed through or close to various Irish-dominated districts such as Bridgeport, Canaryville, Fuller Park, Washington Park, and Englewood. Wentworth was a major thoroughfare at the time; it connected these districts along with Halsted Street to the west and the great boulevards of the South Side to the east. Ragen's Colts and its affiliates ran white gang activity on the street. The Colts were also known in other parts of the South Side as far west as Ashland Avenue and as far east as Cottage Grove. By no means were the Colts and their allies exclusively Irish-American organizations, but, as their sponsor's name testifies, the Irish predominated. Other members were usually second-generation Americans of mixed ethnic origin. The Colts had some 2,000 members who paid two dollars in annual dues in 1919. Their headquarters were at the intersection of 52d and Halsted in an area where two parishes were located, Visitation, an Irish church, and St. John the Baptist, a French-Canadian parish with a large Irish membership. Their extensive headquarters occupied several floors of the building. The organization fitted out the clubhouse with a considerable amount of athletic equipment. It also contained various "parlors," an assembly hall, and a pool and billiard room. Jimmie O'Brien served as the organization's president in 1919. Frank Ragen, a South Side politician and member of the Board of County Commissioners, sponsored the so-called athletic club. His political connections were often used to protect members of the club who came into conflict with the police. The Colts had long been identified with lawlessness and racial clashes even before the riot. According to O'Brien, members had to be at least eighteen years of age. The president claimed that the Colts had not taken part in the riot and that they had gotten a bad reputation because some five hundred new members had been recruited during World War I to make up for those who had left to serve in the armed forces. It was these members who caused the trouble. O'Brien claimed that the club had expelled the younger recruits, and that the Colts now enforced the minimum-age-of-eighteen rule.[13]

Mary McDowell, of the University of Chicago Settlement House, testifying before the Chicago Commission on Race Relations, said that politicians had extended their patronage to gangs of boys as young as thirteen and fourteen in order to exploit them. McDowell claimed that the athletic clubs provided one of the most dangerous problems that the city faced. Certainly, Frank Ragen was not the only politician supporting a club. Alderman Joseph McDonough of Bridgeport backed the Hamburg Athletic Club, which counted the young Richard J. Daley, the future mayor of Chicago, among its members.[14]

According to the Chicago Commission on Race Relations, these white gangs became bolder in the spring of 1919. The commission pointed out various clashes in the Washington Park and Englewood areas. Once again these clashes occurred within the boundaries of the Irish middle-class crescent. As a result of the inability of the police to find witnesses, or the perceived intervention of politicians on behalf of the athletic clubs, African Americans had little faith in the Chicago police or the judicial system in the summer of 1919.[15]

The police came under suspicion from the beginning of the racial conflict. They arrested African Americans in large numbers and killed seven blacks during the riot but no whites. George Flemming, the lone white killed by a law enforcement officer, was bayonetted, along with another white named Fennesey, by a militiaman. In contrast to the Chicago police, the militia proved to be a well-trained and disciplined force that quickly cracked down on the athletic clubs.[16]

The presence of the militia after July 30 proved crucial to the restoration of order. While many of the troops originally thought that they would be fighting blacks, they quickly changed their opinions once in the field. The militia soon identified the white athletic clubs as the major problem. The troops were not tainted by any personal or political connection with the white athletic clubs. They moved especially hard against these groups. Gang members, in turn, showed a good deal of contempt for the militia. The troops, however, remained well disciplined and quelled the riot.[17]

The use of automobiles and trucks in raids in the Black Belt also is of interest in tracking down the gangs. The police definitely tied the automobiles to the athletic clubs. In the investigation after the riot, witnesses told the police that the gangs met in club headquarters and were furnished "auto trucks" to speed through the Black Belt to throw what the police called "grenade torches"—bricks that were tightly wrapped in wastepaper and saturated with oil. They could be easily thrown through a window to cause a conflagration. The police noted that the gangs also used stolen railroad gasoline torches to start the fires. Many of those involved in the firebombings were under the age of twenty. On August 14 the police arrested fifteen-year-old Matthew Walsh and eighteen-year-old Joseph Touhy, both of 59th and La Salle in the Washington Park neighborhood, for their involvement in the firebombings.[18]

The automobile gave a good deal of geographic mobility to the rioters. At first consideration, the use of cars would imply that whites driving through the Black Belt could come from any place in the city. The automobile attacks would seem to cloud the identity of the assailants. Yet, looked at in another way, the use of cars points once again to the middle- and lower middle-class origins of the gangs. In 1919 the automobile was still a middle-class luxury. Widespread use of cars and trucks by gang members indicated that these were not the children of newer immigrants but of older, more established groups. This conclusion fits well with the outbreak of violence in the zone distinguished by middle- and lower middle-class Irish parishes.

By the end of World War I, Irish Americans had started to experience upward mobility. Most still lived in a working-class world, but they had begun to move into the higher strata of that world and out of it into the middle class. Their aspirations were high, and the prosperity of the war years gave them a taste of a better future. It was here that their clash with the city's expanding black community would occur. African Americans, too, had witnessed at least the promise of prosperity. The geographic and economic history of the city put these two groups on a collision course.[19]

Polish Americans, on the other hand, were still settling in Chicago and becoming acculturated into American society. In 1919 the Polish community remained firmly entrenched in the lower levels of the working class. Most labored as unskilled or semiskilled workers. They made up a large number of the membership of the emerging unions in the steel and meatpacking industries. Poles had learned the importance of class and communal solidarity in Poland. That appreciation became intensified in industrial Chicago.[20]

Much has been said concerning the clash between white and black workers over the issue of organized labor in the stockyards. Many African Americans harbored negative views of the unions. Black leaders often spoke out against the folly of joining the "white" union. Job competition was a major source of conflict as the country attempted to adjust to peace. If the Poles and blacks were to clash in 1919, it would be over this subject. After all, few middle-class African Americans looked to the Polish tenement district in Back of the Yards for relief from the ghetto. Also, few Poles thought of moving into Washington Park, Englewood, or Hyde Park far from the communal institutions they had established in Back of the Yards, Western Bridgeport, McKinley Park, or the steel mill district in South Chicago. Unlike the Irish, the Poles had not yet made a commitment to moving out of the working-class neighborhoods. They were still in the process of making these districts their own.[21]

Since before the turn of the century blacks and whites had clashed over labor issues. Black strikebreakers arrived in the stockyards in 1894. They reappeared ten years later. The 1905 teamsters' strike resulted in twenty deaths and over four hundred injuries. The strike had turned into a race riot before it ended. All African Americans on the street became targets of mobs. In turn, blacks began to defend themselves. The 1905 strike in many ways presaged the 1919 conflict. There was plenty of historical fuel to stoke the fires after World War I.[22]

It is interesting, therefore, to note the reaction of the Polish community to the outbreak of the riot. On July 28, 1919, the *Dziennik Związkowy*, Chicago's leading Polish newspaper, ignored the riot. The first news of the racial conflict appeared the next day in a short article discussing the tumult and offering a short history of the African-American experience in the United States. It ended with the question, "Is it not right that they should hate the whites?"[23] As the riot raged on, the *Dziennik Związkowy* continued to cover the fighting. Until August 2 the paper generally took a neutral, if not pro-black, stance. By that date, however, it began to identify black interests with those of the meatpackers. The paper claimed that the packers planned to use the riot to crush the union in the stockyards.[24]

The *Dziennik Chicagoski*, the city's other leading Polish newspaper, with a point of view considerably to the right of the *Dziennik Związkowy*, covered the riot extensively from the beginning. The newspaper blamed Mayor William H. Thompson for the riot. In an editorial the paper accused Thompson of favoring African Americans over whites and of making an error in not calling out the militia earlier. The *Dziennik Chicagoski*'s editorial cartoons criticized America for its racial problems.[25]

The *Naród Polski*, the official organ of the Polish Roman Catholic Union, took the most violent stand on the race riots. The newspaper compared East European pogroms to America's race riots and took a much more anti-Semitic and anti-black stand. The newspaper wrote that both groups deserved the treatment they received. The *Naród Polski* went on to claim that both blacks and Jews were controlled by Germans and Bolsheviks. After this, like the other Polish newspapers, the *Naród Polski* warned the Polish community to remain calm.[26]

While the Polish newspapers encouraged the community to be quiet and stay out of the fighting, events continued to run their course. The calling out of the militia seemed to quell the fighting until another tragic episode took place, one that directly involved the Polish and Lithuanian community in Back of the Yards. On Saturday morning, August 2, a fire broke out in the Polish and Lithuanian neighborhoods just west of the stockyards. Forty-nine tenements eventually burned in the Polish parish of the Sacred Heart and the neighboring Lithuanian parish of the Holy Cross. These fires are crucial for understanding the role played by the Polish community in the riot. The Polish press again gives insight into the reaction of the immigrant community to the fires. The civil authorities never established the blame for the fires. Later the grand jury investigation made the argument that the white athletic clubs started the fires in an attempt to incite the East Europeans against the blacks. The Polish community did not have to deliberate. It quickly made up its mind as to who the perpetrators were. The Rev. Louis Grudzinski of St. John of God Parish in Back of the Yards openly blamed the Irish.[27]

The Poles were still a new immigrant group. They looked at American events through European eyes. Spokesmen referred to whites as a separate group from the Poles. This peculiar usage implied that Poles and whites were two different and distinct groups, that whites were Americans. When Polish leaders spoke about blacks and whites not getting along together or of the correctness of black feelings toward whites, they did not see their own group as included. Poles viewed themselves as still outside the web of race relations in American society.

Others agreed. Mary McDowell claimed that the Polish immigrants did not take part in the riot. The chief offenders were Ragen's Colts and the other athletic clubs that attacked black workers outside the stockyards and throughout the South Side. McDowell further claimed that skin color did not concern foreign-born Chicagoans as much as it did native whites. The assertion that the Polish community took no part in the riot is probably not completely true. Still, the evidence of their participation in the fighting is not overwhelming. This lack may primarily be a result of geography. The Poles in general did not live next to large black populations. Streetcar attacks did take place in Polish neighborhoods, but these were ethnically mixed areas within the boundaries of Irish working-class parishes. Among those listed as either killed or as perpetrators of these assaults, no distinctly Polish names appear. There are, however, a few Slavic names, and these may have been Poles. Two of these died on their way to work in the Black Belt, and two others attacked a black man in the livestock-pen riot on the Thursday after the fighting peaked, and just before the fires in Back of the Yards. That some Poles hated blacks goes without question. Police arrested a local resident, John Lendki of 4640 South Lincoln, along with W. E. Jones, who lived in Englewood, for trying to incite a riot after the Back of the Yards fires. They both attempted to address a crowd of victims of the Saturday morning fires. Lendki and Jones harangued the crowd telling them that African Americans wanted to take their jobs and that blacks had set their homes on fire.[28]

The fires of August 2 actually give credence to the view that the East European community had generally stayed out of the fighting. If the grand jury and the Polish leadership were correct, the gangs set the homes on fire to arouse the Poles and Lithuanians against blacks. The ploy did not work. Also, while the *Dziennik Związkowy* should not be taken as the sole voice of the Polish community, the paper reflected much weaker antiblack sentiment than might have been expected. Certainly its attitude was very different from the major English-language newspapers. Perhaps Polish Chicagoans in 1919 had not yet been acculturated into the American tradition of racism.

The question of why the Irish participated in the riots in large numbers and the Poles did not has to be asked. Was it simply a result of geography, or were there other socioeconomic factors? A closer look at the riot in terms of its nature and of the Irish-American community may give some answers.

Chicago's race riot can be broadly defined as a "collective action"—that is, an action by a number of persons with a set of specific goals in mind. Samuel Clark in his study of the Irish Land War points out that participants in such an action might be voluntary or involuntary, so long as the set of goals remains constant.[29] As studies of urban crowds have shown, European crowds acted with specific goals in mind. The definition of the 1919 race riot as a collective action, following Clark's model, leads to the question of the social relationships that created the riot, which in turn leads to the question of goals. How did individuals become involved in the riot? What institution made that participation possible?

The institution that readily comes to mind is obviously the athletic clubs, which were really gangs. The clubs, however, were not the only unifying factor in the white neighborhoods. Various "integrating" factors existed, to use once again a term of Clark's. Included were Catholicism, level of and type of education, familiarity with the city and its local institutions, socioeconomic status, and level of acculturation. All of these factors provided a sense of unity for white Chicagoans. Fragmentation resulted from various "cleavage" factors, which included religious differences, ethnicity, language, and length of stay in Chicago and therefore acculturation. It is a combination of integrating and cleavage factors that point to the division between Polish and Irish South Siders and explain their different responses to the riot.[30]

Here, once again, arises the problem of the ethnic and class complexity of the city. Integrating factors are based, according to Clark and others, on both communal and associational structures. Although Catholicism predominated among both the Irish and the Poles, they lived very separate religious lives. Although the two groups could be called co-religionists, this hardly provided a unifying factor between them. In 1919 religion and ethnicity went hand in hand.

Still, it cannot be claimed that Poles remained totally isolated from the Irish and other groups. Integrating factors that were associational in nature brought these groups together at least in a superficial manner. These links could hardly be otherwise in an intensely multiethnic city such as Chicago. In 1919 organized labor provided the associational structure that predominated on the South Side and brought various ethnic groups together. The Poles enthusiastically supported the labor unions. In many ways their militancy outshone even that of the Irish, who had a longer relationship with the union movement in the United States. One historian has pointed to the very important Americanizing role that unions, especially those in meatpacking, played on the South Side.[31]

Cleavage factors can also be defined as being of two types. There are those that arise out of isolation and those that come from opposition.[32] While integrating factors between Chicago's Polish and Irish communities were few, cleavage factors based on opposition were many. These differences revolved around Catholic hierarchical rivalries, local party politics, and socioeconomic competition. The absence of frequent social interaction also compounded the division between the two groups. It is obvious that one group's internal integrating factor acted as a cleavage factor between the two. It is not surprising, then, that the Poles and Irish did not act in concert in 1919.

The question of the relationship between Polish-, Irish-, and African-American communities then becomes central to understanding the riot. What cleavage factors were most intense between the three groups to lead to violence? If these cleavage factors can be identified, the nature of the riot can be found. Except at the workplace, Poles and African Americans remained basically isolated from each other. The question of organized labor did divide the two groups, but in early 1919 this did not yet seem to be an insurmountable problem. In fact, black union membership had been growing. Indeed, the argument could be made that it was the riot itself that made organizing among African Americans impossible. The Irish and black communities, on the other hand, faced off against each other on various levels that included cleavage factors rooted both in opposition and isolation.

The Irish-American community, though based on the Catholic parish system, tended to be more diffuse than that of the Poles. The Irish were more integrated into the larger society as the result not only of a common language but also of historical chance.[33] The Irish had arrived in Chicago very early in the city's history. In a very real way the Irish community and the city grew up together. By 1919, Irish Americans could be found throughout the city's various neighborhoods. Their length of stay in the United States was much longer than that of the Poles and other new immigrant groups. Therefore, they were more acculturated into both life in industrial cities and American culture.

As is obvious from map 7.1, the Irish no longer lived simply in a working-class ghetto. In many ways they had already "arrived" in American society. One is reminded of James T. Farrell's fictional Lonigan family. Mr. Lonigan had worked his way out of the Stock Yard District and into Washington Park's middle class. By the World War I era, the Irish had moved up the ladder of mobility. As sociologists and historians have pointed out, expectations are a key toward social attitudes. Discontent is often based on a group's expectations for the future rather than on the current situation. The Irish, who already dominated the American Catholic Church and who were powerful in American urban politics, expected continued success in the United States. African Americans posed a possible threat to this success, at least insofar as the way in which the Irish middle and lower middle classes perceived that success.

James Davies's well-known "J-curve" is important here. Davies argued that revolutions were most likely to occur when socioeconomic advances were followed by a sharp reversal—that is, when expectations were frustrated.[34] The World War I period can be interpreted as such a period for Chicago's Irish. In fact, this era is also a period of tribulation for the growing African-American community in the city. The postwar economic collapse threatened the expectations of both groups who now faced each other on the streets of the South Side. The riot saw those expectations clash in a time-honored American orgy of racism.

The Irish- and African-American communities had clashed before. Even before the Civil War the Irish saw blacks as economic competitors. During the sectional conflict, New York City's Irish engaged in the Draft Riots of 1863, which turned quickly into a race riot in which working-class and middle-class white New Yorkers pursued African Americans through the streets. The Irish played a major role in this conflict. In his study of the riot, Adrian Cook pointed out the helplessness of local authorities to act against the mobs that roamed the city. One persistent motive of the draft rioters was a deep-seated hatred for blacks. Cook asserted that the Irish had a tradition of violence and that many saw violence as the only means of asserting their rights. The local government in New York did not command respect. All of these factors were also present in Chicago in 1919. Even streetcar attacks and the burning and looting of black homes presaged the Chicago experience nearly sixty years later. Another historian of New York's Irish has also pointed out that they often found themselves in conflict with other ethnic groups.[35]

Certainly there was a precedent for the violence of 1919 in Irish history. Ireland had a tradition of local magistrates patronizing gangs for political purposes, much like the patronage of Frank Ragen and Joseph McDonough in Chicago. Much of the agrarian protest in Ireland in the nineteenth century was of a defensive nature—that is, in defense of perceived rights and economic relationships. Irish historians often speak of the inseparable link between collective action and peasant society. Once again the roles of personalism, political families, and patron-client ties remain important. Irish mobs followed particular aims and resorted to violence in order to secure them. Obviously, Irish and Irish-American society had a rich tradition of protest, violence, and collective action from which to draw in 1919.[36]

The riot's typology further explains the reaction of both the Irish and Polish communities to the events of the summer of 1919. What kind of riot was the race riot? Some have called it a communal or ideal-type riot. William Tuttle pointed out that it was hardly a pogrom as some claimed; rather, it was a pitched battle. Over the last decade or so there has been a good deal of study concerning European forms of collective action. Charles Tilly discussed European violence over the last three hundred years in terms of three broad categories: primitive violence, reactionary violence, and modern collective violence. The first two of these tend to be communally based and are resistant to change. The third promotes change. It seems obvious that the 1919 rioters resisted change. The very nature of the institution involved, the social athletic clubs, also spoke to its communal nature. This kind of reactionary violence, localized and communally based, remained important in Ireland itself early into the twentieth century, which, of course, could be said for any place going through traumatic change. It certainly was true for Chicago at the end of World War I.[37]

Both Charles Tilly and George Rudé have discussed the nature of crowds. Rudé made a distinction between backward- and forward-looking groups. Tilly reformulated these terms as proactive and reactive forms of collective action. In 1919 the white rioters responded to what they saw as a threat to their economic well-being.[38]

The Chicago housing market provided a major source of conflict. Violence here was not essentially working-class in nature. Before the riot some twenty-four racially motivated bombings took place in the middle-class wards of the city. During the riot, whites attacked African Americans wherever they lived outside of the Black Belt. White Chicagoans saw the expansion of the Black Belt as aggressive behavior aimed at their economic investments—a type of land-grabbing by blacks and those whites who profited from Chicago's tense racial housing market. The bombings were often aimed at real estate agents and landlords, both black and white, who dealt in racially changing neighborhoods. Of course, assailants also attacked tenants.[39]

Chicago's Irish had the most to lose from an expanding Black Belt. In fact, blacks threatened the city's Irish on three basic fronts. First, housing competition was most acute for these two groups. This fact is obvious from the sections of the city where the two groups overlapped each other. Housing competition was particularly severe in the middle- and lower middle-class neighborhoods of Washington Park and Englewood. Second, with the emergence of the Republican organization of Mayor Thompson, in which African Americans played an important role, blacks threatened Irish domination of the city's political structure. Finally, competition for employment threatened the older and economically less successful Irish neighborhoods such as Canaryville and Fuller Park, out of which the middle- and lower middle-class Irish Americans had already emerged and where they feared they might be driven back.

Poles and blacks, however, did not compete on these three fronts. The Poles generally did not look to the areas east of the Polish crescent for housing. They themselves had more to fear from the Irish politically than from African Americans. It was only in the packinghouses and steel mills that competition between blacks and Poles seemed obvious. The Poles called for unionization as a solution to this problem. Labor leader John Kikulski directed many of his speeches toward this end. He spoke of interracial cooperation, as did Father Grudzinski. These leaders had a class-based appeal that did not reach the Irish. In fact, shortly after the riot, Irish union leader Dennis Lane accused Kikulski and other non-Irish labor leaders, including blacks, of being demagogues. Later, Kikulski supported the Irish, but this was after the demise of the union movement in the ashes of the race riot. It was obvious to all involved that the riot could not help the labor movement.[40]

The Polish response to the African-American community remained class based. The Irish response was also class based. However, it was founded on middle-class expectations and fears of economic slippage. The Irish, and their allied older immigrant groups, thought that they might slip downward on the economic ladder as black neighbors brought perceived economic devaluations of their investments in real estate and helped to dismantle their political and organized labor machines. The Irish middle-class goal was the removal of African Americans from their neighborhoods.

While the Irish sought the removal of blacks, Polish workers wanted to bring them into the unions. The Poles knew the riot could not accomplish that.

In order to understand the riot, it is not enough to look for typologies based on the European model. The realities of American immigrant and migrant society have to be investigated. The dominant culture in the United States in 1919 was racist. The question of what it meant to be assimilated, or at least acculturated, into that society is important. To be acculturated meant to accept the dominant theme of racism. By 1919 the Irish-American community had become American. The Irish, along with other older ethnic groups, had accepted basic middle-class American values. The dead and the wounded among the active white rioters seemed to have shared membership in older ethnic groups. The interaction of middle-class expectations and racism proved to be deadly in the summer of 1919. In many ways the riot was not a working-class confrontation, as implied by various studies, but rather a middle- and lower-middle-class conflict.

The Poles and other newer ethnic groups quickly became assimilated into the web of middle-class expectations and race. The riot of that summer became an acculturating event for the Polish community. Combined with the packinghouse strike of the winter of 1921–1922, it solidified, if not formed, Polish opinions toward African Americans. Not surprisingly, the black community did not support the largely Polish and Lithuanian strike, whose failure ended the role of organized labor in the stockyards for nearly twenty years. In fact, the Chicago Urban League provided African-American strikebreakers during that industrial conflict. By 1928 the Poles of Back of the Yards took part in a meeting of the 14th Ward Citizens Club held at Pulaski Hall at 4831 South Throop Street, in the parish of St. John of God. The club called the meeting to discuss the gradual arrival of "other" races in the district and their negative impact on real estate values.[41]

Despite the fact that Polish and Irish Chicagoans pursued fundamentally different goals at the time of the riot, that event subsequently shaped the relationship between African and Polish Americans on much the same basis as Irish and black relations. Poles became acculturated into the dominant middle-class racist ideology. The riot then should be seen within the dynamics not simply of black-white relations but also within the historical context of the particular ethnic groups involved. The riot and the later strike were major factors in the acculturation of East Europeans on the South Side.

The black-white dichotomy is useful only to a point. In a pluralistic society, investigators must look beyond it to understand more deeply ethnicity and acculturation and their role in the history of conflict in the United States. Subtle shadings of gray can help historians to understand more clearly the tragic history of race relations in the United States. Acculturation did not bring the Poles and Irish closer, but, unfortunately, it did provide them with a common enemy.

NOTES

1. Department of Development and Planning, City of Chicago, *The People of Chicago: Who We Are and Who We Have Been* (Chicago: City of Chicago, 1976); James R. Grossman, *Land of Hope: Chicago, Black Southerners, and the Great Migration* (Chicago: University of Chicago Press, 1989).

2. Dominic A. Pacyga and Ellen Skerrett, *Chicago: City of Neighborhoods* (Chicago: Loyola University Press, 1986), 458; Rev. Msgr. Harry C. Koenig, S.T.D., ed., *A History of the Parishes of the Archdiocese of Chicago*, 2 vols. (Chicago: Archdiocese of Chicago, 1980), I:135; Joseph John Parot, *Polish Catholics in Chicago, 1850–1920* (DeKalb: Northern Illinois University Press, 1981), 133–60; Victor Greene, *For God and Country: The Rise of Polish and Lithuanian Ethnic Consciousness in America, 1860–1910* (Madison: State Historical Society of Wisconsin, 1975), 133–42.

3. William M. Tuttle Jr., *Race Riot: Chicago in the Red Summer of 1919* (New York: Atheneum, 1972) offers the best overview of the riot.

4. Chicago Commission on Race Relations, *The Negro in Chicago: A Study of Race Relations and a Race Riot* (Chicago: University of Chicago Press, 1922), 5–6, 8; Tuttle, *Race Riot*, 35.

5. Grossman, *Land of Hope*, 164, 178. For a discussion of the ethnic development of the Stock Yard District, see Pacyga and Skerrett, *Chicago: City of Neighborhoods*, chap. 13; and James R. Barrett, *Work and Community in the Jungle: Chicago's Packinghouse Workers, 1894–1922* (Urbana: University of Illinois Press, 1987), chap. 2, which deals with the ethnicity of Chicago's packinghouse workers.

6. Mary E. McDowell, "Prejudice," in Caroline M. Hill, ed., *Mary McDowell and Municipal Housekeeping: A Symposium* (Chicago: Millar Publishing Company, n.d.), 27–32.

7. Chicago Commission on Race Relations, *Negro in Chicago*, 7, 27.

8. Koenig, ed., *History of the Parishes*, I:454–61; Koenig, ed., *Caritas Christi Urget Nos: A History of the Offices, Agencies, and Institutions of the Archdiocese of Chicago*, 2 vols. (Chicago: Archdiocese of Chicago, 1981), I:450.

9. Chicago Commission on Race Relations, *Negro in Chicago*, 656–62; *Chicago Daily News*, July 29, 30, 1919; *Chicago Tribune*, July 31, 1919.

10. Chicago Commission on Race Relations, *Negro in Chicago*, 656–62; *Chicago Daily News*, July 29, 30, 1919, August 5, 1919; *Lakeside Directory of the City of Chicago* (Chicago: Chicago Directory Company, 1917).

11. "Emily Frankenstein Diary, 1918–1920," Special Collections, Chicago Historical Society.

12. Sterling Morton, "The Illinois Reserve Militia during World War One and After," Special Collections, Chicago Historical Society.

13. *Chicago Daily News*, August 2, 1919; Chicago Commission on Race Relations, *Negro in Chicago*, 12–15.

14. Chicago Commission on Race Relations, *Negro in Chicago*, 55.

15. Ibid., 53–57.

16. Tuttle, *Race Riot*, 10; Chicago Commission on Race Relations, *Negro in Chicago*, 42.

17. Testimony of Henry McName, Illinois State Militiaman, before the Chicago Commission on Race Relations Meeting, February 25, 1920, Minutes, Microfilm Rolls 30–78, Chicago Commission on Race Relations Papers, Illinois State Archives, Springfield, Illinois; Chicago Commission on Race Relations, *Negro in Chicago*, 42–43.

18. *Chicago Daily News*, August 14, 1919.

19. James T. Farrell, *Studs Lonigan* (New York: Avon Books, 1977). For a discussion of the accuracy of Farrell's novels concerning the South Side Irish, see Charles Fanning and Ellen Skerrett, "James T. Farrell and Washington Park: The Novel as Social History," *Chicago History* 8, no. 2 (Summer 1979): 80–91.

20. *Chicago Daily News*, August 5, 1919. For a discussion of the contribution of Polish workers to organized labor in Chicago, see Dominic A. Pacyga, *Polish Immigrants and Industrial Chicago: The Back of the Yards and South Chicago, 1880–1922* (Columbus: Ohio State University Press, 1991).

21. Grossman, *Land of Hope*, 210–22.

22. Tuttle, *Race Riot*, 109–19.

23. *Dziennik Związkowy*, July 29, 1919.

24. Ibid., August 2, 1919.

25. *Dziennik Chicagoski*, August 1, 1919.

26. *Naród Polski*, August 6, 1919.

27. *Dziennik Związkowy*, August 5, 1919.

28. *Chicago Daily News*, August 2, 1919.

29. Samuel Clark, *Social Origins of the Irish Land War* (Princeton, NJ: Princeton University Press, 1979), 4.

30. Ibid., 7.

31. Edward R. Kantowicz, "Polish Chicago: Survival through Solidarity," in Melvin G. Holli and Peter d'A. Jones, eds., *Ethnic Chicago* (Grand Rapids, MI: Eerdmans Publishing Company, 1984), 214–38. For Polish participation in labor unions, see Pacyga, *Polish Immigrants and Industrial Chicago*; and Barrett, *Work and Community*, chap. 4.

32. Clark, *Irish Land War*, 9.

33. Michael F. Funchion, "Irish Chicago: Church, Homeland, Politics, and Class: The Shaping of an Ethnic Group, 1870–1900," in Holli and Jones, *Ethnic Chicago*, 17.

34. Clark, *Irish Land War*, 12; James C. Davies, "Toward a Theory of Revolution," *American Sociological Review* 27 (February 1962): 5–19; James C. Davies, "The J-Curve of Rising and Declining Satisfactions as a Cause of Some Great Revolutions and a Contained Rebellion," in Hugh Davis Graham and Ted Robert Gurr, eds., *Violence in America: Historical and Comparative Perspectives* (New York, 1969), 671–709.

35. Adrian Cook, *The Armies of the Streets: The New York City Draft Riots of 1863* (Lexington: University of Kentucky Press, 1974), 30, 77, 82; Ronald H. Bayor, *Neighbors in Conflict: The Irish, Germans, Jews, and Italians of New York City, 1929–1941* (Baltimore: Johns Hopkins University Press, 1979), 1.

36. S. J. Connolly, "Violence and Order in the Eighteenth Century," in Patrick O'Flanagan, Paul Ferguson, and Kevin Whelan, eds., *Rural Ireland, 1600–1900: Modernization and Change* (Cork: Cork University Press, 1987), 48, 53; Samuel Clark and James S. Donnelley Jr., eds., *Irish Peasants: Violence and Political Unrest, 1780–1914* (Madison: University of Wisconsin Press, 1983), 25, 421–27.

37. Tuttle, *Race Riot*, 65; Connolly, "Violence and Order," 58.

38. George Rudé, *The Crowd in History: A Study of Popular Disturbances in France and England, 1730–1848* (New York: Wiley and Company, 1964), 48–55; Clark, *Irish Land War*, 353.

39. Chicago Commission on Race Relations, *The Negro in Chicago*, 3.

40. *Butcher Workman*, November 1919.

41. Grossman, *Land of Hope*, 239; *Dziennik Chicagoski*, January 7, 1928.

Chapter 8

Pittsburgh's Three Rivers: From Industrial Infrastructure to Environmental Asset

Timothy M. Collins, Edward K. Muller, and Joel A. Tarr

Like most river cities in Europe and America, Pittsburgh has looked upon its three principal waterways—the Allegheny, the Monongahela, and the Ohio—as invaluable natural resources to be used in support of economic development and municipal services. These urban rivers have always been as much a part of Pittsburgh's infrastructure as its highways, railroads, mass transportation lines, or electrical grids. For decades many of the natural features of these river systems were subsumed and in some cases destroyed by human activities. Despite these losses, the riparian ecosystems adapted, survived, and now flourish as part of a new vision for the region's future.

Over the course of more than two centuries, the city has forged very different relationships with its rivers, corresponding with three distinct periods of economic life. During its initial hundred years or so, Pittsburgh depended on the rivers for transporting the trade that was its lifeblood; nevertheless, its attempts to manage them physically were minimal and largely ineffective. The city's headlong embrace of industrialism, commencing around the middle of the nineteenth century, radically transformed the rivers' hydrology and ecology. In order to sustain rapid growth, Pittsburgh elites sought to regulate the rivers' flow, shape their banks, and augment the floodplains. They also used river water for both household and manufacturing consumption. In so doing, they conceived of the rivers in this second period as an integral part of the city's infrastructure. Thus the rivers were harnessed, managed, and rationalized for the smooth functioning of the city and its industrial machine.

Turning the rivers into aqueous infrastructure had negative consequences for their ecosystems as well as for the public's health and safety. A second riverine nature evolved as a result of the altered hydrology and massive amount of pollutants that degraded water quality and greatly diminished the diversity and abundance of flora and fauna. In the first half of the twentieth century, progressive reformers sought to

Reprinted from Christof Mauch and Thomas Zeller, eds., *Rivers in History: Perspectives on Waterways in Europe and North America* (University of Pittsburgh Press, 2008), 41–62. Reprinted by permission of the University of Pittsburgh Press.

mitigate the conditions most hazardous for humans due to water pollution and flooding. They employed additional engineering and conservation measures in their efforts. The subsequent improvements in water quality gradually renewed interest in the rivers' scenic beauty and recreational potential, especially after 1950.

Federal water quality legislation passed in the 1970s and the massive collapse of the region's traditional industries in the 1980s provided the impetus for Pittsburgh to rethink its connection to the rivers. Impressed by the revitalization of urban waterfronts elsewhere in the United States, civic leaders began to recognize Pittsburgh's rivers as potential sites for profitable scenic and recreational enterprises and thus as part of a new regional development strategy. At the same time, community activists began to advocate restoration of the rivers' damaged ecosystems. Promoting a view of the riverine environment—air, water, riverbanks, and the many organisms they support—as a public commons, this group sought to restore that environment to its preindustrial state. While these commercial and conservation agendas sometimes came into conflict, together they inaugurated a third phase in the relationship between the city and its rivers, which have once again become vital to Pittsburgh's economic future.

THE RIVERS BEFORE INDUSTRIALIZATION

Flying into Pittsburgh today, a traveler readily spots from the airplane the city's outstanding physical feature—the convergence of two broad rivers to form a third, even larger river. At this junction the tall buildings of Pittsburgh's downtown rise up from a small peninsula formed by the confluence of the Allegheny and Monongahela rivers. These skyscrapers stand like sentinels over the Ohio River, as it begins its westward journey of nearly a thousand miles to the Mississippi River.[1] Far to the south the sources of the Monongahela lie in the Appalachian Mountains of West Virginia. The Tygart and West Fork rivers come down from the mountains and join at Fairmont, West Virginia, to form the Monongahela, which leisurely flows northward for 128 miles to Pittsburgh. In contrast, the swiftly moving Allegheny River begins in the mountains of north-central Pennsylvania and flows briefly north and westward into New York state before turning southwest for 325 miles through western Pennsylvania for its meeting with the Monongahela. These three rivers and the point of land they create together comprise the physical structure around which the Pittsburgh region developed. Three secondary rivers—the Beaver, Kiskiminetas, and Youghiogheny—as well as dozens of tributary streams, creeks, or runs augment this riverine structure.[2]

Before the invasion of western Pennsylvania by French and English military expeditions, traders, and colonists, these river valleys were occupied at different times by various tribes of Amerindians, including the Delaware, the Shawnee, and several tribes from the Iroquois nation.[3] By the turn of the nineteenth century, settlers (with the assistance of military troops) had largely displaced the native population and taken over the land. The rivers supplied the primary organizational framework for this new settlement, providing a transport corridor in drought-free years, an abundance of fish, and fertile land in the floodplains. Moreover, Pittsburgh's location at the head of the Ohio River presented the young city with an opportunity to become the commercial gateway to the newly opened midwestern frontier. Thus the three rivers were not only central to the city's economic vitality and aspirations but also an integral part of people's everyday lives.[4]

Despite their significant role in supporting Pittsburgh's economy, the rivers presented serious impediments to navigation. Water provided an ideal means of transportation, but the fluctuations in flow, dangerous snags and boulders, treacherous riffles, and shifting sandbars all limited commercial uses. At the urging of politically connected local residents, both the state and federal governments funded modest attempts to clear the rivers of obstacles and deepen the channels. They contracted private companies to dynamite rocks in riffles, remove flotsam and jetsam, and establish small "wing" dams to ensure sufficient depth for transport. These efforts to make the rivers more navigable produced only minimal improvements by the end of the Civil War.[5]

One solution was to create a network of canals, which regulated water flow in separate, often parallel waterways. Among the many miles of canalized waterways that the state constructed, the most important was the Pennsylvania Main Line system, built in 1834. It was a combination of inclined plane, railroad, and canal extending from Philadelphia to Pittsburgh. For almost twenty years Pittsburgh's commercial life benefited enormously from this awkward system as it snaked into the city along the northern floodplain of the Allegheny River. The value of Monongahela River traffic, especially coal shipping, persuaded the state of Pennsylvania to commission the Monongahela Navigation Company in the mid-1840s to construct the first dams and locks between Pittsburgh and the West Virginia state line. This modestly successful slackwater venture established privatized toll navigation.[6]

The rivers fulfilled essential functions for the growing city, such as providing water for households and industry and a sink for municipal sewage, storm water, and commercial and industrial wastes. Pittsburgh residents used the rivers for recreation and annually coped with the cleanup required by spring and fall floods that inundated low-lying neighborhoods. Private companies erected bridges to replace the slower, less reliable ferries as urban development emerged on the banks of the Allegheny and Monongahela across from the city at the Point. As a result of the city's expansion in the first half of the nineteenth century, the wooded banks of all three rivers gave way to wharves, docks, and other infrastructure that aided mercantile sales, commercial navigation, and early industries.[7] Nevertheless, the human impact on the natural ecosystem was negligible compared to what it would be in the coming decades.

THE TRANSFORMATION TO URBAN INDUSTRIAL INFRASTRUCTURE

Pittsburgh's hope of becoming a gateway to westward migration and commerce via its rivers and canals evaporated in 1852 when the Pennsylvania Railroad brought the first rail service to the city. This event was the catalyst for a dramatic long-term shift in how civic leaders perceived the three rivers. Instead of transportation routes, they were increasingly regarded as essential infrastructure for industrial production and urban development, and engineers shaped and managed them accordingly.

Industrialization supplanted the city's river-based mercantilism in the three-quarters of a century following the railroad's arrival. The most intensive development occurred in the region's mines and iron- and steelworks. After 1875 the explosive growth of the mass-production steel industry defined the city's transformation. Industrialists sited their mills on the broad river floodplains nestled within the sweeping river meanders. Railroad tracks ran along the mills' landward side. Other capital-intensive firms dealing with glass, aluminum, railroad equipment, food processing, and electrical equipment, to name the most prominent, also spread to sites along the three rivers' floodplains, stretching for thirty to forty miles from the Pittsburgh Point. By providing cheap transportation for fuel from the region's coalfields and for other natural resources, such as timber and oil, the rivers were critical to the region's industrialization.[8]

Although the total number of people and vessels engaged in commercial river traffic shrank steadily during the remainder of the nineteenth century, the actual tonnage of goods shipped along the rivers increased. Bulk commodities, such as oil, sand, gravel, and especially coal, along with some finished iron and steel products, dominated this traffic. After the Civil War, the U.S. Army Corps of Engineers took over management of the rivers from private interests and the state. Reshaping them into stable, efficient infrastructure systems produced significant economic returns, since each additional six inches of channel depth allowed boats and barges to increase their cargo by seventy tons. Under pressure from Ohio Valley business interests, Congress in 1875 authorized the construction of locks and dams for the Ohio River. Measurable improvement in river traffic, attributable to the Davis Island Lock and Dam, located five miles below the Point, intensified political pressure for the "canalization" of the entire three-river system. By the turn of the century, locks had been constructed up both the Allegheny and Monongahela rivers and down the Ohio as far as Marietta. The Army Corps of Engineers finally completed the Ohio River system to Cairo, Illinois, in 1929. All three rivers now consisted of a series of pools connected by navigation channels whose depth was maintained at between six and nine feet.[9]

Controlled river flow and the concomitant growth of industry along the waterfronts changed the river edges nearly as dramatically as the rivers themselves had been altered. The "pools" permanently raised water levels, drowning mudflats and establishing new riverbanks. Industries constructed wooden and cement bulkheads for shipping terminals and flood management. They built large round mooring cells; sprinkled the banks with cranes, conveyor belts, and loading chutes; and added water-intake and waste-discharge pipes. Some companies raised the height of the banks with extensive fill, much of it slag from the iron and steel mills, and a few even closed back channels to nearby islands. Boat-building firms erected launching facilities, and repair yards sprang up along the banks in several places. Shanty boats, sunken watercraft, and abandoned barges littered the edges of the waterway. Railroads lined the riverfronts as well, and in many places steep hillsides narrowed the floodplains so that only the railroads occupied them.[10]

Both municipalities and industries used prodigious amounts of water. They pumped water for household consumption and commercial production while discharging wastewater contaminated with human and industrial wastes back into the rivers. Writing in 1912, N. S. Sprague, superintendent of the Pittsburgh Bureau of Construction, observed that "rivers are the natural and logical drains and are formed for the purpose of carrying the wastes to the sea," expressing with admirable economy the attitude of most municipal officials and local manufacturers toward Pittsburgh's rivers between 1850 and 1940.[11]

This attitude was codified into administrative law for Pittsburgh in 1923 when the Pennsylvania Sanitary Water Board created a classification system that designated each stream in the state as belonging to one of three categories: clean and pure; polluted but not hazardous to public health; or unsafe for drinking and recreational uses, including fishing. Streams in this last category could continue to be used for the discharge of untreated wastes—that is, as open sewers. Pittsburgh's three rivers fell into this third category.[12]

Pollution flows were of three principal kinds: municipal sewage, industrial wastewater, and mine acid drainage. Cumulatively, they all degraded water quality, but their effects differed somewhat with respect to public health and stream ecology. In terms of public health, municipal sewage had the most devastating impact.

Beginning in the second quarter of the nineteenth century, Pittsburghers began to rely on local rivers for their water supply, although residents of some working-class areas continued to depend on groundwater and pumps into the twentieth century. By 1915 the municipal system included 743 miles of distribution pipes.[13] The provision of running water to households and the widespread adoption of water-using appliances such as sinks, showers, and water closets benefited households in many ways, but these developments also exacerbated the problem of wastewater disposal.

For much of the nineteenth century, Pittsburghers placed household wastes and wastewater in cesspools and privy vaults, not in sewers. They continued this practice even after the availability of running water greatly increased the volume of wastewater. In 1881, for instance, about four thousand of the city's sixty-five hundred water closets were connected to privy vaults and cesspools, with only about fifteen hundred linked to street sewers that the city had begun constructing at midcentury. The Pittsburgh Board of Health noted that overflowing privies were a constant nuisance and presented the city with a major health issue.

Such conditions raised the likelihood of epidemics from infectious disease and highlighted the need for improved sanitation and construction of a sewage system. In the 1880s a fierce debate arose over whether the sewer system should be a separate system carrying only household and some industrial wastes (the plan physicians favored) or a combined system that could accommodate both wastewater and storm water in one pipe (the design preferred by engineers). The engineers triumphed, primarily for reasons of cost, and the city began constructing a combined sewer system, building more than 412 miles of combined sewers between 1889 and 1912. That design decision had large implications for the rivers' water quality in the future.[14]

Like other cities, Pittsburgh discharged its untreated sewage from public sewer outlets (145 of them) directly into neighboring waterways on the theory that running water purified itself, diluting and dispersing the wastes. Simultaneously, upstream communities were also building sewers and discharging their wastes into the same rivers. By 1900, more than 350,000 inhabitants in seventy-five upstream municipalities discharged their untreated sewage into the Allegheny, the river that provided drinking water for most of the city of Pittsburgh's population. Even some of Pittsburgh's own sewers discharged into the river at locations above its water-supply intake pumping stations. The resulting pollution gave Pittsburgh the highest death rate from typhoid fever of the nation's large cities—well over 100 deaths per 100,000 people from 1873 to 1907. By contrast, in 1905 the average death rate for northern cities was 35 per 100,000 persons.[15]

Concerned over the growing typhoid mortality and morbidity rates, several professional groups and the Pittsburgh Ladies Health Protective Association formed a citizens' Joint Commission in the 1890s to study the issue of water pollution. Their report of 1894 indicated that Pittsburgh and Allegheny City water supplies were "not only not up to a proper standard of potable water but . . . actually pernicious," and it recommended filtering the water supply of both cities. In 1896 the mayor established the Pittsburgh Filtration Commission, which made a similar recommendation. After several years of delay caused by political infighting and technical problems, the municipal water department delivered the first filtered water to the city in December 1907. Pittsburgh thus joined cities such as Philadelphia and Cincinnati, which took water from their local rivers and filtered it, while cities such as Boston and New York chose to rely on supplies from a protected watershed. Almost immediately Pittsburgh's typhoid rates began to decline, and by 1912, after chlorination of the water supply, the city's typhoid death rate dropped to the level of the national average for large cities.[16]

Filtration provided one safeguard against polluted water, but many sanitation specialists and public-health physicians believed that a further measure—sewage treatment—was required for effective protection. In 1905, responding to a severe typhoid epidemic, the Pennsylvania General Assembly passed the Purity of Waters Act "to preserve the purity of the waters of the State for the protection of the public health." This act forbade the discharge of any untreated sewage into state waterways by new municipal systems, and although it permitted existing systems to continue the practice, it required cities to secure a permit from the state commissioner of health for any expansion of those systems.

In 1910 Pittsburgh sought a permit that would allow it to extend its sewerage system, thus setting up a confrontation with the state agency. The Pennsylvania Department of Health, headed by Dr. Samuel G. Dixon, a follower of the New Public Health doctrine, then ordered a "comprehensive sewerage plan for the collection and disposal of all of the sewage of the municipality." In addition, the department argued that, in order to ensure efficient treatment, the city should consider changing from a combined system to separate sewer systems. The municipality responded by hiring the renowned engineering firm of Hazen and Whipple to study the issue. The report produced by Allen Hazen and George C. Whipple in 1912 asserted that a new sewage treatment plant would not eliminate the need for users downstream to filter their water supplies, since other communities would continue to discharge raw sewage into the rivers. The method of disposal by dilution, they maintained, would suffice to prevent nuisances, particularly if storage reservoirs were constructed upstream from Pittsburgh to augment flow during periods of low stream volume.[17]

Dixon, the health commissioner, found the Hazen and Whipple report an insufficient response to his original order for a long-range plan for a comprehensive regional sewerage system, but most members of the engineering community agreed with its premises. The issues for them were controlling costs and avoiding nuisance. Dixon countered that streams should not be allowed to "become stinking sewers and culture beds for pathogenic organisms." Given the political context, however, and the city's financial limitations, Dixon had no realistic means by which to enforce his order. In 1913 he capitulated and issued Pittsburgh a temporary discharge permit, thus continuing the use of Pittsburgh's rivers as open sewers.[18]

While demands for sewage treatment had been rising, another major pollutant, mine acid, had escaped regulation. Other industrial pollutants caused problems, but the sulfuric acid discharge from coal mines was the most ecologically damaging water contaminant in western Pennsylvania's industrial history. Mine acid destroyed fish life, altered the flora in and along small streams and major rivers, caused millions of dollars' worth of damage to domestic and industrial water users, and raised the costs of water and sewage treatment.[19]

The economic importance of coal production in southwestern Pennsylvania impeded attempts by government to counter the burden of mine acid drainage. The coal industry contended that no "suitable" method existed for the treatment of mine water. In addition, the courts had granted the industry legal protection in the infamous case of *Pennsylvania Coal Company v. Sanderson and Wife* (1886), which concerned the destruction by mine acid of the water supplies of a farm near Scranton, Pennsylvania. In this case the Pennsylvania Supreme Court maintained that "the right to mine coal is not a nuisance in itself" and that the acidic substances had entered the stream via natural forces that were beyond company control. The justices also noted the economic importance of the coal industry, arguing that "the trifling inconvenience to particular persons must sometimes give way to the necessities of a great community." In 1905, when the Pennsylvania legislature passed the Purity of Waters Act, it specifically exempted "waters pumped or flowing from coal mines," as it did again in 1937 in the Clean Streams Act.[20] In general, therefore, as reflected in the failure to regulate sewage disposal and mine acid, the three rivers and their valleys had become and remained industrial infrastructure, engineered and utilitarian. By the 1920s they had been so altered that few older Pittsburgh residents would have recognized the rivers they had known a half century earlier.

REFORMING INDUSTRIAL NATURE

The rapid growth and unbridled development of the Pittsburgh region left in its wake a number of social, political, and, as noted above, environmental problems that many early-twentieth century Pittsburghers believed threatened the city's civic order and long-term economic welfare. As with the nation as a whole, local progressive reformers viewed improving the built and natural environments as a means to uplift the society's moral character and health conditions as well as to create a more efficient and successful business community. Although often emphasizing different aspects of the reform agenda, both voluntary citizens' groups such as the Civic Club of Allegheny County and business organizations such as the Pittsburgh Chamber of Commerce agreed on the importance of addressing problems associated with the rivers and riverfronts. Never challenging the primacy of business prerogatives and private property rights, these reform efforts did represent a modification of the prevailing view of the rivers as industrial infrastructure, which was consistent with progressive reform and the conservation movement then gaining momentum at the national level. Pittsburgh's elites increasingly participated in national networks in which they encountered campaigns to conserve forest resources and watersheds, preserve land for parks, and adopt urban planning.

Following the disastrous flood of 1907 and the threat of another a year later, the Pittsburgh Chamber of Commerce appointed a flood commission, chaired by industrialist H. J. Heinz and consisting of representatives from local government, reform groups, and business as well as individuals with engineering expertise. The Flood Commission of Pittsburgh hired an executive director who was strongly identified with national concerns for planned watershed development. In its massive technical report published four years later, the commission projected both pragmatic local thinking and a vision for regional conservation. Predicting that continued urban industrial development and clear-cut logging in the mountainous watersheds of the Allegheny and Monongahela rivers would exacerbate the frequency and intensity of flooding, the commission recommended constructing a floodwall to protect the downtown area, filling in back channels of islands near the city's center, creating seventeen regional impoundment reservoirs, and establishing forest preserves in the headwater areas.

The Flood Commission persuaded the federal government to purchase land for reforestation in the upper watersheds, mirroring the conservation triumphs of President Theodore Roosevelt and his chief forester, Gifford Pinchot. However, it soon became embroiled in a protracted struggle with Congress and federal agencies. In particular, the Army Corps of Engineers resisted broadening its mandate to manage inland rivers for more than navigational purposes. Only successive years of drought, economic depression, and the ruinous floods of 1936 and 1937 impelled local and federal leaders to prevail on Congress to authorize a comprehensive flood-control program.[21]

At the same time that the Flood Commission tackled its work, the Pittsburgh Civic Commission contracted with landscape architect Frederick Law Olmsted Jr. to prepare a plan for Pittsburgh's roadways. Olmsted's work focused primarily on issues of traffic congestion and future highway development, but in his report in 1910 he also lamented the dilapidated condition of downtown riverfronts and urged the city to rethink their possibilities. While he advocated modernization of the Monongahela Wharf cargo-handling facilities, incorrectly predicting a resurgence of general merchandise commerce on the rivers, he also envisioned the rivers as a potential amenity for their picturesque qualities. Modeling his vision on European cities, he proposed promenades and overlooks above the waterfronts, which would coexist with an expanded roadway to channel traffic rapidly around the periphery of the congested downtown area. Moreover, the Boston planner tapped into an ongoing discussion about reclaiming the land where the three rivers converged in order to create a symbolic park and monument at this historical and geographical inception point. Probably recalling the various plans for the preservation of open spaces and riverscapes in Boston, he also urged that several undeveloped tributary stream valleys be preserved and designated as public parks.[22]

For the next three decades Olmsted's successors in planning for Pittsburgh kept these ideas for the waterfronts alive in one form or another, but the industrial and infrastructural utility of the rivers and riverfront lands precluded their implementation. In 1923, for example, a subcommittee on waterways of the Citizens Committee on the City Plan (an elite volunteer group that put forth a city plan in six parts) summed up the business community's view of the rivers when it reported that "navigation interests have a prior right to the use of those portions of the City's water front which can be advantageously used for water transportation, and that no encroachments should be permitted thereon which will interfere with such activities."[23] Further, the subcommittee recommended development of several rail-to-river terminals on the waterfronts in and around downtown.

While a few decades into the century civic leaders still wished to manage the rivers for flood control and city planners envisioned the redesign of riverfront lands, other reformers and conservationists continued to worry about the disposal of waste in the rivers and the hazards it posed to public health. They refocused their energies on the question of water quality. Although by 1934 the drinking water supplies of 80 percent of the state's population were treated, 85 percent of Pennsylvania waterways suffered from various degrees of degradation attributable to raw sewage and industrial wastes. For instance, only 18 percent of the sewage from a population of 920,000 in the Allegheny River basin was treated, and it was the Allegheny from which the city of Pittsburgh drew most of its water supply. Sewage from Pittsburgh and other communities overwhelmed the oxidation capacity of the streams, creating offensive sights and smells on the rivers. Gross pollution levels in streams threatened public health, and while water treatment had sharply reduced typhoid deaths, the death rates from diarrhea and enteritis remained above the national average. Fish were absent from long dead stretches of the rivers, and chemical pollution fouled the taste of many drinking water supplies. In addition, mine acid drainage increased the costs of water filtration for Pittsburgh residents.[24]

By the end of the 1930s, public concern over these conditions had united environmental groups and associations of outdoor sports enthusiasts in demanding that state and local authorities initiate conservation efforts. In 1937 the Pennsylvania General Assembly passed the Clean Streams Act, giving the Sanitary Water Board power to issue and enforce waste treatment orders to all municipalities and most industries except for coal mines. In 1944 the Sanitary Water Board announced comprehensive plans to reduce the pollution of Pennsylvania streams, requiring all municipalities to treat their sewage "to a primary degree." The following year the board issued orders to the City of Pittsburgh and 101 other municipalities, as well as to more than 90 Allegheny County industries, to cease discharging untreated wastes into state waterways.

The state authorized the formation of the Allegheny County Sanitary Authority (ALCOSAN) in 1946, but political interests prevented any real progress until October 1, 1958, when ALCOSAN's centralized, activated sludge treatment plant located on the northern bank of the Ohio River below the Point began treating the wastewater of

Pittsburgh and eighty-one county boroughs and towns. A major step had finally been taken to improve the water quality of Pittsburgh's rivers.[25]

THE PITTSBURGH RENAISSANCE AND THE RIVERS

Despite the economic revival during World War II after years of depression, Pittsburgh's leaders feared that peace would bring back the declining industrial prospects the city had experienced since 1920. The desire to retain existing firms and attract new companies, especially ones that diversified the region's industrial base, dominated the postwar civic agenda. In 1945, the city initiated a twenty-five-year redevelopment program, the so-called "Renaissance" program, under the leadership of Richard King Mellon, Mayor David Lawrence, and the newly formed Allegheny Conference on Community Development, a nonprofit organization controlled by the presidents of the region's largest corporations. This public/private partnership addressed issues of economic development, renewal of infrastructure, downtown redevelopment, and environmental pollutants such as smoke. By 1960 the national media were heralding the revitalization of the "Smoky City." Even the three rivers received some attention in the Renaissance program. Besides the construction of sewage treatment facilities and implementation of flood-control measures, the city cleared the railroad yards, warehouses, and last remaining residences from the Point and undertook construction of a state park there, which invited contemplation of both the aesthetic and historical significance of the three rivers' confluence. Moreover, recreational boating began to return to the city's waters.[26]

These steps toward the rehabilitation of the rivers proved to be relatively small ones, however, and the flood-protection program only expanded the type of river management begun in the nineteenth century. Despite Olmsted's dreams, prewar proposals by pragmatic urban planners to use downtown's waterfronts for highways and parking lots were implemented during the Renaissance program. The continued inflows of industrial wastes, mine acid, and sewage from the overflow pipes of the combined sewer system of Pittsburgh and other county municipalities prevented any real ecological recovery of the rivers.[27]

In the 1970s the failure to exploit the rivers' aesthetic and public relations potential for two major developments demonstrated the persistent grip of the industrial mind-set on the perceptions of civic leaders. Despite its name and its location across from the historic Point, Three Rivers Stadium, which opened in 1970 and became a nationally recognized sports venue, offered no views of either the rivers or downtown Pittsburgh. Similarly, the new convention center that opened in 1977 was designed facing away from the Allegheny and with the rear of the building and its loading docks oriented toward the river.[28] Even the region's principal conservation organization, which emerged in conjunction with the national movement for the preservation of wilderness lands, abjured the city's rivers. The elite-sponsored Western Pennsylvania Conservancy, increasingly active and influential after World War II, focused mainly on protecting environments either well beyond the city limits or on the metropolitan fringe.[29]

Having achieved success with the Renaissance program's smoke-abatement efforts, new sewage-treatment facility, flood-control project, and extra-urban preservation work, the city proudly assumed a leadership role in the national environmental movement of the 1960s. But a plan for the riverfronts called this leadership into question in 1959, at least as far as the rivers were concerned. Pittsburgh's urban planners noted that the Renaissance program had neglected the conservation of the rivers and riverfronts. They recommended several possible sites for riverfront parks and recreation areas. Nevertheless, they still argued that "most of the flat land adjacent to the rivers must continue to be occupied by the industry and commerce which support the City." At best they hoped to "balance" the diverse interests in the rivers, because "the rivers can provide an additional opportunity for recreation without detracting anything from industry."[30] Thus, despite the dramatic postwar renewal program, municipal leaders persisted in viewing the three rivers as engineered, infrastructural systems for industry and urban development. Conservation measures implemented beginning early in the twentieth century had ameliorated only the worst health consequences of this conception and marginally improved water quality and some riverfront lands.

REINVENTING THE RIVERS
AS ENVIRONMENTAL INFRASTRUCTURE

The collapse of Pittsburgh's industrial base in the last quarter of the twentieth century forced a reconceptualization of the city's economic and social life. Although at the time it seemed as though civic leaders were slow to rethink the city's relationship to the rivers, in fact they began to develop a new understanding in a little more than a decade. After initially scrambling to attract any sort of job-creating businesses to former industrial sites, civic leaders, some developers, and community activists began to envision the rivers as settings for scenic, recreational, and environmental amenities that would improve residents' quality of life. The city would thus become more attractive to new businesses, especially advanced technology firms and the professionals they employ. This revised conception of the rivers repositioned them as a key component, once again, of the region's economic development strategy. However, as this view became generally accepted, a new tension surfaced between environmentalists and municipal boosters. Appeals for the restoration and preservation of river ecosystems conflicted with development proposals that sought to exploit the region's recreational and tourism potential.

In the late 1970s earlier predictions of absolute decline in Pittsburgh's industrial base began to come true. By the early 1980s, older steel mills, factories, and coal mines were permanently shuttered, leaving the region in crisis. Seemingly all at once, thousands of acres of formerly vital industrial riverfront turned into vacant and often polluted brownfields, commercial river traffic plummeted, and river infrastructure fell into disrepair. Under intense pressure to replace the many thousands of lost manufacturing jobs with new sources of employment, civic leaders cast about for all kinds of development opportunities and governmental support. Pittsburgh's weakened economy and Rust Belt image, the real and perceived toxic condition of brownfields, the outdated character of the industrial areas' highway networks, and the lack of a unified development strategy among the region's many local governments stymied new investment, especially along the older industrial riverfronts.[31] Ironically, this failure saved these critical sites from the prospect of redevelopment without adequate consideration of the rivers' potential in the "new" Pittsburgh.

Although generally greeted by civic leaders with polite indifference, several studies by governmental agencies and nonprofit organizations in the 1980s explored the question of how the rivers might be used to improve the region's quality of life. Most Pittsburghers dismissed the recommendations of these reports as impractical and elitist because of the region's cascading underemployment and unemployment that spelled hard times for thousands of families. Nevertheless, a few new waterfront projects indicated that the rivers might become popular with the public and eventually with investors, just as other such developments had already demonstrated in Baltimore, Portland (Oregon), and several other American cities. A small public boat-launching ramp and linear park along the city's South Side riverbank attracted hordes of weekend boaters. The new, high profile annual River Regatta, featuring Formula One speedboat races, drew large crowds. A marina, riverfront park, and hike-and-bike trail similarly enlivened the depressed industrial city of McKeesport several miles south of Pittsburgh, while a waterslide amusement park flourished on the edge of a riverfront brownfield in run-down West Homestead, which had formerly housed a massive industrial-machinery works. Finally, a small sculpture park and office development called Allegheny Landing spruced up the riverfront across from downtown on that river's north shore.[32]

By the early 1990s, the attitudes of investors and public officials toward the development prospects of the riverfronts for scenic and recreational opportunities had clearly shifted. The successful redevelopment of an industrial island in the Allegheny River (Herr's Island, renamed Washington's Landing a couple of miles above downtown) into a complex of offices, light industry, a large marina, and townhouses with a circumferential walking and biking trail overlooking the water showed how important the rivers were to the region's future economic growth and stability. Recreational boating along with the attendant marinas and yacht clubs proliferated throughout the river valleys. The revival of rowing added another dimension to river participation, while river tours and commercial party boats attracted other clienteles. Most important, civic leaders and government officials embraced the idea of turning the north shore of the Allegheny River across from Pittsburgh's downtown area into a signature development dependent on the river ambience. The North Shore Corridor, as it has been called, became the site of two new baseball and football stadiums oriented to the river with views of downtown. The Aluminum Company of America (ALCOA) built its new headquarters along the river, where office buildings, entertainment venues, retail shops, and private residences have since been developed with support from the city. On the south (downtown) bank of the Allegheny, the newly rebuilt and enlarged "green" convention center was oriented to face the waterfront. The adjacent cultural district that has been emerging for more than twenty years contributed to the North Shore Corridor with new buildings, signage, and lighting as well as a linear park along the river's edge. A group of civic leaders and foundations formed the Riverlife Task

Force, which conceived of a Three Rivers Park consisting of public spaces along the city's central riverfronts. The Riverlife Task Force has taken it upon itself to steward the development of these public spaces, coordinating with private developers and public agencies as well as negotiating for appropriate designs.[33]

Not all development of the brownfields has taken advantage of their location alongside the rivers. For example, the new development on the former site of Homestead Steel Works, which stretches for nearly three miles along the Monongahela about eight miles from downtown Pittsburgh, generally ignores the river despite being named "The Waterfront." The developers designed the complex as a suburban-style retail, restaurant, and office mall; only the walking trail on the riverbank and a few townhouses and other buildings face the river.[34]

The collapse of industry and the diminution of associated pollution and traffic from the rivers, along with state and federal clean-water regulations, have markedly improved both water quality and the river ecology. Biologists have determined that in the past "the upper Ohio River drainage basin was so grossly degraded that these systems were completely devoid of fish life."[35] The ecological recovery has been surprisingly rapid and extensive. Fish have returned to the rivers. In one recent study of tributaries of the three rivers, twenty-nine species of fish were discovered in streams flowing to the Allegheny, sixteen species in tributaries of the Monongahela, and thirty-two species in a tributary of the Ohio River. This significant recovery had sports enthusiasts, environmentalists, and Pennsylvania State Fish and Boat Commission employees cooperating to bring the Bass Master Classic fishing tournament to Pittsburgh for the first time.[36]

The woody vegetation along the region's riverbanks was also severely degraded, but as with the fish, woody plants have made a vigorous return to the rivers' once-bare and eroded edges. A recent study of the Monongahela and Allegheny rivers identified the existence of four native woody-plant communities and one native herbaceous-plant community typical of large rivers in North America. It also determined that the frequency of invasive species decreases with distance from the city's Point.[37] This rapid regeneration of riparian vegetation has taken observers by surprise. Organizations concerned with riverine ecology such as the Friends of the Riverfront, the Pennsylvania Environmental Council, 3 Rivers 2nd Nature, and the Western Pennsylvania Field Institute held several workshops to discuss the creation of water trails and in the process discovered several local sites of intense natural diversity. For instance, Sycamore Island, a large wooded island in the Allegheny River nine miles from downtown Pittsburgh, has few sycamore trees today, but its silver maples are so large and so tall that people seeing photographs of these maple groves assume that the setting is a national forest.

The ability of the rivers and streams to support life and the return of typical riparian vegetation reveal a natural potential that has been dormant for more than a century and suggest the possibility for human intervention to aid the process. Planning is under way for the restoration of natural riverine systems at several regional sites. The U.S. Army Corps of Engineers, for example, is engaged in the process of restoring an urban stream called Nine Mile Run. This stream flows from creeks that have long been directed into sewer pipes and from springs in a city park through a three-hundred-acre reclaimed brownfield site into the Monongahela River.[38] Additional plans and activities are under way to restore, conserve, and preserve local ecosystems. Recent river restoration studies by the U.S. Army Corps of Engineers, island studies by the U.S. Fish and Wildlife Service, and land conservation along the rivers by the Allegheny Land Trust reveal the gradual shift in thinking from traditional conservation of the hinterlands to conservation and restoration of land along the region's most industrialized waterways.[39]

Ecological restoration is difficult despite the remarkable recovery of natural systems. Riverine ecological systems encounter wet-weather threats to water quality from outdated sewage systems; the Pittsburgh region has the highest number of combined sewer outfalls in the country. Recurring episodes of mine-acid drainage also endanger ecological rejuvenation. Furthermore, some of Pittsburgh's forested hills and slopes near the rivers are once again being considered for rezoning to spur development. There has also been a proposal to construct an expressway through four Monongahela waterfront communities, which would affect two miles of reforested riverbank—the longest undeveloped stretch within the city limits. Clearly, the old development values still tug at Pittsburghers, even as natural systems have begun regenerating in the brief twenty-year respite from intense industrial use.

The ecological recovery has nevertheless spawned a growing interest in the aesthetics of river viewing. Public spaces with panoramic river views from walkways, bridges, hills, parks, and the water itself create outstanding opportunities to enjoy the rivers, their recovering banks, and the forested hillsides. Real estate developers are erecting townhouses with water views as a means of capturing the rising economic value created by this aesthetic. This ecological recovery thus enhances the city's intention to become known as a place where residents and visitors are able to play in, on, and along the rivers and riverbanks.

The postindustrial view of nature emphasizing preservation and restoration of riverine ecologies, however, clashes at times with development that leverages the rivers' recreational and scenic attributes. Intensive housing and office complexes, manicured landscaping of banks, and noisy, high-speed boats roiling river waters all contrast with the aesthetic of ecological preservation. Rowers and power boaters uneasily share the water; birders despair at the managed vegetation of developers' complexes; and commercial shipping still has navigational priority.

The concepts of the environment as an amenity and as an ecological aesthetic both depend on a physical, sensual relationship to place, appealing to fashionable values of youth and an active, healthy lifestyle. Clean rivers with green edges and trails, it is argued, support this kind of lifestyle. Both concepts rely in distinct ways on continued management of the three rivers, and despite their inherent contradictions, the combination of these concepts has become critical environmental infrastructure that is essential for Pittsburgh to compete with other regions.

URBAN RIVERS

Throughout the city's history, Pittsburgh's succession of civic leaders has defined the rivers with respect to the three periods of its economic life. These periods conform generally with the experiences of other American river cities. Although the timing and specifics vary, Pittsburgh's river story also resonates with those of many European cities. The experiences of older industrial cities such as Newcastle-on-Tyne in England closely parallel those of Pittsburgh, but even Paris's relationship with the Seine, as suggested by Isabelle Backouche, shares many of the same general characteristics.[40] Like Pittsburgh's three rivers, the Seine supported multiple functions and the "ordinary" life of Parisians until the late eighteenth century. After 1760, business elites and government officials increasingly regulated and reshaped this famous river according to a "mono-functional" vision of it as a national trade artery in an industrializing economy. Slowly the Seine became a stranger to residents, writes Backouche, though not to tourists. Finally, Parisian leaders in recent years have tried to reconnect the river to the lives of citizens in hopes of again making the Seine part of Paris's public space.

In some ways the segments of rivers that flow through urban areas shared many characteristics with their country cousins. Farmers, loggers, millers, and country merchants also regarded rivers as natural resources critical to their economic enterprises; if needed be, these rural entrepreneurs endeavored to regulate and manage them with, for example, dams or diversion canals. These rivers generally were not as intensively managed and exploited as the urban segments, where greater waste loads, hardening of edges, and filling or "reclamation" often drastically altered the ecology.[41]

Such intense intervention in urban rivers readily invites a historical interpretation that emphasizes the now-familiar dichotomy between nature and culture.[42] While now discredited in academic literature, this dichotomy was clearly reflected in public perceptions. Until recently the heavily engineered three rivers did not seem like "real" rivers to most Pittsburgh residents. Just as the Seine became a stranger to Parisians, the three rivers became inaccessible and unusable to ordinary Pittsburghers. Human activity had so degraded both water quality and riparian flora and fauna in pursuit of urban industrial development that most citizens had ceased to think of the rivers as part of nature. As infrastructure, the rivers might as well have been buried in culverts or concrete channels to do their job. In the search for nature's scenic and recreational amenities, Pittsburghers left the city for rural rivers or more distant sites of recreation. This industrial nature was "unnatural."[43]

Today the ecological rejuvenation of the three rivers and their rediscovery as part of the public commons depends on continuing regulation and management by those with the power to make policy, effect development, and enforce laws. The return of the rivers to their preindustrial state is, of course, no less a cultural construct than was the riverine ecology during the period of the rivers' industrialization. As environmental historian William Cronan has noted, nature "is a profoundly human construction . . . the way we describe and understand [it] is so entangled with our own values and assumptions that the two can never be fully separated."[44] The restoration of a preindustrial ecology will be only partially achievable. The maintenance of industrial-era infrastructure such as locks, dams, and hard edges; the alterations caused by dredging for sand and gravel; and the presence of invasive species will prevent complete restoration. Furthermore, the pressure for development, even of some river-friendly recreational and residential projects, will introduce highly managed landscapes. Nonetheless, with riverfront trails; increased boating, rowing, and fishing; and the renewed pleasure of river viewing, the three rivers, as reconceptualized and shaped by humans, are again part of the public commons and critical to Pittsburgh's reinvention of itself.

NOTES

1. Edward K. Muller, "The Point," in *Geographical Snapshots of North America,* ed. Donald G. Janelle (New York: Guilford Press, 1992), 231–34.

2. David J. Cuff et al., *The Atlas of Pennsylvania* (Philadelphia: Temple University Press, 1989), 52–67. Some have questioned whether there are in fact three rivers, arguing that the Allegheny and the Ohio are one river, which the Monongahela joins. However, ever since Europeans first explored this region, most people have viewed these as three separate rivers.

3. Paul A. W. Wallace, *Indians in Pennsylvania* (Harrisburg: Pennsylvania Historical and Museum Commission, 1981).

4. Leland D. Baldwin, *Pittsburgh: The Story of a City, 1750–1865* (Pittsburgh: University of Pittsburgh Press, 1937).

5. Shera A. Moxley, *From Rivers to Lakes: Engineering Pittsburgh's Three Rivers,* 3 Rivers 2nd Nature History Report (Pittsburgh: STUDIO for Creative Inquiry, Carnegie Mellon University, 2001), 18, available at http://3r2n.cfa.cmu.edu/history/engineer/index.htm; Leland R. Johnson, *The Headwaters District: A History of the Pittsburgh District, U.S. Army Corps of Engineers* (Pittsburgh: Pittsburgh District, U.S. Army Corps of Engineers, 1978), 1–101.

6. Catherine Elizabeth Reiser, *Pittsburgh's Commercial Development, 1800–1850* (Harrisburg: Pennsylvania Historical and Museum Commission, 1951); Richard C. Wade, *The Urban Frontier: Pioneer Life in Early Pittsburgh, Cincinnati, Lexington, Louisville, and St. Louis* (Chicago: University of Chicago Press, 1964), 39–46. Wade's study was originally issued in 1959 by Harvard University Press under the title *The Urban Frontier: The Rise of Western Cities, 1790–1830.*

7. Edward K. Muller, "River City," in *Devastation and Renewal; An Environmental History of Pittsburgh and Its Region,* ed. Joel A. Tarr (Pittsburgh: University of Pittsburgh Press, 2003), 41–63, esp. 45–51.

8. John N. Ingham, *Making Iron and Steel: Independent Mills in Pittsburgh, 1820–1920* (Columbus: Ohio State University Press, 1991).

9. Moxley, *From Rivers to Lakes,* 10–25; Leland R. Johnson, *The Davis Island Lock and Dam, 1870–1922* (Pittsburgh: U.S. Army Corps of Engineers, 1985).

10. Muller, "River City," 51–56; Edward K. Muller and Joel A. Tarr, "The Interaction of Natural and Built Environments in the Pittsburgh Landscape," in *Devastation and Renewal: An Environmental History of Pittsburgh and Its Region,* ed. Joel A. Tarr (Pittsburgh: University of Pittsburgh Press, 2003), 11–40.

11. Quoted in Joel A. Tarr and Terry F. Yosie, "Critical Decisions in Pittsburgh Water and Wastewater Treatment," in *Devastation and Renewal: An Environmental History of Pittsburgh and Its Region,* ed. Joel A. Tarr (Pittsburgh: University of Pittsburgh Press, 2003), 64–88, esp. 76.

12. Ibid.

13. Erwin E. Lanpher and C. F. Drake, *City of Pittsburgh, Pennsylvania: Its Water Works and Typhoid Fever Statistics* ([n.p.], 1930), 23–25. An online edition of this work, published

in 1999 by the University of Pittsburgh Digital Research Library, is available at http://digital
.library.pitt.edu/cgi-bin/t/text/textidx?idno=ooabv4381m;view=toc;c=pitttext.

14. Tarr and Yosie, "Critical Decisions," 69.

15. Ibid., 70–72.

16. Ibid., 70–74. Allegheny City was a separate city directly across the Allegheny River
from Pittsburgh until annexed by its larger neighbor in 1907.

17. Ibid., 74–77. Hazen had been the key engineer on the Pittsburgh Filtration Commission.

18. Ibid., 76–77.

19. Nicholas Casner, "Acid Mine Drainage and Pittsburgh's Water Quality," in *Devastation
and Renewal: An Environmental History of Pittsburgh and Its Region,* ed. Joel A. Tarr (Pittsburgh: University of Pittsburgh Press, 2003), 89–109.

20. Ibid.

21. Pittsburgh Flood Commission, *Report of the Flood Commission of Pittsburgh, Penna.
Containing the results of the surveys, investigations and studies made by the Commission for
the purpose of determining the causes of, damage by and methods of relief from floods in the
Allegheny, Monongahela, and Ohio rivers at Pittsburgh, Penna., together with the benefits
to navigation, sanitation, water supply and water power to be obtained by river regulation*
(Pittsburgh: Murdoch, Kerr & Co., 1912); Roland M, Smith, "The Politics of Pittsburgh Flood
Control, 1908–1936," *Pennsylvania History* 42 (1975): 5–24.

22. Frederick Law Olmsted Jr., *Main Thoroughfares and the Down Town District* (Pittsburgh:
Pittsburgh Civic Commission, 1911), 19–30, also available at http://pghbridges.com/articles/
olmsted/oointro/olmoooa.htm; John F. Bauman and Edward K. Muller, *Before Renaissance:
Planning in Pittsburgh, 1889–1943* (Pittsburgh: University of Pittsburgh Press, 2006), 72–86.

23. Citizens Committee on the City Plan of Pittsburgh, "Waterways: A Part of the Pittsburgh
Plan," Report No. 6 (Pittsburgh: Citizens Committee on the City Plan of Pittsburgh, 1923),
13–15, esp. 13; also available at http://digital.library.pitt.edu/cgi-bin/t/text/text-idx?idno=oohc
02396m;view=toc;c=pitttext.

24. Tarr and Yosie, "Critical Decisions," 78–79.

25. Ibid., 77–86.

26. Roy Lubove, *Twentieth-Century Pittsburgh,* 2nd ed., 2 vols. (Pittsburgh: University of
Pittsburgh Press, 1996), I: 106–41; Shelby Stewman and Joel A. Tarr, "Four Decades of Public-
Private Partnerships in Pittsburgh," in *Public-Private Partnerships in American Cities,* ed. R.
Scott Fosler and Renee A. Berger (Lexington, MA: Lexington Books, 1982), 59–127; Sherie
R. Mershon, "Corporate Social Responsibility and Urban Revitalization: The Allegheny Con-
ference on Community Development, 1943–1968" (Ph.D. diss., Carnegie Mellon University,
2000); Roland M. Smith, "The Politics of Pittsburgh Flood Control, 1936–1960," *Pennsylvania
History* 44 (1977): 3–24; Robert C. Alberts, *The Shaping of the Point: Pittsburgh's Renaissance Park* (Pittsburgh: University of Pittsburgh Press, 1980).

27. Muller, "River City," 57–63.

28. Lubove, *Twentieth-Century Pittsburgh,* II: 201–2.

29. M. Graham Netting, *50 Years of the Western Pennsylvania Conservancy* (Pittsburgh:
Western Pennsylvania Conservancy, 1982), 19.

30. Griswold, Winters, and Swain, *A Master Plan for the Development of Riverfronts and
Hillsides in the City of Pittsburgh: An Analysis of Their Best Possible Uses, for the Enhance-
ment of the City, and the Enjoyment of Its Citizens* (Pittsburgh: Department of Parks and Recreation, 1959), 3–5, esp. the dedication.

31. Edgar M. Hoover, *Economic Study of the Pittsburgh Region,* 3 vols. (Pittsburgh: University of Pittsburgh Press, 1963); John P. Hoerr, *And the Wolf Finally Came: The Decline of
the American Steel Industry* (Pittsburgh: University of Pittsburgh Press, 1988).

32. Lubove, *Twentieth-Century Pittsburgh,* II: 5–23.

33. For more on this project, see Chan Krieger & Associates et al., *A Vision Plan for Pittsburgh's Riverfronts* ([Pittsburgh]: Riverlife Task Force, [2001]), also available at http://www.riverlifetaskforce.org/about/news/publications.

34. Muller, "River City," 62–63.

35. Robert Hoskin, Michael Koryak, and Linda Stafford, *Fishes of Small Tributaries to the Allegheny and Monongahela Rivers in Allegheny County, Pennsylvania,* 3 Rivers 2nd Nature Fish Report: Monongahela and Allegheny (Pittsburgh: STUDIO for Creative Inquiry, Carnegie Mellon University, 2002), pt. III, sec. A, also available at http://3r2n.cfa.cmu.edu/water/fish/monAlleg/index.htm.

36. Robert Hoskin, Michael Koryak, et al., "The Impact of Above Grade Sewerline Crossing on the Distribution and Abundance of Fishes in Recovering Small Urban Streams of the Upper Ohio River Valley," *Journal of Freshwater Ecology* 164 (2001): 591–98, esp. 594.

37. Susan Kalisz and Jessica Dunn, *Riverbank Vegetation,* 3 Rivers 2nd Nature Botany Report: Allegheny River (Pittsburgh: STUDIO for Creative Inquiry, Carnegie Mellon University 2002), pt. IV, also available at http://3r2n.cfa.cmu.edu/land/bot/alleg/index.htm. See also Pennsylvania Economy League, *Investing in Clean Water: A Report from the Southwestern Pennsylvania Water and Sewer Infrastructure Project Steering Committee* (Pittsburgh: Southwestern Pennsylvania Water and Sewer Infrastructure Project, 2002). Attempts to resolve the mine acid problem included state and federal mine sealing programs, but these achieved only limited success. Not until the passage of state and federal legislation requiring active mining operations to treat polluted water prior to discharge did conditions finally improve; see Casner, "Acid Mine Drainage." In addition, see Jan Ackerman, "Mount Washington Residents Question Development Plans," *Pittsburgh Post Gazette,* May 29, 2003, http://www.post-gazette.com/neigh_city/20030529hillsidec5.asp; and Tom Barnes, "Council OKs Mining Project as Precursor to Hays Development," *Pittsburgh Post Gazette,* July 31, 2003, http://www.post-gazette.com/neigh_city/20030731miningc2.asp.

38. United States, *Nine Mile Run Ecosystem Restoration Project* ([Pittsburgh]: U.S. Army Corps of Engineers, Pittsburgh District, 2000); see also http://www.lrp.usace.army.mil/pm/9mile.htm.

39. For more information on these projects, see the U.S. Army Corps of Engineers' Web site for information on the *Ohio River Mainstem Systems Study (ORMSS) Interim Feasibility Report: Ohio River Ecosystem Restoration Program,* 7 vols., (2000), at http://www.lrl.usace.army.mil/ORMSS/; the U.S. Fish and Wildlife Service's Web site on its Ohio River Islands National Wildlife Refuge, at http://northeast.fws.gov/planning/ORIWEB/chap1.htm; and the Allegheny Land Trust's Web site, especially the pages related to the Whetzel Preserve, at http://www.alleghenylandtrust.org/properties/whetzel/overview/index.html.

40. Dieter Schott, "Rivers as Urban Environments: Cycles and Constellations in the Management and Perception of British Cities," lecture delivered at "The Making of European Contemporary Cities: An Environmental History," Third International Round Table on Urban Environmental History of the 19th and 20th Century, University of Siena, June 24–27, 2004, 89–96; Isabelle Backouche, "From Parisian River to National Waterway: The Social Functions of the Seine, 1750–1850," in *Rivers in History: Perspectives on Waterways in Europe and North America*, ed. Christof Mauch and Thomas Zeller (University of Pittsburgh Press, 2008), chap. 3.

41. For a comparison of rural and urban river development, see Susan Q. Stranahan, *Susquehanna: River of Dreams* (Baltimore: Johns Hopkins University Press, 1993); and Ari Kelman, *A River and Its City: The Nature of Landscape in New Orleans* (Berkeley: University of California Press, 2003). For an extreme example of an urban river, see Blake Gumprecht, *The Los*

Angeles River: Its Life, Death, and Possible Rebirth (Baltimore: Johns Hopkins University Press, 1999).

42. Eva Jakobsson, "How Do Historians of Technology and Environmental Historians Conceive the Harnessed River?" lecture delivered at "Rivers in History: Designing and Conceiving Waterways in Europe and North America" conference, Dec. 4–7, 2003, German Historical Institute, Washington, DC.

43. Edward K. Muller, "The Legacy of Industrial Rivers," *Pittsburgh History* 72 (1989): 46–75.

44. William Cronan, "Introduction: In Search of Nature," in *Uncommon Ground: Toward Reinventing Nature,* ed. William Cronan (New York: Norton, 1995), 23–66, esp. 25.

Part III

THE MODERN METROPOLIS

Introduction

The patterns of American urbanization and urban life shifted, often dramatically, in the years after 1920. As in the industrial era, dynamic growth and change remained a constant feature of the urban landscape. Some ninety years later, by the beginning of the second decade of the twentieth-first century, large central cities—some dynamic and growing, others troubled by declining populations and aging economies—had come to anchor sprawling metropolitan areas. Suburbia dominated the American residential pattern throughout the late twentieth century. By 2010, more than 150 million Americans, or just about 50 percent of the nation's total population, resided in the suburbs—a larger proportion than for those who lived in central cities or rural areas. Suburban home builders and home buyers had pushed out the residential periphery far beyond anything imagined in the nineteenth century. Nationwide, the percentage of metro population residing outside city boundaries continued to grow into the twenty-first century, while central city populations, with a few exceptions, declined further or remained relatively stable. By 2010, some fifty-one metropolitan areas in the United States each had more than one million residents. The rising population of giant metros also expanded urban peripheries and filled in empty spaces between existing cities and metropolitan areas.[1]

Vast metropolitan areas of cities and sprawling suburbs thus came to characterize urban America by the beginning of the twenty-first century. Unevenly distributed across the nation, metropolitan population has increasingly concentrated on the east and west coasts, in the Midwest industrial belt from Pittsburgh to Chicago, and in growing sunbelt regions such as Florida, Texas, and Arizona. In 2010, for instance, the New York City metropolitan region contained almost 19 million people spread over three states and 3,600 square miles, while the sprawling Los Angeles urbanized area of about 2,200 square miles was home to almost 13 million. A densely settled urbanized area of over 5.5 million people emerged along the southeast coast of Florida, a narrow elongated metropolis situated between the Atlantic Ocean and the Everglades and stretching about 110 miles from south of Miami north to Fort Pierce. The urbanized northeastern seaboard of the

United States—or "megalopolis," as it has been called—spread across twelve states from Virginia to Maine. This new monster metropolis included the Boston, New York, Philadelphia, and Washington, D.C., metropolitan areas and contained more than 50 million people by 2010. These statistics barely begin to suggest the consequences of volatile demographic change since the mid-twentieth century.[2]

DEMOGRAPHIC TRANSFORMATIONS

Huge population shifts within metropolitan regions have reshaped the United States since about 1940. Most of the older cities of the Northeast and Midwest—cities shaped economically and physically by the industrial revolution of the late nineteenth century—began losing substantial numbers of residents to suburban regions. The classic example is Saint Louis, which suffered a 63 percent population loss between 1950 and 2010, leaving the city with considerably fewer people than it had more than a century earlier in 1890. Similarly, by 2010 Detroit had lost 61 percent of its 1950 population of about 1.8 million. Cleveland and Pittsburgh lost 58 percent and 55 percent, respectively, of their 1950 populations by 2010. Most of the big "rustbelt" or "snowbelt" cities experienced similar population declines (see table P3.1). Boston lost 23 percent of its population between 1950 and 2010, while Baltimore dropped by 35 percent; Philadelphia and Chicago each lost 26 percent of their populations over the same sixty-year period. For smaller industrial snowbelt cities, the trend of central city population decline was much the same: Buffalo, Youngstown, Newark, Rochester, Providence, and Akron lost between 27 percent and 60 percent of 1950 population by 2010. During the same fifty-year period, however, other snowbelt cities, such as Columbus and Indianapolis, defied the pattern of decline and doubled or nearly doubled in population, suggesting differential demographic outcomes depending on economic or administrative functions. Both cities are state capitals that have developed as important regional and national centers of banking, insurance, information technology, and similar new economy businesses. Both cities host large urban public universities and advanced medical centers.

These demographic shifts in the older cities of the Northeast and Midwest reflected the significant economic changes, cultural transformations, and migration patterns that reshaped urban America in the late twentieth century. Beginning in the immediate postwar era, most of those fleeing the cities were middle-class and working-class whites, who found in the suburbs a more pleasant lifestyle and opportunities to demonstrate their upward economic mobility. The suburbs were appealing as well, because in the early postwar years they offered racial homogeneity and social exclusivity—a means of escaping the cramped housing, rising poverty, and racial diversity of the central cities. Real estate developers recognized the suburbanizing trend soon after World War II and transformed the home-building industry to meet the surging demand for new homes with garages, backyards, and green grass. Thus, while the central cities suffered the consequences of a declining population base, the suburban rings surrounding the cities expanded at an enormous rate, even as early as midcentury. Generally, most but not all central city populations in the Northeast and

Table P3.1. Representative Snowbelt Cities, 1950–2010

City and Year	Central City Population	Metropolitan Area Population	Percentage Metro Population in Central City	Percentage City Black	Percentage City Hispanic	Percentage City Foreign-Born
Baltimore						
1950	949,708	1,337,373	71.0	23.7	N/A	5.4
1980	786,775	2,172,757	36.2	54.8	1.0	3.1
1990	736,014	2,382,052	30.9	59.2	1.0	3.2
2000	651,154	2,552,994	25.5	64.3	1.7	4.6
2010	620,961	2,710,489	22.9	63.7	4.2	6.2
Boston						
1950	801,444	2,369,986	33.8	5.0	N/A	18.0
1980	562,994	2,943,747	14.3	22.5	6.5	15.5
1990	574,283	4,133,028	13.9	25.6	10.8	20.0
2000	589,141	4,391,344	13.4	25.3	14.4	25.8
2010	617,594	4,552,402	13.6	24.4	17.5	26.7
Chicago						
1950	3,620,962	5,495,364	65.9	13.6	N/A	14.5
1980	3,005,078	7,906,475	38.0	39.8	14.1	14.5
1990	2,783,726	8,182,041	34.0	39.1	19.6	16.9
2000	2,896,016	9,098,316	31.8	36.8	26.0	21.7
2010	2,695,598	9,461,105	28.5	32.9	28.9	21.0
Cleveland						
1950	914,808	1,465,511	62.4	16.2	N/A	14.5
1980	573,822	2,169,998	26.4	43.8	3.1	5.8
1990	505,616	2,102,177	24.1	46.6	4.6	4 1
2000	478,403	2,148,143	22.3	51.0	7.3	4.5
2010	385,890	2,077,240	18.6	54.9	10.2	4.9
Detroit						
1950	1,849,568	3,016,197	61.3	16.3	N/A	14.9
1980	1,203,339	4,353,243	27.6	63.0	2.4	5.7
1990	1,027,974	4,248,535	24.2	75.7	2.8	3.4
2000	951,270	4,452,557	21.4	81.6	5.0	4.8
2010	713,777	4,296,250	16.6	82.7	6.8	6.5
New York						
1950	7,891,957	12,911,994	61.1	9.5	N/A	22.6
1980	7,071,639	16,342,593	43.3	25.3	19.9	23.6
1990	7,322,564	16,844,432	43.5	28.7	24.4	28.4

2000	8,008,278	18,323,002	43.7	26.6	27.0	35.9
2010	8,175,133	18,897,109	43.3	24.6	28.6	35.9
Philadelphia						
1950	2,071,605	3,671,048	56.4	18.2	N/A	11.2
1980	1,688,210	5,238,957	32.2	37.8	3.8	6.4
1990	1,585,577	5,433,079	29.2	39.9	5.6	6.6
2000	1,517,550	5,687,147	26.7	43.2	8.5	9.0
2010	1,526,006	5,965,343	25.6	43.4	12.3	11.0
Pittsburgh						
1950	676,806	2,213,236	30.6	12.2	N/A	9.6
1980	423,938	2,441,781	17.6	24.0	0.8	5.2
1990	369,879	2,468,268	15.0	25.8	0.9	4.6
2000	334,563	2,431,087	13.8	27.1	1.3	5.6
2010	305,704	2,356,285	13.0	26.1	2.3	7.0
Saint Louis						
1950	856,796	1,681,281	51.0	18.0	N/A	4.9
1980	453,085	2,393,503	19.0	45.4	1.2	2.6
1990	396,685	2,600,058	14.1	47.5	1.3	2.5
2000	348,189	2,721,491	12.8	51.2	2.0	5.6
2010	319,294	2,812,896	11.4	49.2	3.5	6.3

Sources: U.S. Census, 1950, 1980, 1990, 2000, and 2010. Metropolitan area data for 1980 through 2010 are adapted from sociologist John Logan's Brown University project, "US 2010: Discover America in a New Century." For comparative purposes, metropolitan area populations are projected backward to 1980 based on 2010 Metropolitan Statistical Area boundaries. See http://www.s4.brown.edu/us2010/Data/Data.htm. For 2010, population data for foreign-born in cities are taken from the 2009 American Community Survey. See http://www.census.gov/acs.

Midwest were on the downswing, but virtually all major industrial cities witnessed a large population increase in their metropolitan area after 1950. The decentralizing trend slowed or began reversing slightly in a few northeastern and midwestern metropolises during the 1970s but surged forward again in the decades after 1980. For the entire period 1950 to 2010, the general trend of metropolitan population was upward as well as outward, countered only by a slight population shift back to some central cities such as Boston, New York, Philadelphia, and Washington, D.C., by the twenty-first century (see table P3.1).[3]

As urban whites fled for the suburban frontier, the shrinking central cities came to be more heavily populated by poor and low-income people, including greater percentages of blacks, Hispanics, and other new immigrant groups. The rapid turnover of urban population left the industrial snowbelt cities with a declining population base, and with people often characterized by precarious economic circumstances. A 1982 study by investigative journalist Ken Auletta demonstrated, for example, that almost two million middle-income people abandoned New York City between 1945 and 1980, while at least that many low-income people moved in. As a result, Auletta suggested, New York City developed "a permanent underclass."[4] As the population turned over and the cities aged, housing stock and infrastructure deteriorated. Every major American city faced rising social problems of poverty, unemployment or underemployment, welfare dependency, and social conflicts. An intense pattern of economic deindustrialization was occurring at the same time, as factories shut down or moved away. For example, in his important book *The Origins of the Urban Crisis* (1996), historian Thomas J. Sugrue documented the devastating social impact of automation and deindustrialization on automobile workers in Detroit during the immediate postwar years. Over several decades, the combination of a declining tax base and higher social service costs pushed some cities such as New York and Cleveland to the brink of bankruptcy in the 1970s; still other cities experienced serious fiscal dangers in the 1980s.[5]

During the twentieth century, U.S. central cities became home to heavy concentrations of African Americans. A great black migration from the rural and urban South to the urban North began during and after World War I. The human flow from the South slowed during the depression era of the 1930s but surged forward again after 1940. About 1.5 million blacks migrated from the South to the North and West each decade between 1940 and 1970. Central-city whites began moving to the expanding suburbs after World War II, aided by favorable federal housing, mortgage, tax, and highway programs. Black migration to the North created severe housing pressures in existing black communities. The white exodus to more distant suburbs opened up opportunities for blacks to break the racial housing barrier in aging, white neighborhoods in the inner city and older first-ring suburbs. This process of population turnover or displacement—the creation of what urban historians have called the "second ghetto"—dramatically altered the demographic character of the modern American city. Consequently, black population majorities or near majorities now prevail in such northern cities as Detroit, Baltimore, Washington, Cleveland, Saint Louis, Newark, and Gary. In Chicago and Philadelphia, the proportion of African Americans now stands at 33 percent and 43 percent, respectively. Blacks also became numerically dominant in many southern cities, including Atlanta, Birmingham, Richmond, and New Orleans. In 1890, about 90 percent of black Americans lived in the South, but by 1970 less than half of the black population remained in the region. Similarly, early in the twentieth century, blacks were heavily rural, but by the 1980s they had become the most urbanized of all racial groups in the United States. However, as jobs began disappearing in the urban and industrial heartland over the past few decades, blacks began moving back to southern states and cities.[6]

A working-class white migration from the South to northern and western destinations paralleled the black migration in the postwar decades. According to James N. Gregory's important book *The Southern Diaspora* (2005), an astonishing fifteen million white southerners moved out of the region between 1940 and 2000, more than double the black migration totals of about six million during the same sixty-year period. Coal miners from Appalachia and farmers from Kentucky, Tennessee, Alabama, and Arkansas, the white southern migrants sought to escape the poverty, low wages, and economic displacement that characterized the rural and small-town South. Like African Americans, they primarily headed for industrial jobs in Detroit, Cleveland, Chicago, and smaller industrial cities in Michigan, Ohio, Indiana, and Illinois.[7]

The twentieth-century American city has other newcomers, too. An enormous Hispanic migration, initially to the urban Southwest and more recently to most other parts of the nation, has added to the ethnic, linguistic, and political complexity of urban America. By 2010, more than one million Hispanics lived in Miami-Dade County, almost half of the entire population. The arrival of massive waves of Cubans after the success of Fidel Castro's Cuban Revolution in 1959 initiated a virtual demographic revolution in south Florida—a process intensified in more recent years with the emergence of large south Florida communities of Nicaraguans, Colombians, Dominicans, and others from the Caribbean basin. Hispanics made up almost 29 percent of New York City's population in 2010. Puerto Ricans began coming to New York in sizable numbers by midcentury, and in more recent years they have been joined by hundreds of thousands of Colombians, Dominicans, and other Latin newcomers. In Los Angeles, Hispanics—largely Mexican and Mexican-American—totaled almost half of the city's entire population of 3.8 million in 2010. In Houston, Dallas, San Antonio, El Paso, Albuquerque, Phoenix, San Diego, and other southwestern cities, the proportion of Hispanic residents has been rising rapidly. Even in Chicago, in the center of the industrial snowbelt, Mexican, Cuban, and Puerto Rican newcomers pushed the Hispanic population to 29 percent in 2010 (see tables P3.1 and P3.2). Southern states and cities, especially Atlanta, Charlotte, Nashville, Memphis, and Birmingham, have also become new immigrant destinations since the 1990s, reflecting the rising tide of Latino migration to the United States, primarily from Mexico and Central America. According to the 2010 census, the nation's largest minority comprised some fifty million Latinos, surpassing African Americans by a sizable amount. No longer primarily rural agricultural workers, Latinos have carved out a huge presence in the contemporary American city.[8]

Urban America, like its industrial era counterpart, has also exercised a magnetic attraction for millions of new immigrants. European immigrants provided the manpower to propel the industrial revolution in nineteenth-century America, but newcomers have been arriving from all over the globe. From Central America, South America, Asia and the Pacific region, the Caribbean, Africa, and the Middle East, immigrants have been pouring into the United States, driven by war, revolution, oppression, famine, natural disaster, and especially by thwarted economic aspiration. As in the past, cities have provided the widest range of opportunities for social adjustment and economic advancement. By the early 1980s, Los Angeles fully reflected this new pattern of immigrant and ethnic diversity. By that time, according to *Time* magazine writer Kurt Andersen, the largest ethnic and immigrant groups in the California metropolis, in addition to Mexicans, were Iranians, Salvadorans, Japanese, Chinese, Filipinos, Koreans, Vietnamese, Palestinians, Israelis, Colombians, Hondurans, Guatemalans, Cubans, East Indians, Pakistanis, and Samoans and other Pacific Islanders. According to the U.S. Census Bureau's American Community Survey in 2008, the foreign-born population of the City of Los Angeles stood at 39 percent of the total. Much of urban America now shares at least some of the ethnic and cultural complexity of Los Angeles. Among the larger cities, Boston, New York, Dallas, Houston, Miami, San Francisco, San José, and San Diego all had foreign-born populations above 25 percent in 2008 (see tables P3.1 and P3.2).[9]

Table P3.2. Representative Sunbelt Cities, 1950–2010

City and Year	Central City Population	Metropolitan Area Population	Percentage Metro Population in Central City	Percentage City Black	Percentage City Hispanic	Percentage City Foreign-Born
Albuquerque						
1950	98,815	145,673	67.8	1.2	N/A	2.6
1980	331,767	454,499	73.0	2.3	33.8	4.5
1990	384,736	599,416	64.2	3.0	34.5	5.5
2000	448,607	729,649	61.5	3.1	39.9	8.9
2010	545,842	887,077	61.5	3.3	46.7	10.9
Atlanta						
1950	331,314	671,797	49.3	36.6	N/A	1.3
1980	425,022	2,029,710	20.9	66.6	1.4	2.3
1990	394,017	3,069,425	12.8	67.1	1.9	3.4
2000	416,474	4,247,981	9.8	61.4	4.5	6.6
2010	420,003	5,268,860	8.0	54.0	5.2	7.8
Dallas						
1950	434,462	614,799	70.7	13.1	N/A	1.9
1980	904,074	2,957,091	30.6	29.3	12.2	6.1
1990	1,006,877	3,989,294	25.2	29.5	20.9	12.5
2000	1,188,580	5,161,544	23.0	25.9	35.6	24.4
2010	1,197,816	6,371,773	18.8	25.0	42.4	25.4
Houston						
1950	596,163	806,701	73.9	20.9	N/A	2.9
1980	1,595,167	3,157,072	50.5	27.6	17.6	9.8
1990	1,630,553	3,767,166	43.3	28.1	27.6	17.8
2000	1,953,631	4,715,407	41.4	25.3	37.4	26.4
2010	2,099,451	5,946,800	35.3	23.7	43.8	27.9
Los Angeles						
1950	1,970,358	4,367,911	45.1	8.7	N/A	12.5
1980	2,966,850	9,414,035	31.5	17.0	27.5	27.1
1990	3,485,398	11,266,628	30.9	14.0	39.9	38.4
2000	3,694,820	12,365,627	29.9	11.2	46.5	40.9
2010	3,792,621	12,828,837	29.6	9.6	48.5	39.5
Miami						
1950	249,276	495,084	50.4	16.2	N/A	10.8
1980	346,865	3,220,447	10.8	25.1	56.0	53.7
1990	358,548	4,055,975	8.8	27.4	62.5	59.7
2000	362,470	5,007,564	7.2	22.3	65.8	59.5
2010	399,457	5,564,635	7.2	19.2	70.0	56.5

Phoenix

1950	106,818	331,770	32.2	4.9	N/A	6.7
1980	789,704	1,599,970	49.4	4.8	14.8	5.7
1990	983,403	2,238,480	43.9	5.2	19.7	8.6
2000	1,321,045	3,251,876	40.6	5.1	34.1	19.5
2010	1,445,632	4,192,887	34.5	6.5	40.9	22.8

San Antonio

1950	408,442	500,460	81.6	7.0	N/A	8.0
1980	785,809	1,071,954	73.3	7.3	53.7	8.3
1990	935,933	1,407,745	66.5	7.0	55.6	9.4
2000	1,144,646	1,711,703	66.9	6.8	58.7	11.7
2010	1,327,407	2,142,508	62.0	6.9	63.2	13.4

San Diego

1950	334,387	556,808	60.1	4.5	N/A	7.0
1980	875,538	1,833,340	47.8	8.9	14.8	15.0
1990	1,110,549	2,476,568	44.8	9.4	20.7	20.9
2000	1,223,400	2,813,833	43.5	7.9	25.4	25.7
2010	1,307,401	3,095,313	42.2	6.7	28.9	25.5

Sources: U.S. Census, 1950, 1980, 1990, 2000, and 2010. Metropolitan area data for 1980 through 2010 are adapted from sociologist John Logan's Brown University project, "US2010: Discover America in a New Century." For comparative purposes, metropolitan area populations are projected backward to 1980 based on 2010 Metropolitan Statistical Area boundaries. See http://www.s4.brown/us2010/Data/Data.htm. For 2010, population data for foreign-born in cities are taken from the 2009 American Community Survey. See http://www.census.gov/acs.

SUBURBANIZATION

The central cities became new melting pots, while the suburban periphery continued to be mostly, but not completely, white and middle class. The suburban phenomenon dates back to the middle years of the nineteenth century, when new transit technology permitted a more widespread spatial distribution of urban population. Changing conceptions of the role of family and home emphasized the salutary effect of domesticity and private residential space, encouraging those who could afford it to abandon increasingly congested cities. At the same time, romanticized views of nature led some Americans to distance themselves from the commercialism, industrial pollution, and other problems of the rapidly growing cities. Early urban decentralization found further support with the introduction in the mid-nineteenth century of a cheap new building technology—the balloon-frame house—which transformed home building into a profitable industry for land speculators and suburban developers.[10]

The suburban pattern intensified in the twentieth century. By the 1940s, the automobile had displaced urban mass transit systems, and road building opened up distant fringe areas for suburban development. The real estate industry played a major role as well, mass-producing houses in look-alike communities from New York to California, typified by the well-known Levittowns in New York, New Jersey, and Pennsylvania. Having developed a series of new assembly-line building techniques during World War II, William Levitt rapidly erected affordable homes in the late 1940s and early 1950s to meet the intense demand for new housing. Levitt's construction crews completed 150 houses per week by 1948, eventually putting up 17,400 look-alike homes on former potato farms on Long Island and additional thousands in his New Jersey and Pennsylvania Levittown projects. Developers throughout the country followed Levitt's lead. In 1955, Houston developer Frank Sharp built a similar large planned community of several thousand homes and apartments. Like many other housing developers, Sharp consciously modeled his suburban creation on Levittown, even naming it after himself—Sharpstown. Similar mass-produced suburban communities sprouted in Illinois, Michigan, California, and Arizona. Also important in the twentieth-century development of suburbia, however, was the shaping role of the federal government after the mid-1930s. Federal highway, housing, mortgage, and tax policies all helped promote the dispersal of the urban population, particularly the white population, in the years after World War II.[11]

Although most of the poor and racial minorities remained behind in the deteriorating central cities, growing numbers of African Americans, and later other minorities, joined the postwar suburban movement. Like their white middle class counterparts, blacks fled inner cities in search of newer housing, more living space, better schools, and less crime. Just as they had historically met resistance when trying to move from racial ghettos into all-white inner-city neighborhoods, blacks typically encountered opposition from white suburbanites. As whites moved farther out to the metropolitan fringe, blacks bought homes in older, inner-ring suburbs bordering central cities, where they often found the same underfunded schools, high crime rates, and substandard municipal services left behind by departing white families. The rate of African-American suburbanization increased, but as historian Andrew Wiese noted in his landmark book *Places of Their Own* (2004), segregation generally persisted throughout metropolitan regions.[12]

In Los Angeles, Houston, and other cities with rapidly changing ethnic populations, Latinos and Asians followed the American dream of suburban homeownership. One such community, Monterey Park, a city of 60,000 in Los Angeles County, has been described as the first suburban Chinatown. Taiwanese immigrants first began arriving in the 1970s, followed in the 1980s by mainland Chinese immigrants. Asians made up 67 percent of the city's 2010 population, while Hispanics numbered about 27 percent and white Americans 19 percent. In 2010, in the small city of Chamblee just outside Atlanta, Latinos, Asians, and blacks made up 74 percent of the population. In two huge suburban counties just outside Washington, D.C.—Fairfax County, Virginia (2010 population: 1,081,726) and Montgomery County, Maryland (2010 population: 971,777)—the proportion of minority residents in 2010 reached 45 percent and 51 percent, respectively. Beginning in the 1990s, blacks, Latinos, and Asians gradually began replacing whites in Houston's Sharpstown. In the Miami metropolitan area, the suburban city of Hialeah began in the 1920s as a white working-class community of modest homes, but by 2010 Hispanics made up 95 percent of its population. Multiethnic and multiracial suburban communities are no longer unusual in many parts of the nation, reflecting the way in which migration, immigration, and intermarriage have been changing the United States.[13]

In recent years, suburbs have experienced many of the problems that their new residents hoped to leave behind in the cities. A 1995 special report in *Newsweek* titled "Bye-Bye, Suburban Dream," highlighted the ingredients of this emerging suburban dilemma: crime, drugs, traffic congestion, overcrowded schools, poor planning, environmental damage, declining governmental revenues, and rising expenses for social programs, among other problems. Ultimately, *Newsweek* seemed to suggest, suburbia provided no panacea for those seeking to escape big-city life. And suburbia's problems have persisted into the twenty-first century. The mortgage and foreclosure crisis that began in 2008 has pushed hundreds of thousands of families out of their homes, decimated suburban neighborhoods, and left banks in possession of abandoned and declining properties.[14]

DECENTRALIZATION AND DEINDUSTRIALIZATION

Following those who departed inner cities for the crabgrass frontier, industry, retail, and jobs moved to the metropolitan fringe as well. Alongside the acres of suburban housing subdivisions, massive factories, office parks, and sprawling shopping malls sprang up outside core city areas. The decentralization of business began right after World War II, when major corporations in New York City began relocating their corporate offices from Manhattan to suburban Westchester County, just north of the city. By 1955, IBM, General Electric, General Foods, Union Carbide, Pepsico, AT&T's long-distance division, and other business behemoths pioneered postwar corporate decentralization to Westchester. In contrast to the congested streets, high real estate prices, and cramped quarters of central cities, suburban relocation provided many advantages to corporate businesses. Large tracts of land available on the urban fringe allowed for the construction of sprawling office parks or one-story factories, ideally suited to assembly-line production, with plenty of parking for workers. The enormous interstate highway system provided trucks easy access to manufacturing plants and warehouses. At the same time, taking advantage of good roads and the proliferation of automobiles, retailers followed population to the suburbs. Department stores, once the anchors of the central business district, opened branches in distant shopping centers and often closed their flagship downtown stores as customer numbers declined. Retail trends favored suburban shopping malls with acres of parking. The loss of residents and businesses leeched tax dollars from aging central cities, which increasingly possessed fewer resources to support municipal services.[15]

The metropolitan decentralization following World War II, spearheaded by the proliferation of suburbia, has taken many forms. Joel Garreau of the *Washington Post* coined the term "edge cities" to describe the urban nodes of office buildings, hotels, shopping malls, and high-rise residential buildings that developed at the intersections of interstate highways outside large central cities. Garreau counted two hundred edge cities across the nation by the late 1980s.[16] In the 1970s and 1980s, demographers also noted the growth of rural and nonmetropolitan areas, labeled by some as "exurbia."

During the 1970s, for instance, rural and small-town America grew more rapidly than the urban and suburban regions of the nation. A 1983 demographic analysis in *Scientific American* pointed out that the rate of urbanization slowed for the first time during that decade. Some nonmetropolitan growth reflected lifestyle choices among more affluent or retired Americans who could afford to move to Nevada, Colorado, Idaho, or Utah. There was a perception at the time that the fast-growing mountain and northwestern states did not share the problems of urban-centered life in California or New York. Yet, as the *Scientific American* study suggested, these new population clusters represented only "small centers of urban culture transplanted to the country-side and enabled to survive by recent advances in communications, transportation, and methods of industrial production." Nevertheless, the migration to the mountain states persisted into the 1990s and beyond. By the early twenty-first century, the nation's fastest-growing metropolitan areas included Las Vegas; Greeley, Colorado; St. George, Utah; Bend, Oregon; and Boise, Idaho. All were growing primarily from internal migration.[17]

To a certain extent, the rise of nonmetropolitan America reflected the shifting character of the nation's urban and industrial economy. In recent decades, the manufacturing economies of the urban industrial heartland experienced dramatic transformation, even significant decline in many cases. The deindustrial pattern began soon after World War II, as New England cotton, wool, and textile mills began closing down and moving to small towns in southern states where nonunion labor prevailed, and where wages, taxes, and other costs were considerably lower. By the 1950s, industrial plants began relocating to the South, as well. Northern unions and the liberal media coined the term "runaway plants" to describe what later became known as deindustrialization.[18]

Industrial relocation to the South and to nonmetropolitan America continued for years, sucking the economic life out of northern factory cities and towns. By the 1970s and 1980s, large multinational corporations began shutting down factories in the old industrial belt and transferring production overseas to South Korea, China, Taiwan, Mexico, and Third World nations. High labor costs in the United States, stiff foreign competition, higher energy costs, corporate mergers and buyouts, and extensive employee downsizing all resulted in a massive reorganization of the American economy during the late twentieth century. The powerful drive for productivity and profit that led to factory closings caused heavy blue-collar unemployment, middle-management layoffs, and troubled times in such basic industries as textiles, automobiles, and steel. Large cities with diverse economies adjusted to change, but many single-industry cities, such as steel-producing Gary and Youngstown, rubber-tire-city Akron, and auto-city Detroit, withered economically. As early as the 1980s, some observers began predicting the obsolescence of the nation's aging industrial cities.[19]

As more traditional forms of manufacturing and production declined, a postindustrial and service-oriented economy rose to take its place. This process of economic transformation was well under way in the aftermath of World War II. As early as 1955, service and professional workers outnumbered blue-collar manufacturing laborers. The industrial sector employed fewer than half as many workers as the growing service economy by the 1980s. Over the past thirty to forty years, the American economy has been powered by tremendous expansion in the postindustrial service sector. Many of these service jobs are now held by women, who entered the labor force in large numbers in the postwar era. By 2007, nearly 60 percent of all women over age sixteen held jobs, all but 6 percent of them in service occupations. In the same year, the service economy employed an astonishing 83 percent of the entire labor force of about 150 million, while manufacturing workers had dropped to 10 percent. The rapidly growing service economy involved huge job gains in education, medical care, computer technology, information and data processing, business services, recreational activities, shopping malls, big-box retail, fast-food and motel chains, airline travel, and the like. Such new service businesses, mostly concentrated in urban areas, have become essential ingredients in the new American economy. Government employment and government services have become especially important in the new scheme of things. By 2007, government at all levels in the United States employed more than 22 million civilian workers.[20]

Responding to deindustrialization and the rising service economy, many cities promoted new forms of economic development and urban revitalization. Once the home of both the manufacturing and administrative sectors of American business, industrial cities suffered the loss of factories to suburban, sunbelt, and foreign locations. However, by the last decades of the twentieth century, business activity involving government, finance, law, and communications monopolized office space in new downtown skyscrapers. Expanding urban universities and medical complexes ("eds and meds") gobbled up central city space and frequently employed the largest number of workers in the cities. Local governments invested in new venues such as ballparks, convention centers, theaters, concert halls, museums, and gambling casinos to bring suburbanites, conventioneers, and tourists downtown. Municipal officials engaged in intense competition with other cities and resorts for entertainment dollars, aggressively seeking visitors to stay in new luxury hotels, dine at fancy restaurants, and attend cultural and sporting events during their stay. New Urbanist planning and design that emphasized urban sustainability and pedestrian-friendly community development caught on in many places. Similarly, cities encouraged gentrification of aging homes and businesses so that well-educated and affluent workers could choose downtown residences close to work rather than commute from distant suburbs. Despite the complaints of critics who questioned downtown economic redevelopment at the expense of neighborhood concerns, local governments continued to invest in revenue-producing enterprises believed to ease the strain on beleaguered municipal budgets.[21]

THE RISE OF SUNBELT CITIES

Linked to the shifting American economy is the dramatic rise of the sunbelt cities of the South and Southwest. In 1920, nine of the ten largest U.S. cities were located in the Northeast and Midwest. The same was true in 1950. Only Los Angeles was able to break into the top ten cities in population during that period. With a little more than 600,000 people in 1950, Minneapolis was larger than Atlanta, Dallas, Houston, Phoenix, San Antonio, or San Diego—all future megacities. But several decades of shifting demographic and economic activity made a huge difference in the regional distribution of urban and metropolitan population. In 2000, six of the ten largest American cities were located in the Southwest—Los Angeles, Houston, Dallas, Phoenix, San Diego, and San Antonio. According to the 2010 census, San José joined the list, replacing Detroit as the nation's tenth-largest city. Among metropolitan areas in 2000, five of the ten largest had sunbelt zip codes: Los Angeles, Dallas, Houston, Atlanta, and Phoenix. By 2010, the sunbelt still had five of the largest metros, but Miami had displaced Phoenix, primarily because the Census Bureau had adjusted the boundaries of metro Miami from two to three counties (see tables P3.1 and P3.2).

These sunbelt cities and metro areas never experienced the nineteenth-century industrial revolution. They are twentieth-century automobile cities, less densely settled and more widely extended over the urban and suburban landscape. Aided by mid-twentieth-century highway building and widespread automobile ownership in the postwar era, sunbelt city populations pushed out the boundaries of the urban and metropolitan periphery. Annexation of surrounding territory, which had virtually ceased for older cities by the early twentieth century, became a way of life in the urban Southwest. Between 1950 and 2010, for instance, Houston grew from 160 to 579 square miles, and Oklahoma City from 51 to 621 square miles. By 2010 Phoenix had expanded by annexation to 519 square miles from 17 in 1950. By contrast, with 130 square miles in the 1850s, Philadelphia only marginally increased by 5 square miles in 2010. Similarly, New York City's 299 square miles of territory has barely changed since 1898. Boston, a city of 48 square miles, has been hemmed in by inner-ring suburbs since the late nineteenth century. Aggressive acquisition of peripheral land by southwestern cities has resulted in sprawling, low-density urban living. For instance, 2010 population densities in Phoenix and Houston stood at 3,072 and 3,897 per square mile, respectively. By comparison, within a much smaller municipal footprint, New York City's density surpassed 27,500 people per square mile. In several ways, however, newer sunbelt cities are similar to the older northern cities. Despite massive central-city annexations, the peripheral suburban regions of the metropolitan sunbelt have been growing more rapidly than the central city areas since the 1980s.[22]

The explosive postwar urban development of the sunbelt South and Southwest stemmed largely from deep structural changes in the American economy and consequent new migration flows. Urban growth in the sunshine regions began in earnest during World War II, when the federal government built dozens of new air bases, naval bases, and military training facilities in the southern and western states. From San Francisco, Los Angeles, and San Diego on the west coast to Pensacola, Tampa, Miami, and Jacksonville in Florida, the sunbelt cities profited from the federal military connection. Military airfields surrounded San Antonio, aircraft production boosted Seattle and Los Angeles, the aerospace industry propelled Houston's post-1950 expansion, and big U.S. Navy facilities fueled growth and prosperity in San Diego, Jacksonville, and Norfolk. Initiated during the World War II era, this vast federal defense spending established the foundation for economic prosperity and urban growth in the region, and it persisted through the Cold War era and beyond.[23]

At the same time, the emerging sunbelt cities were benefiting from the changing nature of the modern American economy. With little inherited from the industrial era, the sunbelt cities grew as the nation's economy moved away from factory production toward a technology-based, informational, and service economy. In the sunbelt cities and states, high-tech industries such as aerospace, electronics, and computers, along with energy development in the southwestern "oil patch," attracted new workers and provided important stimuli to urbanization. As postwar prosperity roared ahead during the 1950s, the amenities factor also came into play. Americans with more leisure time, paid vacations, and higher disposable incomes avidly pursued recreational interests. Every American child wanted a trip to Disneyland in California or Disney World in Florida. The completion of the federal interstate highway system permitted even working-class Americans to become winter vacationers in the sunshine regions of the country. As Americans lived longer and retired earlier, the elderly as early as the 1950s began a migration of their own to Florida, Arizona, and other retirement havens in the urban sunbelt—an early internal migration to the nation's sunshine regions, partially facilitated by monthly Social Security checks. The mass production of air-conditioned homes by the 1950s also undergirded sunbelt expansion by facilitating comfortable year-round residence in humid tropical or arid desert climes such as Florida and Arizona. For whatever reason, 5.5 million Americans migrated from the Northeast and Midwest to the sunbelt regions during the 1970s and ever since, as reflected in the growth patterns of states like Florida, Arizona, and Nevada.[24]

The shifting pattern of the American economy provided a major impetus to sunbelt city growth. In the postindustrial era, the looming, almost interchangeable glass and steel skyscrapers of Atlanta, Miami, Houston, Dallas, and Los Angeles suggested the power and the persistence of the information age. Yet the rising trajectory of sunbelt regions experienced some setbacks, such as the oil bust of the 1980s that hammered Houston and other Gulf Coast cities. Hurricane Katrina devastated New Orleans in 2005, and the housing bubble and mortgage crisis beginning in 2008 financially decimated homeowners in sunbelt states such as Florida, Arizona, Nevada, and California. Nevertheless, the new urban America of the South and Southwest benefited enormously from the growth of the postindustrial service economy.

Some of the older northern cities with diverse economies adjusted to economic change. Still economically vital, Chicago, New York, Philadelphia, Boston, and Minneapolis nurtured important cultural, educational, and medical services and industries, even as their peripheral areas surged ahead as well. Some older industrial-era cities transformed themselves in the postindustrial age: Pittsburgh and Birmingham, once grimy steel-producing cities, are now known primarily for higher education and medical services, key elements in the new economy. Washington, D.C., remains in a class of its own. The city and its huge nineteen-county metro area has surged ahead in recent decades, largely due to the vast expansion of federal government agencies and employment, but also because of the powerful political, intellectual, and global service activities attracted to the nation's capital. The shifting urban pattern of the last half century or so, in short, reflected both the changing nature of the American economy and the enormous new migration flows to the sunbelt South and Southwest.

URBAN POLICY AND POLITICS

Important transformations in urban policy and politics accompanied urban demographic and economic change. Beginning in the New Deal era of the 1930s, the federal government initiated for the first time a political partnership with the cities. President Franklin D. Roosevelt built a new Democratic Party coalition, relying heavily on the urban electorate for his political success. As federal intervention, initiative, and activism became the order of the day, social legislation and public works programs flowed out of Washington, D.C., much of it aimed at city residents and metropolitan problems. New Deal agencies such as the Works Progress Administration (WPA) and the Public Works Administration (PWA) put millions of the urban unemployed to work and saved municipalities from bankruptcy. Moreover, federal agencies built roads, bridges, airports, schools, parks, municipal buildings, and other public works that became an indispensable part of the nation's urban infrastructure for decades thereafter. Since the age of Roosevelt, the cities have sought out and become reliant on the federal financial connection. Massive infusions of federal dollars funded public housing, urban renewal, mass transit, highway and public works construction, public health, and public welfare. In the 1960s, President Lyndon B. Johnson revived the New Deal spirit with his Great Society initiatives. The War on Poverty, the Model Cities programs, community development efforts, and the civil rights crusade all had their roots in the cities. At about the same time, social scientists and journalists discovered an "urban crisis," as explosions of racial violence rocked cities across the nation, from Harlem to Watts, and from Chicago and Detroit to Newark and Washington, D.C.[25]

The burned-out ghettos of the late 1960s suggested to many the failure of federal urban policy. In fact, the federal programs that shaped urban America after the mid-1930s did not always have positive effects. A national transportation policy emphasizing highways and the automobile ultimately siphoned population and economic activities away from the central city and toward the urban periphery. Urban expressways tore through existing neighborhoods, destroyed housing, and left huge empty spaces in the urban cores. Federal mortgage policies, especially those provided by the Federal Housing Administration and the Veterans Administration, made it possible for working-class urbanites to obtain their dream house in the suburbs. However, a residential appraisal system initiated by the Home Owners Loan Corporation, another New Deal agency, resulted in redlining by banks and mortgage companies and the ultimate physical decay of many inner-city urban neighborhoods. Federal public housing programs promoted residential segregation of the races and encouraged the image of suburbia as a haven from the problems of the city. Urban renewal often disrupted or demolished low-income neighborhoods and generally benefited urban real estate interests. The high-rise public housing projects that went up in many cities in the 1950s became unlivable vertical ghettos, and many such projects—in Newark, Chicago, and Saint Louis, for example—have been dynamited to the ground in recent years. Thus, some federal programs had negative consequences for the cities.[26]

On the other hand, heightened federal activism beginning in the 1930s brought many positive advances for American cities. New Deal agencies not only put millions of unemployed people to work, but financed the construction of needed airports, bridges, subway systems, modern water and sewer systems, parks and recreational facilities, and, according to one recent estimate, more than 500,000 miles of streets and 110,000 public buildings such as schools and post offices. To get access to federal funding, city governments had to modernize their operations and develop planning procedures and more efficient management practices. In the 1960s, President Johnson's urban policies were plagued by mismanagement and political infighting; nevertheless, antipoverty programs such as Head Start, community action initiatives, and various neighborhood-based services brought important benefits to the urban poor.[27]

The difficulties of urban policy making, along with a changing national political climate, brought a dramatic reversal of public policy and federal activism beginning in the 1970s with the Nixon, Ford, and Carter administrations. In the 1980s, the Reagan administration initiated massive federal cutbacks in the public works and social programs that had moved the cities forward in the 1960s. Seeking to turn back the governmental intervention that marked the New Deal and the Great Society, presidents Ronald Reagan and George H. W. Bush, along with their conservative Republican supporters, attempted to return social policy to the marketplace. Reagan's idea of urban policy was to urge the unemployed in declining cities to seek new jobs in more prosperous regions of the nation. During the Reagan era, tens of thousands of unemployed Michigan autoworkers migrated to Texas cities, where the "blue platers" (a reference to Michigan's blue auto license plate) arrived just in time for the big oil bust of the 1980s. Nationally and locally, a powerful conservative political movement surged to the surface during the 1970s and 1980s, bringing budget cuts, retrenchment, and privatization to the forefront of urban policy making.[28]

The policy dilemmas of the Reagan era persisted into the 1990s and beyond. Committed to finding a "third way" for American cities as part of a centrist political agenda that had wide political appeal, Democratic president Bill Clinton continued the push for decentralization by supporting enterprise zones. Pledging to achieve a balanced budget, he signed bills that revamped the nation's welfare system and required public housing residents to perform community service to retain their lodging subsidies. His successor, Republican George W. Bush, did little for cities except promote the idea of "faith-based" solutions, and he generally subscribed to the pro-business policies prevalent since the Reagan years. The election of Democrat Barack Obama in 2008 offered big-city mayors and urban interest groups hope that the federal government would devote greater attention to the worsening plight of the cities. But war, recession, and political battles over health-care and financial services reforms diverted Obama's attention from urban policy during his first term.[29]

Changes in urban policy have paralleled major transformations in the urban political pattern. After the mid-twentieth century, local politics increasingly reflected the shifting racial demography of the cities. With the black migration from the South and the simultaneous white exodus to the suburbs, blacks eventually came to dominate urban politics in many cities, large and small. Since 1967, when black mayors were first elected in Cleveland and Gary, blacks have succeeded to the mayoralty in numerous cities, including New York, Detroit, Philadelphia, Chicago, Baltimore, Newark,

Camden, New Orleans, Los Angeles, Atlanta, Richmond, Birmingham, Memphis, Charlotte, Hartford, and Washington, D.C. Even cities with relatively small black populations, such as Denver, Seattle, and Minneapolis, have elected black mayors in recent years. In Miami, Los Angeles, Albuquerque, San Antonio, and Denver, Hispanic politicians rose to the mayoralty. And beginning in the 1990s, reflecting changing patterns of gender relations and the power of the women's movement, voters elevated women to mayoralty positions in San Francisco, Pittsburgh, Houston, Dallas, San Diego, Minneapolis, Portland, San José, Tulsa, Fort Worth, and Washington, D.C. Tempering the unprecedented electoral successes of minorities and women, however, was the realization that the new mayors often faced a host of intractable financial and social problems that made control of city hall a hollow prize. Elected to the highest local offices at a time of rapid urban decline, early black mayors especially found their cities depleted by deindustrialization and population loss; with municipal coffers empty, they relied upon declining state and federal dollars to deliver services and balance budgets.[30]

It seemed clear by the 1980s that the old political machines that dominated such cities as Chicago and Detroit had fallen into disarray, at least for a time, as black political leaders built new coalitions with Hispanic voters and white liberals. For instance, the old Chicago Democratic machine that kept Mayor Richard J. Daley in office for twenty years collapsed in the early 1980s, permitting a black former Congressman, Harold Washington, to rise to the mayoralty. However, urban politics had become much more complex by the end of the twentieth century. Minority political power in the cities seemed on the wane in some places, as white politicians regained power in Chicago, Philadelphia, New York, and Los Angeles. Even in Gary, Indiana, where the minority population surpassed 86 percent in 1990, voters in 1995 sent a white candidate to the mayor's office when several black candidates divided the African-American vote. By 2006, however, black voters reclaimed Gary's mayoralty.[31]

Sweeping political transformations affected rising sunbelt cities, too. Lacking powerful ethnic voting blocs and a machine tradition, these cities mostly had been controlled politically by local business and professional elites. Motivated by the booster mentality, the urban elites sought to govern in the interests of the central-city business community, at least until the 1960s. The rapid growth of suburbia, however, resulted in newer forms of urban political conflict in which city and suburb struggled for dominance and control. Many of the issues were spatial or territorial, such as where highways or public housing would be located, what areas would be annexed, or which schools would be integrated by busing. Some places resolved these conflicts with experiments in new governmental structures: the creation of a powerful metropolitan government for Miami-Dade County in 1957; the establishment of a metropolitan service district with wide-ranging regional power in Portland, Oregon, in 1992; and city-county consolidations in Nashville, Jacksonville, Indianapolis, Lexington, Anchorage, and Louisville since the 1960s. In southern California, where suburban bedroom communities mushroomed after World War II, Los Angeles County pioneered the Lakewood Plan, contracting to supply a package of services and utilities to Lakewood and numerous other municipalities. Elsewhere, political leaders in Memphis,

Birmingham, and Charlotte sought city-suburban consolidations, but voters rejected these metropolitan government solutions.[32]

The vast demographic transformations of the cities in the late twentieth century eventually pushed urban politics into a new and more participatory phase. City-suburban battles have long since been supplanted by issues revolving around race, ethnicity, and neighborhood. Neighborhoods and local communities, urban historian Carl Abbott has written, have become "focal points for political action."[33] In Miami, for instance, with its "tri-ethnic" population of whites, blacks, and Hispanics, virtually every local political issue is now perceived in terms of race and ethnicity. As the immigrant newcomers to the cities—people from Asia and Latin America, from the Caribbean and the Pacific Basin—become citizens and voters, this new pattern of pluralistic urban politics will certainly intensify in the future. But as former Albuquerque mayor David Rusk pointed out in 1995, only metropolitan government can enable cities and suburbs to effectively confront areawide problems such as urban transit, water supply, and environmental regulation that cut across municipal boundaries.[34] The need to address issues affecting entire metropolitan regions could be seen clearly in the concern over rising energy costs at the close of the twentieth century. Reliance on petroleum products for transportation and the expense of heating and cooling homes and businesses made conservation and the development of new energy sources a concern for all residents of metropolitan America.

As in the industrial era, modern metropolis served as a crucible of growth, diversity, and dynamic change. Despite evidence of decline in some areas, the American city has demonstrated a remarkable capacity for adaptation to new circumstances. Many contemporary central cities face entrenched problems, but a new urban vitality can be found in renewal efforts for downtown development and in the edge cities out on the fringes of metropolitan areas. Although fragmented socially, urban America seems to be periodically regenerated, as new population groups come to make cities their home. The traditional industrial economy has faded, but newer forms of economic activity appropriate to new technologies and a service economy have taken the place of older patterns of production. The changing urban political structure has reflected the dramatic demographic and economic shifts of recent decades. Progressive reformers of the early twentieth century thought of the American city as "the hope of the future."[35] As the history of the modern American city suggests, tension has always existed between utopian visions and urban reality. Nevertheless, it is quite likely that, although the details will surely be different, the twenty-first-century American metropolis will continue to offer the nation a threshold for growth, change, and renewal.

In the following essays, urban historians pursue some of the diverse strands of twentieth-century urban life in the United States. The Great Depression of the 1930s brought serious problems of unemployment and relief to cities throughout the United States. Most interpretations of President Franklin D. Roosevelt's New Deal program build on the proposition that urban America benefited enormously from an energetic and expansive federal government. That may have been true for cities in the Northeast and Midwest, but Roger Biles demonstrates that things were considerably different in the South. In his chapter on the New Deal in Dallas, Biles challenges the now dominant view that FDR's new federal programs brought significant modernization and reform to the urban South. In Dallas, an autonomous local business elite, shaped by a conservative political culture, generally ignored the human and social consequences of the depression. City welfare expenditures were sharply cut back despite rising unemployment. Few gains were made by organized labor, as the Dallas business community supported the antiunion open shop movement. Little was accomplished in the way of new infrastructure and public works projects. Existing "Jim Crow" racial customs persisted, and African Americans suffered high rates of joblessness, political exclusion, and segregated housing. Moreover, New Deal agencies in Washington condoned racial segregation in Dallas and elsewhere in the South. In the final analysis, Biles contends, the New Deal had a strikingly minimal impact on Dallas. Local business elites demonstrated little support for new federal innovations, and the weight of traditional social customs such as racial segregation remained unchallenged. Most New Deal programs depended on local implementation, but where local officials were hostile to federal intrusion into local affairs, little could be accomplished. New Deal activism has often been portrayed as beneficial to urban America, but this Dallas case study suggests a more complex alternative interpretation.

The racial transformation of U.S. metropolitan regions after World War II resulted from the Second Great Migration, in which millions of African Americans left the South and resettled in northern and western cities. The black migration coincided with a postwar exodus of urban whites to mushrooming new suburbs, facilitated by the mass production of housing subdivisions and the construction of urban interstates. These demographic shifts produced racial conflict in the cities. Blacks sought to break out of rigidly segregated neighborhoods in search of housing, while remaining whites resisted housing transitions. These events took place in dozens of cities against a backdrop of civil rights protest and a repudiation of New Frontier / Great Society liberalism. However, as historian Thomas J. Sugrue explains in his case study of race and politics in Detroit, Michigan, racial cleavages existed well before white working-class voters in northern cities deserted the Democratic New Deal coalition and embraced the racist candidacy of Alabama governor George C. Wallace. Sugrue finds the seeds of the white political backlash in the 1940s and 1950s. These were tumultuous decades for the cities, a time when deindustrialization, job loss, and rapid demographic change threatened the economic and social well-being of embattled white homeowners. Forming homeowners' associations and neighborhood protective organizations, Detroit's whites employed the language of rights to safeguard their communities against what they perceived to be an invasion by blacks whose arrival threatened racial mixing and deflated real estate values. In particular, white opposition to public housing for low-income African Americans especially helped build the case against activist government, undermined white working-class loyalty to the New Deal, and fostered hostility toward the liberalism of the 1960s. Seeing how the combustible issue of race and housing in Detroit and other cities shaped local politics at a time of economic contraction allows historians to understand the conservative challenge to liberal reform nationally that surfaced later in the postwar era.

In the decades following World War II, U.S. metropolitan areas experienced significant changes as older industrial central cities lost population, industry, and retail to suburbs and the sunbelt. Urban historians, geographers, and other social scientists have carefully documented the economic, political, and demographic transformations caused by postwar decentralization and deindustrialization, but they have given relatively short shrift to the cultural manifestations of urban change. Eric Avila's essay considers these dramatic changes in the context of a rising political conservatism that rejected the city's heterogeneity and embraced a new suburban ideal based upon white homeownership, traditional gender roles, and racial exclusion. The resultant "chocolate cities and vanilla suburbs," he contends, stemmed from the deliberate actions of local officials, planners, developers, and policy makers in Washington, D.C., who responded to the fears and desires of a public fleeing the cities in search of jobs and housing in a more inviting environment. The author looks at two examples of the interplay between popular culture and alterations in urban form during the post–World War II era. First, he discusses the motion picture genre of the late 1940s and early 1950s characterized as film noir, a series of hard-boiled crime tales set in dark and uninviting urban settings. Film noir linked the deterioration of urban America with rising social disorder, especially the declining state of race and sexual relations. Second, he posits California's Disneyland as the archetypal suburban antidote to the racial and sexual upheaval threatening the traditional order of the industrial city. Nestled in booming Orange County and tied politically to the rising tide of Reagan Republicanism, Disneyland presented an idealized vision of suburbia as a safe haven from the urban evils graphically depicted in film noir fare. Avila's essay reminds us how popular culture can both reflect and shape historical change.

The interstate highway system, mostly completed between 1956 and 1973, had a powerful stimulating effect on American economic growth and suburban development. The interstates did more than just link the major cities in a national transportation network. They also penetrated the central cities and encircled them with beltways. Big city mayors, planners, and business interests believed that urban expressways would "save" the central cities from the negative consequences of economic deconcentration and suburban decentralization. Actually, the new highway system sucked the life out of already declining central cities by boosting access to suburban shopping malls and housing developments. The urban expressways that penetrated the hearts of the cities also had other negative consequences. They destroyed housing, divided neighborhoods, gobbled up parks and prime riverfront land, and brought noise and air pollution in their wake. Raymond A. Mohl's essay, "Planned Destruction," notes that the urban interstates cleared huge swaths of inner-city land for expressway corridors and access ramps. Highway engineers and local decision makers generally targeted lower-income and African-American neighborhoods for expressway construction. Urban highway building became a form of slum clearance and urban renewal, as well as a method of urban redevelopment. Neighborhood groups in many cities challenged the highway decision making that destroyed entire housing districts, organizational efforts that eventually led to the so-called Freeway Revolt of the 1960s and early 1970s. Some such community efforts were successful, but the highway builders prevailed in most cities. The destruction of inner-city neighborhoods during the interstate era had broad consequences, as dislocated black families usually moved to nearby white working-class areas already being affected by suburbanization. The racial transitions that resulted during the 1950s and 1960s created new "second ghettoes" in many cities.

Post–World War II demographic changes ultimately transformed big-city politics in the United States. By the 1960s, as blacks migrated to the cities and as whites moved to the sprawling new suburbs, urban political power began shifting to African-American voters. In his essay on black urban politics, Arnold R. Hirsch provides a comparative case study of two black mayors—Ernest "Dutch" Morial of New Orleans and Harold Washington of Chicago—comparing their rise to prominence and power, their electoral success, their exercise of power, and the consequences of their respective mayoralties. There are fascinating parallels in the political careers of the two men, as well as major differences between the political structures and practices of the two cities. In New Orleans, blacks had been excluded from a major political role until the civil rights movement. Morial served his political apprenticeship in the National Association for the Advancement of Colored People (NAACP), which provided his political power base. In Chicago, Washington slowly climbed the ladder of the city's Democratic political machine and built a base of African-American electoral support in the city's South Side wards. Both were elected with overwhelming support of black voters, but in both cases it was division among white opponents that made their election possible. Once in power, each faced new problems in governing, in challenging old power structures, and in achieving reforms. Expectations for positive change were high among black citizens in both cities, but political realities made reform difficult to achieve, especially in such important areas as housing and schooling. Hirsch's comparison continues through the issue of succession, as in each city a second black mayor came to power. But the politics were different. In New Orleans, Morial's successor had little commitment to reform and little support among black voters. In Chicago, white machine politicians expediently, and temporarily, supported an African American as Washington's replacement. And things continued to change in succeeding years: In 1989, Chicagoans elected as mayor Richard M. Daley, son of the legendary five-term mayor Richard J. Daley; and in New Orleans in 1994, voters chose Marc Morial, son of Dutch Morial, in a bitterly contested mayoralty election.

Immigration shaped the industrial cities of the late nineteenth and early twentieth centuries. Now, more than a hundred years later, immigration has once again brought dramatic social and cultural change to the modern American metropolis. Atlanta, Georgia, the subject of Mary E. Odem's essay, has emerged as one of the new immigrant destinations for Latino immigrants from Mexico and Central America. Historically, Latinos settled primarily in Texas, California, and the Southwest, but since the 1980s the cities and small towns of the Southeast have become a major destination for new immigrants, attracted by work in construction, landscaping, service, carpet factories, and poultry plants. For a quarter of a century, Latino newcomers have poured into the Atlanta area, where by 2008 they numbered just over 517,000, or about 10 percent of the entire twenty-eight-county Atlanta metro population. Odem's essay documents the creation of strong Latino communities and especially the persistence of traditional religious practice, but also a pattern of discriminatory "spatial regulation" by government agencies that limited the ability of Latinos to obtain a driver's license, find employment, or sustain community life. Odem applies a modern theory of space to her discussion, suggesting that government authorities at various levels have sought to curb Latino access to various spaces, such as day-labor hiring spots. Social scientists have used such spatial concepts to understand and explain how groups of people use specific places or social spaces to pursue community goals. In Atlanta, street corners, shopping plaza parking lots, and neighborhoods have become contested areas where Latinos have asserted their claims to public and social space. Odem turns to Latino religious practice for her prime example of spatial contestation. In 1991, the Catholic hierarchy in Atlanta closed a small mission church where hundreds of Latinos regularly worshiped, urging them to integrate with American Catholic parishes. Latinos collectively resisted the Church's decision and, with the support of a sympathetic Hispanic priest, began holding weekly outdoor services in parking lots and other public spaces. Latino determination to pursue their own forms of religiosity in this public way finally persuaded the Church to open an official Misión Católica, another urban space they could claim for themselves. Spatial regulations or restrictions, whether by government or Church authorities, reflected anti-immigrant attitudes—but ironically, as Odem points out, the new Catholic mission church actually contributed to Latino integration into American society and culture through its English language classes and other educational programs. In this new era of immigration, spatial contestations similar to those in Atlanta have become commonplace throughout urban America.

In the concluding essay, historian Michael B. Katz assesses the condition of the American city in the early twenty-first century and concludes that a host of economic, demographic, and physical alterations have created an entirely new set of urban forms. These changes have blurred the distinction between types of cities, between cities and suburbs, and between types of suburbs. Consequently, historians, sociologists, planners, and urbanologists now struggle to find new typologies to explain or understand the places where people gather to live and work. Terms such as *inner city*, *edge city*, *dual city*, *postindustrial city*, *galactic city*, *global city*, *city of knowledge*, and *informational city* all have provided useful insights but ultimately have been found wanting. No metaphor has comprehensively described the diverse configuration of urban forms that have developed in recent decades following the demise of industrial cities. Whereas nineteenth- and twentieth-century cities looked to city halls and sought state and federal funds to solve their problems, the new urban forms increasingly spurned activist government and relied upon market-based initiatives—even contracting with private entities to provide security, street cleaning, and other basic services traditionally supplied by municipalities. The emasculation of government, Katz notes, has produced a number of regrettable outcomes such as a growing incidence of poverty and homelessness, the collapse of public education, an antiquated urban infrastructure, and a loss of open space in metropolitan areas. These worrisome developments, along with the widespread squalor outside of the handsomely redeveloped downtowns and the persistent fiscal uncertainty plaguing municipal budgets, contradict optimistic reports of an urban renaissance at the beginning of the twenty-first century. The author's provocative essay impels us to think critically about recent developments in urban form and to contemplate the future of American cities.

The essays gathered in part III exemplify recent historical scholarship on the twentieth-century American city. They touch upon important interpretive issues and identify some of the powerful forces and shaping influences that have brought urban America to its present condition. They also suggest directions for the reader seeking a more detailed exploration of twentieth-century urban development and change.

NOTES

1. U.S. Census Bureau, *Current Population Survey, Annual Social and Economic Supplement, 2009* (Internet release October 20, 2010).

2. Robert E. Lang and Dawn Dhavale, *Beyond Megalopolis: Exploring America's New "Megapolitan" Geography* (Blacksburg: Virginia Tech Metropolitan Institute, 2005), 15.

3. Larry Long and Diana DeAre, "The Slowing of Urbanization in the U.S.," *Scientific American* 249 (July 1983): 31–39; Edward L. Glaeser and Jesse M. Shapiro, *City Growth and the 2000 Census: Which Places Grew, and Why* (Washington, DC: Brookings Institution, Center on Urban and Metropolitan Policy, 2001).

4. Ken Auletta, *The Underclass* (New York: Random House, 1982), 17. The work of sociologist William Julius Wilson popularized the term "underclass." See, for example, Wilson's books *The Truly Disadvantaged: The Inner City, the Underclass, and Public Policy* (Chicago: University of Chicago Press, 1987) and *When Work Disappears: The World of the New Urban Poor* (New York: Knopf, 1996).

5. Thomas J. Sugrue, *The Origins of the Urban Crisis: Race and Inequality in Postwar Detroit* (Princeton, NJ: Princeton University Press, 1996); William K. Tabb, *The Long Default: New York City and the Fiscal Crisis* (New York: Monthly Review Press, 1982); Todd Swanstrom, *The Crisis of Growth Politics: Cleveland, Kucinich, and the Challenge of Urban Populism* (Philadelphia: Temple University Press, 1985).

6. On the black migration, see Nicholas Lemann, *The Promised Land: The Great Black Migration and How It Changed America* (New York: Knopf, 1991); James N. Gregory, *The Southern Diaspora: How the Great Migrations of Black and White Southerners Transformed America* (Chapel Hill: University of North Carolina Press, 2007). On the second ghetto, see Arnold R. Hirsch, *Making the Second Ghetto: Race and Housing in Chicago, 1940–1960* (Cambridge, UK: Cambridge University Press, 1983). On black return migration to the South, see William H. Frey, *The New Great Migration: Black Americans Return to the South, 1965–2000* (Washington, DC: Brookings Institution, 2004); William H. Frey et al., *State of Metropolitan America* (Washington, DC: Brookings Institution, 2010), 51–63.

7. Gregory, *The Southern Diaspora.*

8. Alejandro Portes and Alex Stepick, *City on the Edge: The Transformation of Miami* (Berkeley: University of California Press, 1993); Melanie Shell-Weiss, *Coming to Miami: A Social History* (Gainesville: University Press of Florida, 2009); Mike Davis, *Magical Urbanism: Latinos Reinvent the U.S. City* (London: Verso, 2000); Raymond A. Mohl, "Globalization, Latinization, and the Nuevo New South," *Journal of American Ethnic History* 22 (Summer 2003): 31–66; Jeffrey S. Passel et al., "Hispanics Account for More Than Half of the Nation's Growth in Past Decade," News Release, Pew Research Center, March 25, 2001.

9. David M. Reimers, *Still the Golden Door: The Third World Comes to America* (New York: Columbia University Press, 1985); Reimers, *Other Immigrants: The Global Origins of the American People* (New York: New York University Press, 2005); Kurt Andersen, "The New Ellis Island," *Time* (June 13, 1983): 18–25; Roger Waldinger and Mehdi Bozorgmehr, eds., *Ethnic Los Angeles* (New York: Russell Sage Foundation, 1996); U.S. Census Bureau, *Statistical Abstract of the United States: 2011* (Washington, DC: U.S. Department of Commerce, 2011), 43.

10. Kenneth T. Jackson, *Crabgrass Frontier: The Suburbanization of the United States* (New York: Oxford University Press, 1985); Robert Fishman, *Bourgeois Utopias: The Rise and Fall of Suburbia* (New York: Basic Books, 1987); Delores Hayden, *Building Suburbia: Green Fields and Urban Growth, 1820–2000* (New York: Pantheon, 2003).

11. Mark S. Foster, *From Streetcar to Superhighway: American City Planners and Urban Transportation, 1900–1940* (Philadelphia: Temple University Press, 1987); Barbara M. Kelly, *Expanding the American Dream: Building and Rebuilding Levittown* (Albany: SUNY Press, 1993); Marc A. Weiss, *The Rise of the Community Builders: The American Real Estate Industry and Urban Land Planning* (New York: Columbia University Press, 1987); Jordan Bauer, "Urban Village or Burb of the Future? The Racial and Economic Politics of a Houston Neighborhood," *Houston History* 6 (Summer 2009): 39–45.

12. Andrew Wiese, *Places of Their Own: African American Suburbanization in the Twentieth Century* (Chicago: University of Chicago Press, 2004).

13. Timothy P. Fong, *The First Suburban Chinatown: The Remaking of Monterey Park, California* (Philadelphia: Temple University Press, 1994); Audrey Singer, ed., *Twenty-First Century Gateways: Immigrant Incorporation in Suburban America* (Washington, DC: Brookings Institution Press, 2008); Sabrina Tavernise and Robert Gebeloff, "Immigrants Make Paths to Suburbs, Not Cities," *New York Times*, December 15, 2010.

14. Jerry Adler, "Bye-Bye, Suburban Dream," *Newsweek* (May 15, 1995): 40–53; William H. Lucy, *Foreclosing the Dream: How America's Housing Crisis Is Reshaping Our Cities and Suburbs* (Washington, DC: American Planning Association, 2011).

15. Sharon Zukin, *Landscapes of Power: From Detroit to Disney World* (Berkeley: University of California Press, 1991), 153–64; Richard Longstreth, *City Center to Regional Mall: Architecture, the Automobile, and Retailing in Los Angeles, 1920–1950* (Cambridge, MA: MIT Press, 1997); William Severini Kowinski, *The Malling of America: An Inside Look at the Great Consumer Paradise* (New York: Morrow, 1985).

16. Joel Garreau, *Edge City: Life on the New Frontier* (New York: Doubleday, 1991); Jon C. Teaford, *Post-Suburbia: Government and Politics in the Edge Cities* (Baltimore: Johns Hopkins University Press, 1997).

17. Larry Long and Diana DeAre, "The Slowing of Urbanization in the U.S.," *Scientific American* 249 (July 1983): 33–41, quotation on p. 36; Amos H. Hawley and Sara Mills Mazie, eds., *Nonmetropolitan America in Transition* (Chapel Hill: University of North Carolina Press, 1981), 3–115; U.S. Census Bureau, *Population Change in Metropolitan and Micropolitan Statistical Areas, 1990–2003* (Washington, DC: U.S. Department of Commerce, 2005), 12.

18. "War on Runaway Plants," *National Guardian*, January 18, 1954; "Union Fights Yonkers Plant's 'Dixie Runaway,'" *National Guardian*, June 12, 1954. The "runaway" label continued in use as late as 1980. See Harry Brill, "The Runaway Steel Industry," *The Nation* 230 (February 9, 1980): 138–39.

19. Barry Bluestone and Bennett Harrison, *The Deindustrialization of America: Plant Closings, Community Abandonment, and the Dismantling of Basic Industry* (New York: Basic Books, 1982).

20. Marlene A. Lee and Mark Mather, "U.S. Labor Force Trends," *Population Bulletin* 63 (June 2008): 4, 7.

21. Bernard J. Frieden and Lynne B. Sagalyn, *Downtown, Inc.: How America Rebuilds Cities* (Cambridge, MA: MIT Press, 1989); Peter Calthorpe, *The Next American Metropolis: Ecology, Community, and the American Dream* (New York: Princeton Architectural Press, 1993); Andres Duany and Elizabeth Plater-Zyberk, *Suburban Nation: The Rise of Sprawl and the Decline of the American Dream* (New York: North Point Press, 2001).

22. Raymond A. Mohl, "Metropolitan Government," in *Encyclopedia of American Urban History*, ed. David R. Goldfield (2 vols.; Thousand Oaks, CA: Sage Publications, 2007), II: 460–64; Jon C. Teaford, *City and Suburb: The Political Fragmentation of Metropolitan America, 1850–1970* (Baltimore: Johns Hopkins University Press, 1979).

23. Roger W. Lotchin, ed., *The Martial Metropolis: U.S. Cities in War and Peace* (New York: Praeger, 1984); Gerald D. Nash, *The American West Transformed: The Impact of the Second World War* (Bloomington: Indiana University Press, 1985); James C. Cobb, *Industrialization and Southern Society, 1877–1984* (Lexington: University of Kentucky Press, 1984); Carl Abbott, *The New Urban America: Growth and Politics in Sunbelt Cities* (rev. ed.; Chapel Hill: University of North Carolina Press, 1987).

24. Edward Ullman, "Amenities as a Factor in Regional Growth," *Geographical Review* 44 (1944): 119–32; Raymond Arsenault, "The End of the Long Hot Summer: The Air Conditioner and Southern Culture," *Journal of Southern History* 50 (November 1984): 597–628. See also Richard M. Bernard and Bradley R. Rice, eds., *Sunbelt Cities: Politics and Growth since World War II* (Austin: University of Texas Press, 1983); Raymond A. Mohl, ed., *Searching for the Sunbelt: Historical Perspectives on a Region* (Knoxville: University of Tennessee Press, 1990); Kirkpatrick Sale, *Power Shift: The Rise of the Southern Rim and Its Challenge to the Eastern Establishment* (New York: Random House, 1975).

25. Mark I. Gelfand, *A Nation of Cities: The Federal Government and Urban America, 1933–1965* (New York: Oxford University Press, 1975); G. Calvin Mackenzie and Robert Weisbrot, *The Liberal Hour: Washington and the Politics of Change in the 1960s* (New York: Penguin Press, 2008); James Q. Wilson, ed., *The Metropolitan Enigma: Inquiries into the Nature and Dimensions of America's "Urban Crisis"* (Cambridge, MA: Harvard University Press, 1968).

26. For critiques of federal urban policy, see Jane Jacobs, *The Death and Life of Great American Cities* (New York: Random House, 1962); Martin Anderson, *The Federal Bulldozer: A Critical Analysis of Urban Renewal, 1949–1962* (Cambridge, MA: MIT Press, 1964); William Moore Jr., *The Vertical Ghetto: Everyday Life in an Urban Project* (New York: Random House, 1969). See also John F. Bauman, Roger Biles, and Kristin Szylvian, eds., *From Tenements to the Taylor Homes: In Search of an Urban Housing Policy in Twentieth-Century America* (University Park: Penn State University Press, 2000), especially the essays by Gail Radford, Roger Biles, Alexander von Hoffman, Arnold R. Hirsch, and Raymond A. Mohl.

27. Jason Scott Smith, *Building New Deal Liberalism: The Political Economy of Public Works* (Cambridge, UK: Cambridge University Press, 2009); Charles H. Trout, "The New Deal and the Cities," in *Fifty Years Later: The New Deal Evaluated*, ed. Harvard Sitkoff (New York: Knopf, 1985), 133–53; Raymond A. Mohl, "Shifting Patterns of Urban Policy since 1900," in *Urban Policy in Twentieth-Century America*, ed. Arnold R. Hirsch and Raymond A. Mohl (New Brunswick, NJ: Rutgers University Press, 1993), 1–45; Alice O'Connor, "Swimming against the Tide: A Brief History of Federal Policy in Poor Communities," in *Urban Problems and Community Development*, ed. Ronald F. Ferguson and William T. Dickens (Washington, DC: Brookings Institution Press, 1999), 77–137.

28. For a detailed overview of urban policy from the Nixon years to the early 1990s, see Roger Biles, *The Fate of Cities: Urban America and the Federal Government, 1945–2000* (Lawrence: University Press of Kansas, 2001). More specifically, see Thomas J. Sugrue, "Carter's Urban Policy Crisis," in *The Carter Presidency: Policy Choices in the Post–New Deal*

Era, ed. Gary M. Fink and Hugh Davis Graham (Lawrence: University Press of Kansas, 1998), 137–57; President's Commission for a National Agenda for the Eighties, *Urban America in the Eighties: Perspectives and Prospects* (Washington, DC: U.S. Government Printing Office, 1980); Thomas Bender, "A Nation of Immigrants to the Sun Belt," *The Nation* 232 (March 28, 1981): 359–61; U.S. Department of Housing and Urban Development, *The President's National Urban Policy Report, 1982* (Washington, DC: U.S. Government Printing Office, 1982); George E. Peterson and Carol W. Lewis, eds., *Reagan and the Cities* (Washington, DC: Urban Institute Press, 1986); Robert Wood, "Cities in Trouble," *Domestic Affairs*, no. 1 (Summer 1991): 221–38; Demetrios Caraley, "Washington Abandons the Cities," *Political Science Quarterly* 107 (Spring 1991): 1–30.

29. Biles, *The Fate of Cities*, 318–47; Avis C. Vidal, "Clinton Administration Urban Policy," in *Encyclopedia of American Urban History* (2 vols.; Thousand Oaks, CA: Sage Publications, 2007), I:164–65; Kimberly Hendrickson, "Bush and the Cities," *Policy Review*, no. 126 (August/September 2004); William R. Barnes, "Beyond Federal Urban Policy," *Urban Affairs Review* 40 (May 2005): 575–89; Alan Greenblatt, "Obama and the Cities," *Governing Magazine* (April 2009), available at http://www.governing.com/topics/economic-dev/Obama-and-the-Cities.html.

30. David R. Colburn and Jeffrey S. Adler, eds., *African-American Mayors: Race, Politics, and the American City* (Urbana: University of Illinois Press, 2001); F. Chris Garcia, ed., *Latinos and the Political System* (Notre Dame, IN: University of Notre Dame Press, 1988). On the hollow prize that faced new black mayors, see Thulani Davis, "Black Mayors: Can They Make the Cities Work?" *Mother Jones* 9 (July 1984): 30–41, 51; Robert A. Catlin, *Racial Politics and Urban Planning: Gary, Indiana, 1980–1989* (Lexington: University Press of Kentucky, 1993); and Alison Isenberg, *Downtown America: A History of the Place and the People Who Made It* (Chicago: University of Chicago Press, 2004), 203–54.

31. Paul Kleppner, *Chicago Divided: The Making of a Black Mayor* (DeKalb: Northern Illinois University Press, 1985); Gary Rivlin, *Fire on the Prairie: Chicago's Harold Washington and the Politics of Race* (New York: Henry Holt, 1992).

32. Amy Bridges, *Morning Glories: Municipal Reform in the Southwest* (Princeton, NJ: Princeton University Press, 1997); James F. Horan and G. Thomas Taylor Jr., *Experiments in Metropolitan Government* (New York: Praeger, 1977); Gary Miller, *Cities by Contract: The Politics of Municipal Incorporation* (Cambridge, MA: MIT Press, 1981); Raymond A. Mohl, "Metropolitan Government," in *Encyclopedia of American Urban History*, ed. David R. Goldfield (2 vols.; Thousand Oaks, CA: Sage Publications, 2007), II: 460–464.

33. Carl Abbott, *The New Urban America: Growth and Politics in Sunbelt Cities* (rev. ed.; Chapel Hill: University of North Carolina Press, 1987), 185–243, quotation on p. 214.

34. Raymond A. Mohl, "Ethnic Politics in Miami, 1960–1986," in *Shades of the Sunbelt: Essays on Ethnicity, Race, and the Urban South* (Westport, CT: Greenwood Press, 1988), 143–60; David Rusk, *Cities without Suburbs* (2nd ed., Washington, DC: Woodrow Wilson Center Press, 1995).

35. Frederick C. Howe, *The City: The Hope of Democracy* (New York: Scribners, 1906).

Chapter 9

The New Deal in Dallas

Roger Biles

Historians continue to analyze the New Deal and its impact on U.S. history. Did Franklin D. Roosevelt's innovative responses to hard times constitute a watershed in the nation's past? How new, in other words, was the New Deal? William E. Leuchtenburg stated the case for change, arguing in his seminal *Franklin D. Roosevelt and the New Deal*: "The New Deal, however conservative it was in some respects and however much it owed to the past, marked a radically new departure." Similarly, Carl Degler called the New Deal "a revolutionary response to a revolutionary situation." Especially since the mid-1960s, however, historians have begun to focus on the lack of reform achieved in the 1930s. New Left historians like Barton Bernstein and Paul Conkin emphasized the degree to which the New Deal overlooked the plight of the downtrodden in its desire to preserve capitalism. Although many scholars stopped short of characterizing Roosevelt's presidency as counter-revolutionary, most acknowledged the shortcomings of the New Deal in effecting meaningful economic and social reform. Clearly not a radical bent on the destruction of free enterprise capitalism, they believed, Roosevelt naturally sought limited reform within the American political consensus. The New Deal could accomplish only so much because of conservative forces in Congress and the courts. Further, James T. Patterson added, the American system of federalism bolstered the states at the expense of the national government, and the New Deal made few inroads against states' rights and strict constructionism.[1]

Historians have also noted the limited impact of the New Deal in cities. In Pittsburgh, Bruce Stave concluded, the New Deal relieved unemployment and improved the housing situation somewhat, but had little effect on the more lasting problems of economic stagnation and physical decay. A number of studies suggest that, rather than undermine the strength of big city political machines, Roosevelt supported those bosses loyal to national Democratic platforms and policies. Charles H. Trout found

Reprinted from *Southwestern Historical Quarterly* 95 (July 1991): 1–19. Reprinted with the permission of the Texas State Historical Association.

that "during the entire New Deal policies from Washington altered Boston, but just as surely Boston modified federal programs." Or, as Zane Miller summarized: "The federal response to depression in the cities was conservative. The New Deal's urban policy neither envisaged nor produced a radical transformation of metropolitan form and structure."[2]

In recent years, however, some historians concerned with the exceptionalism of southern cities have designated the 1930s as the time when sweeping changes engendered by the New Deal began to narrow the gap between urban Dixie and northern municipalities. Although emphasizing the distinctiveness of southern cities overall, David R. Goldfield conceded that the pace of change accelerated rapidly in the twentieth century. The watershed, he contended, was the New Deal, since "the federal government paid for the capital facilities in southern cities that northern cities had paid for themselves in earlier decades and on which they were still paying off the debt. The almost-free modernization received by southern cities would prove to be an important economic advantage in subsequent decades." In *The New Deal in the Urban South*, Douglas L. Smith looked at four southern cities—Atlanta, Birmingham, Memphis, and New Orleans—and suggested that the involvement of the federal government in local affairs during the 1930s resulted in significant changes. He concluded that public works and housing initiatives altered southern cityscapes, New Deal relief agencies paved the way for the establishment for the first time of social welfare agencies, organized labor established new footholds, and black communities mobilized to make possible significant breakthroughs in later years. Moreover, according to Smith, the New Deal helped sever the ties to the Old South and develop among southerners an urban consciousness.[3]

An earlier study of Memphis, Tennessee, during the 1930s saw little evidence of sweeping change or, for that matter, of substantial preparation for later departures. This study of Dallas, Texas, looking at local government, relief, labor, and race relations, similarly finds minimal impact by the New Deal. In Dallas the federal government worked through city hall but exerted no influence over who made policy there, and the rise of the Citizens' Council made the control of the city's corporate regency explicit and unmistakable. No appreciable increase in social welfare activity ensued to reflect an expanded commitment to relief. To a great extent, management successfully preserved the open shop and regional wage differentials, two ingredients local businessmen viewed as essential for industry to compete effectively with northern concerns. Black residents of Dallas survived the depression in somewhat better fashion because of federal aid, but their status remained largely unchanged. In short, New Deal largess provided welcome assistance but did not alter appreciably the traditional way of life.[4]

In Dallas the business community brought local government more firmly under its control in the 1930s. Agitation for political reform dated back to the first decade of the twentieth century with the founding of the nonpartisan Citizens Association. Interest flagged, however, and by the 1920s the association was dormant. In 1927 the *Dallas News* published a series of muckraking articles exposing inefficiency in city government and proposing the city manager plan as an alternative. In 1929 over thirty men ran for mayor, nine of whom constituted one-man "parties." The eventual winner, self-styled populist J. Waddy Tate, lambasted the wealthy, removed all "keep off the grass" signs from city parks, and promised to allow "plain folks" to camp there. Largely because of Tate's eccentric behavior, Dallasites began to consider seriously the *News*'s arguments for change. The remnants of the old Citizens Association formed the Citizens Charter Association (CCA) in 1930 and joined in the battle for new municipal government. Tate delayed and dissembled, but finally presented the question of charter amendments to the people in a 1930 referendum. By a two-to-one margin, the voters jettisoned the mayor-commission government for council-city manager rule. Under the new system, the nine-member council (six chosen from districts and three elected at-large) chose a mayor from its own ranks and appointed a city manager.[5]

In 1933 the CCA's slate of candidates ran unopposed, but resistance quickly formed among the ranks of the suddenly deposed politicians. They accused the CCA of being "organized . . . financed and controlled by Wall Street trusts," and unsuccessfully sought the recall of the new council. In 1935 an opposition faction composed of seasoned pols, known as the Catfish Club, bested the CCA's candidates to gain control of the city council. A haphazardly planned counteroffensive by the CCA never got off the ground in 1937, and the brief reign of the business elite seemed finished. At that time, however, two hundred of the city's corporate presidents and chief executive officers formed the Dallas Citizens' Council to breathe new life into the dying CCA. In 1939 the candidates of the fledgling Citizens' Council parlayed rumors of graft in Mayor George Sprague's parks department into a resounding victory. The council's 1941 slate won without opposition, and its dominance of local government continued into the 1970s.[6]

The Dallas Citizens' Council sprang from the imagination of Robert Lee Thornton. A former tenant farmer who mismanaged several businesses into bankruptcy, Thornton finally struck it rich as a banker. Thornton was a maverick in the local financial community; while other banks avoided risky ventures, he had the prescience to invest in the automobile industry and gave hotel tycoon Conrad Hilton his first loan. He became one of the city's most visible and esteemed philanthropists and in later years a four-time mayor who refused to keep a desk in city hall, continuing to operate from his desk at the Mercantile Bank. By the mid-1930s he had grown tired of the ineffectiveness of local government and resolved to seize authority for the city's "natural leadership." In 1936 Thornton helped persuade the Texas Centennial Commission to hold the celebration in Dallas and then served as a member of the executive committee that planned and conducted the gala. Serving on that committee convinced him that only a small, manageable group of the city's best people could effectively make decisions about such a massive undertaking as the Texas Centennial—or for that matter, he concluded, govern the city. Therefore, Thornton set out to make the emerging Citizens' Council in the form best suited to get things done.[7]

Thornton wanted to call the Citizens' Council the "Yes or No Council," but others thought the title a bit unseemly and overruled him. Thornton did prevail on a number of other matters, however, including his insistence that membership be limited to chief executive officers of major corporations—no doctors, lawyers, educators, clergymen, or intellectuals who might temporize when hasty action was needed.

Similarly, Thornton's no-nonsense attitude predominated with the exclusion of proxy voting. "If you don't come," the rough-hewn banker said, "you ain't there." The Citizens' Council, sometimes called "Thornton's oligarchy," centralized power in an open and complete fashion. A local newspaper observed: "In many cities, power descends from a small group of influential businessmen to the city council. What distinguishes the Dallas power group from others is that it is organized, it has a name, it is not articulately opposed and it was highly publicized." If anything, local autonomy, concentrated in the hands of a relatively few influential citizens, increased during the depression decade; the bureaucracy-laden state and federal governments held no truck with the "yes or no" men of Dallas. Other southern city halls showed equally sparse evidence of federal presence. President Roosevelt made no effort to unseat political machines in Memphis or New Orleans, and local elites continued to predominate in countless other southern communities. In Houston, for example, four-time mayor Oscar Holcombe faithfully acted upon the concerns of the business community as represented by New Dealer and financial tycoon Jesse Jones. Just as Roosevelt kept hands off the steel barons who wielded such influence in Birmingham and the commercial elite in Atlanta, he declined to support or oppose the ascendance of the Citizens' Council in Dallas.[8]

In the months following the stock market crash, no widespread panic ensued in Dallas. The *Dallas Morning News* dismissed the significance of the stock market collapse, noting: "Many individuals, undoubtedly have suffered a loss far heavier than they could afford. Yet economic conditions in general are sound . . . and, after the storm, the sun of prosperity will again shine on thrift, hard work and efficient effort." Nor did city officials appreciate discouraging talk of economic setbacks; when a local lawyer spoke on a radio broadcast about rising unemployment, the city commission enacted a statute requiring that any such negative remarks be submitted in advance for approval. In fact, hard times were not all that hard in Dallas for the first year of the depression. According to 1930 data, the city's jobless rate stood at only 4.7 percent. The merger of North Texas Bank with Republic National Bank and Trust Company constituted the largest merger of financial institutions in the state's history. Also, thanks in large part to the booster efforts of Industrial Dallas, Incorporated, a total of 802 new businesses located in the city in 1929, and some 600 more followed suit during the first nine months of 1930.[9]

Dallas seemed to suffer less than many other cities due to the discovery of oil in East Texas at the outset of the decade. In October 1930 wildcatter Columbus M. Joiner found two hundred square miles of land floating on a veritable lake of oil about 120 miles southeast of Dallas. By 1933 over nine thousand producing oil wells operated in that field. Almost immediately Dallas profited from the newfound economic opportunity a major oil strike provided. Industrial Dallas, Incorporated, launched a promotional campaign to portray the city as headquarters of the new oil field by printing advertisements in *Oil Weekly* and *Oil and Gas Journal* and mailing over five thousand reprints to oil companies. The city quickly installed telephone and telegraph service to Tyler, Kilgore, Gladewater, Longview, and the other fledgling communities of the oil field. Several Dallas banks, most notably the First National, introduced new methods of oil financing such as production loans made against oil still in the ground. As a result of these efforts, hundreds of petroleum-related businesses came to Dallas, including several oil companies that located their executive headquarters or southwest branch offices there. Several local firms, such as the Magnolia and Sun Oil companies, and individuals, like H. L. Hunt and Clint W. Murchison, prospered from the beginning. In short order, Dallas established itself as the financial and service center for the greatest oil strike since the legendary Spindletop strike of 1901.[10]

Although the fortuitous oil discovery no doubt mitigated the economic crisis of the early depression years, Dallas did not escape hard times altogether. Unemployment became a grave problem; more than 18,500 jobless men and women applied for relief at city hall by the end of 1931. Employers discharged married female employees, and retail stores cut back to five-day workweeks. Ironically, the federal government reported in 1931 that the most serious unemployment problem in the state existed in the East Texas oil fields, where an estimated ten thousand of the many thousands who arrived from around the country to get work found none. As the federal government noted, the care of these new arrivals fell on local communities, including nearby Dallas.[11]

Other economic indicators reflected the city's troubles. Dallas building permits for 1931 totaled only $7.5 million, down from $11 million the year before. By 1933 the slowdown in construction led the Dallas Carpenters' Union to offer a 50 percent reduction on all repair and remodeling work. Dallas boasted of being the merchandising capital of the South and, therefore, suffered severely when net retail sales plummeted from $189 million in 1929 to $130 million in 1935. Wholesale business in 1929 totaled $729 million but only $48 million a decade later. A persistent decline in bank deposits and loans led to frequent reorganizations and mergers. In the most notable case the city's three largest banks pooled their resources to save a smaller state bank from closing. Clearly, Dallas suffered from the weight of the Great Depression.[12]

Faced with unprecedented demands on local resources, the city responded minimally. Burdened by reduced tax collections, Dallas cut expenditures—including relief—to keep from going heavily in the red. In 1931 the city stood over $32.5 million in arrears. After its initial year the newly instituted city manager government trimmed the overdraft by more than $400,000. In its second year city hall refunded the remainder of the deficit, and the budget maintained a cash surplus for the duration of the decade. By and large, this owed to the cutting of municipal workers' salaries from 5 percent to 20 percent and the release of hundreds of employees. New city manager John Edy refused to allocate funds for street paving or building a levee sewer along the Trinity River downtown—despite significant pressure from the business community. Teachers received their monthly paychecks without interruption, but the sums decreased; in the 1931–1932 school year, for example, teacher salaries averaged $1,669, and in the 1932–1933 year only $1,463. The Board of Education reduced the number of faculty by demanding the automatic resignation of married women employees.[13]

As the monthly case load of the city welfare department rose to an average of 2,800 in 1931, city officials instituted a plan whereby the unemployed labored one day per week on public works projects and were paid in groceries bought by the city wholesale. After a prolonged campaign the Laboring Men's Relief Association persuaded the welfare department to issue some cash payments in addition to food, but the city continued to focus its efforts on encouraging self-sufficiency by subsidizing the planting of four hundred acres of vegetable gardens and distributing over one thousand packages of seeds to the unemployed. The welfare department also operated a cannery so that vegetables could be preserved for winter consumption. Noting that the thirty cents an hour it currently paid day laborers "cost the city about 40 percent more than if the work were done by private contract," the municipal government cut the pay to eighteen cents an hour, to be discharged in groceries. As in other southern cities, economy continued to be the first priority.[14] (Table 9.1 compares Dallas, the fourth largest southern city in 1930, with the other largest cities with respect to sources of relief funding.)

With an enervated municipal government, local social welfare institutions were called on to provide relief. Their resources disappeared rapidly, however, and philanthropic activity lagged as well. An American Public Welfare Association survey concluded that "analysis of Community Chest giving in Dallas . . . indicates an unusually small proportion, both in number and amount, of gifts, by individuals as compared with business firms and corporations. . . . This is not to indicate that business firms and corporations in Dallas give too much to the Community Chest. Some should give much more." The *Dallas Morning News* editorialized: "The richest of the rich in Dallas have fallen down on the task. They have shirked in the face of the winter's desperate need."[15]

With city halls closely cleaving to a policy of low taxes and limited expenditures, private giving insufficient, and state government bereft of resources, the federal government became the last resort. In the early days of the depression, the *Dallas Morning News* rejected the idea of federal relief, saying: "The News has steadfastly set its face against tin-cup-and-blue-goggles trips to Washington for 'relief' for Texans." But the prospect of desperately needed aid proved too attractive to spurn. The *Dallas Morning News* supported the National Recovery Administration, and the Chamber of Commerce responded so quickly and energetically that NRA chief Hugh Johnson singled out the organization for commendation. Similarly, the paper encouraged com-

Table 9.1.   Relief Expenditures by Government and Private Organizations, January 1–March 31, 1931

City	Municipal ($)	%	Private ($)	%	Total ($)
Atlanta	20,493	26.7	56,183	73.2	76,676
Birmingham	74,544	50.4	73,326	49.6	147,870
Dallas	34,622	48.3	37,109	51.7	71,731
Houston	12,329	20.4	48,224	79.6	60,553
Memphis	11,190	8.8	115,317	91.2	126,507
New Orleans	0	0	27,103	100.0	27,103
Total	153,178	30.0	357,262	70.0	510,440

Source: U.S. Bureau of the Census, *Relief Expenditures by Government and Private Organizations, 1929 and 1931* (Washington, DC: Government Printing Office, 1932), 6, 32–33.
Note: Nationwide, local governments provided 60.4% and private sources, 39.6%.

pliance with the Agricultural Adjustment Act, a reflection of the community's concern with deflated cotton prices.[16]

Of most immediate concern to Dallas, to be sure, was unemployment and the resultant relief crisis. In May 1933, Congress created the Federal Emergency Relief Administration (FERA), authorizing it to distribute $500 million for direct and work relief as well as transient care. The federal government provided funds for distribution by state and local governments, with emphasis on decentralization. In spring 1933 the state legislature created the Texas Rehabilitation and Relief Commission to distribute the largess through county agencies. From its inception in July 1933 to 1935, when the federal government turned unemployment relief over to state and local authorities, FERA general relief aided thousands of jobless in Dallas. At its peak the agency dispensed relief to 14,125 city residents monthly. Workers paved roads, dug ditches, and performed hundreds of other tasks that improved the city's appearance. And the federal government paid for over 80 percent of the relief appropriations.[17]

The Public Works Administration (PWA) opened its offices in Dallas in 1933. Unlike the other New Deal agencies concerned with unemployment, which concentrated on short-term, low-cost projects, the PWA awarded grants to cities for large-scale efforts. (The cities had to augment these grants with sizable contributions of their own.) In PWA projects, about 70 percent of funds went for materials and the remaining 30 percent for wages. Since "make work" was never the primary goal, the agency directly employed relatively few men; moreover, PWA hired indiscriminately, not just from the relief rolls, so it had only an incidental impact on gross unemployment figures. In Dallas the PWA built the Museum of Natural History and added 130 beds to city-owned Parkland Hospital. In 1939 the city completed negotiations with the U.S. Housing Authority (negotiations originating with PWA) for its first slum clearance project, providing shelter for 626 black families.[18]

Such programs as FERA and PWA provided some succor for Dallas's destitute, but by 1935 the relief crisis remained just as critical. That year President Roosevelt created the Works Progress Administration (WPA) to employ men in greater numbers and at a wage higher than the relief rate. Recognizing that "make work" often had little intrinsic value, he nonetheless favored it to the dole. (At the same time the federal government created WPA, it turned unemployment relief back over to state and local governments.) Unlike the PWA, the WPA focused its resources on smaller scale jobs with little cost for materials so that most of the funds could be spent paying wages.[19]

By 1938 when Congress mandated draconian cuts in relief appropriations, WPA had spent thousands of dollars in Dallas, a substantial contribution but somewhat less than might have been possible. Several reasons accounted for WPA's limited success. Small payments to reliefers underscored community values. The federal government divided the nation into four regions to establish variable pay rates, and laborers in the Southwest division (which included Dallas) received the second lowest wages. Certainly relief stipends fell short of desirable levels nationwide, but workers in southern cities suffered most, receiving from 33 to 65 percent at the national average emergency standard of living expense identified by federal authori ties. In 1939 in Dallas 8,939 persons received certification for relief employment, but only 4,973 actually obtained assignments. A local social worker observed that, as a result, "a large though undetermined number of individuals in varying degrees of need were thus left unprovided for by any existing agency, public or private." Without federal funds after 1935, relief virtually vanished altogether; in 1935 Dallas spent approximately $350,000 to augment federal money but in 1936 appropriated nothing. Like other southern cities Dallas increasingly relied upon external sources for care of its dependents.[20] (See tables 9.2 and 9.3.)

Indeed, substandard pay rates, paltry contributions to public relief, and the virtually total reliance on federal funds indicate a minimal commitment to social welfare by the community. The *Dallas Morning News* called WPA "evil but necessary," a succinct

Table 9.2.   Sources of Funding for Relief Programs, 1935–1936

City	Year	Total Spent on Relief ($)	Federal Dollars Spent on Relief ($)	Percent of Total from Federal Sources
Atlanta	1935	5,910,810	5,051,153	86
	1936	0	0	0
Birmingham	1935	5,452,319	5,072,506	93
	1936	140,209	51,996	37
Dallas	1935	1,776,400	1,429,494	81
	1936	0	0	0
Houston	1935	2,422,159	1,931,037	80
	1936	0	0	0
Memphis	1935	2,280,031	2,123,861	93
	1936	0	0	0
New Orleans	1935	9,241,949	8,973,956	97
	1936	0	0	0

Source: United States Federal Emergency Relief Administration, *Final Statistical Report of the Federal Emergency Relief Administration, prepared under the direction of Theodore E. Whiting, Work Projects Administration* (Washington, DC: Government Printing Office, 1942), 327, 335, 343, 374, 376, 377.

Table 9.3.   Emergency Relief by Sources of Funds, July 1933–December 1935

City	Total ($)	Federal Funds ($)	Total (%)	State Funds ($)	Total (%)	Local Funds ($)	Total (%)
Atlanta	12,955,483	11,138,002	86.0	0	0.0	1,817,481	14.0
Birmingham	11,486,481	10,915,435	95.0	64,898	0.6	506,148	4.4
Dallas	4,733,623	3,814,125	80.6	891,230	18.8	28,268	0.6
Houston	5,742,238	4,490,605	78.2	1,241,315	21.6	10,318	0.2
Memphis	4,119,607	3,963,437	96.2	0	0.0	156,170	3.8
New Orleans	17,422,059	16,990,480	97.5	0	0.0	431,579	2.5
Total	56,459,491	51,312,084	90.9	2,197,443	3.9	2,949,964	5.2

Source: Arthur E. Burns, "Federal Emergency Relief Administration," in Clarence E. Ridley and Orin F. Nolting (eds.), *The Municipal Year Book, 1937* (Chicago: The International City Managers' Association, 1937), 413–14.

statement of how the agency fared in the public's esteem. The acceptance of New Deal funds provided a way to preserve traditional customs related to relief while temporarily expanding coverage to meet an emergency. Far from being infused with any new spirit of social welfare, Dallas seems not to have altered its policies on indigent care at all during the Great Depression.[21]

In Dallas resistance to labor emanated from respectable, influential businessmen's groups committed to the preservation of open shops. The Chamber of Commerce boasted that Dallas was one of the first open-shop cities in the country and advertised nationally the virtues of the city's docile labor force. The chamber's Open Shop Bureau took an active role in politics, supporting candidates of antiunion persuasion. The Dallas Open Shop Association, formed in 1919 by a coterie of local businessmen, guaranteed the solvency of all its members in case of work-stopping strikes through the use of its rumored $2 million to $3 million reserve fund. Further, it subjected any member who knowingly hired union workers to a $3,000 fine. The success of the business community in safeguarding the open shop resulted in total capitulation by the local AFL leadership, as witnessed by the Central Labor Council offering to help the Chamber of Commerce keep the CIO out of the community.[22]

The *Dallas Morning News* consistently took a hostile position toward labor unionization, opposing the National Labor Relations Act and the Fair Labor Standards Act. Moreover, it flaunted compliance of New Deal labor laws in its own business affairs, refusing to pay its employees an hourly wage with time-and-a-half for overtime. In short, the newspaper continued to treat its workers in the frankly paternalistic way it always had. It guaranteed employees a certain wage in its contracts with them and disregarded federal requirements for minimum pay levels. Nobody at the *News* ever punched a time clock, federal strictures notwithstanding. The company felt so strongly about management's right to deal freely with its own workers that it successfully withstood legal challenges by the U.S. government, first in the Fifth Circuit Court of Appeals and finally in the U.S. Supreme Court. As the most influential newspaper in Dallas, its victory lent special authority to its regular anti-labor fulminations.[23]

As in other southern cities violence against union organizers in Dallas was frequent, brutal, and shockingly open. In 1937 the United Auto Workers (UAW) initiated a campaign to organize a local Ford plant. Several union members, labor lawyers, and sympathizers suffered beatings near the automobile factory and downtown in broad daylight. Socialist Herbert Harris was knocked out, stripped, tarred and feathered, and deposited on a downtown street. A few days later several men took a UAW attorney from a downtown drugstore and beat him severely. Police did nothing. In 1939 and 1940 the UAW filed unfair labor practice charges against Ford with the National Labor Relations Board, which accused company officials in Dallas with "brutality unknown in the history of the Board." Brutal, but effective—the 1930s ended with Ford still free of UAW representation.[24]

Similar violence developed when textile unions sought to penetrate the substantial Dallas clothing industry. Hat, Cap, and Millinery Workers vice president George Baer lost sight in one eye when three men wielding blackjacks waylaid him on a busy downtown street. Baer identified his attackers, but police took no action. Sporadic violence interrupted an ILGWU strike in which hooligans stripped ten women before a crowd of hundreds in the central business district. The bitter strike dragged on for over eight months before collapsing in defeat. By 1940 several hundred garment workers belonged to two ILGWU locals, representing the signal accomplishment of labor in the city. "Nevertheless," writes labor historian George Green, "the union rated Dallas as the only Southwestern city with a considerable dress production market that was still unorganized."[25]

Both the AFL and the CIO won significant victories in the 1930s, though primarily in the smokestack cities of the Northeast and Midwest. In the tradition-laden South success came more grudgingly. Major breakthroughs, achieved earlier in other parts of the nation, were forestalled by the opposition of local authorities like Memphis's Boss Crump and organizations like the Dallas Open Shop Association. The drive to unionize the South persisted for decades; in 1946 the CIO's Operation Dixie, a comprehensive drive for closed shops from the Piedmont to Texas, commenced with great fanfare. In 1953 it ceased operation, conceding defeat. Only 14.4 percent of the region's nonagricultural workers belonged to unions as late as the mid-1960s (compared to 29.5 percent nationally). The situation in Dallas confirmed historian George Tindall's conclusion that despite nominal gains in membership and the laying of a foundation for future success, "the South remained predominantly nonunion and largely antiunion."[26]

Dallas blacks suffered severely from the economy's collapse in the 1930s. Traditionally "last hired and first fired" and confined to the lowest paying jobs, they constituted fully one-half of the city's unemployed by 1932. The few black-owned businesses faced extinction; no banks and one black insurance company (Excelsior Mutual) survived by 1937. Residential segregation continued to be the rule, despite court rulings outlawing discriminatory municipal ordinances. Expanding black communities in "Oak Cliff" and "Elm Thicket" were situated in the least desirable areas of the city, inching across the landscape only as bordering white residents surrendered their homes. But racial turnover occurred very slowly and construction nearly ceased in the Depression years, so inadequate housing remained a serious problem. Whites also used violence to keep blacks from occupying homes in white neighborhoods. The *Dallas Express* reported a dozen bombings during the winter of 1940–1941 and criticized Mayor Woodall Rodgers, who blamed blacks for inciting violence by not accepting residential segregation. A 1938 Dallas housing survey reported 86 percent of black homes substandard. Given the squalor in which so many blacks lived, the fact that in 1930 black mortality rates more than doubled those of whites is not surprising.[27]

The drive for equal rights and improved living conditions met formidable opposition in the courts. In Texas the white primary formed the major obstacle to black voting. In 1923 the state legislature revised the election laws to prohibit explicitly black participation in Democratic primaries. When the U.S. Supreme Court ruled the statute a violation of the Fourteenth Amendment's equal protection clause in *Nixon v. Herndon*, the state legislature rewrote the law deleting references to blacks and empowering the State Democratic Executive Committee to approve voting qualifications. In 1935 the nation's highest court approved the revision in *Grovey v. Townsend*, arrogating disfranchisement to the political party by virtue of its being a nongovernmental voluntary association.[28]

In 1936 a group of the state's most influential blacks, including Antonio Maceo Smith and Maynard H. Jackson of Dallas and Clifford Jackson and Richard Grovey of Houston, reorganized the defunct Independent Voters League as the Progressive Voters League to continue the battle against white primaries. In 1938 several blacks filed a class action suit in U.S. District Court seeking an injunction against the Houston Democratic Executive Committee to prevent the exclusion of black voters in that year's primary election. The court refused to grant the injunction; the black petitioners considered an appeal but finally did nothing. Not until 1944 did the U.S. Supreme Court rule the white primary unconstitutional in the landmark *Smith v. Allright* decision. In the 1930s black efforts at contesting the Democratic party's exclusive policies fell consistently short.[29]

The inability to participate in Democratic primaries severely limited the political role played by Texas blacks in the 1930s. The Dallas Progressive Voters League remained active, registering black voters and endorsing the white candidates who seemed least objectionable. Nonetheless, few blacks voted or even paid their poll taxes—only 3,400 in Dallas and just 400 in Houston in 1935. Since neither city possessed a political machine that relied on black patronage for continued electoral success, local Democratic leaders had no reason to liberalize their voting requirements. Few blacks bothered to seek elective office. In 1935 A. S. Wells did in Dallas, in a special election to fill a vacancy in the state legislature. He placed fifth with 1,001 votes as many black registered voters stayed home, allegedly in response to the Ku Klux Klan's campaign of intimidation. In 1939 black businessman James B. Grigsby ran for election to the Houston school board but received only 689 votes. In an electorate dominated by whites, blacks' efforts consistently failed to alter election outcomes.[30]

Dallas had a black chamber of commerce, an NAACP chapter, and other voluntary associations that sought to improve conditions of their constituents. Generally, their impact was unremarkable, their achievements few. Limited local resources and the overwhelming bulwark of custom, coupled with community demoralization, meant that any attempt to improve conditions for blacks would be an uphill struggle. Most blacks had only the New Deal's relief and recovery programs to fall back on. Unfortunately, in the tradition-laden southern cities the New Deal made few inroads. Nor did southern-based federal bureaucrats launch unpopular reform campaigns. Southerners feared the New Deal's reputation as liberal on the issue of race, even though Roosevelt initiated few efforts designed specifically to aid blacks, and his administration's celebrity can best be attributed to the unofficial efforts of a few activists such as Harold Ickes, Aubrey Williams, and Eleanor Roosevelt. And as in politics, local administrators exercised considerable autonomy in the application of New Deal programs and policies.[31]

Segregation also proved unassailable by New Deal agencies. Many programs enforced separation, as did the WPA in its sewing rooms and the Civilian Conservation Corps in its camps. The inchoate public housing program preserved racial segregation, first under the aegis of the PWA and subsequently, the U.S. Housing Authority. Under the PWA's Harold Ickes, about half the federal housing projects in the South went to blacks, and PWA housing contracts required the hiring of black workers. Dallas began construction of public housing projects during the 1930s, designating most of them for black occupation. No question ever arose about the suitability of segregated housing units—no one, black or white, called for integrated projects—but implementation of the program aroused considerable controversy nevertheless. Construction delays developed when black projects fell too near white neighborhoods, and despite PWA and USHA housing contract stipulations that blacks be employed in construction, local authorities often failed to do so.[32]

The New Deal provided new housing, jobs, and relief for many destitute blacks in Dallas but always under the vigilant control of local authorities. Municipal officials set guidelines and implemented policies to reinforce existing racial norms—with little or no federal incursions. Even the blacks helped by New Deal programs lived in a community where segregation and second-class citizenship went largely unquestioned. In Dallas, as throughout the South, few blacks voted and none held elective office. The assault on Jim Crowism and political disfranchisement, a post–World War II movement, received little impetus from the New Deal.

The Great Depression struck hard in Dallas. Although the city fared better than some others because of the oil bonanza, problems arose to tax local resources. Businesses shut down, workers lost jobs, productivity declined, trade ebbed, and the demands for relief skyrocketed. Reduced tax collections, no heritage of social welfare, and city government's insistence upon fiscal "responsibility" combined to curtail the amount of relief offered the needy in Dallas and other southern cities. The New Deal provided some aid but, even when most generously funded, only for a fraction of the needy and at wage levels below the standards in other regions. New Deal alphabet agencies allowed Dallas to minimize its welfare contributions, not expand them. City leadership rested more firmly than ever in the city's business elite by the end of the decade. The defenders of the status quo preserved the community's independence from union influence, at least for the immediate future. New Deal programs never excluded blacks from benefits, and occasionally explicitly included them—on paper, anyway. But the Roosevelt administration had neither the desire nor the capacity to challenge the South's rock-ribbed racial mores. The federal government's impact on Dallas in the 1930s favored continuity; resistance to change resulted from the influence of powerful elites, unvarnished fealty to long-standing values and institutions, the political powerlessness of the have-nots, and the New Deal's admittedly modest reform agenda. Comparisons with other large southern cities call into question the significance of the New Deal's impact. The forces of conservatism in Dallas and its sister cities in the South appear to have resisted—or at least slowed—the dissolution of traditional political, social, and economic customs.

NOTES

1. William E. Leuchtenburg, *Franklin D. Roosevelt and the New Deal, 1932–1940* (New York: Harper and Row, 1963), 336 (1st quotation); Carl N. Degler, *Out of Our Past: The*

Forces That Shaped Modern America (New York: Harper and Brothers, 1959), 416 (2nd quotation); James T. Patterson, *The New Deal and the States: Federalism in Transition* (Princeton: Princeton University Press, 1969), 206–207. Also see Barton J. Bernstein, "The New Deal: The Conservative Achievements of Liberal Reform," in Barton J. Bernstein (ed.), *Towards a New Past: Dissenting Essays in American History* (New York: Pantheon Books, 1968), 263–288; Paul K. Conkin, *The New Deal* (Arlington Heights, IL.: Harlan Davidson, Inc., 1967); Barry D. Karl, *The Uneasy State: The United States from 1915 to 1945* (Chicago: University of Chicago Press, 1983); and Robert S. McElvaine, *The Great Depression: America 1929–1941* (New York: Times Books, 1984). On New Deal historiography, see Richard S. Kirkendall, "The New Deal as Watershed: The Recent Literature," *Journal of American History*, 54 (Mar. 1968), 839–852; Jerold S. Auerbach, "New Deal, Old Deal, or Raw Deal: Some Thoughts on New Left Historiography," *Journal of Southern History*, 35 (Feb. 1969), 18–30; Alonzo L. Hamby (ed.), *The New Deal: Analysis and Interpretation* (New York: Longman, 1981); and Harvard Sitkoff (ed.), *Fifty Years Later: The New Deal Evaluated* (New York: Alfred A. Knopf, 1985).

2. Bruce M. Stave, "Pittsburgh and the New Deal," in John Braeman, Robert H. Bremner, and David Brody (eds.), *The New Deal: The State and Local Levels* (Columbus: Ohio State University Press, 1975), 376–402; Lyle W. Dorsett, "Kansas City and the New Deal," in Braeman, Bremner, and Brody (eds.), *The New Deal*, 407–418; Roger Biles, *Big City Boss in Depression and War: Mayor Edward J. Kelly of Chicago* (DeKalb: Northern Illinois University Press, 1984); Charles Hathaway Trout, *Boston, the Great Depression, and the New Deal* (New York: Oxford University Press, 1977), 315 (1st quotation); Zane L. Miller, *The Urbanization of Modern America: A Brief History* (New York: Harcourt Brace Jovanovich, 1973), 168–169 (2nd quotation).

3. David R. Goldfield, *Cotton Fields and Skyscrapers: Southern City and Region, 1607–1980* (Baton Rouge: Louisiana State University Press, 1982), 181–182 (quotation); Douglas L. Smith, *The New Deal in the Urban South* (Baton Rouge: Louisiana State University Press, 1988). Also see David R. Goldfield, "The Urban South: A Regional Framework," *American Historical Review*, 86 (Dec., 1981), 1009–1034.

4. Roger Biles, *Memphis in the Great Depression* (Knoxville: University of Tennessee Press, 1986).

5. *Dallas Morning News*, Jan. 26, 1967; Ann P. Hollingsworth, "Reform Government in Dallas, 1927–1940" (M.A. thesis, North Texas State University, 1971), 10–16; *New York Times*, Oct. 19, 1930; Roscoe C. Martin, "Dallas Makes the Manager Plan Work," *The Annals of the American Academy of Political and Social Science*, 199 (Sept. 1938), 64; Louis P. Head, "Dallas Joins Ranks of Manager Cities," *National Municipal Review*, 19 (Dec. 1930), 806–809; W. D. Jones, "Dallas Wins a Place in the Sun," *National Municipal Review*, 24 (Jan. 1935), 11–14; Work Projects Administration Writers' Project, *Dallas Guide and History* (Dallas: n.p., 1940), 193–194, 202–203; *New York Times*, Apr. 12, 1931.

6. *Dallas Morning News*, Mar. 23, 27, 1967; "'N.M.L.' Charged With Traitorous Propaganda to Install Imperialistic Government," *National Municipal Review*, 21 (Mar. 1932), 140 (quotation); Robert B. Fairbanks, "The Good Government Machine: The Citizens Charter Association and Dallas Politics, 1930–1960," in Robert B. Fairbanks and Kathleen Underwood (eds.), *Essays on Sunbelt Cities and Recent Urban America* (College Station: Texas A&M University Press, 1990), 127–132.

7. Michael C. D. Macdonald, *America's Cities: A Report on the Myth of Urban Renaissance* (New York: Simon and Schuster, 1984), 114; Transcript of interview with R. L. Thornton, Jr., Nov. 8, 1980 (quotation), Dallas Mayors Oral History Project, Dallas Public Library; Stanley Walker, *The Dallas Story* (Dallas: Dallas Times Herald, 1956), 33–35.

8. Warren Leslie, *Dallas, Public and Private* (New York: Grossman Publishers, 1964), 64 (2nd quotation), 69, 84 (1st quotation); Lyle W. Dorsett, *Franklin D. Roosevelt and the City Bosses* (Port Washington, NY: National University Publications, Kennikat Press, 1977). Dallas remains the largest city in the nation with a city-manager form of government. Stephen L. Elkin, "State and Market in City Politics: Or, the 'Real' Dallas," in Clarence N. Stone and Heywood T. Sanders (eds.), *The Politics of Urban Development* (Lawrence: University Press of Kansas, 1987), 50n; Biles, *Memphis in the Great Depression*, especially chap. 4; T. Harry Williams, *Huey Long* (New York: Alfred A. Knopf, 1969), 425–427, 675, 849–853; Betty Marie Field, "The Politics of the New Deal in Louisiana, 1933–1939" (Ph.D. diss., Tulane University, 1973), 83–85, 109–112, 286–287; Edward Shannon LaMonte, "Politics and Welfare in Birmingham, Alabama: 1900–1975" (Ph.D. diss., University of Chicago, 1976), 135–136; Douglas L. Fleming, "Atlanta, the Depression, and the New Deal" (Ph.D. diss., Emory University, 1984).

9. *Dallas Morning News*, Nov. 13, 1929 (quotation), June 23, 1930; Bureau of the Census, Fifteenth Census of the United States: 1930. Unemployment (Washington, DC: Government Printing Office, 1932), II, 135; *Dallas Morning News*, Oct. 13, 1929, Oct. 12, 1930.

10. James Howard, *Big D Is For Dallas: Chapters in the Twentieth-Century History of Dallas* (Austin: University Cooperative Society, 1957), 43, 89; Dorothy De Moss, "Resourcefulness in the Financial Capital: Dallas, 1929–1933," in Robert C. Cotner et al., *Texas Cities and the Great Depression* (Austin: Texas Memorial Museum, 1973), 119–121; Dallas Chamber of Commerce, "Report of Industrial Dallas, Inc., 1928–1929–1930," Dallas Public Library (Dallas: n.p., 1931).

11. *Dallas Morning News*, Dec. 11, 1931; Work Projects Administration Writers' Project, *Dallas Guide and History*, 195; J. F. Lucey to Walter S. Gifford, telegram, Oct. 27, 1931, State File: Texas, President's Organization For Unemployment Relief, Record Group 73 (National Archives).

12. Dorothy Dell De Moss, "Dallas, Texas, During the Early Depression: The Hoover Years, 1929–1933" (M.A. thesis, University of Texas, 1966), 70–81; *Dallas Morning News*, Jan. 5, 1933; Howard, *Big D Is For Dallas*, 15–16.

13. Roscoe C. Martin, "Dallas Makes the Manager Plan Work," *The Annals of the American Academy of Political and Social Science*, 199 (Sept. 1938), 65; *Dallas Morning News*, Apr. 28, 1932; Fairbanks, "The Good Government Machine," 127–128; De Moss, "Dallas, Texas, During the Early Depression," 119–122.

14. De Moss, "Resourcefulness in the Financial Capital," 124, 125 (quotation), 126; *Dallas Morning News*, Apr. 12, 1932. See also American Public Welfare Association, "Dallas Welfare Survey," Southern Methodist University Library, Dallas, Texas (n.p., 1938).

15. American Public Welfare Association, "Dallas Welfare Survey," 84 (1st quotation); *Dallas Morning News*, Dec. 4, 1931 (2nd quotation).

16. Donald W. Whisenhunt, *The Depression in Texas: The Hoover Years* (New York: Garland Publishing, 1983), 9 (quotation); *Dallas Morning News*, July 23, Aug. 11, 1933; Dallas Chamber of Commerce, "Departmental Reports for 1933," *Dallas*, 12 (Dec. 1933), 6.

17. Lionel V. Patenaude, *Texans, Politics, and the New Deal* (New York: Garland Publishing, 1983), 88; United States Federal Emergency Relief Administration, *Final Statistical Report on the Federal Emergency Relief Administration*, prepared under the direction of Theodore E. Whiting, Work Projects Administration (Washington, DC: Government Printing Office, 1942), 177–192; Arthur E. Burns, "Federal Emergency Relief Administration," in Clarence E. Ridley and Orin F. Nolting (eds.), *The Municipal Year Book*, 1937 (Chicago: The International City Managers' Association, 1937), 413–414.

18. Otis L. Graham, Jr., and Meghan Robinson Wander (eds.), *Franklin D. Roosevelt, His Life and Times: An Encyclopedic View* (Boston: G. K. Hall, 1985), 336–337; Work Projects

Administration Division of Information, "Texas," Appraisal Report File, County Reports DE, Record Group 69 (National Archives); Work Projects Administration Writers' Project, *Dallas Guide and History,* 508.

19. Graham and Wander (eds.), *Franklin D. Roosevelt, His Life and Times,* 461–464.

20. Donald S. Howard, *The WPA and Federal Relief Policy* (New York: Russell Sage Foundation, 1943), 84, 95, 178; Work Projects Administration Writers' Project, *Dallas Guide and History,* 494, 495 (quotation); *Final Statistical Report of the Federal Emergency Relief Administration,* 343. The city did employ 8,000 men in construction and landscaping work on the Texas Centennial Exposition. Work Projects Administration Writers' Project, *Dallas Guide and History,* 199.

21. *Dallas Morning News,* Mar. 30, 1935.

22. *New York Times,* Jan. 5, 1930; George Lambert, "Dallas Tries Terror," *The Nation,* 145 (Oct. 9, 1937), 377. *The Craftsman,* local AFL organ, protested the Chamber of Commerce's depiction of a pliable labor force. *The Craftsman* (Dallas), Mar. 28, 1930.

23. Stanley Walker, "The *Dallas Morning News,"* *American Mercury,* 65 (Dec., 1947), 708–711. Also see Ernest Sharpe, G. B. Dealey of the *Dallas News* (New York: Henry Holt & Co., 1955).

24. Work Projects Administration Writers' Project, *Dallas Guide and History,* 283–284; John J. Granberry, "Civil Liberties in Texas," *Christian Century,* 54 (Oct. 27, 1937), 1326–1327; Lambert, "Dallas Tries Terror," 376–378; F. Ray Marshall, *Labor in the South* (Cambridge, MA.: Harvard University Press, 1967), 191 (quotation).

25. *The Craftsman* (Dallas), Feb. 22, Mar. 8, 1935; Work Projects Administration Writers' Project, *Dallas Guide and History,* 284; John J. Granberry, "Civil Liberties in Texas," 1327; George N. Green, "The ILGWU in Texas, 1930–1970," *Journal of Mexican American History,* 1 (Spring 1971), 154 (quotation). Also see George N. Green, "Discord in Dallas: Auto Workers, City Fathers, and the Ford Motor Company, 1937–1941," *Labor's Heritage,* 1 (July 1980), 20–33.

26. Billy Hall Wyche, "Southern Attitudes Toward Industrial Unions, 1933–1941" (Ph.D. diss., University of Georgia, 1969), 167; George Brown Tindall, *The Emergence of the New South, 1913–1945* (Baton Rouge: Louisiana State University Press, 1967), 515, 522 (quotation). On unionization efforts since World War II, see Robert Emil Botsch, *We Shall Not Overcome: Populism and Southern Blue Collar Workers* (Chapel Hill: University of North Carolina Press, 1980); Marshall, *Labor in the South*; and Merl E. Reed, Leslie S. Hough, and Gary M. Fink (eds.), *Southern Workers and Their Unions, 1880–1975: Selected Papers/The Second Labor History Conference,* 1978 (Westport, CT: Greenwood Press, 1981). Outlining the failures of the CIO in the immediate post–World War II period is Barbara S. Griffith, *The Crisis of American Labor: Operation Dixie and the Defeat of the CIO* (Philadelphia: Temple University Press, 1988).

27. Bureau of the Census, *Fifteenth Census of the United States: 1930. Unemployment* (Washington, DC: Government Printing Office, 1931), I, 952–953; "Minutes of the Annual Meeting, Texas Commission on Interracial Cooperation," Dec. 6, 7, 1940, Houston Metropolitan Research Center, Houston Public Library; Alwyn Barr, *Black Texans: A History of Negroes in Texas, 1528–1971* (Austin: Jenkins Publishing Co., Pemberton Press, 1973), 154–155; Work Projects Administration Writers' Project, *Dallas Guide and History,* 507, 517; *Dallas Express,* Jan. 18, Mar. 1, 1941.

28. Robert Haynes, "Black Houstonians and the White Democratic Primary, 1920–1945," in Francisco A. Rosales and Barry J. Kaplan (eds.), *Houston: A Twentieth Century Urban Frontier* (Port Washington, NY: Associated Faculty Press, 1983), 122–137; James Martin SoRelle, "The Darker Side of 'Heaven': The Black Community in Houston, Texas, 1917–1945" (Ph.D. diss., Kent State University, 1980), 172–196.

29. Barr, *Black Texans*, 136; SoRelle, "The Darker Side of 'Heaven,'" 203–205. Also see Darlene Clark Hine, *Black Victory: The Rise and Fall of the White Primary in Texas* (Millwood, NY: KTO Press, 1979).

30. Fairbanks, "The Good Government Machine," 130–133; Ralph J. Bunche, *The Political Status of the Negro in the Age of FDR*, ed. Dewey W. Grantham (Chicago: University of Chicago Press, 1973), 95, 466, 557; SoRelle, "The Darker Side of 'Heaven,'" 302–303.

31. Tempie Virginia Strange, "The Dallas Negro Chamber of Commerce: A Study of a Negro Institution" (M.A. thesis, Southern Methodist University, 1945); Barr, *Black Texans*, 147; Leedell W. Neyland, "The Negro in Louisiana Since 1900: An Economic and Social Study" (Ph.D. diss., New York University, 1958), 66.

32. Tindall, *The Emergence of the New South, 1913–1945*, 546; Charles S. Johnson, *Patterns of Negro Segregation* (New York: Harper and Brothers, 1943), 37.

Chapter 10

Crabgrass-Roots Politics: Race, Rights, and the Reaction against Liberalism in the Urban North, 1940–1964

Thomas J. Sugrue

The dominant narratives of twentieth-century United States history depict the rise of a triumphant liberal state, shaped by the hopeful marriage of government and expertise and validated by a "liberal consensus" of workers, corporations, southerners and northerners, whites and blacks, Catholics and Jews. Conservative critics of the state have remained on the fringes of historiography, as Alan Brinkley has recently argued, a "largely neglected part of the story of twentieth-century America." One of the unexamined ironies of recent American history is that the most influential critics of the liberal state came neither from the ranks of the Republicans nor from such radical rightist organizations as the Liberty League, the Black Legion, and the John Birch Society, nor from the ranks of Communists and socialists. The most vocal—and ultimately the farthest-reaching challenge to liberalism—came from within the New Deal coalition itself. Southern whites, whether die-hard Democrats or disaffected Dixiecrats, constrained New Deal liberalism from its inception. Corporate leaders and business unionists limited the possibilities for social democratic reform in the workplace. Their stories are well known. But crucial to the fate of liberalism and antiliberalism in mid-twentieth-century United States were northern, urban whites. They were the backbone of the New Deal coalition; their political views and their votes limited the possibilities of liberal reform in the mid-twentieth century and constrained the leading liberal social movement, the extension of civil rights and liberties to African Americans.[1]

The New Deal may have been, as Lizabeth Cohen and others have argued, a unifying moment in American political history, at least in the urban North. Industrial workers discovered common political goals in the Democratic party, built class solidarity through the Congress of Industrial Organizations (CIO), and expressed their grievances through an inclusive language of Americanism. Yet beneath the seeming unity of the New Deal order were unresolved questions of racial identity and racial politics.

Reprinted from *Journal of American History* 82 (September 1995): 551–78. Reprinted with the permission of the Organization of American Historians.

Eating away at the "liberal consensus," just as it reached its postwar apotheosis, was a newly assertive working-class whiteness.[2] As early as the 1940s, white politicians in the urban North began to identify the hot-button issues that motivated urban working-class and middle-class white voters. In the crucible of postwar northern cities undergoing profound racial and economic transformation, they fashioned a new politics that combined racial antipathy with a growing skepticism about liberalism. The white rebellion against the New Deal had its origins in the urban politics of the 1940s and 1950s. The local politics of race and housing in the aftermath of World War II fostered a grass-roots rebellion against liberalism and seriously limited the social democratic and egalitarian possibilities of the New Deal order.

POSTWAR DETROIT

The history of politics in the post–New Deal era has been told primarily at the national level. The values, ideals, and social movements that formed the political world of the mid-twentieth century can be seen most clearly, however, at the local level, where political and social history intersected in the day-to-day lives of ordinary Americans. An examination of post–World War II Detroit, Michigan, offers insights into the travails of liberalism at the grass-roots level. Dominated by a blue-collar workforce, heavily unionized, and predominantly Catholic, Detroit was a stronghold of the Democratic party, a bastion of support for New Deal liberalism. Detroit workers—both white and black—benefited tremendously from New Deal programs. By providing temporary work during the Great Depression, the Works Progress Administration cemented the loyalty of the unemployed of all races to the New Deal. The National Labor Relations Act of 1935 facilitated unionization, which brought tangible gains to Detroit's blue-collar population. By the 1940s Detroit's heavily unionized workforce commanded high wages and generous benefits. In addition, federal housing subsidies, under the aegis of the Home Owner's Loan Corporation, the Federal Housing Administration, and the Veterans Administration, protected homeowners from foreclosure and made homeownership possible for much of the city's working class.

Detroit's voters turned out in droves for Democratic presidential candidates in every election after 1932, most prominently supporting Franklin D. Roosevelt, whose portrait graced working-class clubs, bars, and homes throughout the city. Detroiters provided the crucial margin of votes in gubernatorial elections for the New Dealer Frank Murphy (later appointed to the United States Supreme Court by FDR) and for liberals such as G. Mennen "Soapy" Williams. Only once after 1932 did Detroiters fail to rally behind the Democratic candidate for governor. But just as support for the New Deal reached its zenith at the state and national levels, social and demographic changes began to erode support for the liberal agenda in Detroit.[3]

The Second Great Migration of southern Blacks to the city set into motion political tremors. Detroit was a magnet for African-American migrants during and after World War II. The city's black population increased by over five hundred thousand between 1940 and 1970, growing from 9 percent of the city's population in 1940 to 45 percent in 1970. Aspiring black workers, many of whom found stable and relatively high-paying employment in the city's defense and automobile industries, began to look for housing outside Detroit's small and crowded inner-city area, which had held most of the city's African-American population in 1940. In the postwar decades, the city's racial geography changed dramatically. Upwardly mobile blacks sought better housing in predominantly white sections of the city. Poorer blacks also put pressure on the real estate market. Between 1940 and 1960, the first African Americans moved into 110 previously white census tracts.[4]

In the wake of this influx of blacks, racial tensions mounted. World War II brought a wave of hate strikes against black defense workers, a riot at the site of the Sojourner Truth Homes, a public housing project for blacks, and the 1943 race riot, the bloodiest civil disorder in the United States since the draft uprisings of the Civil War. Although Detroit did not experience another major race riot until 1967, race relations in the period after World War II were not tranquil. One city race relations official called the postwar period "the dark ages of Detroit."[5]

Postwar Detroit was not unique in its history of racial tension. The post–World War II decades witnessed a profound transformation in the politics, urban geography, and economies of dozens of northern industrial cities. Urban whites responded to the influx of millions of black migrants to their cities in the 1940s, 1950s, and 1960s by redefining urban geography and urban politics in starkly racial terms. In Chicago and Cicero, Illinois, working-class whites rioted in the 1940s and 1950s to oppose the construction of public housing in their neighborhoods. White Chicagoans fashioned a brand of Democratic party politics, especially under mayors Martin H. Kennelly and Richard J. Daley, that had a sharp racial edge. In Newark, New Jersey, in the 1950s, blue-collar Italian and Polish Americans harassed African-American newcomers to their neighborhoods. And in the postwar period, white Philadelphians and Cincinnatians attacked blacks who moved into previously all-white enclaves and resisted efforts to integrate the housing market. Countless whites retreated to suburbs or neighborhoods on the periphery of cities where they excluded blacks by federally sanctioned redlining, real estate steering, and restrictive zoning laws.[6]

While the racial demography of Detroit was changing, the economy of the Motor City and other older industrial centers began to decline. On the surface, Detroit seemed an embodiment of the postwar affluent society. Detroit's workers, especially in the automobile and auto parts industries, were among the best paid in the country. They used their relatively high wages, along with federal mortgage subsidies, to purchase or build modest single-family houses on Detroit's sprawling northeast and northwest sides. The proportion of homes in the city that were occupied by their owners rose from 39.2 percent in 1940 to 54.1 percent in 1960. Yet the working-class hold on affluence was tenuous. The postwar boom was punctuated by periodic layoffs and four recessions, which painfully evoked memories of the Great Depression. Beginning in the early 1950s, the industrial bases of almost every major city in the North began to atrophy, and Detroit was no exception. Large and small companies relocated outside cities to suburban and rural areas, reduced the number of workers in newly automated plants, and closed dozens of central city factories altogether. Between 1954 and 1960, Detroit lost more than eighty thousand manufacturing jobs. The vagaries of the economy jeopardized workers' most significant, usually their only substantial investment—their homes.[7]

The simultaneous black migration and economic dislocation in postwar Detroit created a sense of crisis among the city's white homeowners. As they endured layoffs, plant closings, and downsizing, some working-class homeowners feared that they would lose their homes to foreclosure. Auto worker Bill Collett, reacting to news of layoffs at the Ford Motor Company's River Rouge plant in 1951, worried about the effect of unemployment on his homeowning fellow workers: "What will happen to the thousands who will be let out? What is going to happen to the thousands who are buying homes?" Even those who held steady employment found that mortgage or land contract payments stretched family budgets to the breaking point. In a comprehensive survey of Detroit residents conducted in 1951, the Wayne University sociologist Arthur Kornhauser found that white Detroiters ranked housing needs as the most pressing problem in the city. Homeownership required a significant financial sacrifice for Detroit residents: the most frequent complaint (voiced by 32 percent of respondents) was that the cost of housing was too high.[8]

The issues of race and housing were inseparable in the minds of many white Detroiters. Homeowners feared, above all, that an influx of blacks would imperil their precarious economic security. A self-described "average American housewife" wrote: "What about us, who cannot afford to move to a better location and are surrounded by colored? . . . Most of us invested our life's savings in property and now we are in constant fear that the neighbor will sell its property to people of different race." Kornhauser found that race relations followed a close second in Detroiters' ranking of the city's most pressing problems. Only 18 percent of white respondents from all over the city expressed "favorable" views toward the "full acceptance of Negroes," and 54 percent expressed "unfavorable" attitudes toward integration. When asked to discuss ways in which race relations "were not as good as they should be," 27 percent of white respondents mentioned "Negroes moving into white neighborhoods." Among white respondents 22 percent answered that the "Negro has too many rights and privileges; too much power; too much intermingling." Another 14 percent mentioned "Negroes' undesirable characteristics." Only 14 percent mentioned discrimination as a problem in race relations.[9]

Whites in Kornhauser's sample regularly spoke of the "colored problem" or the "Negro problem." In their responses to open-ended questions, Kornhauser's informants made clear what they meant by the "colored problem." "Eighty percent of [blacks] are animals," stated one white respondent. "If they keep them all in the right place there wouldn't be any trouble," responded another. "Colored treat the whites in an insolent way," added a third white. "They think they own the city." A majority of whites looked to increase segregation as the solution to Detroit's "colored problem." When asked "What do you feel ought to be done about relations between Negroes and whites in Detroit?" a remarkable 68 percent of white respondents called for some form of racial segregation—56 percent of whites surveyed advocated residential segregation. Many cited the Jim Crow South as a model for successful race relations.[10]

Class, union membership, and religion all affected whites' attitudes toward blacks. Working-class and poor whites expressed negative views toward blacks more frequently than other respondents to Kornhauser's survey. Among poor and working-class whites, 85 percent supported racial segregation, in contrast to 56 percent among middle-income and 42 percent among upper-income whites. Union members were slightly "less favorable than others towards accepting Negroes." CIO members were even more likely than other white Detroiters to express negative views of African Americans—65 percent—although more CIO members were also likely to support full racial equality (18 percent) than ordinary white Detroiters. And finally Catholics were significantly more likely than Protestants to express unfavorable feelings toward blacks.[11]

In reaction to the postwar transformation of the city, Detroit's whites began fashioning a politics of defensive localism that focused on threats to property and neighborhood. They directed their political energy toward the two groups they believed were the agents of change: blacks and their liberal allies. Acting on their perception of the threat of black newcomers to their stability, economic status and political power, many of Detroit's working- and middle-class whites banded together in exclusive neighborhood organizations, in what became one of the largest grass-roots movements in the city's history. By moving the politics of race, homeownership, and neighborhood to center stage, they reshaped urban politics in the 1940s and 1950s and set in motion the forces that would eventually reconfigure national politics.[12]

Between 1943 and 1965, whites throughout Detroit founded at least 192 neighborhood organizations, variously called "civic associations," "protective associations," "improvement associations," and "homeowners' associations." Their titles reveal their place in the ideology of white Detroiters. As civic associations, they saw their purpose as upholding the values of self-government and participatory democracy. They offered members a unified voice in city politics. As protective associations, they fiercely guarded the investments their members had made in their homes. They also paternalistically defended neighborhood, home, family, women, and children against the forces of social disorder that they saw arrayed against them in the city. As improvement associations, they emphasized the ideology of self-help and individual achievement that lay at the very heart of the American notion of homeownership. Above all, as home- and property-owners' associations, these groups represented the interests of those who perceived themselves as independent and rooted rather dependent and transient.

The surviving records of homeowners' associations do not, unfortunately, permit a close analysis of their membership. From the hundreds of letters that groups sent to city officials and civil rights groups, from neighborhood newsletters, and from improvement association letterheads, it is clear that no single ethnic group dominated most neighborhood associations. Names as diverse as Fadanelli, Csanyi, Berge, and Watson appeared on the same petitions. Groups met in public school buildings, Catholic and Protestant churches, union halls, Veterans of Foreign Wars clubhouses, and parks. Letters, even from residents with discernibly "ethnic" names, seldom referred to national heritage or religious background. Organizational newsletters and neighborhood newspapers never used ethnic modifiers or monikers to describe neighborhood association members—they reserved ethnic nomenclature for "the colored" and Asians (and occasionally Jews). The diversity of ethnic membership in neighborhood groups is not surprising, since by the 1940s, Detroit had few ethnically homogeneous neighborhoods. But the heterogeneity of Detroit's neighborhoods only partially explains the absence of ethnic affiliation in remaining records. Members of homeowners' and neighborhood groups shared a common bond of whiteness and Americanness—a bond that they asserted forcefully at public meetings and in correspondence with public officials.[13]

Neighborhood associations had a long history in cities such as Detroit. Real estate developers had originally created them to enforce restrictive covenants and, later, zoning laws. Frequently, they sponsored community social activities and advocated better public services, such as street lighting, stop signs, and traffic lights. During and after World War II, these organizations grew rapidly in number and influence. Increasingly, they existed solely to wage battles against proposed public housing sites and against blacks moving into their neighborhoods.

Beginning in the 1940s, the threat of a black influx became the raison d'être of community groups. One new group, the Northwest Civic Association, called its founding meeting "So YOU will have first hand information on the colored situation in this area," and it invited "ALL interested in maintaining Property Values in the NORTH-WEST section of Detroit." The Courville District Improvement Association gathered residents of a northeast Detroit neighborhood to combat the "influx of colored people" into the area and rallied supporters with its provocatively entitled newsletter, *Action!* The founders of the Connor-East Homeowners' Association promised to "protect the Area from undesirable elements." Members of the San Bernardo Improvement Association pledged to keep their neighborhood free of "undesirables"—or "Niggers"—as several who eschewed euphemism shouted at the group's first meeting. Existing organizations took on a new emphasis with the threat of black mobility. In 1950 Orville Tenaglia, president of the Southwest Detroit Improvement League, recounted his group's history: "Originally we organized in 1941 to promote better civic affairs, but now we are banded together just to protect our homes." The league was engaged in a "war of nerves" over the movement of blacks into the community.[14]

As the racial demography of Detroit changed, neighborhood groups demarcated racial boundaries with great precision and, abetted by federal agencies and private real estate agents, divided cities into strictly enforced racial territories. From the 1940s through the 1960s, white urban dwellers fiercely defended their turf. They referred to the black migration in military terms: they spoke of "invasions" and "penetration" and plotted strategies of "resistance." White neighborhoods became "battlegrounds" where residents struggled to preserve segregated housing. Homeowners' associations helped whites to "defend" their homes and "protect" their property.[15]

Their militancy was more than rhetorical. As a former Detroit race relations official remarked of the postwar period, the city "did a lot of firefighting in those days." White Detroiters instigated over two hundred incidents against blacks attempting to move into formerly all-white neighborhoods, including mass demonstrations, picketing, effigy burning, window breaking, arson, vandalism, and physical attacks. Most incidents followed improvement association meetings. A potent mixture of fear and anger animated whites who violently defended their neighborhoods. All but the most liberal whites who lived along the city's racial frontier believed that they had only two choices. They could flee, as vast numbers of white urbanites did, or they could hold their ground and fight.[16]

Neighborhood groups responded to the threat of "invasion" with such urgency because of the extraordinary speed of racial change. Most blocks in changing neighborhoods went from all-white to predominantly black in three or four years. The movement of a single black family to a white block fueled panic. Real estate brokers canvassed door to door in areas bordering black neighborhoods warning fearful white homeowners that if they did not sell quickly, the value of their houses would plummet. Realtors created a climate of fear by ostentatiously showing houses to black families, waiting a day or two for rumors to spread throughout the neighborhood, and then inundating residents with leaflets and phone calls urging them to sell. One broker paid a black woman to walk her baby down an all-white block, to spark fears that "Negroes [were] 'taking over' this block or area" and that the residents "had best sell now while there was still a chance of obtaining a good price." Such sales tactics, while often despised by white homeowners, were remarkably effective. Whites living just beyond "racially transitional" neighborhoods witnessed rapid black movement into nearby areas. They feared that without concerted action, their neighborhoods would turn over just as quickly.[17]

White Detroiters also looked beyond transitional neighborhoods to the "slum," a place that confirmed their greatest fears. Whites saw in the neighborhoods to which blacks had been confined in the center city area a grim prophecy of their neighborhoods' futures. They focused on places like Paradise Valley, Detroit's first major ghetto, which housed two-thirds of the city's black population during World War II. Housing in Paradise Valley consisted mainly of run-down rental units, most built in the 1860s and 1870s, owned by absentee white landlords. White Detroiters also noticed the striking class difference between blacks and whites. Through 1960 the median family income of blacks in Detroit was, at best, two-thirds that of whites there. Although the poorest blacks were seldom the first to move into formerly white neighborhoods (in fact, black "pioneers" were often better off than their white neighbors), whites feared the incursion of a "lower-class element" into their neighborhoods.[18]

To white Detroiters, the wretched conditions in Paradise Valley and other poor African-American neighborhoods were the fault of irresponsible blacks, not of greedy landlords or neglectful city officials. Wherever blacks lived, whites believed, neighborhoods inevitably deteriorated. "Let us keep out the slums," admonished one east-side homeowners' group. If blacks moved into white neighborhoods, they would bring with them "noisy roomers, loud parties, auto horns, and in general riotous living," thus depreciating real estate values and destroying the moral fiber of the community. A northwest-side neighborhood association poster played on white residents' fears of the crime that, they believed, would accompany racial change: "Home Owners Can You Afford to . . . Have your children exposed to gangster operated skid row saloons? Pornographic pictures and literature? Gamblers and prostitution? You Face These Issues Now!"[19]

The most commonly expressed fear was not of "riotous living" or crime, but of racial intermingling. Black "penetration" of white neighborhoods posed a fundamental challenge to white racial identity. Again and again, neighborhood groups and letter writers referred to the perils of rapacious black sexuality and race mixing. The politics of family, home, and neighborhood were inseparable from the containment of uncontrolled sexuality and the imminent danger of interracial liaisons. Proximity to blacks risked intimacy. As one opponent of a proposed Negro housing project stated: "We firmly believe in the God-given equality of man. He did not give us the right to choose our brothers . . . but he did give us the right to choose the people we sleep with." Newspaper accounts ominously warned of the threat of miscegenation. One northwest-side newspaper praised a city council candidate in a banner headline: "Kronk Bucks Mixing Races." Neighborhood defense became more than a struggle for turf. It was a battle for the preservation of white womanhood. Men had a duty, as the Courville District Improvement Association admonished, to "pitch for your civic rights and the protection of your women."[20]

The prevention of interracial residential and sexual contact was not just a masculine responsibility. Women also policed the boundaries of race and sex. The overlapping concerns of neighborhood integrity, racial purity, and domestic tranquility gave particular urgency to demonstrations led by women against Edward Brock. Brock, the white owner of two houses on Detroit's lower west side, had sold them to black families in 1948. Groups of ten to twenty-five women, many pushing baby strollers, gathered at Brock's workplace every day for a week, carrying hand-painted signs that read: "My home is my castle, I will die defending it"; "We don't want to mix"; and "Ed Brock sold to colored in white neighborhood." Passersby were taken aback by a picket line of white mothers and babies, an uncommon sight at a time when most demonstrations in Detroit were labor-oriented and male-led. Replete with the symbols of motherhood and family, these protests touched a deep, sympathetic nerve among onlookers, many of whom saw black movement into a neighborhood as a threat to virtuous womanhood, innocent childhood, and the sanctity of the home.[21]

"RIGHTS," HOUSING, AND POLITICS

Neighborhood associations resorted to pickets, harassment, and violence in the days and weeks of desperation that followed black "invasions" of their neighborhoods. More commonly, however, they relied on traditional political means—the ballot box, constituent letters, and testimony at city hearings—to stem racial change. Neighborhood associations became the most powerful force in postwar Detroit politics. They backed conservative politicians who opposed public housing, tax increases, and racial integration. Their members turned out in huge numbers on election day. In moments of crisis, they sent an extraordinary volume of mail to city officials and packed city plan commission and common council hearings on public housing and zoning. Issues of race and homeownership dominated local politics in postwar Detroit. White homeowners forged an extraordinarily well organized grass-roots conservative coalition in local politics, constrained public housing policy, and thwarted attempts to integrate the private housing market.

Perhaps the issue that most visibly galvanized neighborhood groups was the threat of "socialized housing," especially government-sponsored developments for low-income blacks. Public housing became the first significant wedge between white voters and New Deal liberalism in Detroit. Federal officials made public hosing a centerpiece of New Deal social policy, beginning with the Federal Public Housing Act in 1937 and culminating in the Taft-Ellender-Wagner Housing Act of 1949. New Deal and Fair Deal legislation allocated over a billion dollars in federal resources to provide shelter for the poorest Americans.[22] Black migrants, entrapped in crowded center-city neighborhoods, suffered the brunt of the postwar urban housing shortage. As Detroit's relatively small center-city ghetto grew overcrowded and as black inner-city residents were displaced by highway and urban renewal construction, the proportion of blacks seeking public housing increased dramatically. To alleviate the shortage, city officials, social welfare advocates, and civil rights organizations proposed the construction of public housing projects on open land throughout the city. White Detroiters, however, vehemently opposed public housing during and after World War II, largely on racial grounds. Between 1942 and 1950 neighborhood associations resisted public housing proposed for outlying white sections of the city, and they succeeded in preventing the building of almost all the projects.

In 1942 whites in northeast Detroit tried unsuccessfully to prevent black occupancy of the Sojourner Truth defense housing project, and whites and blacks battled on the streets when the first black families arrived at the site. In 1944 whites living near the site of a proposed temporary wartime project for blacks, on Algonquin Street, flooded city officials with angry petitions. In 1944 and 1945, residents of suburban Dearborn and Ecorse, cooperating with the Ford Motor Company, had prevented the construction of public housing in their communities, and white Detroiters in the Oakwood district in southwest Detroit blocked the construction of a public housing project for blacks in their neighborhood. In 1948 and 1949, neighborhood group members packed city plan commission and common council hearings on proposals to locate twelve public housing projects on sites on Detroit's periphery. They won a mayoral veto of all outlying public housing projects in 1950. Through intensive lobbying efforts, they succeeded in restricting Detroit's public housing to neighborhoods with sizable African-American populations.[23]

In the battles over public housing in the 1940s, neighborhood groups fashioned a potent political language of rights, a language that they refined and extended in the 1950s and 1960s. As one observer noted, "the white population has come to believe that it has a vested, exclusive, and permanent 'right' to certain districts." Civic associations cast their demands for racially segregated neighborhoods in terms of entitlement and victimization. Homeowners' groups were by no means alone in couching their political demands in the language of rights. They were part of a New Deal–inspired rights revolution that empowered other groups, including African Americans, trade union members, and military veterans, to use rights talk to express their political discontent and their political vision.[24]

The notion of the white entitlement to a home in a racially homogeneous neighborhood was firmly rooted in New Deal housing policy. Supporters of the Home Owners' Loan Corporation (HOLC) and the Federal Housing Administration (FHA) argued that national security and self-preservation required the stability of private homeownership. President Franklin Delano Roosevelt frequently alluded to the ideal of a nation of free homeowners in his speeches, and he included the right to a decent home in his 1944 "Second Bill of Rights." This New Deal rhetoric touched a deep nerve among white Detroiters who had struggled, usually without the benefit of loans or mortgages, to build meager homes of their own in the city. With government-backed mortgages and loans, they were able to attain the dream of property ownership with relative ease. They welcomed government assistance; in fact, by World War II, they began to view homeownership as a perquisite of citizenship. The FHA and HOLC's insistence that mortgages and loans be restricted to racially homogeneous neighborhoods also resonated strongly with Detroit's homeowners. They came to expect a vigilant government to protect their segregated neighborhoods.[25]

The rhetoric linking homeownership and citizenship echoed in the newsletters and petitions of neighborhood associations. The Federated Property Owners of Detroit, for example, was founded in 1948 to "promote, uphold and defend the rights of home and property ownership and small business as the cornerstone of American opportunity and prosperity." The promise of government-sanctioned racial homogeneity also resounded in neighborhood association rhetoric. In 1949, the Greater Detroit Neighbors Association, Unit No. 2, rallied its members around "the right to live in the type of neighborhood that you chose." Homeowners' rights were precarious and needed to be defended vigorously from grasping blacks and acquiescent federal officials who threatened to usurp them. The slogan "Help Stamp Out Oppression—Fight for Our Rights" inspired organizers of a "Vigilantes Organizational Meeting" in 1945; they appealed to "the oppressed Homeowners" of Detroit.[26]

The experience of World War II solidified white Detroiters' belief in their right to racially homogeneous neighborhoods. Flyers produced by neighborhood improvement associations couched the grievances of whites struggling against public housing in the language of Americanism and wartime patriotism. In the immediate aftermath of World War II, petitioners highlighted the theme of wartime sacrifice, appealing to the sentiments that undergirded federal entitlements for returning veterans. In 1945 Michael J. Harbulak, who opposed the construction of a public housing project in his neighborhood, Oakwood, wrote: "Our boys are fighting in Europe, Asia, and Africa to keep those people off our soil. If when these boys return they should become refugees who have to give up their homes because their own neighborhood with the help of our city fathers had been invade[d] and occupied by the Africans, it would be a shame which our city fathers could not outlive." Testifying against public housing, Louis J. Borolo, president of the Oakwood Blue Jackets Athletic Club, appealed to the city council using the patriotic language that many of his neighbors had used in their petition letters. "There are 1,500 blue stars in the windows of homes of that neighborhood," he testified. "Those stars represent soldiers waiting to come back to the same neighborhood they left." Acknowledging the "moral and legal right" of blacks to adequate housing, he nonetheless contended that "we have established a prior right to a neighborhood which we have built up through the years—a neighborhood which is entirely white and which we want kept white."[27]

"Homeowners' rights" was a malleable concept that derived its power from its imprecision. Some whites described their rights in humble "bootstraps" terms. They had acquired property and earned their rights through hard work and responsible citizenship. Homeowners' rights were, in this view, a reward for sacrifice and duty. Others drew from an idiosyncratic reading of the Declaration of Independence and Bill of Rights to justify their neighborhood defensiveness. Public housing for blacks in a white neighborhood was a violation of white "rights" to "peace and happyness." Some defined homeowners' rights as an extension of their constitutional right of freedom of assembly. They had a right to choose their associates. That right would be infringed if their neighborhoods were racially mixed.[28]

In an era of growing civil rights consciousness, many white letter writers and petitioners made grudging acknowledgments of racial equality. Many petitions in opposition to the Oakwood housing project included the formula "I have nothing against the colored" or "I believe in the God-given equality of man." The writers qualified these shibboleths with such statements as "But I wouldn't want them for a neighbor nor growing up with my children." Rights for blacks were acceptable in the abstract, as long as blacks remained in their own neighborhoods and kept to themselves. But many whites believed that civil rights for blacks were won only at the expense of white rights. One opponent of a public housing project slated for black occupancy stated succinctly, "It looks as if, we the white people are being discriminated against. Let the colored people make their own district, as we had to."[29]

In the crucible of Detroit's racial and economic transformation, not all rights were equal. Neighborhood groups criticized public housing as a handout to the undeserving poor, who demanded rights without bearing the burden of responsibilities. Politicians on the right (Democrat and Republican alike) were quick to pick up that theme. Mayor Edward Jeffries staunchly opposed public housing on the grounds that "good government is the kind of government that takes unusual steps to give people opportunities, not to give them hand-outs." Jeffries's rhetoric found a sympathetic hearing in white Detroit neighborhoods. An opponent of public housing noted in 1949 that "taxpayers and home-owning groups are rising in wrath against subsidizing homes." Why should government compel hardworking whites to pay for housing for the poor? And why should it "force" white neighborhoods to accept housing for poor blacks?[30]

In the wake of public housing disputes, white Detroiters grew increasingly critical of what they perceived as the growing disjuncture between federal social policy and their own interest, and the apparent acquiescence of an activist government in the demands of those who sought racial and economic leveling. Detroit's whites began to view public housing as "Negro housing," and they grew increasingly skeptical of the federal agenda that called for the provision of shelter for America's poor. Erosion of support for public housing on grounds of race also eroded support for New Deal programs more generally. One astute observer noted in 1946:

> In the field of housing, there has tended to develop a tie-up in our thinking between Negroes and government. Public housing and housing for Negroes is synonymous or nearly so in the minds of many people. This is bad for public housing and bad for Negroes. Many people are concerned about government interference of all kinds. This tends to create a separation in their minds between themselves and "the government."[31]

Alienated Detroit whites increasingly directed their animus against local public officials, whom they saw as active agents in the transformation of their neighborhoods.

"We must stop the wasting of the taxpayers money on public housing, or any other wasteful planning," warned a west-side chapter of the National Association of Community Councils in 1945. In the same year, a "Group of Taxpayers" complained to the city of the "insurmountable tax, housing, hospitalization and social problems facing taxpayers" because of the influx of "colored" moving to the city to collect welfare benefits denied them in the South. Equally blameworthy were the black poor who depended on government assistance and the bureaucrats who fostered that dependence through social welfare programs. In an ambiguously worded letter (its pejorative references could refer to either black welfare recipients or to welfare administrators), the "Group of Taxpayers" argued that in city welfare offices "stink has reached to high heaven for years" and railed against the "polysyllabic patter" that they heard there. Speaking for the neighborhood associations that he advocated, Karl H. Smith, a local realtor, praised groups who fought "unjust tax levies for the benefit of shiftless drifters who have not the guts to want to own a home of their own."[32]

As domestic anticommunism rose to political prominence, neighborhood groups began to articulate their concerns in McCarthyite terms. A growing number of white Detroiters believed in a conspiracy of government bureaucrats, many influenced by communism or socialism (terms used interchangeably), who misused tax dollars to fund experiments in social engineering for the benefit of pressure groups. In so doing, the government repudiated property rights and democratic principles. Behind the scenes was a cabal of public housing officials, city planning committees, civil rights groups, labor activists, and socialist agitators who worked to defraud honest taxpayers and destroy the city.

Homeowners' groups and sympathetic politicians used McCarthyite rhetoric against liberal politicians and advocates of public housing and open housing. Red-baiting was a crass smear tactic, but in the perfervid atmosphere of the anticommunist crusade, many whites believed that a sinister conspiracy was afoot. In their minds, the issues of race, left-wing politics, and government action became inextricably linked. Public housing projects were part of the conspiratorial effort of well-placed Communists and Communist sympathizers in the government to destroy traditional American values through a carefully calculated policy of racial and class struggle. Floyd McGriff, the editor of a chain of northwest-side neighborhood newspapers, warned that multiple-family homes "threatened local areas with additional blight." He blamed the "fringe disruptionists, the political crack-pots, and the socialist double-domes" who "injected racial issues" into housing debates. Reds in the city government planned to "move the slum-area residents into city-built housing projects in Northwest Detroit" and "to force pioneering families to move out." Open housing was the product of a "leftist political brigade" that had as its mission "political activity to provide colored persons with homes they cannot afford to live in." Small neighborhood struggles against the "Black invasion" and against public housing were really skirmishes in a larger battle against communism itself.[33]

The pro-homeowner and anti-integrationist sentiments unleashed by public housing debates had a profound impact on local mayoral elections. The political career of Detroit mayor Edward Jeffries (1941–1947) revealed the power of crabgrass-roots politics and the fragility of liberalism in Detroit. Jeffries was first elected mayor in

1941 as a New Dealer, prolabor and racially liberal. He garnered the endorsements of labor unions and civil rights groups and swept both black and white working-class precincts. After the wartime riots and hate strikes and the emergence of a powerful homeowners' movement, Jeffries refashioned his racial politics. He combined red-baiting and race-baiting in his successful reelection bid in 1945 against the liberal candidate backed by the United Automobile Workers (UAW), Richard Frankensteen. In the wake of the Algonquin Street and Oakwood debates, Jeffries turned his opponent's support of federal public housing policy into a political liability. In a campaign laden with racial innuendo, he flooded neighborhoods on the northwest and northeast sides with literature highlighting Frankensteen's ties to black organizations. Handbills reading "Increasing Negro Housing" and "Negroes Can Live Anywhere With Frankensteen Mayor. Negroes—Do Your Duty Nov. 6" were widely distributed in white neighborhoods during the election. Jeffries supporters sounded the ominous warning that Frankensteen was a "red" who, if elected, would encourage "racial invasions" of white neighborhoods.[34]

The electoral choice was stark. Jeffries would uphold white community interests. An editorial in the *Home Gazette*, a newspaper in the virtually all-white, predominantly homeowning northwest side, stated, "There is no question where Edward J. Jeffries' administration stands on mixed housing." It praised the Detroit Housing Commission's policy of segregation in public housing for "declaring that a majority of the people of the city of Detroit do not want the racial character of their neighborhoods changed" and for reiterating "its previous stand against attempts of Communist-inspired Negroes to penetrate white residential sections." Black observers of the election and union supporters of Frankensteen were appalled by the blatant racial claims of the Jeffries campaign, and they attempted to use economic populist and anti-Nazi rhetoric to deflate Jeffries's charges. The black journalist Henry Lee Moon, writing in the National Association for the Advancement of Colored People (NAACP) monthly *Crisis*, accused Jeffries of appealing "to our more refined fascists, the big money interests and the precarious middle class whose sole inalienable possession is a white skin." Racial appeals bolstered the flagging Jeffries campaign and gave him a comfortable margin in November against a UAW-backed candidate in a solidly union city. On the local level, the link between black and red was a clever strategy for attracting white Democrats, suspicious of liberalism and its capacity for equalitarian political and social rhetoric.[35]

The political tensions over race and housing came to a head in the mayoral election of 1949. The liberal common council member George Edwards faced the conservative city treasurer, Albert Cobo. Edwards, a onetime UAW activist, former public housing administrator, and New Deal Democrat, was the political antithesis of Cobo, a corporate executive, real estate investor, and Republican. Cobo focused his campaign on the issues of race and public housing. Armed with the endorsement of most white neighborhood improvement associations, Cobo swept the largely white precincts on the northeast and northwest sides, where voters were especially concerned about the threat of public housing. The distinction between Cobo and Edwards was crystal clear. Cobo adamantly opposed "Negro invasions" and public housing, whereas Councilman Edwards had consistently championed the right of blacks to decent housing anywhere in the city and had regularly voted for proposals to locate public housing in outlying areas.[36]

Liberal leaders were baffled that the conservative Cobo had beaten the prolabor Edwards in a heavily Democratic city and that Cobo did particularly well among union voters. The Edwards campaign was coordinated by the UAW and other CIO unions, which provided him with nearly $30,000 in funding, printed and distributed over 1.3 million pro-Edwards pamphlets, and sent union members canvassing door to door throughout the city. Pamphlets in English, Polish, and Hungarian lambasted Cobo for his connections with bankers and slumlords who "live in Grosse Pointe, Birmingham, and Bloomfield Hills." Radio spots featured a "snotty woman's voice" urging voters to "vote Republican in the Detroit election for mayor," and UAW sound trucks blasted pro-Edwards messages at local unemployment offices. Yet despite the massive and well-organized union effort, Edwards lost to Cobo even in heavily blue-collar precincts.[37]

Stunned by the overwhelming defeat of Edwards, UAW political activists met to discuss the election. On the east side, one organizer reported, many union members refused to place Edwards placards in their windows. In one heavily Democratic ward on the west side, blue-collar voters told a UAW canvasser that they supported Edwards, yet on election day, they turned out for Cobo two to one. A west-side coordinator explained the seeming paradox of union support for Cobo: "I think in these municipal elections we are dealing with people who have a middle class mentality. Even in our own UAW, the member is either buying a home, owns a home, or is going to buy one. I don't know whether we can ever make up this difficulty." The problem was that "George was beaten by the housing program."[38]

The 1949 election revealed the conflict between the politics of home and the politics of workplace, a conflict exacerbated by racial tensions in rapidly changing neighborhoods. Blue-collar workers, one activist lamented, failed to "see the relationship between their life in the plant and their life in the community." Racial fears and neighborhood defensiveness made the political unity of home and workplace impossible. East-side UAW shop stewards, many of whom were open Cobo supporters, told one UAW Political Action Committee organizer that "the Union is okay in the shop but when they buy a home they forget about it. You can tell them anything they want to but as long as they think their property is going down, it is different." The Edwards defeat marked the beginning of a UAW retreat from labor politics in the city; the disillusioned UAW Political Action Committee continued to endorse liberal candidates, but it offered only half-hearted support to Cobo's opponents in Detroit's biennial mayoral races in the 1950s. The combination of racial resentment and homeowners' politics that defeated Edwards dimmed future hopes for the triumph of labor liberalism on the local level in Detroit.[39]

The new Cobo administration was sympathetic to neighborhood associations. Cobo offered prominent housing and city plan commission appointments to movement leaders. He established an advisory council of civic groups and regularly addressed neighborhood improvement association meetings. In his first weeks of office, he vetoed eight proposed public housing sites in outlying, predominantly white sections of the city. By putting brakes on all public housing development outside heavily black inner-city neighborhoods, Cobo single-handedly killed public housing as a controversial political issue. Orville Tenaglia, the southwest Detroit community leader who had fought public housing through the 1940s, wrote Cobo that "we who have come to look upon this community as 'our home,' living with people of our 'own kind,' do most humbly . . . thank you for the courageous stand you have taken" on the housing issue. With the support of grateful homeowners' groups, Republican Cobo won reelection easily in 1951, 1953, and 1955. By advocating and defending "homeowners' rights," he brought the majority of Detroit's whites into a powerful, bipartisan antiliberal coalition.[40]

CIVIL RIGHTS AND "CIVIL WRONGS"

The neighborhood movement's monopoly on Detroit politics was short-lived. Huge numbers of white Detroiters fled the city for the booming suburbs in the 1950s. Detroit's white population fell by more than 23 percent in the 1950s, while its African-American population rose by more than 180,000, to nearly one-third of the city's population. By the mid-1950s, blacks had become an increasingly large bloc of voters in Detroit, electing black candidates to citywide offices for the first time and providing a crucial swing vote in many local elections. As black electoral power grew, homeowners' associations lost their stranglehold on the city government and struggled for power against an emerging alliance uniting blacks and a small but vocal population of liberal white activists. Cobo's successor, Louis Miriani—sympathetic to the homeowners' movement when elected in 1957—recognized the changing balance of power in the city and tried, unsuccessfully, to accommodate both white neighborhood groups and blacks. His successor, Jerome Cavanagh, a little-known insurgent, won an upset victory in 1961 over Miriani with the support of an unlikely alliance of African Americans and white neighborhood groups, both alienated (for different reasons) by Miriani's equivocal, middle-of-the-road position on race, civil rights, and housing.[41]

As the racial balance of power in Detroit began to change, civil rights organizations found a new voice and began to challenge the conservative politics of neighborhood associations. Initially stunned by the Cobo victory and weakened by organizational infighting, advocates of racial equality slowly began to regroup in the early and mid-1950s. A coalition of labor activists, religious groups, and African-American organizations directed their energies toward racial integration and open housing. They found a powerful ally in the Detroit Mayor's Interracial Committee (MIC), which had been founded after the race riot of 1943 to monitor racial tension in the city and to advocate civil rights reform. Dominated by liberal whites and blacks close to civil rights organizations, the MIC consistently opposed segregation in public housing and other facilities, worked to abolish restrictive covenants, and investigated incidents of racial conflict in the city. The MIC, despite its name, was a largely independent city agency whose members were protected by civil service laws. Under Jeffries and Cobo it became a refuge for a small, dedicated band of integrationists, who maintained close ties with civil rights groups through the country. When the MIC became an increasingly vocal supporter of open housing in the early 1950s, the neighborhood movement counterattacked, railing against what its members saw as an unholy alliance between government and blacks. Homeowners' groups began an attack on "pressure groups, be they labor, government, or other impractical idealists," who supported the civil rights agenda.[42]

Empowered by the conservative climate of the Cobo administration, neighborhood improvement associations targeted the city's race relations agency. In 1951, a neighborhood association–backed group, which called itself the Legislative Research Committee, issued a report calling for the abolition of the MIC. It attempted to taint MIC director George Schermer with charges of leftism by noting his membership in the liberal Americans for Democratic Action. The report argued that under his leadership, the race relations agency fostered racial animosity in the city: "instead of lessening and assuaging interracial tensions, Schermer's outfit, by devious means has accentuated them, stirring up racial strife." Joining the cry against the MIC, Ralph Smith, president of the Michigan Council of Civic Associations, warned Cobo of the danger of "minority pressure groups."[43]

The anti-MIC campaign combined an anti–civil rights stance with antibureaucratic and antitax sentiments. Neighborhood group representatives charged that the MIC wrongfully used public funds to assist civil rights organizations. C. Katherine Rentschler, a member of the Warrendale Improvement Association and chair of Home-Owner Civic and Improvement Associations, accused the "watch-dog commission" of "using our TAX MONEY to create agitation." According to Rentschler, "a review of the work of the Mayor's Interracial Committee indicates that it has continually functioned solely for the Negro race." As an alternative to the MIC, she called for a "Home Owner Participation Ordinance" that would give neighborhood associations "a voice in planning and regulating the activities" of city agencies. The campaign against the Mayor's Interracial Committee met with success: in 1953, Mayor Cobo restructured the MIC, purged its most liberal members, and appointed two prominent white neighborhood association members to the board. The neighborhood associations did not win a "homeowners' participation ordinance," but they opened a new chapter in the struggle for homeowners' rights that would culminate in the early and mid-1960s.[44]

Even with the temporary defeat of their ally in city government, civil rights groups continued to battle for open housing in Detroit throughout the 1950s. Inspired by the United States Supreme Court's 1948 ruling in *Shelley v. Kraemer* that racially restrictive covenants were legally unenforceable, they launched a campaign to integrate Detroit's neighborhoods. At first their attempts were primarily educational. Civil rights groups, including the Urban League, the Metropolitan Detroit Council of Churches, and the Catholic Interracial Committee, led seminars on open housing in churches throughout the city, wrote articles and letters for local newspapers on the benefits of racial integration, and published materials attempting to assuage homeowners' fears that property depreciation and crime would follow black movement. By the late 1950s, open housing groups moved beyond advocacy to political action. In the mid-1950s, they lobbied the Federal Housing Administration and Home Owners' Loan Corporation to allow blacks to purchase foreclosed houses in white neighborhoods. In 1959, they persuaded the Michigan Department of State to revoke the licenses of real estate brokers who refused to support open housing.[45]

As civil rights groups began to agitate for open housing, neighborhood groups began a counterattack. The Federated Property Owners of Detroit, an umbrella organization of neighborhood protective associations, lambasted those who breached the now unenforceable racial covenants. "Property owners violating these principles have larceny in their hearts. They are worse than outlaw hoodlums who hold you up and steal your money. They have blood on their hands for having cut deep into their hearts and home life." The East Side Civic Council, like many whites in the city, blamed the Supreme Court decision on a conspiracy led by the NAACP and noted with disdain "the organization and cooperation of the Colored groups" on the covenant issue. Throughout the 1950s, neighborhood groups pressured "block-busting" real estate agents who sold homes to blacks in predominantly white neighborhoods, petitioned the city government to preserve racially segregated areas, and harassed black newcomers to formerly all-white blocks.[46]

In the early 1960s, the struggle between civil rights and homeowners' rights culminated at the ballot box. At the urging of civil rights groups, the city council drafted and passed a mild Fair Housing Practices Ordinance that restricted the display of For Sale signs to deter blockbusting real estate agents and prohibited references to race in real estate ads. Open housing groups, however, drafted a stronger ordinance that would outlaw all discrimination in real estate transactions.[47] In response, neighborhood groups proposed a "Homeowners' Rights Ordinance" that would preserve their "rights" to segregated neighborhoods. The competing ordinances pitted blacks, white racial liberals, and civil rights groups against a solidly white, bipartisan, antiliberal coalition.

Leading the anti–open housing movement was Thomas Poindexter, a founder of the Greater Detroit Homeowners' Council. Poindexter, an unsuccessful labor-liberal candidate for the city council in the 1950s, abandoned liberalism in the early 1960s and adopted crabgrass-roots politics with all the fervor of a convert. In August 1963, he testified on behalf of "99 percent of Detroit white residents" to the United States Senate Committee on Commerce (invited by Dixiecrat senator Strom Thurmond) against Kennedy administration civil rights legislation. Poindexter warned that "when integration strikes a previously all-white neighborhood . . . there will be an immediate rise in crime and violence . . . of vice, of prostitution, of gambling and dope." With a "general lowering of the moral standards," racially mixed neighborhoods "will succumb to blight and decay, and the residents will suffer the loss of their homes and savings."[48]

Advocates of the Homeowners' Rights Ordinance linked class resentments with an indictment of civil rights groups and government. Organizers of the Butzel-Guest Property Owners' Association railed against "the 'Civil Wrongs' that are being forced on us more and more every day" and pledged to "put out of office those who are working just for the minority and put in someone who will work for all the people." Many whites directed a populist rage against both civil rights organizations and their allegedly well-off white supporters. "The hypocrites who scream about the homeowners' refusal to be dictated to by pressure groups and who advocate open housing," wrote one angry woman, "are the very ones who live in ultraexclusive neighborhoods." Another chastised the hypocrisy of "Bishops, ministers, and union leaders [who] lecture about brotherhood . . . confident that their means of income will never force them to live among their black brothers." The open housing movement, in their view, elevated minority rights over the rights of the majority. "You can't ram people down people's throats," argued another angry white Detroiter who opposed open housing.[49]

Drawing from the rights rhetoric of the neighborhood movement, the Homeowners' Rights Ordinance pledged to protect the individual's "right to privacy," the "right to choose his own friends and associates," "the right to freedom from interference with his property by public authorities attempting to give special privileges to any group," the "right to maintain what in his opinion are congenial surroundings for himself, his family, and his tenants," and the "right" to choose a real estate broker and tenants and home buyers "for his own reasons." More was at stake than the preservation of rights, for, Poindexter contended, the ordinance would stop "the spread of crime, disease, and neighborhood blight" and the takeover of the city by "persons living on public assistance."[50]

Supporters of the Homeowners' Rights Ordinance quickly collected over forty-four thousand signatures to put it on the 1964 primary ballot, more than twice the number required for ballot initiatives. On Detroit's northeast side, more than two thousand volunteers assisted the campaign. The campaign was remarkably successful. Voter turnout, over 50 percent, was especially high for a local primary election. The ordinance passed by a 55-to-45 margin. In the city's two largest, predominantly white wards, the ordinance passed by a 2-to-1 margin; it lost by nearly 4-to-1 in predominantly African-American wards in the inner city.[51] Poindexter capped his efforts by winning a seat on the Common Council, the top vote getter in a thirty-six-candidate field. Although he called himself a "moderate liberal," Poindexter built a base of support among working-class Democrats and middle-class Republicans alike.[52]

The Homeowners' Rights Ordinance was declared unconstitutional by the Wayne County District Court in 1965 and never implemented. But the language of homeowners' rights remained potent long after the campaign. In the mid-1960s, stalwart northern Democratic voters turned out in cheering crowds of thousands at rallies for Gov. George C. Wallace of Alabama, who derided civil rights, open housing, welfare spending, urban crime, and big government. A UAW local in Flint, Michigan, endorsed Wallace, and Ford workers at the company's flagship River Rouge plant supported Wallace in a straw poll. The politician whose most famous declaration was "Segregation now, segregation forever" found a receptive audience among supposedly liberal northern urban voters. He won the 1972 Michigan Democratic primary, sweeping every predominantly white ward in Detroit. Wallace found some of his most fervent support on Detroit's northwest and northeast sides, the remaining bastions of homeowners' association activity in a city that was 45 percent African American. Following the lead of Wallace, Richard M. Nixon and Spiro Agnew repudiated their party's moderate position on civil rights and wooed disaffected urban and southern white Democrats. They swept predominantly white precincts in Detroit in 1968 and 1972.[53]

The timing of the New Right insurgency gives credence to the thesis of many recent commentators that the Democratic party made a grievous political error in the 1960s by ignoring the needs of white working-class and middle-class voters, in favor of the demands of the civil rights movement, black militants, the counterculture, and the "undeserving" poor. "The close identification of the Democratic party with the cause of racial justice," argues Allen J. Matusow, "did it special injury." Jonathan Rieder contends that the 1960s rebellion of the "silent majority" was in part a response to "certain structural limitations of liberal reform," especially "black demands" that "ran up against the limits of liberalism." Wallace's meteoric rise seems to sustain the argument of Thomas Byrne Edsall and Mary D. Edsall that the Alabama independent "captured the central political dilemma of racial liberalism and the Democratic party: the inability of Democrats to provide a political home for those whites who felt they were paying—unwillingly—the largest 'costs' in the struggle to achieve an integrated society."[54]

The Edsalls, Rieder, and Matusow, although they correctly emphasize the importance of white discontent as a national political force, err in their overemphasis on the role of the Great Society and the sixties rebellions in the rise of the "silent majority." To view the defection of whites from Democratic ranks simply as a reaction to the War on Poverty and the civil rights and Black Power movements ignores racial cleavages that shaped the local politics of the North well before the tumult of the 1960s. Urban antiliberalism had deep roots in a simmering politics of race and neighborhood defensiveness that divided northern cities well before Wallace began his first speaking tours in the snowbelt, well before Lyndon B. Johnson signed the Civil Rights Act of 1964, well before the long, hot summers of Watts, Harlem, Chicago, Newark, and Detroit, and well before affirmative action and busing began to dominate the civil rights agenda.

The view of postwar urban politics from Detroit (and from other cities) shows the importance of the politics of race and neighborhood in constraining liberal social reform. From the 1940s through the 1960s, Detroit whites fashioned a language of discontent directed toward public officials, blacks, and liberal reformers who supported public housing and open housing. The rhetoric of George Wallace, Richard M. Nixon, Spiro Agnew, and Ronald Reagan was familiar to the whites who supported candidates such as Edward Jeffries, Albert Cobo, and Thomas Poindexter.[55]

The "silent majority" did not emerge de novo from the alleged failures of liberalism in the 1960s; it was not the unique product of the white rejection of the Great Society. Instead it was the culmination of more than two decades of simmering white discontent and extensive antiliberal political organization. The problem of white backlash in the urban North is longer-lived and far more intractable than recent analyses would suggest. Until we have a greater understanding of the deeply entrenched politics of race in the urban North, our understanding of the deeply entrenched politics of race in the urban North, and our solutions to the problems of the nation's divided metropolises inadequate.

NOTES

1. Alan Brinkley, "The Problem of American Conservatism," *American Historical Review*, 99 (April 1994), 410. See also the important review essay, Michael Kazin, "The Grass-Roots Right: New Histories of U.S. Conservatism in the Twentieth Century," *ibid.*, 97 (Feb. 1992),

136–55. On southern whites and the role of southern Democrats in limiting New Deal social programs, see James C. Cobb and Michael Namorato, eds., *The New Deal and the South* (Jackson, 1984). On the post–World War II South, see Numan V. Bartley, *From Thurmond to Wallace: Political Tendencies in Georgia, 1948–1968* (Baltimore, 1970); Jill Quadagno, "From Old Age Assistance to Supplemental Security Income: The Political Economy of Relief in the South, 1935–1972," in *The Politics of Social Policy in the United States*, ed. Margaret Weir, Ann Shola Orloff, and Theda Skocpol (Princeton, 1988), 235–64; and Bruce J. Schulman, *From Cotton Belt to Sunbelt: Federal Policy, Economic Development, and the Transformation of the South, 1938–1980* (New York, 1991). On the limits on reform in the workplace, see Nelson Lichtenstein, "From Corporatism to Collective Bargaining: Organized Labor and the Eclipse of Social Democracy in the Postwar Era," in *The Rise and Fall of the New Deal Order, 1930–1980*, ed. Steve Fraser and Gary Gerstle (Princeton, 1989), 122–52; and Elizabeth A. Fones-Wolf, *Selling Free Enterprise: The Business Assault on Labor and Liberalism, 1945–60* (Urbana, 1994).

2. Lizabeth Cohen, *Making a New Deal: Industrial Workers in Chicago, 1919–1939* (New York, 1990); Gary Gerstle, *Working-Class Americanism: The Politics of Labor in a Textile City, 1920–1960* (New York, 1989); Gary Gerstle, "Working-Class Racism: Broaden the Focus," *International Labor and Working-Class History*, 44 (Fall 1993), 33–40; Bruce Nelson, "Class, Race, and Democracy in the CIO: The 'New' Labor History Meets the 'Wages of Whiteness,'" *International Review of Social History*, 41 (1996), 351–75; David Roediger, *Towards the Abolition of Whiteness: Essays on Race, Politics, and Working Class History* (London, 1994).

3. For a distillation of election returns, see Melvin G. Holli, ed., *Detroit* (New York, 1976), 274.

4. U.S. Department of Commerce, Bureau of the Census, *U.S. Census of Population and Housing, 1940, Census Tract Statistics for Detroit, Michigan and Adjacent Area* (Washington, 1942), table 1; U.S. Department of Commerce, Bureau of the Census, *U.S. Census of Population, 1950, Census Tract Statistics, Detroit Michigan and Adjacent Area* (Washington, 1952), table 1; U.S. Department of Commerce, Bureau of the Census, *U.S. Census of Population and Housing, 1960, Census Tracts, Detroit, Michigan Standard Metropolitan Statistical Area*, Final Report PHC(1)-40 (Washington, 1962), table P-1.

5. Dominic J. Capeci Jr., *Race Relations in Wartime Detroit: The Sojourner Truth Housing Controversy of 1942* (Philadelphia, 1984); August Meier and Elliott Rudwick, *Black Detroit and the Rise of the UAW* (New York, 1979), 192–97; Nelson Lichtenstein, *Labor's War at Home: The CIO in World War II* (New York, 1982); Martin Glaberman, *Wartime Strikes: The Struggle against the Nonstrike Pledge in the UAW during World War II* (Detroit, 1980); Harvard Sitkoff, "The Detroit Race Riot of 1943," *Michigan History*, 53 (Fall 1969), 183–206; Alan Clive, *State of War: Michigan in World War II* (Ann Arbor, 1979), 157–62; Alfred McClung Lee and Norman Daymond Humphrey, *Race Riot* (New York, 1943); Robert Shogan and Tom Craig, *The Detroit Race Riot: A Study in Violence* (Philadelphia, 1964); B.J. Widick, *Detroit: City of Race and Class Violence* (Chicago, 1972), 99–112; Dominic J. Capeci Jr. and Martha Wilkerson, *Layered Violence: The Detroit Rioters of 1943* (Jackson, 1991). For the official's statement, see Joseph Coles interview by Jim Keeney and Roberta McBride, July 8, 1970, transcript, p. 17, Blacks in the Labor Movement Collection (Archives of Labor and Urban Affairs, Walter P. Reuther Library, Wayne State University, Detroit, Mich.).

6. There is a voluminous literature on the Great Migration of African Americans to the North between 1914 and 1929, but no comparable historiography for the post–World War II period. Arnold R. Hirsch, *Making the Second Ghetto: Race and Housing in Chicago, 1940–1960* (New York, 1983), 40–99; Arnold R. Hirsch, "Massive Resistance in the Urban North: Trumbull Park, Chicago, 1953–1966," *Journal of American History*, 82 (Sept. 1995), 522–50; John T. Cumbler, *A Social History of Economic Decline: Business, Politics, and Work in Trenton*

(New Brunswick, 1989), 153; John F. Bauman, *Public Housing, Race, and Renewal: Urban Planning in Philadelphia, 1920–1974* (Philadelphia, 1987), 160–64; Kenneth S. Baer, "Whitman: A Study of Race, Class, and Postwar Public Housing Opposition" (senior honors thesis, University of Pennsylvania, 1994); Charles F. Casey-Leininger, "Making the Second Ghetto in Cincinnati: Avondale, 1925–1970," in *Race and the City: Work, Community, and Protest in Cincinnati, 1820–1970*, ed. Henry Louis Taylor Jr. (Urbana, 1993), 239–40, 247–48; Kenneth T. Jackson, *Crabgrass Frontier: The Suburbanization of the United States* (New York, 1985), esp. 190–218; Patricia Burgess Stach, "Deed Restrictions and Subdivision Development in Columbus, Ohio, 1900–1970," *Journal of Urban History*, 15 (Nov. 1988), 42–68.

7. U.S. Department of Commerce, Bureau of the Census, *U.S. Census of Population and Housing, 1940, Population and Housing Statistics for Census Tracts: Detroit, Michigan and Adjacent Areas* (Washington, 1942), table 4; Bureau of the Census, *U.S. Censuses of Population and Housing, 1960, Census Tracts, Detroit, Michigan Standard Metropolitan Statistical Area*, table H-1. On the economy of postwar Detroit, see Thomas J. Sugrue, "The Structures of Urban Poverty: The Reorganization of Space and Work in Three Periods of American History," in *The "Underclass" Debate: Views from History*, ed. Michael B. Katz (Princeton, 1993), 100–117. Detroit's loss of manufacturing jobs in the postwar period was not atypical of older northeastern and Midwestern cities. See John Kasarda, "Urban Change and Minority Opportunities," in *The New Urban Reality*, ed., Paul E. Peterson (Washington, 1985), 43–47, esp. tables 1 and 2.

8. "Open Letter to Henry Ford II," *Ford Facts*, Sept. 15, 1951; Arthur Kornhauser, *Detroit as the People See It: A Survey of Attitudes in an Industrial City* (Detroit, 1952), 68–69, 75, 77–82. Kornhauser's team interviewed 593 adult men and women randomly selected from all sections of the city. On the survey's methodology, see *ibid.*, 189–96.

9. "Integration Statement," anonymous letter, [c. mid-1950s], box 9, part 1, Metropolitan Detroit Council of Churches Collection (Archives of Labor and Urban Affairs); Kornhauser, *Detroit as the People See It*, 95.

10. The term "colored problem" was used most frequently by whites to describe black movement into their neighborhoods. See, for example, Property Owners Association, flyer, 1945, box 66, Civil Rights Congress of Michigan Collection (Archives of Labor and Urban Affairs), and the newsletter of the Courville District Improvement Association, *Action!*, Feb. 15, 1948, attached to Mayor's Interracial Committee, Minutes, April 5, 1948, box 10, part 1, Detroit Commission on Community Relations Collection, *ibid.*; Kornhauser, *Detroit as the People See It*, 85, 185, 100. There was virtually complete residential segregation in Detroit when Kornhauser conducted his survey. In 1950, the index of dissimilarity between blacks and whites (a measure of segregation calculated on the percentage of whites who would have to move to achieve complete racial integration) was 88.8; the index of dissimilarity in 1940 had been 89.9. Respondents to the survey supported even stricter racial segregation than already existed. For the figures, see Karl E. Taeuber and Alma F. Taeuber, *Negroes in Cities: Residential Segregation and Neighborhood Change* (Chicago, 1965), 39.

11. Kornhauser, *Detroit as the People See It*, 87, 90, 91. On the importance of Catholic parish boundaries in preserving the racial homogeneity of neighborhoods and in shaping Catholic attitudes toward blacks, see John T. McGreevy, "American Catholics and African-American Migration, 1910–1970" (Ph.D. diss., Stanford University, 1992); and Gerald Gamm "Neighborhood Roots: Institutions and Neighborhood Change in Boston, 1870–1994" (Ph.D. diss., Harvard University, 1994).

12. I borrow the term defensive localism from Margaret Weir, "Urban Poverty and Defensive Localism," *Dissent*, 31 (Summer 1994), 337–42. She uses it in a context of city-suburban relations.

13. On the ethnic heterogeneity of Detroit neighborhoods, see Olivier Zunz, *The Changing Face of Inequality: Urbanization, Industrial Development, and Immigrants in Detroit, 1880– 1920* (Chicago, 1982), 340–51. In arrest records of whites involved in anti-public housing riots in Chicago, Arnold Hirsch found great diversity in ethnic affiliations. See Hirsch, *Making the Second Ghetto*, 81–84. For examples of ethnic diversity in Detroit, see letters to Mayor Edward Jeffries, regarding the Algonquin Street and Oakwood defense housing projects, Housing Commission Folder, box 3, Detroit Archives—Mayor's Papers, 1945 (Burton Historical Collection, Detroit Public Library, Detroit Mich.). See also Exhibit A, Oct. 22, 1948, pp. 1–2, attached to Charles H. Houston to Charles S. Johnson et al., memorandum, Michigan: *Swanson v. Hayden* Folder, box B133, group II, National Association for the Advancement of Colored People Papers (Manuscript Division, Library of Congress, Washington, D.C.); newsletter of the Greater Detroit Neighbors Association—Unit No. 2, *Neighborhood Informer* (Dec. 1949), 2, folder 4-19, box 4, United Automobile Workers, Community Action Program Collection (Archives of Labor and Urban Affairs). For a derogatory reference to Jews, see "Demonstrations Protesting Negro Occupancy of Homes, September 1, 1945–September 1, 1946: Memorandum J," p. 31, box 3, part 1, Detroit Commission on Community Relations Collection. For a reference to "niggers, chinamen, and Russians," see William K. Anderson to Herbert Schultz, Oct. 17, 1958, South Lakewood Area Association Papers, 1955–1960 (Burton Historical Collection). For incidents involving an Indian family, a Chinese family, and a Filipino family who moved into white neighborhoods, see Chronological Index of Cases, 1951 (51-31) and (51-58), box 13, Detroit Commission on Community Relations Collection; Detroit Police Department Special Investigation Bureau, Summary of Racial Activities, April 30, 1956–May 17, 1956, folder A2-26, box 38, Detroit Urban League Papers (Michigan Historical Collections, Bentley Library, University of Michigan, Ann Arbor). Detroit was a magnet for southern white migrants, but I have found little evidence of an extensive southern white presence in neighborhood organizations. Although southern whites were frequently blamed for racial tension in the city, their role was greatly exaggerated. In the postwar years, many southern whites continued to live in racially mixed neighborhoods and did not actively resist black residential mobility. See Capeci and Wilkerson, *Layered Violence*, and John M. Hartigan Jr., "Cultural Constructions of Whiteness: Racial and Class Formations in Detroit" (Ph.D. diss., University of California, Santa Cruz, 1995).

14. "OPEN MEETING . . . for Owners and Tenants," poster (c. 1945), Property Owners Association Folder, box 66, Civil Rights Congress of Michigan Collection; *Action!*, Feb. 15, 1948, p. 2; Guyton Home Owners' Association and Connor-East Home Owners' Association, leaflets, 1957–1960 Folder, South Lakewood Area Association Papers; Richard J. Peck, Community Services Department, Detroit Urban League, "Summary of Known Improvement Association Activity in Past Two Years, 1955–1957," box 2, Pre-1960, Community Organization 1950s Vertical File (Archives of Labor and Urban Affairs); *Southwest Detroiter*, May 11, 1950, Housing Commission Folder, box 5, Detroit Archives—Mayor's Papers, 1950.

15. *Neighborhood Informer* (Dec. 1949), 1, 3, folder 4-19, box 4, United Automobile Workers, Community Action Program Collection; "Emergency Meeting, March 11, 1950," handbill, folder 25-107, box 25, part III, Detroit Commission on Community Relations Collection; Ruritan Park Civic Association, "Dear Neighbor," folder 25-101, *ibid*.

16. John G. Feild interview by Katherine Shannon, Dec. 28, 1967, transcript, p. 11, Civil Rights Documentation Project (Moorland-Spingarn Research Center, Howard University Library, Washington, D.C.). The finding guide and interview transcript mistakenly spell Feild as Fields. I calculated the number of racial incidents by surveying records in the Detroit Commission on Community Relations Collection; the Detroit Branch, National Association for the Advancement of Colored People Collection (Archives of Labor and Urban Affairs); the Detroit Urban League Papers; and Detroit's three black newspapers: *Michigan Chronicle, Detroit*

Tribune, and *Pittsburgh Courier* (Detroit edition). On racial violence in postwar Detroit, see Thomas J. Sugrue, "The Origins of the Urban Crisis: Race, Industrial Decline, and Housing in Detroit, 1940–1960" (Ph.D. diss., Harvard University, 1992), 208–78.

17. Mel Ravitz, "Preparing Neighborhoods for Change," July 13, 1956, folder A8-1, box 44, Detroit Urban League Papers; William Price, "Scare Selling in a Bi-Racial Housing Market," June 11, 1957, *ibid.*; "Incident Report," July 6, 1950, folder 50-23, box 6, Detroit Commission on Community Relations Collection; Mary Czechowski to Mayor Albert Cobo, Oct. 8, 1950, folder 50-57, box 7, *ibid.*

18. Detroit Housing Commission and Work Projects Administration, *Real Property Survey of Detroit, Michigan* (Detroit, 1939), II, III, maps and data for Area K. See Sugrue, "Origins of the Urban Crisis," 316–17. Gloster Current, "Paradise Valley: A Famous and Colorful Part of Detroit as Seen through the Eyes of an Insider," *Detroit* (June 1946), 32, 34.

19. Outer-Van Dyke Home Owners' Association, "Dear Neighbor," [1948], folder 25-94, box 25, part III, Detroit Commission on Community Relations Collection; interview with Six Mile Road–Riopelle area neighbors in Incident Report, Aug. 30, 1954, folder A7-13, box 43, Detroit Urban League Papers; Longview Home Owners Association, poster, n.d., Housing— Homeowners Ordinance—Friendly Folder, box 10, part I, Metropolitan Detroit Council of Churches Collection. Ellipsis in original.

20. Alex Csanyi and family to Jeffries, Feb. 20, 1945, Housing Commission 1945 Folder, box 3, Detroit Archives—Mayors' Papers 1945. Ellipsis in original. *Home Gazette,* Oct. 25, 1945, Charles Hill Papers (Archives of Labor and Urban Affairs); Gloster Current, "The Detroit Elections: A Problem in Reconversion," *Crisis,* 52 (Nov. 1945), 319–21; *Action!,* Feb. 15, 1948, p. 2. On the politics of sexual containment, see Elaine Tyler May, "Cold War, Warm Hearth: Politics and the Family in Postwar America," in *Rise and Fall of the New Deal Order,* ed. Fraser and Gerstle, 153–81.

21. Attachment to letter, Miss James, Detroit Branch NAACP, to George Schermer, Aug. 23, 1948, folder 48-125A, box 5, part I, Detroit Commission on Community Relations Collection. See photographs and description in "Constable Sells Home to Negro—Picketed," *Michigan Chronicle,* Aug. 21, 1948; "Three Families Move into Homes on Harrison as Police Stand By to Prevent Violence," *ibid.,* Aug. 28, 1948; and "Mayor Guarantees Protection for Negro Home-Owner," *Detroit Tribune,* Aug. 28, 1948. For other female-led protests, see "Memorandum J," p. 31, attached to "Demonstrations, 1945–1946," folder 47-54, box 4, part I, Detroit Commission on Community Relations Collection; "Case Report: Case No. 54," *ibid.*; George Schermer, "Report of Incident, Subject: Neighborhood Protest to Sale of House on 13933 Maine Street," June 23, 1947, *ibid.*; Schermer to John F. Ballenger, commissioner, Department of Police, June 23, 1947, *ibid.*; John Feild to Director, "Neighborhood Protest to Sale of House on 13933 Maine Street," memo, June 1947, *ibid.*; "Police Action Averts Riot," *Pittsburgh Courier* (Detroit edition), June 28, 1947; and "White Neighbors Threaten Negroes Moving into Home," *Michigan Chronicle,* June 28, 1947. For a case of female-initiated vandalism, see *Pittsburgh Courier* (Detroit edition), June 18, 1955. On the role of women in neighborhood protests and local politics in the postwar period, see Sylvie Murray, "Suburban Citizens: Domesticity and Community Politics in Queens, New York, 1945–1960" (Ph.D. diss., Yale University, 1994). On white fears of black sexuality in Chicago, see Hirsch, *Making the Second Ghetto,* 195–96.

22. Robert Moore Fisher, *Twenty Years of Public Housing: Economic Aspects of the Federal Program* (New York, 1959); Richard O. Davies, *Housing Reform during the Truman Administration* (Columbia, Mo., 1966).

23. On Dearborn and Ecorse, see *Dearborn Press,* Nov. 22, 1944; *Detroit Times,* May 24, 1945; *Detroit News,* May 15, 1945; and David L. Good, *Orvie: The Dictator of Dearborn: The*

Rise and Reign of Orville L. Hubbard (Detroit, 1989), 142. On Oakwood, see *Detroit News*, Feb. 16, 28, March 20, 1945.

24. On the expansion of rights language in the New Deal, see Sidney M. Milkis, *The President and the Parties: The Transformation of the American Party System since the New Deal* (New York, 1993), esp. 41–43, 48–50; and Alan Brinkley, *The End of Reform: New Deal Liberalism in Recession and War* (New York, 1995), 10–11, 164–70. More generally, see Rogers M. Smith, "Rights," in *A Companion to American Thought*, ed. Richard Wightman Fox and James Kloppenberg (Oxford, Eng., 1995); and Mary Ann Glendon, *Rights Talk: The Impoverishment of Political Discourse* (New York, 1991).

25. Franklin Delano Roosevelt, "Message to Congress on the State of the Union," Jan. 11, 1944, in *The Public Papers and Addresses of Franklin D. Roosevelt*, vol. XIII: *Victory and the Threshold of Peace, 1944–45* (New York, 1950), 41; Henry Lee Moon, "Danger in Detroit," *Crisis*, 53 (Jan. 1946), 28; Seven Mile–Fenelon Improvement Association, "WE DEMAND OUR RIGHTS," poster, Property Owners Association Folder, box 66, Civil Rights Congress of Michigan Collection. On the New Deal and home ownership, see Ronald Tobey, Charles Wetherell, and Jay Brigham, "Moving Out and Settling In: Residential Mobility, Home Owning, and the Public Enframing of Citizenship, 1921–1950," *American Historical Review*, 95 (Dec. 1990), 1395–1422, esp. 1415–20; and Cohen, *Making a New Deal*, 272–77. On immigrants and home ownership in Detroit, see Zunz, *Changing Face of Inequality*, 129–76. On the discriminatory nature of federal housing programs, see Kenneth T. Jackson, "Race, Ethnicity, and Real Estate Appraisal: The Home Owners Loan Corporation and the Federal Housing Administration," *Journal of Urban History*, 6 (Aug. 1980), 419–52.

26. *Michigan Chronicle*, Dec. 4, 1948; *Neighborhood Informer* (Dec. 1949), 1; "Join the Fight," flyer, Nov. 1945, folder 20-37, box 20, part III, Detroit Commission on Community Relations Collection.

27. Michael J. Harbulak to Jeffries, Feb. 21, 1945, Housing Commission 1945 Folder, box 3, Detroit Archives—Mayors' Papers 1945; "Negro Homes Vote Delayed," *Detroit News*, March 9, 1945; Current, "Detroit Elections," 325. See also *Action!*, March 15, 1948. On popular patriotism and Americanism, see, especially, Gerstle, *Working-Class Americanism*; Gary Gerstle, "The Working Class Goes to War," *Mid-America*, 75 (Oct. 1993), 303–22; Michael Kazin and Steven J. Ross, "America's Labor Day: The Dilemma of a Workers' Celebration," *Journal of American History*, 78 (March 1992), 1294–1323; and James R. Barrett, "Americanization from the Bottom Up: Immigration and the Remaking of the Working Class in the United States, 1880–1930," *ibid.*, 79 (Dec. 1992), 996–1020.

28. Harbulak to Jeffries, Feb. 21, 1945, Housing Commission 1945 Folder, box 3, Detroit Archives—Mayors' Papers 1945.

29. Mr. and Mrs. Fred Pressato to Jeffries, March 6, 1945, *ibid.*; William Leuffen to Jeffries, March 6, 1945, Housing / Bi-Racial Letters Folder, *ibid.*; John Watson to Jeffries, March 6, 1945, *ibid.*

30. The remarks appear in an editorial, *Brightmoor Journal*, Oct. 27, 1949. (I wish to express my gratitude to the staff of Bentley Historical Library, University of Michigan, who allowed me to consult their yet uncataloged and unprocessed collection of northwest-side neighborhood newspapers, including the *Brightmoor Journal*.) See also *Action!*, March 15, 1948, p. 2.

31. "Fourth Meeting of the Speaker's Study Group of Intercultural Affairs," Feb. 4, 1946, p. 2, Interracial Resolutions / Intercultural Council Folder, box 74, Citizens Housing and Planning Council Papers (Burton Historical Collection).

32. "Join the Fight," flyer, Nov. 1945, folder 20-37, box 20, part III, Detroit Commission on Community Relations Collection; "A Group of Taxpayers" to the councilmen of the City of Detroit, April 12, 1945, Common Council Folder, box 23, Citizens Housing and Planning

Council Papers; "Survey of Racial and Religious Conflict Forces in Detroit," Sept. 30, 1943, box 71, Civil Rights Congress of Michigan Collection.

33. *Brightmoor Journal*, Feb. 3, May 12, Jan. 12, 1950, April 21, 1966. See also *Action!*, March 15, 1948. On Floyd McGriff and his anticommunist activity in the 1940s, see Floyd McGriff Papers (Michigan Historical Collections).

34. On Edward Jeffries, see Capeci, *Race Relations in Wartime Detroit*, 17–27. Handbills, folder 3-8, box 3, Donald Marsh Papers (University Archives, Wayne State University, Detroit, Mich.). See also "The 1945 Mayoral Campaign—National Lawyers Guild," Jan. 10, 1946, attached to Gloster Current to Thurgood Marshall, memo, Racial Tension in Detroit, Mich., 1944–46 Folder, box A505, group II, National Association for the Advancement of Colored People Papers; "Mayor Jeffries is Against Mixed Housing," flyer, Politics, Michigan, 1945–1953 Folder, box A475, *ibid.*

35. "White Neighborhoods Again in Peril: Frankensteen Policy Up On Housing Negroes Here," *Home Gazette*, Oct. 11, 1945, clipping, Clippings File, Hill Papers; Moon, "Danger in Detroit," 12.

36. On Albert Cobo, see Melvin G. Holli and Peter d'A. Jones, *Biographical Dictionary of American Mayors, 1820–1980: Big City Mayors* (Westport, 1981), 69–70. On George Edwards, see *Detroit News*, Oct. 31, 1947, clipping, folder 10-4, box 10, United Automobile Workers, Research Department Collection (Archives of Labor and Urban Affairs). See also "Biographical Data, George Edwards," Vertical File—Biography, *ibid. Brightmoor Journal*, Sept. 22, 1949; newsletter of the Outer-Van Dyke Home Owners Association, *"Hi" Neighbor*, 1 (Nov. 1949), copy, folder 5-5, box 5, United Automobile Workers, Community Action Program Department Collection; *Detroit News*, Nov. 8, 1949; Coles interview, 17.

37. Labor's Municipal Campaign Committee, "Schedule 1: Liabilities," folder 62-10, box 62, United Automobile Workers, Political Action Committee—Roy Reuther Collection (Archives of Labor and Urban Affairs). Labor spent $28,455.51 on George Edwards's campaign; see Al Barbour to Roy Reuther, Nov. 17, 1949, folder 62-19, *ibid.* "East Side Meeting, Thursday, November 17, 9:00 a.m.," notes, folder 62-13, *ibid.*; "Material for Sound Trucks and Leaflets at MUCC Offices," folder 62-7, *ibid.*; "Suggested Slot Announcements," folder 62-16, *ibid.*; "Housewives—Don't Stay Home Nov. 8th," poster, folder 62-10, ibid.; "750,000 Detroiters *Did Not Vote* in the Primary Election," flyer, *ibid.* According to analysis of returns from selected precincts by the United Automobile Workers, Edwards did better in blue-collar areas than in "middle class" white districts, although he lost in both. Edwards won only among black voters (82%) and white public housing project residents (59%). The only other group that came close to majority support (49%) for Edwards was "hillbillies," presumably recent southern white migrants to the city. Untitled tables, folder 63-2, box 63, *ibid.*

38. "West Side Coordinators Meeting, Wednesday, November 16, 1949," notes, folder 62-11, box 62, United Automobile Workers, Political Action Committee—Roy Reuther Collection.

39. "East Side Meeting, Thursday November 17, 9:00 a.m.," notes, p. 6, folder 62-13, box 62, *ibid.* On Detroit politics in the 1950s, see J. David Greenstone, "A Report on the Politics of Detroit," unpublished paper, Harvard University, 1961 (Purdy-Kresge Library, Wayne State University). On the 1949 election and its legacy, see Kevin G. Boyle, "Politics and Principle: The United Automobile Workers and American Labor-Liberalism, 1948–1968" (Ph.D. diss., University of Michigan, Ann Arbor, 1991), 94–100. On the separation of home and work as an important constraint on American radical politics, see Ira Katznelson, *City Trenches: Urban Politics and the Patterning of Class in the United States* (New York, 1981). It is important not to overstate the contrast between neighborhood and union politics; research on Congress of Industrial Organizations (CIO) unions in the North shows that shop floor conflicts over racial is-

sues such as upgrading and seniority lists continued well into the 1950s. See, especially, Kevin G. Boyle, "'There Are No Union Sorrows That the Union Can't Heal': The Struggle for Racial Equality in the United Automobile Workers, 1940–1960," *Labor History*, 36 (Winter 1995), 5–23; Bruce Nelson, "Race Relations in the Mill: Steelworkers and Civil Rights, 1950–1965," paper delivered at the conference "Toward a History of the 1960s," Madison, Wisconsin, April 1993 (in Thomas J. Sugrue's possession).

40. On Albert Cobo's appointments, see box 2, Detroit Archives—Mayors' Papers 1951. Detroit Housing Commission, "Monthly Report," Dec. 1949, 1–2, Detroit Housing Commission Folder, box 2, Detroit Archives—Mayors' Papers 1950; Detroit City Plan Commission, Minutes, vol. 16 (1950–1951), 44, Detroit City Plan Commission Collection (Burton Historical Collection); *Detroit Free Press*, March 14, 1950; Orville Tenaglia to Cobo, March 28, 1950, Civic Associations Folder, box 2, Detroit Archives—Mayors' Papers 1950; "Degree of Voting in Detroit Primary," Sept. 11, 1951, folder 62-25, box 62, United Automobile Workers, Political Action Committee—Roy Reuther Collection.

41. On the changing balance of power in Detroit politics, see Greenstone, "Report on the Politics of Detroit," 68; Dudley W. Buffa, *Union Power and American Democracy: The UAW and the Democratic Party, 1935–1972* (Ann Arbor, 1984), 140–41; James Q. Wilson, *Negro Politics: The Search for Leadership* (New York, 1960), 28–30; and Sidney Fine, *Violence in the Model City: The Cavanagh Administration, Race Relations, and the Detroit Riot of 1967* (Ann Arbor, 1988), 3, 6, 16. Louis Miriani had enjoyed neighborhood association support as a city council member. See, for example, *Small Property Owner* (Nov. 1949), folder 5-2, box 5, United Automobile Workers, Community Action Program Collection.

42. On the weakness of the civil rights movement in Detroit in the late 1940s and early 1950s, see Robert Korstad and Nelson Lichtenstein, "Opportunities Found and Lost: Labor, Radicals, and the Early Civil Rights Movement," *Journal of American History*, 75 (Dec. 1988), 786–811. *Brightmoor Journal*, April 20, 1950.

43. *Brightmoor Journal*, April 5, 1951; Ralph Smith to Cobo, March 23, 1950, Civic Associations Folder, box 2, Detroit Archives—Mayors' Papers 1950.

44. Home-Owner Civic and Improvement Associations, "Memorandum to Home-Owner Presidents," March 13, 1953, Civic Associations Folder, box 1, Detroit Archives—Mayors' Papers 1953; C. Katherine Rentschler, "Request to Abolish the Present Mayor's Interracial Committee and to Refrain from Authorizing the Proposed Commission on Community Relations," April 7, 1953, *ibid*,; C. Katherine Rentschler to Detroit Common Council, Aug. 17, 1953, *ibid*.; *Detroit Focus* (March–April 1954), folder 8-1, box 8, Detroit Urban League Papers; "Statement of the Detroit Branch NAACP Board of Directors Regarding the City of Detroit Commission on Community Relations," Feb. 22, 1954, *ibid*.; Detroit Urban League, Board of Directors, Minutes of Special Meeting, Jan. 27, 1954, folder 11-18, box 11, *ibid*.; Cobo to Father John E. Coogan, Jan. 18, 1954, Freedom Agenda Folder, box 71, Citizens Housing and Planning Council Papers.

45. *Shelley v. Kraemer*, 334 U.S. 1 (1948); William H. Boone, "Major Unmet Goals that Suggest Continuing Attention," March 9, 1956, folder A2-16, box 38, Detroit Urban League Papers; United Automobile Workers Legal Department to Thomas Kavanagh, Michigan Attorney General, Draft of letter, July 18, 1956, folder A2-17, *ibid.* On Michigan House and Senate bills to prevent real estate discrimination, see Housing Folder, box 10, part I, Metropolitan Detroit Council of Churches Collection. On open housing efforts in the 1950s and early 1960s, see Rose Kleinman Papers (Michigan Historical Collections); and Rose Kleinman Papers (Archives of Labor and Urban Affairs).

46. *Michigan Chronicle*, Dec. 4, 1948; Eastside Civic Council, Meeting announcement, May 24, 1948, Restrictive Covenants Folder, box 66, Civil Rights Congress of Michigan Pa-

pers. On activities of neighborhood groups, see, for example, "Report on Ruritan Park Civic Association Meetings, September 20, 1956 and November 29, 1956," folder A7-13, box 43, Detroit Urban League Papers; Detroit Commission on Community Relations, Minutes, March 17, 1958, pp. 4–6, Minutes—Jan. March 1958 Folder, box 2, part IV, Detroit Commission on Community Relations Collection; "Racial Appeals in Primary Election," Aug. 18, 1958, folder 13-28, box 13, part III, *ibid*.

47. *Detroit News*, July 14, 1963; Mayor Jerome P. Cavanagh, Statement, Sept. 26, 1963, folder A18-11, box 54, Detroit Urban League Papers; Detroit Commission on Community Relations, Annual Report, 1963, box 2, Kleinman Papers (Archives of Labor and Urban Affairs).

48. *Ford Facts*, July 10, 1954; *Detroit Free Press*, Nov. 3, 1963, Nov. 27, 1964; U.S. Congress, Senate, Committee on Commerce, *Civil Rights—Public Accommodations Hearings*, 88 Cong., 1 sess., Aug 1, 1963, part 2, esp. pp. 1085, 1088.

49. Annual Meeting of the Butzel-Guest Property Owners' Association, Housing—Michigan, Detroit, 1956–1964 Folder, box A160, group III, National Association for the Advancement of Colored People Papers; Glenna Stalcup to *Detroit News*, Jan. 11, 1965. On class resentment in other cities, see Ronald P. Formisano, *Boston against Busing: Race, Class, and Ethnicity in the 1960s and 1970s* (Chapel Hill, 1991); and James R. Ralph Jr., *Northern Protest: Martin Luther King, Jr., Chicago, and the Civil Rights Movement* (Cambridge, Mass., 1993), 114–30. Anonymous letter, n.d., Civil Rights Activity Folder, box 9, part I, Metropolitan Detroit Council of Churches Collection; Albert Nahat to *Detroit News*, May 28, 1964.

50. "Exhibit of Petition, Ordinance, and Ballot Proposed by Greater Detroit Homeowner's Council," Housing—Homeowners' Ordinance—Friendly Statements Folder, box 10, Metropolitan Detroit Council of Churches Collection; *Detroit News*, July 1, July 14, 1963; "Home Owners Ordinance," transcript of WBTM discussion with Thomas Poindexter and Leonard Gordon, [c. summer 1964], *NAACP v. Detroit*—Background Material Folder, box 59, group III (Legal Department Cases), National Association for the Advancement of Colored People Papers.

51. *Michigan Chronicle*, Sept. 12, 1964; *East Side Shopper*, Sept. 12, 1964; *Detroit Daily Press*, Sept. 3, 1964. "Primary Election Results, City of Detroit," Sept. 1, 1964, *NAACP v. Detroit*—Background Material Folder, Box 59, group III (Legal Department Cases), National Association for the Advancement of Colored People Papers. Similar ordinances passed in other parts of the country.

52. *Detroit Daily Press*, Sept. 3, 1964. Some of Thomas Poindexter's votes undoubtedly went to an unknown candidate, Charley Poindexter, who did not campaign and picked up 8,082 votes in the primary election. See also *ibid*., Nov. 11, 1964.

53. *New York Times*, Oct. 6, 1968, p. 75; *ibid*., May 18, 1972, p. 36; Election Returns, Wayne County, Michigan, Primary Election 1972, microfilm (Office of the Wayne County Clerk, City-County Building, Detroit, Mich.).

54. Allen J. Matusow, *The Unraveling of America: A History of Liberalism in the 1960s* (New York, 1984), 438; Jonathan Rieder, "The Rise of the 'Silent Majority,'" in *Rise and Fall of the New Deal Order*, ed. Fraser and Gerstle, 254; Thomas Byrne Edsall and Mary D. Edsall, *Chain Reaction: The Impact of Race, Rights, and Taxes on American Politics* (New York, 1991), 77. Similar views pervade the scholarly and popular literature on the 1960s. See also Frederick F. Siegel, *The Troubled Journey: From Pearl Harbor to Ronald Reagan* (New York, 1983), esp. 152–215; Jim Sleeper, *The Closest of Strangers: Liberalism and the Politics of Race in New York City* (New York, 1990); Jonathan Rieder, *Canarsie: The Jews and Italians of Brooklyn against Liberalism* (Cambridge, Mass., 1985); and Edward G. Carmines and James A. Stimson, *Issue Evolution: Race and the Transformation of American Politics* (Princeton, 1989). Important critical reviews of this literature include James R. Grossman, "Traditional

Politics or the Politics of Tradition?," *Reviews in American History*, 21 (Sept. 1993), 533–38; Adolph Reed and Julian Bond, "Equality: Why We Can't Wait," *Nation*, Dec. 9, 1991, pp. 723–37; and Adolph Reed, "Review: Race and the Disruption of the New Deal Coalition," *Urban Affairs Quarterly*, 27 (Dec. 1991), 326–33.

55. See Arnold R. Hirsch, "Chicago: The Cook County Democratic Organization and the Dilemma of Race, 1931–1987," in *Snowbelt Cities: Metropolitan Politics in the Northeast and Midwest since World War II*, ed. Richard M. Bernard (Bloomington, 1988), 63–90; Richard M. Bernard, "Milwaukee: The Death and Life of a Midwestern Metropolis," *ibid.*, esp. 173–75. Especially perceptive on the rhetoric of George Wallace, Richard M. Nixon, Spiro Agnew, and Ronald Reagan is Michael Kazin, *The Populist Persuasion: An American History* (New York, 1995), 221–66.

Chapter 11

Popular Culture in the Age of White Flight: Film Noir, Disneyland, and the Cold War (Sub)Urban Imaginary

Eric Avila

Urban life in the United States underwent a dramatic transformation toward the middle of the twentieth century. To the extent that one can think of the history of the American city as a series of successive but overlapping paradigms, the 1930s marked the beginnings of a transition from the modern, industrial, centralized city, which emerged around the turn of the century, to the postwar, decentralized urban region. The shifting concentration of public resources and private capital, coupled with federal incentives toward suburban homeownership among broader segments of the population, accelerated the pattern of decentralized urbanization in postwar America and decimated the economic and social life of the inner city. The regional biases of such development were manifest in the postwar ascendance of the Sun Belt, which cradled a compelling vision of the suburban good life, whereas an "urban crisis" took shape within the Rust Belt cities of the industrial Northeast.[1]

This transition accompanied a profound reconfiguration of social relations. In the second half of the twentieth century, after a wave of labor strikes during the mid-1940s, class gradually subsided as the discursive basis of social conflict, whereas racial and gendered divisions assumed greater prominence.[2] What role the spatial transformation of American society at midcentury played in this development, how-ever, requires additional exploration. The postwar suburban boom created a space, literally and figuratively, for reinstating racial and sexual barriers that weakened within an ascendant urban liberalism that reached its zenith during the 1930s and 1940s. As the racially exclusive patterns of postwar suburbanization facilitated the "blackening" of American inner cities, white flight reflected and reinforced the racial resegregation of the United States. And whereas the modern city incorporated women into public life—as workers and consumers—postwar suburbanization placed greater demands on women to return to the private sphere to resume their traditional responsibilities as mothers and wives. Creating a space for a return to

Reprinted from *Journal of Urban History* 31 (November 2004): 2–22. Reprinted with the permission of Sage Publications.

normalcy, the postwar suburban boom offered a setting in which to restore traditional divisions between the races and the sexes.[3]

Urban historians, geographers, and sociologists have measured and mapped the political, economic, and social transition from the modern industrial city to the decentralized urban region, but the cultural corollary to this process has been overlooked. White flight during the postwar period necessitated the formation of a new cultural order, one that marked an exchange of the heterogeneous, anonymous, promiscuous spaces of the centralized city for the contained, segregated, homogeneous experiences of the decentralized urban region.[4] This article explores that transformation through the lens of popular culture, considering the mid-1940s debut of film noir as a popular genre of film and the successive opening of Disneyland in 1955. Both cultural productions posited a critique of the modern city and its typical pattern of social relations, and both arrived alongside the heightened thrust of postwar suburbanization. If film noir situated its indictment of the racial and sexual promiscuity within the spatial context of the modern city, Disneyland offered a suburban antithesis, modeling a new sociospatial order that took shape along the fringes of the urban core. The juxtaposition of film noir and Disneyland within their historical context illustrates a key cultural tension between a reinvigorated suspicion of urban modernity, on one hand, and a suburban retreat from the black city and its disordered culture, on the other. This tension underscored the post–World War II construction of a white suburban ethos and encompassed the political unconscious of a "silent majority" still in its formative years.[5]

THE MODERN CITY, ITS NEW MASS
CULTURE, AND THEIR MIDCENTURY DECLINE

Not too long ago, a generation of historians discovered the culture of the modern city as a rich field of historical inquiry and illustrated how diverse groups of Americans collectively experienced the transition to urban modernity through a burgeoning set of cultural institutions. In world's fairs, expositions, movie palaces, amusement parks, spectator sports, and night clubs, urban Americans reveled in the "new mass culture" that electrified the landscape of the American city at the turn of the century. As the preeminent metropolis of the nineteenth century, New York City dominated this discussion as the city's cultural institutions facilitated the transition from a Victorian social order, with its strict separation of classes, races, and sexes, to a new cultural order, one that promoted a promiscuous set of interactions among a motley crowd of urban strangers. In New York City, as well as in its urban counterparts at the turn of the century, the crowded venues of the new mass culture reflected the ways in which urban Americans negotiated the perils and pleasures of the modern city.[6]

The vitality of the new mass culture, however, rested in no small part on the economic fortunes of the great industrial centers of the Northeast and Midwest, but such fortunes began to contract toward the middle of the twentieth century. The Great Depression crippled the urban economies of New York City, Philadelphia, Detroit, and Chicago, but perhaps more than any other singular event, World War II undermined the hegemony of urban industrial society and culture by initiating the deconcentration of public resources and private capital. Beginning in the early 1940s, the federal government actively promoted industrial decentralization as a strategy to protect a burgeoning military-industrial infrastructure from the event of an air attack. When the Chrysler Warren Tank Plant took advantage of federal incentives to open on an undeveloped tract of land some fifteen miles north of downtown Detroit in 1941, for example, it augmented the suburban model of postwar industrial development that weakened the economic vitality of traditional urban centers.[7]

The urban crisis initiated during the war years was as much social as it was economic. World War II unleashed a wave of racial violence in the nation's cities, demonstrating the level of discomfort that accompanied the sudden diversification of urban society. The great migration of African Americans from the rural South to wartime centers of employment in the Northeast, Midwest, and Far West "blackened" the face of American cities considerably and aroused hostility from local whites, whose sense of entitlement to defense jobs rested on an entrenched conviction of white supremacy. On June 6, 1944, for example, ten thousand white workers at Cincinnati's Wright aircraft engine plant staged a wildcat strike to protest the integration of the machine shop. Race riots exploded in cities elsewhere. The year 1943 delivered a moment of intense racial violence for the nation's cities, as race riots erupted in New York City, Detroit, and Los Angeles, where the infamous Zoot Suit Riots between white sailors and Chicano youth demonstrated the extent to which other racial groups besides African Americans were implicated within wartime racial tensions.[8]

As American cities festered with racial violence during the war years, an emergent pattern of suburbanization materialized during and after World War II and offered a setting removed from such tensions. Again, the federal government played no small part in this development. Housing policy under the New Deal administration set the stage for the postwar suburban boom and offered incentives to industrialists and aspiring homeowners to abandon the nation's urban centers. In particular, the creation of the Homeowners Loan Corporation, the Federal Housing Administration, and, later, the Veterans Administration stimulated the national market for housing construction by shifting the focus of urban development away from the inner city and toward the suburbs. But, as historians have demonstrated, the discriminatory measures built into federal housing policy created the basis for the racial resegregation of postwar America. The urbanization of African Americans throughout and beyond the war years coincided with the largest phase of mass suburbanization in American history, in which millions of Americans who qualified themselves or were qualified as white realized their dream of suburban homeownership. Generally, excluded from the greatest mass-based opportunity for wealth accumulation in American history, African Americans and other minority groups largely remained concentrated within decaying cores of urban poverty. The racial dimensions of the postwar urban crisis thus gave rise to "chocolate cities and vanilla suburbs," which became the dominant paradigm of race and space after World War II.[9]

As a generation of white Americans pursued their dreams of homeownership in the suburbs and as the face of the American city blackened considerably in the aftermath of that exodus, it is not difficult to understand how the culture of industrial urbanism entered a period of decline. Reports of the demise of the new mass culture circulated throughout the networks of public discourse in postwar America, and not surprisingly race emerged as a primary explanation for this development. For example, though Coney Island at the turn of the century reigned as the capital of modern urban culture, the *New York Times* reported in 1962 "Coney Island Slump Grows Worse," drawing attention to the postwar plight of the amusement park. Amidst the many reasons cited for Coney Island's decline, "concessionaire after concessionaire" agreed "the growing influx of Negro visitors [to the park] discouraged some white persons to the area." Three years later, Steeplechase Park, the first of Coney Island's great amusement parks, became the last, closing its doors forever.[10]

Chicago's Riverview Park experienced a similar fate. Once billed as the world's largest amusement park, Riverview stood on 140 acres of land in the city's northwest region. Whereas Riverview enticed an ethnically diverse array of pleasure seekers throughout its sixty-four-year popularity, the amusement park could not withstand the changing demographics that ensued in the era of racial desegregation. By the 1960s, Riverview entered a period of rapid decline, and on October 3, 1967, Riverview closed its doors forever. The *Chicago Tribune* explained that the park's "natural defenses began to crumble. Racial tension ran rampant inside the park."[11]

Amusement parks were not the only genre of popular amusement that fell by the wayside. Urban baseball parks that grew alongside amusement parks encountered similar difficulties during the postwar period. Philadelphia's Shibe Park, for example, once hailed as the crown jewel of ballparks, lost much of its appeal among baseball fans during the 1950s. In 1970, Bob Carpenter, owner of the Philadelphia Phillies, removed his team from its inner-city locale, convinced that baseball was "no longer a paying proposition" at Shibe Park and that its location in "an undesirable neighborhood" meant that white baseball fans "would not come to a black neighborhood" to see a ball game.[12] Similarly, in the aftermath of Walter O'Malley's infamous decision to move the Dodgers from Brooklyn to Los Angeles, one disappointed fan pointed to Brooklyn's changing racial profile to explain O'Malley's decision: "I guess O'Malley was like everybody else, as long as you're not my neighbor, it was okay. But once [blacks] started to live in the neighborhood, it was time to move out."[13]

Clearly, a complex interplay of factors contributed to the decline of these cultural landmarks, but in the era of desegregation, a perception emerged that black urbanization facilitated a retreat from the modern city and its culture among a white public. Such a perception informed the tenor of American popular culture as far back as the early postwar period. Take, for example, that body of American film that critics and historians have identified as film noir. Coined by French film critics in the late 1940s, film noir describes a cycle of American filmmaking roughly spanning the ten years following the end of World War II. Defined as a genre, a mood, a sensibility, and a movement, film noir eludes precise definition but includes a diverse array of crime dramas ranging from individual case studies of murder and criminal deviance to more general treatments of gangsters and organized crime.[14]

Historical assessments of film noir tend to emphasize the experience of the war and its effects on the nation's psyche, but when viewed through the lens of urban history, the genre reveals some striking perceptions about the American city and its culture at midcentury. One of film noir's defining characteristics, after all, is its use of the modern city as setting and subject. Unlike the gleaming spires of the *Wizard of Oz*, however, the noir city exposed the seedy side of urban life. Noir's dark urban vision resonated throughout its titles: *Dark City*, *City of Fear*, *The Naked City*, and *Cry of the City*. The noir vision of urban life drew on a representational tradition in Western culture. In contrast to the Enlightenment view of the Western city as the summit of social progress, film noir emphasized the social and psychological consequences of urban modernity. Based initially on the writings of Dashiell Hammett, Raymond Chandler, and James Cain, and with striking parallels to the paintings of Reginald Marsh, George Bellows, and Edward Hopper, noir's erotic portrait of an urban wasteland intonated a deep ambivalence toward the midcentury American metropolis. By the 1940s, as the postwar urban crisis took shape, film noir translated the literary and artistic visions of urban malaise into a more popular cinematic discourse that paralleled the midcentury fate of the American city.[15]

Film noir targeted those urban spaces that best conveyed its vision of urban malaise. The tenement, for example, is a recurrent noir setting, identified as an appropriate milieu for noir's gallery of urban deviants. Its peeling walls, dingy lighting, and rickety stairs frame the encounters between prostitutes and their johns in *Act of Violence* and hide the monstrous fetishes of child molesters in *M*. Film noir featured other spaces of the modern city in its blighted urban landscape. Desolate train stations and abandoned warehouses, vacant streetcars and late-night diners, deserted alleys and empty sewers, seedy nightclubs and tawdry amusement parks: these were the landmarks of film noir and they symbolized the brand of industrial urbanism that entered a period of decline at the outset of the postwar period.

Noir's portrait of urban life focused on the social disorder that ensued within the spatial context of the modern city. In particular, as film historians have demonstrated, noir emphasized the degraded state of sexual relations at the outset of the postwar period. Similar to African Americans, women entered urban public life in unprecedented numbers in the early 1940s, as the female workforce in the United States rose from eleven million to nearly twenty million during the war years.[16] But the very public profile of "Rosie the Riveter," particularly within the nation's cities, aroused animosity toward women who abandoned traditional social roles. As men returned from the war front to resume the routines of work and family, film noir channeled such animosities into its alluring yet disturbing portrait of a new breed of public woman—sassy, conniving, and out to undermine masculine authority through her many misdeeds. The femme fatale resurfaced with a vengeance in American culture vis-à-vis film noir, but the urban context in which she debuted underscored the dangers of a promiscuous urban world where the gendered divisions between public and private life dissolved. Film noir saw the ascendance of such actors as Joan Crawford, Barbara Stanwyck, and Veronica Lake, who perfected the image of the public woman and modeled a clear contempt for the traditional role of women as guardians of the private sphere.[17]

Noir's urban vision of sexual disorder had a racial corollary as well. By the mid-1940s, amidst the blackening of American cities, film noir—translated from French as "black film"—offered a recurring portrait of the promiscuous mixing of the races. Film noir dramatized a larger discourse of race that likened the denigrated condition of blackness to white criminality. In this capacity, film noir echoed a larger discursive affinity between white deviance and black identity. For example, the National Association of Real Estate Boards issued *Fundamentals of Real Estate Practice* in 1943, which advised real estate agents to be wary of those living on the margins of respectability:

> The prospective buyer might be a bootlegger who could cause considerable annoyance to his neighbors. a madam who had a number of call girls on her string, a gangster who wants a screen for his activities by living in a better neighborhood, a colored man of means who was giving his children a college education and thought they were entitled to live among whites. . . . No matter what the motive or character of the would-be purchaser, if the deal would instigate a form of blight, then certainly the well-meaning broker must work against its consummation.[18]

Within the discourse of the real estate industry at midcentury, race and deviance went hand in hand. In their marketing of a suburban alternative to urban blight, real estate agents likened blacks to the city's deviants: bootleggers, madams, call girls, and gangsters. But within their definition of "blight," the racial distinctions between black people and white deviants disappear. To real estate agents and presumably their white clientele, blacks are akin to the white criminals who reside within the noir city: all are equally undesirable as neighbors.

Film noir deploys a similar discourse. In the noir city, white criminality and black identity are mutually constitutive. The morally corrupt white folks who inhabit the noir city, for example, often are viewed alongside black service workers—servants, custodians, garage attendants, shoe shine boys, Pullman porters, and jazz musicians—suggesting their ease within the city's black underworld. In *Double Indemnity*, for example, arguably the quintessential film noir, Walter Neff depends on a colored woman to look after him. After he executes his plans for murder, he relies on the black janitor of his apartment building for an airtight alibi. Throughout his many crimes, Neff's whiteness is compromised by his conspicuous position alongside African Americans. Moreover, noir's innovative and masterful use of light and shadow reinforced the symbolic blackening of white deviants. Darkness pervades the noir screen, always encroaching on the sources of light within the frame. Noir's deviants often are mired in blackened cinematic compositions as if to illuminate their corrupt souls. Throughout *He Walked by Night*, for example, the face of a violent psychopath, never seen in its totality, is marred by dark shadows, reinforcing the black connotations of white criminality.[19]

As film noir coincided with a general retreat from the blackening spaces of industrial urbanism, the genre honed in on those spaces that sanctioned racial and ethnic transgression. The nightclub and its exotic music offer a quintessential noir setting where the boundaries between whiteness and blackness blur. In *Criss Cross*, Steve Thompson wanders through downtown Los Angeles, stumbling into "the old club," where he is hypnotized by the haunting music of Esy Morales and his Rhumba Band. There, Thompson reignites a relationship with an old flame that leads him to his demise. In *D.O.A.,* as Frank Bigelow sacrifices his engagement by swinging with "jive crazy" women in a San Francisco nightclub, the camera focuses tightly on the black face of a trumpeter, reinforcing the racialized milieu of urban nightlife. And in *T-Men*, as two undercover agents from the treasury department venture into a Chinatown nightclub to pursue a mob moll who fancies silk kimonos and fastens tiger lilies to her hair, vaguely Asian music enhances the mood of mystery and danger. The nightclub, a prominent cultural institution of the Swing Era that sanctioned racial intermingling, figured prominently with noir's portrait of urban malaise.[20]

Ultimately, film noir identified a crisis of white masculinity at the outset of the postwar period, but the spatial context of that crisis demands an awareness of how filmmakers and their audiences at midcentury shared a perception of the modern city as a detriment to traditional models of social order. Noir's parade of "weak men," rendered so memorably by the acting of Fred MacMurray, Robert Mitchum, and Burt Lancaster, underscored the destabilization of the white male identity within the topsy-turvy world of the modern city. Duped by conniving women at every turn and mired within the shadows of the black city, noir's white male antiheroes met their demise within the culture of urban modernity. As many Americans craved some semblance of normalcy after the social turmoil of depression and war, and as they satisfied that yearning by removing themselves, physically, from the racialized spaces of the new mass culture, film noir prefigured the need for a "new" new mass culture, one that offered an alternative to the modern city and its degraded culture.

DISNEYLAND AND THE "NEW" MASS CULTURE OF POSTWAR AMERICA

Recent scholarship emphasizes the degree to which black urbanization and white suburbanization belonged to a larger set of social, economic, and political processes that enabled the transition from the centralized metropolis to the decentralized urban region. For this reason, popular culture in the age of white flight included a suburban antithesis to its noir vision of urban life. If film noir dramatized the degraded condition of the black city, Disneyland premiered the cultural mythography of suburban whiteness. Arguably the preeminent cultural impresario of postwar America, Walt Disney took deliberate steps to model his theme park as the very antithesis of its New York predecessor, Coney Island. In its proximity to freeways, its highly disciplined ordering of space, its validation of patriarchy and the nuclear family, and its thematic emphasis on racial distinctions, Disneyland provided a spatial articulation of a new suburban ethos that millions of Americans adopted in their claim to homeownership after World War II.

Disney's decision to locate his new theme park in Orange County, California, underscores the significance of that region to the shifting basis of cultural capital in postwar America. Whereas Detroit suffered the most severe effects of the postwar urban crisis, Orange County profited handsomely from the westward migration of federal defense expenditures during the Cold War. In the decades following World War II, the region sheltered the development of a vast military-industrial complex that for decades provided Orange County's main source of income. The growth of a regional defense industry, in turn, spurred suburban development, as ranchers turned property developers and real estate speculators marketed affordable, suburban tract housing units for an expanding middle-class population. Orange County's expansion during the postwar period was nothing short of spectacular. While in 1940, 130,760 people made their homes in Orange County, that total reached nearly 1.5 million by 1970.[21]

The very newness of Orange County's suburban communities created a cultural space for the resurrection of traditional social values that seemed to dissipate within the promiscuous spaces of the noir city. Removed from Southern California's dominant urban center and far distant from the cosmopolitan culture of eastern cities, Orange County fostered a distinctive political identity that increasingly appealed to groups of Americans disaffected from decades of New Deal liberalism. In a region sustained by a militarized economy, a staunch nationalism and a rigid defense of the American way took shape against the presence of un-American outsiders, whereas the privatized nature of suburban growth in the region nurtured a homegrown appreciation for the values of privacy, individualism, and property rights. The region's remarkable social homogeneity, moreover, coddled an antipathy toward the expansion of a collectivist welfare state and a repudiation of federal interventions on behalf of civil rights activists and other special interest groups. By the 1960s, Orange County sheltered a conservative populism that catapulted New Right ideologues such as Ronald Reagan into California's and ultimately, the nation's, highest public office. With 72 percent of its electorate voting for Reagan in California's 1966 gubernatorial election, Orange County first emerged as "Reagan Country" toward the end of the postwar period.[22]

Orange County sustained a political culture amenable for not only Reagan's postwar metamorphosis from a crusader for the New Deal to an ideologue of the New Right, but also Walt Disney's foray into other cultural enterprises besides filmmaking. In fact, as if to underscore the ideological affinities between the two men, Reagan "starred" at the opening ceremonies of Disneyland held on June 17, 1955. Both Reagan and Disney emerged as men of their time, embracing a set of values that resonated with an expanding middle class that sought refuge from the disordered culture of the modern city within the well-ordered landscapes of suburbia. Not unlike Reagan, Disney underwent a political transformation during the Cold War, in which his hostility grew toward those groups whose gains during an era of New Deal reform threatened to undermine the postwar prospects for resurrecting the American way: intellectuals, racial and ethnic groups, labor unions, and, most of all, Communists. After an embittering experience with labor unions during the war years and at the height of Cold War anxiety, Disney retreated into a vision of a homogeneous WASP folk who for him embodied the traditional values of hard work, rugged individualism, tightly knit families, and traditional gender roles. Such values inspired the basis for not only a spate of Disney films including *Davy Crockett*, *The Swiss Family Robinson*, and *Pollyanna* but also the creation of Disneyland.[23]

As postwar Americans withdrew from the racialized spaces of the modern city, Disney labored to create a cultural alternative to its noir culture. The war years left Walt Disney Productions in financial disarray, prompting company executives to seek alternate venues in which to market Disney products. Following his foray into television, Disney began to think seriously about the creation of an amusement park, and he expressed the "need for something New" but admitted that he "didn't know what it was." He was clear, however, about his aversion toward that paragon of urban industrial culture: Coney Island. The showman once remarked that Coney Island and its generation of amusement parks were "dirty, phoney places run by tough looking people." After visiting a dilapidated Coney Island in the course of planning Disneyland in the mid-1950s, Disney recoiled from "its tawdry rides and hostile employees." Subsequent admirers of Disneyland affirmed Disney's indictment of Coney Island. *New York Times* reporter Gladwin Hill asserted that Disneyland marked a departure from "the traditionally raucous and ofttimes shoddy amusement park," delighting in the fact that Disneyland eliminated the "ballyhoo men to assault [the visitor's] ears with exhortations to test his strength, skill, courage, digestion or gawk at freaks or cootch dancers."[24]

Disney repudiated the slick cynicism of the noir city and sought to restore the innocence and wonder that seemed lost on generations of urban Americans. Raised by a strict father who cautioned against the "corruptive influences of a big city," Disney remained suspicious of modern urban culture throughout his life. His disdain for New York City, for example, became public after the success of Disneyland. When asked by a reporter to consider New York as the site for a second theme park, he dismissed that suggestion in large part because he doubted the capacity of New Yorkers to embrace the Disney worldview.[25] "He said that audience is not responsive," recalled Disneyland's chief architect and Disney's close associate, John Hench, "that city is different." Hench also elaborated on Disney's conviction that urban modernity preyed on the moral conscience of Americans:

In modern cities you have to defend yourself constantly and you go counter to everything that we've learned from the past. You tend to isolate yourself from other people . . . you tend to be less aware. You tend to be more withdrawn. This is counter life . . . you really die a little. . . . I think we need something to counteract what modern society—cities—have done to us.[26]

Having to "defend yourself constantly" became a hallmark experience of the noir city, especially at places like Coney Island, where women, particularly unescorted women, were forced into a defensive posture against the unwanted advances of lustful men. As Kathy Peiss discovered in her study of working women and popular amusements in New York at the turn of the century, the typical shopgirl at Coney Island was "keen and knowing, ever on the defensive . . . she distrusts cavaliers not of her own station."[27]

Disney deplored modernity's sacrifice of innocent virtue. The average citizen, he once remarked, "is a victim of civilization whose ideal is the unbotherable, poker-faced man and the attractive, unruffled woman." Disney's revulsion toward the poker-faced man and the unruffled woman echoed earlier cultural anxieties about "confidence men" and "painted women" in antebellum America. Much like the trickster figure of various folk cultures, the confidence man was the seducer who preyed on the naïveté of the strangers, particularly women, for self-aggrandizement. The confidence man, however, unlike the trickster, owed his existence to the modern city in the first half of the nineteenth century, where individuals could lay claim to new and higher social status through deceit and manipulation. In her study of middle-class culture in nineteenth-century America, Karen Haltunnen located cultural anxieties about confidence men and painted women within the rapid expansion of the city and its ambiguous social milieu. "Hypocrisy," the art of deceit and manipulation mastered by the confidence man, "paid off in an urban environment." Though removed from the historical context in which middle-class moralists denounced the rise of confidence men and painted women, Disney, in his critique of phony amusement parks, poker-faced men, and unruffled women, shared a similar antipathy toward the hypocrisy and deception that defined social relations in the urban world of strangers.[28]

To combat the dissonance and heterosociality of the noir city, Disneyland presented a counterculture of visual order, spatial regimentation, and social homogeneity. Re-acting against what Disney criticized as the "diffuse, unintegrated layout" of Coney Island, the park's designers sought to maximize control over the movement of the crowd through the meticulous organization of space. Whereas Coney Island had mul-tiple entrances and exits, Disneyland offered only one path by which visitors could come and go. Upon entering the park, visitors began their day in Main Street, USA, a central corridor built as a replica of a small-town commercial thoroughfare that channeled pedestrians toward the central hub of the park, "from which the other lands radiate out like spokes in a wheel"—Tomorrowland, Fantasyland, Frontierland, and Adventureland. The spatial organization of Disneyland reflected the designers' inten-tions to direct the continual movement of people with as little indecision as possible. "Each land is easy to enter and easy to exit," asserted one Disney official in a speech to the Urban Land Institute, a national organization of urban developers, "because everything leads back to the central hub again. The result is a revelation to anyone who has ever experienced the disorientation and confusion built into world's fairs and other expositions."[29]

Disneyland's location alongside the Interstate 5 freeway, moreover, underscored the degree to which park designers situated Disneyland within the burgeoning spatial order of the postwar urban region. As Southern California garnered state and federal monies toward highway construction during the 1950s, freeways increasingly dictated regional patterns of development. Following the advice of the Stanford Research Institute—a think tank promoting industrial development in California—Disney strategically situated his theme park alongside the proposed route of the Santa Ana freeway and built what was the largest parking lot in the nation at the time. So vital was the freeway to the success of Disneyland that it earned a permanent place inside the park. Among the thirteen original attractions included in the park's opening in 1955, the Autopia Ride in Tomorrowland was a "real model freeway," not unlike the "motorways of the world of tomorrow" that highlighted the "Futurama" exhibit of the 1939 New York World's Fair. Situated between a rocket-ship ride and the "Voyage to the Moon" attraction, the Autopia Ride demonstrated Disney's optimistic vision of the future and how freeways constituted an integral part of that vision. Like almost every other attraction within the park, and very much unlike the titillating sensations of Coney Island rides, the Autopia Ride had a didactic function, "constructed to acquaint youngsters with traffic conditions on the highways of tomorrow."[30]

The location and layout of Disneyland reflected a larger spatial culture that took shape within the myriad suburban communities that sprouted across the terrain of the decentralized urban region. Lakewood, for example, emerged alongside Disneyland in the early 1950s, and it reflected the intense preoccupation with order that followed the heyday of the noir city. Like the designers of Disneyland, the builders of Lakewood positioned their development in between the proposed routes for two major freeways and incorporated the principles of efficiency, uniformity, and predictability into its design. Typical of postwar suburban development, Lakewood was built on the grid system, a fraction of a larger grid on which Southern California's decentralized urban region took shape. At the center of Lakewood's grid stood Lakewood Center, an outdoor pedestrian mall featuring one hundred retail shops and a major department store. Similar to the way in which the designers of Disneyland organized space to exert maximum control over the vision and movement of the crowd, the architects of Lakewood Center implemented a rigid spatial order to create a self-contained environment dedicated wholly to consumption.[31]

Lakewood also implemented a set of innovations in municipal government that effected a more homogeneous social environment. In 1954, the developers of Lakewood struck a deal with the county of Los Angeles. For minimal costs, Los Angeles County would provide vital services (fire, police, library) to Lakewood, which incorporated as an independent municipality. Contracting services from county government without submitting to its authority, the citizens of Lakewood escaped the burden of supporting county government and enjoyed a greater degree of control over the social composition of their community. "Local control" became a mantra among suburban Southern Californians, whose widespread use of the Lakewood Plan minimized the kind of racial heterogeneity that characterized the modern city and its culture. Given the degree to which the Lakewood Plan effected racial segregation within the context of Southern California's increasingly diverse urban region, one policy expert concluded, "The Lakewood Plan cities were essentially white political movements."[32]

If the Lakewood Plan enforced a literal distance between white and nonwhite people within the postwar urban region, Disneyland underscored that development by asserting a figurative distinction between suburban whiteness and racial otherness. Race and racial difference figured prominently among Disneyland's many themes. Frontierland, for example, described by publicity materials as "a land of hostile Indians and straight shooting pioneers," featured Indians among its main attractions. There one also could find Aunt Jemima's Pancake House, a recreation of a southern plantation where an African-American woman, dressed as "Aunt Jemima did . . . on the plantation . . . was on hand everyday to welcome visitors warmly." Aside from featuring a southern mammie, Disneyland included other stereotypes of African Americans. Adventureland, for example, beckoned visitors to "the sound of native chants and tom-tom drums," where the Jungle Cruise attraction featured "wild animals and native savages [that] attack your craft as it cruises through their jungle privacy."[33]

The racial dimensions of the Disneyland experience surfaced not only in those places of the park where images of blacks and Indians prevailed but also where such images did not appear. Main Street, USA, promoted as "everybody's hometown," and "the heartline of America," reiterated Disney's populist idealization of a WASP folk. Richard Hofstaeder noted in the *Age of Reform* the latent xenopho-

bia within the populist sensibility, which, although seeking to maintain "the primary contacts of country and village life" also cherished a vision of "an ethnically
more homogeneous nation." That vision guided the design of Main Street, USA,
where the absence of mammies, Indians, and savages reified Disney's racialized
and deeply nostalgic vision of the American "folk." The exclusion of African
Americans and their history from the representational landscape of Main Street
was most glaring in the "Great Moments with Mr. Lincoln" exhibit, which debuted in Disneyland in 1966. The "Audio Animatronic" Lincoln recited a speech
designed to elicit patriotic sentimentality, although making no mention of such
divisive conflicts as slavery or the Civil War.[34]

The point here is not to elicit scorn or indignation but rather to understand such
racialized representations within their spatial and historical context. White Americans have long maintained a fascination with race and its representation in popular
culture, but the contours of race relations had changed significantly in postwar
America. After World War II, which brought unprecedented levels of racial cohabi-
tation in American cities, a new generation of white Americans, or at least those
who qualified themselves as such, looked to the decentralized urban region as a
place that could maintain separate and not necessarily equal communities. In the aftermath of the Supreme Court's 1948 ruling against racially restrictive covenants in
Shelley v. Kraemer, and amidst an explosion of civil rights activism, cultural stereotypes of nonwhite racial groups affirmed the racial distinctions that seemed to dissipate within the politically charged climate of a nascent civil rights era. Disneyland,
removed from the "darker" shades of the inner city in Orange County yet permeated
with representations of racial difference, provided a space where white Southern
Californians could reaffirm their whiteness against the fictions of the racial other.[35]
Given the battles that Southern California's white homeowners subsequently waged
against such public initiatives as fair housing, busing, and affirmative action, it is
not difficult to comprehend how Disneyland's racial representations prefigured the
racial underpinnings of a white suburban identity.

If the presence of Aunt Jemima at Disneyland signaled the subordinate position
of blacks within Disney's vision of social order, it also symbolized the subservient
position of women in that order as well. Disneyland's delineation of a social order
appropriate to the tastes and values of an expanding suburban middle class included
an emphasis on patriarchal social relations and the centrality of the nuclear family.[36]
Suburbanization provided a setting in which postwar Americans could confront their
anxieties about the changing position of women in American society, seeking comfort
in cultural representations of domesticated housewives and stable nuclear families.
Disney's effort to position the "typical family of four" at the center of the Disneyland
experience signaled yet another departure from amusement parks of Coney Island's
generation. The *New York Times*, for example, described Disneyland "not as a place
where anyone would casually go to take a roller coaster ride or buy a hot dog, but as
the goal of a family adventure."[37]

Paradoxically, it was in that section of the theme park touted as a "show world of
the future" where park designers chose to insert a traditional vision of gender roles.
Tomorrowland featured as its centerpiece the "Monsanto House of the Future," which

invited park visitors to preview "how the typical American family of four will live in ten years from now." When the house opened to the public on June 12, 1957, models Helen Bernhart and John Marion acted the part of the model couple at home. Photographs depicted the husband relaxing in the "psychiatric chair," which afforded "therapeutic relief after a hard day at the office," with his aproned wife standing in the "Atoms for Living Kitchen." Adhering to the reigning vision family life in postwar America, the interior space of the House of the Future was divided according to the individual needs of family members. The home's cruciform plan ensured "added privacy for various family activities," separating the children's room from the master bedroom. A step-saver kitchen opened onto the family dining room, an arrangement "convenient and perfect for party entertainment." As postwar Americans looked to suburban homeownership as means of restoring some sense of normalcy, Disneyland's House of the Future depicted a futuristic setting where women could return to traditional gender roles.[38]

Moreover, the emphasis on domesticity and private life at Disneyland signaled a shifting cultural focus away from the urban spaces of working-class culture and toward the suburban spaces of middle-class homeownership. In the modern city of the nineteenth and early twentieth centuries, private life belonged to those privileged enough to enjoy the comforts of a townhouse, a carriage, or a private club, whereas the city's working class crowded within the congested spaces of tenement houses, streetcars, and entertainment venues. In the postwar urban region, as greater numbers of Americans attained suburban homeownership through a generous set of public policies, the focus of American popular culture, as Disneyland demonstrated, gradually shifted away from the public venues of the noir city to the private spaces of the home. Thus the park's emphasis on familial domesticity reflected not only a desire to return to traditional gender roles but also a more general valorization of private life that appealed to growing numbers of Americans who entered, or at least aspired to, the ranks of the middle class after World War II.

Disneyland is a complex cultural phenomenon, and there are other aspects of the theme park that underscore its significance to the transformation of urban culture and society at midcentury. Nonetheless, when viewed comparatively alongside simultaneous cultural developments, the theme park illustrates a broader cultural transformation that accompanied the changing configuration of the postwar American city. In its spatial organization, as well as in its thematic emphases, Disneyland asserted a repudiation of the noir sensibility that captivated the American public at the outset of the postwar period. By the mid-1950s, as the heyday of film noir began to wane, a new set of film genres won favor with the public—science fiction, musicals, westerns—that not only upheld traditional models of social order but also delivered the kind of happy endings that were absent from film noir. Disneyland appeared at this cultural moment, delivering its own happy ending to the midcentury transformation of urban life, at least for those who acquired the privileges and comforts of suburban homeownership. As film noir rendered its obituary for the modern city and its new mass culture, Disneyland heralded a new spatial culture that stressed order without complexity, pleasure without danger, and sociability without diversity.

The new suburban cultural order exhibited in film noir and at Disneyland also included other cultural institutions. Television's ascendance as a dominant cultural medium during the 1950s lowered the curtain on the grand movie palaces of the nation's inner cities and rendered the experience of going out on the town an inconvenient waste of time. Suburban shopping malls similarly offered a car-friendly alternative to the downtown department store, where the dire shortage of parking repelled a generation of Americans increasingly wedded to their automobiles. Freeways emerged on top of defunct streetcar lines, introducing a more privatized means of moving rapidly through urban space. The interior settings of the "new" new mass culture provided that very refuge that film noir dramatized a necessity for. Its disciplined, contained, and detached spaces removed consumers from the public realm of decaying cities and modeled idealizations of a new cultural order that captivated a new generation of homeowners eager to create their own suburban retreat from the noir city.[39]

These idealizations, moreover, delivered more than mere entertainment. They also provided a blueprint for a nascent political subjectivity that surfaced in places like Southern California during the 1960s, where a new conservative idealism took shape that aimed to restore traditional patterns of racial and gendered relations. No one better personified that new subjectivity than Ronald Reagan, who championed such principles as property rights, private enterprise, law and order, family values, and small government in his political metamorphosis from New Deal Democrat to New Right Republican. Well attuned to the dawning sensibilities of an expanding suburban public, and affiliating himself with the spectacles of the "new" new mass culture, Reagan fashioned a new political agenda by channeling the values hovering within the larger culture. Film noir, fixated on the disordered culture of the black city, corroborated Reagan's claim in the aftermath of Los Angeles's Watts riots that the urban "jungle is waiting to take over" white suburban communities, whereas Disneyland modeled the very order that his core constituency aspired to.[40] Both cultural productions articulated a deep-seated hostility to urban modernity, both stressed a return to traditional patterns of social order, and both pandered to the political aspirations of an emerging silent majority that retreated from the public culture of the noir city into the private realm of suburban homeownership.

Popular culture in the age of white flight thus exposed the linkages between structure and culture during the post–World War II period. Disneyland, like film noir, owed its existence to the very real transformations that wrought new patterns of urban life in postwar America. Disneyland's calculated proximity to new freeways and its suburban location underscored the park's anticipation of accelerated patterns of decentralized development, whereas film noir refined its techniques of on-location shooting to capture an authentic portrait of urban malaise. In their vital relationship to the postwar transformation of the American city—and it is well to remember that that process happened not simply through the collusion of unseen, abstract social forces but rather through the very conscious efforts of developers, planners, policy makers, and homeowners—film noir and Disneyland codified the anxieties and ambitions, as well as the perceptions and assumptions, widely shared by a public who abandoned their cities for suburban jobs and housing. Their relationship to the postwar emergence of "chocolate cities and vanilla suburbs" was neither incidental nor merely reflective. In modeling popular aspirations toward a new sociospatial order, popular culture in the age of white flight thus enabled the very realization of that order.

The cultural history of the American city illuminates how previous generations of Americans have imagined city form, social order, and the proper relations between the two. Urban imaginings are indeed slippery subjects for the historian to grasp, but popular idealizations of urban life often shape the very real process of making cities. Daniel Burnham's *White City*, for example, which debuted so triumphantly at Chicago's Columbian Exposition in 1893, inspired a generation of urban planners who brought the classical imagery of the Beaux Arts style to bear on the landscape of the American city at the turn of the century. And for better or for worse, few can doubt the impact Disneyland has had on the contours of contemporary urbanism in the United States. Urban cultural history provides a window onto the urban mythography of the past and present—that catalog of simulations and hallucinations that contain our deep-seated fantasies and anxieties about the metropolis and its place in American society.[41]

NOTES

1. Sam Bass Warner, *Streetcar Suburbs: The Process of Growth in Boston, 1870–1900* (Cambridge. MA: Harvard University Press, 1962); Kenneth Jackson, *Crabgrass Frontier: The Suburbanization of the United States* (New York: Oxford University Press, 1985); Mark I. Gelfand, *A Nation of Cities: The Federal Government and Urban America, 1933–1965* (New York: Oxford University Press, 1975); Carl Abbott, *The Metropolitan Frontier: Cities in the Modern American West* (Tucson: University of Arizona Press, 1993); and Thomas Sugrue, *The Origins of the Urban Crisis: Race and Inequality in Postwar Detroit* (Princeton, NJ: Princeton University Press, 1996).

2. The heightened racial consciousness of postwar America, though typically associated with African Americans and the civil rights struggles of racialized minority groups, also encompassed a new generation of white suburban homeowners who defended their interests in racial terms. Becky Nicolaides, for example, argues that suburban homeowners, "grasping willfully for middle class lives in a town with working-class roots," evoked "the language of white rights" to offset racial encroachment by the early 1960s. Similarly, Lisa McGirr locates the origins of a conservative populism in Orange County, which asserted a white backlash to the civil rights gains won by African Americans and other racialized minorities. See Becky Nicolaides, *My Blue Heaven: Life and Politics in the Working Class Suburbs of Los Angeles, 1920–1965* (Chicago: University of Chicago Press, 2002); and Lisa McGirr, *Suburban Warriors: The Origins of the New American Right* (Princeton, NJ: Princeton University Press, 2001). Other social historians recognize the national bases by which racial and gender division attained greater recognition. See chapter 10, Sugrue, "Crabgrass-Roots Politics"; see also Nelson Lichtenstein, "From Corporatism to Collective Bargaining: Organized Labor and the Eclipse of Social Democracy in the Postwar Era," in *The Rise and Fall of the New Deal Order, 1930–1980*, ed. Steve Fraser and Gary Gerstle (Princeton, NJ: Princeton University Press, 1989); Jonathan Reider, "The Rise of the 'Silent Majority,'" in *The Rise and Fall of the New Deal Order, 1930–1980*; and Elaine Tyler May, *Homeward Bound: American Families in the Cold War Era* (New York: Basic Books, 1988).

3. On postwar urbanization and racial segregation, see Michael N. Danielson, *The Politics of Exclusion* (New York: Columbia University Press, 1976); Douglas Massey and Nancy Denton, *American Apartheid: Segregation and the Making of an Underclass* (Cambridge, MA: Harvard University Press, 1993); Arnold Hirsch, *Making the Second Ghetto: Race and Housing in Chicago, 1940–1960* (Chicago: University of Chicago Press, 1998); and Sugrue, *The Origins of the Urban Crisis*. For a contrast between the role of women within a changing urban context, see Kathy Peiss, *Cheap Amusements: Working Women and Leisure in Turn-of-the-Century New York* (Philadelphia: Temple University Press, 1986); and May, *Homeward Bound*.

4. To a certain extent, this new cultural order provides the focus of John Findlay's rigorous study, *Magic Lands*. Although Findlay identifies the distinct spatial character of postwar culture and its relationship to new modes of urbanization in the Far West, his analysis does not emphasize the dynamics of race, class, and gender embedded within these cultural forms and their significance to the shifting (geographic and ideological) bases of national political power. See John M. Findlay, *Magic Lands: Western Cityscapes and American Culture after 1940* (Berkeley: University of California Press, 1992).

5. Frederic Jameson deployed the term "political unconscious" to describe the political meanings embedding within literary forms. Subsequently, the term has been applied to other cultural forms. See Frederic Jameson, *The Political Unconscious: Narrative as a Socially Symbolic Act* (Ithaca, NY: Cornell University Press, 1981). For the relationship between postwar popular culture and the formation of a new white suburban identity, see Eric Avila, *Popular Culture in the Age of White Flight: Suburbanism in Postwar Los Angeles* (University of California Press, 2004).

6. John Kasson identifies Coney Island as exemplifying the new mass culture that emerged within the context of industrial urbanization, and Kathy Peiss describes the "heterosocial" nature of urban popular culture at the turn of the century, emphasizing the role of women within that culture. See John Kasson, *Amusing the Million: Coney Island at the Turn of the Century* (New York: Hill and Wang, 1978); and Peiss, *Cheap Amusements*. Other scholars who have surveyed the history of the new mass culture include David Nasaw, *Going Out: The Rise and Fall of Public Amusements* (New York: Basic Books, 1993); Gunther Barth, *City People: The Rise of Modern City Culture in Nineteenth Century America* (New York: Oxford University Press, 1982); Neil Harris, *Cultural Excursions: Marketing Appetites and Cultural Tastes in Modern America* (Chicago: University of Chicago Press, 1990); Lawrence Levine, *Highbrow/Lowbrow: The Emergence of Cultural Hierarchy in America* (Cambridge, MA: Harvard University Press, 1988); Timothy J. Gilfoyle, *City of Eros: New York City, Prostitution and the Commercialization of Sex, 1790–1920* (New York: Norton, 1992); George Chauncey, *Gay New York: Gender, Urban Culture, and the Making of the Gay Male World, 1890–1940* (New York: Basic Books, 1994); and Karen Haltunnen, *Confidence Men and Painted Ladies: A Study of Middle-Class Culture in America, 1830–1870* (New Haven, CT: Yale University Press, 1982).

7. Sugrue, *The Origins of the Urban Crisis*, 127–30.

8. Howard Chudacoff and Judith Smith, *The Evolution of American Urban Society*, 5th ed. (Upper Saddle River, NJ: Prentice Hall, 2000), 263–67; John Teaford, *The Twentieth Century American City*, 2nd ed. (Baltimore: Johns Hopkins, 1993), 94–95.

9. The terms "chocolate city" and "vanilla suburbs" are taken from George Clinton, leader of the outrageous funk ensemble, Parliament, which issued its hit "Chocolate City" on Casablanca Records in 1975. The song celebrates black political power in American cities, describing black urbanization as a takeover of the nation's cities. In contrast to the disparaging and often dehumanizing portraits of the racialized inner city issued by the nation's lead-

ing social scientists, "Chocolate City" asserts the strength of the black ghetto as a bulwark against the hostility of a racist society. Subsequently, the geographer Reynolds Farley used the term "chocolate city" to frame his account of racial segregation within urban America. See Reynolds Farley, Howard Schuman, Suzanne Bianchi, Diane Colasanto, and Shirley Hatchett, "'Chocolate City, Vanilla Suburbs': Will the Trend toward Racially Separate Communities Continue?" *Social Science Research* 7 (1978): 319–44; and William H. Frey, "Central City White Flight: Racial and Nonracial Causes," *American Sociological Review* 44 (1979): 425–48. On the racial barriers built into postwar suburbanization, see Kenneth T. Jackson, "Race, Ethnicity, and Real Estate Appraisal: The Home Owners Loan Corporation and the Federal Housing Administration," *Journal of Urban History* 6 (1980): 419–52. See also Melvin L. Oliver and Thomas M. Shapiro, *Black Wealth/White Wealth: A New Perspective on Racial Inequality* (New York; Routledge, 1995), 15–18; George Lipsitz, *The Possessive Investment in Whiteness: How White People Profit from Identity Politics* (Philadelphia: Temple University Press, 1998), 5–7.

10. "Coney Island Slump Grows Worse," *New York Times*, July 2, 1964, 1.

11. *Chicago Tribune Magazine*, May 16, 1976.

12. Quoted in Nasaw, *Going Out*, 252. For a more in-depth analysis of the fate of Shibe Park, see Bruce Kuklick, *To Everything a Season: Shibe Park and Urban Philadelphia, 1909–1976* (Princeton, NJ: Princeton University Press, 1991).

13. Peter Golenbock, *An Oral History of the Brooklyn Dodgers* (New York: Putnam, 1984), 38.

14. The literature on film noir is extensive and growing. Foster Hirsch, *Film Noir: The Dark Side of the Screen* (New York: Da Capo, 1981); Paul Schrader, "Notes on Film Noir," in *Film Noir: A Reader*, ed. Alain Silver and James Ursini (New York: Limelight Editions, 1997), 53–64; A. M. Karimi, *Toward a Definition of the American Film Noir (1941–1949)* (New York: Arno, 1976); Alain Silver and Elizabeth Ward, eds., *Film Noir: An Encyclopedic Reference to the American Style* (New York: Overlook Press, 1979); Spencer Selby, *Dark City: The Film Noir* (Jefferson, NC: McFarland, 1984); James Naremore, *More Than Night: Film Noir in Its Contexts* (Berkeley: University of California, 1998); and Frank Krutnik, *In a Lonely Street: Film Noir, Genre, Masculinity* (London: Routledge, 1991).

15. Hirsch, *Film Noir*, 82.

16. American Social History Project, *Who Built America? Working People and the Nation's Economy, Politics, Culture and Society, Volume Two: From the Gilded Age to the Present* (New York: Pantheon Books, 1992), 457.

17. Hirsch, *Film Noir*, 152–57; and May, *Homeward Bound*, 62–63.

18. Quoted in Arnold R. Hirsch, "With or without Jim Crow: Black Residential Segregation in the United States," in *Urban Policy in Twentieth Century America*, ed. Arnold R. Hirsch and Raymond A. Mohl (New Brunswick, NJ: Rutgers University Press, 1993), 75.

19. Eric Lott, "The Whiteness of Film Noir," in *Whiteness: A Critical Reader*, ed. Mike Hill (New York: New York University Press, 1997), 93–94. Lott draws on the work of film historian and critic Richard Dyer, who argues that film noir is part of a broader "culture of light" in the West, in which light and dark are invested with social meanings. In a racialized democracy that values "white over black," to borrow Winthrop Jordan's famous characterization of Anglo-American social values, the delineation of light in the representation of the social world is structured by racial hierarchies that place a moral premium on whiteness and light. The cinematic combination of white skin and light evokes that ethical connotations associate whiteness with moral purity and spiritual hygiene and, conversely, the absence of light, or the abundance of shadows, conveys a denigrated state of moral ambiguity. Within the history of portraiture, photography, film, and other aspects of Western visual culture, the uses of light

speak not only to Western notions of the racial other but also to the West's conception of itself. See Richard Dyer, *White* (London: Routledge, 1997).

20. On the jazz and the urban nightclub, see Louis Erenberg, *Swingin' the Dream: Big Band Jazz and the Rebirth of American Culture* (Chicago: University of Chicago Press, 1998).

21. Security First National Bank, *The Growth and Economic Stature of Orange County*, May 1967, 12–15.

22. McGirr, *Suburban Warriors*, 209.

23. Richard Schickel, *The Disney Version: The Life, Times, Art and Commerce of Walt Disney* (Chicago: Ivan R. Dee, 1997); and Stephen Watts, "Walt Disney: Art and Politics in the American Century," *Journal of American History* 100, no. 2 (1995): 84–110.

24. Schickel, *The Disney Version*, 310; *New York Times*, February 2, 1958; "The Never-Never Land Khrushchev Never Saw," *New York Times*, October 4, 1959, 22.

25. Schickel, *The Disney Version*, 47.

26. John Hench, interview by Jay Horan, December 3, 1982, transcript, Walt Disney Archives, Burbank, CA.

27. Quoted in Peiss, *Cheap Amusements*, 127.

28. "The Wisdom of Walt Disney," *Wisdom* 32 (December 1959): 77; and Haltunnen, *Confidence Men and Painted Women*, 192–93.

29. "Disney's 'Magical Little Park' after Two Decades," *Los Angeles Times*, July 6, 1975, pt. 10, 1; Carl Walker, speech to Urban Land Institute, October 5, 1975, quoted in Findlay, *Magic Lands*, 84.

30. *Disneyland News*, n.d., Regional History Archives, Anaheim Public Library.

31. Richard Longstreth, *From City Center to Regional Mall: Architecture, the Automobile and Retailing in Los Angeles, 1920–1950* (Cambridge, MA: MIT Press, 1997), 336–40.

32. Gary Miller, *Cities by Contract: The Politics of Municipal Incorporation* (Cambridge, MA: MIT Press, 1981), 135; and Mike Davis, *City of Quartz: Excavating the Future in Los Angeles* (New York: Vintage, 1992), 165–69.

33. *News from Disneyland*, Walt Disney Productions 1965, Anaheim History Room, Anaheim Public Library; *Disneyland News*, August 7, 1956; *News from Disneyland*, n.d., Public Relations Division, Disneyland, Inc., Anaheim History Room, Anaheim Public Library.

34. Hofstadter, quoted in Stephen Watts, "Walt Disney: Art and Politics in the American Century," 97; and "Moving Right Along: Disneyland Grows Ever More Sophisticated," *Los Angeles Times Magazine*, July 13, 1986, 8. Text of speech from "Great Moments with Mr. Lincoln," Anaheim Public Library, Anaheim History Room.

35. Disneyland's symbolic delineation of racial hierarchy suited cold war conceptions of racial difference. By contrast, when the City of Los Angeles commissioned local artist Bernard Rosenthal to create a sculpture for the new downtown police department building, the resulting piece incited a local uproar among conservative groups. Rosenthal's piece—titled *The Family*—depicted human figures without a specific racial character. The racial vagueness of Rosenthal's figures led one public official to denounce *The Family* as a "shameless, soulless, faceless, raceless, gutless monstrosity that will live in infamy." In Los Angeles, abstract art aroused intense opposition among cold warriors for its subversive potential, but humanistic representations of racial ambiguity also aroused considerable protest. See Sarah Schrank, "Art and the City: The Transformation of Civic Culture in Los Angeles, 1900–1965" (Ph.D. diss., Department of History, University of California, San Diego, 2002).

36. May, *Homeward Bound*, 3–15.

37. *New York Times*, February 2, 1958, sec. 2, pt. 2, 1.

38. "Monsanto Chemical Co.," *Disneylander*, March 1958, 2, Disneyland Collection, Anaheim History Room, Anaheim Public Library. See also "Disneyland's First Ten Million,"

New York Times, February 2, 1958. For an illuminating analysis of the gendered assumptions built into residential architecture after World War II, see Dolores Hayden, "Model Houses for the Millions: Architect's Dreams, Builder's Boasts, Residents' Dilemmas," in *Blueprints for Modern Living: History and Legacy of the Case Study Houses* (Cambridge. MA: MIT Press, 1989), 197–212.

39. Avila, *Popular Culture in the Age of White Flight*.

40. Reagan, quoted in Lisa McGirr, *Suburban Warriors*, 204.

41. Mike Davis, *Ecology of Fear: Los Angeles and the Imagination of Disaster* (New York: Metropolitan Books, 1998). 392. On the relationship between cultural history and urban history, see Timothy J. Gilfoyle, "White Cities, Linguistic Turns, and Disneylands: The New Paradigms of Urban History," *Reviews in American History* 26 (1998): 175–204.

Chapter 12

Planned Destruction: The Interstates and Central City Housing

Raymond A. Mohl

Few public policy initiatives have had as dramatic and lasting an impact on modern America as the decision to build the Interstate Highway System. Virtually completed over a fifteen-year period between 1956 and the early 1970s, the building of the new Interstates had inevitable and powerful consequences for U.S. urban housing policy — consequences that ranged from the rapid growth of suburban communities to the massive destruction of inner-city housing in the path of the new urban expressways. Housing and highways were intimately linked in the post–World War II United States. In fact, this chapter contends that postwar policymakers and highway builders used interstate construction to destroy low-income and especially black neighborhoods in an effort to reshape the racial landscapes of the U.S. city.

In metropolitan areas, the coming of urban expressways led very quickly to a re-organization of urban and suburban space. The interstates linked central cities with sprawling postwar suburbs, facilitating automobile commuting while undermining what was left of inner-city mass transit. They stimulated new downtown physical development and spurred the growth of suburban shopping malls, office parks, and residential subdivisions. Oriented toward center cities, urban expressways also tore through long-established inner-city residential communities, destroying low-income housing on a vast and unprecedented scale. Huge expressway interchanges, clover leafs, and on-off ramps created enormous areas of dead and useless space in the central cities. The new expressways, in short, permanently altered the urban and suburban landscape throughout the nation. The interstate system was a gigantic public works program, but it is now apparent that freeway construction had enormous and often negative consequences for the cities. As Mark I. Gelfand noted, "No federal venture spent more funds in urban areas and returned fewer dividends to central cities than the national highway program."[1]

Reprinted from John F. Bauman, Roger Biles, and Kristin Szylvian, eds., *From Tenements to the Taylor Homes: In Search of an Urban Housing Policy in Twentieth-Century America* (University Park: Pennsylvania State University Press, 2000), 226–45. Reprinted by permission of Pennsylvania State University Press.

Almost everywhere, the new urban expressways destroyed wide swaths of existing
housing and dislocated people by the tens of thousands. Highway promoters and highway builders envisioned the new interstate highways as a means of clearing "blighted"
urban areas. These plans actually dated to the late 1930s, but they were not fully
implemented until the late 1950s and 1960s. Massive amounts of urban housing were
destroyed in the process of building the urban sections of the Interstate Highway System. According to the 1969 report of the National Commission on Urban Problems, at
least 330,000 urban housing units were destroyed as a direct result of federal highway
building between 1957 and 1968. In the early 1960s, federal highway construction dislocated an average of 32,400 families each year. "The amount of disruption," the U.S.
House Committee on Public Works conceded in 1965, was "astoundingly large."[2] A
large proportion of those dislocated were African Americans, and in most cities the
interstates were routinely routed through black neighborhoods.

Dislocated urbanites had few advocates in the state and federal road-building
agencies. The federal Bureau of Public Roads and the state highway departments
believed that their business was to finance and build highways and that any social
consequences of highway construction were the responsibility of other agencies.[3] One
federal housing official noted in 1957: "It is my impression that regional personnel
of the Bureau of Public Roads are not overly concerned with the problems of family relocation."[4] Indeed, during most of the expressway-building era, little was done
to link the interstate highway program with public or private housing construction
or even with relocation assistance for displaced families, businesses, or community
institutions such as churches and schools.

The victims of highway building tended to be overwhelmingly poor and black.
A general pattern emerged, promoted by state and federal highway officials and by
private agencies such as the Urban Land Institute, of using highway construction to
eliminate "blighted" neighborhoods and to redevelop valuable inner-city land. This
was the position of Thomas H. MacDonald, director of the U.S. Bureau of Public
Roads (BPR) during the formative years of the interstate system. It was also the policy
of New York's influential builder of public works projects, Robert Moses. Highway
builders were clearly conscious of the social consequences of interstate route location. It was quite obvious that neighborhoods and communities would be destroyed
and people uprooted, but this was thought to be an acceptable cost of creating new
transportation routes and facilitating urban economic development. In fact, highway
builders and downtown redevelopers had a common interest in eliminating low-
income housing and, as one redeveloper put it in 1959, freeing "blighted" areas "for
higher and better uses."[5]

The federal government provided most of the funding for interstate highway construction, but state highway departments working with local officials selected the
actual interstate routes. The consequence of state and local route selection was that
urban expressways could be used specifically to carry out local race, housing, and residential segregation agendas. In most cities, moreover, the uprooting of people from
central-city housing triggered a spatial reorganization of residential neighborhoods.
Black population pressure on limited inner-city housing meant that dislocated blacks
pushed into neighborhoods of "transition," generally working-class white neighbor-

hoods on the fringes of the black ghetto where low-cost housing predominated. These newer "second ghettos" were already forming after World War II, as whites began moving to the suburbs and as blacks migrated out of the South into the urban North. Interstate highway construction speeded up this process of second-ghetto formation, helping mold the sprawling, densely populated ghettos of the modern American city. Official housing and highway policies, taken together, helped to produce the much more intensely concentrated and racially segregated landscapes of contemporary urban America.[6]

EARLY EXPRESSWAY PLANNING

The linkage between inner-city expressways and the destruction of urban housing actually originated in the BPR, the federal agency established in 1919. Thomas H. MacDonald, a highway engineer from Iowa, headed the BPR from its founding until early 1953. Over many decades, MacDonald relentlessly promoted his agency's road-building agenda.[7]

The automobile era demanded hard-surfaced roads. By the 1930s, mass transit was on the decline almost everywhere, as Americans seemingly preferred the convenience, flexibility, and privacy of automobile travel. Eyeing the enormous untapped urban market, the automobile industry had a major interest in express highways and in federal highway legislation. In particular, the extremely popular General Motors Futurama exhibit at the 1939 New York World's Fair, as Mark I. Foster noted, "stimulated public thinking in favor of massive urban freeway building." Norman Bel Geddes, the designer of the Futurama exhibit, also promoted the idea of a "national motorways system connecting all cities with populations of more than one hundred thousand."[8]

By the end of the 1930s, Thomas MacDonald and the BPR pushed for an interregional highway system linking the nation's largest metropolitan areas, an idea given initial form by President Franklin D. Roosevelt himself. According to Secretary of Agriculture Henry A. Wallace, at a 1938 meeting with MacDonald, the president sketched out on a map "a system of east-west, north-south transcontinental highways" and then requested that MacDonald make a report on the possibilities of building such a highway system. The BPR's subsequent report, *Toll Roads and Free Roads* (largely written by MacDonald and his assistant H. S. Fairbanks), completed in 1939, represented the first comprehensive effort to conceptualize what later became the Interstate Highway System. Significantly, the report acknowledged the obvious link between express highways and urban reconstruction. It made a strong case that highway planning should take place in the context of an ongoing program of slum clearance and urban redevelopment.[9]

Wallace reported to Roosevelt that the BPR's plan established nothing less than the basis for the complete physical rebuilding of American cities. The big problem, Wallace noted, was not transcontinental automobile traffic, but automobile congestion in the cities themselves. If new express highways penetrated and traversed the cities, traffic flow to the business centers would be facilitated. More than that, careful routing of these arterial highways could cut through and clear out blighted housing areas:

"There exists at present around the cores of the cities, particularly of the older ones, a wide border of decadent and dying property which has become, or is in fact becoming, a slum area." Land acquisition in these slum areas for highway construction and urban redevelopment would result in "the elimination of unsightly and unsanitary districts where land values are constantly depreciating." As Wallace portrayed the situation, the BPR's highway construction plan could become a central element in the reconstruction and revitalization of the central cities.[10]

A second major highway report, *Interregional Highways*, was completed in 1944. It was prepared by the National Interregional Highway Committee, appointed by President Roosevelt, and headed by Thomas MacDonald. This report, which recommended an "interregional" highway system of 40,000 miles, actually mapped out a highway network that looks remarkably like the present Interstate Highway System. The 1944 report also made it clear that the new interregional or interstate highways would penetrate the heart of metropolitan areas. Larger cities would be encircled by inner and outer beltways and traversed by radial expressways tying the urban system together. MacDonald believed these urban expressways essential to the future growth and development of the American city, especially modern slum clearance and urban reconstruction.[11]

Throughout the 1940s and into the early 1950s, MacDonald campaigned tirelessly for inner-city expressways that would clear out low-income housing and tenement districts, eliminating the "blighted districts contiguous to the very heart of the city." Dislocated urban residents, MacDonald suggested, could move to the new suburbs and commute to city jobs on new high-speed, multifunctional expressways.[12] In a 1947 speech to the U.S. Chamber of Commerce Conference on Urban Problems, MacDonald whimsically dismissed the inevitable housing destruction that accompanied urban expressway building: "It is a happy circumstance that living conditions for the family can be re-established and permit the social as well as economic decay at the heart of the cities to be converted to a public asset."[13]

To his credit, MacDonald also pushed for local planning policies and Congressional legislation requiring new housing construction for those displaced from their homes by expressway building. In an important statement in 1947, he made the case for relocation housing: "No matter how urgently a highway improvement may be needed, the homes of people who have nowhere to go should not be destroyed. Before dwellings are razed, new housing facilities should be provided for the dispossessed occupants." Ultimately, however, MacDonald's effort to forge a linkage between urban expressway construction and relocation housing was unsuccessful. In 1949, President Harry S. Truman rejected the coordination of highway and housing programs, citing anticipated high costs and difficulty of Congressional passage. By the early 1950s, the BPR had seemingly lost interest in the broader implications of highway building and focused instead on facilitating automobile and truck transportation. Highway engineers with their narrowly technical concerns were left in control of the BPR. MacDonald halted his speaking and writing crusade, and, after President Dwight D. Eisenhower failed to reappoint him director, he left the agency in 1953. Not until 1965, when most of the interstates had already been built, did the federal government require advance relocation housing for families and businesses displaced by interstate highway construction.[14]

EXPRESSWAYS AND THE CENTRAL CITIES

The federal government rejected an urban policy that integrated highways and housing. However, other powerful interest groups were quick to recognize the implications of interstate expressway construction at the cities' cores. Those interested at the time in the future of the central city—urban policymakers and planners, big city mayors, urban real estate interests, central city business groups—all sought a general rebuilding of the central cities during the contemplated postwar reconstruction. Urban expressway building was considered a necessary component of such urban policy and planning. The absence of any official interest in rebuilding inner-city housing for those displaced meant that huge sections of central-city land could be cleared for other uses. Expressway building was seen as a way of saving the central city from the creeping blight of an older and deteriorating housing stock. Because such housing accommodated mostly poor and minority residents, highway building often meant black removal from the central-city area. As early as 1949, one black housing official predicted—quite correctly, as it turned out—that "the real masters of urban redevelopment will be the forces intent on recapturing Negro living space for the 'right' people."[15]

Among the interest groups seeking to save the central business district, few were more important than the Urban Land Institute (ULI). Founded in 1936 to serve the interests of downtown real estate owners and developers, the ULI consistently pushed for central-city redevelopment. From the 1930s, downtown real estate professionals feared that suburbanization, and especially the decentralization of retailing, would ultimately sap the vitality of central-city economic activities. The automobile was largely to blame, because it both facilitated suburban growth and clogged downtown traffic arteries. As the respected urban planner and architect Victor Gruen put it in the mid-1950s, "the rotting of the core has set in in most American cities, in some cases progressing to an alarming degree." In the decade following World War II, the ULI's Central Business District Council focused on freeways as "the salvation of the central district, the core of every city."[16]

In a stream of pamphlets, newsletters, and technical bulletins, the Urban Land Institute sought to pave the way for central-city expressways. For James W. Rouse, a Baltimore real estate developer involved with the Urban Land Institute in the 1950s and later well known as a builder of "new towns" and festival marketplaces, the pattern of inner-city decay threatened the future of the central business district. According to Rouse, the solution for downtown America was clear: "Major expressways must be ripped through to the central core" as an integral aspect of extensive redevelopment efforts. Urban developer James H. Scheuer, in a 1957 ULI publication, envisioned inner-belt expressways inevitably slicing through "great areas of our nation's worst slums." The ULI's monthly newsletter, *Urban Land*, urged urban governments to survey the "extent to which blighted areas may provide suitable highway routes." ULI consultant James W. Follin saw the 1956 Interstate Highway Act providing "wide open opportunity" to eliminate blighted housing and recapture central-city land for redevelopment. For the ULI, expressway building promised the salvation of the central business district.[17]

Using highways for slum clearance and urban redevelopment excited representatives of other interest groups, as well. The American Road Builders' Association (ARBA) served as the major trade association for the nation's highway construction firms. As early as 1949, in a letter to President Truman, the ARBA defended the use of highway construction in slum clearance. Urban express highways, the ARBA contended, were necessary to alleviate traffic congestion, but through proper right-of-way planning they also could "contribute in a substantial manner to the elimination of slum and deteriorated areas." The elimination of urban slums would stimulate downtown businesses, contribute to an appreciation of property values, and counter the threat posed by slum housing to "the public health, safety, morals, and welfare of the nation." Similarly, as early as 1943 the American Concrete Institute (ACI), which had an obvious interest in highway construction, championed the use of urban expressways in "the elimination of slums and blighted areas." Build highways through the city slums, urged the ARBA and the ACI, and solve the problems of urban America.[18]

The automobile lobby joined the chorus touting the role of expressways in rebuilding urban America. Typically, in a 1956 pamphlet entitled *What Freeways Mean to Your City*, the Automotive Safety Foundation assured readers that freeways were desirable, beneficial, and beautiful; they stimulated rising land values and prevented "the spread of blight and . . . slums." Forward-looking communities used "the transportation potential of freeways to speed redevelopment of run-down sections along sound lines and to prevent deterioration of desirable sections." Similarly, in a 1962 article, the Highway Research Board contended that interstate expressways were "eating out slums" and "reclaiming blighted areas." The inner-city freeway, in short, represented a "positive social good," especially if it was routed through blighted slum neighborhoods that might be reclaimed for more productive civic uses.[19]

The downtown developers, the automobile lobby, highway officials, and planners and politicians at every level shared the urban expressway dream. Echoing his boss Thomas MacDonald, the BPR's urban road division chief, Joseph Barnett, suggested in 1946 that properly located urban expressways would help immeasurably in "the stabilization of trade and values in the principal or central business district." New York's Robert Moses pushed such ideas vigorously. In a 1954 statement to the President's Advisory Committee on a National Highway Program (generally known as the Clay Committee), Moses argued that new urban expressways "must go right through cities and not around them" if they were to accomplish their purpose. Expressways not only addressed urban traffic problems, but through proper coordination they could advance slum clearance plans and other aspects of urban redevelopment. Moses concluded somewhat prophetically that city expressway mileage would be "the hardest to locate, the most difficult to clear, the most expensive to acquire and build, and the most controversial from the point of view of selfish and shortsighted opposition." In other words, people whose homes would be taken for expressways represented a highway problem, not a housing problem.[20]

Like New York, Detroit in the 1940s found expressways an "essential step in slum clearance" that would "open up blighted areas and fit them for more productive uses."

Detroit's depressed inner-city expressways, Mayor Albert E. Cobo told the Clay Committee in 1954, not only enhanced property values along their right-of-way, but also were positively "a picture of beauty." A writer in the *Western Construction News* in 1943 contended that urban expressways, "usually and best built through blighted areas," would solve traffic congestion, provide postwar employment, and revitalize city centers through slum clearance. A 1950 plan for expressways in Cleveland predicated revitalization of the central business district on redevelopment of blighted "central residential areas." In the early 1950s, Kansas City's city manager, L. P. Cookingham, stated that "no large city can hope for a real future" without expressways that cleared slums and preserved the central business district.[21]

Working within federal traffic engineering guidelines, highway builders at state and local levels routed new urban expressways in directions of their own choosing. Local agendas often dictated such decisions; the result was to drive the interstates through black and poor neighborhoods. Urban blacks were heavily concentrated in areas with the oldest and most dilapidated housing, where land acquisition costs were relatively low, and where organized political opposition was weakest. Displaying a "two birds with one stone" mentality, cities and states sought to route interstate expressways through slum neighborhoods, using federal highway money to reclaim downtown urban real estate. Inner-city slums could be cleared, blacks removed to more distant second-ghetto areas, central business districts redeveloped, and transportation woes solved all at the same time—and mostly at federal expense.[22]

It seems clear, then, that the interstates were conceived of as more than just traffic arteries. To be sure, the highway engineers in the BPR and at the state level were interested in building highways that would move traffic efficiently, although many of them also shared the "two birds" theory. But business interests and government officials in the cities anticipated expressways as part of a larger redevelopment of the city centers. This rebuilding of the central city in many cases came at the expense of African Americans in the inner cities, whose neighborhoods—not just housing but churches, business districts, even entire urban renewal areas—were destroyed in the process of interstate construction. In other instances, highway builders routed urban interstates through white working-class and ethnic neighborhoods, historic districts, and parks, but building an expressway through a black community was the most common choice in the interstate-building era.

Highway builders rarely mentioned African Americans specifically in their discussions about blight and slums. The massive migration of southern blacks to northern and midwestern cities was well under way during the war years. Black newcomers moved into urban neighborhoods abandoned by whites as they departed for the suburbs. Southern cities already had large black populations. When the highwaymen talked about clearing out central-city blight in the postwar era, everyone knew what they meant. The intent, the goal, was clear to most, even if it was rarely stated directly. Their intentions were clear from their statements, actions, and policies—and the visible consequences of the highways they built are the best evidence of their intended goals. As one former federal highway planner conceded in a 1972 interview, the urban interstates gave city officials "a good opportunity to get rid of the local niggertown."[23]

EXPRESSWAYS AND INNER-CITY HOUSING DESTRUCTION

From the late 1950s and well into the 1960s, urban expressway construction meant massive family dislocation and housing and community destruction. State highway engineers and consultants, usually working with local civic elites, determined the interstate routes into the central cities. The routes they chose were consistent with perceptions and policies of the past. Highway builders had traditionally made clearing out housing blight at the center of the cities one of their goals. By the mid-1950s, after a decade and a half of heavy black migration into urban areas, most of those inner-city neighborhoods targeted by the highway planners' maps were predominantly African American. Consequently, most American cities faced serious community disruption and racial strife as the interstate expressways ripped through urban neighborhoods and leveled wide swaths of inner-city housing. A few examples should serve to demonstrate the destructive impact of urban expressways.

In Miami, Florida, state highway planners and local officials deliberately routed Interstate 95 directly through the inner-city black community of Overtown. An alternative route using an abandoned railroad corridor was rejected, as the highway planners noted, to provide "ample room for the future expansion of the central business district in a westerly direction," a goal of the local business elite since the 1930s. Even before the expressway was built, and in the absence of any relocation planning, some in Miami's white and black press asked: "What About the Negroes Uprooted by Expressway?" The question remained unanswered, and when the downtown leg of the expressway was completed in the mid-1960s, it tore through the center of Overtown, wiping out massive amounts of housing as well as Overtown's main business district, the commercial and cultural heart of black Miami. One huge expressway interchange took up twenty square blocks of densely settled land and destroyed the housing of about 10,000 people. By the end of the 1960s, Overtown had become an urban wasteland dominated by the physical presence of the expressway. Little remained of the neighborhood to recall its days as a thriving center of black community life, when it was known as the Harlem of the South.[24]

In Nashville, Tennessee, highway planners went out of their way to put a "kink" in the urban link of Interstate 40 as it passed through the city. The expressway route gouged a concrete swath through the North Nashville black community, destroying hundreds of homes and businesses and dividing what was left of the neighborhood. The decision for the I-40 route had been made quietly in 1957 at a nonpublic meeting of white business leaders and state highway officials. By 1967, after years of denying that the expressway would adversely affect the community, the state highway department began acquiring right of way, displacing residents, and bulldozing the route. Outraged blacks in Nashville organized the Nashville I-40 Steering Committee to mount an opposition campaign, charging that routing an interstate expressway through a black community could be legally classified as racial discrimination.[25]

The I-40 Steering Committee won a temporary restraining order in 1967, the first time a highway project had been halted by claims of racial discrimination. The Steering Committee's attorney alleged that "the highway was arbitrarily routed through the North Nashville ghetto solely because of the racial and low socio-economic character of the ghetto and its occupants without regard to the widespread adverse effects on the land uses adjoining the route." Ultimately, the I-40 Steering Committee lost its case in federal court, and the I-40 expressway was completed through Nashville's black community. However, the legal controversy in Nashville starkly revealed, if not a racial purpose, at least a racial outcome experienced by many cities.[26]

In New Orleans, enraged freeway opponents successfully waged a long battle against an eight-lane elevated expressway along the Mississippi River and through the edges of the city's historic French Quarter. The Riverfront Expressway originated in a 1946 plan proposed for New Orleans by the New York highway builder Robert Moses. The planned expressway was part of an inner-city beltway of the type that Moses favored and that the BPR had incorporated into its interstate planning. After several years of hot debate and controversy, historic preservationists succeeded in fighting off the Riverfront Expressway plan. In 1969, the Department of Transportation secretary, John A. Volpe, terminated the I-10 loop through the Vieux Carré.[27]

However, while white New Orleans residents were fending off the highway builders, the nearby midcity black community along North Claiborne Avenue was less successful. Highway builders there leveled a wide swath for Interstate 10. At the center of an old and stable black Creole community, boasting a long stretch of magnificent old oak trees, North Claiborne served a variety of community functions such as picnics, festivals, and parades. The highway builders rammed an elevated expressway through the neighborhood before anyone could organize or protest. Some of the preservationists who fought the Riverfront Expressway gladly suggested North Claiborne as an alternative. By the 1970s, Interstate 10 in New Orleans rolled through a devastated black community, a concrete jungle left in the shadows by a massive elevated highway.[28]

Interstate construction in Montgomery, Alabama, also devastated a black community. In 1961, state highway officials recommended a route for Interstate 85 that traversed the city's major African-American community. George W. Curry, a black minister and head of a Property Owners Committee, sent a petition with 1,150 signatures to local, state, and federal highway officials protesting that the expressway route would destroy an estimated 300 homes in black Montgomery and proposing an alternative route through mostly vacant land. At a public hearing, 650 people stood up to signify their opposition to the expressway. Curry argued that the route "was racially motivated to uproot a neighborhood of Negro leaders." An internal BPR "memorandum for record" spelled out the details:

> Rev. Curry alleges that the routing of this highway will uproot a Negro community, which has no place to relocate, and two Negro churches. It is claimed that there is a nearby alternate route which would cost $30,000 less. Rev. Curry charges that the proposed routing of the highway is designed by State and local officials to purposely dislodge this Negro community where many of the leaders of the fight for desegregation in Montgomery reside. Rev. Curry said that in a recent conversation with a Mr. Sam Englehardt, Alabama's Highway Director, Mr. Englehardt stated that it was his intention to get Rev. Abernathy's church.

Ralph Abernathy, a close adviser of Martin Luther King in the Montgomery bus boycott of 1956 and in other desegregation struggles, also complained about the Interstate

85 route in a telegram to President John F. Kennedy in October 1961. Abernathy's home stood in the path of the highway project, obviously targeted by Alabama highway officials.[29]

In Birmingham, Alabama, where three interstates intersected, a black citizens' committee complained to the Alabama state highway department and the BPR in 1960 that proposed interstate freeways "would almost completely wipe out two old Negro communities [in] eastern Birmingham with their 13 churches and three schools." Moreover, the public hearing held on the highway proposal had been segregated, and blacks were unable to present their grievances.[30] In 1963, as the start of interstate construction neared in Birmingham, opposition flared again in the city's black community. A resident, James Hutchinson, protested to Alabama senator John Sparkman that the interstate (I-59) "bisects an exclusive colored residential area. In addition, it has a large interchange in the heart of this area." In the early days of the interstates, the racial routing of the Birmingham expressway noted by Hutchinson was rather typical. So was the response of Federal Highway Administrator Rex M. Whitton to Senator Sparkman. The route had been chosen by the Alabama state highway department and approved by the Bureau of Public Roads, Whitton wrote, "based on a thorough evaluation of all engineering, economic, and sociological factors involved." If that was the case, then it would seem that the destruction of the Birmingham black community was indeed a planned event.[31]

A similar pattern of planned destruction took place in Camden, New Jersey, bisected in the 1960s by Interstate 95, with the usual consequences for low-income housing. In 1968, the Department of Housing and Urban Development sent a task force to Camden to study the impact of highway building and urban renewal. It found that minorities made up 85 percent of the families displaced by the North-South Freeway—some 1,093 of a total of 1,289 displaced families. For the five-year period 1963 to 1967, about 3,000 low-income housing units were destroyed in Camden, but only about 100 new low-income housing units were built during that period.[32]

The Civil Rights Division of the New Jersey State Attorney General's Office prepared a second report on Camden. Entitled "Camden, New Jersey: A City in Crisis," the report made a similar case for the racial implications of expressway construction in Camden. As the report stated: "It is obvious from a glance at the renewal and transit plans that an attempt is being made to eliminate the Negro and Puerto Rican ghetto areas by two different methods. The first is building highways that benefit white suburbanites, facilitating their movement from the suburbs to work and back; the second is by means of urban renewal projects which produce middle and upper income housing and civic centers without providing adequate, decent, safe, and sanitary housing, as the law provides, at prices which the relocatee can afford." The central argument of the New Jersey civil rights report was that this outcome was purposely planned and carried out.[33]

The experience of Camden during the expressway-building era of the late 1950s and 1960s was duplicated in cities throughout the nation. A Kansas City, Missouri, midtown freeway originally slated to pass through an affluent neighborhood ultimately sliced through a racially integrated Model City area. It destroyed 1,800 buildings there and displaced several thousand people.[34] In Charlotte, North Carolina, Interstate 77 leveled an African-American community, including four black schools.[35] Highway officials pushed ahead with a three-and-one-half-mile inner-city expressway in Pittsburgh, even though it was expected to dislocate 5,800 people.[36] In St. Paul, Minnesota, Interstate 94 cut directly through the city's black community, displacing one-seventh of St. Paul's black population. As one critic put it, "very few blacks lived in Minnesota, but the road builders found them."[37] Despite the fact that the Century Freeway in Los Angeles would dislocate 3,550 families, 117 businesses, and numerous schools and churches, mainly in black Watts and Willowbrook, the Department of Transportation approved the new expressway in 1968.[38]

The story was much the same in other cities. In Florida, expressways in Tampa, Saint Petersburg, Jacksonville, Orlando, and Pensacola routinely ripped through, divided, and dislocated black neighborhoods.[39] In Columbus, Ohio, an inner-city expressway leveled an entire black community.[40] In Milwaukee, the North-South Expressway cleared a path through sixteen blocks in the city's black community, uprooting 600 families and ultimately intensifying patterns of racial segregation.[41] A network of expressways in Cleveland displaced some 19,000 people by the early 1970s.[42] In Atlanta, according to the historian Ronald H. Bayor, highways were purposely planned and built "to sustain racial ghettos and control black migration" in the metropolitan area.[43]

African Americans were not alone in suffering the destructive consequences of urban expressway construction. In Chicago, a whole range of ethnic neighborhoods gave way to expressways as they headed south, southwest, west, and northwest out of the downtown Loop area.[44] In Boston, an inner-city expressway tore through and destroyed the Chinatown district and part of the city's Italian North End.[45] In New York City, the Cross-Bronx Expressway ripped through a massive "wall of apartment houses" that stretched for miles, gouging "a huge trench" across a primarily working-class Jewish community.[46] As one transportation specialist suggested, "almost every major U.S. city bears the scars of communities split apart by the nearly impenetrable barrier of concrete."[47]

The devastating human and social consequences of urban expressway construction ultimately produced widespread opposition and citizen activism. Beginning in San Francisco in 1959, freeway revolts gradually spread throughout the country by the late 1960s.[48] State and federal highway planners accepted citizen opposition as one of the costs of building roads, but by the mid-1960s Congress became more sensitive to the political backlash created by massive housing destruction and the difficulties of relocating displaced families. Political pressure on top staffers in the Federal Highway Administration and the new U.S. Department of Transportation (created in 1966) gradually led to a softening of the narrowly technocratic engineering mentality that had dominated the Bureau of Public Roads. As a result, some routes were altered to avoid neighborhood destruction, while other expressway projects were canceled altogether. In addition, new Congressional legislation required that for highway projects after 1965, relocation housing had to be provided in advance of construction. By that time, however, most of the urban interstates had already been put into place; most of the damage had already been done.[49]

CONCLUSION

The historical record has demonstrated that highways and housing were closely linked in postwar urban policymaking. Early interstate advocates conceived of new urban expressways as a means of rebuilding the central city by clearing away blighted housing. The Bureau of Public Roads advocated such ideas as early as the 1930s, and many of the pre-1956 urban expressways put these ideas into practice. After the landmark 1956 interstate legislation, highway officials at every level implemented expressway plans that destroyed enormous amounts of low-income, inner-city housing, especially in black neighborhoods where land acquisition costs were generally cheaper and where political opposition was minimal, particularly in southern cities. Thus, massive housing destruction—planned destruction—was the natural concomitant of expressway building in the central cities.

Highway planners and local officials did not carefully think through the problem of new housing for hundreds of thousands of dislocated African Americans. In some cities, the large-scale, high-rise public housing projects of the 1950s, such as the Robert Taylor Homes in Chicago or the Pruitt-Igoe Project in Saint Louis, absorbed some dislocated families. However, highways and urban renewal destroyed more inner-city housing than was being built. In many cities, public housing construction slowed in the politically reactionary 1950s. The new lily-white suburbs that sprouted in the postwar automobile era rarely welcomed new black residents. Essentially, most uprooted African American families found new housing in nearby low- and middle-income white residential areas, which themselves were experiencing the transition from white to black. The expressway building of the 1950s and 1960s ultimately produced the much larger, more spatially isolated, and more intensely segregated second ghettos characteristic of late-twentieth-century American cities.

NOTES

1. Mark I. Gelfand, *A Nation of Cities: The Federal Government and Urban America, 1933–1965* (New York: Oxford University Press, 1975), 222.

2. National Commission on Urban Problems, *Building the American City* (Washington, D.C.: U.S. Government Printing Office, 1969), 81; U.S. House of Representatives, Committee on Public Works, *Study of Compensation and Assistance for Persons Affected by Real Property Acquisition in Federal and Federally Assisted Programs* (Washington, D.C.: U.S. Government Printing Office, 1965), 24, 26, 105; Michael Sumichast and Norman Farquar, *Demolition and Other Factors in Housing Replacement Demand* (Washington, D.C.: National Association of Home Builders, 1967), 47–48, 76.

3. National Commission on Urban Problems, *Building the American City*, 91.

4. John P. McCollum to Albert M. Cole, May 23, 1957, Housing and Home Finance Agency Records (hereafter cited as HHFA Records), RG 207, Subject Correspondence Files, Albert Cole, Administrator, 1953–58, Box 18, National Archives II, College Park, Maryland.

5. William H. Claire, "Urban Renewal and Transportation," *Traffic Quarterly* 13 (July 1959): 417; Thomas H. MacDonald, "The Case for Urban Expressways," *The American City*

62 (June 1947): 92–93; Robert Moses, "Slums and City Planning," *Atlantic Monthly* 175 (January 1945): 63–68.

6. On the second ghetto, see Arnold R. Hirsch, *Making the Second Ghetto: Race and Housing in Chicago, 1940–1960* (Cambridge: Cambridge University Press, 1983), esp. 1–39; Raymond A. Mohl, "Making the Second Ghetto in Metropolitan Miami, 1940–1960," *Journal of Urban History* 21 (March 1995): 395–427.

7. W. Stull Holt, *The Bureau of Public Roads: Its History, Activities, and Organization* (Baltimore: Johns Hopkins University Press, 1923); Bruce E. Seely, *Building the American Highway System: Engineers as Policy Makers* (Philadelphia: Temple University Press, 1987).

8. Mark I. Foster, *From Streetcar to Superhighway: American City Planners and Urban Transportation, 1900–1940* (Philadelphia: Temple University Press, 1981), 153; Norman Bel Geddes, *Magic Motorways* (New York: Random House, 1940).

9. Henry A. Wallace to Franklin D. Roosevelt, February 13, 1939, copy in Bureau of Public Roads Records (hereafter cited as BPR Records), RG 30, Classified Central Files, Box 4107, National Archives II, College Park, Maryland; "Report of the Chief of BPR on the Feasibility of a System of Superhighways," undated typescript [1939]; BPR Records, RG 30, Classified Central Files, Box 1949; U.S. Bureau of Public Roads (BPR), *Toll Roads and Free Roads*, U.S. House of Representatives, 76th Congress, 1st Session, 1939, House Document No. 272. The Department of Agriculture initially administered the Bureau of Public Roads, but in 1939 the BPR was transferred to the newly established Federal Works Agency. During the Truman administration, the BPR was shifted again, this time to the Department of Commerce.

10. Wallace to Roosevelt, February 13, 1939, BPR Records, RG 30, Classified Central Files, Box 4107.

11. U.S. National Interregional Highway Committee, *Interregional Highways* (Washington, D.C.: U.S. Government Printing Office, 1944), Thomas H. MacDonald to Albert B. Chandler, with accompanying notes, November 18, 1943, BPR Records, RG 30, Classified Central Files, Box 1892.

12. Thomas H. MacDonald, "Proposed Interregional Highway System as It Affects Cities," January 21, 1943, Thomas H. MacDonald Speeches, U.S. Department of Transportation Library, Washington, D.C.; Thomas H. MacDonald, "The Case for Urban Expressways," *The American City* 62 (June 1947): 92–93; idem, "Future of the Highways," *U.S. News and World Report*, December 29, 1950, 30–33.

13. Thomas H. MacDonald, "The Federal-Aid Highway Program and Its Relation to Cities," September 11, 1947, speech typescript, BPR Records, RG 30, Classified Central Files, 1912–59, Box 1942.

14. MacDonald, "The Case for Urban Expressways," 92–93; Gelfand, *A Nation of Cities*, 225–30, quotation on 226; Mark H. Rose, *Interstate: Express Highway Politics, 1941–1956* (Lawrence: Regents Press of Kansas, 1979), 61–62.

15. George B. Nesbitt, "Relocating Negroes from Urban Slum Clearance Sites," *Land Economics* 25 (August 1949): 285; George B. Nesbitt, "Break Up the Black Ghetto?" *The Crisis* 56 (February 1949): 48–52.

16. Victor Gruen, "The City in the Automobile Age," *Perspectives* 16 (Summer 1956): 48; Hal Burton, *The City Fights Back* (New York: Citadel, 1954), 78.

17. James W. Rouse, "Will Downtown Face Up to Its Future?" *Urban Land* 16 (February 1957): 4; James H. Scheuer, "Highways and People: The Housing Impact of the Highway Program," in *The New Highways: Challenge to the Metropolitan Region*, Technical Bulletin no. 31 (Washington, D.C.: Urban Land Institute, 1957); James W. Follin, "Coordination of Urban Renewal with the Urban Highway Program Offers Major Economies in Cost and Time," *Urban Land* 15 (December 1956): 3, 5.

18. Charles M. Upham to President Truman, February 16, 1949, and accompanying "Resolution of the American Road Builders' Association," BPR Records, RG 30, Classified Central Files, 1912–50, Box 183; "Planning for the Postwar Period: A Report of the Committee on Postwar Planning of the American Concrete Institute," n.d. (c. 1943), BPR Records, RG 30, Classified Central Files, Box 1892.

19. Automotive Safety Foundation, *What Freeways Mean to Your City* (Washington, D.C.: Automotive Safety Foundation, 1956), 32; Floyd I. Theil, "Social Effects of Modern Highway Transportation," *Highway Research Board Bulletin*, no. 327 (1962): 6–7; Gary T. Schwartz, "Urban Freeways and the Interstate System," *Southern California Law Review* 49 (March 1976): 484–85.

20. Joseph Barnett, "Express Highway Planning in Metropolitan Areas," *Transactions of the American Society of Civil Engineers* 112 (1947): 650; Robert Moses to Thomas H. MacDonald, June 11, 1946, BPR Records, RG 30, Classified Central Files, Box 2662; Statement of Robert Moses, Hearings, President's Advisory Committee on a National Highway Program, October 7, 1954, 47–51, in BPR Records, RG 30, Records Relating to National Highway and Defense Highway Programs, 1940–55, Box 1.

21. G. Donald Kennedy, *A Comprehensive Plan of Motorways for Detroit* (Lansing: Michigan State Highway Department, 1941), 14–15, copy in BPR Records, RG 30, Classified Central Files, Box 2448; Statement of Albert E. Cobo, Hearings, President's Advisory Committee on a National Highway Program, October 8, 1954, 249–75, in BPR Records, RG 30, Records Relating to National Highway and Defense Highway Programs, 1940–55, Box 1; Lynn Atkinson, "Freeways Solve Two Problems," *Western Construction News* (January 1943): 20–25, quotation on 22, reprint in BPR Records, RG 30, Classified Central Files, Box 1944; William B. Blaser, "Right-of-Way and Its Effect on Design," Proceedings of the Urban Highway Design Conference, February 13–17, 1950, mimeo, in BPR Records, RG 30, Reports of Highway Studies, Box 19; L. P. Cookingham, "Expressways and the Central Business District," *American Planning and Civic Annual* (1954): 140–46.

22. An extensive literature substantiates these generalizations. See, for example, Jon C. Teaford, *The Rough Road to Renaissance: Urban Revitalization in America, 1940–1985* (Baltimore: Johns Hopkins University Press, 1990); Bernard J. Frieden and Lynne B. Sagalyn, *Downtown, Inc.: How America Rebuilds Cities* (Cambridge, Mass.: MIT Press, 1989), 15–37.

23. Schwartz, "Urban Freeways and the Interstate System," 485.

24. Raymond A. Mohl, "Race and Space in the Modern City: Interstate-95 and the Black Community in Miami," in Arnold R. Hirsch and Raymond A. Mohl, eds., *Urban Policy in Twentieth-Century America* (New Brunswick: Rutgers University Press, 1993), 100–158.

25. Richard J. Whalen, "The American Highway: Do We Know Where We're Going?" *Saturday Evening Post*, December 14, 1968, 22–27, 54–64; John E. Seley, "The Kink in Nashville's Interstate-40," in John E. Seley, *The Politics of Public-Facility Planning* (Lexington, Mass.: Lexington Books, 1983), 57–66; Ben Kelley, *The Pavers and the Paved* (New York: Donald W. Brown, 1971), 97–107.

26. "Bias Is Charged in Highway Suit," *The New York Times*, November 27, 1967; Alan S. Boyd to Flournoy A. Coles Jr., April 8, 1968, Federal Highway Administration Records (hereafter cited as FHWA Records), RG 406, Central Correspondence, 1968–69, Box 131.

27. Priscilla Dunhill, "An Expressway Named Destruction," *Architectural Forum* 126 (March 1967): 54–59; Richard O. Baumbach Jr. and William E. Borah, *The Second Battle of New Orleans: A History of the Vieux Carré Riverfront-Expressway Controversy* (Tuscaloosa: University of Alabama Press, 1981).

28. *Vieux Carré Courier*, January 22, 1965, Claiborne Avenue Design Team, *I-10 Multi-Use Study* (New Orleans: Claiborne Avenue Design Team, 1976).

29. George W. Curry and the Property Owners Committee, A Petition Appeal, April 28, 1960, BPR Records, RG 30, General Correspondence, 1912–65, Box 1665; Berl I. Bernhard to Hyman Bookbinder, June 29, 1961, BPR Records, RG 30, General Correspondence, 1912–65, Box 1664; John W. Roxborough, Memorandum for Record, June 23, 1961, BPR Records, RG 30, General Correspondence, 1912–65, Box 1664; Ralph D. Abernathy to John F. Kennedy, October 3, 1961, telegram, BPR Records, RG 30, General Correspondence, Box 1664.

30. Lala Palmer to Alabama State Highway Department, April 11, 1960, telegram, BPR Records, RG 30, General Correspondence, 1912–65, Box 1665; Joe Davis to Luther Hodges, February 17, 1961, BPR Records, RG 30, General Correspondence, 1912–65, Box 1664.

31. James Hutchinson to John Sparkman, November 3, 1963, FHWA Records, RG 406, Federal-Aid System Correspondence, Box 3; Rex M. Whitton to John Sparkman, November 20, 1963, FHWA Records, RG 406, Federal-Aid System Correspondence, Box 3.

32. Steven H. Leleiko to Lowell K. Bridewell, December 4, 1968, FHWA Records, RG 406, F. C. Turner Files, Box 7.

33. Ibid.

34. Richard Leverone to Lowell K. Bridewell, May 16, 1968, FHWA Records, RG 406, L. K. Bridewell Files, Box 11.

35. *Charlotte Observer*, May 14, May 15, 1968, clippings, in FHWA Records, RG 406, L. K. Bridewell Files, Box 7.

36. Richard Leverone to Lowell K. Bridewell, May 21, 1968, FHWA Records, RG 406, L. K. Bridewell Files, Box 11.

37. Alan A. Aultshuler, *The City Planning Process: A Political Analysis* (Ithaca: Cornell University Press, 1965), 17–83; F. James Davis, "The Effects of a Freeway Displacement on Racial Housing Segregation in a Northern City," *Phylon* 26 (Fall 1965): 209–15; Frieden and Sagalyn, *Downtown, Inc.,* 28–29.

38. F. C. Turner to Lowell K. Bridewell, July 19, 1967, FHWA Records, RG 406, Central Correspondence, 1968–69, Box 140; Lowell K. Bridewell to Gordon C. Luce, March 20, 1968, FHWA Records, RG 406, Central Correspondence, 1968–69, Box 140; Kathleen Armstrong, "Litigating the Freeway Revolt: Keith v Volpe," *Ecology Law Journal* 2 (Winter 1972): 761–99.

39. Mohl, "Race and Space in the Modern City," 135.

40. Mark H. Rose and Bruce E. Seely, "Getting the Interstate Built: Road Engineers and the Implementation of Public Policy, 1955–1985," *Journal of Policy History* 2 (1990): 37.

41. Patricia A. House, "Relocation of Families Displaced by Expressway Development: Milwaukee Case Study," *Land Economics* 46 (February 1970): 75–78.

42. "Toward the Postindustrial City: 1930–1980," in David D. Van Tassel and John J. Grabowski, eds., *The Encyclopedia of Cleveland History* (Bloomington: Indiana University Press, 1987), xlix–li.

43. Ronald H. Bayor, "Roads to Racial Segregation: Atlanta in the Twentieth Century," *Journal of Urban History* 15 (November 1988): 3–21.

44. Elliott Arthur Pavlos, "Chicago's Crosstown: A Case Study in Urban Expressways," in Stephen Gale and Eric G. Moore, eds., *The Manipulated City* (Chicago: Maaroufa Press, 1975), 255–61.

45. Kenneth R. Geiser, *Urban Transportation Decision Making: Political Processes of Urban Freeway Controversies* (Cambridge, Mass.: Department of Urban Studies and Planning, Massachusetts Institute of Technology, 1970), 258–64; Alan Lupo, Frank Colcord, and Edmund P. Fowler, *Rites of Way: The Politics of Transportation in Boston and the U.S. City* (Boston: Little, Brown, 1971)

46. Robert A. Caro, *The Power Broker: Robert Moses and the Fall of New York* (New York: Knopf, 1974), 839–94; Marshall Berman, *All That Is Solid Melts into Air: The Experience of Modernity* (New York: Simon and Schuster, 1982), 290–312; Jill Jonnes, *We're Still Here: The Rise, Fall, and Resurrection of the South Bronx* (Boston: Atlantic Monthly Press, 1986), 117–26.

47. David Hodge, "Social Impacts of Urban Transportation Decisions: Equity Issues," in Susan Hanson, ed., *The Geography of Urban Transportation* (New York: Guilford, 1986), 303.

48. William H. Lathrop Jr., "The San Francisco Freeway Revolt," *Transportation Engineering Journal of the American Society of Civil Engineers* 97 (February 1971): 133–43; "The Revolt Against Big City Expressways," *U.S. News and World Report* 52, January 1, 1962, 48–51; James Nathan Miller, "Stop Choking Our Cities," *Reader's Digest* 89 (August 1966): 37–41; Priscilla Dunhill, "When Highways and Cities Collide," *City* 1 (July 1967): 48–54; "The War over Urban Expressways," *Business Week*, March 11, 1967, 4–5; Jack Linville, "Troubled Urban Interstates," *Nation's Cities* 8 (December 1970): 8–11; Juan Cameron, "How the Interstate Changed the Face of the Nation," *Fortune* 84 (July 1971): 78–81, 124–25; and, for a general critique of the automobile culture, Jane Holtz Kay, *Asphalt Nation: How the Automobile Took Over America and How We Can Take It Back* (New York: Crown, 1997).

49. On these points, see Raymond A. Mohl, "The Interstates and the Cities: The U.S. Department of Transportation and the Freeway Revolt, 1966–1973," *Journal of Policy History* 20/2 (2008): 193–226.

Chapter 13

Harold and Dutch: A Comparative Look at the First Black Mayors of Chicago and New Orleans

Arnold R. Hirsch

Since the 1967 elections of Richard Hatcher in Gary, Indiana, and Carl Stokes in Cleveland, Ohio, the emergence of black mayors in major American cities has been one of the distinguishing characteristics of local politics in the United States. Since then, African Americans have been elected as chief executives in every corner of the nation. In the industrial Northeast and Midwest, blacks presently occupy, or in the recent past have occupied, city halls in New York, Chicago, Detroit, Cleveland, Philadelphia, and Newark. In the South, they have run Washington, Baltimore, Richmond, Atlanta, New Orleans, and Birmingham, among others—places where elected black officials would have been unthinkable even a single generation before. Even in the Far West where African Americans proportionately have settled more sparsely, Los Angeles and Seattle have had black mayors representing overwhelmingly white cities. Such staggering change would seem to herald the ultimate success of the civil rights revolution. Was this not, after all, what it was all about?

It is clear, however, that if the pattern of municipal office holding has undergone a dramatic shift, the conditions that initially sparked black protest and political mobilization remain stubbornly persistent. Certainly, rates of unemployment for African Americans living in the urban core have not dropped below those of the Vietnam era. And compared to the so-called pathologies of contemporary inner-city life—such as rates of crime, illegitimacy, illiteracy, and single-parent households—the violent 1960s look almost like a "golden age" whose problems seem manageable. While there is no denying the mushrooming growth of an expansive black middle class, the emergence of a seemingly chronically dependent urban black "underclass" (as it came to be called in the 1980s) seems equally undeniable.

The black community, in short, is more complex and diverse today than it was a generation earlier. If the ghetto has been gilded for some and escaped by others, it now presents the dual problems of race and poverty in a new and concentrated form.

Original essay published by permission of Arnold R. Hirsch.

If there is legitimate concern over the implicit political and ideological content of the concept of the underclass, the term's popularity stems, at least in part, from its descriptive utility. The elevation of a new class of African-American officeholders has not, in short, substantially altered the social structure of urban America.

This essay will offer a brief examination of two black mayors—Ernest Nathan "Dutch" Morial of New Orleans and Harold Washington of Chicago—in an effort to shed some light on the problems and forces they confronted. Certainly it is helpful to scrutinize African-American administrations in a northern city and a southern one to see if any regional differences come into play, but there should be no easy supposition that the individuals at the focus of this chapter are necessarily representative of black mayors as a class. If anything, Dutch Morial and Harold Washington were among the toughest and smartest of those municipal executives dedicated to attacking the status quo; each was concerned more with pursuing and exercising power than accumulating mere honors. In sum, if individual, local officeholders could shape their immediate environments, these two would be likely candidates for producing visible results.

There are three points at which the careers of each of these figures might be usefully examined. First, there is the acquisition of power. In looking at Morial's rise to the mayor's chair in 1978 and Washington's in 1983, one first sees that each reached that pinnacle at a time when blacks represented both population and voting minorities in New Orleans and Chicago. That simple fact, ultimately, had serious implications for their ability to govern. Second, there is the actual exercise of power. How did each of them govern? What obstacles did they confront and how successful were they in overcoming them? Finally, the succession of power might be revealing if scrutinized. Morial left City Hall in 1986, turned out of office after two consecutive terms by a city charter term limitation that he tried and failed to repeal. Washington, having been reelected to a second term in a city that honored a tradition of extended, multiple terms for its mayors, died, suddenly, in his office, in 1987. How permanent were the advances made during their administrations? Could those advances dictate the direction of change once Morial and Washington were out of office? Had they, in other words, set their respective cities on new courses?

The rise of Dutch Morial and Harold Washington must be understood within their local political contexts. There is a tendency in the study of American race relations to homogenize everything into simple matters of black and white. A study of African-American mayors, however, reveals that within the framework provided by the American racial dichotomy, an understanding of local cultures is critical to an understanding of the individuals themselves.

Atlanta's Andrew Young, for example, entered City Hall through the ministry, and Coleman Young became industrial Detroit's chief executive officer following an extended stint as a labor radical and organizer for the United Auto Workers. The first black mayors of New Orleans and Chicago similarly launched their early careers in the most powerful local black institutions available. Local variables conditioned, if they did not dictate, the channels through which talented and ambitious African-American leaders developed their skills and became prominent figures.

In New Orleans and Chicago, those institutions were neither the black church, although it was not without influence, nor the labor movement. For Morial that central institution was the National Association for the Advancement of Colored People (NAACP). Not only was it the most important vehicle for protest and the civil rights movement in New Orleans, but it also was the institutional home for the remnants of a radical black Creole community that provided much of the city's leadership during the era of Reconstruction and kept alive a tradition of resistance to the color line since the dawning of the Jim Crow era. Personified by Homer Plessy's moral and legal challenge at the end of the nineteenth century, that Creole radicalism survived in New Orleans to tie the first and second Reconstructions together.[1]

Morial was born and raised in New Orleans's Seventh Ward, the very epicenter of the downtown Creole community. He was an integral part of it and assumed the presidency of the local branch of the NAACP during the height of the civil rights agitation of the early 1960s. The New Orleans chapter of the NAACP, created in 1915, was one of the first branches established in the Deep South and displayed roots similar to Morial's. Its chief legal counsel, through the middle of the twentieth century, was A. P. Tureaud, another Seventh Ward Creole and Morial's senior partner and mentor.

Tureaud and Morial, more than any other individuals in the Crescent City, became identified with the dismantling of the legalized system of segregation. It was a fitting role for Morial, who was himself a walking civil rights revolution. The first black to graduate from the Louisiana State University Law School, in 1952, he went on to accumulate an impressive array of other "firsts"; he was the first black assistant U.S. attorney in New Orleans (1965), the first elected to the state legislature in the modern era (1967), the first named to the Juvenile Court bench (1970), the first to serve on the state's Fourth Circuit Court of Appeals (1974), and, ultimately, the first elected mayor. In short, Dutch Morial made his career by opposing, as Rodolphe Desdunes, another black Creole, put it, the "fanaticism of caste." More than a vehicle for the legal assault on Jim Crow, the local branch of the NAACP also carried out, under Morial's direction, voter registration campaigns that proved instrumental in the successful launching of his political career. Initially locked out of the system, Morial mounted an assault from outside, demolishing racial barriers while building an institutional base within the black community.[2]

In Chicago the NAACP was incapable of performing similar services. When, early in the civil rights era, it had threatened to become an activist protest organization, black political boss William Levi Dawson simply had his precinct captains infiltrate the organization as new voting members. A moderating change in leadership followed. That episode, however, gave a clue as to where the path to political power could be found in Chicago—it was in the Cook County Democratic Organization, the famed Chicago "machine" itself.

Indeed, Harold Washington had been raised in the very bosom of the organization that he would later defeat. The Democratic political machine in Chicago, and its subordinate black branch, provided a wealth of opportunity for those who could gather concentrated black votes in the city's highly segregated neighborhoods. Demography, geography, and the peculiar features of its political landscape made that arena an attractive one for skilled and ambitious players. Chicago's South Side Black Belt proved a veritable political hothouse, developing a sophisticated cadre of movers and shakers by the turn of the twentieth century. Indeed, it was that scarred battleground on the South Side, not larger New York, that produced, by 1928, the first black representative to the U.S. Congress elected from a northern district.[3]

Harold Washington's father, Roy Washington, was an attorney, an African Methodist Episcopal preacher, a dabbler in real estate, and a precinct captain in the Democratic organization. Active at the beginning of the 1930s, he was one of the earliest black Democratic stalwarts. Politics formed the core of the dinner table discussions that Harold Washington recalled from his childhood. And Harold did more than absorb stories about the machine. He watched it operate at close hand as when, in 1947, his father strapped a gun on his hip and went looking for the Democratic ward committeeman who had covertly undermined his campaign for the city council.[4]

If Harold Washington was never quite an unthinking machine loyalist (he characterized himself, at one point, as an "independent machine politician"), he paid it enough obeisance early in his career to emerge as one of its most promising stars. He had taken over the South Side Third Ward precinct worked by his father and filled the elder Washington's slot in the corporation counsel's office following his death in 1953 (Harold Washington's law degree came from Northwestern University in 1952). Though considerably younger than the Third Ward's Democratic committeeman (committeemen were the key political officers in each ward), former Olympic star and rising machine politician Ralph Metcalfe, Washington possessed political skills that were more finely honed, and it is not entirely clear who, exactly, was mentoring whom.

Finally rewarded with a seat in the state legislature, Washington became something of a renegade after his posting to Springfield (first in the state House of Representatives and, later, in the Senate) in 1964. Confronting Mayor Richard J. Daley directly on the issue of police brutality and wandering away from the party line on a host of lesser concerns, Washington soon found himself beyond Metcalfe's protective mantle and on his own. He made a longshot's futile run for City Hall in 1977 following Daley's death and fought off the organization's subsequent attempted purge. In the party primary the following year he had to survive an election in which the organization slated three opponents—two of them named Washington—against him. The attempt to confuse Washington's electoral base into submission fell barely 200 votes short of success. Washington then confirmed his independence by successfully challenging the machine-slated nominee for the U.S. House of Representatives in his district in 1980. Displaying the power to outdraw the machine in his home district, he became a vocal critic of the Reagan administration, further ingratiating himself with his South Side constituency.

Both Dutch Morial and Harold Washington, consequently, succeeded in building solid black political bases. In Morial's case it was rooted in the downtown Creole community but extended uptown into the old "American" sector of the city. As attorney and legislative candidate, he mined those neighborhoods for supporters in both the NAACP's civil rights crusades and in his race for the state House of Representatives. For Washington, home was Chicago's massive South Side Black Belt, particularly those growing middle-class wards that were proving less than reliable for the machine. That provided the base from which he could reach out to whites (he ultimately settled in the integrated Hyde Park community that surrounded the University of Chicago) and to the newer, growing ghetto on the West Side. It is important to note also that neither Morial nor Washington emerged overnight. In both cases long years of service and an extended political apprenticeship forged an organic unity between the community and the candidates. The extraordinarily high levels of black voter turnout and solidarity that they enjoyed in their surprising initial victories were testimonies, ultimately, to their long-established credibility as well as to the magic of their respective moments.

In each case, the assertiveness of the black candidates and their ability to forge solid African-American electoral bases allowed them to surprise divided white communities that did not take them seriously as political threats. In dissecting their winning coalitions, however, analysts have divided over the relative significance of the solid black base as opposed to the essential white fragment that provided, in theory, their margins of victory. Often rooted in political or racial interests, at least some of this attention is misplaced. The key factor, it seems, is the black base in combination with the ignorance and arrogance that led to the underestimation of the African-American candidates in the white community and the internal white divisions that opened the door for seemingly quixotic challenges.

In New Orleans, in 1977, Morial faced three major white opponents who sharply divided the white vote in an open (nonpartisan) primary that would pit the top two finishers against one another if no one earned a majority of the ballots cast. Morial was seen as nothing more than a spoiler at the outset, and his relative lack of financial resources and grass-roots campaign in the black community led mainstream analysts to dismiss his prospects in a city in which black registrants amounted to no more than 43 percent of the vote. His impact on the campaign was discussed primarily in terms of how he would affect the tallies of Nat Kiefer and Toni Morrison, the "serious" white candidates who were actively courting black supporters. The fourth candidate, Joseph DiRosa, ran a white populist campaign that made no pretense of seeking black votes.[5]

In the end, the traditional paternalistic ties that linked white political elites to African-American "leaders" and voters were no match for the communal ties forged by Morial over his long career. Morial's base returned a sizable majority of the black vote in the primary, eviscerating the campaigns of both Kiefer and Morrison. Having split the white vote with DiRosa, they were left dueling over a small slice of the minority pie. Morial thus squeezed into the runoff with DiRosa, a candidate who had thoroughly alienated the business community and carried his own ethnic baggage. In the final showdown, Morial swept 97 percent of an exceptionally high black turnout and just enough whites, about 20 percent, to enable him to win a close contest.[6]

Similarly, Washington was given no chance to win when he announced his candidacy in the 1983 mayoralty. After all, he had won only 11 percent of the vote in his 1977 warm-up, and blacks still represented less than 40 percent of Chicago's electorate. The "real" race would be in the Democratic primary between the incumbent, Jane Byrne, and her major white challenger, Richard M. Daley, the son of Chicago's legendary Richard J. Daley. Washington, until the final days of the primary campaign, enjoyed nearly a free ride. The mainstream white press virtually ignored his prospects while concentrating its closest scrutiny on Byrne and Daley. For their part, the mayor and her Irish challenger similarly refrained from attacking Washington. Seeking some portion of the black vote for themselves in the primary, they certainly did not wish to alienate that constituency and hoped to pick it back up in the general election. Only in the closing days of the campaign did it become clear that, indeed, it was Washington, not Daley, who was Byrne's most threatening opponent. That turn of events prompted Democratic party chairman Ed Vrdolyak's now famous dictum that the election had become a "racial thing." Calling on whites to desert Daley in defense of racial interests, his raw appeal backfired. With Byrne and Daley neatly dividing the white ballots almost in half, Washington won the Democratic nomination for mayor with only 36 percent of the total primary vote. His showing in the black community—he had won 85 percent of a 70 percent turnout there following a massive increase in voter registration—carried the day. Part political campaign, part religious crusade, the Washington movement capitalized on a long series of racial provocations by Mayor Byrne and Ronald Reagan that had energized black Chicagoans.[7]

Historically, the Democratic nomination for mayor in Chicago was tantamount to election. No Republican had been elected mayor since 1927, and their numbers were so few that Democrats often were pressed into service as nominally "Republican" election judges so that the precincts might be properly staffed. Washington's seizure of the Democratic nomination, however, suddenly reinvigorated the city's Republicanism.

The national Republican party raised hundreds of thousands of dollars for the campaign, provided media expertise, and furnished advice on how to run a racially divisive campaign without mentioning race—all of this to secure the election of the man who won his party's nomination with only 11,000 votes (in contrast, Washington's 424,131 outpolled Byrne's 387,986 and Daley's 344,590). More important, of the fifty Democratic ward committeemen, more endorsed Washington's opponent in the general election, Bernard Epton, than supported the nominee of their own party; and even those nominally in Washington's corner often provided Epton with covert assistance in the attempt to undermine Washington. Still, in a bitter, racially charged campaign, Washington took just under 52 percent of the vote, winning by less than 50,000 out of nearly 1.3 million ballots cast. He managed to eke out about 12 percent of the white vote and 62 percent of the city's growing Hispanic vote (if Hispanics are counted as "whites," Washington's "white" vote increased to 16 to 18 percent). That support supplemented the 97 to 99 percent of the black voters who backed Washington with an astounding 85 percent turnout. He won every black vote in the city, as one Epton supporter put it, "except for the accidents."[8] If Morial's victory seemed characteristic of an outsider's ferocious storming of dearly protected battlements, Washington's rise seemed more like an "insider's" palace coup.

Whites in New Orleans and Chicago, who had initially taken neither the Morial nor the Washington campaign seriously and were hardly prepared even to share power, now found that they had actually lost control of City Hall to aggressive black challengers. A great deal of fear, uncertainty, and resentment were, consequently, primary political realities facing the victors. Having mobilized little more than one in ten, or, at best, less than one in five white voters on their behalf, Washington and Morial faced white communities seemingly unprepared to deal with powerful black political figures. Moreover, those whites who supported their campaigns often viewed themselves as "kingmakers" and were not well prepared for the independence displayed by the new mayors or their determination to address the needs of their "base."

Once in office, both Morial and Washington also had to deal with certain structural political realities that prevented them from having free hands with which to retool their cities. Morial had to confront not only the atavistic racial attitudes still characteristic of a majority of the white population in his southern city but also a fragmented governmental structure designed precisely to keep mayors weak and the public sector under the control of a conservative economic and social elite.

Beginning nearly one century before, in the late nineteenth century, the pillars of the New Orleans commercial community began to pull key powers out of City Hall as the ethnic Irish were coming to control the electoral arena and flexing their political muscle. No longer in control of the local ballot box, the Crescent City's economic and social elite sought alternatives given the emergence of the Regular Democratic Organization (RDO), one of the few big-city machines to appear in the South. They succeeded in making a series of end runs to the governor and state legislature and, largely through the use of those vehicles, succeeded in creating a network of appointed, nonelected boards and commissions from which they could effectively protect their interests. Controlling key city functions such as tax rates, riverfront development, and drainage, they could still dictate the pace and nature of urban development from perches on the Board of Liquidation, City Debt (created in 1880), the Sewerage and Water Board (created in 1900), and the Board of Commissioners of the Port of New Orleans (created in 1896 and known simply as the "Dock Board"), among others. When coupled with a later city charter provision that limited the mayor to two terms, such structures placed the city's elected chief executive at a considerable disadvantage. The attempt to defuse one ethnic challenge from below at the end of the nineteenth century produced a governmental structure that impeded another one a hundred years later.[9]

In Chicago, Washington's chief obstacle was not the formal structures of government but the informal political structure of the city. It was the Democratic machine, the Cook County Democratic Organization, that controlled the city council and virtually every other city agency that confronted the new black mayor. Washington's entire first term, therefore, was taken up with political battles and the struggle for control of the city's government and its budget. This was the era of Chicago's stalemated "Council Wars" that matched an antagonistic white city council (it controlled twenty-nine of the council's fifty votes, enough to frustrate mayoral initiatives but not sufficient to overcome executive vetoes) under the leadership of "Darth" Vrdolyak against Harold "Skywalker," his largely black supporters, and a handful of "reform" representatives. The white majority controlled the powerful and patronage-rich council committees and refused to approve hundreds of Washington appointments that would have threatened the status quo in other city agencies. The factionalism and infighting became so intense that the *Wall Street Journal* branded Chicago "Beirut on the Lake."[10]

It is crucial to understand that these political difficulties meant that both Morial and Washington confronted deep structural problems that transcended narrow or immediate issues of race and that their attempts at reform, even absent the race issue, would have provoked tenacious resistance. The race issue greatly added to their burdens, of course, and provided cynical political manipulators with a powerful club that they did not hesitate to employ. It also meant that both mayors had to work hard at democratizing their cities and that they each necessarily referred frequently to the need to "open" the political and economic structures of their respective towns.

In Morial's case the concept of an "open" New Orleans included a redefinition of the mayor's role that was sharply at odds with traditional practice. In asserting a primary role in urban governance for the city's democratically elected chief executive, Morial's race—or at least the public's fascination with it—obscured the real dynamics of a fundamental political challenge to the social and economic oligarchy that dominated public affairs from their seats of social privilege on those primarily nonelected boards and commissions. Indeed, in a speech before the Metropolitan Area Committee, Morial let the city know what was coming. He made pointed reference to Tulane University political scientist Charles Chai's 1971 study, "Who Rules New Orleans?" and informed his audience that he was "astounded" that the mayor was not included among the list of "influentials" compiled after discussions with community leaders. It was inconceivable to him that "a majority of the people [consulted] failed to even mention the mayor as a man essential to the communal equation." He added diplomatically that he "would like to think that that perception has changed." What he meant, of course, was that it would be changed. No longer of that class, nor willing to serve its narrow ends, a democratically responsive, independent chief executive represented a real threat to the traditional elite's interests; it was a challenge that would have set off a political firestorm for any mayor, black or white, who dared to stake out such a position.[11]

Indeed, Morial's long-standing efforts to democratize New Orleans's government—his support for a 1975 lawsuit challenging the exclusive composition of the Board of Liquidation, City Debt antedated his election as mayor—continued once he attained office. Believing a revitalized system of public education held the key to economic growth, he attacked the city's Board of Education and the "anachronism" that "separate[d] the schools from the public consensus as expressed in the powers and person of the office of mayor." Similarly, the deteriorating position of the Port of New Orleans led him to go after the Dock Board as well, and he raised "the serious question as to whether this management, set so distinctly apart from the public consensus, will not eventually bear the same bitter fruit as the antiquity of our school board policy." Although the lawsuit against the Board of Liquidation ultimately proved successful, efforts to extend mayoral influence over the Board of Education (Morial sought to add two mayoral appointees to an otherwise elected board) and Dock Board were distinctly less so. Combined with a long, acrimonious public dispute with the Sewerage and Water Board over affirmative action access to its jobs and contracts (a bitter struggle in which Morial eventually prevailed), the mayor's efforts produced mixed results.[12]

The tenor of the times, however, is perhaps best revealed by the fact that Morial also found himself forced to play defense. Using the powers of the state to attack the office of the mayor and the city of New Orleans was a well-worn strategy in Louisiana that constituted the primary thrust of earlier Progressive-era "reforms" as well as both Huey and Earl Long's bids to dominate the state. Whether legislative initiatives advanced by ostensible "good government" forces or brutal frontal assaults launched by ambitious governors, they were all self-serving power grabs that threatened the city's independence. In the early 1980s, Morial had to fight off attempts to remove the mayor as president of the Sewerage and Water Board and an effort to strip the city's authority over the metropolitan airport and Aviation Board. Successful in these defensive battles, he also fought off multiple attempts by the uptown social elite to wrest Audubon Park out of the city's hands. Morial's city attorney, Sal Anzelmo, bluntly linked this last dispute to changing demographic realities and a broader pattern of conduct when he stated that

> the State takeover is an effort by those in the Uptown establishment to keep blacks from getting control of the Zoo Commission. . . . They want to keep it under white control. They don't want blacks to sit on the Zoo Commission, the Aviation Board, . . . the Sewerage and Water Board or anything. They say they want to "regionalize" everything. Well, that just means they want a controlling majority of whites who aren't even from Orleans Parish.[13]

Unable to extend his authority to areas he deemed vital, Morial had to expend considerable time and energy fighting to retain what powers he had.

In Chicago, Washington defeated the Cook County Democratic Organization by energizing an unprecedentedly large black base and by plugging into a long-standing stream of antimachine reform politics that brought a significant number of white voters to his coalition. Jane Byrne had done much the same four years before but returned to the machine fold as she pondered the difficulty of transforming an electoral majority into a governing one. Indeed, the organization's success in recapturing Byrne led several of the ward leaders to hope that the same could be done with Washington. It was Washington's resistance to this scenario—"I'm not going to pull a Byrne," he declared at one point—that precipitated the showdown with the machine's leadership. His continued attacks on patronage led one organization stalwart, Northwest Side alderman Roman Pucinski, to claim that he could support a machine-oriented African American for mayor but that Washington's desire to dismantle the organization asked too much. "Why should I give him the guillotine with which to cut off my head?" Pucinski asked. Finally, when Washington moved against party chairman Vrdolyak by attempting to oust him from his powerful leadership post on the zoning committee, Vrdolyak solidified the twenty-nine council members in opposition. There is no doubt that he and his retinue would have done the same to Byrne had she had the courage of her stated convictions, or that they would have been able to "play ball" with a more compliant and subservient Washington.[14]

Stalemated legislatively, Washington took a number of executive actions that placed him firmly in the "reform" camp. He cut his own salary by 20 percent and mothballed the limousine traditionally placed at the mayor's disposal. He also issued a "freedom of information" executive order that opened the city's records to public scrutiny, held budget hearings in the neighborhoods, and signed the Shakman decree that prohibited the hiring or firing of city employees for political reasons. He also announced a self-imposed cap of $1,500 on campaign contributions by companies doing business with the city and cut the payroll by 700 employees in an attempt to resolve the city's fiscal crisis.[15]

In the end, Washington's antimachine crusade was given an incomparable boost by the federal courts. Finding that the city council's ward reapportionment under Byrne was an outrageous racial gerrymander that discriminated against blacks and Hispanics, the courts ordered a new map and special elections in seven wards in 1986. The machine threw everything it had into these contests, but it could not prevent Washington from garnering four new supporters. The city council was now divided 25 to 25, with Mayor Washington casting all tie-breaking votes; he had pieced together his governing majority on his own terms.[16]

Changes followed rapidly. The mayor either stripped the machine's ward barons of their leadership posts in the council or diluted their authority and then watched as the council passed a new ethics ordinance and a tenants' bill of rights, amended taxi regulations to break up an existing near monopoly, and approved his executive appointments that had literally been held hostage for years. This last development was of the utmost importance, for it finally gave Washington control of such agencies as the Chicago Park District, a quasi-independent power base and source of patronage for machine opponent Edmund Kelly. Soon stripped of his powers, Kelly resigned.[17]

As was the case in New Orleans, Chicago's black mayor also had to play defense. Like Dutch Morial, Harold Washington proved largely successful in this endeavor. Hostile interests introduced measures in the state legislature that would strip the city of its control over the Park District, the McCormick Place convention centers, Navy Pier, and the Port Authority. Another proposal called for the creation of a regional airport authority (taking O'Hare and Midway airports away from the city), and the opposition-controlled Finance Committee in the city council tried to arrogate unto itself the right to approve all city contracts. There was even a sudden, expressed desire for an elected school board.[18] Even as Dutch Morial struggled, unsuccessfully, to put a couple of mayoral appointees on New Orleans's elected board, Harold Washington's presence led some Chicagoans to question the merit of their mayorally appointed body.

The most telling episode, however, involved the effort, inspired by mayoral hopeful Richard M. Daley, to institute an "open," nonpartisan primary that would be followed by a runoff, given the likelihood that no candidate would win an outright majority in the next election. Stung by the charge that he had been the white "spoiler" who paved the way for Washington's victory, Daley wanted to make certain that the strongest white candidate in 1987 would be able to face Washington one-on-one.

Petitions circulated throughout the city as sponsors of the measure hoped to get enough signatures to place it quickly before the people in a referendum. The Washington forces in the city council countered by placing three other innocuous referenda on the ballot before the nonpartisan primary petitions could be collected and validated. Under an obscure Illinois law, no more than three such propositions could be considered by a city at one time; Washington's council majority had preempted the ballot and blocked the attempt to change the rules in the middle of the game. Even his enemies grudgingly admired his deft political touch and the act of parliamentary legerdemain that left them standing in the dust. He had learned his lessons well.[19]

Washington's coup set the stage for his reelection in 1987 and a second term that promised, finally, substantive accomplishments. Having watched his first term consumed by endless political wrangling, Washington ultimately consolidated his position and prepared to move forward. It was in this realm, however, in the symmetry between their first and second terms, that the experiences of Dutch Morial and Harold Washington sharply diverged.

Morial's most notable achievements were primarily confined to his first term. The short-lived oil boom of the early 1980s and the Morial administration's management skills kept the city afloat despite underlying weaknesses and the beginning of federal retrenchment; a burst of new downtown construction and the steady growth of tourism contributed to the early sense of well-being. The mayor clearly recognized that the city's long-term health demanded greater economic diversification and fiscal reform, and he tried to nudge it in that direction. The optimism of the moment, however, and the political ethos of the city and the state proved impossible to overcome, and the city's fortunes declined radically in the mid-1980s. Still, his successful handling of a police strike, the streamlining of government, and a record of scandal-free, sound administration all graced his first term.

It was during his second term that Morial found himself constrained. The two-term limit placed on mayors by the city charter made him a "lame duck" as soon as he was reelected. Furthermore, the incoming city council included what Morial later called the Gang of Five. In the New Orleans seven-member city council (five elected by districts, two at large), the five representatives who rose in opposition could not only blunt his initiatives but override his vetoes as well. Consisting of three whites elected from districts and two black opponents (one of whom was elected at large), Morial's antagonists harassed him at every turn. When combined with the full weight of Ronald Reagan's budget cuts, Morial's second term was characterized more by stagnation than progress. Unseemly controversies regarding a pay raise for the mayor, a shopping mall near the Superdome, and, particularly, Morial's unsuccessful efforts to remove the two-term limitation from the city charter provided less than edifying public theater.[20]

The trajectory of Washington's reign was exactly the opposite. Beset with difficulties in the beginning, he enjoyed more freedom toward the end of his administration. Having gained control of the city council, he made particular strides in retiring the city debt through a combination of payroll reductions and new taxes and succeeded in restoring Chicago's favorable credit rating. Equally significant, feeling politically secure, the mayor extended an olive branch to his adversaries, endorsing candidates Richard M. Daley and Aurelia Pucinski (Roman Pucinski's daughter) for high county offices and retaining eight former Vrdolyak supporters as council committee chairs. Former adversaries, believing Washington when he claimed that he would occupy City Hall longer than Daley, began to move into his orbit following his reelection early in 1987; the most recalcitrant, such as Vrdolyak, simply left the Democratic party altogether. Preparing to move forward in building a genuine biracial coalition, Washington then died on the day before Thanksgiving, little more than a half-year after his second victorious campaign.[21]

Politically unassailable within their respective communities, Morial and Washington nonetheless endured significant undercurrents of black opposition that proved of great importance for their successions. Some of the opposition had to be due, at least in part, to the impossibility of meeting inflated expectations and the enormous difficulty in dealing with deep-seated urban problems and institutions. Few areas were of greater concern to New Orleans's and Chicago's African Americans, for example, than housing, particularly public housing, and education. Yet it was precisely in these areas that Morial and Washington proved unable or unwilling to stimulate progressive change. The political resistance that manifested itself when Morial tried to tinker with the Crescent City's school board apparently convinced him that the risks were not worth a bitter battle with uncertain outcomes; he quickly backed off and did not pick up the issue again.

In dealing with the Chicago Housing Authority, however, Washington inherited a political wasteland that, for the previous generation, served as little more than a dumping ground for the black poor and a patronage trough for the machine. It clearly demanded more attention and resources than he was willing to commit.[22] Less than forceful leadership thus combined with the inertia of these large bureaucracies and a deteriorating economic climate beyond mayoral control—long-standing trends toward deindustrialization in Chicago and the oil bust in New Orleans (not to mention federal cutbacks that impacted both)—to increase poverty and the demands placed on already inadequate and dysfunctional systems of public service.[23] Problems in these areas, if anything, got worse rather than better. Still, the overwhelming popularity of both Morial and Washington with the poor and with public housing residents meant that their opposition was rooted in more than their inability to address successfully long-standing urban ills.

In each city, machine or "machine-style" patronage politicians within the black community existed in an uncomfortable relationship with Morial and Washington, as did those who might be considered racial nationalists or ethnic chauvinists. In New Orleans, Morial's predecessor, Moon Landrieu, had cultivated his own coterie of black officials, and Morial found them already in place on the public payroll and with strong ties to city government. They certainly expected to be treated no less well by the city's first black mayor and, in fact, were stunned and embittered when Morial staffed his administration with blacks and whites from private business, academia, and the professions. Conducting a mini purge, Morial even discharged large numbers of those who had entered public employment under the aegis of their former white patron. They were confused by the radical Creole who stressed "merit" and tried to transcend traditional racial divisions; and they accused the mayor of only hiring "superblacks" who had been held to unrealistically high standards.[24]

Washington similarly had to deal with a number of black ward committeemen and members of the city council who found themselves tied to his cause by an aroused constituency but who felt distinctly ill at ease with the mayor's reform posture. Creatures of the Democratic machine for most of their careers, they saw no reason to eschew "spoils" politics at the very moment that one of their own earned the keys to the city vault. Unable to oppose Washington openly—to do so would have been racial treason, as defined by the nationalists, and political suicide—they bided their time as nominal converts to a crusade in which they had no faith.[25]

The New Orleans and Chicago experiences differ at this point to the extent that a segment of the black spoils politicians in the southern metropolis embraced the rhetoric and goals of racial nationalism in their thirst for the emoluments of office. The novelty of the black presence in New Orleans's political life meant that the patronage seeker's racial "militance" could hold the ring of plausibility. In Chicago, however, the African-American machine politicians had been affiliated so long with

Daley's organization that they could not credibly rattle the racial saber. Instead, Chicago displayed a larger, more institutionalized, more vocal nationalist community that had played its own distinct role in Washington's initial campaign and placed its own demands on his administration. No less distressed than the machinists (albeit for quite different reasons) by Washington's transition team, cabinet of advisers, patronage policies, political priorities, and campaign endorsements, they increasingly found themselves distanced from his administration.[26] That the mayor's "Dream Slate" for county elections in 1988 included names such as Daley and Pucinski bespoke the grave differences in their agendas.

Indeed, the democratization of Chicago and New Orleans, pursued ardently by both Washington and Morial, offered something less to those seeking favor due to an "insider's" positioning—whether defined politically or racially—than either the machinists or the nationalists wanted. As far as conventionally, and more narrowly, defined racial interests were concerned, however, both mayors apparently made an impact in moderating the behavior of their respective police departments (long a primary irritant in the relations between black communities and successive municipal administrations and an achievement not to be underestimated) and in vigorously pursuing affirmative action initiatives in the granting of public jobs and contracts. If their efforts in the latter instance were denounced by their white opponents as mere patronage in disguise and by black dissenters as meager and insufficient, their attempt to open up the municipal polity and bring African Americans into the "mainstream" apparently had the approval of the vast majority of black voters who swept each of them into a second term.

Finally, the sheer strength of their personalities, their combative, aggressive, "tell-it-like-it-is" styles of governance and politics undoubtedly provided an enormous psychological boost to communities that identified closely with their travails and, apparently, values. In Chicago, those pursuing a chauvinistic black agenda found themselves further hemmed in by their own success in making support for Washington a litmus test for "blackness" during his first campaign; they could hardly oppose him later without appearing to undermine their community's "champion."

The chaos surrounding Washington's succession and the more deliberate, systematic procedures that orchestrated Dutch Morial's illustrate one last dimension of the racial struggle for political power in urban America. In each case, white opponents of the first black mayors demonstrated the resourcefulness and resolve to catapult themselves back into control by dominating the processes through which Chicago and New Orleans selected their second black mayors. And the African American communities of the two cities, fearful and fragmented following the deaths of their most historic political figures (Morial died in December 1989, in the midst of his successor's reelection campaign), retreated to a narrower brand of racial politics that left them more isolated from power than before.

In Chicago, the white ethnic bloc on the city council won over a handful of former black allies who had been tied to the machine but could not openly oppose Washington while he lived. After failing to negotiate the recapture of City Hall for themselves, they threw their support to a compliant black machine operative who accepted their backing. In a raucous city council meeting that ran past four a.m. With blacks and whites gathered in the streets in the predawn hours outside City Hall chanting "No deals," waving dollar bills, and throwing coins at him, a majority vote of the city council anointed Eugene Sawyer Chicago's second black mayor.[27] Shamelessly donning blackface to salvage its fortunes, what remained of the machine selected a candidate who became immediately and irredeemably tainted in the eyes of the black community. Unable to survive politically, His Conveniency's administration separated nationalists from machinists and both of those from Washington's reform heirs. In a city where black voters still constitute a minority, Daley reclaimed the office on the fifth floor of City Hall in 1989.

In New Orleans, regular electoral procedures made Sidney Barthelemy, another Creole of color, mayor after Dutch Morial failed in his attempts to change the city charter. Barthelemy, a leading opponent of Morial's campaign for unlimited terms as well as his second effort to permit "Just 3," represented a strong assimilationist tendency among some New Orleans Creoles and was the antithesis to the fading Creole radicalism personified by Morial. A Moon Landrieu protégé, he had strong ties to the local Urban League and enjoyed close contact with the white civic and economic leadership. Running against another black candidate in what had become, during the Morial era, a majority black city, Barthelemy turned Morial's winning electoral coalition inside out. Where Morial had been elected with solid and massive black support combined with a liberal fragment of white backing, Barthelemy went into office with 85 percent of the white vote and the support of barely one in four black voters. Morial's progressive biracial coalition had been transformed into a conservative one that knit together whites and a patronage-oriented black leadership that had no agenda beyond its own perpetuation. White New Orleans had found itself a black mayor it could live with—one who would protect, rather than challenge, the status quo.[28]

Ironically, when Barthelemy ran for reelection in 1990, he campaigned, this time, as the hope of the black community. In facing a white candidate with a good civil rights record, Barthelemy ran (in the weeks immediately following Morial's unexpected death) as a racial champion. As was the case with Sawyer, another emergent black politician who had left no tracks in the snow of the civil rights revolution, Barthelemy's campaign exploited symbolic racial issues and fears. But unlike Sawyer, he ran in what was now a majority black city and won. His second winning coalition appeared, then, as an unlikely combination that mixed reactionary whites at the top of his campaign structure with a mass of black voters at the bottom. It was a shotgun marriage of the rankest sort, and one bound to leave its partners unfulfilled.

It would, however, be a mistake to think that nothing had changed as a result of the Morial and Washington administrations. Black access to city jobs and services certainly improved, as did relations with local police departments that had earlier earned reputations for brutality within their respective black communities, although this relationship could easily slide back to that of an earlier age. Opportunities for individual African Americans within the political system also improved dramatically. But fundamental change proved more elusive. Changes in the global economy, as well as the federal government's retreat from urban affairs, obviously made purely local responses to challenges experienced on the municipal level problematic at best. To the extent that such solutions might have an ameliorative impact, it is apparent that they must await new strategies for forging governing coalitions in a multiethnic society.

NOTES

1. For an introduction to the concept of Creole radicalism, see Arnold R. Hirsch and Joseph Logsdon, eds., *Creole New Orleans: Race and Americanization* (Baton Rouge: Louisiana State University Press, 1992), esp. 189–319.

2. A somewhat more detailed look at Dutch Morial's political career is offered in Arnold R. Hirsch, "Race and Politics in Modern New Orleans: The Mayoralty of Dutch Morial," *Amerikastudien/American Studies* 35 (December 1991): 461–84.

3. For early black politics in Chicago, see Charles Branham, "Black Chicago: Accommodationist Politics before the Great Migration," in Melvin G. Holli and Peter d'A. Jones, eds., *The Ethnic Frontier: Essays in the History of Group Survival in Chicago and the Midwest* (Grand Rapids: William B. Eerdmans Publishing Co., 1977), 211–62; see also Branham's dissertation, "A Transformation of Black Political Leadership in Chicago, 1864–1942" (Ph.D. dissertation, University of Chicago, 1981). Other important works are St. Clair Drake and Horace Cayton, *Black Metropolis: A Study of Negro Life in a Northern City* (New York: Harper and Row, 1945, 1962, 1970); Harold F. Gosnell, *Negro Politicians: The Rise of Negro Politics in Chicago* (Chicago: University of Chicago Press, 1935, 1967); Allan H. Spear, *Black Chicago: The Making of a Negro Ghetto, 1890–1920* (Chicago: University of Chicago Press, 1967); William M. Tuttle, Jr., *Race Riot: Chicago in the Red Summer of 1919* (New York: Atheneum, 1970); and John M. Allswang, *A House for All Peoples: Ethnic Politics in Chicago, 1890–1936* (Lexington: University Press of Kentucky, 1971).

4. For Washington's early life and career, see Florence Hamlish Levinsohn, *Harold Washington: A Political Biography* (Chicago: Chicago Review Press, 1983); Gary Rivlin, *Fire on the Prairie: Chicago's Harold Washington and the Politics of Race* (New York: Henry Holt and Company, 1992); Robert McClory, "Up from Obscurity: Harold Washington," in Melvin G. Holli and Paul M. Green, eds., *The Making of the Mayor: Chicago, 1983* (Grand Rapids: William B. Eerdmans Publishing Co., 1984), 3–16; William J. Grimshaw, *Bitter Fruit: Black Politics and the Chicago Machine, 1931–1991* (Chicago: University of Chicago Press, 1992); and Dempsey Travis, *An Autobiography of Black Politics* (Chicago: Urban Research Press, 1987).

5. For the primary election, see Hirsch, "Race and Politics in Modern New Orleans," 465–68; for a broader context and essential background, see also Hirsch, "Simply a Matter of Black and White: The Transformation of Race and Politics in Twentieth-Century New Orleans," in *Creole New Orleans*, 262–319; and "New Orleans: Sunbelt in the Swamp," in Richard M. Bernard and Bradley R. Rice, eds., *Sunbelt Cities: Politics and Growth Since World War II* (Austin: University of Texas Press, 1983), 100–137; see also Edward M. Haas, *DeLesseps S. Morrison and the Image of Reform: New Orleans Politics, 1946–1961* (Baton Rouge: Louisiana State University Press, 1974).

6. *New Orleans Times-Picayune*, October 3, November 13, 14, 1977; *Figaro*, May 4, August 3, October 5, 12, 19, November 16, 1977; *Louisiana Weekly*, November 12, 1977.

7. For Washington's first mayoral triumph, see Grimshaw, *Bitter Fruit*, 167–96; Holli and Green, *Making of the Mayor*; Levinsohn, *Harold Washington*, 189–300; Travis, *Autobiography of Black Politics*, 528–610; and Paul Kleppner, *Chicago Divided: The Making of a Black Mayor* (DeKalb: Northern Illinois University Press, 1985).

8. Rivlin, *Fire on the Prairie, 196.*

9. Joy J. Jackson, *New Orleans in the Gilded Age: Politics and Urban Progress, 1880–1896* (Baton Rouge: Louisiana State University Press, 1969); Peirce F. Lewis, *New Orleans: The Making of an Urban Landscape* (Cambridge: Ballinger Publishing Co., 1976).

10. For Chicago's "Council Wars," see Grimshaw, *Bitter Fruit*, 184–86, 189, 191, 213; Rivlin, *Fire on the Prairie*, 205–344; and Melvin G. Holli and Paul M. Green, *Bashing Chicago Traditions: Harold Washington's Last Campaign* (Grand Rapids: William B. Eerdmans Publishing Co., 1989), 166.

11. Morial's speech is reprinted in its entirety in *Figaro*, January 25, 1978; Charles Y. W. Chai, "Who Rules New Orleans?" *Louisiana Business Survey* 2 (October 1971): 2–7.

12. Hirsch, "Race and Politics in Modern New Orleans," 469–70, 472, 473, and passim.

13. *Louisiana Weekly*, September 18, 1982; July 23, 1983.

14. Rivlin, *Fire on the Prairie*, 187, 222.

15. Ibid., 235–36.

16. Grimshaw, *Bitter Fruit*, 189–90; Kleppner, *Chicago Divided*, 140; Rivlin, *Fire on the Prairie*, 348–58.

17. Rivlin, *Fire on the Prairie*, 357–61; Holli and Green, *Bashing Chicago Traditions*, 35–36.

18. Rivlin, *Fire on the Prairie*, 400–401.

19. Alderman Ed Burke, a bitter Washington foe, denounced the derailment of the nonpartisan primary proposition as a political "ploy." With knowing appreciation, however, he added that he had to "compliment whoever thought of it." See Holli and Green, *Bashing Chicago Traditions*, 36–43.

20. A more detailed summary of Morial's two terms can be found in Hirsch, "Race and Politics in Modern New Orleans," 461–84.

21. Holli and Green, *Bashing Chicago Traditions*, 170, 187–88; Rivlin, *Fire on the Prairie*, 400.

22. Hirsch, "Race and Politics in Modern New Orleans," 473; Rivlin, *Fire on the Prairie*, 384–90.

23. The social and economic trends for Chicago are closely examined in Gregory D. Squires, Larry Bennett, Kathleen McCourt, and Philip Nyden, *Chicago: Race, Class and the Response to Urban Decline* (Philadelphia: Temple University Press, 1987).

24. Hirsch, "Simply a Matter of Black and White," 310–16.

25. Grimshaw, *Bitter Fruit,* 133–36; Rivlin, *Fire on the Prairie*, 403–20.

26. The black nationalists' role in Washington's campaigns, his administration, and their growing sense of estrangement is handled in depth and throughout in Rivlin, *Fire on the Prairie.* See also Abdul Alkalimat and Doug Gills, *Harold Washington and the Crisis of Black Power in Chicago* (Chicago: Twenty-First Century Books, 1989); and Dianne M. Pinderhughes, *Race and Ethnicity in Chicago Politics* (Urbana: University of Illinois Press, 1987).

27. For some background and context, see Hirsch, "Chicago: The Cook County Democratic Organization and the Dilemma of Race, 1931–1987," in Richard M. Bernard, ed., *Snowbelt Cities: Metropolitan Politics in the Northeast and Midwest Since World War II* (Bloomington: Indiana University Press, 1987), 63–90. For Sawyer's rise (and fall), see Grimshaw, *Bitter Fruit*, 197–224, and Rivlin*, Fire on the Prairie*, 403–20.

28. Hirsch, "Simply a Matter of Black and White," 317–18.

Chapter 14

Latino Immigrants and
the Politics of Space in Atlanta

Mary E. Odem

In the fall of 1990 more than two hundred Latino immigrants, mostly Mexicans and Central Americans, gathered for Mass in the middle of New Peachtree Road in the Chamblee-Doraville area of Atlanta to protest the closing of a Catholic center that had served Latino immigrants for the previous two years. The crowd, which included men, women, and children, many of them undocumented immigrants, blocked traffic for an hour as they took part in the Mass led by a Colombian priest who worked for the Atlanta archdiocese. Over the next several weeks, the immigrant Mass moved from the street to a parking lot of an apartment complex, and when the cold weather came it moved inside, first to a local Mexican tortilla factory and then to a nearby Baptist church.

Immigrants continued to hold Mass and other church-related activities in streets, parking lots, and restaurants of the Chamblee-Doraville neighborhood for several months until the archdiocese agreed to provide funding for a new meeting place for the group. A prefabricated building formerly used as a warehouse was purchased and converted into a Latino Catholic mission and named La Misión Católica de Nuestra Señora de Las Américas in honor of Our Lady of Guadalupe. The Misión Católica quickly became a major religious and community center for thousands of Mexican and Central American immigrants in the Atlanta metropolitan area.[1]

The formation of the Misión Católica was an early sign of the major demographic transformation taking place in metropolitan Atlanta. By 1990 tens of thousands of Latin Americans had migrated to Atlanta to work in its thriving construction and service industries and in the nearby carpet and poultry processing plants. Most of the early immigrants were young Mexican men who had moved from Texas, California, and northern Mexico. They were soon joined by migrants from other regions of Mexico and from Central American countries, principally Guatemala and El Salvador.

Reprinted from Mary E. Odem and Elaine Lacy, eds., *Latino Immigrants and the Transformation of the U.S. South* (Athens: University of Georgia Press, 2009), 112–25. Reprinted with the permission of the University of Georgia Press.

At the same time, an increasing number of women and children joined male workers, resulting in a greater Latin American presence in schools, churches, and neighborhoods of the Atlanta area. During the 1990s the metropolitan region was one of the fastest growing Latino immigrant destinations in the country. Fueled primarily by foreign immigration, Atlanta's Latino population grew from 25,000 in 1980 to 57,000 in 1990 to nearly 270,000 in the year 2000, a growth rate of 370 percent in the decade from 1990 to 2000.[2]

The founding of the Misión Católica and its role among Latino newcomers in Atlanta draw our attention to the issue of social space in the process of immigration and settlement. Influenced by the work of cultural geographers and theorists, I pay particular attention to the spatial aspects of Latino immigrants' experiences in this southern metropolis. Henri Lefebvre, one of the first to develop a critical theory of space, holds that throughout history each society has produced a distinct social space that meets its demands for economic production and social reproduction. Particularly relevant to this chapter is his analysis of the space of social reproduction, the spaces created to perpetuate social and class relations, including housing, neighborhoods, schools, and the public spaces of the city.[3] In *The Power of Place* Delores Hayden uses Lefebvre's theoretical framework to explore the social and spatial history of the American urban landscape. Hayden proposes that we examine urban spaces as "political territories" where boundaries have been established to restrict marginal groups such as women, workers, and ethnic and racial minorities. "One of the consistent ways to limit the economic and political rights of groups," she argues, "has been to constrain social reproduction by limiting access to space."[4]

Drawing on the work of Hayden and Lefebvre, I suggest that a central form of regulation of Latino immigrants in U.S. urban areas occurs at the level of space. By restricting immigrants' movements within and excluding them from certain spaces (neighborhoods, roads, housing, etc.), authorities limit their ability to sustain social life in the new place of settlement. Mexican and Central American immigrants have struggled in various ways against these spatial barriers to appropriate the spaces they need to maintain families and communities in the face of discrimination and uncertain legal status.

I examine how this struggle was played out in Atlanta during the period of dramatic growth of the Latino immigrant population. A significant way that Latinos have claimed space in U.S. urban landscapes has been through religious practice and institution building. In Chamblee-Doraville immigrants created a Latino religious place that provided social and spiritual resources to help them deal with the hardships of migration and adaptation to life in the U.S.[5] I focus on the period 1988 to 2004, when the Misión Católica was located in the Chamblee-Doraville neighborhood. (In 2006, the Atlanta archdiocese moved the misión ten miles to a new neighborhood in Gwinnett County, marking a new stage in its development.)

My analysis is based on varied sources: interviews with public officials and immigrant leaders and advocates in Atlanta; participant observation of religious and social activities in the Misión Católica; archival records of the Catholic Archdiocese of Atlanta; local newspapers (*Atlanta Journal-Constitution, Mundo Hispanico, Georgia Bulletin*); county and municipal records and reports; and U.S. census data for 1980, 1990, and 2000.

LATIN AMERICAN SETTLEMENT IN ATLANTA

One of the earliest and now most concentrated centers of immigrant settlement in metro Atlanta is in northern DeKalb County in the neighboring small cities of Chamblee and Doraville. Prior to 1970 the Chamblee-Doraville area was home to mostly white, blue-collar workers who labored in the factories nearby, including General Motors, Frito-Lay, Kodak, and General Electric. The economic slowdown of the 1970s resulted in factory closings and layoffs and the departure of many working-class residents from the area. As the number of housing and rental vacancies climbed, apartment managers began marketing to Vietnamese refugees and later to Chinese, Korean, and Latin American migrants.[6]

Immigrants were initially drawn to the Chamblee-Doraville area because of the availability of low-cost housing, especially the large number of moderately priced rental units. The opening of two subway stops in the 1980s made the area even more attractive to immigrant workers dependent on the low-wage jobs scattered throughout the metropolitan region. By 1990 the Chamblee-Doraville area had become one of the most ethnically diverse in the Southeast (excluding Florida). The ethnic transformation was particularly pronounced in Chamblee. In 1980 non-Hispanic whites composed 89 percent of Chamblee's population; African Americans, Asians and Latinos together composed only 11 percent. In 2000 whites composed only 24 percent of the Chamblee population, while Latinos had become the majority group with 54 percent of the population; Asians made up another 14.5 percent and African Americans 5 percent.[7]

In contrast to previous U.S. historical patterns in which immigrants settled in urban neighborhoods, recent immigrants in Atlanta have settled in suburban areas outside the inner city. They are living in apartment complexes located on multilane highways, alongside shopping plazas and convenience stores. Buford Highway, a busy six-lane highway that runs through Chamblee and Doraville, is the commercial center of the area. Numerous aging strip malls that line the highway have been converted to large ethnic and multiethnic shopping plazas with names like Chinatown Square, Asian Square Mall, Plaza Fiesta, and Plaza Latino. In many ways immigrants have breathed new economic, social, and cultural life into an area that had suffered economic stagnation and population decline.[8]

The Latino population in Chamblee and the rest of metro Atlanta has diverse national and regional origins. The largest group by far is Mexican, but there are significant numbers of Central American, South American, and Caribbean newcomers. According to the 2000 census Mexicans made up 61 percent of metro Atlanta's Latino population; Central Americans, mostly from Guatemala and El Salvador, formed 8 percent; Puerto Ricans made up another 7 percent; and South Americans 6 percent.[9] A significant portion of the Latino immigrant population is undocumented. A 2004 report by the Urban Institute estimated that between 40 and 49 percent of all immigrants in the state of Georgia in 2000 were undocumented.[10] The percentage would be noticeably higher if only Latino immigrants were counted. Jeffrey Passel's 2005 report, "Unauthorized Migrants," estimates that nationally Latin Americans make up 81 percent of the unauthorized population.[11]

Latinos, regardless of legal status, have formed an integral part of the labor force in metropolitan Atlanta since 1990. Most have worked as laborers in the construction and service industries. More than 60 percent of Latino workers were employed in these industries in 2000, with 30 percent in construction and 35 percent in services, which includes hotel and restaurant work, landscaping, and janitorial service. Another 12 percent of Latino workers are employed in manufacturing, largely in carpet and poultry-processing factories.[12] The growth and prosperity of key economic sectors in Atlanta has depended on the labor of Mexican and Central American workers.

SPATIAL REGULATION OF LATINO IMMIGRANTS

Despite their importance to the region's economy, many Latin Americans in Atlanta, particularly the large number of undocumented immigrants, lead precarious lives. Although immigrant workers provide a crucial source of labor to employers, U.S. immigration policies prohibit the legal entry of most Mexican and Central American workers and deny them a legitimate role in U.S. social and civic life. According to David Bacon, U.S. labor and immigration policies in effect create a "special category of residents in the U.S. who have significantly fewer rights than the population as a whole; they cannot legally work or receive social benefits, and can be apprehended, incarcerated, and deported at any time."[13]

A central way of limiting the rights of Latino immigrants has been to restrict their access to social space and thereby limit their ability to build and sustain social and community life. Regulation of immigrants' access to space has taken various forms in metropolitan Atlanta. Federal immigration officials have conducted periodic raids of workplaces, apartment complexes, and other gathering spots to round up and deport undocumented immigrants. Surveillance and control of immigrants has also occurred at the level of local government: the growing presence of Latino immigrants in metro Atlanta has unsettled many residents and local authorities and prompted numerous measures to restrict their movement and exclude them from particular places and neighborhoods. The various ordinances and policies limit immigrants' access to housing, higher education, employment, and transportation. Not all are directed explicitly against undocumented immigrants, but the reality is that the populations of legal and unauthorized residents among Latino immigrants are so intertwined (e.g., undocumented parents with U.S.-born children) that laws affecting one group necessarily affect the other.

A closer look at the regulation of day laborers and access to driver's licenses illuminates the conflicts over social space between Latino immigrants and local authorities. A drive through metropolitan Atlanta on any weekday morning starting at seven o'clock will reveal numerous street corners where groups of Latino immigrant men wait to be hired by local employers to perform a range of labor-intensive jobs: painting walls, building homes, clearing debris, moving furniture, weeding, and mowing lawns. Most of the men who wait for work are undocumented; immigrants with work permits have access to steadier and more secure forms of employment. Many local employers in the lawn maintenance, construction, and restaurant industries depend on day laborers for their businesses to survive. Although they provide a needed source of labor, these workers are often viewed with suspicion by local residents and merchants who complain that laborers scare off customers and threaten the peace and security in their neighborhoods.

As a result of such complaints, a number of city councils have passed ordinances forbidding laborers from gathering on street corners: The city of Chamblee passed an ordinance in 1996 prohibiting people from "assembl[ing] on private property for the purpose of soliciting work as a day laborer without the permission of the property owner." In 1998 the city of Roswell in Fulton County passed a similar law, followed in 1999 by Marietta in Cobb County.[14] In March 1999 police in Roswell arrested five workers waiting at a day-labor pickup spot in front of an apartment complex after the managers of the complex complained to authorities. That same year Immigration and Naturalization Service (INS) agents conducted a raid at a day-labor site in Marietta, arresting sixty-four migrant workers with the help of local police. Undercover agents had posed as contractors looking for workers.[15] Such mass arrests do not happen often, but they underscore the vulnerability of undocumented workers in public spaces.

In an attempt to address the tensions around day laborers, a Methodist church group established a day-labor center in Gwinnett County, initially located in a church basement, to provide a safe, legal place for workers to wait for employers. In 2001 the city of Roswell opened Georgia's first publicly financed center for day laborers, devoting $40,000 to the project. The center came about through the efforts of Latino community leaders, especially Jose Bernal, a local businessman who provided additional financial support for the center and led the formation of the Roswell Intercultural Alliance, a nonprofit organization created to address immigrant labor issues. The center provided a waiting area for workers, matched employers with laborers, and provided English classes and "seminars on state laws and other issues to help Hispanics assimilate."[16]

Despite the promising initial collaboration between Latino immigrants and city and police officials, the Roswell City Council bowed to public opposition and closed the center after just one year of operation. The Georgia Coalition for Immigration Reform (one of several anti-immigrant organizations established in the state since the late 1990s) protested the opening of the center in letters to Roswell city leaders, as well as to federal immigration officials in Atlanta. Coalition members complained about the use of public funding for a center that served "illegal" workers and called on immigration officials to uphold the law by arresting and deporting the workers who gathered there.[17] Even though the day-labor center no longer exists, workers continue to gather on street corners and local employers continue to hire them.

The use of automobiles and public roads has been another arena of struggle between Latino immigrants and local authorities. Latino immigrants frequently use buses and taxi services, but the South's low-density suburban development, dispersed job locations, and limited public transportation systems virtually require the use of personal vehicles. Many immigrant workers in metro Atlanta have to travel long distances to get to job sites; they depend heavily on automobiles to go shopping, visit health facilities, and take children to and from school. Yet Georgia, like most states in the country, has prohibited unauthorized immigrants from obtaining driver's licenses by requiring proof of legal residence or valid social security cards as identification. Thousands of immigrants in Georgia have been arrested, fined, and sometimes jailed for driving without a valid license.

Latino community leaders and immigrant advocacy groups in Atlanta have engaged in political efforts to legalize driving for unauthorized immigrants in Georgia. State Representative Pedro Marin of Gwinnett County, one of the first Latino legislators in the state, coauthored a bill in the house in 2003 (Ga. HB 578) that would have enabled unauthorized immigrants to obtain a driver's license with certain restrictions. Under the proposed act immigrant drivers would have to renew their license annually and could use it only for transportation to work, school, church, and medical clinics.

The measure provoked such public opposition that it was soundly defeated, and two years later state legislators passed Ga. HB 501, which mandated that only legal residents of the state could obtain driver's licenses.[18] Federal legislation passed in 2005 reinforced Georgia's stance on the issue. Legislators in the U.S. House of Representatives attached a provision (called the Real ID Act) to a military spending bill that prohibits states from offering driver's licenses to immigrants who cannot provide identification approved by the U.S. Department of Homeland Security, effectively barring unauthorized residents from obtaining driver's licenses.[19]

CLAIMING SOCIAL SPACE

For immigrants the roads, neighborhoods, and public places in Atlanta have been arenas of conflict where they have struggled in various ways against the spatial restrictions imposed by local and federal authorities. During the late 1980s and early 1990s immigrants in Chamblee-Doraville challenged these restrictions by claiming a Latino religious space. Through a process of negotiation and struggle with local government officials and the Catholic Archdiocese of Atlanta, immigrants formed a Latino Catholic mission where they could practice their faith in a familiar, welcoming environment and develop social and material resources to support their families and communities.

The Catholic Church, in contrast to federal immigration laws and local policies and ordinances that restrict and exclude undocumented immigrants, officially opens its doors to all people, regardless of nationality or legal status. The archdiocese was one of the first and continues to be one of the central institutions in the metropolitan area to address the problems confronting Latin American immigrants. Catholic Social Services provides job referral services, immigration counseling, and numerous other services, while the St. Vincent de Paul Society collects and sells clothing and household goods to immigrants at inexpensive prices.[20] Still the church—at both the archdiocese and parish levels—has had its own difficulties accepting an increasingly diverse immigrant Catholic population.

Most church officials have advocated the integration of immigrants into existing parishes. Although clearly more welcoming to immigrants than exclusion, the policy of integration as practiced in the Atlanta archdiocese still constituted a form of spatial restriction. Just as certain local and federal policies exclude immigrants and demand their invisibility from some public places, most church officials and priests in the Atlanta archdiocese expected immigrants to enter existing parishes, which are predominantly white, middle-class, and suburban, and conform to U.S. Catholic traditions and styles of worship.

Numerous barriers, however, stood in the way of this integration plan for Mexican and Central American immigrants in the late 1980s and 1990s. Many immigrants did not own cars and thus often relied on public transportation to go to Mass, yet few churches were located on convenient public transportation routes. Language, cultural, and class barriers also discouraged the participation of Latin American immigrants in existing churches. Many could not understand or speak English and did not feel welcome among the more prosperous, white members of suburban Catholic churches. Moreover, mainstream Catholic churches discouraged the different religious practices and styles of worship of Mexican and other Latin American Catholics: the intense devotions to regional and national patron saints; the processions, celebrations, and other forms of religious expression that take place outside of the church in the streets and neighborhoods; and the more informal, noisy atmosphere of Sunday Masses with families with young children and infants.[21]

Immigrants felt unwelcome at local Catholic churches, yet greatly desired a place where and community with whom they could practice their faith. In the summer of 1988 several young Mexican men asked one of the few Spanish-speaking priests in the archdiocese, Father Jorge Christancho from Colombia, to visit their apartment complex in Chamblee to say Mass for the Spanish-speaking men, women, and children who lived there. More than fifty people gathered to meet with the Latin American priest in the patio of one family's apartment. Father Christancho, who was assigned to a church some distance from Chamblee, tried to persuade the priests in the two nearby parishes to provide Spanish religious services for the immigrants in the neighborhood. When this attempt failed he decided to continue to meet with immigrants in Chamblee in addition to his regular duties.[22]

As the numbers of participants quickly expanded, the group found a larger space to meet: the basement of a small, Latino-owned grocery store in a local shopping plaza. Immigrants used the space to address the social and material needs of participants as well as their religious needs—by collecting and storing food and clothing to distribute to those in need and by renting a small apartment to provide temporary shelter for newly arrived immigrants. After a few months in this location, attendance at the Mass had grown to more than two hundred people.[23]

In summer 1989, due to complaints from local residents and other tenants in the shopping plaza, the owners of the plaza sought to prohibit the gatherings. At this point Father Christancho attempted once again to gain the support of Catholic Church officials. At his invitation, in August 1989 the newly appointed archbishop, Eugene Marino, who was the first African-American Roman Catholic archbishop in the United States, celebrated Mass for the Latino community in Chamblee. Archbishop Marino was so impressed by the number of people and their commitment and faith that he promised to provide archdiocesan support for a "Hispanic mission." In December 1989 the archdiocese rented a small hall in Chamblee for this purpose, which became known among immigrants as El Centro Católico de Chamblee.[24]

After almost two years in the new location, El Centro faced a growing number of complaints to the archdiocese from local residents and city officials that the religious gatherings violated noise and crowd ordinances. By this time Archbishop Marino had resigned. The new archbishop, also African American, was less sympathetic to the concerns of immigrants in Chamblee. More tied to the church's model of ethnic integration, he closed the Latino Catholic center and instructed immigrants to attend the churches in the parishes closest to Chamblee.[25]

Latino migrants did not passively accept the archdiocese's decision. In response to the closing of El Centro, they took the Mass to the streets. The crowds of Latino Catholics meeting in public roads, parking lots, and the local Baptist church for the next several months eventually convinced the archdiocese to provide a new meeting place for the group.[26] In fall 1992 the Misión Católica de Nuestra Señora de Las Américas opened its doors in a converted warehouse convenient to a subway stop. The misión soon became a major religious and community center for Mexican and Central American immigrants in Chamblee, Doraville, and surrounding towns and suburbs. By 1999, it was holding four Masses every weekend with standing-room-only crowds (more than five hundred people per Mass) and performing hundreds of marriages and baptisms for its members each year. With a small paid staff and close to a hundred volunteers, the misión also offered English, computer, and job training classes, sponsored a health clinic and free job bureau, and collected food and clothing for needy immigrants.[27]

Appropriating this space enabled immigrants to develop collective resources to sustain their communities and to challenge the confines of discrimination, economic hardship, and legal marginality in the United States. Often discriminated against and excluded in the broader society, immigrants found a welcoming place in the misión. They came together not only to pray and attend Mass, but also to socialize, to celebrate important events, to get needed resources (food, clothing, health care) and to exchange information about jobs and housing.

For young male workers from Mexico and Central America, the misión offered a place where they could gather together without raising the suspicions of law enforcement officials. Whereas U.S. authorities often perceive young Latino men as potential criminals and restrict their movement in public, people at the misión recognized them as decent, hardworking men struggling to support their families. For undocumented migrants in particular the misión has been a haven. In the words of Father Carlos García-Carreras, a Cuban American priest who served the misión from 1994 to 2000: "It's a place where they can say, 'I'm not afraid.' . . . [This] is the only place where they can feel more at home, more understood, more among their own people . . . because they feel so bad . . . in the rest of their surroundings here in Atlanta."[28]

Participation in the misión also has helped immigrants integrate into U.S. social and civic life. Since its founding the Latino mission has offered free English classes, one of the most sought-after services among its members. Immigrants have taken part in a number of other activities at the Misión Católica that encourage their integration into U.S. society, such as computer classes, driving lessons, and various job training courses.[29]

Equally important are the possibilities for political participation that immigrants have pursued in the misión. They have joined petition drives to voice their opinions on various immigration laws and policies. Many participated in a region-wide petition drive in support of a proposal before the Georgia legislature to allow driver's licenses for undocumented immigrants. In July 1999 more than eight hundred people from the misión signed a letter protesting the arrest of the sixty-four day laborers in Marietta in an INS raid. The signers expressed their support for an expanded and improved guest worker program in the United States as a solution to the problem of "labor shortages, especially in jobs most Americans recoil from, and the presence of thousands of hard-working, undocumented immigrants from south of the border." Excluded from standard avenues of political participation in the United States, immigrants use the misión as an alternative public space from which to engage in political debate over issues that affect their lives.[30]

While the misión has facilitated immigrants' incorporation into U.S. religious and social life, it also has fostered ties with their homelands. They have sustained connections to their homelands through the practice of familiar faith devotions and rituals. According to Father García-Carreras many immigrants attended the misión instead of other Catholic churches in the metro area in order to honor and pray to their specific national and regional saints there. Such practices are "a remembrance for them of their own devotions in their country. . . . People would tell you when they come over here, 'Everything changes in our lives. The only thing that doesn't change is God.' So, religion for them is a relation with their own country or with their own traditions and being able to teach their children about the traditions in their country and being able to celebrate them over here."[31]

Initially mainstream Catholic parishes in Atlanta were uncomfortable with the diverse religious devotions of Mexican and other Latin American immigrants and discouraged their efforts to display images of patron saints in church, with the explanation that the devotions are private, rather than parishwide.[32] The misión, by contrast, encouraged the display of and devotions to Latin American saints. The Blessed Sacrament Chapel in the misión displayed statues and images of at least ten different patron saints from Latin America including Our Lady of Guadalupe and Our Lady of Juan de los Lagos from Mexico, Our Lady of Peace from El Salvador, Our Lady of Suyapa from Honduras, Our Lady of Copacabana from Bolivia, Our Lady of Charity from Cuba, Lord of Miracles from Peru, and Our Lady of Altagracia from the Dominican Republic. People visited the chapel regularly to pray and leave offerings for their saints.

The largest Catholic devotion among immigrants in the Chamblee-Doraville area is to Our Lady of Guadalupe. Although known originally and primarily as the patroness of Mexico, the Virgin of Guadalupe has also come to be known as the patron saint of all of Latin America. This devotion dates from the sixteenth century, when the Virgin Mary miraculously appeared to an indigenous man, Juan Diego, at Tepeyac, a place near Mexico City that had been sacred to an Aztec goddess. The Virgin appeared as an Indian and spoke to Juan Diego in his native language, Nahuatl. According to historian Jeffrey Burns, "To the Indian and Mestizo population. Guadalupe instilled a sense of personal dignity in the face of the affronts of the Spanish colonizers. She was not only a religious figure, but a national figure who gave birth to the Mexican faith and people. . . . To generation after generation the apparition of Our Lady of Guadalupe affirmed the Mexican people and provided solace to a people whose existence was often quite harsh, particularly in the United States."[33]

Mexican immigrants have carried this religious devotion with them to Atlanta. Images of Guadalupe adorn walls, T-shirts, trucks, and store windows throughout the neighborhoods where Mexicans have settled. Our Lady of Guadalupe has been a prominent presence at the *Misión*. A statue of the brown-skinned Virgin surrounded by golden rays greeted people as they entered the building and a colorful painting of her hung in the Blessed Sacrament Chapel. Since the founding of the mission lay leaders have organized an impressive annual celebration and procession in honor of Our Lady of Guadalupe on her feast day. During the celebration in 1999 hundreds of people gathered on the evening of December 11 to celebrate Mass and sing the traditional songs. "las mañanitas," led by a mariachi band. The following morning a procession with decorated trucks, one carrying the large painting of Guadalupe, traveled from the *Misión* down Shallowford Road for several blocks, marking a Latino immigrant presence in the neighborhood. Local police held back traffic to enable the truck floats and marchers to pass safely through the streets of Chamblee-Doraville.

With the formation of the Misión Católica, Latino immigrants challenged the policies of exclusion and restriction they faced from federal and local authorities, as well as the policy of assimilation promoted by the Catholic archdiocese. The appropriation of social space has been a critical means of empowerment for Latino immigrants in Atlanta. The need for social space has been especially pressing for undocumented immigrants who are most vulnerable to the laws, policies, and practices restricting immigrants' social and political rights. In the face of current immigration policies at the federal and local levels, ethnic religious institutions like the Misión Católica will continue to be an important means of immigrant community building and empowerment in Atlanta and elsewhere in the country.

NOTES

1. "IHM Ministers at Centro Católico," *Georgia Bulletin,* April 11, 1991; "Hispanic Mission Serves Newcomers," *Georgia Bulletin,* Dec. 5, 1991; interview with Father Carlos García-Carreras, Jan. 21, 2000; interview with Gonzalo Saldaña, June 20, 2000.

2. Mary E. Odem, "Unsettled in the Suburbs: Latino Immigration and Ethnic Diversity in Metro Atlanta," in Audrey Singer et al., *Twenty-first Century Gateways: Immigrant Incorporation in Suburban America* (Washington, D.C.: Brookings Institution, 2008), 105–36; Audrey Singer, "The Rise of New Immigrant Gateways" (Washington. D.C.: Brookings Institution, Feb. 2004); U.S. Census Bureau, *Census of Population, 1980, 1990, 2000.*

3. Henri Lefebvre, *The Production of Space,* trans. Donald Nicholson-Smith (Oxford and Cambridge, Mass: Oxford University Press, 1974, 1991); see also Edward Soja, *Postmodern Geographies: The Reassertion of Space in Critical Social Theory* (London and New York; Verso. 1989); David Harvey, *Spaces of Capital: Towards a Critical Geography* (New York: Routledge, 2001).

4. Delores Hayden, *The Power of Place: Urban Landscapes as Public History* (Cambridge, Mass.: MIT Press, 1995, 1999), 22–23.

5. For a study that situates Latino Catholics in Atlanta in the broader history of immigrants in the U.S. Catholic Church, see Mary E. Odem, "Our Lady of Guadalupe in the New South:

Latin American Immigrants and the Politics of Integration in the Catholic Church," *Journal of American Ethnic History* 23 (Fall 2004): 29–60. Although I focus on Latino immigrants' involvement in the Catholic Church, immigrants have also participated in large numbers in evangelical Protestant churches in Atlanta.

6. Odem, "Unsettled in the Suburbs"; Judith Waldrop, "The Newest Southerners," *American Demographics* 15 (1993): 38–43; Audrey Singer and Jill H. Wilson, *From "There" to "Here": Refugee Resettlement in Metropolitan America* (Washington, D.C.: Brookings Institution, 2006). 7. U.S. Census Bureau, *Census of Population, 1980, 1990, 2000.*

8. Odem, "Unsettled in the Suburbs"; Singer, "Rise of New Immigrant Gateways"; Susan M. Walcott, "Overlapping Ethnicities and Negotiated Spaces: Atlanta's Buford Highway," *Journal of Cultural Geography* 20, no. 1 (Fall/Winter 2001): 51–75.

9. U.S. Census Bureau, *Census of Population, 2000,*

10. Jeffrey S. Passel, Randolph Capps, and Michael E. Fix, "Undocumented Immigrants: Facts and Figures" (Washington, D.C.: Urban Institute, 2004). See www.urban.org/url.cfm?ID=1000587.

11. Jeffrey S. Passel, "Unauthorized Migrants: Numbers and Characteristics" (Washington, D.C.: Pew Hispanic Center, 2005). See http://pewhispanic.org/files/reports/46.pdf.

12. Rakesh Kochhar, Roberto Suro, and Sonya Tafoya, "The New Latino South: The Context and Consequences of Rapid Population Growth" (Washington, D.C.: Pew Hispanic Center, 2005).

13. David Bacon, "For an Immigration Policy Based on Human Rights," in *Immigration: A Civil Rights Issue for the Americas,* eds. Susanne Jonas and Suzanne Dodd Thomas (Wilmington, Del.: Scholarly Resources, 1999), 157.

14. *City Code of Marietta, Georgia,* sec. 10-4-130, www.municode.com, accessed June 20, 2007; City of Duluth, Georgia, *Code of Ordinances,* sec. 10-13, www.municode.com, accessed June 20, 2007.

15. Mark Bixler, "Day Laborers in Roswell Get a Place to Call Their Own," *Atlanta Journal-Constitution,* Dec. 19, 1999, 1D; Rick Badie, "Gwinnett Mulls Rules for Laborers," *Atlanta Journal-Constitution,* June 2, 2000, 1D; Pilar Verdes, "Roswell pone manos a la obra," *Mundo Hispanico,* Aug. 5, 1999.

16. Martha Durango, "Centro está por abrir sus puertas," *Mundo Hispánico,* Dec. 21, 2000; Rick Badie, "Gwinnett Seeks Rules for Laborers," *Atlanta Journal-Constitution,* June 2, 2000, D1; Mark Bixler, "Few Employers Know about Day Laborers Center," July 9, 2001, B1.

17. Bixler, "Few Employers Know about Day Laborers Center."

18. Mark Bixler, "Illegal Immigrants' License Try Revs Up," *Atlanta Journal-Constitution,* Aug. 27, 2001, IB; Georgia House Bill 501, enacted May 2, 2005. This was an amendment to Title 40, "Motor Vehicles and Traffic" of the Official Code of Georgia Annotated: the bill can be found at http://www.legis.ga.gov/legis/2005-06/fulltext/hb501.htm.

19. Eunice Moscoso, "Driver's Licenses for Illegals to End," *Atlanta Journal-Constitution,* May 5, 2005, A1.

20. Helen Blier, "A 'Catholic' Catholic Church: The Roman Catholic Community of Atlanta," in *Religions of Atlanta: Religious Diversity in the Centennial Olympic City,* ed. Gary Laderman (Atlanta: Scholars Press, 1996), 68.

21. Interview with Father Jorge Christancho, July 30, 1999; interview with Gonzalo Saldaña, June 20, 2000; Martha Woodson Rees and T. Danyael Miller, *Quienes Somos? Que Necesitamos?: Needs Assessment of Hispanics in the Archdiocese of Atlanta* (Atlanta: Hispanic Apostolate of the Archdiocese of Atlanta, 2002).

22. Father Jorge Christancho, "Perspectives on the Hispanic Ministry," March 16, 1992, box 014/2, folder 15, Catholic Archdiocese of Atlanta Archives; "Brief History of Our Lady of

the Americas Catholic Mission" (Doraville, Ga., Feb. 1999), prepared by staff members of the misión (copy in author's collection).

23. See both references in the previous note.

24. "Catholic Center Seeks a Home," *DeKalb Extra,* March 28, 1991; "Brief History of Our Lady of the Americas Catholic Mission."

25. "Catholic Center Seeks Home," *DeKalb Extra,* March 28, 1991; Most Rev. James Lyke to Rev. Jorge Christancho, March 14, 1991, box 014/2, folder 12, Archdiocese of Atlanta Archives; Interview with Father Jorge Christancho, July 30, 1999.

26. "IHM Ministers at Centro Católico," *Georgia Bulletin,* April 11, 1991; "Hispanic Mission Serves Newcomers," *Georgia Bulletin,* Dec. 5, 1991; interview with Father Carlos García-Carreras, Jan. 21, 2000; interview with Gonzalo Saldaña, June 20, 2000.

27. Interview with Father Carlos García-Carreras, Jan. 21 and 27, 2000; "Ideario de la Misión" (Doraville, Ga.: n.d.), prepared by staff members of the mission (copy in author's collection).

28. Interview with Father Carlos García-Carreras, Feb. 11, 2000.

29. Interview with Sister Ricarda, March 13, 2001; Rees and Miller, *Quienes Somas?*

30. *Atlanta Journal Constitution,* July 12, 1999, A8.

31. Interview with Father Carlos García-Carreras, Jan. 27, 2000.

32. Ibid.

33. Jeffrey Burns, "The Mexican Catholic Community in California," in *Mexican Americans and the Catholic Church, 1900–1965*, eds. Jay P. Dolan and Gilberto M. Hinojosa (Notre Dame, Ind.: University of Notre Dame Press, 1994); Timothy Matovina, "Guadalupan Devotions in a Borderlands Community," *Journal of Hispanic/Latino Theology* 4 (Aug. 1996): 6–26.

Chapter 15

What Is an American City?

Michael B. Katz

For many years I have argued that in the decades after the Second World War, economic, demographic, and spatial transformations in the United States resulted in an urban form unlike any other in history. Recently, I realized that in one important way this formulation of recent urban history misleads, for it reports the outcome of history as singular when it should be plural. "Form" should be "forms"—what we have today is an unprecedented configuration of urban places that calls into question the definition of city itself.

The April 25, 2006, death of Jane Jacobs was one of the events that prompted me to rethink my narrative of recent urban history. If any one person can be anointed patron saint of urban studies, Jacobs deserves the crown. Her 1961 *The Death and Life of Great American Cities* must be the most widely read and influential book ever written about American cities. After more than forty years, it retains its powerful impact. I have assigned it often to students, who invariably find it moving and convincing. *Death and Life* resonates with their ideal of urbanism and gives them a set of criteria for identifying a good city. With the book as a yardstick, they find that current-day cities come up short. Although the book has the same effect on me—new delights emerge every time I read it—recently, I wonder if it does as much to inhibit as to advance our grasp of American cities today. Its identification of mixed use, short blocks, multi-age dwellings, and density as defining a healthy neighborhood is based on models of old cities like Philadelphia, New York, Boston, or many of the cities of Europe. At least implicitly, this makes recapturing the past the goal of urban reform. Yet, the growing, dynamic, vibrant components of urban America are more like Phoenix and Los Angeles than the old East Coast cities. With Jacobs's criteria, they never can qualify as good cities; mutant forms of urbanism, they repel rather than attract anyone who loves cities. But is this a useful assessment? Is the fault with these cities or with the criteria? Did Jacobs bequeath us a definition of urbanism or do we

Reprinted from *Dissent* (Summer 2009): 19–26. Reprinted with the permission of the University of Pennsylvania Press.

need a different set of markers to characterize what makes a city—and a good city—in early-twenty-first-century America? Certainly, the former view—the belief in a core set of ideas defining healthy urbanism—underlies one of the most influential urban design movements of today: new urbanism. New urbanism does not take Jacobs's criteria literally, although her spirit is visible in its emphasis on density, mixed residential and commercial use, pedestrian-friendly streets, and vibrant public spaces. Its charter defines a set of principles it considers adaptable to a wide array of places from suburbs to shopping malls. The other view, which finds new urbanism an exercise in nostalgia out of touch with the forces driving urban change, is represented by Robert Bruegmann in his 2005 *Sprawl: A Compact History*. He cites approvingly a writer who "persuasively argues that the New Urbanism is only the latest version of a long-standing desire by cultural elites to manage middle-class urban life."

Even more than Jacobs's death, what forced me to confront the protean quality of today's urbanism and the inadequacy of singular definitions was my research on a book, *One Nation Divisible: What America Was and What It Is Becoming*, co-authored with Mark J. Stern. Stern and I set out to examine how the 2000 U.S. Census reflected social and economic trends during the preceding century. We concluded that America is living through a transformation as profound as the industrial revolution—one that reshapes everything, from family to class, from race and gender to cities. Events on the ground have undermined the standard concepts with which we interpret public life: work, city, race, family, nationality. All of them have lost their moorings in the way life is actually lived today. Their conventional meanings lie smashed, badly in need of redefinition.

The same situation occurred during the transition from the nineteenth to the twentieth century, when an emergent industrial civilization, based on a global economy, shattered existing ideas, producing, among other changes, a new urban form: the industrial city. "'Modern industry,' is almost equivalent to 'city life,'" observed University of Chicago sociologist Charles Henderson in 1909, "because the great industry, the factory system, builds cities around the chimneys of steam engines and electric plants." The emergence of this new urban form energized late-nineteenth- and early-twentieth-century social science and reform. With their focus on applied research, social scientists in both Europe and the United States tried to figure out how to respond to the problems of housing, poverty, public health, employment, and governance posed by this new entity, which they understood only imperfectly. Others, like Max Weber and Georg Simmel, searched for its essence as they advanced new theories of the city. In the United States, the attempt to define the industrial city culminated in the work of the Chicago School, which based its model on the interaction of industrial change, immigration, and social geography. The geographer Peirce Lewis calls this urban form, described "in any sixth grade geography book written before the [Second World] war" as the "nucleated city." This nucleated city and its compact suburbs no longer exist. What has taken their place?

My point that we need new answers to the question of what constitutes an American city is hardly original. If you poke around just a little in current writing about cities it pops up, either explicitly or by implication. A keen observer, in fact, could find the dissolution of conventional urban form described much earlier than the closing decades of the twentieth century. In his monumental 1961 jeremiad, *The City in History*, Lewis Mumford asked, "What is the shape of the city and how does it define itself? The original container has completely disappeared: the sharp division between city and country no longer exists." In the same year (also, remarkably, the same year as *Death and Life*), geographer Jean Gottman used the term Megalopolis, the title of his massive book, to describe the "almost continuous stretch of urban and suburban areas from southern New Hampshire to northern Virginia and from the Atlantic shore to the Appalachian foothills." Within this territory, the "old distinctions between rural and urban" no longer applied. As a result, within Megalopolis, "we must abandon the idea of the city as a tightly settled and organized unit in which people, activities, and riches are crowded into a very small area clearly separated from its nonurban surroundings." Although Megalopolis was most developed in the northeastern United States, it represented the future of the world. More recently, in his iconoclastic history of sprawl, Bruegmann observes, "With the penetration of urban functions into the countryside, the old distinctions between urban, suburban, and rural have collapsed."

Pronouncements by authorities are one way to illustrate the need to redefine what city means in the early twenty-first century. Another emerges clearly from contrasting actual cities. Philadelphia and Los Angeles, for instance, provide especially apt comparisons because they embody the old and the new urban America.

In *The Next Los Angeles*, Robert Gottlieb and his colleagues observe, "To understand the future of America, one needs to understand Los Angeles. Nearly every trend that is currently transforming the United States . . . has appeared in some form in Los Angeles." This new megalopolis was shaped by the automobile rather than the railroad, which, along with the streetcar, did so much to define America's industrial cities in the nineteenth and early twentieth centuries. L.A.'s heterogeneous population—far more diverse than Philadelphia's ever was—came from around the globe as well as from all over America. L.A.'s sprawling, multicentered, multiethnic regional development posed a dramatic contrast to the old model of a single, dense core surrounded by residential zones and a suburban periphery, exemplified by the Philadelphia region. Even though service industries dominated its economy to an unprecedented degree, Los Angeles probably was America's most important twentieth-century industrial city. At midcentury, its aerospace industry replaced Pennsylvania's shipbuilders as the heart of the military-industrial complex, while factory jobs migrated from the Northeast and Midwest to the South, West, and overseas. Los Angeles emerged as a major center in the Pacific basin and an important player in the global economy. Philadelphia, on the other hand, could not surmount its place as a second-order city on the international stage.

The contrast between Philadelphia and Los Angeles reflected not only changes in the two cities over time but also America's divergent regional history. Phoenix, Houston, Las Vegas, and other sunbelt cities more or less followed the Los Angeles model and grew rapidly. Old industrial cities, like Philadelphia, Baltimore, and Detroit, lost manufacturing jobs and population. Philadelphia represents a city surrounded by suburbs, Los Angeles a product of "suburban urbanization," where center and periphery meld into sprawling cities that lack a meaningful center. The stark contrasts between Philadelphia and Los Angeles—their diverse regional histories, economic and demographic differences, and divergent social ecologies—pose an unavoidable question: in early-twenty-first-century America, Just what is a city?

TRANSFORMATIONS

Despite their differences, Philadelphia and Los Angeles experienced the common transformations of economy, demography, and space that have led to new American cities. The decimation of manufacturing evident in Philadelphia and other rustbelt cities resulted from both the growth of foreign industries, notably electronics and automobiles, and the corporate search for cheaper labor. Cities with economic sectors other than manufacturing, such as banking, commerce, medicine, government, and education, withstood deindustrialization most successfully—for example, New York, Miami, Los Angeles, the San Francisco Bay Area, Chicago, Boston, and Houston. Those with no alternatives—Baltimore, Cleveland, Buffalo, Saint Louis, Detroit— nearly collapsed. Philadelphia, Pittsburgh, and the Twin Cities struggled with mixed success. Cities such as Las Vegas, Phoenix, Albuquerque, and, in some ways, New Orleans built economies on entertainment, hospitality, and retirement.

As services replaced manufacturing everywhere, office towers became the late twentieth century's urban factories. A broad category, service embraces both demanding and rewarding jobs and low-wage, nonunionized employment that offers few benefits. In the fortunate cities like Los Angeles, new economic functions included the production of the financial and business services and products that served the emergent international economy. They also included, as, again, notably in Los Angeles, the reappearance of small-scale manufacturing drawing on inexpensive immigrant labor.

The first urban demographic transformation was the migration of African Americans from the South to northern and midwestern, even, to some extent, western cities. (As James Gregory has shown, in the same years, more than twice as many white southerners also moved to the North and Midwest.) As African Americans moved into cities, whites moved out. Between 1950 and 1970, overall, the population of American cities grew by ten million people, and the population of suburbs by eighty-five million. Even more than racial change, a severe urban housing shortage, a desire to escape urban congestion, and mass-produced suburban homes made affordable by federally insured, long-term, low-interest mortgages pulled whites from cities. They sped to their suburban homes along the new interstate highway system. Aggressive and often unscrupulous realtors, fanning fears of racial change, played a role as well. In the North and Midwest the number of African-American newcomers often did not equal the number of whites who left. As a result, city populations and density went down, returning swaths of inner cities to empty lots and weed-filled fields where once working-class housing and factories had stood—a process vividly captured by the great photographer Camillo José Vergara, who has documented the emergence of the "green ghetto" in rustbelt America. In the sunbelt, in cities like Los Angeles, population trends went in the opposite direction. Between 1957 and 1990, the sunbelt's urban population, lured by economic opportunity and an appealing climate and boosted by annexation as well as in-migration, climbed from eight-and-a-half to twenty-three million.

Massive immigration following changes to federal law in 1965 also transformed urban demography. More immigrants entered the United States in the 1990s than in any other decade in its history. Mostly from Asia and Latin America, these immigrants altered the ethnic mix of America's population, most notably of its cities, and fueled most of the urban population growth that occurred during the 1990s. Four of five settled in metropolitan areas, clustering in "gateway" cities: New York, Miami, Los Angeles, and, to some extent, Chicago. By 2000, they had begun to spread out across the nation, transforming suburbs and both small and large cities. Thanks to labor market networks in agricultural work, construction, landscaping, low end manufacturing, and domestic service, Hispanics spread out faster than any other ethnic group in American history. In 1910, 84 percent of the foreign born in greater Philadelphia lived in the central city. By 2006, the number had plummeted to 35 percent. Similar trends appeared everywhere. Across the nation, the suburbanization of immigration became a major factor reshaping metropolitan geography.

Suburbanization and racial segregation transformed urban space. Suburban growth, which had begun much earlier, exploded in the years after the Second World War, with suburbs growing ten times faster than cities in the 1950s. Population, retailing, services, and industry all suburbanized. Suburbs remained predominantly white until late in the twentieth century, when immigrants and African Americans began moving out of the center cities in significant numbers—although even in the suburbs African Americans often clustered in segregated neighborhoods or dominated some suburban towns. Within cities, racial segregation increased through 1970, with growing numbers of African Americans clustered in districts of concentrated poverty. Racial segregation was much higher in late- than in early-twentieth-century American cities. In the 1990s, although segregation in cities declined by an average of 5.5 percentage points, the average African American still lived in a census tract more than half black, while affluent African Americans were more likely to live near African Americans with modest incomes than near comparably well-off whites. Growing economic as well as racial inequality reconfigured urban space as well. Economic segregation among whites, for instance, grew notably after the 1970s.

In the decades after the Second World War, redevelopment also transformed city space, as urban renewal displaced poor residents, usually without relocating them to alternate housing, and cleared downtown land for reuse as offices, retailing, and homes for the affluent. Public housing, by and large, remained confined to segregated districts and never matched existing needs. Gentrification, the rehabilitation of working-class housing for use by a wealthier class, played a modest counterpoint to urban renewal. Movement into gentrified neighborhoods was not large enough to reverse overall population decline outside of select neighborhoods, but it did transform cityscapes as it attracted young, white professionals with above-average incomes and empty-nesters who demanded new services and amenities.

At the same time, married couples with children made up a shrinking percentage of suburban populations. In a sample of fourteen representative metropolitan areas, between 1970 and 2000, the proportion of suburban census tracts where married couples and their children composed more than half of all households plummeted from 59 percent to 12 percent. In the same years, the share of the suburban population living in census tracts where young, unmarried people between eighteen and thirty-five living alone or without relatives predominated rocketed from 8 percent to 35 percent. These changes subverted the suburbs' historic function as providers of housing for families with children. The result was a new domestic landscape that increasingly called into question the meaning of "suburb" as well as "city."

URBAN METAPHORS

By the early twenty-first century, economic, demographic, and spatial transformations had undercut all the existing definitions, and a variety of new urban metaphors competed to replace them. One set of metaphors looks inward toward central cities; another set looks outward to metropolitan areas, regions, and, indeed, the world. The two sets are not mutually exclusive. Sometimes the same writers use different metaphors to capture the increasingly fractured reality of "urban" or "city." All of them, however, try to make sense of the patterns of inequality that grew out of the economic, demographic, and spatial transformation of American cities in the second half of the twentieth century. The inward-looking metaphor that still comes first to mind is "inner city," which, since the 1960s, has served as shorthand for a bundle of problems—disorder, crime, drugs, poverty, homelessness, out-of-wedlock births. As a metaphor, inner city was colored poor and black. So pervasive did the image become that it spawned a new genre of popular culture that diffused outward from inner cities to the American heartland. According to *Maclean's*, "Urban music," a category that includes "funk, soul, and hip hop, as well as R and B" became "the biggest selling genre in the United States."

"Postindustrial," another inward-looking metaphor, focused on the loss of urban manufacturing rather than on demography and social structure. Political scientist John H. Mollenkopf identified a "profound transformation" that had

> seriously eroded the nineteenth-century industrial city. For lack of a better term, it might be called "the postindustrial revolution." This second urban revolution grew out of and in many ways constituted a reaction against the first. If labor and capital concentrated into factories defined the industrial city, the postindustrial city is characterized by the geographic diffusion of production and population. The office building, not the factory, now provides the organizing institution of the central city.

Vivid though it was, analytic usefulness of the metaphor "postindustrial" was limited. It defined the city by what it was not rather than by what it had become.

"Dual City," a third inward-looking metaphor, focused on the social structure that had emerged from economic and demographic transformation abetted by governments—federal, state, and local—that remapped the distribution of classes and functions across urban space and, through funding cuts, decimated services. Growing class polarization, a problem everywhere in the nation (and, indeed, as Mike Davis shows, in even more extreme forms around the globe), appeared most vividly in big cities. Increasingly bereft of their middle class, city populations divided between rich and poor, the former buoyed by jobs in finance, information, and high-end services, the latter barely sustained by low-end service jobs, the informal economy, or government assistance.

This was the dual city. Its two worlds, the gleaming office towers and condos and the rundown housing and public ghettos of the poor, were not two separate spheres. Indeed, dual-city theorists stressed the links that joined them: they produced and depended on one another. Although the dual-city metaphor, as its theorists recognized, oversimplified a very complicated situation, it had the virtue of directing attention to the new inequalities that define current-day cities, just as Jacob Riis's depiction in *How the Other Half Lives* captured the emerging industrial social structure a century ago.

A variety of outward-looking metaphors—"city region," "metropolitan area," "elastic/inelastic city," "galactic city"—try to capture the extension of cities beyond their legal boundaries. Three public intellectuals—David Rusk, Myron Orfield, and Bruce Katz—have led the effort to substitute metropolitan for narrowly bounded definitions of current-day cities. For them, the exercise is more than theoretical, because policies needed to counteract the baneful effects of metropolitan political fragmentation require an expanded definition of "city." No less concerned with inequality than dual-city theorists, they focus more on economic and political disparities between central cities and their suburbs than on income gaps among city residents. Grossly unequal public services and tax burdens, environmental degradation, sprawl, racial segregation, anemic job growth: these, they argue, can be countered only through metropolitan-wide actions.

Where city and suburb rubbed up against each other, they were becoming more alike. As urban problems spread outward, distinctions lessened, and the real differentiation separated older inner suburbs from those further out on the periphery of metropolitan areas, which, themselves, could not remain immune from the urban problems attendant on growth. Just what a suburb was, what made it distinct, was no longer clear. Recognizing the inadequacy of the conventional city/suburb/rural distinction, the U.S. Census Bureau began to develop a reclassification of municipalities based on a sophisticated mathematical model, which, if it works, should greatly facilitate comparative urban research and policy development.

Historian Robert Fishman proclaimed the end of the era of the suburb defined as a sylvan residential enclave for affluent male-headed families, a "bourgeois utopia" of commuters. By the 1980s, he held, the classic suburb had been replaced by the "post-suburb" or "technoburb." Others reclassified suburbs differently. Orfield divided metropolitan areas into six categories of municipalities based on their financial capacity and age. "Suburbia conceals as well as reveals its complexity," observes historian Delores Hayden in *Building Suburbia*. "For years, when urban historians wrote about the 'city,' they meant the center, the skyline, downtown." Looking closely, she identifies seven suburban patterns. Although the earliest date from before the Civil War, vestiges of all of them still exist. The most famous, or notorious, new suburban forms are Joel Garreau's "edge cities," massive configurations of office towers and malls at the crossroads of exurban highways, "[a] new frontier being shaped by the freeways, in a constantly reinvented land." Recently, Robert E. Lang and his colleagues identified "boomburbs," the "ultimate symbol of today's sprawling postwar metropolitan form." These are places "with more than one hundred thousand residents that are not the largest cities in their respective metropolitan areas and that have maintained double-digit rates of population growth in recent decades." Others, like geographer Wei Li, focusing on the new suburbanization of immigration, have identified a suburban variant they call "ethnoburbs," which "serve as bridges between historical ethnic neighborhoods and the broader region." Peirce Lewis has termed the new urban form that developed "far beyond the old urban fringe" the "galactic city," defined as "a city where all the traditional urban elements float in space like stars and planets in a galaxy, held together by mutual gravitational attraction but with large empty spaces in between. . . . This new galactic city is an urban creation different from any sort Americans have ever seen before." With chain migration linking towns and villages in Latin America and the Caribbean with U.S. cities, Mike Davis writes of the creation of new suburban forms extending across national boundaries as "transnational suburbs."

Metropolitan metaphors linked cities to their regions; global metaphors joined them to the world. Saskia Sassen, whose work set the agenda for debate on global cities, identifies a set of such cities at the pinnacle of new urban hierarchies, detached from their regions and connected, instead, to the world of international finance and trade. As "transnational market 'spaces,'" global cities have "more in common with one another than with regional centers in their own nation-states, many of which have declined in importance." The "finance and producer services complex in each city," she asserts, "rests on a growth dynamic that is somewhat independent of the broader regional economy—a sharp change from the past, when a city was presumed to be deeply articulated with its hinterland." Rather than regional centers, global cities are "command points in the organization of the world economy." Economic globalization has made great cities more relevant and important than ever, a point reinforced by a July 2006 report describing the movement of corporate headquarters back to New York City.

A second outward-looking metaphor defines modern cities by what they produce. For Manuel Castells, the late-twentieth-century "informational city" replaces the early-twentieth-century "industrial city." To be sure, knowledge and information processing have been important to every mode of production. What distinguishes the informational mode "is the action of knowledge upon knowledge itself as the main source of productivity." The informational city differs from Garreau's edge city, whose "primitive technological vision that sees the world through the simplified lenses of endless freeways and fiber-optic networks" misses "the core of the new urbanization process" in the United States. Unlike Garreau and Sassen, Castells stresses the interdependence of edge cities and the "functional interdependence" among "different units and processes in a given urban system over very long distances, minimizing the role of territorial contiguity and maximizing the communication networks in all their dimensions. Flows of exchange are at the core of the American edge city." The second point missed by Garreau's metaphor is the multiple dependencies at the heart of America's distinctive informational city: "the profile of America's informational city is not fully represented by the edge city phenomenon but by the relationship between fast exurban development, inner-city decay, and obsolescence of the suburban built environment." Castells's informational city is better understood as a network than a place, a process rather than an object. In the United States, the Information Age also has given rise to a distinctive suburban form, what Margaret Pugh O'Mara identifies as "cities of knowledge," residential and high-tech industrial nodes built around major research universities.

In the early twenty-first century, these metaphors—inner city, postindustrial city, dual city, city-region, edge city, galactic city, global city, informational city, city of knowledge—compete to answer the question, What is an American city? All of them are both useful and partial. Their utility depends on the angle of interest—inward vs. outward, national vs. global—and the concern—inequality, environmental degradation, aesthetic value, political fragmentation, the possibility of community, for instance. They are, moreover, not entirely consistent. Garreau's cheerful optimism about the future of edge cities contrasts with Hayden's withering attack, and Sassen's emphasis on the importance of place and contiguity in global cities contrasts with Castells's stress on a-geographic networks. The work of assessing and reconciling multiple metaphors and exploring their implications is a central and urgent task for interdisciplinary urban studies. Economic, demographic, and spatial transformation have exploded old ideas of cities and suburbs, turning them into encumbrances to the reformulation of helpful public policies.

At both ends of the twentieth century, profound economic change forced redefinitions of "city." In the late nineteenth and early twentieth centuries, the industrial city emerged as the new urban form, and a host of commentators tried to define its character. The problems they identified, and the issues on which they concentrated, are remarkably similar to those on the agenda of urbanists in the early twenty-first century. Only now, as we have seen, the model of the old industrial city is gone forever. The question, then, is how to characterize what has taken its place. What is an American city? The answer remains far from clear.

One point about this history requires emphasis. A huge difference between the early and late twentieth century lies in the response to urban redefinition. Early-twentieth-century reformers, struggling to define and tame industrial cities, grappled with the consequences of massive immigration by people with different cultures, the lack of affordable housing, the growth of poverty and homelessness, crises in public health and sanitation, and the impact of growing concentrations of wealth on society and politics.

They worried about the role of privatization in municipal services, the heavy hand of state government, the weakness of mayoral authority, the corruption of machine politics, the inefficiencies and inequities of the courts, and the regressive and inadequate foundation of city finances on property taxes.

In the late nineteenth and early twentieth centuries, cities tried to respond to these issues with active government—what historians have labeled progressivism. Despite the persistence of corruption, widespread poverty, and racial discrimination, cities increased municipal expenditures, professionalized their administrations, and constructed buildings and infrastructures that supported the most vibrant and successful era in American urban history. In the late twentieth century, by contrast, the response to similar issues was the withdrawal of active government, evident in reduced federal funds, reliance on market-based solutions to urban problems, and the need to turn to private initiatives, like special service districts, to carry out public functions, such as street cleaning and security. The results are everywhere to be seen, in homeless-ness on city streets, poverty spreading outward to inner suburbs, uncontrolled sprawl eating up open space, crumbling infrastructure, gross inequity in spending on public education, the future of urban finance mortgaged to casino gambling, the incapacity to prevent or respond effectively to the devastation of Hurricane Katrina in 2005, and the subprime mortgage crisis. The widely heralded comeback of American cities is thin and fragile. If you move away from shiny center cities, it is not nearly so visible. Look at city budgets, and it does not seem nearly so robust. The question, "What is an American city?" has begun to elicit both a cacophony of definitions and an array of intelligent and promising ideas about how to respond. But we have yet to see a power-ful and pervasive new urban progressivism. Clearly, though, without the will to forge an effective and coordinated political response, the future of American cities, however defined, is unlikely to be as buoyant as their past.

Part IV

THE HISTORIOGRAPHY
OF URBAN AMERICA

New Perspectives on American Urban History

Raymond A. Mohl and Roger Biles

The writing of American history has been transformed dramatically over the past several decades. In particular, a new interest in social and cultural history has energized the field and substantially altered the way historians research, conceptualize, and interpret the past. In the field of urban history, scholars have brought exciting new perspectives to the study of the American city. New methods, new approaches, and new interpretations have illumined dim corners of the urban past and pushed back the frontiers of historical understanding.

The rise of the American industrial city became one of the dominant characteristics of the late nineteenth century. Since the turn of the twentieth century, the city in its various permutations continued to reflect or to shape modern social, economic, and political life. Yet American historians, Richard C. Wade suggested, "arrived at the study of the city by slow freight."[1] Historians lagged far behind scholars in other disciplines, who by 1900 began to apply the tools of the emerging social sciences to the examination of urban America. Indeed, American urban history as a distinctive field of scholarly inquiry does not date much earlier than 1940, when Arthur M. Schlesinger published his landmark article "The City in American History."[2] But interest in the field grew rather slowly, and by the mid-1950s only a half dozen or so universities offered courses on the subject. Progress in urban history research was also less than dynamic, the chief accomplishments in the early postwar period being several fine urban biographies and a handful of monographs. Important early studies included the works of Carl Bridenbaugh on the colonial seaport cities, Oscar Handlin's study of Boston's immigrants, and Wade's pioneering book *The Urban Frontier* (1959).[3]

The decade of the 1960s, however, brought powerful changes to the historical profession—changes that affected research and writing in urban history in significant ways. The mainstream consensus history that grew out of the conditions of the Great Depression, World War II, and the Cold War peaked in the Eisenhower era of the 1950s but began to crack amid the social strains and political conflicts of the 1960s. The ghetto riots of the 1960s and the social-crusading spirit of the Kennedy-Johnson years riveted attention on the American city and its discontents. The writing of history generally reflects the climate of opinion at any particular moment in time, and certainly this occurred in the 1960s. Traditional interest in political and diplomatic history—a form of elitist history concerned with the ideas and activities of decision makers, opinion shapers, and power wielders—gave way to a new and invigorated commitment to social history broadly considered. American historians began to examine with new interest such subjects as race, ethnicity, gender, and class and the ways in which people ordered their lives in the family, at work, and in various group and community settings; they began to explore the social values, behaviors, and processes that shaped the lives of people and communities; and they began to pay attention to the local as well as the national level, and to the people at the bottom of the social and economic hierarchy as well as at the top. In addition, many historians began to move away from narrative history toward a more critical analytical history influenced by social theory and the social sciences. As historian Olivier Zunz has suggested, the appearance of this newer form of social history "generated great excitement in the progressive and eclectic intellectual atmosphere of the sixties."[4]

These shifts in historiographical tradition coincided with two other powerful changes in 1960s America. First, the computer revolution made possible a more careful and exact social science history based on analysis of massive amounts of information collected, stored, sorted, and manipulated by computer. Second, the arrival of the baby boom generation at the college gates spurred an explosion of graduate education, generating in turn a substantial amount of new research as young historians wrote dissertations, articles, and books. By the end of the 1960s, the historiographical landscape had been altered considerably from the mid-1950s, the heyday of the consensus historians.[5]

The convergence of these changing social patterns and historiographical trends energized research and writing in American urban history. The ferment of scholarly innovation and shifting interests pushed urban history in at least two new directions in the early 1960s. Each new path was illuminated by an important and innovative book—one path by Sam Bass Warner's *Streetcar Suburbs: The Process of Growth in Boston, 1870–1900* (1962) and the other by Stephan Thernstrom's *Poverty and Progress: Social Mobility in a Nineteenth-Century City* (1964).

Sam Warner's work had an ecological slant, focusing on the process of urbanization and population redistribution in the Boston metropolitan area in response both to technological innovation in urban transit and to the rural appeal of suburbia. Warner also used an inventive methodology. Examination of some 23,000 building permits for three Boston inner-ring suburbs enabled Warner to draw conclusions about construction patterns, architectural and building styles, and the class structure underlying neighborhood formation. Warner's *Streetcar Suburbs* pushed well beyond the established perimeters of urban history and provided powerful insights into the physical expansion of the late-nineteenth-century American city.[6]

In *Streetcar Suburbs* and in some of his other work, Warner primarily dealt with the processes of urban growth. In rejecting more traditional approaches to urban history, such as urban biography or the study of social problems or political movements within an urban context, he demonstrated that fresh thinking could be historiographically liberating. Warner was not entirely alone in this emphasis on the process of urbanization in the early 1960s. Eric Lampard, who published several important articles over thirty years, advocated the study of urbanization as a "societal process." Studying urbanization from this perspective, Lampard argued, required urban historians to examine such "interacting elements" as population, topography, economy, societal organization, political process, civic leadership, and urban imagery.[7] In a similar vein, Roy Lubove suggested the utility of the "city-building process" as a conceptual framework for analyzing decision making, social organization, and urban change. Lubove illustrated this methodology in a little-heralded but nevertheless important book, *Twentieth-Century Pittsburgh: Government, Business, and Environmental Change* (1969).[8]

Stephan Thernstrom staked out a second new path in American urban history in the early 1960s. In *Poverty and Progress*, he tested the widely asserted conception of nineteenth-century America as a land of opportunity for the urban working class. Drawing samples from manuscript census schedules for Newburyport, Massachusetts, between 1850 and 1880, Thernstrom pioneered in the use of new kinds of sources and in quantitative analysis, although he did not ignore more traditional literary sources. Thernstrom focused on the relatively narrow question of social mobility rather than the larger process of urbanization, or city building. Nevertheless, his research methodology was widely imitated and came to be associated with a "new urban history."[9]

Younger historians began pumping out a stream of books and articles replicating Thernstrom's work for other cities. By the early 1970s, the new urban history had been taken over by the quantifiers in the Thernstrom tradition who studied mobility and related issues.[10] Indeed, when Thernstrom catalogued the achievements of the new urban history in a 1971 article, he wrote primarily of findings about mobility. These included tremendously high rates of urban population turnover, positive correlations between economic failure and spatial mobility, and a general fluidity in rates of occupational and social mobility, although rates varied for different economic classes and ethnic groups, and blacks had considerably fewer opportunities.[11]

Thernstrom's approach rather than Warner's came to dominate among practitioners of the new urban history by the early 1970s. Michael Frisch has suggested that the popularity and influence of Thernstrom's *Poverty and Progress* "stemmed less from the book's substance than from the way it brought together a number of diverse concerns central to the moment." These included a methodology conducive to quantification at the beginning of the computer age, a model that could be applied easily to other communities, and, finally, a concern for nonelitist history, or history from the bottom up, at the height of the political radicalism of the 1960s. As Frisch put it, "quantification, as applied by Thernstrom . . . came to be invested with an aura of social and political relevance," making this particular approach appealing to a younger generation of urban historians.[12]

Thus, the new urban history came to be perceived as a special sort of quantitative history. Yet, ironically, at about the same time that he was carrying his quantitative methodology to a new level of sophistication in his prize-winning book *The Other Bostonians* (1973), Thernstrom had begun having second thoughts about the term "new" urban history. Indeed, as he confessed in an interview in the *Journal of Urban History* in 1975, he had not only given up the term, but he also had even stopped labeling himself as an urban historian. Rather, Thernstrom preferred to be known as a social historian, contending that "the modern city [was] so intimately linked to the society around it, and [was] so important a part of the entire social order that few of its aspects [could] safely be examined in isolation."[13]

Always difficult to categorize, Warner, too, rejected the emerging notion of a new urban history. In a 1977 article, he labeled the narrow mobility studies "a bare-boned empiricism" and "a quantitative antiquarianism," the purpose behind such studies "lost in technique." Nothing, he suggested, was "more likely to put a researcher on a false track than the advertisement: new urban history." Building on his earlier emphasis on the process of urbanization, Warner asserted that the central focus of urban history should be the spatial distribution of population, institutions, activities, and artifacts—the basic elements in all human communities that are continuously evolving in relation to each other over time.[14] By the mid-1970s, therefore, the two chief pioneers of new ways of doing urban history had abandoned or rejected the notion altogether.

The new urban history made one last stand, however. Theodore Hershberg and others associated with the Philadelphia Social History Project promoted the continued viability of a new, quantified urban history. In an important article in 1978 and in the introduction to a collection of essays on Philadelphia, Hershberg provided yet another prescriptive statement about urban history. For him, the old and the new urban history differed in treating the city as site or as process. By site, Hershberg meant "the conceptual treatment of the city as a passive backdrop to whatever else [was] the subject of central concern." By contrast, he wrote, "urban as process should be thought of as the dynamic modeling of the interrelationships among environment, behavior, and group experience—three basic components in the larger urban system." Such an approach, Hershberg contended, would explain what was distinctively different or unique about life and change in the city. By Hershberg's account, neither Warner nor Thernstrom had been pursuing a new urban history; they were simply working within the older tradition of urban as site rather than urban as process.[15] Thus, at about the same time that Warner and Thernstrom abandoned the idea of a new urban history as unsatisfying and incomplete, a new band of purists tossed the pioneers off the team, consigning their work to the historiographical scrap heap.

Through the 1970s, then, debates over the new urban history held center stage within the discipline. This apparent absorbing interest, however, tended to mask the fact that an extensive urban history literature was pouring from university presses and filling the pages of scholarly journals—a literature that often paid little attention to the new urban history controversy.[16] Indeed, for some areas of urban history the new quantitative or social science approaches had little relevance or application. The microlevel analysis of work, residence, family, and group experience typical of the Hershberg school offered important and informative conclusions, but many dimensions of the urban experience could not be addressed in exactly that way. In addition, the new urban history seemed particularly unhelpful in suggesting alternative ways of approaching the twentieth-century American city. Hershberg's book on Philadelphia, for instance, concentrated almost exclusively on the years 1850 to 1880, and only one of its fourteen chapters ventured into the twentieth century. This concentration on the nineteenth century clearly reflected the reliance of the new urban history on manuscript census data, which at that time was not available for early decades of the twentieth century.

The perceived weaknesses of an exclusively quantitative approach to urban history research liberated urban historians to pursue many diverse paths of the urban experience, to follow their instincts and their interests. The results have been fruitful and stimulating. Historians of the American city have begun to carve out an array of new and exciting areas of urban research. Meanwhile, as Bruce M. Stave noted, the heavy emphasis on quantification diminished considerably by the early 1980s. Students and scholars, Stave wrote in 1983, "will be less overtly confronted by the numbers as historians increasingly recognize the problems of sometimes imprecise data and flawed methodology. Qualitative rather than quantitative analysis will be the historian's prime goal."[17]

Stave's epitaph for the new urban history sparked surprisingly little comment, which suggested that his observation was right on target. But if the now old, quantitative urban history is long gone, the larger field itself is brimming with new approaches, new interpretations, and new ideas. The remainder of this essay will survey more than a dozen of these new perspectives on American urban history.

CITY AND REGION

Much of the published work on American urban history takes the form of case studies of specific topics or processes in specific cities. As early as the 1950s, however, a few urban historians adopted a regional framework in analyzing the links between American cities and the wider regions of which they were a part. Perhaps the first of the American urban historians to fully conceptualize the city as integrally linked to its regional hinterland was Richard C. Wade. In *The Urban Frontier: The Rise of Western Cities, 1790–1830* (1959), Wade analyzed the formative years of early-nineteenth-century river cities Pittsburgh, Cincinnati, Louisville, and Saint Louis, as well as Lexington, Kentucky. He identified the important role of transportation and economic development as central to frontier urbanization. This approach led to Wade's main thesis—that the cities "were the spearheads of the frontier," a challenge to the famous frontier thesis of historian Frederick Jackson Turner. Turner portrayed towns and cities as the end product of a linear development process. Wade, by contrast, contended that the cities facilitated the settlement and development of the agricultural frontier, serving marketing and processing functions, providing capital and credit, and supplying goods, services, and cultural amenities.[18] Wade followed a few years later with *Slavery in the Cities: The South, 1820–1860* (1964), a regional analysis that countered the notion of slavery as a rural institution. Urban bondage was typified by slaves who hired themselves out, worked in industrial or skilled occupations, lived separate from their masters, and developed their own forms of independent community. Thus, Wade contended that urban life and work increasingly blurred the distinction between slavery and freedom, contributing to a weakening of the institution as the Civil War approached.[19] Wade wrote ambitious books on big subjects, demonstrating important connections between city and region, but his work had little impact in the 1960s as urban history researchers turned to new methodologies.

More than twenty years later, the city-region concept was revived by David Goldfield, whose book *Cotton Fields and Skyscrapers: Southern City and Region, 1607–1980* (1982) analyzed southern urbanization within the context of southern history and regional culture. Goldfield challenged earlier views that the pattern of southern urban development matched the national urban experience. He suggested instead that "the southern city is different because the South is different." More specifically, he argued that three distinctive aspects of southern regional history and culture shaped southern urbanization: first, a rural lifestyle in which the cities maintained a symbiotic relationship with staple agriculture, cotton especially; second, the importance of race and the reality of a biracial society; and third, a colonial economy dominated by northern business and financial interests. The application of this regionalist model of explanation resulted in a stimulating reinterpretation of southern urban history.[20]

William Cronon's powerful book *Nature's Metropolis: Chicago and the Great West* (1991) offered still another innovative regional interpretation of American urban history. Primarily known as an environmental historian, Cronon demonstrated that late-nineteenth-century Chicago was at the center of a vast economic ecosystem that stretched from the Ohio Valley to the Pacific Coast. The Midwest metropolis, he contended, was built not so much by the work of individual entrepreneurs but by the functioning of impersonal economic forces, especially the enormous flows of raw materials and commodities such as meat, timber, and grain. Chicago became a major processing center, with great grain elevators, immense stockyards for cattle and pigs, and numerous timber yards, sawmills, and furniture factories. New technology and machinery, as well as the creation of a commodities futures market, made Chicago's rural-based industries possible and profitable. The commodity flows, facilitated by Chicago's immense railroad transportation system, inextricably linked the city and the hinterland. City and farm developed a symbiotic relationship: As commodities flowed into Chicago, outward-bound trains carried farm machinery, lumber, processed meat, and mail-order-catalog items. Cronon also documented the economic exploitation of the natural environment—the degradation of the forests, the plowing of the tallgrass prairies, and the slaughtering of the bison herds. Farming, grazing, and lumbering eventually destroyed the natural ecosystem of the "Great West" as new and more wide-ranging economic relationships emerged between city and region. Indeed, the linkage between Chicago and its hinterland ultimately pulled the Great West into the orbit of the world capitalist system, with powerful modernizing influences. Urban and rural history blended together in this original study, demonstrating the value of a regionalist perspective for urban history.[21]

Cronon and Goldfield presented the most fully developed regional interpretations of U.S. urban history in recent years. A number of other urban histories—most dealing with the West and the South—also provided imaginative insights into the linkages between cities and regions. Eugene P. Moehring's *Urbanism and Empire in the Far West, 1940–1890* (2004) presented a deeply researched analysis of the role of urbanism in developing networks of small western towns linked together and to larger cities that facilitated exploitation of the region's natural resources. Moehring applied the concept of colonialism to frame his effort "to trace the dynamics of network formation" within the vast and empty expanses of the nineteenth-century mountain, desert, and Pacific coastal West. Similarly, Gray Brechin's *Imperial San Francisco* (2006) demonstrated the regional reach of powerful San Francisco interests in controlling and exploiting a vast western hinterland, often with costly environmental consequences.[22]

Other studies also suggested the utility of a regional research strategy. Timothy R. Mahoney's *River Towns in the Great West* (1990) analyzed the development of a network of river cities in the upper Mississippi River region; Jeffrey S. Adler's *Yankee Merchants and the Making of the Urban West* (1991) documented the important role of Saint Louis in commanding the economic linkages to the West in the antebellum period; and Gunther Barth's *Instant Cities* (1975) compared the nineteenth-century rise of San Francisco and Denver within a western regional context.[23] Carl Abbott's *The Metropolitan Frontier* (1993) surveyed the urban West in the rapid growth years after 1940, noting that the West had long been the most heavily urbanized region of the nation, even though it was also the emptiest region. Abbott contended that "it is western cities that organize the region's vast spaces and connect them to the even larger sphere of the world economy." Abbott's more recent book *How the Cities Won the West* (2008) explored the contours of western urbanization over four centuries, echoing Wade's "spearhead" thesis but once again linking the modern West's cities to the theme of globalization.[24] Earl Pomeroy's *The American Far West in the Twentieth Century* (2008) contains two long chapters on western urbanization that explored, among other subjects, the challenges of distance. Bradford Luckingham's *The Urban Southwest* (1982) examined the common patterns in the growth and development of Albuquerque, El Paso, Phoenix, and Tucson, while Michael F. Logan's *Fighting Sprawl and City Hall* (1995) considered resistance to urban growth in Tucson and Albuquerque. Gerald D. Nash's *The American West Transformed* (1985) emphasized the importance of World War II in promoting the economic and population growth of western cities.[25]

The West has received considerable attention, but the regionalist urban historians have found other subjects as well, including the Midwest. Carl Abbott's *Boosters and Businessmen* (1981) focused on popular economic thought in four midwestern cities during the period of rapid regional growth between 1840 and 1860. In *Chicago Dreaming* (2005), Timothy B. Spears used contemporary fiction to explore the cultural consequences of the enormous number of rural migrants to late-nineteenth-century Chicago, who helped shape the city's life and institutions but still dreamed of their hometowns. Books on urbanism in the Midwest by Jon C. Teaford and Anthony M. Orum focused primarily on the rise and fall of the midwestern industrial economy.[26] Finally, in a class by itself, Carl Abbott's *Political Terrain* (1999) offered a provocative interpretation of the multiple and overlapping regional, national, and international roles of Washington, D.C.[27]

David Goldfield was not the only historian writing about the South in a regional context. Don H. Doyle's *New Men, New Cities, New South* (1990) examined patterns of post–Civil War growth and change in four New South cities: Atlanta, Nashville, Charleston, and Mobile. Doyle was especially interested in the role of a new urban business elite that pursued a modernizing "New South creed" but found resistance from old planter elites and small-town mill owners. New South cities, Doyle wrote, formed "the nerve centers of a changing economy and culture that penetrated the rural hinterland and remade the South in the decades following the Civil War." Over a fifty-year period from 1860 to 1910, the South advanced economically and developed a regional urban system linked by railroads, steamships, and the telegraph. Yet southern cities remained burdened by chronic poverty, poor housing, and racism, lagging behind the modernizing development that characterized the rest of the nation. Doyle's New South cities, it seems, represented only a partial challenge to the regional pattern identified by Goldfield.[28]

Several books with a regionalist perspective focused on the rural areas influenced or changed by widening urban orbits. Don Kirschner's *City and Country* (1970) explored rural responses in the midwestern corn belt to urbanization during the 1920s. Farmers relied on urban markets, but they held hostile attitudes toward cities and fought in state legislatures to protect their cultural values and curb the growth of state taxes and bureaucracies. David R. Danborn's *The Resisted Revolution* (1979) recounted the history of the Country Life Movement, which hoped to modernize agricultural regions, make farmers more productive, and incorporate them more fully into the urban-industrial society—goals that were achieved during and after World War I.[29]

In the 1970s, some journalists began thinking and writing about the South and the West as part of a new regional phenomenon they labeled the "sunbelt." Books by Kevin Phillips and Kirkpatrick Sale launched the sunbelt into popular parlance as a catchy journalistic phrase describing the political conservatism and the dynamic economic and population growth of the two regions.[30] In particular, the postwar growth of southern and western cities attracted attention. By 1980, five of the nation's ten largest cities were located in the Southwest: Houston, Dallas, Phoenix, San Diego, and Los Angeles. By the 1980s, as well, some urban historians began engaging sunbelt conceptualization, generally disputing the convergence of the traditionally distinctive areas into a single sunbelt region with shared characteristics. Carl Abbott's *The New Urban America* (1981; rev. ed. 1987) presented the first full-scale historical study of sunbelt city growth. In a complex analysis, Abbott identified two distinct growth regions—a seven-state sunbelt Southeast, and a ten-state sunbelt West. The cities of these areas mostly shared common patterns of economic and population growth, but they also experienced the same forces of automobile-driven decentralization and metropolitan political fragmentation that affected cities nationwide. Sunshine had little to do with Abbott's sunbelt boundaries, since they included Denver, Baltimore, and Portland, Oregon.[31] Other sunbelt urban histories, especially a collection of essays edited by Richard M. Bernard and Bradley R. Rice, *Sunbelt Cities* (1983), demonstrated the incredible variety in the demographic, cultural, economic, and political patterns in the urban sunbelt. Urban historians drew similar conclusions in two other sunbelt anthologies that challenged the utility of sunbelt conceptualization: Raymond A. Mohl, ed., *Searching for the Sunbelt* (1990); and Randall M. Miller and George E. Pozzetta, eds., *Shades of the Sunbelt* (1988).[32]

Urban historians working within the regionalist framework produced some strongly argued books, such as those by Wade, Goldfield, Cronon, and Abbott. But for whatever reason, this sort of urban historical research has languished over the past decade, as historians of the American city have moved off in many different directions.[33]

SUBURBANIZATION

Reflecting the fact that more Americans now live in the extensive metropolitan areas surrounding big cities than in the urban cores and rural areas combined, historians in recent years have devoted increasing attention to suburban history. Sam Warner initiated this sort of study nearly fifty years ago in *Streetcar Suburbs* (1962), but few followed his lead at the time. The subject has been revitalized since the mid-1980s by the publication of a number of books and articles, most importantly Kenneth T. Jackson's synthesis of two centuries of suburbanization, *Crabgrass Frontier: The Suburbanization of the United States* (1985). Beginning with the preindustrial "walking city" of the eighteenth and early nineteenth centuries, Jackson described a residential pattern altered by transit innovations and the romantic allure of suburbia. He likewise emphasized the political dimension to suburbanization, as cities sought in the late nineteenth century to recapture population through the annexation of adjacent municipalities. For the twentieth century, Jackson focused on the impact of the automobile and the role of the federal policy affecting cities. Government highway construction, federal housing programs, and federal mortgage and tax policies propelled the suburban drift of population and economic activities. Although Jackson's study has been widely acclaimed as the most thorough and sophisticated account of these subjects, some critics have suggested that he has overemphasized the federal role in metropolitan decentralization while ignoring important racial and class dimensions of widespread suburban growth.[34]

Jackson's *Crabgrass Frontier* was accompanied by a number of studies of specific suburbs and suburbanization. Henry C. Binford's *The First Suburbs: Residential Communities on the Boston Periphery, 1815–1860* (1985) pushed suburbanization back well before the development of mass transit in the mid-nineteenth century. Binford's study of Cambridge and Somerville saw the suburbanization process stemming from a variety of fringe economic activities, an emerging sense of middle-class domesticity, and the rise of new commuter patterns.[35] In *Borderland: Origins of the American Suburb, 1820–1939* (1988), landscape historian John R. Stilgoe offered a richly descriptive account of the presumed Edenic attractions of the suburban "borderlands." Distant from the cities but still within commuting range, the nineteenth-century suburban village offered an escape from the evils of the city. By the mid-twentieth century, such places increasingly were being swallowed up by a seemingly unstoppable urban sprawl.[36] In *City and Suburb* (1979), Jon C. Teaford provided the first sustained historical analysis of the politics of metropolitan deconcentration, governmental fragmentation, annexation, and consolidation. With a wealth of detail on city-suburban political conflicts from 1850 to 1970, Teaford's book opened up important new territory for urban historians.[37] Margaret Marsh's *Suburban Lives* (1990) explored the nineteenth-century merger of the suburban ideal with the new ideology of domesticity. Her book charted the changing meanings of suburban life for families and for women as the domestic ideal experienced transformation over time.[38]

Since the 1990s, suburban historians have moved off in several directions. For instance, John Archer's *Architecture and Suburbia* (2005) explored the cultural history of suburban domestic architecture, demonstrating British influences from the eighteenth-century pastoral to the early-twentieth-century Garden City movement. Robert Fogelson's *Bourgeois Nightmares* (2007) portrayed suburbia between 1870 and 1930 as racially and economically exclusive. Fogelson contended that suburban subdividers and homeowners associations, fearing unwanted neighborhood change, promoted residential restrictions, racial covenants, zoning ordinances, and aesthetic standards for suburban property and homes, hoping thereby to maintain racial and class exclusivity.[39] Not to be overlooked are studies of planned suburban communities such as Radburn, New Jersey, and Forest Park, Ohio, and of such classic suburbs as Scarsdale, New York, Chestnut Hill near Philadelphia, the Country Club District of Kansas City, the North Shore communities of Chicago, and Westchester County just north of New York City.[40] In addition, recent works have explored the activities of suburban builders, subdividers, and developers, providing new perspectives on the explosive development of the suburban fringe.[41]

Contributing to the debate among historians about the nature of suburbanization, Robert Fishman and Joel Garreau wrote provocative books that portrayed modern suburbs as perimeter cities that developed simply as the most recent stage of urbanization. Fishman's *Bourgeois Utopias* (1987) offered a quick, comparative study of Anglo-American suburbanization ranging from London in the eighteenth century to Los Angeles in the twentieth century. Fishman noted how the classic suburb represented the expression of deeply embedded middle-class values, such as homeownership, family life, communion with nature, and isolation from the urban-industrial world. But in the past half century, a still newer urban form—what Fishman called the "technoburb"—took shape, created as a consequence of the movement of industry and commerce to new "perimeter cities" on the outskirts of the old urban cores. As Fishman put it, "urban functions disperse across a decentralized landscape that is neither urban nor rural nor suburban in the traditional sense." Old residential suburbs, in short, have begun taking on many of the functions of the cities, dramatically altering their character in the process.[42]

Fishman's basic thesis has been developed at length by Garreau in *Edge City* (1991), which demonstrated the spread of multiple-nuclei urban centers distant from old downtowns. Usually growing up around shopping malls at the intersections of interstate highways, these edge cities expanded still further with the addition of hotels, industrial parks, office buildings, additional retail centers, and eventually, massive new high-rise residential housing. Regional airports often sprouted nearby, and in some cases, as in Chicago, Washington, D.C., or Miami, the edge cities grew up around airports. Most American cities have such new "outer cities," but Garreau focused on particularly pertinent examples on the edges of Washington, D.C., Atlanta, Phoenix, Boston, San Francisco, and a few other places. For Garreau, the edge city increasingly represented the dominant urban form of the future. In *Post-Suburbia: Governments and Politics in the Edge Cities* (1996), Jon C. Teaford considered the political implications of Garreau's findings for metropolitan governance. In *Sprawl: A Compact History* (2006), Robert Bruegmann delivered a ringing defense of rampant suburbanization as a fortunate alternative to the intractable problems of urban life for a growing middle class.[43]

A number of books, beginning with Scott Donaldson's *The Suburban Myth* (1969), challenged the common depiction of postwar suburbs as bland, homogeneous bedroom communities characterized by conformity and upward-striving families. More recent work has emphasized instead the economic, racial, ethnic, and class diversity of American suburbs. Moreover, these new studies portrayed varied and heterogeneous suburbs as crucial battlegrounds over race, class, and politics that have largely determined the contours of twentieth-century American history and politics. These works have emphasized the struggle for power in metropolitan regions, pitting central cities against suburbs and involving public policies made in Washington, D.C., that shaped resource allocation, tax collection, and land use. According to the practitioners of this "new suburban history," the development of metropolitan America has framed the crucial issues of the post–World War II era, including the environment, the rise of the political right, and a host of social movements. *The New Suburban History* (2006), edited by Kevin M. Kruse and Thomas J. Sugrue, provided a useful introduction to this emerging scholarship.[44]

A number of recent studies have examined the extensive African-American suburbanization largely overlooked by urban historians writing in earlier decades. Having thoroughly documented the means by which public authorities and private real estate interests systematically sought to exclude racial minorities from suburbs, scholars long perpetuated the popular image of all-white bourgeois refuges on the metropolitan periphery, thereby ascribing an exaggerated sense of racial homogeneity to the suburban landscape. Providing a useful corrective to this stereotyped picture, Andrew Wiese's *Places of Their Own: African American Suburbanization in the Twentieth Century* (2004) noted that significant numbers of blacks have been leaving inner cities for more than a century—first settling in isolated blue-collar suburbs and increasingly in respectable middle-class communities. Paying particular attention to the post–World War II decades and underscoring the importance of the civil rights movement, Wiese's influential book clearly showed how African Americans and other racial minorities played a large and increasingly vital role in American suburbanization.[45]

Historians have also linked rampant suburbanization and the growth of the sunbelt with the rise of the powerful political conservative movement of the late twentieth century. Kevin M. Kruse's *White Flight: Atlanta and the Making of Modern Conservatism* (2005) is an excellent case study of metropolitan decentralization and politics in the New South's premier city. Matthew D. Lassiter's *The Silent Majority: Suburban Politics in the Sunbelt South* (2006) analyzed the relationship between school desegregation and suburban expansion in Atlanta, Richmond, and Charlotte. The key role played by suburban California is covered in *Postsuburban California* (1991), edited by Rob Kling, Spencer Olin, and Mark Poster; Lisa McGirr's *Suburban Warriors* (2001); and *My Blue Heaven* (2002), by Becky M. Nicolaides.[46]

SPACE AND PLACE

In recent years, urban scholars have devoted considerable attention to the ways in which city residents have used civic plazas, public buildings, cemeteries, streets, parks, homes, and other physical locations for cultural, political, or other purposes. Often such spaces in cities acquired special cultural importance or evoked powerful

historical memories. Scholars also examined urban spatial arrangements from a geographical perspective, exploring the forces that stimulated spatial change across urban
landscapes, as well as the consequences of such change. Thus, various studies have
documented the importance of spatial changes in downtowns, neighborhoods, and
communities; others noted important distinctions between the uses of public and private space. Investing their studies of cities with an important spatial dimension, these
scholars have used interdisciplinary approaches to connect cultural, demographic,
architectural, and economic histories in a way that brings changing cityscapes into
clearer focus.[47]

Several significant works have used spatial analysis in reexamining important
aspects of early American history. For instance, Benjamin L. Carp's *Rebels Rising:
Cities and the American Revolution* (2009) argued that local leaders adeptly used a
variety of public spaces in major colonial cities to build the case among the populace
for insurrection against Great Britain. According to Carp, revolutionaries in five
communities along the Atlantic seaboard successfully appealed to certain audiences
through the careful appropriation of key venues. On the Boston waterfront, in New
York City taverns, among Newport congregations, in Charleston households, and in
Philadelphia's State House and Square, they skillfully proselytized among heterogeneous urban populations and mobilized resistance in the early days of the revolt before
fighting against the British moved into the countryside. Merging political, social, and
cultural history, Carp noted the central role of the cities in the years leading up to the
American Revolution and highlighted the adaptation of urban space to mold revolutionary sentiment.[48]

Studies of the importance of parades, festivals, and other ceremonial occasions
have enhanced our understanding of how urban life played a crucial role in the nation's early history. Simon P. Newman's *Parades and the Politics of the Street* (1999)
argued that participation in parades and street celebrations of national holidays in the
early Republic supported the creation of an indigenous American political culture.
Collective experiences in the cities, according to Newman, became crucial to the
development of the national two-party system that supplanted the unsettled regional
alliances of the colonial years. In a similar vein, David Waldstreicher's *In the Midst
of Perpetual Fetes* (1997) described patriotic parades, festivals, and celebrations
in the early American republic that served as unifying events channeling contested
politics into patriotism and an emerging national identity. In *Parades and Power:
Street Theater in Nineteenth-Century Philadelphia* (1986), Susan G. Davis began
with an examination of the Washington Centennial celebration of 1832, referenced
several relevant European antecedents, and discussed in detail the use of historical
commemorations, celebrations, propaganda, political demonstrations, and protests.
Her account of nineteenth-century Philadelphia underscored how the residents' use
of street theater reflected cultural norms of the time and provided an essential outlet
for public discourse. In *Civic Wars* (1998), Mary P. Ryan described how residents
of mid-nineteenth-century New Orleans, San Francisco, and New York City initially
used parades as patriotic and civic ceremonies that celebrated important holidays and
anniversaries. These elaborate celebrations changed by mid-century, Ryan noted, as
the immigrant working class increasingly predominated and merchants and skilled ar-

tisans participated less often. No longer inclusive unifying events, the parades became opportunities for ethnic groups and the working class to seek power and recognition.[49]

Thinking spatially has provided new understandings about urban growth, change, and development. Dell Upton's *Another City: Urban Life and Urban Spaces in the New American Republic* (2008) focused on efforts of urban elites to bring spatial order to the chaos of early American cities through the use of street grids, uniform architecture, "monumental structures" such as churches and public buildings, and new city spaces for emerging urban functions—all of which, Upton argued, helped to create a "republican spatial imagination." David Henkin's *City Reading: Written Words and Public Spaces in Antebellum New York* (1998) contended that street signs, commercial advertising, newspapers, bulletin boards, showbills, political broadsides, and other "urban texts" posted in key public spaces shaped public discourse. In *Invented Cities: The Creation of Landscape in Nineteenth-Century New York and Boston* (1996), Mona Domosh argued that cultural geography explained alternative trajectories of development in fast-growing New York and mostly stagnant Boston. A regular street grid, large department stores, tall business buildings, an expanding retail district, and an economically aggressive commercial elite characterized New York City, while Boston retained a preindustrial form, an irregular street pattern, a small retail center, a large central open space, and a local elite dedicated to stability and control. Lisa Keller's *Triumph of Order* (2009) compared public spaces in nineteenth-century New York and London that served to promote and regulate democracy by providing acceptable outlets for public discourse. Robin F. Bachin's *Building the South Side: Urban Space and Civic Culture in Chicago, 1890–1919* (2004) looked at a number of public spaces on Chicago's South Side—Comiskey Park, the Black Belt, and the University of Chicago, for example—to illustrate how community leaders in the Progressive Era used physical design principles to mold civic culture. Peter C. Baldwin's *Domesticating the Street: The Reform of Public Space in Hartford* (1999) examined the process by which the homogeneous streets of a nineteenth-century Yankee city changed into contested spaces populated by immigrants and natives, prostitutes and newsboys, ethnic leaders and middle-class reformers. Blanche Linden-Ward's *Silent City on a Hill* (1989, 2007) recounted the creation of Boston's Mount Auburn Cemetery in the 1830s, an urban space that evoked family memories for some but served as an early park and pleasure ground for many others. Books by Setha Low, William David Estrada, and Lydia R. Otero focused on civic plazas as important public spaces invested with cultural memory and meaning.[50]

Scholars interested in twentieth-century urban landscapes have noted the changes in residential and commercial districts that have accompanied metropolitan decentralization. Alison Isenberg's *Downtown America* (2004) explained the commercial decline of central business districts less as the inevitable product of remote market forces than as the outcome of economic and policy decisions made by property owners, developers, government officials, planners, architects, and assorted interest groups. Using a variety of visual sources, Isenberg paid particular attention to race and gender while looking at the main commercial avenues in a host of communities of different sizes throughout the nation. Larry Bennett's *Fragments of Cities* (1990) explained the downtown renaissance of the late twentieth century in terms of the segmentation of urban space with a variety of consequences for public life in the neighborhoods, most of which undermined the capacity of cities to provide good environments for the majority of their residents. *Fortress America* (1997), by Edward J. Blakely and Mary Gail Snyder, and Setha Low's *Behind the Gates* (2003) discussed the increasing popularity of gated communities in metropolitan America as a means by which affluent populations could separate themselves from the urban masses. In *Defensible Space: Crime Prevention through Urban Design* (1973), Oscar Newman explained how careful design could enhance safety in urban locations by maximizing the number of eyes trained on streets and making public spaces less isolated. Essays in *Inventing Times Square*, edited by William R. Taylor, described the cultural significance and economic development of the famed New York City district.[51]

Many recent studies have analyzed the spatial configurations of American cities in the last decades of the twentieth century. Sharon Zukin's *Landscapes of Power* (1991) demonstrated that concentrations of political and economic power shaped the landscapes of leading U.S. cities, citing as key examples the Ford industrial complex in Detroit and Disney World in Orlando. Zukin's *Naked City: The Death and Life of Authentic Urban Places* (2009) lamented the decline of authenticity in several New York City neighborhoods, decades after Jane Jacobs's impassioned plea for the preservation of such places. In *Variations on a Theme Park* (1992), edited by Michael Sorkin, eight authors (architects, architectural critics, and other academics) attributed the deepening urban malaise in the United States to the wholesale devaluation of public space by ravenous developers and public officials. According to many of the volume's contributors, elites responsible for the construction of megamalls, historical re-creations, and gentrification ignored the commonweal and consigned the poor to the margins of American urban life. Mike Davis's provocative *City of Quartz* (1990) painted a bleak picture of a postindustrial landscape in Los Angeles created by a grasping plutocracy that encouraged automobility without regard for the human and environmental consequences. As an optimistic counterpoint to Davis's declension narrative, Dolores Hayden's *The Power of Place* (1995) hailed the use of historic preservation and public art in Los Angeles as means of creating a vernacular urban landscape. Hayden documented the successes of the Power of Place, a nonprofit organization founded in downtown Los Angeles that enlisted historians, artists, planners, designers, and lay volunteers in an effort to enhance the livability of the postmodern city denounced by Davis and other critics.[52]

Spatial analysis derived from a geographical perspective has also informed recent scholarship on space and place in the American city. The literature on one powerful spatial shift—suburbanization—has already been addressed in an earlier section of this essay. Urban histories focused on racial and ethnic changes in city neighborhoods represented another form of urban spatial change. For instance, Arnold R. Hirsch's *Making the Second Ghetto* (1983) focused on the racial turnover of postwar Chicago neighborhoods from white to black. W. Edward Orser's *Blockbusting in Baltimore* (1994) and Amanda I. Seligman's *Block by Block* (2005), on Chicago, also interpreted racial change in spatial terms. All three books found the impetus for such spatial change in public housing policies, instigation by real estate interests, and overcrowding in hemmed-in black neighborhoods. In *Red Lines, Black Spaces*

(2001), Bruce D. Haynes recounted the origins and evolution of a black middle-class suburb in Yonkers, New York. Articles by Raymond A. Mohl and Ronald H. Bayor demonstrated the impact of postwar highway and expressway construction that destroyed housing, triggered neighborhood racial change, and served as barriers separating racial communities. Essays in Daniel D. Arreola's edited collection, *Hispanic Spaces, Latino Places* (2004), elucidated the dramatic growth of an urban Latino population in formerly black and white neighborhoods in places ranging from Las Vegas and San Francisco to Kansas City, Cleveland, and Washington, D.C.[53] Two significant and deeply researched books on Saint Louis—Colin Gordon's *Mapping Decline* (2008) and Eric Sandweiss's *St. Louis* (2001)—provided fine-grained spatial analysis of the city's neighborhoods, housing decline, and racial change over time. Saint Louis has been in decline, but some cities have experienced the redevelopment and gentrification of older neighborhoods. Alexander von Hoffman's optimistic *House by House, Block by Block* (2003) explored the role of new immigrants, housing activists, and community associations in initiating an urban renaissance in the 1990s by preserving and revitalizing aging inner-city communities. Books on gentrification by Neil Smith, Lance Freeman, Derek S. Hyra, and Suleiman Osman offered a good introduction to a large literature.[54] As the foregoing discussion suggests, studies of space and place have assumed an important place in urban historiography.

URBAN ENVIRONMENTAL HISTORY

Over the past few decades, American urban historians have become more conscious of the links between their subfield and an emerging environmental history field.[55] Most historians trace the origins of modern environmentalism to the conservation movement of the Progressive Era, with its concern for preserving nature, safeguarding public lands and forests, and using natural resources efficiently.[56] However, a few historians discovered the beginnings of an urban environmental consciousness in the epidemics of yellow fever and cholera that ravaged American cities beginning in the late eighteenth century. Charles E. Rosenberg, neither an urban nor an environmental historian, published a key early book, *The Cholera Years* (1962, 1987), that illuminated the connections between disease and the urban environment. A specialist in medical history, Rosenberg explored the impact of three nineteenth-century cholera epidemics, primarily in New York City. He demonstrated that in an era prior to the discovery of the bacteriological origins of disease, medical and public health officials recognized that inadequate disposal of human waste, slum housing, and tainted drinking water had something to do with the spread of disease, and thus urged sanitary reforms that cleaned up the urban environment. Other historians of urban public health, especially the medical historian John Duffy, also contributed to an early scholarly literature on urban epidemics and sanitary reform.[57] In a similar vein, Stuart Galishoff contributed two books on sanitary reform and public health in Newark. Barbara G. Rosenkrantz's *Public Health and the State* (1972) and Judith L. Leavitt's *The Healthiest City* (1982) documented sanitary reforms before and after 1900 in urban Massachusetts and Milwaukee, respectively. These works suggest that environmentalism—as opposed to conservation—was an urban movement from very early in American history.[58]

Historians of the Progressive Era have long recognized that the urban reformers of the period between 1890 and 1920 sought to clean up and reshape the urban environment, in the broadest sense. That is, they wanted to eliminate slum housing, improve working and living conditions, and address issues of poverty, unemployment, public health, disease, and social disorder. Robert Bremner's important book *From the Depths* (1956) presented an early argument for the environmental thinking of progressive reformers.[59]

More recent historians have elaborated on these issues. Martin V. Melosi's edited collection *Pollution and Reform in American Cities* (1980) initiated the new urban environmental history. The scholarly essays in Melosi's book dealt with urban water supply, waste disposal, smoke pollution, garbage disposal, noise pollution, and household sanitation practices. Melosi followed up with several other environmental studies, including *Garbage in the Cities* (1981) and *Coping with Abundance* (1985), an analysis of energy usage and the environment. In *The Sanitary City* (2000), Melosi presented one of the most wide-ranging studies of urban environmental history. Moving from the colonial era to the present, the book focused on the ever-advancing infrastructure of urban environmental reform, especially for water supply, sewage systems, and garbage disposal. These varied works established Melosi as a key interpreter of urban environmental history.[60]

Three other urban environmental historians have also helped shape this new research field since the 1970s. Joel A. Tarr has published dozens of research articles on specific aspects of urban environmental history, many collected in his important book *The Search for the Ultimate Sink* (1996). These pieces dealt with urban air, land, and water pollution; wastewater and sewer technologies; smoke control regulation; industrial wastes; and environmental policy. Tarr coedited *Technology and the Rise of the Networked City in Europe and America* (1988), which demonstrated the overlapping interests of historians of cities, technology, and the environment. *The Horse and the City* (2007), by Clay McShane and Joel A. Tarr, provided insight into the negative environmental consequences of thousands of large animals in nineteenth-century American cities, as well as the improvements that accompanied the replacement of horse-drawn transit vehicles by electric streetcars.[61] Samuel P. Hays, a pioneer in urban environmental history, was one of the first scholars to document the shift from an earlier history of conservation to a modern environmental history stemming from the rise of urban and suburban society, the harmful effects of various forms of urban pollution, and a shifting urban political culture that valued healthy ecosystems. Hays published important books and articles on twentieth-century environmental policy and politics, including *Beauty, Health, and Permanence* (1987), *Explorations in Environmental History* (1998), and *A History of Environmental Politics since 1945* (2000).[62] William Cronon's *Nature's Metropolis* (1991), discussed earlier, made a powerful argument for the importance of environmental history for urban historians. Cronon's study of nineteenth-century Chicago and its economic and ecological relationships with rural regions, from forested Michigan to the plains of the Great West, provided an early example of capitalist exploitation of the natural environment.[63] Taken together, the work of Melosi, Tarr, Hays, and Cronon launched urban historical research in new and exciting directions.

Since the 1990s, a second generation of urban environmental historians has produced a substantial monographic literature on urban pollution and environmental reform. For example, Andrew Hurley published *Environmental Inequalities* (1995), a sophisticated piece of research that documented persistent patterns of air, water, and industrial waste pollution generated by the steel industry in Gary, Indiana, throughout the twentieth century. However, differential environmental consequences based on class, racial, and residential patterns prevented any cohesive community opposition, and the U.S. Steel Corporation staved off effective regulation for decades. David Stradling's *Smokestacks and Progressives* (1999) analyzed the "smoke problem" of coal-based industrial cities, as well as the debate among activists and engineers involved in an early environmental movement. Adam Rome's *The Bulldozer in the Countryside* (2001) linked the rise of American environmentalism to the postwar suburban sprawl and its many negative consequences: septic tank effluvia, the decimation of landscapes, the failure of solar energy, the disappearance of open space, damage to water supplies, disappearing wildlife habitats, and soil erosion. In *Concrete and Clay* (2002), an environmental study of New York City, Matthew Gandy explored the transformation of nature into engineered landscapes. Gandy focused on the development of the city's water supply system, the creation of Frederick Law Olmsted's Central Park, and the building of Robert Moses's parkways and expressways, as well as the emergence of an environmental justice movement and an ongoing crisis in disposing of New York's garbage.[64] Robert D. Bullard's *Dumping in Dixie* (1990, 2000) opened up the discussion of environmental justice, now the subject of an extensive literature.[65]

The second generation of environmental historians also contributed several important books on the environmental history of New Orleans, Los Angeles, and Saint Petersburg, Florida. For example, Ari Kelman's *A River and Its City* (2003) and Craig E. Colton's *An Unnatural Metropolis* (2005) both considered how natural landscapes, especially the Mississippi River, shaped the development of New Orleans. In *Smogtown* (2008), Chip Jacobs and William J. Kelly documented the long and frustrating battle against smog in Los Angeles, the city of freeways and gas guzzlers. Also on metropolitan Los Angeles, Mike Davis's *Ecology of Fear* (1998) blamed developers for ignoring the region's natural limitations, as they built housing subdivisions on earthquake faults, mountainsides, and desert landscapes. Natural disasters often followed: devastating earthquakes, flash floods, mudslides, wildfires, water shortages, carnivorous "neighbors" in distant suburbs, even killer bees. Jared Orsi's *Hazardous Metropolis* (2004) echoed Davis as he focused on ineffective river management, regular flooding, and the slow emergence of environmental consciousness in Los Angeles. R. Bruce Stephenson's *Visions of Eden* (1997) emphasized the failures of early urban planning in Saint Petersburg, Florida, with severe ecological consequences, until the implementation of new, environmentally friendly plans in the 1970s that emphasized growth management and restored natural landscapes.[66]

Recent interest in the field led to several important case studies of urban environmental history. Matthew Klingle's *Emerald City* (2007) presented a complex analysis of Seattle's environmental history—a history shaped by development that reorganized landscapes, engineering that tamed nature for urban progress, policies that damaged waterfronts and watersheds and native salmon, and community conflicts over nature, space, and power. Harold L. Platt's *Shock Cities* (2005) contributed a comparative environmental history of Chicago and Manchester, England, during the industrial age. Platt demonstrated how economic elites in both cities reshaped urban space for their own needs and consigned the urban poor to slum housing, but also how community activists and public health reformers seeking environmental justice challenged those with power in the political arena.[67] The University of Pittsburgh Press has published a series of books on the environmental history of individual cities. These include Char Miller's *On the Border* (2001), a study of San Antonio; Joel A. Tarr's *Devastation and Renewal* (2005), a study of Pittsburgh; William Deverell and Greg Hise's *Land of Sunshine* (2005), a study of Los Angeles; Michael F. Logan's *Desert Cities* (2006), a study of Phoenix and Tucson; Martin V. Melosi and Joseph A. Pratt's *Energy Metropolis* (2007), a study of Houston; Anthony N. Penna and Conrad E. Wright's *Remaking Boston* (2009); and Jeffrey Craig Sanders's *Seattle and the Roots of Urban Sustainability* (2010).[68] Similarly, Andrew Hurley edited *Common Fields* (1997), an environmental history of Saint Louis; Kathleen A. Brosnan wrote *Uniting Mountain and Plain* (2002), an environmental history of Denver and nearby Pueblo and Colorado Springs; Richard A. Walker's *The Country in the City* (2008) and Philip J. Dreyfus's *Our Better Nature* (2009) both analyzed the environmental history of San Francisco and the Bay Area; Michael Rawson's *Eden on the Charles* (2010) linked Boston's urban growth with the city's ecological history; and Scott W. Swearingen's *Environmental City* (2010) recounted the rise of an environmental movement in Austin. Char Miller's edited collection, *Cities and Nature in the American West* (2010), gathered environmental essays on Seattle, Portland, San Jose, New Orleans, and Los Angeles, among other topics. Taken together, these case studies—virtually all published within the last decade and a half—have reworked traditional urban narratives in ways that demand the attention of urban historians.[69]

The growth of American cities and suburbs altered nature dramatically. However, a few books have documented ways in which urban residents historically sought to remain connected with natural environments. In *Back to Nature* (1969), Peter J. Schmitt contended that the "back to nature" movement of the early twentieth century—involving summer vacations and summer camps, bird watching, Campfire Girls and Boy Scouts, wilderness novels and movies, and the like—represented an effort to reinvigorate city life. David Stradling's *Making Mountains* (2007) argued the importance of the Catskill Mountains for urban New Yorkers. Hudson River School artists of the nineteenth century created ideal landscapes that shaped city people's understandings of nature, eventually turning the Catskill region into a major vacation resort. In the renderings of Schmitt and Stradling, city and country environments remained deeply interconnected.[70]

TECHNOLOGY, TRANSPORTATION, AND INFRASTRUCTURE

From the nineteenth century, technological innovation has been one of the main stimulants to urban growth and change. Railroads and new transit technologies linked far-flung cities and promoted spatial demographic shifts within cities; new or improved municipal utilities and services made urban life safer and more convenient; dramatic advances in communications telescoped time and space, contributing to the modernization of urban life; and new engineering and building technologies permitted the construction of skyscrapers, bridges, tunnels, airports, and other important infrastructure. After the 1830s, railroads revolutionized transportation patterns in the United States, a subject documented in two classic histories: George Rogers Taylor's *The Transportation Revolution, 1815–1860* (1951) and Edward C. Kirkland's *Men, Cities, and Transportation* (1948). Subsequent case studies of Kansas City, New Orleans, Louisville, and Chicago demonstrated the varied ways in which railroad promotion facilitated land speculation, urban growth, rivalries among cities, and urban economic control of vast hinterlands. John R. Stilgoe's *Metropolitan Corridor* (1983) traced the impact of the coming of the railroads on urban and rural landscapes.[71]

A number of important books elaborated on the significance of transit innovations beginning in the mid-nineteenth century—the horsecar in the 1850s, the electric streetcar in the 1890s, and subways in the largest east coast cities in the early twentieth century. Sam Warner paved the way on this topic with his *Streetcar Suburbs* (1962), a study of the impact of urban transit on the development of three inner suburbs in late-nineteenth-century Boston. In separate books, Clay McShane and Joel A. Tarr contributed concise analyses of the connections between urban transit and suburban growth in Milwaukee and Pittsburgh. Charles W. Cheape's *Moving the Masses* (1980) provided an excellent analysis of the financial, political, and technological context of new city transit systems in Boston, New York, and Philadelphia. John Franch's *Robber Baron* (2006) discussed the work of Charles Tyson Yerkes, the business tycoon who developed Chicago's mass transit system. Clifton Hood's *722 Miles* (1993) and Peter Derrick's *Tunneling to the Future* (2001) demonstrated the ways in which the construction of the world's largest subway system transformed New York City in the early twentieth century. Zachary M. Schrag's *The Great Society Subway* (2008) documented the complex history of the Washington, D.C., subway system, initiated during the administration of President Lyndon B. Johnson.[72]

The electric streetcar was the technological innovation of the late nineteenth century that most stimulated the physical growth of the American city. In the twentieth century, the automobile served that function. In *From Streetcar to Superhighway* (1981), Mark S. Foster studied the role of city planners involved with urban transportation between 1900 and 1940 and attributed the decline of mass transit to the perceived flexibility and economy of the automobile. Case studies of Chicago by Paul Barrett, of Atlanta by Howard L. Preston, and of Los Angeles by Scott L. Bottles also detailed the decline of the electric streetcar systems and the rise of the automobile after 1900. In *Mass Motorization and Mass Transit* (2008), David W. Jones provided a detailed history of the rise and decline of transit and the subsequent emergence of "pervasive motorization."[73] Clay McShane's *Down the Asphalt Path* (1994) analyzed the introduction of the automobile in urban life, contending that an emerging culture of consumption valued cars as symbols of status and liberation. In *Fighting Traffic* (2008), Peter D. Norton outlined the early-twentieth-century contest for control of the streets between cars and older uses by street railways, pedestrians, and even children playing games; the automobile, Norton argued, required a "social reconstruction of the city street." Jeremiah B. C. Axelrod's *Inventing Autopia* (2009) explored the multifaceted impact of the automobile on the early-twentieth-century development of metropolitan Los Angeles. Automobiles and highways also featured in important ways in Robert M. Fogelson's important study of early Los Angeles, *The Fragmented Metropolis* (1967), and in his more recent book *Downtown* (2001). Tom McCarthy's *Auto Mania* (2007) detailed the links between automobiles, the consumer society, and the environmental consequences of automobility. Brian Ladd's *Autophobia* (2008) explored the complex relationship of Americans with their cars. These last two books, despite their contrasting titles, were not all that different in their interpretive arguments about America's powerful automobile culture.[74] *The Best Transportation System in the World* (2006), coauthored by Mark H. Rose, Bruce E. Seely, and Paul F. Barrett, focused on railroads, trucking, and aviation and offered an important overview of twentieth-century transportation policy.[75]

Technology revolutionized not only urban transit and highway transportation, but also many other types of urban systems. Essays in *Technology and the Rise of the Networked City in Europe and America* (1988), edited by Joel A. Tarr and Gabriel Dupuy, explored varied dimensions of urban infrastructure (sewers, water lines, transit, power and energy, and communication systems), particularly the speed at which these new systems became available in the late nineteenth century and the impact of such innovations on the modernizing city.[76] Books by Joel A. Tarr and Martin V. Melosi have provided detailed overviews of new technological and public health breakthroughs in urban sewer, sanitation, and water systems. Other historians have recounted the evolution of water supply systems in New York City, Boston, Chicago, Milwaukee, Oakland, and Los Angeles.[77] The dramatic impact of electricity on American urban life has been documented in Harold L. Platt's *The Electric City* (1991), David E. Nye's *Electrifying America* (1990), and John A. Jakle's *City Lights* (2001). Mark H. Rose's *Cities of Light and Heat* (1995) offered an innovative analysis of the domestication of gas and electricity in Kansas City and Denver.[78] New industrial-era communications systems such as the telegraph and the telephone had a powerful and shaping impact on nineteenth-century cities, especially business and industry, as suggested in studies by Joel A. Tarr, Edwin Gabler, Gregory J. Downey, Claude S. Fischer, and most recently, by Richard R. John.[79]

Engineering advances and new technologies contributed immeasurably to the development of new urban infrastructure, utility systems, and modern urban services. For example, Eugene P. Moehring's *Public Works and the Pattern of Urban Real Estate Growth in Manhattan, 1853–1894* (1981) traced the impact of publicly funded improvements in New York City, including water supply and sewers, as well as docks, streets, schools, hospitals, parks, and bridges. Several works have recounted the history and significance of one of those bridges, the famous Brooklyn Bridge completed in 1883 that linked Manhattan and its first suburb.[80] Harold L. Platt's *City Building in the New South* (1983) documented the Gilded Age transformation of urban services in Houston, as modern infrastructure and utility systems became a normal function of city government. By 1900, according to Jon C. Teaford's *The Unheralded Triumph* (1984), technological and engineering advances had become institutionalized throughout much of urban America. The New Deal period of the 1930s witnessed an enormous expansion in the construction of public works and other infrastructure, much of which was built in cities, as discussed in Jason Scott Smith's *Building New Deal Liberalism* (2009).[81]

The coming of the automobile created demands for long-distance paved highways, a subject treated in great detail in Bruce E. Seely's *Building the American Highway System* (1987). Michael Fein's *Paving the Way* (2008) examined the pattern of road building in New York State between 1880 and 1956, as well as the rising importance of highway engineers and their expertise in planning and building highway networks. Of course, the interstate highway system initiated in 1956 has reshaped late-twentieth-century metropolitan America, as urban expressways cut through central city neighborhoods and dislocated hundreds of thousands of residents, while at the same time stimulating a vast and continuous suburban expansion. Mark H. Rose's *Interstate* (1979, 1990), explored the congressional politics that produced the interstates, while several articles on the interstates and the cities by Raymond A. Mohl demonstrated the social consequences of road building and the local opposition movements to elevated expressways that penetrated and damaged local communities. Using three case studies, Owen D. Gutfreund's *Twentieth-Century Sprawl* (2004) noted the powerful role of highway infrastructure in undergirding metropolitan sprawl.[82]

Technology and innovation facilitated important advances in the built environment of the modernizing city. New sources of energy and new building technologies—electricity and steel-frame construction—ended the era of the low-rise city and permitted the rapid spread of skyscrapers with elevator access. New York and Chicago led the way, as demonstrated in Carol Willis's *Form Follows Finance* (1995), Carl W. Condit's *The Rise of the Skyscraper* (1952), and Paul Goldberger's *The Skyscraper* (1981). More recent books by Daniel Bluestone, Pauline A. Saliga, and Joanna Merwood-Salisbury on Chicago and by Sarah Bradford Landau and Carl L. Condit, John Tauranac, Mark Kingwell, Eric Darton, Gail Fenske, and Benjamin Flowers on New York City have reprised skyscraper historiography. *The American Skyscraper* (2005), edited by Roberta Moudry, gathered a group of important scholarly skyscraper essays, primarily on Chicago and New York.[83]

Like the skyscraper, the central-city railroad terminal became an important physical symbol of urban growth and achievement in the Gilded Age and Progressive Era. Encouraged by city leaders, railroad companies built opulent terminals in cities across the nation—structures that served as urban gateways for millions of travelers and visitors. Many of these rail stations have since been demolished, but books by Carl Condit, Kurt Schlicting, and Jill Jonnes documented the histories of rail terminals in Cincinnati and New York City.[84] Twentieth-century technological advances also introduced aviation and air conditioning, two innovations that had shaping impacts on urban development. Early studies opening up these subjects include Janet Bednarek's *America's Airports: Airfield Development, 1918–1947* (2001), Gail Cooper's *Air Conditioning America* (2002), and Marsha E. Ackerman's *Cool Comfort* (2002).[85] The invention of the camera in the mid-nineteenth century has provided twenty-first-century scholars with an important photographic record of the city and the built environment through time. Peter Bacon Hales's *Silver Cities* (1984; rev. ed. 2006),

Thomas Campanella's *Cities from the Sky* (2001), and Eric Gordon's *The Urban Spectator* (2010) supplied powerful visual evidence of the American urban tradition.[86] The central achievement of all the studies noted above has been to demonstrate the significant role of new technological innovations and networked systems in stimulating urban growth and change—a point made in several important historiographical surveys of the literature.[87]

PLANNING

Technology is related closely to the ways in which Americans planned and built their cities. Technological innovations established the parameters of what was possible and feasible in the built environment, although politics usually determined what actually was accomplished. Studies of planning history published in the 1960s and 1970s focused inordinately on the nineteenth-century roots of urban planning. These works emphasized the landscape architecture tradition, in which Frederick Law Olmsted played such a major role, and the emergence of the City Beautiful Movement under the leadership of such Chicago figures as architect and planner Daniel Burnham and architect Louis Sullivan.[88] These nineteenth-century traditions—and Olmsted's work especially—continue to attract scholarly interest. Olmsted's latest biographer, Witold Rybczynski, author of *A Clearing in the Distance* (1999), has written a fascinating account of the multitalented and visionary landscape architect who designed and supervised the building of New York City's magnificent Central Park.[89]

Beginning in the last decades of the twentieth century, most scholars abandoned the "great planner" tradition and presented more comprehensive analyses of planning history that discussed the implementation of zoning policies, urban transit, highway building, public utilities, and central city development and redevelopment, in addition to city plans and urban parks. The wide-ranging collection of essays in *Planning the Twentieth-Century American City* (1996), edited by Mary Corbin Sies and Christopher Silver, analyzed a variety of issues and influences in large and small metropolitan areas to explain the development of the twentieth-century built environment; the volume's introduction provided an especially useful overview of the history of planning history. The essays in *The American Planning Tradition* (2000), edited by Robert Fishman, are similarly eclectic in their approach to planning history, both at the national and local levels.[90] Jon A. Peterson's *The Birth of City Planning in the United States, 1840–1917* (2003) offered a balanced overview that fit comfortably between Mel Scott's celebratory *American City Planning since 1890* (1969) and M. Christine Boyer's highly critical *Dreaming the Rational City* (1983). While giving full attention to nineteenth-century developments, Peterson's highly readable volume concentrated on the critical planning breakthroughs of the Progressive Era.[91]

Several specialized studies have also attempted to place urban planning in a broad political and social context. William H. Wilson's *The City Beautiful Movement* (1989) presented the most detailed study of the turn-of-the-twentieth-century campaign to beautify urban America. Wilson's case studies of Kansas City, Seattle, Denver, and Dallas shifted the focus away from the heavily studied eastern cities. Planning activity in these cities demonstrated that the City Beautiful Movement depended on wide pop- ular support and that it had appeal throughout the United States. Stanley K. Schultz's *Constructing Urban Culture* (1989) linked city planning with new technological in- novations that made the modernizing city possible. In *The Mysteries of the Great City* (1993), a study of New York, Chicago, and Cincinnati, John D. Fairfield emphasized the connections between urban political power and new patterns of urban design. In separate books, Mansell Blackford and Greg Hise challenged the idea that the rapid growth of the Los Angeles metropolitan area stemmed from chaotic and unplanned sprawl; rather, they documented the systematic work of planners, community builders, and industrialists in creating the first spread-out automobile city. Pierre Clavel's *The Progressive City* (1986) recounted the emergence between 1969 and 1984 of partici- patory planning in cities ranging from Hartford and Cleveland to Berkeley and Santa Monica. Howard Gillette Jr.'s *Civitas by Design* (2010) surveyed urban planning from the Progressive Era to the New Urbanism.[92]

Other studies have also framed planning decisions and outcomes more broadly. In *The Urban Idea in Colonial America* (1977), Sylvia D. Fries demonstrated how contemporary conceptions of cities shaped the early planning of Boston, New Haven, Philadelphia, Savannah, and Williamsburg. Case studies that also located urban plan- ning within a political and social context included June Manning Thomas on Detroit, Howard Gillette Jr. on Washington, D.C., Judd Kahn on San Francisco, Christopher Silver on Richmond, Lawrence W. Kennedy on Boston, Robert A. Catlin on Gary, Carl Abbott on Portland, John F. Bauman and Edward K. Muller on Pittsburgh, Zane L. Miller and Bruce Tucker on Cincinnati, Charles E. Connerly on Birmingham, and R. Bruce Stephenson on Saint Petersburg, Florida.[93]

Disastrous urban fires prompted urban citizens to plan and rebuild. Christine M. Rosen's significant book *The Limits of Power* (1986) compared planned and un- planned rebuilding efforts after great fires in Chicago, Boston, and Baltimore. These destructive events provided opportunities for rational redevelopment, but Rosen found powerful barriers to effective planning, including competing power groups, political corruption, and the complexity of real estate markets. Ross Miller, Karen Sawislak, and Carl Smith published works on the rebuilding of Chicago after the great fire of 1871; Sawislak echoed Rosen on divisive responses, while Miller and Smith focused on architectural issues and Smith on the "urban disorder" that resulted from the fire.[94]

A number of scholars have examined attempts to construct planned communities in the United States as alternatives to troubled industrial cities. In *Building the Working- man's Paradise* (1995), Margaret Crawford documented the planning and design of company towns from Massachusetts to New Mexico. Stanley Buder's *Pullman* (1967) and James Gilbert's *Perfect Cities* (1991) chronicled the failed attempt of industrial- ist George M. Pullman to build a utopian community south of Chicago.[95] Buder's *Visionaries and Planners* (1990) presented a comparative study of the Garden City Movement in Great Britain and the United States, suggesting as well the continuing influence of such planning ideals in the contemporary "new towns" on both sides of the Atlantic. Carol A. Christensen in *The American Garden City and the New Towns Movement* (1986) made a similar connection between the garden cities of the Progres- sive Era and the new towns of the late twentieth century. Daniel Schaffer's *Garden*

Cities for America (1982) examined the role of the Regional Planning Association of America (RPAA) in building Radburn, a garden city in northern New Jersey, on the eve of the Great Depression. Roy Lubove's *Community Planning in the 1920s* (1963) and Edward K. Spann's *Designing Modern America* (1996) discussed the intellectual influences that shaped the work of the RPAA. Michael Simpson's *Thomas Adams and the Modern Planning Movement* (1985) analyzed the work of a trans-Atlantic planner centrally involved in the Regional Plan of New York in the 1920s and 1930s. The New Deal's planned communities are described in Joseph Arnold's *The New Deal in the Suburbs* (1971), Paul K. Conkin's *Tomorrow a New World* (1959), and Cathy Knepper's *Greenbelt, Maryland* (2001). Patrick D. Reagan's *Designing a New America* (1999) provides considerable attention to city and regional planning in the New Deal era.[96]

The postwar era was notable for large, mass-produced, mass-marketed, planned residential communities such as New York's Levittown. However, according to Marc A. Weiss's *The Rise of the Community Builders* (1987), this pattern of large-scale home building actually began in the Los Angeles area early in the twentieth century. These early community builders incorporated important planning principles in their residential subdivisions and sought the support of local planning commissions to regulate land uses to protect property values. In *Planning for the Private Interest* (1994), Patricia Burgess analyzed the differential impacts of private and public land use controls (private residential covenants vs. public zoning ordinances) in Columbus, Ohio, between 1900 and 1970. William S. Worley's *J. C. Nichols and the Shaping of Kansas City* (1990) documented the work of an early-twentieth-century builder who planned and developed Kansas City's exclusive Country Club District between 1910 and 1940.[97]

Large-scale community building intensified after World War II, as developers sought to satisfy the pent-up demand for new housing. Barbara M. Kelly's *Expanding the American Dream* (1993) described the planning, design, construction, and marketing of the first Levittown just east of New York City on Long Island, an enormous undertaking that built 17,500 homes between 1946 and 1951. Rosalyn Baxandall and Elizabeth Ewen's *Picture Windows* (2000) and David Kushner's *Levittown* (2009) filled in additional details regarding the politics of the private housing market and black exclusion from Levittown homes. In *The Levittowners* (1967), sociologist Herbert J. Gans reported on his role as a participant observer living in Levittown, New Jersey, for two years. Dianne Harris's edited collection of essays on Levittown, Pennsylvania, *Second Suburb* (2010), included discussions of community planning. In *The Merchant Builders* (1982), Ned Eichler reflected on his experience as a developer of planned residential communities in postwar California. Gregory C. Randall's *America's Original GI Town* (2000) explored the history of Park Forest, Illinois, a planned postwar residential community in the Chicago suburbs. William H. Wilson's *Hamilton Park* (1998) traced the history of a planned black subdivision in the Dallas area, initially built to accommodate middle-class blacks who might otherwise have sought housing in white neighborhoods.[98] In the 1960s and 1970s, "new town" community development revitalized the planning profession. Nicholas Dagen Bloom's *Suburban Alchemy* (2001) provided a broad overview of the new towns movement of

New Perspectives on American Urban History

the period. Individual studies of new towns include George T. Morgan Jr. and John O. King's *The Woodlands* (1987) and Frederick Steiner's *The Politics of New Town Planning* (1981).[99]

The new towns movement of the 1960s and 1970s gave way in the 1990s and after to a movement for a "new urbanism." The new urbanists drew inspiration from Jane Jacobs, a key midcentury urban thinker, writer, and activist. Her powerful book *The Death and Life of Great American Cities* (1961) presented a withering critique of contemporary urban policy, planning, and architecture. Jacobs skewered urban renewal that destroyed thriving neighborhoods, elevated expressways that laid wide swaths of concrete that cut through built-up communities, and modernist architecture that imposed a sterile conformity on the nation's central cities. Instead, she argued the merits of traditional low-rise, pedestrian-friendly city neighborhoods, with their mix of residential, retail, commercial, and recreational land uses. Jacobs also believed that public transit, not the automobile and the highway, helped maintain traditional neighborhoods. The Congress for the New Urbanism, founded in 1993, sought to incorporate these principles into the design of new suburban communities, as well as in redesigned older urban neighborhoods. New urbanist architects, planners, environmentalists, and builders have argued their case in a number of books on the subject. These include Peter Calthorpe, *The Next American Metropolis* (1993); Peter Katz, *The New Urbanism* (1994); James Howard Kunstler, *Home from Nowhere* (1996); John O. Norquist, *The Wealth of Cities* (1998); Andres Duany, Elizabeth Plater-Zyberk, and Jeff Speck, *Suburban Nation* (2000); and Emily Talen, *New Urbanism and American Planning* (2005). One such new urbanist community, Celebration, Florida, was built by the Walt Disney Corporation as a model new town of the future. Following the pattern set by Herbert Gans in *The Levittowners*, two separate participant observer books on Celebration have appeared, evaluating the first years of the new urbanist village.[100]

HOUSING

One aspect of urban planning that generally received short shrift in the United States was housing. In European nations, from the late nineteenth century, the provision of housing was linked integrally to all other facets of planning.[101] Not so in the United States, where historically housing has generally been a matter for building entrepreneurs, the real estate industry, landlords, and individual renters and home buyers. As a result, housing city people in urban America more often than not became a serious social issue. The problem began early in American history. Gary Nash's *The Urban Crucible* (1979) and Billy G. Smith's *The "Lower Sort"* (1990) described the deplorable state of housing for the working class in eighteenth-century American cities.[102] Bernard L. Herman's *Town House* (2005) provided detailed discussion of house architecture and material life in the early American city to about 1830. Donna J. Rilling's *Making Houses, Crafting Capitalism* (2001) documented the important urban role of Philadelphia's house builders in the early nineteenth century. Elizabeth Blackmar's *Manhattan for Rent, 1750–1850* (1989) emphasized the linkages between the urban housing market and the emerging capitalist economy.[103]

A number of books detailed different urban housing forms common during the nineteenth century. For example, Elizabeth Hawes and Elizabeth C. Cromley published works that addressed the new apartment construction of the late nineteenth century that altered living styles for middle-class and wealthy New Yorkers. Books by Sam Warner and Douglass Shand-Tucci examined new building styles in Boston and its streetcar suburbs. Books by Charles Lockwood, Mary Ellen Hayward, and Andrew Dolkart recounted the emergence and evolution of the popular urban row house in New York City and Baltimore.[104] The proliferation of urban tenements in the nineteenth century received attention in Jacob Riis, *How the Other Half Lives* (1890); Robert H. Bremner, *From the Depths* (1956); and Tyler Anbinder, *Five Points* (2001), a study of the notorious New York City immigrant slum neighborhood.[105] Detailed accounts of Progressive Era tenement-house reform can be found in Roy Lubove, *The Progressive and the Slums*, on New York City (1962); Thomas L. Philpott, *The Slum and the Ghetto*, on Chicago (1978); and Robert B. Fairbanks, *Making Better Citizens*, on Cincinnati (1988). Books by Ronald Lawson and Jared Day on tenant and landlord activism complicated the history of New York City tenement housing.[106]

The housing situation changed during the course of the twentieth century because of internal migration to cities, rapid suburbanization, enhanced homeownership due to federal government subsidies, and the nation's experiments with public housing. Gwendolyn Wright placed housing history in the broad context of modern urban and suburban development in *Building the Dream* (1981). Peter G. Rowe's marvelously illustrated *Modernity and Housing* (1993) emphasized the influence of modernist thinking on housing policy during the 1920s and the 1970s.[107] The various essays in John F. Bauman, Roger Biles, and Kristin M. Szylvian, *From Tenements to the Taylor Homes* (2000) provided a wide-ranging overview of federal housing policy.[108] New Deal reforms in the 1930s both underwrote metropolitan decentralization and, on a much smaller scale, initiated the building of public housing. Gail Radford's *Modern Housing for America* (1996) described the development of a two-tiered federal housing program during the New Deal era that failed to realize the hopes of reformers.[109]

A substantial literature has developed in recent decades about the ill-fated history of public housing in America. Among the best studies of public housing in particular cities are John F. Bauman, *Public Housing, Race, and Renewal*, on Philadelphia (1987); D. Bradford Hunt, *Blueprint for Disaster*, on Chicago (2009); and Don Parson, *Making a Better World* (2005), which detailed the political controversy over public housing in Los Angeles during the Cold War era. A. Scott Henderson's *Housing and the Democratic Ideal* (2000) recounted the life and important work of housing policy expert and reform advocate Charles Abrams from the New Deal era through the 1960s.[110] In *Public Housing That Worked* (2008), Nicholas Dagen Bloom argued that effective management, careful tenant selection, and regular maintenance explained the success of public housing in New York City. Several books by historians and sociologists utilized interviews and oral histories to understand the lives of public housing tenants. See, for example, William Moore Jr., *The Vertical Ghetto* (1969); Sudhir Venkatesh, *American Project* (2000); Alex Kotlowitz, *There Are No Children Here* (1991); Susan J. Popkin et al., *The Hidden War* (2000); and Rhonda Y. Williams, *The Politics of Public Housing* (2004).[111]

In many twentieth-century cities, racial conflict and violence accompanied black efforts to seek better housing. Kevin Boyle's *Arc of Justice* (2005) provided a dramatic early example of racial confrontation over housing in 1920s Detroit. David M. P. Freund's *Colored Property* (2007) critically analyzed the long history of official racial exclusivity in twentieth-century urban and suburban real estate. For the postwar period, Arnold R. Hirsch's path-breaking *Making the Second Ghetto* (1983) recounted the violent resistance met by African Americans in all-white neighborhoods as they moved out of the overcrowded initial areas of black settlement. Hirsch detailed the role played by government agencies and real estate power brokers in creating Chicago's second ghetto. Amanda I. Seligman's *Block by Block* (2005) discussed the white response to residential desegregation in Chicago, complementing Hirsch's study of racial transformation. Also focused on postwar Chicago, Beryl Satter's *Family Properties* (2009) traced the work of slumlords and speculators, as well as of community organizers and housing reformers, in reshaping Chicago's housing market for African Americans.[112]

Housing issues in the postwar era remained prominent in many other cities as well. Thomas J. Sugrue's *The Origins of the Urban Crisis* (1996) found the seeds of Detroit's urban decline in the 1940s and 1950s rather than the 1960s. Sugrue especially emphasized the role of white homeowners' associations in provoking racial conflict. Robert O. Self's *American Babylon* (2003) sensitively analyzed the black struggle for housing and white resistance to neighborhood change in post–World War II Oakland. W. Edward Orser's *Blockbusting in Baltimore* (1994) explored the conduct of the real estate industry in stimulating neighborhood racial change in a Baltimore streetcar community. Books by Stephen Grant Meyer, Gerald Gamm, Hillel Levine and Lawrence Harmon, and Antero Pietila presented detailed analyses of racially changing neighborhoods in postwar American cities. Wendell Pritchett's *Brownsville, Brooklyn* (2002) explored the role of racial and ethnic conflict in the decline of a New York City neighborhood. Walter Thabit's *How East New York Became a Ghetto* (2003) attributed the decline of another New York City community to new internal migration patterns, ruthless real estate practices, and failed government policies.[113]

Several books have discussed the struggle to preserve urban neighborhoods. Patricia Mooney Melvin's *The Organic City* (1987) examined early examples of neighborhood preservation efforts. Alexander von Hoffman's *Local Attachments* (1994) detailed the growth of a strong community culture in Boston's Jamaica Plain neighborhood until well into the twentieth century; von Hoffman's *House by House, Block by Block* (2004) offered an optimistic look at the community revitalization movement in late-twentieth-century cities.[114] The best of the housing histories go beyond the purely physical aspect of housing provision and focus on the political, social, and racial context within which housing decisions were made by governments, the housing industry, and individuals.

URBAN POLICY HISTORY

As urban history began to focus on the twentieth century, the increasingly powerful role of the federal government in urban policy making came under scrutiny. Two important books in the 1970s initiated research on this subject—Mark I. Gelfand's *A Nation of Cities: The Federal Government and Urban America, 1933–1965* (1975) and Philip J. Funigiello's *The Challenge to Urban Liberalism: Federal-City Relations during World War II* (1978). These volumes demonstrated the hesitant effort of the federal government to grapple with urban issues during the economic disaster of the 1930s and the wartime emergency of the early 1940s. While government did embark on a range of new programs for relief, employment, and wartime planning—programs especially welcomed in America's big cities—what is remarkable is the lack of any coherent national urban policy. Indeed, government initiatives were usually undermined by the enduring strength of a localist tradition, the power of the corporate sector, and destructive competition among various interest groups for governmental favoritism.[115]

In subsequent years, urban scholars developed urban policy history themes in greater detail. Roger W. Lotchin's edited collection *The Martial Metropolis* (1984) captured the connection between federal military spending and urban development. In Lotchin's recounting, the city and the sword became inextricably linked in such cities as Norfolk, San Francisco, San Diego, Los Angeles, San Antonio, and Seattle. Lotchin's *Fortress California* (1992) offered a massively detailed analysis of the metropolitan-military complex in the nation's largest state. In *The Rise of the Gunbelt: The Military Remapping of Industrial America* (1991), Ann Markusen and others expanded on the military urbanization theme, focusing on the enormous federal funding for military contractors in the late twentieth century, especially those located in Los Angeles, Seattle, Chicago, Boston, and smaller cities such as Colorado Springs and Huntsville, Alabama.[116] John Mollenkopf's *The Contested City* (1983) provided an ambitious overview of the development of urban public policy after the New Deal era. Mollenkopf argued that the Democratic Party put together a national progrowth coalition that altered the urban policy environment and, not incidentally, kept the party in power throughout much of the period between the 1930s and 1980. Mollenkopf also demonstrated that the Democrats' urban liberalism sometimes made conditions worse for inner-city residents, while stimulating conservative countermovements at the same time. In *Metropolitan America: Urban Life and Urban Policy in the United States, 1940–2000* (1986), Kenneth Fox contended that social science research, government data, and rational argument played a more significant role than politics in the shaping of urban public policy. Looking at policy battles in Washington, D.C., especially the political leadership provided by the White House, Roger Biles's *The Fate of Cities: Urban America and the Federal Government, 1945–2000* (2011) argued that the federal government's commitment to the cities peaked during the Great Society era and then declined during the remainder of the twentieth century.[117]

In examining the impact of federal policies on twentieth-century American cities, scholars have paid attention to a variety of topics, including urban redevelopment, housing, highway building, social welfare, and the environment. The essays in *Urban Policy in Twentieth-Century America* (1993), edited by Arnold R. Hirsch and Raymond A. Mohl, provided an overview of these subjects. In *The Metropolitan Revolution: The Rise of Post-Urban America* (2006), Jon C. Teaford noted the critical effect of federal policies in transforming U.S. cities and suburbs into a new metropolitan form. R. Allen Hays's *The Federal Government and Urban Housing* (1985, 1995) assessed changing patterns in federal housing policy from the New Deal era to the 1990s. Robert Halpern's *Rebuilding the Inner City* (1995) analyzed the history of public housing, urban renewal, and economic development initiatives, especially the War on Poverty. Robert A. Beauregard's *Voices of Decline: The Postwar Fate of U.S. Cities* (2nd ed., 2003) gave a good introduction to key urban policy issues.[118]

Urban renewal began in the 1950s with great optimism, but hopes that this federal program would reverse the fortunes of declining inner cities faded by the late 1960s. Martin Anderson provided a thorough contemporary critique of the program in his unsparing book *The Federal Bulldozer* (1964). Jon C. Teaford provided a more dispassionate account in *The Rough Road to Renaissance* (1990), which systematically explored the efforts of twelve northeastern and midwestern cities to revitalize their downtowns in the decades after 1940. Samuel Zipp's *Manhattan Projects* (2010) documented the complexity of urban renewal in New York City. Zipp focused on four major renewal projects—the United Nations building on the East River, Lincoln Center for the Performing Arts, public housing in Harlem, and Metropolitan Life's huge middle-class Stuyvesant Town apartment project in lower Manhattan, which housed 24,000 people in thirty-five twelve- and thirteen-story buildings.[119]

The Model Cities program, widely criticized as an expensive failure, still lacks a definitive national history. However, Sidney Fine's *Violence in the Model City* (1967) provided a detailed analysis of local implementation of the new federal urban programs of the 1960s, including the War on Poverty and the Model Cities program. Two other books provided additional detail: Charles M. Haar's *Between the Idea and the Reality* (1975), an insider's account of Model Cities by a housing expert who served in the Department of Housing and Urban Development; and Mandi Isaacs Jackson's useful case study, *Model City Blues* (2008), an analysis of the program in New Haven (2008).[120]

In recent decades, the focus of scholarship on urban policy history has shifted from the national to the local level. Books by Charles H. Trout, Roger Biles, Thomas Kessner, Jo Ann E. Argersinger, and William H. Mullins analyzed urban policy issues in a variety of cities during the Great Depression and New Deal years.[121] In *Downtown: Its Rise and Fall, 1880–1950* (2001), Robert M. Fogelson demonstrated that the rapid physical growth of twentieth-century cities led to bitter policy disputes in most big cities, especially over such local issues as rapid transit, skyscraper height, zoning, automobile parking, elevated highways, urban blight, and redevelopment. By shifting the focus to the local level, Fogelson's research challenged the existing city narrative and altered the interpretive framework.[122] Fogelson dealt with several big cities, while other scholars produced individual case studies of policy decision making and implementation. For instance, Joel Schwartz's *The New York Approach* (1993) revised the devastating portrait of New York City public works czar Robert Moses presented in Robert A. Caro's *The Power Broker* (1974). Schwartz attributed the calamitous consequences of urban renewal in that city not so much to Moses but to various liberal groups willing to sacrifice the interests of working-class neighborhoods. In *Robert Moses and the Modern City*, Hilary Ballon and Kenneth T. Jackson gathered essays that aimed largely at rehabilitating the memory of Moses as a great public works builder. In *The Assassination of New York* (1993), Robert Fitch added new dimensions to the story of New York's decline through his indictment of the city's financial and real estate interests. Books by John H. Mollenkopf and Vincent Cannato assessed New York City's fortunes during the Edward Koch and John Lindsay mayoralties.[123]

New York's policy history is well documented, but historians also turned the spotlight on key policy initiatives in other cities. For example, Howard Gillette's *Between Justice and Beauty* (1995) reported a long record of urban policy failures in Washington, D.C. Policies designed to make the nation's capital more beautiful and efficient usually conflicted with programs to improve housing, welfare, and social conditions. Consequently, many of the city's neighborhoods began to undergo physical and social decay, despite many programs for public works and redevelopment. Gregory J. Crowley's *The Politics of Place* (2005) recounted the political battles touched off by five major redevelopment projects in Pittsburgh during the 1950s and after, projects often successful because they had the support of the city's major business interests.[124] In *Race and the Shaping of Twentieth-Century Atlanta* (1996), Ronald H. Bayor demonstrated the crucial role of race in the making of urban policy decisions on such issues as highways, housing, development, and employment.[125] Kent B. Germany's *New Orleans after the Promises* (2007) examined the local implementation of the War on Poverty, which coincided in creative ways with the civil rights movement and the beginnings of black political mobilization.[126] Douglas W. Rae's *City: Urbanism and Its End* (2003) traced the history of New Haven, focusing especially on the mayoralty of Richard C. Lee (1954–1970) and his ability to obtain a disproportionate amount of federal urban renewal funding for his city. Rae's title refers to the decline and fall of manufacturing and the need to develop new forms of urbanism in the twenty-first century.[127]

Dealing with deindustrialization, in fact, became a dominant issue for urban policy makers in the last decades of the twentieth century. Thomas Sugrue's *The Origins of the Urban Crisis* (1996) argued that the process of economic decline began in the immediate postwar years when the auto companies in Detroit began shedding jobs and whites began fleeing the city for the suburbs. Recent books by Roy Lubove, Howard Gillette, and Guian McKee analyzed the decline of manufacturing and its consequences in Pittsburgh, Camden, and Philadelphia, respectively. Each author described the ways in which local governments and community organizations responded to factory shutdowns and job losses by developing alternative strategies for economic development. In *Beyond the Ruins: The Meanings of Deindustrialization* (2003), edited by Jefferson Cowie and Joseph Heathcott, various authors traced community responses to urban decline in less-studied places ranging from Yonkers and Atlantic City to Gary and Youngstown. A similar gathering of essays, *Revitalizing Urban Neighborhoods* (1996), edited by Dennis Keating, Norman Krumholz, and Philip Star, emphasized the importance of neighborhood organizing and the role of local activists and community development corporations in reversing urban job losses and rebuilding communities.[128]

Urban policy initiatives often stemmed from the arguments and writings of policy experts and intellectuals. Daniel T. Rodgers brilliantly addressed this subject in *Atlantic Crossings* (1998), which elaborated extensively on the trans-Atlantic intellectual currents that shaped American social reform and social policy from the Progressive Era through the New Deal.[129] In the 1960s, Jane Jacobs, Daniel P. Moynihan, and Lewis Mumford took strong positions on urban policy matters in their writings. Jacobs challenged the thinking behind urban renewal and elevated expressways, as well as the entire drift of modern city planning.[130] Moynihan critiqued interstate expressways that penetrated central cities, challenged existing welfare policies, and asserted the importance of developing a coherent national urban policy.[131] A wide-ranging thinker on urban history and culture, Mumford took strong stands in his writing against the direction of federal urban policy.[132]

In the past decade, urban historians have rediscovered the seemingly forgotten role of urban policy intellectuals. Alice O'Connor's *Poverty Knowledge* (2001) analyzed changing social science conceptions about poverty and its causes and cures—ideas that molded social policy in different ways throughout the twentieth century.[133] In *From Warfare to Welfare* (2003), Jennifer S. Light documented how the ideas of "defense intellectuals" shaped government approaches to cities in the Cold War era, from promoting dispersal of population and industry as a defense against nuclear attack to the adoption of GIS systems by city planners and urban governments. In a second book, *The Defense of Nature* (2009), Light linked the rise of ecological thinking in the early twentieth century to subsequent patterns of urban-related research and policy.[134] Margaret Pugh O'Mara's *Cities of Knowledge* (2005) discussed new forms of urbanism and economic development centered on urban research universities, high-tech industries, and scientific research centers, typified by California's Silicon Valley. In particular, O'Mara emphasized the role of urban research universities in shaping and implementing urban public policy.[135]

URBAN POLITICAL HISTORY

Studies of urban political history traditionally focused on the political machines that emerged in the late nineteenth century and on the reformers and reform organizations that challenged the city bosses. The traditional view was highly moralistic; the bosses and machines were corrupt and venal, while the reformers upheld the democratic ideal. In the 1950s and 1960s, sociologists, political scientists, and historians reversed these widely accepted stereotypes, suggesting instead that the bosses extended democratic politics down to the neighborhood level, provided needed services, supported urban growth and development, and centralized power and decision making at a time of rapid urbanization and social change. As one of these bosses, George B. Cox of Cincinnati, had argued in 1892, the boss was "not necessarily a public enemy."[136]

The defense of the machine reached its epitome in Leo Hershkowitz's *Tweed's New York* (1977), a study of Tammany stalwart William M. Tweed in the middle decades of the nineteenth century. Often singled out as the most notorious of the bosses, Tweed became in Hershkowitz's account "a pioneer spokesman for an emerging New York" and "a progressive force in shaping the interests and destiny of a great city and its people."[137] Few historians carried the revisionist argument that far. More recent studies of the urban political machine and its origins have made fewer expansive claims for the city boss, seeking instead to locate the machine within the broader patterns of American political development and urban growth.[138] Studies of machine politics have been supplemented by numerous biographies of urban politicians, revealing a considerable amount of diversity among them.[139]

Meanwhile, historians began revising the traditional picture of urban reformers. Increasingly, scholars perceived urban reform as badly splintered, a congeries of separate movements devoted to single issues like saloons, playgrounds, public baths, or civil service reform. The general thrust of recent research portrayed urban reform as a complex, constantly shifting, multidimensional set of movements that occasionally cooperated on larger goals. Reformers, it seems, came from all social and economic classes, and they supported a diversity of often conflicting reform legislation, programs, and causes. Some reformers, it appears, took extremely elitist and undemocratic positions in their attack on the electoral base of the machine. At the same time, other reformers supported social causes dear to the heart of the bosses; indeed, some reformers were bosses and vice versa. As a result of several decades of new scholarship, the traditional practice of portraying urban politics simply as a sharply defined struggle between bosses and reformers became less useful than in earlier years.[140]

The acknowledged weakness of the boss-reformer interpretive model forced urban historians to pose new questions and view the evidence in alternative ways. The work of Samuel P. Hays, in particular, shifted the focus away from the boss-reformer debate toward the "social analysis" of urban political history. In a series of important articles beginning in the 1960s, Hays moved beyond the study of political institutions and policies toward the study of underlying structural and socioeconomic forces that produced political change. In the industrial city, Hays argued, political struggle was less a battle between machine and reform than between "forces making for decentralization and forces making for centralization." The old decentralized ward system worked in favor of the immigrant working class, while schemes for citywide centralization, such as the city commission or city manager systems, concentrated political power in the hands of urban elites.[141]

Historians have also challenged the functional view of the boss as a provider of positive government. Jon C. Teaford argued the need for additional research to determine "to what degree the boss actually bossed." Teaford's important book *The Unheralded Triumph: City Government in America, 1870–1900* (1984) demonstrated the powerful and decisive role of urban professionals and experts in managing the industrial city. More important than bosses and reformers, Teaford contended, the growing army of bureaucrats and technicians may have been the real shapers of the city. Public policy making depended on what was technically or financially feasible. Thus, the politicians came to rely on the experts, who by the twentieth century staffed the administrative departments in city government. They were civil engineers, landscape architects, city planners, public health officials, accountants, attorneys, educators, even librarians. Neither the bosses nor the reformers, this new interpretation suggested, had as much power or influence as historians once believed.[142]

Subsequent scholars pursued Teaford's research agenda and filled in additional substantive details. For example, Kenneth Finegold seconded Teaford's emphasis on the importance of an emerging class of urban professionals in his book *Experts and*

Politicians (1995), a study of Progressive Era reform challenges to machine politics in New York, Chicago, and Cleveland. Finegold found that the experts enjoyed temporary success in New York and more sustained reform in Cleveland but met abject failure in Chicago. Keith D. Revell's *Building Gotham* (2003) also echoed Teaford, demonstrating how experts in various fields—engineering, architecture, planning, public health, public finance, and others—took on the enormous task of building, managing, and incorporating the newly acquired boroughs into a consolidated Greater New York City between 1898 and 1938.[143] Similarly, in a number of studies, Terrence J. McDonald and Eric Monkkonen concluded that urban politicians were sharply limited by financial constraints and paid more attention to property-owning taxpayers than to immigrant voting blocs. Likewise, in *Property Rules: Political Economy in Chicago, 1833–1872* (1991), Robin L. Einhorn placed property holders at the center of political decision making. Einhorn posited the replacement of a decentralized, segmented municipal government in mid-nineteenth-century Chicago with a form of urban governance characterized by broader political participation that reformers criticized as corrupt and ineffective. In *The Origin and Resolution of an Urban Crisis* (1977), a study of Progressive Era Baltimore, Alan D. Anderson argued that urban budgets were insufficient to maintain effective services in the expanding city. According to Anderson, new technological innovations, such as streetcars and automobiles, dramatically improved services despite the city's financial weakness. Each of these studies found the boss-reformer model lacking in explanatory power.[144]

Historical studies written in the 1970s and 1980s offered alternatives to political science models that posited either elitist or pluralist interpretations of political power—that is, models that pictured political power as concentrated either among powerful elites or widely distributed among competing social groups. In *Political Power in Birmingham, 1871–1921* (1977), for instance, Carl V. Harris focused on two interrelated aspects of political power, office holding and governmental decision making. He concluded that the elitist model did fit electoral patterns in Birmingham, where office holding was concentrated heavily among the richest 20 percent of the city's population. But these office-holding patterns did not always dictate public policy outcomes. Indeed, decision-making power in Birmingham was distributed in complex ways. Depending on the policy issue involved, the city's politics were complicated by shifting alliances among and within economic groups, and by religious, ethnic, and racial influences. Neither the power-elite thesis nor the pluralist interpretation matched perfectly the political reality in this growing industrial city of the New South. Nevertheless, by abandoning the boss-reformer framework and by posing new questions, Harris brought a fresh perspective to urban political history.[145]

Similar conclusions were reached by David C. Hammack in his important study *Power and Society: Greater New York at the Turn of the Century* (1982). Hammack examined both the pattern of mayoral politics and the conflicts surrounding three big public policy issues: the consolidation of greater New York City in 1898, the building of the first subway, and the centralization of the public school system. The city's increasing ethnic and economic heterogeneity, Hammack argued, stimulated a shift from elitist politics "to a politics of competing elite and nonelite economic, social, and cultural interest groups mediated and managed by specialized professional politicians." In Hammack's

New York, elites splintered along economic and political fault lines; community-based political parties representing a variety of interest groups siphoned off power from elites; and technical experts, professionals, and bureaucrats exercised increasing amounts of governmental authority. These newer studies emphasized that political decision making reflected the economic, ethnic, and cultural complexity of the cities. The new industrial city, according to this argument, was shaped by the continual political interaction of competing elites, pluralistic interest groups, and urban technicians.[146]

Discussion of the urban political machine has also been revived, albeit in different ways. The work of political scientists Amy Bridges, Martin Shefter, and Ira Katznelson in particular has been especially important in developing a more theoretically based discussion of the urban political machine. In *A City in the Republic* (1994), Bridges advanced a class analysis of the growth of New York City's Tammany machine. Mass immigration in the pre–Civil War era coincided with the extension of the vote to the working class, effectively excluding the formerly dominant elites from political power. At the same time, Bridges posited, industrialization brought social and economic issues into the political arena, providing the nascent machine the means for political mobilization of the working class. Focusing on a later era in his book *Political Parties and the State* (1994), Shefter sought to revive the centrality of the "machine/reform dialectic" in urban political history. In *Urban Trenches* (1981), Katznelson applied class analysis to late-twentieth-century New York City machine politics.[147]

In *The Public City: The Political Construction of Urban Life in San Francisco, 1850–1900* (1994), Philip Ethington advanced still another perspective on urban political history. Moving beyond an ethnocultural or class-based political model, Ethington drew on Jürgen Habermas's theories about the public sphere in offering new ways of "reconstructing" urban history. He was particularly interested in exploring an expansive concept of urban politics—one that focused primarily on public discussion and political communication rather than on the more narrow and traditional issues of voting and government policy. Thus, Ethington found that women, although excluded from voting, entered the public sphere, challenged male political dominance, organized a myriad of voluntary associations, and actively engaged in political discourse. A "maternalist" ideology shaped women's political activity in the nineteenth century, leading to many of the Progressive Era social reforms of the early twentieth century. The growth of mass journalism and other new forms of communication at the end of the nineteenth century made possible an extraordinary expansion of popular political participation. In the "public city," a new political culture emerged that transformed American political and social life.[148]

Other recent scholars have expanded on Ethington's arguments about new forms of politics in the public sphere. David Quigley's *Second Founding* (2004), a study of New York City politics during the Reconstruction era, found a similar cacophony of competing political voices. Many New Yorkers resisted the political implications of black enfranchisement, but a loose coalition of various reformers, editors, labor groups, suffragettes, black activists, and some machine politicians pushed, unsuccessfully, for an interracial democracy. In *The Triumph of Ethnic Progressivism* (1998), James J. Connolly revived the ethnocultural interpretation of urban politics, but with a difference.

In earlier decades, it was argued that the new immigrant vote put machine politicians in office. Connolly rejected that position, contending instead that in Progressive Era Boston the mobilized ethnic vote represented a populist and democratic alternative to the structural reforms of business interests. In a second book, *An Elusive Unity* (2010), Connolly applied this model more broadly to urban America in the industrial period.[149]

Class and labor activism in American cities during the Gilded Age and Progressive Era brought new groups into the political arena. Eric L. Hirsh's *Urban Revolt* (1990) analyzed Chicago's fractured ethnic politics of the late nineteenth century. For Irish and German immigrants, class consciousness was less important than ethnic identity. Old-country conflicts with the British absorbed the Irish, who also controlled much of Chicago's machine apparatus, while German immigrants moved toward a radical socialist politics. Leon Fink's *Workingmen's Democracy* (1993) documented the participation of the Knights of Labor in American politics, including chapters on such diverse cities as Richmond, Milwaukee, and Kansas City. Sheldon Stromquist's *Re-inventing "The People"* (2006) portrayed the politics of the Progressive movement as deeply contested, as middle-class reformers "crafted a common language of social reconciliation," a modern liberalism that essentially excluded immigrants and African Americans.[150]

Urban reform has often been portrayed as a recurring struggle against big-city political machines in the Northeast and Midwest. Recent research has provided alternative historiographical models of urban politics drawn from southern and western cities. Amy Bridges's *Morning Glories: Municipal Reform in the Southwest* (1997) detailed how business-oriented municipal reformers governed southwestern cities throughout the twentieth century, replacing powerful political organizations with nonpartisanship and mayors with commissioners and city managers. Books by Robert B. Fairbanks on Dallas; Bradford Luckingham on Phoenix; David R. Johnson, John A. Booth, and Richard J. Harris on San Antonio; and Leonard E. Goodall on the urban Southwest also discussed the powerful role of council-manager city governments controlled by elite business leaders focused on good government and city planning that encouraged urban growth. Generally, politics and policy in these southwestern cities driven by urban boosterism rarely benefited workers, Latinos, and African Americans. In Tampa, Florida, white, black, and immigrant women activists pursued a variety of political and social reforms during the Progressive Era, as documented in Nancy A. Hewitt's *Southern Discomfort* (2001). Raphael Sonenshein's study of urban politics in modern Los Angeles, *The City at Stake* (2006), culminated in struggles over charter reform among different reform coalitions during the 1990s. Competing charter reform commissions eventually cooperated in drafting, and then shepherding through a referendum, a new unified charter that established a stronger mayor and greater authority at the neighborhood level.[151] New work on urban political history has revealed a reinvigorated field of research moving in diverse but fascinating directions.

CLASS

Building on the insights of the British historian E. P. Thompson, students of the American working class have been revamping our understanding of workers and of class relations in the city. Herbert Gutman's important study *Work, Culture, and Society in Industrializing America* (1976) led the way. His research on the first generation of industrial workers in America demonstrated the surprising strength and persistence of communal, preindustrial work patterns, even in the midst of the drive toward industrialization. The chief thrust of Gutman's work has been that workers exercised some control over their lives and over the workplace.[152]

Historians have pushed the rise of working-class activism back into the preindustrial era. In *The Urban Crucible* (1979), historian Gary Nash concluded that social and economic distinctions developed very early in New York, Philadelphia, and Boston. During the economic dislocations of the mid-eighteenth century, Nash contended, the urban working class developed an increasingly radical and participatory politics. As a sense of class consciousness emerged, urban workers began to take charge of their lives in new and dramatic ways. Crowd action in the cities, for instance, became an instrument of collective power, the means by which cohesive colonial communities protected their perceived interests. The American Revolution, Nash asserted, was one result.[153]

Several other studies fleshed out our knowledge of preindustrial working-class history. For instance, in a detailed and important study of New York City's working class, *Chants Democratic* (1984), Sean Wilentz carried the class analysis into the early nineteenth century. Adhering fiercely to an egalitarian ideology, the urban artisans emerged after the American Revolution as a powerful anticapitalist force with a strong sense of working-class consciousness. In *New York City Cartmen, 1667–1850* (1986), Graham R. Hodges explored the dynamics of working-class culture among a highly politicized group of unskilled urban workers. Howard B. Rock, Ronald Schultz, and David A. Zonderman documented city workers' difficult transition from artisanal life to industrial capitalism in New York, Philadelphia, and New England, respectively.[154] David R. Roediger in *The Wages of Whiteness* (1991) and Eric Lott in *Love and Theft* (1995) explored the emergence of racism among white workers in industrializing America. Peter Way, in *Common Labour* (1993), detailed the difficult experiences of Irish immigrant canal workers prior to 1860.[155]

During the industrialization process, urban artisans became factory workers; skilled craftsmen suffered loss of status and economic position as the production process was mechanized and skill became less important. A number of studies have focused on the ways in which the urban working class resisted, protested, and adapted to the changes brought about by industrialization. In *Worker City, Company Town* (1978), Daniel J. Walkowitz traced the divergent patterns in Troy and Cohoes, New York. In separate books, Alan Dawley and Paul G. Faler analyzed the workers' response to industrialization in Lynn, Massachusetts. Other studies have examined the industrializing process and its impact on the working class in Newark, Philadelphia, Pittsburgh, Cincinnati, San Francisco, Detroit, Albany, Chicago, Denver, and Woonsocket, Rhode Island.[156] Books by Dominic A. Pacyga, James R. Barrett, Louise C. Wade, and Rick Halpern considered the experiences of workers in Chicago's meatpacking plants and the surrounding Packingtown neighborhood. A key interpretive argument of this scholarship is that workers did not accept industrialization passively, that they resisted the new work disciplines of the industrial era, that preindustrial values and traditions persisted, and that workers exerted some control over their own lives.[157] As Daniel Rodgers suggested in *The Work Ethic in Industrial America, 1850–1920* (1978), "there is ample evidence that large numbers of industrial workers failed to internalize the faith of the factory masters." Closely allied to this position is David Montgomery's argument in *Workers' Control in America* (1979) that trade unions ultimately became the mechanism for maintaining craft-worker autonomy and for enforcing work rules.[158]

Historians have also written widely about the radical trade unions and political organizations in urban America that challenged the emerging industrial order. Violence often flared in the cities as the International Workers of the World (Wobblies), the Knights of Labor, socialists, anarchists, communists, and other radical groups demanded a host of changes ranging from more humane treatment for workers to a fundamental alteration of the relationship between management and labor.[159] Richard Schneirov's *Labor and Urban Politics* (1998) described how workers influenced politics in Chicago as a result of the 1877 railroad strike, the struggle for the eight-hour workday in 1886, and the 1894 Pullman Strike. David O. Stowell's *Streets, Railroads, and the Great Strike of 1877* (1999) placed the railroad strike in an urban context in his examination of Buffalo, Syracuse, and Albany, New York. Similarly, books by Paul Avrich, Carl Smith, and James Green underscored the significance of the Haymarket Affair in local and national politics. Separate books by Eric Arnesen and Daniel Rosenberg on New Orleans dockworkers revealed a pattern of biracial unionism that challenged post–Civil War southern workforce segregation.[160] Other case studies have chronicled the importance of radical groups in a variety of American cities, including anarchists and socialists in New York City, Milwaukee, Minneapolis, Oklahoma City, Schenectady, Bridgeport, Flint, and Dayton, and communists in Chicago, Philadelphia, and New York. Joshua B. Freeman's *Working-Class New York* (2000) analyzed the rise and fall of a once-powerful urban labor movement in the post–World War II era, a movement that fell victim to Cold War politics in the 1950s and the urban fiscal crisis of the 1970s.[161]

Working-class history traditionally focused on male workers, but recent research has demonstrated that women workers played an increasingly important role in the urban economy. In the late nineteenth century, for instance, women entered the urban workforce on a large scale, taking jobs in offices, as telephone operators, and as department store clerks; simultaneously, the proportion of women in factory and domestic service jobs began to decline. Alice Kessler-Harris's *Out to Work* (2003) is a sweeping history of wage-earning women with a heavy emphasis on those who worked in urban settings. Lisa M. Fine's *The Souls of the Skyscraper* (1990), a study of Chicago, documented the gender shift from male to female in clerical jobs. In separate books, Sharon H. Strom and Margery W. Davies linked the "feminization" of office work to the implementation of principles of scientific management. Stephen H. Norwood's *Labor's Flaming Youth* (1990) and Venus Green's *Race on the Line* (2001) discovered a pattern of militancy among telephone operators, while Susan P. Benson's *Counter Cultures* (1986) analyzed the world of women with jobs in the new department stores in the late nineteenth century, and Dorothy Sue Cobble's *Dishing It Out* (1991) considered the work of waitresses and their efforts to unionize.[162] Some women continued to perform industrial work at home as well, a subject treated in great detail in Eileen Boris's *Home to Work* (1994). Large numbers of other women worked in urban domestic service jobs, as documented in books by David M. Katzman and Tera W. Hunter.[163] Joanne J. Meyerowitz explored the role of single women workers in Chicago in *Women Adrift* (1988). In *Workshop to Office* (1993), Miriam Cohen showed a generational shift among Italian women workers in New York City, while S. J. Kleinberg researched the impact of industrialization on families in Pittsburgh in *The Shadow of the Mills* (1989).[164] Women workers became active in labor unions, as a number of books have demonstrated.[165] All of these volumes on women in the workplace suggest that urban history cannot be entirely disconnected from labor history and, more generally, from social history.

Most of the research on class has concentrated on urban workers, but some studies analyzed the experience of urban middle-class and elite groups. Richard L. Bushman's *The Refinement of America* (1992) discovered that the quest for urban gentility began in the colonial era and spread to the middling levels of society after 1800. E. Digby Baltzell's *The Protestant Establishment* (1964) described the development of an eastern urban elite and noted the tension that developed during the nineteenth century between the aristocracy and the growing number of immigrants. Baltzell's *Puritan Boston and Quaker Philadelphia* (1979) traced the lives of fifty leading families in two eastern cities from colonial times into the twentieth century. Frederic C. Jaher's compendious *The Urban Establishment* (1982) concentrated on the rich and wellborn in Boston, New York, Charleston, Chicago, and Los Angeles in the nineteenth and twentieth centuries. In contrast to the numerous studies of working-class culture, his perspective offered an alternative analysis of political, social, and economic change in urbanizing America.[166] A number of books elucidated the connections between class, money, and power in New York City. Edward Pessen's *Riches, Class and Power before the Civil War* (1973) focused on a relatively small group of wealthy New Yorkers whose careers linked financial and political power in the early nineteenth century. Sven Beckert's *The Monied Metropolis* (1993) documented the emergence of a powerful economic elite in New York City that wielded national power and influence. Books by Thomas Kessner and Eric Homberger also explored the role of social and economic elites in Gilded Age New York City.[167]

Middle-class urbanites have not been ignored. Stuart M. Blumin's *The Emergence of the Middle Class* (1989) and Mary P. Ryan's *The Cradle of the Middle Class* (1981) analyzed the growth of a distinctive middle-class society in the early-nineteenth-century city. John S. Gilkeson Jr.'s *Middle Class Providence, 1820–1940* (1986) examined changes in the middle class in Providence, Rhode Island, over more than a century. Cindy S. Aron's *Ladies and Gentlemen of the Civil Service* (1987) examined the emergence of a bureaucratic federal workforce in Gilded Age Washington, D.C. In *The Web of Progress* (1985), a comparative study of Boston and Charleston during the 1830s, William H. Pease and Jane H. Pease noted differences in class, social mobility, and values between northern and southern cities.[168] In *New York Intellect* (1987) and in several essays on urban and professional and intellectual elites, Thomas Bender provided still another perspective on class in American urban history.[169]

IMMIGRATION AND ETHNICITY

Immigration has long been an important subject for urban historians. Even before the industrial era, immigrants poured into American cities, searching for the opportunity they found lacking in their home countries, and this pattern has persisted to the present day. What has changed is the way in which historians have interpreted the American immigrant experience. The traditional interpretation was ably summarized in Oscar Handlin's *The Uprooted* (1951), a prize-winning book that brought social science conceptualization to the study of immigration history. Handlin depicted immigrants as displaced peasants wrenched from communal roots and thrust into the industrial city in a harsh, foreign land. In the immigrant ghettos of industrial America, Handlin wrote, the newcomers suffered the destruction of their traditional cultures, social breakdown and disorganization, and eventual assimilation. Since the 1980s, however, historians have extensively revised virtually every aspect of Handlin's "ghetto hypothesis" of immigrant arrival and adjustment.[170]

The historical research of the past several decades has provided important new perspectives on the migration process, the creation of ethnic villages in the American city, the geographical spread of immigrant communities across the nation, the development of immigrant institutional life, and the construction of ethnic identities. Along the way, historians discovered the significance of "chain migration"—the family- and community-based process that brought most immigrants to specific places in America.[171] Once in the new land, immigrant family structure remained a powerful determinant of community, work, and culture. For the Irish, Italians, Germans, Poles, French-Canadians, Jews, and most others, the family bolstered ethnic culture and aided in the adaptation to industrial work. Old-country cultural, religious, and folk patterns did not disappear but persisted as vital ingredients of ethnic life in America. Immigration scholars have also recognized the emergence of new forms of transnationalism among late-twentieth-century immigrants, as modern methods of transportation and communication reshape persisting links to the nations of origin.[172]

Thus, rather than weakening under the strains of migration and urban life, historians have concluded that the ties of family, kinship, and community remained strong in the American industrial city and in the postindustrial era as well. Ethnic churches, parochial schools, and a bewildering variety of cultural and fraternal groups kept nationality, ethnicity, and cultural identity alive despite the powerful forces of assimilation. Drawing on the strength of their old-world cultures, immigrants sought both to preserve their traditions and adapt to the new urban environment.[173]

Moreover, as historian Rudolph J. Vecoli argued, the immigrants demonstrated "a powerful tendency to reconstitute community in accordance with Old World origins." Thus, Chicago's "Little Italies" were in reality dozens of old-country village groups reorganized and reconstituted in the American city. Similarly, in his study *Ethnics and Enclaves: Boston's Italian North End* (1981), historian William DeMarco noted the importance of old-country village and regional loyalties and concluded that "in terms of subcultural neighborhoods, the North End resembled the Italian countryside by 1920." Among the Poles in Philadelphia, Caroline Golab wrote in *Immigrant Destinations* (1977), settlement and work patterns "strongly reflected their feudal past and peasant culture." The most sophisticated summary of the revisionist urban immigration history argument was presented by John Bodnar in *The Transplanted: A History of Immigrants in Urban America* (1985), which pulled together in a seamless account the many and varied strands of a new immigration history, setting the research agenda for subsequent scholars.[174]

Many of the new immigrant urban histories focused on a single group in a single community—microhistories that provided detail and added insight into the larger processes of migration, adjustment, and change over time.[175] Most immigrant urban histories initially concentrated on the industrial era, a period in which immigration to the United States surged dramatically. But several studies also looked back to the colonial era, demonstrating the remarkable degree of ethnic diversity in early American cities, especially New York City and Philadelphia.[176] A number of studies of immigrant labor history demonstrated immigrant commitment to worker solidarity and union activism. However, David M. Emmons's *The Butte Irish* (1990) revealed a different pattern, as the Irish in the Montana mining city displayed a striking degree of indifference to union militancy and working-class radicalism.[177] Several important books explored the shaping role of immigrant women in the family and community.[178] Reflecting the considerable recent interest in "whiteness," books by David R. Roediger, Noel Ignatiev, Stefano Luconi, and Thomas A. Guglielmo showed how Irish and Italian immigrants speeded their assimilation by embracing white supremacy.[179]

An important group of books examined the interaction among different immigrant and ethnic groups in American cities. A significant early study of this sort was *Beyond the Melting Pot* (1959), by Nathan Glazer and Daniel P. Moynihan, a study of the ethnic groups in post–World War II New York City that revealed the persistence of ethnic identification across several generations, especially in culture and politics, and the weakness of the melting pot model of immigrant assimilation. Putting the Glazer-Moynihan book in historical perspective, Ronald H. Bayor's *Neighbors in Conflict* pushed back the multiethnic analysis of conflict and resolution in New York City to the years of the Great Depression and the New Deal. Over time, the American political system, in particular, facilitated not just immigrant acculturation but also cooperative efforts among ethnic and nationality groups.[180]

During the past two decades, historians and other immigration scholars have explored the histories and migration patterns of more recent immigrant groups generally ignored in traditional histories of American immigration. For instance, a growing historical literature has filled in our knowledge about black immigrants. Irma Watkins-Owens's *Blood Relations* (1996) explored the emergence of a West Indian immigrant community in New York's Harlem between 1900 and 1930. Marilyn Halter's *Between Race and Ethnicity* (1993) traced the history of Portuguese-speaking black immigrants from the Cape Verde islands, mostly whalers and ocean-going fishermen who settled in New England port cities such as New Bedford and Boston. Philip Kasinitz's *Caribbean New York* (1992) and Nancy Foner's edited collection *Islands in the City* (2001) demonstrated the enormous diversity within the late-twentieth-century black immigration to New York City. Two other Foner books, *From Ellis Island to JFK* (2000) and *New Immigrants in New York* (2001), documented the immigrant patterns of

Haitians, Jamaicans, Dominicans, and West Africans, among other groups. Susan D. Greenbaum's *More Than Black* (2002) traced the history of black Cuban immigrants in Tampa, Florida. Books by Sherri Grasmuck and Patricia R. Pessar and by Jesse Hoffnung-Garskof covered the Dominican migration to New York City.[181]

In 2003, according to the U.S. Census, Latinos surpassed African Americans as the largest minority in the United States. Reflecting shifting ethnic realities, historians and social scientists have produced an enormous recent literature on the Hispanic diaspora in American cities, including numerous studies of Hispanic groups in Los Angeles, New York, Chicago, Miami, and other cities. A representative sample of this work includes Ricardo Romo's *East Los Angeles* (1983), George Sanchez's *Becoming Mexican American* (1993), Edward J. Escobar's *Race, Police, and the Making of a Political Identity* (1999), Douglas Monroy's *Rebirth* (1999), Matt Garcia's *A World of Its Own* (2001), and Stephanie Lewthwaite's *Race, Place, and Reform in Mexican Los Angeles* (2009)—all on Mexicans and Mexican Americans in Los Angeles.[182] For Latinos in other cities, representative studies include Mario Garcia, *Desert Immigrants* (1981), on El Paso; Zaragosa Vargas, *Proletarians of the North* (1993), on Detroit and other midwestern cities; Robert C. Smith, *Mexican New York* (2005); Roberto R. Trevino, *The Church in the Barrio* (1996), on Houston; Gabriela F. Arredondo, *Mexican Chicago* (2008); and Raul A. Ramos, *Beyond the Alamo* (2008), on San Antonio. On very recent Latino migration, *Hispanic Spaces, Latino Places* (2004), edited by Daniel D. Arreola, contains essays on San Francisco, San Diego, Los Angeles, New York, Phoenix, Cleveland, and Kansas City.[183] Key works on the Puerto Rican migration that began in the 1940s are Virginia E. Sanchez Korrol, *From Colonia to Community* (1994), on New York City; Carmen T. Whalen, *From Puerto Rico to Philadelphia* (2001); and Felix M. Padilla, *Latino Ethnic Consciousness* (1985), on Mexicans and Puerto Ricans in Chicago.[184] The post-1960 Cuban exile migration, largely destined for Miami and urban South Florida, can be traced in Alejandro Portes and Alex Stepick, *City on the Edge* (1993); Maria Christina Garcia, *Havana, USA* (1996); and Maria de los Angeles Torres, *In the Land of Mirrors* (2001).[185]

In recent decades, historians and other social scientists have uncovered the long history and growing contemporary significance of Asian immigration to American cities. An extensive bibliography has charted Asian immigration, but a relative handful have focused specifically on urban America. Books by Yong Chen, Judy Yung, John Kuo Wei Tchen, Peter Kwong, Adam McKeown, and Timothy Fong documented the history of Chinese immigrants to San Francisco, New York City, Chicago, Honolulu, and suburban Los Angeles.[186] For Korean immigration to American cities, begin with Illsoo Kim, *New Urban Immigrants: The Korean Community in New York* (1981), and Nancy Abelmann and John Lie, *Blue Dreams: Korean Americans and the Los Angeles Riots* (1995).[187] Books by Mitzika Sawada, L. Kurashige, and Jacalyn D. Harden offered insight into the Japanese in New York, Chicago, and Los Angeles.[188] Padma Rangaswamy provided a key case study of Asian Indians in the American city—in this case, Chicago.[189] Urban immigration history has pushed out in many new directions over the past two decades, energizing the field while also complicating the traditional immigration narrative.

AFRICAN-AMERICAN URBAN HISTORY

Over the past several decades, scholars working on black history, race, and race relations have reinterpreted key elements of the American urban past. Many early studies of African Americans in the city emphasized the degree to which segregation and white racism shaped the physical and institutional structures of the black community. This was the "ghetto synthesis model" applied in the 1960s and 1970s by Gilbert Osofsky, Allan H. Spear, Thomas Lee Philpott, David M. Katzman, and Kenneth L. Kusmer in their books on New York City, Chicago, Detroit, and Cleveland.[190] By contrast, more recent scholarship in the field has moved in a much different direction—one emphasizing the ways in which African Americans established communities and pursued activism and agency in defense of their own interests. This newer work also has emphasized an internal focus on kinship and communal networks, class and culture, the important role of women, and the diversity and complexity of black communities.

The beginnings of a new approach to African-American urban history can be found in the mid-1970s. Challenging contemporary social science literature, Herbert G. Gutman, in *The Black Family in Slavery and Freedom, 1750–1925* (1976), contended that the black family had a long history as a strong and vital institution, both in the South and in the North. In a study of late-nineteenth-century black migration to Boston, Elizabeth Pleck confirmed the existence of stable, two-parent black families supported by extended kinship networks. In his innovative book *Alley Life in Washington* (1980), James Borchert found a remarkable persistence of black folklife in the capital city. Over more than a century after 1850, blacks retained their old cultural patterns and "were able to maintain stability through their primary groups of family, kinship, neighborhood, community, and religion." These cultural patterns, Borchert concluded, sustained black migrants in their "adjustment to a harsh and difficult urban experience." Howard Rabinowitz's *Race Relations in the Urban South* (1978) analyzed the structures of racial segregation in the post–Civil War South, but also demonstrated the beginnings of black community life, especially organized around urban churches, as blacks moved off the plantations to southern cities.[191] The key transitional work setting forth a new research agenda was Joe William Trotter Jr.'s *Black Milwaukee: The Making of an Industrial Proletariat, 1915–45* (1985). Trotter specifically rejected the ghetto model and emphasized the diversity of Milwaukee's black community, the importance of black activism, the role of black women, and especially the emergence of black urban working-class consciousness. Trotter's "proletarianization model" never fully caught on, but other elements of his reinterpretation of black urban history helped shape subsequent historiography.[192]

From the mid-1980s, most new work in black urban history pursued the agency/community model. These histories conveyed a sense of active involvement, of people empowered, engaged in struggle, building communities, and shaping their own lives despite the constraints of segregation and racism. This new scholarship suggested that agency, resistance, and community building began early in American urban history. For example, Gary B. Nash's *Forging Freedom* (1988) portrayed blacks in Revolutionary-era Philadelphia as actively creating community and institutions, building political consciousness, and energetically advocating the abolition of slavery.

Colonial New York City, which had a much larger black population than Philadelphia, has been the subject of a number of recent books. Influenced by critical race theory with its emphasis on white supremacy and racial power, Thelma W. Foote's *Black and White Manhattan* (2004) focused on the patterns of racial formation, black slavery, and anti-black racism in New York City over almost two centuries prior to the American Revolution. Shane White articulated the agency/community model in two books—*Somewhat More Independent* (1991) and *Stories of Freedom in Black New York* (2002)—studies of New York City from the Revolutionary era to the 1820s. Leslie M. Harris's *In the Shadow of Slavery* (2003) uncovered a dynamic black community—slave and free—in New York City from the early seventeenth century to the Civil War. Harris focused especially on the city's sizable black working class, arguing that black New Yorkers developed an ability to survive, build a diverse community, and resist white repression. Covering some of the same ground as Harris, Leslie M. Alexander's *African or American?* reconstructed a black activist community in early New York City that challenged slavery and inequality but remained divided by class and by uncertainty about whether their future lay in claiming an American identity or in emigration to Haiti or Africa. Also on blacks in early New York City (and neighboring New Jersey), Graham Russell Hodges's *Root and Branch* (1999) emphasized the role of religion and black culture in sustaining community and withstanding slavery. Seth Rockman's *Scraping By* (2008) recounted the struggles of slave and free black workers in post-Revolutionary Baltimore.[193]

These patterns of agency, resistance, and community persisted over time. In studies of the late nineteenth and early twentieth centuries, Robin Kelley, Kenneth W. Goings, and Gerald L. Smith documented new patterns of black resistance to white racism in Birmingham and Memphis. In *Race Rebels* (1994), Kelley described a tradition of "infrapolitics"—a pattern of daily behavior, an oppositional culture, in which African Americans in Birmingham demanded recognition and respect in daily encounters with whites in the streets, on streetcars, on the job, in the courts, and elsewhere. Goings and Smith, in their work on Memphis, revealed a record of violent encounters as blacks resisted white supremacy. Kate Masur's *An Example for All the Land* (2010), a study of Washington, D.C., during the Reconstruction era, documented the struggle of African Americans for equality, especially in the areas of jobs, voting, schooling, and local transportation. Michael W. Fitzgerald's *Urban Emancipation* (2002) makes a similar argument about black agency during Reconstruction in Mobile, Alabama. In *Right to Ride* (2010), Blair L. M. Kelley recounted the activism of a "forgotten generation " of black southerners who, between 1900 and 1907, organized and conducted a series of boycotts against segregated streetcars in more than twenty cities, including New Orleans, Richmond, Savannah, Montgomery, Atlanta, and Nashville. Although the streetcar boycotts ultimately failed, Kelley argued that they "planted seeds of resistance" that emerged later in the twentieth century. Writing in the *Journal of Social History* in 1994, Andor Skotnes noted that during the Great Depression of the 1930s, black activists conducted retail boycotts in more than thirty-five cities, urging black residents to "buy where you can work."[194]

Over the past two decades, historians have provided new details on black agency and community building in studies of the great black migrations from the South. For instance, William Cohen's *At Freedom's Edge* (1991) found that in the post–Civil War decades, blacks from the upper South initiated a labor migration to improve their economic position. As Cohen noted, mobility was a key component in their "concept of freedom." Marcy S. Sacks, in *Before Harlem* (2006), traced an early black migration to New York City between 1880 and 1915. Peter Gottlieb's *Making Their Own Way* (1987) documented the black migration to Pittsburgh between 1916 and 1930 and revealed a diverse community of rural folk adapting to the city and industrial work. James R. Grossman's *Land of Hope* (1989) interpreted the difficult adaptation of hundreds of thousands of black southern migrants to Chicago, an adjustment aided by older black settlers but also by new migrant communal institutions and churches. Covering the period to 1945, Kimberley L. Phillips's *Alabama North* (1999) and Gretchen Lemke-Santangelo's *Abiding Courage* (1996) detailed similar black migrations to Cleveland and to Oakland and the East Bay area, respectively. Victoria W. Wolcott's *Remaking Respectability* (2001) elucidated the role of women in shaping black migrant communities in interwar Detroit.[195] Books by two journalists—Nicholas Lemann's *The Promised Land* (1991) and Isabel Wilkerson's *The Warmth of Other Suns* (2010)—heavily based on interviews with black migrants to Chicago, New York, and Los Angeles, provided more personal but nevertheless powerful narratives about leaving the South and accommodating to new urban worlds. James M. Gregory's *The Southern Diaspora* (2005) provided a broad overview of migration, showing that huge numbers of poor and working-class whites also departed the South for jobs and economic opportunity.[196]

Another body of recent literature in the field deals partly with migration, but more extensively with the building of new communities in the city. Richard W. Thomas's *Life for Us Is What We Make of It* (1992) provided an important early statement of the community-building thesis in a comprehensive study of black Detroit between 1915 and 1945. Four books that emphasized the internal development of black community within a segregationist society were Roger Lane's *William Dorsey's Philadelphia and Ours* (1991); Christopher Silver and John V. Moeser's *The Separate City* (1995) on Richmond, Atlanta, and Memphis; Lillian S. Williams's *Strangers in the Land of Paradise* (1999) on Buffalo; and Shirley Ann Wilson Moore's *To Place Our Deeds* (2000) on Richmond, California. Alison Dorsey's *To Build Our Lives Together* (2004) reconstructed the emerging black community in post-Reconstruction-era Atlanta, focusing on such community institutions as businesses and professions, churches, black colleges, and social and fraternal organizations, as well as on activism demanding public schools for black children and curbs on white violence.[197]

Migration and community formed the subject of recent studies on Chicago by Davarian Baldwin and Adam Green. Recent books by Josh Sides and Douglas Flamming explored migration patterns, black activism, and community building in Los Angeles. Marvin Dunn's *Black Miami in the Twentieth Century* (1997) did the same for Miami. Books by Tera Hunter, Elizabeth Clark-Lewis, and Jacqueline Jones analyzed the role of black women workers, especially in domestic and service jobs, in Atlanta, Washington, D.C., and other cities. Joe W. Trotter and Jared N. Day published *Race and Residence* (2010), which focused on the Pittsburgh black community since World War II. Luther Adams's *Way Up North in Louisville* (2010) suggested that despite the appeal of northern or western urban centers, the urban South continued to hold out the promise of opportunity as well. Reflecting the dominant themes of recent historiography, these books all emphasized community, agency, and activism.[198]

An outpouring of studies on black activism for civil rights and racial equality has also shaped new thinking about the African-American experience. Scholars have elaborated a new civil rights history, as bottom-up community studies have moved beyond the top-down nationally focused works of an earlier generation of historians. The new trend began in the 1980s with books on civil rights activism by William H. Chafe on Greensboro, North Carolina; David R. Colburn on Saint Augustine, Florida; and Robert J. Norell on Selma, Alabama. A flood of other urban-based studies followed, including books by Michael K. Honey on Memphis, Alan B. Anderson and George W. Pickering on Chicago, James R. Ralph Jr. on Chicago, Kim Lacy Rogers on New Orleans, Glenn T. Eskew and Diane McWhorter on Birmingham, Glenda A. Rabby on Tallahassee, John A. Kirk on Little Rock, Martha Biondi on New York City, Raymond A. Mohl on Miami, Matthew C. Whitaker on Phoenix, Matthew J. Countryman on Philadelphia, Laurie B. Green on Memphis, Clarence Lang on Saint Louis, Patrick D. Jones on Milwaukee, Shana Bernstein on Los Angeles, and Tomiko Brown-Nagin on Atlanta.[199] J. Mills Thornton's *Dividing Lines* (2005) offered a comparative history of civil rights politics in three Alabama cities: Montgomery, Birmingham, and Selma. Thomas J. Sugrue's *Sweet Land of Liberty* (2008) provided a powerful and sweeping narrative of the civil rights movement in the urban North. Edited collections of original essays by Jeanne Theoharris and Komozi Woodard, *Freedom North* (2003) and *Groundwork* (2005), presented essays on civil rights movements in numerous cities, including Boston, New York City, Newark, Cincinnati, Milwaukee, Oakland, Los Angeles, Detroit, and Chicago. Another book of original essays, Samuel C. Hyde's *Sunbelt Revolution* (2003), drew comparisons among civil rights movements in Gulf South cities such as New Orleans, Biloxi, Tallahassee, and Montgomery.[200]

The recent civil rights literature emphasized the emergence of community activism in response to specific racial grievances at the local level. In addition, several books documented the role of local branches of national racial defense organizations. One early such study, Arvarh E. Strickland's *History of the Chicago Urban League* (1966), traced the development of an important institution often hampered by dependence on white financial support. Christopher Robert Reed's *The Chicago NAACP and the Rise of Black Professional Leadership, 1910–1966* (1997) reported on the early struggles of a parallel organization. Kevin Boyle's *Arc of Justice* (2004) detailed the powerful role of the NAACP in Detroit in a murder trial involving race, housing, and neighborhood violence during the Great Migration of the 1920s. August Meier and Elliott Rudwick's *CORE* (1973) and Gerald Horne's *Communist Front?* (1988) both presented a wealth of material on local branch agencies of the Congress of Racial Equality and the Civil Rights Congress. Claudrena N. Harold's *The Rise and Fall of the Garvey Movement in the Urban South, 1918–1942* (2007) considered the activism of Marcus Garvey's black nationalist Universal Negro Improvement Association, especially in Miami, New Orleans, and several cities in Virginia.[201]

Other scholars have turned the historical spotlight on the nation's long history of racial violence, especially urban race riots. The racial anger directed at blacks during New York City's Draft Riots of the Civil War era established a pattern of urban conflict that persisted into the twentieth century.[202] Two now classic works opened the subject of racial violence in twentieth-century American cities: Elliott Rudwick's *Race Riot at East St. Louis* (1964) and William L. Tuttle's *Race Riot* (1970). Tuttle's work on the Chicago race riot of 1919, in particular, brought new conceptualization to the field of black urban history. He incorporated elements of the prevailing "ghetto model" documenting the structural constraints imposed on recent black migrants to Chicago that led to interracial tension, but he also explored significant elements of black agency and self-defense during the riots.[203] A number of additional books on urban race riots documented persistent racial conflict into the early twentieth century. These works included William Ivy Hair on the New Orleans riot of 1900; Mark Bauerlein, Gregory Mixon, and David Fort Godshalk on the Atlanta riot of 1906; Roberta Senechal on the Springfield, Illinois, riot of 1908; Robert V. Haynes on the Houston riot of 1917; and Scott Ellsworth and James S. Hirsch on the Tulsa riot of 1921. The best of these works incorporated the elements that made Tuttle's *Race Riot* so compelling—essentially placing each riot within the local context of class and community, labor and politics.[204]

Urban racial violence persisted through the twentieth century. In 1943, in the midst of World War II, racial violence exploded in New York, Detroit, and Los Angeles—subjects explored in writings by Dominic J. Capeci, Eduardo Obregon Pagan, and Kevin Allen Leonard.[205] Racial violence ignited again in the mid-1960s, with major riots in Los Angeles, Detroit, and Newark, for which we have historical accounts, and dozens of other cities that remain unexamined by scholars. Key works on the 1960s riots include Gerald Horne's *The Fire This Time* (1995), Sidney Fine's *Violence in the Model City* (1898), and Kevin Mumford's *Newark* (2007).[206] New outbreaks of racial violence occurred in sunbelt cities Miami and Los Angeles through the 1980s and 1990s, analyzed in Bruce Porter and Marvin Dunn's *The Miami Riot of 1980* (1984), Raphael Sonenshein's *Politics in Black and White* (1993), and Nancy Ablemann and John Lie's *Blue Dreams* (1995).[207] In *White Violence and Black Response* (1988), Herbert Shapiro contributed an important overview of racial violence from the 1860s to the 1950s. Janet Abu-Lughod's *Race, Space, and Riots* (2007) abandoned the more typical case study approach and provided a comparative analysis of race riots in Chicago, New York, and Los Angeles from 1919 to the 1990s.[208]

The newer African-American urban history has pursued several other lines of investigation as well. Studies of urban race relations, such as Ronald H. Bayor's *Race and the Shaping of Twentieth-Century Atlanta* (1996), John T. McGreevy's *Parish Boundaries* (1996), and Elizabeth Lasch-Quinn's *Black Neighbors* (1993) provided further evidence of the centrality of race in the modern American city.[209] Historians have documented black involvement in labor and radical movements.[210] They have published important work on black churches, on blacks in sports, and on black women in civil rights activism—studies that have drawn a fuller picture of African-American institutional and cultural life.[211] New scholarship on black politics and the emergence of big-city black mayors has provided historical perspective on the election in 2008 of President Barack Obama, who obtained an early political education in the cauldron of Chicago's race relations and urban politics.[212] The surge of interest in "whiteness" among scholars, beginning with David Roediger's *The Wages of Whiteness* (1991), has provided a new lens through which to view race, ethnicity, politics, and race relations.[213] James W. Loewen's *Sundown Towns* (2005) recounted the long history of racial exclusion that prevailed in many American towns and suburbs through the end of the twentieth century.[214]

Beginning in the 1980s, the contemporary policy debate about the "underclass" had broad implications for African-American urban history. Although widely used in the 1980s and 1990s as a journalistic shorthand for the high levels of crime, poverty, welfare dependency, and social disorganization in the mostly black central cities, the conception of an urban underclass was given scholarly credence by sociologist William Julius Wilson. In his influential book *The Truly Disadvantaged* (1987), Wilson explained the emergence of the black underclass as a consequence of deep structural shifts in the American economy since about 1970—namely, the deindustrialization of industry, the loss of factory jobs, and the rise of a bifurcated postindustrial economy. In Wilson's analysis, central-city blacks were unprepared and untrained for the emerging high-skill, high-tech economy and could never get ahead by relying on the low-skill, low-pay service economy. Wilson refined this argument somewhat in a later book, *When Work Disappears* (1996), but the economic explanation for the emergence of the underclass remained dominant. Wilson's thesis, however, was challenged by sociologists Douglas S. Massey and Nancy A. Denton, whose *American Apartheid: Segregation and the Making of the Underclass* (1993) argued that the persistence of institutional racism was to blame for the continuing plight of the inner cities. Other works, such as Thomas Sugrue's *The Origins of the Urban Crisis* (1996), combined Wilson's structural analysis with the Massey-Denton institutional racism argument. As reflected in the scholarly work included in Michael B. Katz's edited collection, *The "Underclass" Debate* (1993), these arguments stimulated new ways of thinking about African-American urban history.[215]

WOMEN IN THE CITY

Reflecting the limited role ascribed to women in American history, traditional urban histories typically mentioned women only in passing, while emphasizing such topics as the physical growth of cities, suburbanization, race and ethnicity, and urban politics. Social and cultural histories set in cities tangentially included women, and accounts of Progressive Era reform duly noted the contributions of key women such as Jane Addams, but few historians wrote books and articles with women and their contributions to urban life as the centerpiece. In the 1980s, the study of women increased significantly in the discipline overall, and scholarly studies on women in cities proliferated. While refining and challenging older interpretations of women's roles as wives, mothers, and homemakers, these studies also placed women at the heart of important changes in the public sphere.

Increased attention to women can be seen in the number of important books written about the colonial era. Laurel Thatcher Ulrich's *Good Wives* (1982) creatively used such sources as court documents, probate records, wills, church bulletins, sermons, and diaries in describing the important role played by women in New England, as well as in comparing women in colonial communities with those on the frontier. Karin Wulf's *Not All Wives* (2000) considered the lives of widowed, single, and divorced women as well as wives in Philadelphia, the largest community of the era. Wulf challenged the traditional view of passive women, arguing instead that the women, whatever their status, enjoyed remarkable influence in the society. In *Good Wives, Nasty Wenches, and Anxious Patriarchs* (1996), Kathleen Brown noted that ideas about gender and race evolved together in colonial Virginia. In a pair of influential books, *Founding Mothers and Fathers* (1996) and *Liberty's Daughters* (1980), Mary Beth Norton recounted the vital role played by women in politics during the nation's formative years.[216]

Books dealing with the antebellum period likewise argued that women exercised considerable influence in American society, both inside and outside the home. Christine Stansell's *City of Women* (1987), a study of early-nineteenth-century New York City, examined the lives of working-class women as well as the poor, bawdy houses as well as tenements, and prostitutes as well as philanthropists. Stansell's textured portrait identified a distinct female culture in the antebellum city. Susan Strasser provided a broad overview of women's work in the home in *Never Done* (1982). Jeanne Boydston's *Home and Work* (1994) examined the ways that contemporaries viewed the work performed by women as housewives and as wage-earning laborers in the years after the American Revolution. Suzanne Lebsock's *The Free Women of Petersburg* (1984) dealt with the legal status and work lives of black and white women in a southern community, carefully delineating the differences between the experiences of women living in cities and those residing on plantations. Mary P. Ryan's *Women in Public* (1990) analyzed the many ways that women fought to expand their public presence, often against staunch resistance from male authority figures who sought to confine women to their homes.[217] Books by Barbara J. Berg, Nancy A. Hewitt, Teresa Anne Murphy, and Anne M. Boylan explored the crucial role played by women in a variety of benevolent organizations and reform crusades that swept the nation in the antebellum decades.[218]

A spate of studies has examined the crucial role played by women in the various reform movements of the late nineteenth and early twentieth centuries, many such efforts characterized as "municipal housekeeping." That is, historians have theorized that women's interest in public health, clean air and water, childcare, education, sanitary reform, juvenile courts, and other related issues reflected their concerns as mothers and homemakers. In *Seeing with Their Hearts* (2002), Maureen A. Flanagan argued that, unlike male-dominated good government organizations that primarily sought structural changes as the best means of improving urban life, Chicago women advocated a progressive vision that set the welfare of all urban residents as the principal purpose of municipal government. Her detailed case study of Chicago both affirmed the significance of women's contributions and made important distinctions among the reforms advanced by female and male activists.[219] Books by Robyn Muncy, Lori D. Ginsberg, Ruth Bordin, Nancy A. Hewitt, Suellen Hoy, and Sarah Deutsch made a similar case for the distinctiveness of women's reform activities.[220] Studies of leading women reformers in settlement houses, such as Kathryn Kish Sklar's biography of Florence Kelley, Elizabeth Israels Perry's biography of Belle Moskowitz, and several accounts of Jane Addams and Hull House, high-lighted the key role played by women in the Progressive Era.[221] Daphne Spain and Susan Lynn contributed studies of progressive women activists in the Progressive and postwar periods, respectively.[222] Books by Suellen Hoy and Maureen Fitzgerald described the reform activities of Roman Catholic nuns in Chicago and New York City, respectively.[223] In *Women and American Socialism, 1870–1920*, Mari Jo Buhle recounted the work of women who rejected progressive reform in favor of a more thoroughgoing critique of American capitalism.[224]

During the late nineteenth and early twentieth centuries, at a time when the franchise was still widely reserved for males, women reformers frequently exerted political influence through their participation in female clubs, cultural philanthropies, and other voluntary associations. Anne Firor Scott's *Natural Allies* (1991) provided a general history of women's voluntary associations in the United States. Mary P. Ryan's *Civic Wars* (1997), a study of politics and civic discourse in nineteenth-century New York City, New Orleans, and San Francisco, credited women operating through voluntary associations with exerting an important influence in urban governance. Priscilla Murolo's *The Common Ground of Womanhood* (1997) argued that working-class women's clubs as well as middle-class women's organizations served as influential instruments of reform. Books by Anne Meis Knupfer, Dorothy Salem, and Glenda E. Gilmore noted the importance of African-American women's clubs at a time when Jim Crow still held sway in the South and blacks in the North enjoyed very little political or economic power.[225]

Historians have written widely about the experiences of immigrant women in the cities. Donna R. Gabaccia's *From the Other Side* (1994) presented a broad overview of assimilation patterns of immigrant women in the United States. Gabaccia dealt extensively with women's need to reconcile communal and familial traditions with American expectations of individualism. She also compared the challenges facing foreign-born women with those confronting native-born racial minorities. In *The Qualities of a Citizen* (2009), Martha Gardner used the wealth of information contained in U.S. immigration files to chart the evolution of citizenship law pertaining to women immigrants. Scholars have examined in great detail women of different ethnic groups, ascribing the level of difficulty in assimilation to the culture of the immigrants' home-land. Books by Susan A. Glenn, Elizabeth Ewen, Paula Hyman, and Hasia Diner dealt with Jewish women. Diane C. Vecchio considered Italian women, while Judith E. Smith's *Family Connections* (1985) compared Jewish and Italian female immigrants in Providence, Rhode Island. Hasia Diner's *Erin's Daughters in America* (1983) discussed the Irish, and Judy Yung's *Unbound Feet* (1995) explored the conditions facing Chinese immigrant women. Diner's *Hungering for America* (2003) found in the immigrant kitchen useful information about assimilation in American society.[226]

A growing interest in the lives of urban and suburban women has also resulted in more scholarly attention to the activities of housewives and homemakers. Thomas J. Schlereth's *Victorian America* (1997) studied the effects of modernization in all venues, but paid considerable attention to changes within the home. In *"Just a Housewife"* (1987), Glenna Matthews argued that the rise of professionalism in industrializing America and the culture of consumption that came to fruition in the 1920s combined to undermine the "cult of domesticity" that had trapped women in their homes for much of the nineteenth century. In *More Work for Mother* (1985), Ruth Schwartz Cowan demonstrated that new labor-saving devices actually made more work—not less—for housewives and bound them more closely to quotidian household labors. Dolores Hayden's *The Grand Domestic Revolution* (1982) attempted to link alterations in the home with changing circumstances in neighborhoods and entire cities. In *Building a Housewife's Paradise* (2010), Tracey Deutsch examined grocery stores as economic and social institutions that both extended the domestic sphere into the marketplace and revised the nature of women's work. Sylvie Murray's *The Progressive Housewife* (2003) documented the role of activist women in postwar suburban Queens, New York. Such scholarship on housewifery generally ascribed to women a greater agency than traditional histories of domestic life.[227]

SEXUALITY

Since the 1980s, historians have explored themes related to gender and sexuality as well as race, class, and ethnicity in their study of the social complexity and extraordinary diversity of urban America. The anonymity prevalent in large cities provided opportunities for sexual fulfillment to single men and women, gay and lesbian couples, and other marginalized urban residents that they lacked in smaller communities. Distinctive subcultures that blurred traditional gender, ethnic, and racial lines thrived in urban settings; some urban neighborhoods assumed bohemian personalities as recognized centers of sexuality, and a few cities even became widely known for their tolerance of a variety of sexual practices. Histories about the pursuit of sexual freedom, involving heterosexuals as well as gays, lesbians, bisexuals, and transgendered individuals, have largely been written about urban locations. Cities also served as the settings for gendered power struggles in which the ruling classes used sexuality norms to subordinate more vulnerable groups.

The literature on sexuality prior to the twentieth century remains sparse, although some scholars have begun to make inroads into the subject. In *Sex among the Rabble* (2006), Clare A. Lyons described the emergence of a sexual culture in Philadelphia between 1730 and 1830. In Lyons's rendering, the upper class eroticized print culture to establish hegemony over women, blacks, and poor whites. This mix of politics, power, and sexuality shaped the importance of class, race, and gender in early urban America. *The Flash Press* (2008) by Patricia Cline Cohen, Timothy J. Gilfoyle, and Helen Lefkowitz explored the role of the sporting male weeklies that flourished briefly in New York City in the 1840s. Before a reform crusade led to their demise, these salacious newspapers provided pornography, gossip about prostitutes, and editorials condemning homosexuality, along with news about sporting events and theater performances. Donna Dennis's *Licentious Gotham* (2009) dealt with the public outcry against the publication of erotic material in nineteenth-century New York City. Chad C. Heap argued in *Slumming: Sexual and Racial Encounters in American Nightlife, 1885–1940* (2010) that the affluent in New York and Chicago affirmed their whiteness and heterosexuality through the titillation of visiting bohemian haunts.[228]

Urban historians have written extensively about prostitution, studying the social, legal, and political manifestations of the "oldest profession." In *City of Eros* (1994), Timothy J. Gilfoyle showed that prostitution was deeply entrenched in the culture and economy of the nation's largest city. Noting that packs of teenage prostitutes roamed New York's Bowery and that sporting houses proliferated throughout the city, Gilfoyle concluded that joblessness and exorbitant Manhattan rents drove vulnerable women to work in brothels. Always sympathetic to victimized and objectified women, he nevertheless recognized that prostitution created entrepreneurial opportunities and gave some women a degree of agency lacking in other occupations. *City of Eros* explained how economic and social changes in the early twentieth century stopped short of ending prostitution altogether, but reduced its scope and profitability in metropolitan America. Ruth Rosen's *The Lost Sisterhood* (1982) revealed how lower-class women lacking opportunities in more respectable careers turned to prostitution out of economic need, described the prevalence of the institution in the growing communities of the American West, and discussed the views and activities of the progressive reformers determined to eradicate the practice. Jacqueline B. Barnhart's *The Fair but Frail* (1986) documented prostitution in late-nineteenth-century San Francisco as an "economic necessity" for some women but an entrepreneurial opportunity for others. Mark Thomas Connelly's *The Response to Prostitution in the Progressive Era* (1980) and Barbara M. Hobson's *Uneasy Virtue* (1997) detailed the crusade against prostitution in the early decades of the twentieth century. Thomas C. Mackey's *Red Lights Out* (1987) provided a legal history of community efforts to deal with brothels and vice districts. Books by David Langum and Brian Donovan analyzed the crusade against "white slavery" that culminated in the passage of the Mann Act in 1910. Karen Abbott's *Sin in the Second City* (2007) recounted the history of Chicago's most infamous sporting house, highlighting the connections linking madams, respectable clientcles, and local government.[229]

In recent years, scholars have published a number of historical studies about gay and lesbian communities in America's cities. John D'Emilio's pioneering *Sexual Politics, Sexual Communities* (1983) provided extensive background about the changing status of homosexuals in American society, detailing the systematic oppression of the beleaguered minority, the struggle for equality, the increased militancy after the pivotal Stonewall uprising in 1969, and the forging of contemporary gay culture in metropolitan America. The definitive history of the Stonewall episode remains Martin Duberman's *Stonewall: The Riots That Sparked the Gay Revolution* (1993). In *Gay New York* (1994), George Chauncey argued that the boundaries between the behaviors of gay and straight men were far looser in the decades before World War II than they became afterward—especially among working-class males. After sifting through police reports, newspapers, oral histories, medical records, diaries, and, most notably, the Society for the Suppression of Vice papers, Chauncey reported finding remarkably permeable sexual borders in New York City in the decades preceding World War II. Allan Bérubé's *Coming Out under Fire* (1990) primarily recounted the experiences of gay soldiers in World War II training camps and overseas battlefield assignments, but also contained information about the treatment of gays in urban induction centers and seaport cities. Charles Kaiser's *The Gay Metropolis* (2007) focused on New York City and dealt almost exclusively with gay men while devoting comparatively little attention to lesbians.[230]

Recent work has devoted considerable attention to lesbians and lesbian communities. Lillian Faderman's *Odd Girls and Twilight Lovers* (1991) provided a broad introduction to lesbian life in the twentieth century. *Boots of Leather, Slippers of Gold* (1993), by Elizabeth L. Kennedy and Madeline Davis, focused on the history of a lesbian community in Buffalo, New York, from the 1930s through the 1960s. John Howard's *Carryin' On in the Lesbian and Gay South* (1997) and two books by James T. Sears, *Lonely Hunters* (1997) and *Rebels, Rubyfruit, and Rhinestones* (2001), covered the emergence of gay and lesbian communities in the American South, including discussions of New Orleans, Atlanta, Charleston, Memphis, and Louisville.[231]

Several historical studies have described how particular neighborhoods in American metropolises—and indeed, certain cities—became avant-garde communities that fostered sexual freedom. Christine Stansell's *American Moderns* reconstructed the world of bohemian New York City, while books by Judith Schwartz, June Sochen, and Ross Wetzsteon focused on New York City's Greenwich Village as a magnet for free-thinkers and nonconformists. Kevin J. Mumford's *Interzones* (1997) considered interracial sex districts in New York City and Chicago. Beth Bailey and David Farber's *The First Strange Place* (1994) discussed prostitution and interracial sex in Honolulu during World War II.[232] Anthropologist Esther Newton's *Cherry Grove Fire Island* (1995), based largely upon extensive interviews she conducted with current and former residents of the nation's first openly gay and lesbian community, explored the resort's origins as a clandestine getaway spot for New York City vacationers in the 1930s, the battles of its residents with the gay-bashing elements of McCarthyism in the 1950s, and its gradual emergence as an east coast haven for gays and lesbians by the 1970s.[233]

Work on sexuality in urban America has expanded still further in the past decade. Nan Boyd's *Wide Open Town* (2003) recounted the evolution of San Francisco as a center of homosexual life up to 1965; Josh Sides's *Erotic City* (2009) carried the narrative through the remainder of the twentieth century; and Martin Meeker's *Contacts Desired* (2008) dealt especially with the gay press in San Francisco.[234] Daniel Hurewitz's *Bohemian Los Angeles and the Making of Modern Politics* (2007), Moira Kenney's *Mapping Gay L.A.* (2001), and Lillian Faderman and Stuart Timmons's *Gay L.A.* (2009) considered gay life and sexual politics in Los Angeles.[235] Books by Alicia P. Long, Jennifer M. Spear, and Judith Kelleher Schafer detailed New Orleans's status as the libertine city of the South.[236] Beth Bailey's *Sex in the Heartland* (2002) used a small midwestern college town (Lawrence, Kansas) as a lens for viewing the sexual revolution of the 1960s.[237] Howard P. Chudacoff's *The Age of the Bachelor* (1999) described how changing ideals of manhood from the late nineteenth century through the 1920s fostered a bachelor lifestyle in America's cities. Once regarded as misfits in a culture that idealized marriage and stable families, bachelors found acceptance in big cities as they concentrated most notably in such male domains as sporting houses, taverns, barber shops, and YMCAs.[238]

CONSUMPTION

Over the past two decades, new research and conceptualization on consumption encouraged some historians to reinterpret American urban history in startlingly different ways. Lizabeth Cohen's *A Consumer's Republic* (2003), a study of postwar America, offered the most powerful and compelling such work. Cohen noted that periodization and conceptualization in American urban history usually relied on discussions of the role of the preindustrial city, the industrial city, the postindustrial city, and similar phrases dictated by economies of production. Cohen contended that economies of consumption might offer new ways of thinking about cities and urban change. Through the lens of shopping and consuming, Cohen discussed consumer activism of the Progressive Era and the Great Depression, the links between consumption and citizenship encouraged by wartime price controls and rationing, and the consumer revolution of the postwar period—all sustained by rising economic prosperity, the suburban housing boom, the growth of shopping malls, and the mass marketing of everything. Urban America changed in the process, as population and retailing decentralized and downtown shopping declined. The postwar promise of democratized consumption (thus Cohen's phrase the "consumers' republic") was never completely fulfilled, however. Race, class, and gender discrimination determined those who gained and those who lost out in the push for better housing, better jobs, higher wages, more disposable income, and a higher standard of living. Corporate capital and federal policy often dictated the winners and losers, thus politicizing consumption. Cohen's big, wide-ranging, and complex book stimulated a rethinking of postwar urban America.[239]

Cohen's *A Consumer's Republic* provided a critical synthesis of the postwar urban and suburban culture of consumption. Two other synthetic works published about the same time offered more positive analyses of the experience of consumption. Sharon Zukin's *Point of Purchase* (2004) presented a social history of modern American shopping, ranging from department stores and discount chains to ethnic markets and Internet websites—from Woolworth's to Walmart to Amazon.com. In Zukin's analysis, shopping represented Americans' efforts to achieve a better life and the American Dream, but consumption also helped sustain the American economy (at least until lately). In a detailed study, Gary Cross's *An All-Consuming Century* (2000) traced consumption's powerful hold on twentieth-century Americans, concluding that shopping and consumption had beneficial consequences for self and society. Neither Zukin nor Cross addressed the critical issues raised by Lizabeth Cohen. By contrast, Ann Satterthwaite's *Going Shopping* (2001) provided a thoughtful history and critique of the shopping habit, concluding that modern consumption patterns and spaces, such as online shopping, undermined civic culture and community.[240]

Historians of colonial America discovered an early consumer revolution in the mid-eighteenth century. In a key 1988 article in *Past and Present*, Timothy H. Breen emphasized the importance of imported British manufactured goods in the colonial seaport cities. In a subsequent book with a fully elaborated thesis, *The Marketplace of Revolution* (2004), Breen documented British economic reliance on the market for consumer goods among 250,000 British colonists. According to Breen, the lust for such products and the eventual emergence of a consumer politics—basically the boycotts organized in colonial cities and towns in the 1760s and 1770s in response to onerous British taxation—put Americans on the path to independence.[241] Recent research by other scholars on the nation's early industrialization between 1790 and 1840 also emphasized the significance of consumption as a stimulus to manufacturing. Economic historian David R. Meyer argued in his book *The Roots of American Industrialization* (2003) that prosperous eastern farmers who supplied cities with foodstuffs provided a willing market for nascent urban manufacturers, thereby energizing the emerging industrial economy. Suggesting an important link between cities and rural regions, Meyer contended that rural consumer demand and capital accumulated by wealthy farmers fueled the early industrial revolution in eastern cities. Helen Tangires's *Public Markets and Civic Culture in Nineteenth-Century America* (2003) analyzed the shift in mid-century from human-scale public markets with face-to-face exchange, especially for food, to large, privately owned markets reflecting the rise of a capitalist economy.[242]

During the industrial era, marked by technological innovation and the creation of a national railroad network, the nation's consumer market, especially in rapidly growing cities, expanded exponentially. Advertising and mass marketing developed increasingly sophisticated techniques to stimulate consumer demand and produce profit. In *Merchants and Manufacturers* (1971, 1989), Glenn Porter and Harold C. Livesay analyzed manufacturers' responses to "concentrated urban demand" in a vast national market. Initially relying on wholesalers and commission merchants, corporate producers of consumer goods eventually took over distribution, marketing, and advertising functions themselves. By the end of the nineteenth century, popular new magazines such as *Good Housekeeping*, *Cosmopolitan*, and *Ladies' Home Journal* became essential in advertising mass-produced consumer goods for urban markets, a subject discussed in Jennifer Scanlon's *Inarticulate Longings* (1995), Matthew Schneirov's *The Dream of a New Social Order* (1994), and Richard Ohmann's *Selling Culture* (1996).[243] In *Fables of Abundance* (1994), Jackson Lears complicated the cultural history of American advertising, suggesting that nineteenth-century Americans' undisciplined lust for seemingly exotic consumer goods gave way by the twentieth century to rationalized consumers whose tastes and desires were shaped by advertising and corporate marketing campaigns.[244] Susan Strasser's *Satisfaction Guaranteed* (1989) detailed the refinement of new marketing, advertising, and branding practices of makers of consumer products in the early twentieth century. Thomas Hine's *The Total Package* (1995) argued the importance of packaging products in easily recognizable boxes, bottles, cans, and tubes as an essential aspect of successful marketing. Covering the decades between 1920 and 1940, Roland Marchand's *Advertising and the American Dream* (1985) offered a deeply researched, marvelously illustrated, multifaced analysis that linked advertising with consumer desire, changing cultural values, and modernity. Stuart Ewen's *Captains of Consciousness* (1976) focused on the manipulative aspects of advertising in sustaining the capitalist social order.[245]

Advertising trumpeted corporate culture and the consumer economy as signaling an age of progress, and most Americans embraced the outpouring of new products. Targeted by the mass-market magazines and corporate mass-marketing campaigns, American women became early and essential participants in the emergence of the nation's culture of consumption. In an important article in the *Journal for MultiMedia History* (1998) and in her book *Hope in a Jar* (1998), Kathy Peiss elaborated on the important role of women as consumers after 1890. Lisa Jacobson's *Raising Consumers* (2004) demonstrated that in the early twentieth century, advertisers and mass marketers even targeted children as a potentially lucrative consumer market. Purveyors of consumption also found a large and willing market among immigrants to urban America. For example, Andrew R. Heinze's *Adapting to Abundance* (1990) concluded that for Jewish immigrants to New York City's Lower East Side the culture of consumption contributed to the process of assimilation. Jenna Weissman Joselit made a similar argument in *The Wonders of America* (1994).[246]

Not all Americans responded to the culture of consumption with enthusiasm, however. Jackson Lears's complex cultural history *No Place of Grace* (1983) identified a powerful strain of antimodernism among urban bourgeois elites in late-nineteenth-century America. Initially repulsed by the rise of corporate bureaucracy and pervasive consumption, Lears's antimodernists ultimately found "therapeutic" ways to adapt to material progress.[247] Lizabeth Cohen's *Making a New Deal* (1990, 2008), a study of mass consumption among industrial workers in Chicago, found a strong resistance to mass marketing and retail grocery chains in ethnic communities, where residents preferred instead the neighborhood shops that had familiar products.[248] Meg Jacobs's *Pocketbook Politics* (2005) and Charles F. McGovern's *Sold American* (2006) both documented the emergence of consumer activism and consumer advocacy movements after about 1890. Dana Frank's *Purchasing Power* (1994) linked consumer organizing in early-twentieth-century Seattle to gender concerns and labor activism. Robert E. Weems Jr.'s *Desegregating the Dollar* (1998) traced the mass marketers' discovery of the black consumer market in the early twentieth century, the rise of black consumer activism such as boycotts and civil rights sit-ins, and the decline of black small businesses that could not compete with the national marketing of big business.[249]

For middle-class urbanites of the late nineteenth and early twentieth centuries, the department store became the focus of consumer desires and fantasies. William Leach's *Land of Desire* (1993) presented the most comprehensive study of these multistory downtown institutions built by "merchant princes" such as A. T. Stewart in New York City, Marshall Field in Chicago, and John Wanamaker in Philadelphia. Creating desire through ostentatious window displays and appealing floor arrangements of goods, the department store encapsulated the "consumer capitalism" of the decades between 1880 and 1930. Middle-class women were particularly attracted to these shopping palaces, often on a daily basis, suggesting to several scholars that the new shopping venues feminized public space in the cities of the industrial era.[250] Susan Porter Benson's *Counter Cultures* (1986) and Kathy Peiss's *Cheap Amusements* (1986) showed that working-class women found work as department store retail clerks. Elaine S. Abelson's revelatory book *When Ladies Go A-Thieving* (1989) demonstrated the power of desire in a study of middle-class women shoplifters in Victorian era department stores.[251]

The growing popularity of the automobile and the rise of suburbia eventually ended the dominance of downtown department stores. Retailers followed their customers to the suburbs, beginning slowly in the 1920s and then in a rush after 1945, first to shopping centers and then to enclosed suburban malls. Richard Longstreth's *City Center to Regional Mall* (1998) traced this shift in retailing in Los Angeles between 1920 and 1950. Longstreth elaborated in a second book, *The Drive-in, the Supermarket, and the Transformation of Commercial Space in Los Angeles, 1914–1941* (2000). Heavily illustrated, both books provided careful detail on commercial architecture, as well as on the demographic and technological forces for change. Catherine Gudis's *Buyways* (2004) linked the emerging automobile culture to the rapid spread of billboards and roadside advertising in urban and rural America.[252]

A number of other books have also dealt with urban and suburban retailing. M. Jeffrey Hardwick's *Mall Maker* (2004) documented the career of architect Victor Gruen, who designed some of the first postwar shopping centers. Nicholas Dagen Bloom's *Merchant of Illusion* (2004) recounted the career of James W. Rouse, a builder of shopping centers, new towns, and, more famously, festival marketplaces in many cities, including Baltimore, Boston, Miami, Philadelphia, and New York. William Severini Kowinski's *The Malling of America* (1985) reported on the virtual takeover of postwar retailing by shopping centers and enclosed malls.[253] Bernard J. Frieden and Lynne B. Sagalyn's *Downtown, Inc.* (1989) and Alison Isenberg's *Downtown America* (2004) dealt in part with efforts to revitalize downtown shopping districts long abandoned by department stores.[254] In addition to new shopping locations, new forms of advertising emerged in the 1920s with radio and in the 1950s with television, subjects discussed in Susan Smulyan's *Selling Radio* (1994) and Lynn Spigel and Denise Mann's *Private Screenings* (1992). All of this relatively recent scholarship on consumption has provided new historical perspectives on urban life and society in the United States.[255]

SPORTS AND LEISURE

In recent decades, urban historians have displayed an interest in documenting and interpreting how city people used increasing amounts of leisure time in sports, tourism, cultural activities, or simply socializing with others. The best synopsis of urban sports history can be found in Steven A. Reiss, *City Games: The Evolution of American Urban Society and the Rise of Sports* (1989), which recognized both the ways in which sports defined class boundaries (in the early nineteenth century) and promoted a mass spectator culture (beginning in the late nineteenth century).[256] Baseball, in particular, was extremely popular in the city from the late nineteenth century, but other sporting and recreational activities also caught on. Baseball, boxing, and especially horse racing came to be linked to city politics, gambling, and organized crime, as documented in Riess's *The Sport of Kings and the Kings of Crime* (2011).[257] Some Progressive Era playground reformers thought of baseball as a means of socializing and controlling urban and immigrant children, as suggested in Dominick Cavallo's *Muscles and Morals* (1981). Working from the same interpretive framework, Peter Levine's *Ellis Island to Ebbets Field* (1992) contended that sports in America—especially baseball, basketball, and boxing—helped transform immigrant Jews into assimilated Jews. Neil Lanctot's *Negro League Baseball* (2004) provided the most comprehensive research study of a key black cultural institution that did not survive the integration of major league baseball. An excellent case study, Rob Ruck's *Sandlot Seasons: Sport in Black Pittsburgh* (1987), documented the ways in which organized black baseball served as "a forum for symbolic political assertion and an area for real political struggle" but also became centrally involved in the numbers racket in the black community.[258]

Along with sport, taverns and saloons played an extremely important role over time in urban communities. They served as essential places of leisure, but they had other functions as well, such as politicizing patrons in the American revolutionary era, mobilizing voters in the machine-politics era, and socializing immigrants and rural transplants in the industrial period. Books by David W. Conroy, Peter Thompson, and Sharon V. Salinger documented the significance of taverns, saloons, and the drinking culture in the colonial period, revealing the social, economic, and political functions of these key community institutions. Benjamin J. Carp's *Rebels Rising: Cities and the American Revolution* (2007) argued that "taverns were the perfect venues for revolutionaries seeking to surmount the challenges of political mobilization."[259] Books by Roy Rosenzweig, Perry R. Duis, and Thomas J. Noel detailed the multifaceted roles of industrial-era saloons in Worcester, Boston, Chicago, and Denver. These studies contended that such working-class urban institutions had significant social, political, and economic functions. Madelon Powers's study of saloons in several industrial-era cities, *Faces along the Bar* (1998), argued for the critical importance of saloons in community building during a period of social upheaval. Mary Murphy's *Mining Cultures: Men, Women, and Leisure in Butte, 1914–41* (1997) noted that saloons on the mining frontier were "multifunctional institutions" that continued operating despite Prohibition. In *Dry Manhattan* (2007), Michael A. Lerner analyzed the ethnic and religious conflicts over drinking and the nightclub cultures that emerged during the 1920s. Burton W. Peretti's *Nightclub City* (2007) portrayed Manhattan nightclubs of the 1920s and 1930s as "representative of a more general rebellion in American culture against traditional concepts of civic life."[260]

A number of historical studies have examined the variety of public amusements that developed in the industrial city as working men and women with more leisure time and disposable income sought distractions from their workaday worlds. David Nasaw's *Going Out* (1993) concentrated on the significance of amusement parks, vaudeville, world's fairs, baseball, and motion pictures in late-nineteenth- and early-twentieth-century cities. Lengthy discussions about vaudeville houses and baseball parks in Gunther Barth's *City People* (1980) formed an important part of his larger argument about the unifying cultural and institutional forces at work in nineteenth-century American cities. Patricia C. Click's *The Spirit of the Times* (1989) focused on class-based public amusements in nineteenth-century Baltimore, Norfolk, and Richmond. Scott C. Martin and Barbara Berglund wrote on nineteenth-century patterns of leisure in the Pittsburgh area and San Francisco, respectively, emphasizing how such activities fostered class, ethnic, and gender distinctions but also encouraged a sense of community. John Kasson's *Amusing the Million* (1978) noted how the success of New York City's Coney Island mirrored the development of American mass culture. Woody Register's *The Kid of Coney Island* (2001) emphasized the entrepreneurial aspects of popular amusement parks. Robert W. Snyder's *The Voice of the City* (1989) and Robert C. Allen's *Horrible Prettiness* (1991) did the same for two other forms of public entertainment, vaudeville and burlesque theater.[261]

Musical performance and movies increasingly absorbed Americans' leisure time by the early twentieth century. Lewis A. Ehrenberg's *Steppin' Out* (1981), Ehrenberg's *Swingin' the Dream* (1998), and Burton W. Peretti's *The Creation of Jazz* (1992) argued that nightclub jazz musicians and their audiences helped define a new urban culture in the early twentieth century.[262] In *Cheap Amusements* (1986), Kathy Peiss related how young working women took advantage of new opportunities for leisure in industrial cities. In *For the Love of Pleasure* (1998), Lauren Rabinovitz pursued the same theme in documenting women's enthusiasm for movies in turn-of-the-century Chicago. Gregory A. Waller's *Main Street Amusements* (1995) used Lexington, Kentucky, as a case study of how the downtowns of southern communities provided outlets for leisure, amusement, and culture. Richard Butsch's edited collection *For Fun and Profit* (1990) presented essays arguing that by the twentieth century, leisure had become a form of consumption.[263]

Tourism, generally considered a modern form of leisure, has deep urban roots. For instance, John Hope Franklin's *A Southern Odyssey* (1976) followed early-nineteenth-century elite southern travelers to northern cities for business, education, or cultural curiosity. In *Doing the Town* (2001), Catherine Cocks discovered an early pattern of pleasure travel in urban tourism. Angela M. Blake's *How New York Became American, 1890–1924* (2006) documented the role of business leaders and boosters in promoting an exotic public image for New York City that attracted tourists and pleasure seekers. Urban boosters in Atlanta, according to Harvey K. Newman's *Southern Hospitality* (1999), used tourism to help shape the city's development even before 1900. The quintessential tourist destination for most of the first half of the twentieth century was Miami (and Miami Beach). Mark S. Foster's *Castles in the Sand* (2000) recounted the meteoric career of Carl G. Fisher, the builder and chief promoter of Miami Beach. Susan R. Braden's *The Architecture of Leisure* (2002) discussed the significance of the resort hotels built by Florida boosters Henry Flagler and Henry Plant in Miami, Tampa, Palm Beach, and Saint Augustine beginning in the late nineteenth century.[264]

The revenue generated by tourism has become the economic lifeblood of some cities, as detailed in books about New Orleans by J. Mark Souther, Anthony J. Stanonis, and Kevin Fox Gotham. In separate books, Samuel Kinser and Reid Mitchell explored the significance of the New Orleans Mardi Gras tradition.[265] Hal K. Rothman's *Devil's Bargain: Tourism in the Twentieth-Century American West* (1998) analyzed the impact of western travel on such cities as Santa Fe and Las Vegas. John M. Findlay's *Magic Lands: Western Cityscapes and American Culture after 1940* (1992) noted the special importance of urban tourism, with insightful chapters devoted to Disneyland and the 1962 Seattle World's Fair. In *Married to the Mouse* (2001), Richard E. Fogelsong linked the late-twentieth-century growth of Orlando to the arrival of Disney World, now one of the world's top tourist destinations, with consequences that were not always positive for the Orlando metro area.[266]

Beginning in the nineteenth century, American cities periodically sponsored a number of world's fairs and international expositions that celebrated local growth and achievements, showcased new technology, and promoted commercial enterprise.

Robert W. Rydell's influential *All the World's a Fair* (1987) argued that the expositions of the late nineteenth and early twentieth century offered a materialistic vision of progress that supported ruling elites, segregated leisure by social class, promoted racial dominance, and endorsed American imperialism. The Century of Progress expositions held during the Depression-era 1930s, which altogether attracted more than 100 million visitors, sought to affirm faith in capitalism, progress, and government at a time of great anxiety. Rydell's *World of Fairs* (1993) examined fairs held in New York, Chicago, San Francisco, San Diego, Cleveland, and Dallas. James Gilbert's *Whose Fair?* (2009), on the Saint Louis Exposition of 1904, and Cheryl R. Ganz's *The 1933 Chicago World's Fair* (2008) offered good case studies. Chicago's Columbian Exposition of 1893 has attracted a great deal of scholarly attention, most notably including James Gilbert's *Perfect Cities: Chicago's Utopias of 1893* (1991); David F. Burg's *Chicago's White City of 1893* (1976); and R. Reid Badger's *The Great American Fair* (1979).[267]

By the second half of the twentieth century, confronted with deindustrialization, population loss, and budgetary shortfalls, cities frequently emphasized entertainment and tourism to counter financial losses. John Hannigan's *Fantasy City* (1998); *The Tourist City* (1999), edited by Dennis R. Judd and Susan S. Fainstein; and *The Infrastructure of Play* (2003), edited by Dennis R. Judd, offered broad discussion of this phenomenon. Michael N. Danielson's *Home Team* (1997) focused on the significance of professional sports in the post–World War II tourist city. In perhaps the most notable examples of the centrality of tourist revenue for municipal budgets, a few cities have defined themselves almost exclusively as gambling sites. John M. Findlay's *People of Chance* (1986) provided a wide-ranging history of gambling in America. Eugene P. Moehring's *Resort City in the Sunbelt* (1989) and Hal K. Rothman's *Neon Metropolis* (2003) gave insightful histories of the rise of Las Vegas as a gambling mecca. Charles E. Funnell's *By the Beautiful Sea* (1975) and Bryant Simon's *Boardwalk of Dreams* (2004) recounted the transformation of Atlantic City, New Jersey, from a glitzy seaside resort into a tawdry casino town.[268] A different form of gambling—playing the numbers, or bolita—was extremely popular in black communities across the nation from the 1920s onward. Recent studies by Shane White et al. and by Victoria A. Wolcott traced the development and significance of the numbers racket in New York City's Harlem and in Detroit.[269]

CRIME AND VIOLENCE

American cities have long been known as particularly violent places. During the colonial era, seaport communities such as New York, Boston, and Philadelphia endured a high incidence of lawlessness but relied largely on private initiatives to maintain order and deal with crime. Like their British counterparts, these colonial cities maintained night watches and employed a few constables but relied primarily on a limited system of voluntarism. Determined to avoid the tyranny associated with large standing armies, the colonists ardently resisted the establishment of organized police forces. In the decades following the American Revolution, however, the growing and increasingly heterogeneous cities experienced a number of riots, as well as noticeable increases in robbery, drunkenness, and prostitution. The informal arrangements long employed in these cities proved unsatisfactory to growing numbers of urban dwellers who sought a greater degree of safety and security. American cities created police departments in the first decades of the nineteenth century, launching an ongoing and largely unsuccessful attempt to grapple with the lawlessness that continued to characterize urban places in America. *The Civilization of Crime: Violence in Town and Country since the Middle Ages* (1996), edited by Eric H. Monkkonen and Eric A. Johnson, placed the American case into a larger context, considering conditions in Sweden, Holland, and England, among other locations.[270]

Several studies have dealt with urban crime and violence in the colonial and antebellum years. James F. Richardson's *The New York Police: Colonial Times to 1901* (1970) provided one of the best sources on urban crime in the colonial era. Roger Lane's *Murder in America* (1997) dealt with homicide in the nation's early years.[271] Paul A. Gilje's *The Road to Mobocracy* (1987) discussed the scope and importance of civil disorder in early New York City, which he suggested was representative of other communities during those years. Gilje noted that mobs ceased acting as safety valves and social correctives, roles traditionally tolerated by public officials, and became both more autonomous and violent. These changes, he argued, reflected the unsettling influence of industrialization, immigration, and a changing workforce on American cities. Gilje's *Rioting in America* (1996) explored some of the same themes throughout American history, ranging from the colonial era through the late twentieth century. David Grimsted's *American Mobbing, 1828–1861* (1998), Paul O. Weinbaum's *Mobs and Demagogues* (1979), and two books by Michael Feldberg, *The Philadelphia Riots of 1844* (1975) and *The Turbulent Era* (1980), analyzed the rage of violence in early-nineteenth-century American cities. Nigel Cliff's *The Shakespeare Riots* (2007) recounted the Astor Place riot of 1849 in New York City, in which mobs supporting American and British actors faced off, revealing an early American culture war. Michael A. Gordon's *The Orange Riots* (1993) documented patterns of Irish political violence in post–Civil War New York City, as Irish Catholics and Protestants battled in the streets over old-country cultural issues and new-country class divisions. Reflecting the fear of riot and rebellion, Robert M. Fogelson's *America's Armories* (1989) probed circumstances behind the building of massive urban armories in the late nineteenth century as a means of protecting cities and their residents from mass violence. Patricia Cline Cohen's *The Murder of Helen Jewett* (1998) reconstructed the history of a sensational murder of a New York City prostitute in 1836—a case study framed within the larger context of early-nineteenth-century urban life, work, sexuality, and justice.[272]

A number of books explored escalating crime and violence rates in nineteenth-century cities characterized by unchecked population growth, rapid industrialization, and growing ethnic and racial diversity. Roger Lane's *Violent Death in the City* (1979), an analysis of suicides, accidents, and murder in nineteenth-century Philadelphia, relied heavily on obituaries and other published records to uncover the links between urban growth and rising patterns of violence. Lane's *Roots of Violence in Black Philadelphia, 1860–1900* (1989) noted how a black criminal subculture eroded family life and spawned violence; the book demonstrated that modern crime patterns could be traced back to cultural norms established a century earlier. Jeffrey S. Adler's copiously detailed *First in Violence, Deepest in Dirt* (2006), based upon six thousand police reports, courtroom testimony, and commutation petitions, noted a significant change in Chicagoans' violent behavior between 1875 and 1920—that is, the city's inhabitants became less drunken and disorderly and more homicidal. Adler attributed this change to intense job competition, increasing fears of financial instability, and disruptions in family life caused by industrialization and heightened immigration. Eric H. Monkkonen's *Murder in New York City* (2000), an examination of homicide rates in the city beginning in the late 1700s, identified the mid-nineteenth century and the 1920s as particularly lethal periods. Monkkonen considered such variables as age, ethnicity, demographic change, and the availability of weapons, but found no single factor that accounted for fluctuating murder rates.[273]

From the nineteenth century, crime and violence of one kind or another became increasingly threatening in the American city. Analyzing high rates of violent behavior among single men throughout American history, from the frontier era to contemporary inner cities, David Courtwright's *Violent Land* (1996) found the explanation in demography—a shortage of marriageable women and the consequent lack of social control over rootless young men. Kevin J. Mullen's two books on crime in San Francisco, *Let Justice Be Done* (1989) and *Dangerous Strangers* (2005), dealt respectively with vigilante justice in the 1850s and with criminal violence, especially murder committed by new immigrants from 1850 to 2000. Kali N. Gross's *Colored Amazons* (2006), focused on crime, violence, and black women in early-twentieth-century Philadelphia, while Cheryl D. Hicks's *Talk with You Like a Woman* (2010) dealt with black working-class women caught up in the justice system in early-twentieth-century New York City. Studies by Timothy Gilfoyle on New York, John C. Schneider on Detroit, Allen Steinberg on Philadelphia, Michael Willrich on Chicago, and Eric Monkkonen on Columbus, Ohio, explored various aspects of crime and justice in nineteenth-century cities.[274]

Urban scholars have carefully studied the establishment and development of police departments in American cities during the nineteenth century and after. David R. Johnson's *Policing the Urban Underworld* (1979) argued that the behavior of criminals in American cities, rather than the guidance provided by politicians and reformers, determined how fledgling police forces defined their occupation. In Johnson's view, four groups of criminals—professional thieves, street gangs, prostitutes, and gamblers—presented discrete sets of challenges that required different responses from law enforcement authorities. In *Policing the City* (1971), Roger Lane examined the establishment of a uniformed police force in Boston. Lane noted that the city's residents overcame their fears of armed authorities and accepted the necessity of a police department; he also described the political and social tensions that arose between city officials and reformers, between the city and the surrounding countryside, and between urban and rural interests in the Massachusetts legislature. James F. Richardson and Eric H. Monkkonen contributed histories of urban police in the United States, documenting shifts in policing methods, objectives, and levels of success in controlling crime over time. Robert M. Fogelson's *Big City Police* (1979) presented a more sympathetic account of the challenges confronting police departments in the twentieth century.[275] Marilynn Johnson's *Street Justice: A History of Police Violence in New York City* (2003) recounted the sordid history of police brutality from the department's founding in 1845 to the infamous backroom torture of Haitian immigrant Abner Louima in 1997, concluding that the mistreatment of minorities and other vulnerable groups has ebbed and flowed over time, but not necessarily declined. Richard C. Lindberg's *To Serve and Collect* (1991) told an unsavory story of corruption, political influence, and malfeasance in the Chicago police department. In *Black Rage in New Orleans* (2010), Leonard N. Moore documented a history of corruption and police brutality that especially targeted African Americans from World War II to Hurricane Katrina in 2005.[276]

Urban historians who have studied crime in twentieth-century cities have looked especially at the key roles played by organized crime, ethnic gangs, and the influence of the narcotic drug trade. Unlike the sensational popular accounts of organized crime that have proliferated in recent decades, Humbert S. Nelli's *The Business of Crime* (1976) provided a clear-eyed account of the crucial role played by Italians in the development of a national crime cartel in the wake of Prohibition. David Critchley's *The Origin of Organized Crime in America* (2008) pushed back into the late nineteenth century in analyzing the beginnings of New York City's Italian-American criminal underworld. Rufus Schatzberg published two books on African-American organized crime in New York City, demonstrating that although blacks had only partial control of gambling and the numbers racket in the early twentieth century, in the postwar era black criminal organizations took control of gambling and drug distribution in ghetto streets in New York and other cities.[277] In *Vampires, Dragons, and Egyptian Kings* (1999), Eric C. Schneider discussed the importance of masculine identity and an emerging street culture in the rise of youth gangs in post–World War II New York City. In Schneider's account, wrenching economic change, immigration, and dislocations caused by urban renewal pitted African-American, Puerto Rican, and Euro-American adolescents against each other in violent turf battles. Books by James Diego Vigil, Malcolm W. Klein, Martin Sanchez Jankowski, and Andrew J. Diamond likewise described how immigrant and ethnic youths banded together and fought rival gangs to defend their neighborhoods and achieve status. Elijah Anderson's *Code of the Street: Decency, Violence, and the Moral Life of the Inner City* (2000) cited high unemployment, elevated teenage pregnancy rates, and low educational achievement as the principal causes of a deviant street culture that emerged in the postwar years. As Anderson related, the code of the streets sanctioned verbal boasting, sexual prowess, and drug selling, ultimately leading to violence and death. Eric C. Schneider's *Smack: Heroin and the American City* (2008) related an urban history of heroin. The world opiate market consisted of a hierarchy of cities; New York City criminal elements organized national distribution, neighborhoods emerged as retail centers, and increased heroin addiction drove up crime rates.[278]

Historians and social scientists have written on urban crime and violence in other contexts as well. For instance, Kenneth T. Jackson's *The Ku Klux Klan in the City, 1915–1930* (1967) established the strength of the violent KKK in urban settings, especially in northern urban areas in New Jersey, Indiana, Colorado, and Oregon. William D. Jenkins's *Steel Valley Klan* (1990) found the Youngstown, Ohio, region a seedbed of Klan activity. Shawn Lay's *Invisible Empire in the West* (1992) presented essays on the Klan in Denver; El Paso; Salt Lake City; Anaheim, California; and Eugene and La Grande, Oregon. Lay's *Hooded Knights on the Niagara* (1995) outlined the Klan's nefarious activities in Buffalo, New York.[279] Several studies have taken a popular culture perspective. Thus, Nicholas Christopher's *Somewhere in the Night* (1997) and Steve Macek's *Urban Nightmares* (2006) discussed popular perception of cities as particularly violent places in film, fiction, and other media.[280]

THE SEARCH FOR SYNTHESIS

The subject categories discussed in this essay all represent important subfields of urban history research and publication. Knowledgeable readers can probably think of topics that have been omitted, as urban history continues to spread its net more broadly than ever. This historiographical essay has concentrated on books and monographs, but the reader also should be aware of an extensive article literature on all aspects of urban history. The field has been invigorated with an enormous outpouring of scholarly research, especially in the decade and a half since the last edition of this book.

It is also true, however, that the flood of published scholarship in American urban history has fragmented the field and, as in other areas of historical research, prompted calls for synthesis. Few urban historians have responded to the call. The few survey texts in the field—by Charles N. Glaab and A. Theodore Brown, Howard Chudacoff and Judith E. Smith, Zane Miller and Patricia M. Melvin, and David Goldfield and Blaine Brownell—have come the closest to offering a synthesis of the field. Only the Chudacoff and Smith book remains in print at this time.[281] A few others have written interpretive texts of shorter time periods, such as the industrial era, the twentieth century, or the postwar era after 1945.[282]

Fifteen years ago, the second edition of this book predicted that new syntheses of American urban history would probably be produced in the future. That future has not yet arrived. Given the great variations among cities and the enormous published literature of the dozen and a half urban subfields outlined in this essay, it is unlikely that many urbanists will venture into the demanding work of synthesis. What urban history scholars have done, however, has been to enliven the field with many hundreds of engaging, fascinating, and often argumentative books that in the past few decades pushed out the boundaries of urban history in many different directions. Urban history as a research and teaching field has not suffered from the absence of synthetic works. Actually, every teacher of urban history has conceptualized his or her own version of synthesis through lectures and teaching. The editors of this book hope that the mountain of scholarship detailed in this essay will lead interested teachers, students, and researchers into the exciting field of American urban history.

NOTES

1. Richard C. Wade, "Urbanization," in *The Comparative Approach to American History*, ed. C. Vann Woodward (New York, 1968), 203.

2. Arthur M. Schlesinger, "The City in American History," *Mississippi Valley Historical Review* 27 (June 1940): 43–66. See also Schlesinger, *The Rise of the City, 1878–1898* (New York, 1933).

3. Blake McKelvey, "American Urban History Today," *American Historical Review* 57 (July 1952): 919–29; Carl Bridenbaugh, *Cities in the Wilderness* (New York, 1938); Bridenbaugh, *Cities in Revolt* (New York, 1955); Oscar Handlin, *Boston's Immigrants* (Cambridge, MA, 1941); Richard C. Wade, *The Urban Frontier: The Rise of Western Cities, 1790–1830* (Cambridge, MA, 1959). For a model urban biography from this period, see Bayrd Still, *Milwaukee: The History of a City* (Madison, 1948). For outstanding examples of the multivolume genre of urban biography, see Bessie L. Pierce, *A History of Chicago*, 3 vols. (Chicago, 1937–1957); and Constance McLaughlin Green, *Washington*, 2 vols. (Princeton, 1962–1963).

4. Oliver Zunz, "The Synthesis of Social Change: Reflections on American Social History," in *Reliving the Past: The Worlds of Social History*, ed. Oliver Zunz (Chapel Hill, NC, 1985), 54. See also Irwin Unger, "The 'New Left' and American History: Some Recent Trends in United States Historiography," *American Historical Review* 72 (July 1967): 1237–63; Michael Kammen, "The Historian's Vocation and the State of the Discipline in the United States," in *The Past before Us: Contemporary Historical Writing in the United States*, ed. Michael Kammen (Ithaca, NY, 1980), 19–46; Dorothy Ross, "The New and Newer Histories: Social Theory and Historiography in an American Key," in *Imagined Histories: American Historians Interpret the Past*, ed. Anthony Molho and Gordon S. Wood (Princeton, NJ, 1998), 85–106; Harvey J. Graff, "The Shock of the 'New' (Histories): Social Science Histories and Historical Literacies," *Social Science History* 25 (Winter 2001): 483–533.

5. W. O. Aydolette, "Quantification in History," *American Historical Review* 71 (April 1966): 803–25; Edward Shorter, *The Historian and the Computer* (Englewood Cliffs, NJ, 1971); Allan G. Bogue, "Numerical and Formal Analysis in United States History," *Journal of Interdisciplinary History* 12 (Summer 1981): 137–75; Jerome M. Clubb, "Computer Technology and the Source Materials of Social Science History," *Social Science History* 10 (Summer 1986): 97–114. For an early critique of quantitative history, see Jacques Barzun, *Clio and the Doctors* (Chicago, 1974).

6. Sam Bass Warner Jr., *Streetcar Suburbs: The Process of Growth in Boston, 1870–1900* (Cambridge, MA, 1962). See also Warner's other writings: "If All the World Were Philadelphia: A Scaffolding for Urban History, 1774–1930," *American Historical Review* 74 (October 1968): 26–43; *The Private City: Philadelphia in Three Periods of Its Growth* (Philadelphia, 1968); *The Urban Wilderness: A History of the American City* (New York, 1972); *The Way We Really Live: Social Change in Boston since 1920* (Boston, 1977); *Province of Reason* (Cambridge, MA, 1984); and *Greater Boston: Adapting Regional Traditions to the Present* (Philadelphia, 2001).

7. Eric E. Lampard's articles include "American Historians and the Study of Urbanization," *American Historical Review* 67 (October 1961): 49–61; "Urbanization and Social Change: On Broadening the Scope and Relevance of Urban History," in *The Historian and the City*, ed. Oscar Handlin and John Burchard (Cambridge, MA, 1963), 225–47; "Historical Aspects of Urbanization," in *The Study of Urbanization*, ed. Philip M. Hauser and Leo F. Schnore (New York, 1965), 519–54; "Historical Contours of Contemporary Urban Society: A Comparative View," *Journal of Contemporary History* 4 (July 1969): 3–25; "The Dimensions of Urban History: A Footnote to the 'Urban Crisis,'" *Pacific Historical Review* 39 (August 1970): 261–78; "The Pursuit of Happiness in the City: Changing Opportunities and Options in America," *Transactions of the Royal Historical Society* 23 (1973): 175–220; "The Urbanizing World," in *The Victorian City*, ed. H. J. Dyos and Michael Wolff (London, 1973), 1:3–57; "City Making and City Mending in the United States," in *Urbanization in the Americas*, ed.

Woodrow Borah et al. (Ottawa, 1980), 105–118; and "The Nature of Urbanization," in *Visions of the Modern City*, ed. William Sharpe and Leonard Wallock (New York, 1983), 47–96. See also Bruce M. Stave, "A Conversation with Eric E. Lampard," *Journal of Urban History* 1 (August 1975): 440–72.

8. Roy Lubove, "The Urbanization Process: An Approach to Historical Research," *Journal of the American Institute of Planners* 33 (January 1967): 33–39; Lubove, *Twentieth-Century Pittsburgh: Government, Business, and Environmental Change* (New York, 1969); and Lubove, *Twentieth-Century Pittsburgh: The Post-Steel Era* (Pittsburgh, PA, 1996).

9. Stephan Thernstrom, *Poverty and Progress: Social Mobility in a Nineteenth-Century City* (Cambridge, MA, 1964); Thernstrom and Richard Sennett, eds., *Nineteenth-Century Cities: Essays in the New Urban History* (New Haven, CT, 1969); Leo F. Schnore, ed., *The New Urban History: Quantitative Explorations by American Historians* (Princeton, NJ, 1975). See also the extensive discussion of *Poverty and Progress* in *Social Science History* 10 (Spring 1986): 1–44.

10. For a sampling of this mobility literature see Richard J. Hopkins, "Occupational and Geographical Mobility in Atlanta, 1870–1896," *Journal of Southern History* 34 (May 1968): 200–213; Stephan Thernstrom and Peter R. Knights, "Men in Motion: Some Data and Speculations about Urban Population Mobility in Nineteenth-Century America," *Journal of Interdisciplinary History* 1 (Autumn 1970): 7–35; Peter R. Knights, *The Plain People of Boston, 1830–1860: A Study in City Growth* (New York, 1971); Howard P. Chudacoff, *Mobile Americans: Residential and Social Mobility in Omaha, 1880–1920* (New York, 1972); Michael B. Katz, *The People of Hamilton, Canada West: Family and Class in a Mid-Nineteenth-Century City* (Cambridge, MA, 1975); Dean R. Esslinger, *Immigrants and the City: Ethnicity and Mobility in a Nineteenth-Century Midwestern Community* (Port Washington, NY, 1975); Stuart M. Blumin, *The Urban Threshold: Growth and Change in a Nineteenth-Century American Community* (Chicago, 1976); Thomas Kessner, *The Golden Door: Italian and Jewish Mobility in New York City, 1880–1915* (New York, 1977); Gordon W. Kirk Jr., *The Promise of American Life: Social Mobility in a Nineteenth-Century Immigrant Community, Holland, Michigan, 1847–1894* (Philadelphia, 1978); Peter R. Decker, *Fortunes and Failures: White-Collar Mobility in Nineteenth-Century San Francisco* (Cambridge, MA, 1978); Clyde Griffin and Sally Griffin, *Natives and Newcomers: The Ordering of Opportunity in Mid-Nineteenth-Century Poughkeepsie* (Cambridge, MA, 1978); and Knights, *Yankee Destinies: The Lives of Ordinary Nineteenth-Century Bostonians* (Chapel Hill, NC, 1991).

11. Stephan Thernstrom, "Reflections on the New Urban History," *Daedalus* 100 (Spring 1971): 359–75.

12. Michael Frisch, "American Urban History as an Example of Recent Historiography," *History and Theory* 18 (1979): 350–77.

13. Stephan Thernstrom, *The Other Bostonians: Poverty and Progress in the American Metropolis, 1880–1970* (Cambridge, MA, 1973); Bruce M. Stave, "A Conversation with Stephan Thernstrom," *Journal of Urban History* 1 (February 1975): 189–215.

14. John B. Sharpless and Sam Bass Warner Jr., "Urban History," *American Behavioral Scientist* 21 (November–December 1977): 221–44. See also Bruce M. Stave, "A Conversation with Sam Bass Warner, Jr.," *Journal of Urban History* 1 (November 1974): 85–100; and Stave, "A Conversation with Sam Bass Warner, Jr.: Ten Years Later," *Journal of Urban History* 11 (November 1984): 83–113.

15. Theodore Hershberg, "The New Urban History: Toward an Interdisciplinary History of the City," *Journal of Urban History* 5 (November 1978): 3–40; Hershberg, ed., *Philadelphia: Work, Space, Family and Group Experience in the Nineteenth Century* (New York, 1981), 3–35.

16. For historiographical surveys, see Charles N. Glaab, "The Historian and the American City: A Bibliographic Survey," in *The Study of Urbanization*, ed. Philip M. Hauser and Leo F. Schnore, 53–80; Dwight W. Hoover, "The Diverging Paths of American Urban History," *American Quarterly* 20 (Summer 1968): 296–317; Dana F. White, "The Underdeveloped Discipline: Interdisciplinary Directions in American Urban History," *American Studies: An International Newsletter* 9 (Spring 1971): 3–16; Raymond A. Mohl, "The History of the American City," in *The Reinterpretation of American History and Culture*, ed. William H. Cartwright and Richard L. Watson Jr. (Washington, DC, 1973), 165–205; Clyde Griffin, "The United States: The 'New Urban History,'" *Urban History Yearbook* (Leicester, UK, 1977), 15–23; Michael H. Ebner, "Urban History: Retrospect and Prospect," *Journal of American History* 68 (June 1981): 69–84; Bruce M. Stave, "Urban History: A Tale of Many Cities," *Magazine of History* 2 (Winter 1986): 32–37; Howard Gillette Jr. and Zane L. Miller, eds., *American Urbanism: A Historiographical Review* (Westport, CT, 1987); Terrence J. McDonald, "The Burdens of Urban History: The Theory of the State in Recent American Social History," *Studies in American Political Development* 3 (1989): 3–55; Howard Gillette Jr., "Rethinking American Urban History: New Directions for the Posturban Era," *Social Science History* 14 (Summer 1990): 203–28; Timothy J. Gilfoyle, "White Cities, Linguistic Turns, and Disneylands: The New Paradigms of Urban History," *Reviews in American History* 26 (March 1998): 175–204; James Connolly, "Bringing the City Back In: Space and Place in the Urban History of the Gilded Age and Progressive Era," *Journal of the Gilded Age and Progressive Era* 1 (July 2003): 258–78; Mary Corbin Sies, "North American Urban History: The Everyday Politics and Spatial Logics of Metropolitan Life," *Urban History Review* 32 (Fall 2003): 28–42; Clay McShane, "The State of the Art in North American Urban History," *Journal of Urban History* 32 (May 2006): 582–97; Timothy Gilfoyle, "American Urban Histories," in *A Century of American Historiography*, ed. James M. Banner Jr. (Boston, 2010), 156–69. See also Bruce M. Stave, *The Making of Urban History: Historiography through Oral History* (Beverly Hills, CA, 1977), a collection of Stave's *Journal of Urban History* interviews with leading urban historians: Blake McKelvey, Bayrd Still, Constance M. Green, Oscar Handlin, Richard C. Wade, Sam Bass Warner Jr., Stephan Thernstrom, Eric E. Lampard, and Samuel P. Hays.

17. Bruce M. Stave, "In Pursuit of Urban History: Conversations with Myself and Others—A View from the United States," in *The Pursuit of Urban History*, ed. Derek Fraser and Anthony Sutcliffe (London, 1983), 424. For one objection to Stave's conclusion, see Terrence J. McDonald, "The Pursuit of Urban History: To the Rear March," *Historical Methods* 18 (Summer 1985): 116.

18. Richard C. Wade, *The Urban Frontier: The Rise of Western Cities, 1790–1830* (Cambridge, MA, 1959). Some earlier historians conceptualized western urbanization in similar ways. See Bayrd Still, "Patterns of Mid-Nineteenth-Century Urbanization in the Middle West," *Mississippi Valley Historical Review* 28 (September 1941): 187–206; Eric E. Lampard, "The History of Cities in the Economically Advanced Areas," *Economic Development and Cultural Change* 3 (January 1955): 121–23. On the evolution of the city-region concept, see Carl Abbott, "Frontiers and Sections: Cities and Regions in American Growth," in *American Urbanism: A Historiographical Review*, ed. Howard Gillette Jr. and Zane L. Miller (New York, 1987), 271–290; Edward K. Muller, "From Waterfront to Metropolitan Region: The Geographical Development of American Cities," in *American Urbanism*, ed. Gillette and Miller, 105–133; Raymond A. Mohl, "City and Region: The Missing Dimension in U.S. Urban History," *Journal of Urban History* 25 (November 1998): 3–21.

19. Richard C. Wade, *Slavery in the Cities: The South, 1820–1860* (New York, 1964). Claudia D. Goldin, *Urban Slavery in the American South, 1820–1860: A Quantitative History* (Chicago, 1976), employed quantitative methodologies, disputed Wade's findings, and empha-

sized the strength of slavery in urban settings. See also Leonard P. Curry, *The Free Black in Urban America, 1800 1850: The Shadow of a Dream* (Chicago, 1986), which surveyed fifteen southern and northern cities in the antebellum years.

20. David R. Goldfield, *Cotton Fields and Skyscrapers: Southern City and Region, 1607–1980* (Baton Rouge, LA, 1982). See also Goldfield's "The New Regionalism," *Journal of Urban History* 10 (February 1984): 171–86, and his collection of essays, *Region, Race, and Culture: Interpreting the Urban South* (Baton Rouge, LA, 1997). For a critique, see Bradley R. Rice, "How Different Is the Southern City?" *Journal of Urban History* 11 (November 1985): 115–21. Goldfield drew upon an earlier sociological literature on southern regionalism and urbanization. See Howard W. Odum, *Southern Regions of the United States* (Chapel Hill, NC, 1936); Rupert B. Vance and Nicholas J. Demerath, eds., *The Urban South* (Chapel Hill, NC, 1954).

21. William Cronon, *Nature's Metropolis: Chicago and the Great West* (New York, 1991). Cronon's book stimulated considerable discussion and debate. See, for instance, Richard Walker, ed., "William Cronon's *Nature's Metropolis*: A Symposium," *Antipode: A Radical Journal of Geography* 26 (April 1994): 113–76; Peter A. Coclanis, "Urbs in Horto," *Reviews in American History* 20 (March 1992): 14–20; and Paul Barrett, "Chicago and Its Interpreters," *Journal of Urban History* 20 (August 1994): 577–84.

22. Eugene P. Moehring, *Urbanism and Empire in the Far West, 1840–1890* (Reno, NV, 2004), quotation on p. xii; Gray Brechin, *Imperial San Francisco: Urban Power, Earthly Ruin* (Berkeley, CA, 2006).

23. Timothy R. Mahoney, *River Towns in the Great West: The Structure of Provincial Urbanization in the American Midwest, 1820–1870* (Cambridge, UK, 1990); Jeffrey S. Adler, *Yankee Merchants and the Making of the Urban West: The Rise and Fall of Antebellum St. Louis* (Cambridge, UK, 1991); Gunther Barth, *Instant Cities: Urbanization and the Rise of San Francisco and Denver* (New York, 1975). See also Mahoney, "Urban History in a Regional Context," *Journal of American History* 72 (September 1985): 318–39.

24. Carl Abbott, *The Metropolitan Frontier: Cities in the Modern American West* (Tucson, AZ, 1993), quotation on p. xii; Abbott, *How Cities Won the West: Four Centuries of Urban Change in Western North America* (Albuquerque, NM, 2008). See also Abbott's essay "The Metropolitan Region: Western Cities in the New Urban Era," in *The Twentieth-Century West: Historical Interpretations*, ed. Gerald D. Nash and Richard W. Etulain (Albuquerque, NM, 1989), 71-98.

25. Earl Pomeroy, *The American Far West in the Twentieth Century* (New Haven, CT, 2008), 149–224; Bradford Luckingham, *The Urban Southwest: A Profile History of Albuquerque, El Paso, Phoenix, and Tucson* (El Paso, TX, 1982); Michael F. Logan, *Fighting Sprawl and City Hall: Resistance to Urban Growth in the Southwest* (Tucson, AZ, 1995); Gerald D. Nash, *The American West Transformed: The Impact of the Second World War* (Bloomington, IN, 1985).

26. Carl Abbott, *Boosters and Businessmen: Popular Economic Thought and Urban Growth in the Antebellum Middle West* (Westport, CT, 1981); Timothy B. Spears, *Chicago Dreaming: Midwesterners and the City, 1871–1919* (Chicago, 2005); Jon C. Teaford, *Cities of the Heartland: The Rise and Fall of the Industrial Midwest* (Bloomington, IN, 1993); Anthony M. Orum, *City-Building in America* (Boulder, CO, 1995).

27. Carl Abbott, *Political Terrain: Washington, D.C., from Tidewater Town to Global Metropolis* (Chapel Hill, NC, 1999).

28. Don H. Doyle, *New Men, New Cities, New South: Atlanta, Nashville, Charleston, Mobile, 1860–1910* (Chapel Hill, NC, 1990), quotation on p. xiii. For other studies of the urban South in a regional context, see Blaine A. Brownell and David R. Goldfield, eds., *The*

City in Southern History: The Growth of Urban Civilization in the South (Port Washington, NY, 1977); Blaine A. Brownell, *The Urban Ethos in the South, 1920–1930* (Baton Rouge, LA, 1975); David R. Goldfield, *Urban Growth in the Age of Sectionalism: Virginia, 1847–1861* (Baton Rouge, LA, 1977); Howard N. Rabinowitz, *Race Relations in the Urban South, 1865–1890* (New York, 1978); Douglas L. Smith, *The New Deal in the Urban South* (Baton Rouge, LA, 1988); Roger Biles, "The Urban South in the Great Depression," *Journal of Southern History* 56 (February 1990): 71–100.

29. Don S. Kirschner, *City and Country: Rural Responses to Urbanization in the 1920s* (Westport, CT, 1970); David B. Danborn, *The Resisted Revolution: Urban America and the Industrialization of Agriculture, 1900–1930* (Ames, IA, 1979).

30. Kevin Phillips, *The Emerging Republican Majority* (New Rochelle, NY, 1969); Kirkpatrick Sale, *Power Shift: The Rise of the Southern Rim and Its Challenge to the Eastern Establishment* (New York, 1975).

31. Carl Abbott, *The New Urban America: Growth and Politics in Sunbelt Cities* (Chapel Hill, NC, 1981; rev. ed., 1987).

32. Richard M. Bernard and Bradley R. Rice, eds., *Sunbelt Cities: Politics and Growth since World War II* (Austin, 1983); Raymond A. Mohl, ed., *Searching for the Sunbelt: Historical Perspectives on a Region* (Knoxville, TN, 1990); Randall M. Miller and George E. Pozzetta, eds., *Shades of the Sunbelt: Essays on Race, Ethnicity, and the Urban South* (Westport, CT, 1988). For an excellent counterpoint to the sunbelt city studies, see Richard M. Bernard, ed., *Snowbelt Cities: Metropolitan Politics in the Northeast and Midwest since World War II* (Bloomington, IN, 1990). For social science perspectives on the sunbelt, see David C. Perry and Alfred J. Watkins, eds., *The Rise of the Sunbelt Cities* (Beverly Hills, CA, 1977); Robert Jay Dilger, *The Sunbelt/Snowbelt Controversy: The War over Federal Funds* (New York, 1982); Larry Sawers and William K. Tabb, eds., *Sunbelt/Snowbelt: Urban Development and Regional Restructuring* (New York, 1984).

33. An important recent article suggests that there may yet be life in the regionalist approach. See Andrew Needham and Allen Dieterich-Ward, "Beyond the Metropolis: Metropolitan Growth and Regional Transformation in Postwar America," *Journal of Urban History* 35 (November 2009): 943–69.

34. Kenneth T. Jackson, *Crabgrass Frontier: The Suburbanization of the United States* (New York, 1985). Among the best historiographical essays on suburbanization are Michael H. Ebner, "Re-reading Suburban America: Urban Population Deconcentration, 1810–1980," *American Quarterly* 37 (1985): 368–81; and Margaret Marsh, "Reconsidering the Suburbs: An Exploration of Suburban Historiography," *Pennsylvania Magazine of History and Biography* 112 (October 1988): 579–605. Also see Barbara M. Kelly, ed., *Suburbia Reexamined* (Westport, CT, 1989).

35. Henry C. Binford, *The First Suburbs: Residential Communities on the Boston Periphery, 1815–1860* (Chicago, 1985). Also see Tamara Plakins Thornton, *Cultivating Gentlemen: The Meaning of Country Life among the Boston Elite, 1785–1860* (New Haven, CT, 1989), and, for a later period, Matthew Edel, Elliott D. Sclar, and Daniel Luria, *Shaky Palaces: Homeownership and Social Mobility in Boston's Suburbanization* (New York, 1984).

36. John R. Stilgoe, *Borderland: Origins of the American Suburb, 1820–1939* (New Haven, CT, 1988). On similar themes, see Clifford Edward Clark Jr., *The American Family Home, 1800–1960* (Chapel Hill, NC, 1986).

37. Jon C. Teaford, *City and Suburb: The Political Fragmentation of Metropolitan America, 1850–1970* (Baltimore, 1979).

38. Margaret Marsh, *Suburban Lives* (New Brunswick, NJ, 1990). Also see Mary Corbin Sies, "The City Transformed: Nature, Technology, and the Suburban Ideal, 1877–1917," *Journal of Urban History* 14 (November 1987): 81–111.

39. John Archer, *Architecture and Suburbia: From English Villa to American Dream House, 1690–2000* (Minneapolis, 2005); Robert M. Fogelson, *Bourgeois Nightmares: Suburbia, 1870–1930* (New Haven, CT, 2007).

40. Daniel Schaffer, *Garden Cities for America: The Radburn Experience* (Philadelphia, 1982); Zane L. Miller, *Suburb: Neighborhood and Community in Forest Park, Ohio, 1935–1976* (Knoxville, TN, 1981); Carol A. O'Connor, *A Sort of Utopia: Scarsdale, 1891–1981* (Albany, NY, 1983); David R. Contosta, *Suburb in the City: Chestnut Hill, Philadelphia, 1850–1990* (Columbus, OH, 1992); William S. Worley, *J. C. Nichols and the Shaping of Kansas City* (Columbia, MO, 1990); Michael H. Ebner, *Creating Chicago's North Shore: A Suburban History* (Chicago, 1988); Roger Panetta, ed., *Westchester: The American Suburb* (New York, 2006).

41. Ann Durkin Keating, *Building Chicago: Suburban Developers and the Creation of a Divided Metropolis* (Columbus, OH, 1988); Keating, *Chicagoland: City and Suburbs in the Railroad Age* (Chicago, 2005); Marc A. Weiss, *The Rise of the Community Builders: The American Real Estate Industry and Urban Land Planning* (New York, 1987); Barbara M. Kelly, *Expanding the American Dream: Building and Rebuilding Levittown* (Albany, NY, 1993); Dianne Harris, ed., *Second Suburb: Levittown, Pennsylvania* (Pittsburgh, PA, 2010); Joseph L. Arnold, *The New Deal in the Suburbs: A History of the Greenbelt Town Program, 1935–1954* (Columbus, OH, 1971); Arnold R. Alanen and Joseph A. Eden, *Main Street Ready-Made: The New Deal Community of Greendale, Wisconsin* (Madison, WI, 1987); and the early chapters of Mike Davis, *City of Quartz: Excavating the Future in Los Angeles* (London, 1990).

42. Robert Fishman, *Bourgeois Utopias: The Rise and Fall of Suburbia* (New York, 1987); Fishman, "America's New City: Megalopolis Unbound," *The Wilson Quarterly* 14 (Winter 1990): 25–48.

43. Joel Garreau, *Edge City: Life on the New Frontier* (New York, 1991); Jon C. Teaford, *Post-Suburbia: Governments and Politics in the Edge Cities* (Baltimore, 1996); Peter O. Muller, *The Outer City: Geographical Consequences of the Urbanization of the Suburbs* (Washington, DC, 1976); Muller, *Contemporary Suburban America* (Englewood Cliffs, NJ, 1981); Robert Bruegmann, *Sprawl: A Compact History* (Chicago, 2006).

44. Scott Donaldson, *The Suburban Myth* (New York, 1969); Kevin M. Kruse and Thomas J. Sugrue, eds., *The New Suburban History* (Chicago, 2006); Eric Avila, *Popular Culture in the Age of White Flight: Fear and Fantasy in Suburban Los Angeles* (Berkeley, CA, 2004). On industrial suburbs, see Robert Lewis, ed., *Manufacturing Suburbs: Building Work and Home on the Metropolitan Fringe* (Philadelphia, 2004); Lewis, *Chicago Made: Factory Networks in the Industrial Metropolis* (Chicago, 2008); Bennett Berger, *Working-Class Suburb: A Study of Auto Workers in Suburbia* (Berkeley, CA, 1968). For suburban ethnic diversity, see Timothy P. Fong, *The First Suburban Chinatown: The Remaking of Monterey Park, California* (Philadelphia, 1994); Audrey Singer, Susan W. Hardwick, and Caroline B. Brettell, eds., *Twenty-First Century Gateways: Immigrant Incorporation in Suburban America* (Washington, DC, 2008).

45. Andrew Wiese, *Places of Their Own: African American Suburbanization in the Twentieth Century* (Chicago, 2004). Other studies of African-American suburbanization include Bruce B. Williams, *Black Workers in an Industrial Suburb* (New Brunswick, NJ, 1987); Bruce D. Haynes, *Red Lines, Black Spaces: The Politics of Race and Space in a Middle-Class Suburb* (New Haven, CT, 2001); William H. Wilson, *Hamilton Park: A Planned Black Community in Dallas* (Baltimore, 1998); and on efforts to open suburban housing to minorities, Anthony Downs, *Opening Up the Suburbs: An Urban Strategy for America* (New Haven, CT, 1973); and David L. Kirp, John P. Dwyer, and Larry Rosenthal, *Our Town: Race, Housing, and the Soul of Suburbia* (New Brunswick, NJ, 1995).

46. Kevin M. Kruse, *White Flight: Atlanta and the Making of Modern Conservatism* (Princeton, NJ, 2005); Matthew D. Lassiter, *The Silent Majority: Suburban Politics in the Sunbelt South* (Princeton, NJ, 2006); Rob Kling, Spencer Olin, and Mark Poster, eds., *Postsuburban California: The Transformation of Orange County since World War II* (Berkeley, CA, 1991); Lisa McGirr, *Suburban Warriors: The Origins of the New American Right* (Princeton, NJ, 2001); Becky M. Nicolaides, *My Blue Heaven: Life and Politics in the Working-Class Suburbs of Los Angeles, 1920–1965* (Chicago, 2002). Also see Michael Danielson, *The Politics of Exclusion* (New York, 1976); and Stanley B. Greenberg, *Middle Class Dreams: The Politics and Power of the New American Majority* (New Haven, CT, 1996).

47. For a key essay on the modern American metropolis incorporating spatial conceptualization, see Robert O. Self and Thomas J. Sugrue, "The Power of Place: Race, Political Economy, and Identity in the Postwar Metropolis," in *A Companion to Post-1945 America*, ed. Jean-Christophe Agnew and Roy Rosenzweig (Malden, MA, 2002), 20–43. For historiographical discussions of space and place, see James Connolly, "Bringing the City Back In: Space and Place in the Urban History of the Gilded Age and Progressive Era," *Journal of the Gilded Age and Progressive Era* 1 (July 2003): 258–78; Mary Corbin Sies, "North American Urban History: The Everyday Politics and Spatial Logics of Metropolitan Life," *Urban History Review* 32 (Fall 2003): 28–164.

48. Benjamin L. Carp, *Rebels Rising: Cities and the American Revolution* (New York, 2009).

49. Simon P. Newman, *Parades and the Politics of the Street: Festive Culture in the Early American Republic* (Philadelphia, 1997); David Waldstreicher, *In the Midst of Perpetual Fetes: The Making of American Nationalism, 1776–1820* (Chapel Hill, NC, 1997). Susan G. Davis, *Parades and Power: Street Theater in Nineteenth-Century Philadelphia* (Philadelphia, 1986); Mary P. Ryan, *Civic Wars: Democracy and Public Life in the American City during the Nineteenth Century* (Berkeley, CA, 1998).

50. Dell Upton, *Another City: Urban Life and Urban Spaces in the New American Republic* (New Haven, CT, 2008); David Henkin, *City Reading: Written Words and Public Spaces in Antebellum New York* (New York, 1998); Mona Domosh, *Invented Cities: The Creation of Landscape in Nineteenth-Century New York and Boston* (New Haven, CT, 1996); Lisa Keller, *Triumph of Order: Democracy and Public Space in New York and London* (New York, 2009); Robin F. Bachin, *Building the South Side: Urban Space and Civic Culture in Chicago, 1890–1919* (Chicago, 2004); Peter C. Baldwin, *Domesticating the Street: The Reform of Public Space in Hartford* (Columbus, OH, 1999); Blanche Linden-Ward, *Silent City on a Hill: Landscapes of Memory and Boston's Mount Auburn Cemetery* (Columbus, OH, 1989); Setha Low, *On the Plaza: The Politics of Public Space and Culture* (Austin, TX, 2000); William David Estrada, *The Los Angeles Plaza: Sacred and Contested Space* (Austin, TX, 2008); Lydia R. Otero, *La Calle: Spatial Conflicts and Urban Renewal in a Southwest City* (Tucson, AZ, 2010).

51. Alison Isenberg, *Downtown America: A History of the Place and the People Who Made It* (Chicago, 2004); Larry Bennett, *Fragments of Cities: The New American Downtowns and Neighborhoods* (Columbus, OH, 1990); Edward J. Blakely and Mary Gail Snyder, *Fortress America: Gated Communities in the United States* (1997); Setha Low, *Behind the Gates: Life, Security, and the Pursuit of Happiness in Fortress America* (New York, 2003); Oscar Newman, *Defensible Space: Crime Prevention through Urban Design* (New York, 1973); William R. Taylor, ed., *Inventing Times Square: Commerce and Culture at the Crossroads of the World* (New York, 1991). See also Jessica Ellen Sewell, *Women and the Everyday City: Public Space in San Francisco, 1890–1915* (Minneapolis, 2010); Paul Groth, *Living Downtown: The History of Residential Hotels in the United States* (Berkeley, CA, 1994); and Miles Orvell and Jeffrey L. Meikle, eds., *Public Space and the Ideology of Place in American Culture* (New York, 2009).

52. Sharon Zukin, *Landscapes of Power: From Detroit to Disney World* (Berkeley, CA, 1991); Zukin, *Naked City: The Death and Life of Authentic Urban Places* (New York, 2009); Michael Sorkin, ed., *Variations on a Theme Park: The New American City and the End of Public Space* (New York, 1992); Mike Davis, *City of Quartz: Excavating the Future in Los Angeles* (London, 1990); Dolores Hayden, *The Power of Place: Urban Landscapes as Public History* (Cambridge, MA, 1995).

53. Arnold R. Hirsch, *Making the Second Ghetto: Race and Housing in Chicago, 1940–1960* (Cambridge, UK, 1983); W. Edward Orser, *Blockbusting in Baltimore: The Edmondson Village Story* (Lexington, KY, 1994); Amanda I. Seligman, *Block by Block: Neighborhoods and Public Policy on Chicago's West Side* (Chicago, 2005); Bruce D. Haynes, *Red Lines, Black Spaces: The Politics of Race and Space in a Black Middle-Class Suburb* (New Haven, CT, 2001); Raymond A. Mohl, "Race and Space in the Modern City: Interstate-95 and the Black Community in Miami," in *Urban Policy in Twentieth-Century America*, ed. Arnold R. Hirsch and Raymond A. Mohl (New Brunswick, NJ, 1993), 100–58; Ronald H. Bayor, "Roads to Racial Segregation: Atlanta in the Twentieth Century," *Journal of Urban History* 15 (November 1988): 3–21; Daniel D. Arreola, ed., *Hispanic Spaces, Latino Places: Community and Cultural Diversity in Contemporary America* (Austin, TX, 2004). On race and spatial issues, see also John W. Frazier, Florence M. Margai, and Eugene Tetty-Fio, eds., *Race and Place: Equity Issues in Urban America* (Boulder, CO, 2003); Richard H. Schein, ed., *Landscape and Race in the United States* (New York, 2006).

54. Colin Gordon, *Mapping Decline: St. Louis and the Fate of the American City* (Philadelphia, 2008); Eric Sandweiss, *St. Louis: The Evolution of an American Urban Landscape* (Philadelphia, 2001); Alexander von Hoffman, *House by House, Block by Block: The Rebirth of America's Urban Neighborhoods* (New York, 2003); Neil Smith, *The New Urban Frontier: Gentrification and the Revanchist City* (New York, 1996); Lance Freeman, *There Goes the 'Hood: Views of Gentrification from the Ground Up* (Philadelphia, 2006); Derek S. Hydra, *The New Urban Renewal: The Economic Transformation of Harlem and Bronzeville* (Chicago, 2008); Suleiman Osman, *The Invention of Brownstone Brooklyn: Gentrification and the Search for Authenticity in Postwar New York* (New York, 2011).

55. On recent historiography on urban environmental history, see Martin V. Melosi, "The Place of the City in Environmental History," *Environmental History Review* 17 (Spring 1993): 1–23; Harold Platt, "The Emergence of Urban Environmental History," *Urban History* 26 (May 1999): 89–95; Mark H. Rose, "Technology and Politics: The Scholarship of Two Generations of Urban Environmental Historians," *Journal of Urban History* 30 (July 2004): 769–85; Chris Sellers, "Cities and Suburbs," in *A Companion to American Environmental History*, ed. Douglas C. Sackman (New York, 2010), 462–81.

56. Hal Rothman, *The Greening of a Nation? Environmentalism in the United States since 1945* (Fort Worth, TX, 1997); Rothman, *Saving the Planet: The American Response to the Environment in the Twentieth Century* (Chicago, 2000); Thomas R. Wellock, *Preserving the Nation: The Conservation and Environmental Movements, 1870–2000* (Wheeling, IL, 2007).

57. Charles E. Rosenberg, *The Cholera Years: The United States in 1832, 1849, and 1866* (Chicago, 1962, 1987); John Duffy, *Sword of Pestilence: The New Orleans Yellow Fever Epidemic of 1853* (Baton Rouge, LA, 1966); Duffy, *A History of Public Health in New York City, 1625–1866* (New York, 1968); Duffy, *A History of Public Health in New York City, 1866–1966* (New York, 1974); Duffy, *The Sanitarians: A History of American Public Health* (Urbana, IL, 1990); John B. Blake, *Public Health in the Town of Boston, 1630–1822* (Cambridge, MA, 1959). See also Dorceta E. Taylor, *The Environment and the People in American Cities, 1600s–1900s: Disorder, Inequality, and Social Change* (Durham, NC, 2009), a rare overview of U.S.

environmental history that discusses the importance of early epidemics of disease in stimulating environmental thinking.

58. Stuart Galishoff, *Newark, the Nation's Unhealthiest City, 1832–1895* (New Brunswick, NJ, 1988); Galishoff, *Safeguarding the Public Health: Newark, 1895–1918* (Westport, CT, 1975); Barbara Gutman Rosenkrantz, *Public Health and the State: Changing Views in Massachusetts, 1842–1936* (Cambridge, MA, 1972); Judith L. Leavitt, *The Healthiest City: Milwaukee and the Politics of Health Reform* (Princeton, NJ, 1982).

59. Robert H. Bremner, *From the Depths: The Discovery of Poverty in the United States* (New York, 1956). See also Robert Gottlieb, *Forcing the Spring: The Transformation of the American Environmental Movement* (Washington, DC, 1993); Daniel Eli Burnstein, *Next to Godliness: Confronting Dirt and Despair in Progressive Era New York City* (Urbana, IL, 2006); Marilyn Thornton Williams, *Washing "The Great Unwashed": Public Baths in Urban America, 1840–1920* (Columbus, OH, 1991).

60. Martin V. Melosi, ed., *Pollution and Reform in American Cities, 1879–1930* (Austin, TX, 1980); Melosi, *Garbage in the Cities: Refuse, Reform, and the Environment, 1880–1980* (College Station, TX, 1981); Melosi, *Coping with Abundance: Energy and Environment in Industrial America* (New York, 1985); Melosi, *The Sanitary City: Urban Infrastructure in America from Colonial Times to the Present* (Baltimore, 2000). See also Melosi's *Effluent America; Cities, Industry, Energy, and the Environment* (Pittsburgh, PA, 2001), a collection of his key articles on urban environmental history; and an important recent article, "Humans, Cities, and Nature: How Do Cities Fit in the Material World?" *Journal of Urban History* 36 (January 2010): 3–21.

61. Joel A. Tarr, *The Search for the Ultimate Sink: Urban Pollution in Historical Perspective* (Akron, OH, 1996); Tarr and Gabriel Dupuy, eds., *Technology and the Rise of the Networked City in Europe and America* (Philadelphia, 1988); Clay McShane and Joel A. Tarr, *The Horse and the City: Living Machines in Nineteenth-Century America* (Baltimore, 2007). See also Joel A. Tarr, "Urban History and Environmental History in the United States: Complementary and Overlapping Fields," in *Environmental Problems in European Cities of the 19th and 20th Century*, ed. Christoph Bernhardt (New York, 2001), 26–39; Joel A. Tarr and Jeffrey K. Stine, eds., "Technology, Pollution, and the Environment," special issue, *Environmental History Review* 18 (Spring 1994).

62. Samuel P. Hays, *Beauty, Health, and Permanence: Environmental Politics in the United States, 1955–1985* (Cambridge, UK, 1987); Hays, *Explorations in Environmental History* (Pittsburgh, PA, 1998); Hays, *A History of Environmental Politics since 1945* (Pittsburgh, PA, 2000).

63. William Cronon, *Nature's Metropolis: Chicago and the Great West* (New York, 1991).

64. Andrew Hurley, *Environmental Inequalities: Class, Race, and Industrial Pollution in Gary, Indiana, 1945–1980* (Chapel Hill, NC, 1995); David Stradling, *Smokestacks and Progressives: Environmentalism, Engineers, and Air Quality in America, 1881–1951* (Baltimore, 1999); Adam Rome, *The Bulldozer in the Countryside: Suburban Sprawl and the Rise of American Environmentalism* (Cambridge, UK, 2001); Matthew Gandy, *Concrete and Clay: Reworking Nature in New York City* (Cambridge, MA, 2002).

65. Robert D. Bullard, *Dumping in Dixie: Race, Class, and Environmental Quality* (Boulder, CO, 1990; 3rd ed. 2000). On environmental justice, see also Martin V. Melosi, "Environmental Justice, Political Agenda Setting, and the Myths of History," *Journal of Policy History* 12 (2000): 43–71; Maureen Flanagan, "Environmental Justice in the City: A Theme for Urban Environmental History," *Environmental History* 5 (April 2000): 159–64; Colin Fisher, "Race and U.S. Environmental History," in *A Companion to American Environmental History*, ed. Douglas Cazaux Sackman (Malden, MA, 2010), 99–115.

66. Ari Kelman, *A River and Its City: The Nature of Landscape in New Orleans* (Berkeley, CA, 2003); Craig E. Colton, *An Unnatural Metropolis: Wrestling New Orleans from Nature* (Baton Rouge, LA, 2005); Chip Jacobs and William J. Kelly, *Smogtown: The Lung-Burning History of Pollution in Los Angeles* (Woodstock, NY, 2008); Mike Davis, *Ecology of Fear: Los Angeles and the Imagination of Disaster* (New York, 1998); Jared Orsi, *Hazardous Metropolis: Flooding and Urban Ecology in Los Angeles* (Berkeley, CA, 2004); R. Bruce Stephenson, *Visions of Eden: Environmentalism, Urban Planning, and City Building in St. Petersburg, Florida, 1900–1995* (Columbus, OH, 1997).

67. Matthew Klingle, *Emerald City: An Environmental History of Seattle* (New Haven, CT, 2007); Harold L. Platt, *Shock Cities: The Environmental Transformation and Reform of Manchester and Chicago* (Chicago, 2005).

68. Char Miller, *On the Border: An Environmental History of San Antonio* (Pittsburgh, PA, 2001); Joel A. Tarr, ed., *Devastation and Renewal: An Environmental History of Pittsburgh and Its Region* (Pittsburgh, PA, 2003); William Deverell and Greg Hise, eds., *Land of Sunshine: An Environmental History of Metropolitan Los Angeles* (Pittsburgh, PA, 2005); Michael F. Logan, *Desert Cities: An Environmental History of Phoenix and Tucson* (Pittsburgh, PA, 2006); Martin V. Melosi and Joseph A. Pratt, eds., *Energy Metropolis: An Environmental History of Houston and the Gulf Coast* (Pittsburgh, PA, 2007); Anthony N. Penna and Conrad E. Wright, eds., *Remaking Boston: An Environmental History of the City and Its Surroundings* (Pittsburgh, PA, 2009); Jeffrey Craig Sanders, *Seattle and the Roots of Urban Sustainability: Inventing Ecotopia* (Pittsburgh, PA, 2010).

69. Andrew Hurley, ed., *Common Fields: An Environmental History of St. Louis* (St. Louis, MO, 1997); Kathleen A. Brosnan, *Uniting Mountain and Plain: Cities, Law, and Environmental Changes along the Front Range* (Albuquerque, NM, 2002); Richard A. Walker, *The Country in the City: The Greening of the San Francisco Bay Area* (Seattle, WA, 2008); Philip J. Dreyfus, *Our Better Nature: Environment and the Making of San Francisco* (Norman, OK, 2009); Michael Rawson, *Eden on the Charles: The Making of Boston* (Cambridge, MA, 2010); Scott W. Swearingen, *Environmental City: People, Place, Politics, and the Meaning of Modern Austin* (Austin, TX, 2010); Char Miller, ed., *Cities and Nature in the American West* (Reno, NV, 2010).

70. Peter J. Schmitt, *Back to Nature: The Arcadian Myth in Urban America* (New York, 1969); David Stradling, *Making Mountains: New York City and the Catskills* (Seattle, WA, 2007).

71. George Rogers Taylor, *The Transportation Revolution, 1815–1860* (New York, 1951); Edward C. Kirkland, *Men, Cities, and Transportation: A Study in New England History, 1820–1900* (2 vols.; Cambridge, MA, 1948); Charles N. Glaab, *Kansas City and the Railroads: Community Policy in the Growth of a Regional Metropolis* (Madison, WI, 1962); Merl E. Reed, *New Orleans and the Railroads: The Struggle for Commercial Empire, 1830–1860* (Baton Rouge, LA, 1966); Leonard P. Curry, *Rail Routes South: Louisville's Fight for the Southern Market, 1865–1872* (Lexington, KY, 1969); William Cronon, *Nature's Metropolis: Chicago and the Great West* (New York, 1991); David M. Young, *The Iron Horse and the Windy City: How Railroads Shaped Chicago* (DeKalb, IL, 2005); John R. Stilgoe, *Metropolitan Corridor: Railroads and the American Scene* (New Haven, CT, 1983). See also Julius Rubin, *Canal or Railroad? Imitation and Innovation in the Response to the Erie Canal in Philadelphia, Baltimore, and Boston* (Philadelphia, 1961).

72. Clay McShane and Joel A. Tarr, *The Horse and the City: Living Machines in Nineteenth-Century America* (Baltimore, 2007); Anne Norton Greene, *Horses at Work: Harnessing Power in Industrial America* (Cambridge, MA, 2008); Sam Bass Warner Jr., *Streetcar Suburbs: The Process of Growth in Boston, 1870–1900* (Cambridge, MA, 1962); Clay McShane, *Technology and Reform: Street Railways and the Growth of Milwaukee, 1887–1900* (Madison,

WI, 1974); Joel A. Tarr, *Transportation Innovation and Changing Spatial Patterns in Pitts-burgh, 1850–1934* (Chicago, 1978); Charles W. Cheape, *Moving the Masses: Urban Public Transit in New York, Boston, and Philadelphia, 1880–1912* (Cambridge, MA, 1980); John Franch, *Robber Baron: The Life of Charles Tyson Yerkes* (Urbana, IL, 2006); Clifton Hood, *722 Miles: The Building of the Subways and How They Transformed New York* (New York, 1993); Peter Derrick, *Tunneling to the Future: The Story of the Great Subway Expansion That Saved New York* (New York, 2001); Zachary M. Schrag, *The Great Society Subway: A History of the Washington Metro* (Baltimore, 2006). See also George W. Hilton and John F. Due, *The Electric Interurban Railways in America* (Stanford, CA, 1960).

73. Mark S. Foster, *From Streetcar to Superhighway: American City Planners and Urban Transportation, 1900–1940* (Philadelphia, 1981); Paul Barrett, *The Automobile and Urban Transit: The Formation of Public Policy in Chicago, 1900–1930* (Philadelphia, 1983); Howard L. Preston, *Automobile Age Atlanta: The Making of a Southern Metropolis, 1900–1935* (Athens, GA, 1979); Scott L. Bottles, *Los Angeles and the Automobile: The Making of the Modern City* (Berkeley, CA, 1987); David W. Jones, *Mass Motorization and Mass Transit: An American History and Policy Analysis* (Bloomington, IN, 2008).

74. Clay McShane, *Down the Asphalt Path: The Automobile and the American City* (New York, 1994); Peter D. Norton, *Fighting Traffic: The Dawn of the Motor Age in the American City* (Cambridge, MA, 2008); Jeremiah B. C. Axelrod, *Inventing Autopia: Dreams and Visions of the Modern Metropolis in Jazz Age Los Angeles* (Berkeley, CA, 2009); Robert M. Fogelson, *The Fragmented Metropolis: Los Angeles, 1850–1930* (Cambridge, MA, 1967); Tom McCarthy, *Auto Mania: Cars, Consumption, and the Environment* (New Haven, CT, 2007); Brian Ladd, *Autophobia: Love and Hate in the Automobile Age* (Chicago, 2008).

75. Mark H. Rose, Bruce E. Seely, and Paul F. Barrett, *The Best Transportation System in the World: Railroads, Trucks, Airlines, and American Public Policy in the Twentieth Century* (Philadelphia, 2006).

76. Joel A. Tarr and Gabriel Dupuy, eds., *Technology and the Rise of the Networked City in Europe and America* (Philadelphia, 1988); Ann D. Keating, Eugene P. Moehring, and Joel A. Tarr, *Infrastructure and Urban Growth in the Nineteenth Century* (Chicago, 1985).

77. Joel A. Tarr, *The Search for the Ultimate Sink: Urban Pollution in Historical Perspective* (Akron, OH, 1996); Martin V. Melosi, *The Sanitary City: Urban Infrastructure in America from Colonial Times to the Present* (Baltimore, 2000). See also Joanne Abel Goldman, *Building New York's Sewers: Developing Mechanisms of Urban Management* (West Lafayette, IN, 1997); and Maureen Ogle, *All the Modern Conveniences: American Household Plumbing, 1840–1890* (Baltimore, 2000). On urban water supply, see Nelson M. Blake, *Water for the Cities: A History of the Urban Water Supply Problem in the United States* (Syracuse, NY, 1956); Louis P. Cain, *Sanitation Strategy for a Lakefront Metropolis: The Case of Chicago* (DeKalb, IL, 1978); William L. Karl, *Water and Power: The Conflict over Los Angeles' Water Supply in the Owens Valley* (Berkeley, CA, 1982); Sarah S. Elkind, *Bay Cities and Water Politics: The Battle for Resources in Boston and Oakland* (Lawrence, KS, 1998); Kate Foss-Mallon, *Hard Water: Politics and Water Supply in Milwaukee, 1870–1995* (West Lafayette, IN, 2000); Gerard T. Koeppel, *Water for Gotham: A History* (Princeton, NJ, 2000). On water power, see Theodore Steinberg, *Nature Incorporated: Industrialization and the Waters of New England* (Amherst, MA, 1991); Patrick M. Malone, *Waterpower in Lowell: Engineering and Industry in Nineteenth-Century America* (Baltimore, 2009).

78. Harold L. Platt, *The Electric City: Energy and the Growth of the Chicago Area, 1880–1930* (Chicago, 1991); David E. Nye, *Electrifying America: Social Meanings of a New Technology* (Cambridge, MA, 1990); John A. Jakle, *City Lights: Illuminating the American Night* (Baltimore, 2001); Mark H. Rose, *Cities of Light and Heat* (State College, PA, 1995).

79. Joel A. Tarr et al., "The City and the Telegraph: Urban Telecommunications in the Pre-Telephone Era," *Journal of Urban History* 14 (November 1987): 38–80; Edwin Gabler, *The American Telegrapher: A Social History, 1860–1900* (New Brunswick, NJ, 1988); Gregory J. Downey, *Telegraph Messenger Boys: Labor, Technology, and Geography, 1850–1950* (New York, 2002); Claude S. Fischer, *America Calling: A Social History of the Telephone to 1940* (Berkeley, CA, 1992); Richard R. John, *Network Nation: Inventing American Telecommunications* (Cambridge, MA, 2010).

80. Eugene P. Moehring, *Public Works and the Patterns of Urban Real Estate Growth in Manhattan, 1835–1894* (New York, 1981); David McCullough, *The Great Bridge: The Epic Story of the Building of the Brooklyn Bridge* (New York, 1983); Margaret Lattimer, Brooke Hindle, and Melvin Kranzberg, eds., *Bridge to the Future: A Centennial Celebration of the Brooklyn Bridge* (New York, 1984); Alan Trachtenbrg, *Brooklyn Bridge: Fact and Symbol* (2nd ed., Chicago, 1979); Richard Haw, *The Brooklyn Bridge: A Cultural History* (New Brunswick, NJ, 2008). For other iconic urban bridges, see John Van Der Zee, *The Gate: The True Story of the Design and Construction of the Golden Gate Bridge* (New York, 1987); Robert W. Jackson, *Rails across the Mississippi: A History of the St. Louis Bridge* (Urbana, IL, 2001); Louise Nelson Dyble, *Paying the Toll: Local Power, Regional Politics, and the Golden Gate Bridge* (Philadelphia, 2010).

81. Harold L. Platt, *City Building in the New South: The Growth of Public Services in Houston, Texas, 1830–1915* (Philadelphia, 1983); Jon C. Teaford, *The Unheralded Triumph: City Government in America, 1870–1900* (Baltimore, 1984); Jason Scott Smith, *Building New Deal Liberalism: The Political Economy of Public Works, 1933–1956* (Cambridge, UK, 2009); Joel A. Tarr and Josef W. Konvitz, "Patterns in the Development of Urban Infrastructure," in *American Urbanism: A Historiographical Review*, ed. Howard Gillette Jr. and Zane L. Miller (New York, 1987), 195–236.

82. Bruce E. Seely, *Building the American Highway System: Engineers as Policy Makers* (Philadelphia, 1987); Michael R. Fein, *Paving the Way: New York Road Building and the American State, 1880–1956* (Lawrence, KS, 2008); Mark H. Rose, *Interstate: Express Highway Politics, 1939–1989* (rev. ed.; Knoxville, TN, 1990); Raymond A. Mohl, "Ike and the Interstates: Creeping toward Comprehensive Planning," *Journal of Planning History* 2 (August 2003): 237–62; Mohl, "Stop the Road: Freeway Revolts in American Cities," *Journal of Urban History* 30 (July 2004): 674–706; Mohl, "The Interstates and the Cities: The U.S. Department of Transportation and the Freeway Revolt, 1966–1973," *Journal of Policy History* 20/2 (2008): 193–226; Owen D. Gutfreund, *Twentieth-Century Sprawl: Highways and the Reshaping of the American Landscape* (New York, 2004).

83. Carol Willis, *Form Follows Finance: Skyscrapers and Skylines in New York and Chicago* (New York, 1995); Carl W. Condit, *The Rise of the Skyscraper* (Chicago, 1952); Paul Goldberger, *The Skyscraper* (New York, 1981); Daniel Bluestone, *Constructing Chicago* (New Haven, CT, 1991); Pauline A. Saliga, *The Sky's the Limit: A Century of Chicago Skyscrapers* (New York, 1998); Joanna Merwood-Salisbury, *Chicago 1890: The Skyscraper and the Modern City* (Chicago, 2009); Sarah Bradford Landau and Carl L. Condit, *Rise of the New York Skyscraper, 1865–1913* (New Haven, CT, 1996); John Tauranac, *The Empire State Building: The Making of a Landmark* (New York, 1997); Mark Kingwell, *Nearest Thing to Heaven: The Empire State Building and American Dreams* (New Haven, CT, 2006); Eric Darton, *Divided We Stand: A Biography of New York City's World Trade Center* (New York, 1999); Gail Fenske, *The Skyscraper and the City: The Woolworth Building and the Making of Modern New York* (Chicago, 2008); Benjamin Flowers, *Skyscraper: The Politics and Power of Building New York City in the Twentieth Century* (Philadelphia, 2009); Roberta Moudry, ed., *The American Skyscraper: Cultural Histories* (Cambridge, UK, 2005). For a documentary col-

lection on skyscraper history, see Roger Shepherd, *Skyscraper: The Search for an American Style, 1891–1941* (New York, 2003). See also Manfredo Tafuri, "The Disenchanted Mountain: The Skyscraper and the City," in *The American City: From the Civil War to the New Deal*, ed. Giorgio Ciucci et al. (Cambridge, MA, 1979), 389–528.

84. Carl W. Condit, *The Railroad and the City: A Technological and Urbanistic History of Cincinnati* (Columbus, OH, 1977); Condit, *The Port of New York: A History of the Rail and Terminal System from the Beginnings to Pennsylvania Station* (Chicago, 1980); Kurt Schlicting, *Grand Central Terminal* (Baltimore, 2001); Jill Jonnes, *Conquering Gotham: A Gilded Age Epic: The Construction of Penn Station and Its Tunnels* (New York, 2007). See also Keith L. Bryant Jr., "Cathedrals, Castles, and Roman Baths: Railway Station Architecture in the Urban South," *Journal of Urban History* 2 (February 1976): 195–230.

85. Janet R. Daly Bednarek, *America's Airports: Airfield Development, 1918–1947* (College Station, TX, 2001); Gail Cooper, *Air Conditioning America: Engineers and the Controlled Environment, 1900–1960* (Baltimore, 2002); Marsha E. Ackerman, *Cool Comfort: America's Romance with Air-Conditioning* (Washington, DC, 2002). See also Paul Barrett, "Cities and Their Airports: Policy Formation, 1926–1952," *Journal of Urban History* 14 (November 1987): 112–37.

86. Peter Bacon Hales, *Silver Cities: The Photography of American Urbanization, 1839–1915* (Philadelphia, 1984; rev. ed., Albuquerque, NM, 2006); Thomas Campanella, *Cities from the Sky: An Aerial Portrait of America* (New York, 2001); Eric Gordon, *The Urban Spectator: American Concept-Cities from Kodak to Google* (Dartmouth, NH, 2010).

87. Joel A. Tarr and Josef W. Konvitz, "Patterns in the Development of Urban Infrastructure," in *American Urbanism: A Historiographical Review*, ed. Howard Gillette Jr. and Zane L. Miller (Westport, CT, 1987), 195–226; Mark H. Rose, "Machine Politics: The Historiography of Technology and Public Policy," *The Public Historian* 10 (Spring 1988): 27–47; Josef W. Konvitz, Mark H. Rose, and Joel A. Tarr, "Technology and the City," *Technology and Culture* 31 (April 1990): 284–94; Martin V. Melosi, "Cities, Technical Systems, and the Environment," *Environmental History Review* 14 (Spring–Summer 1990): 45–64; Mark H. Rose, "Technology and Politics: The Scholarship of Two Generations of Urban-Environmental Historians," *Journal of Urban History* 30 (July 2004): 769–85; Ann Durkin Keating, *Invisible Networks: Exploring the History of Local Utilities and Public Works* (Malabar, FL, 1994); Gerrylynn K. Roberts and Philip Steadman, *American Cities and Technology: Wilderness to Wired City* (London, 1999). See also special issues of the *Journal of Urban History*, "The City and Technology" (May 1979 and November 1987).

88. Albert Fein, *Frederick Law Olmsted and the American Environmental Tradition* (New York, 1972); Laura Wood Roper, *FLO: A Biography of Frederick Law Olmsted* (Baltimore, 1973); Elizabeth Stevenson, *Park Maker: A Life of Frederick Law Olmsted* (New York, 1977); Thomas S. Hines, *Burnham of Chicago: Architect and Planner* (New York, 1974); Robert Twombly, *Louis Sullivan: His Life and Work* (Chicago, 1986).

89. Witold Rybczynski, *A Clearing in the Distance: Frederick Law Olmsted and America in the Nineteenth Century* (New York, 1999). See also Cynthia Zaitzevsky, *Frederick Law Olmsted and the Boston Park System* (Cambridge, MA, 1982); Galen Cranz, *The Politics of Park Design: A History of Urban Parks in America* (Cambridge, MA, 1982); Irving D. Fisher, *Frederick Law Olmsted and the City Planning Movement in the United States* (Ann Arbor, MI, 1986); Melvin Kalfus, *Frederick Law Olmsted: The Passion of a Public Artist* (New York, 1990); Roy Rosenzweig and Elizabeth Blackmar, *The Park and the People: A History of Central Park* (Ithaca, NY, 1992); David Schuyler, *The New Urban Landscape: The Redefinition of City Form in Nineteenth-Century America* (Baltimore, 1986); David Schuyler, *Apostle of Taste: Andrew Jackson Downing, 1815–1852*

(Baltimore, 1996); Carl Smith, *The Plan of Chicago: Daniel Burnham and the Remaking of the American City* (Chicago, 2006).

90. Mary Corbin Sies and Christopher Silver, eds., *Planning the Twentieth-Century American City* (Baltimore, 1996); Robert Fishman, ed., *The American Planning Tradition: Culture and Policy* (Washington, DC, 2000). See also the earlier essay collections, Donald A. Krueckeberg, ed., *The American Planner: Biographies and Recollections* (New York, 1983); Krueckeberg, ed., *Introduction to Planning History in the United States* (New Brunswick, NJ, 1983); and Daniel Schaffer, *Two Centuries of American Planning* (Baltimore, 1988).

91. Jon A. Peterson, *The Birth of City Planning in the United States, 1840–1917* (Baltimore, 2003); Mel Scott, *American City Planning since 1890* (Berkeley, CA, 1969); M. Christine Boyer, *Dreaming the Rational City: The Myth of American City Planning* (Cambridge, MA, 1983). Also see John W. Reps, *The Making of Urban America: A History of City Planning in the United States* (Princeton, NJ, 1965); Richard E. Fogelsong, *Planning the Capitalist City: The Colonial Era to the 1920s* (Princeton, NJ, 1986); and Peter Hall, *Cities of Tomorrow: An Intellectual History of Urban Planning and Design in the Twentieth Century* (London, 1988).

92. William H. Wilson, *The City Beautiful Movement* (Baltimore, 1989); Stanley K. Schultz, *Constructing Urban Culture: American Cities and City Planning, 1800–1920* (Philadelphia, 1989); John D. Fairfield, *The Mysteries of the Great City: The Politics of Urban Design, 1877–1937* (Columbus, OH, 1993); Mansell Blackford, *The Lost Dream: Businessmen and City Planning on the Pacific Coast, 1890–1920* (Columbus, OH, 1993); Greg Hise, *Magnetic Los Angeles: Planning the Twentieth Century Metropolis* (Baltimore, 1997); Pierre Clavel, *The Progressive City: Planning and Participation, 1969–1984* (New Brunswick, NJ, 1986); Howard Gillette Jr., *Civitas by Design: Building Better Communities, from the Garden City to the New Urbanism* (Philadelphia, 2010).

93. Sylvia D. Fries, *The Urban Idea in Colonial America* (Philadelphia, 1977); June Manning Thomas, *Redevelopment and Race: Planning a Finer City in Postwar Detroit* (Baltimore, 1997); Howard Gillette Jr., *Between Justice and Beauty: Race, Planning, and the Failure of Urban Policy in Washington, D.C.* (Baltimore, 1972); Judd Kahn, *Imperial San Francisco: Politics and Planning in an American City* (Lincoln, NE, 1979); Christopher Silver, *Twentieth-Century Richmond: Planning, Politics, and Race* (Knoxville, TN, 1984); Lawrence W. Kennedy, *Planning the City upon a Hill: Boston since 1630* (Amherst, MA, 1992); Robert A. Catlin, *Racial Politics and Urban Planning: Gary, Indiana, 1980–1989* (Lexington, KY, 1993); Carl Abbott, *Portland: Planning, Politics, and Growth in a Twentieth-Century City* (Lincoln, NE, 1983); John F. Bauman and Edward K. Muller, *Before Renaissance: Planning in Pittsburgh, 1889–1943* (Pittsburgh, PA, 2006); Zane L. Miller and Bruce Tucker, *Changing Plans for America's Inner Cities: Cincinnati's Over-the-Rhine and Twentieth-Century Urbanism* (Columbus, OH, 1998); Charles E. Connerly, *"The Most Segregated City in America": City Planning and Civil Rights in Birmingham, 1920–1980* (Charlottesville, VA, 2005); R. Bruce Stephenson, *Visions of Eden: Environmentalism, Urban Planning, and City Building in St. Petersburg, Florida, 1900–1995* (Columbus, OH, 1997).

94. Christine M. Rosen, *The Limits of Power: Great Fires and the Process of City Growth in America* (Cambridge, UK, 1986); Ross Miller, *American Apocalypse: The Great Fire and the Myth of Chicago* (Chicago, 1990); Karen Sawislak, *Smoldering City: Chicagoans and the Great Fire, 1871–1874* (Chicago, 1995); Carl Smith, *Urban Disorder and the Shape of Belief* (Chicago, 1995).

95. Margaret Crawford, *Building the Workingman's Paradise: The Design of American Company Towns* (London, 1995); Stanley Buder, *Pullman: An Experiment in Industrial Order and Community Planning, 1880–1930* (New York, 1967); James Gilbert, *Perfect Cities: Chicago's Utopias of 1893* (Chicago, 1991).

96. Stanley Buder, *Visionaries and Planners: The Garden City Movement and the Modern Community* (New York, 1990); Carol A. Christensen, *The American Garden City and the New Towns Movement* (Ann Arbor, MI, 1986); Daniel Schaffer, *Garden Cities for America: The Radburn Experience* (Philadelphia, 1982); Roy Lubove, *Community Planning in the 1920's: The Contribution of the Regional Planning Association of America* (Pittsburgh, PA, 1963); Edward K. Spann, *Designing Modern America: The Regional Planning Association of America and Its Members* (Columbus, OH, 1996); Michael Simpson, *Thomas Adams and the Modern Planning Movement: Britain, Canada, and the United States, 1900–1940* (London, 1985); Joseph Arnold, *The New Deal in the Suburbs: A History of the Greenbelt Town Program* (Columbus, OH, 1971); Paul K. Conkin, *Tomorrow a New World: The New Deal Community Program* (Ithaca, NY, 1959); Cathy Knepper, *Greenbelt, Maryland: A Living Legacy of the New Deal* (Baltimore, 2001); Patrick D. Reagan, *Designing a New America: The Origins of New Deal Planning, 1890–1943* (Amherst, MA, 1999).

97. Marc A. Weiss, *The Rise of the Community Builders: The American Real Estate Industry and Urban Land Planning* (New York, 1987); Patricia Burgess, *Planning for the Private Interest: Land Use Controls and Residential Patterns in Columbus, Ohio, 1900–1970* (Columbus, OH, 1994); William S. Worley, *J. C. Nichols and the Shaping of Kansas City: Innovation in Planned Residential Communities* (Columbia, MO, 1990).

98. Barbara M. Kelly, *Expanding the American Dream: Building and Rebuilding Levittown* (Albany, NY, 1993); Rosalyn Baxandall and Elizabeth Ewen, *Picture Windows: How the Suburbs Happened* (New York, 2000); David Kushner, *Levittown: Two Families, One Tycoon, and the Fight for Civil Rights in America's Legendary Suburb* (New York, 2009); Herbert J. Gans, *The Levittowners: Ways of Life and Politics in a New Suburban Community* (New York, 1967); Dianne Harris, ed., *Second Suburb: Levittown, Pennsylvania* (Pittsburgh, PA, 2010); Ned Eichler, *The Merchant Builders* (Cambridge, MA, 1982); Gregory C. Randall, *America's Original GI Town: Park Forest, Illinois* (Baltimore, 2000); William H. Wilson, *Hamilton Park: A Planned Black Community in Dallas* (Baltimore, 1998). See also the key article by Barry Checkoway, "Large Builders, Federal Housing Programmes, and Postwar Suburbanization," *International Journal of Urban and Regional Research* 4 (March 1980): 21–45.

99. Nicholas Dagen Bloom, *Suburban Alchemy: 1960s New Towns and the Transformation of the American Dream* (Columbus, OH, 2001); George T. Morgan Jr. and John O. King, *The Woodlands: New Community Development, 1964–1983* (College Station, TX, 1987); Frederick Steiner, *The Politics of New Town Planning: The Newfields, Ohio, Story* (Athens, OH, 1981).

100. Jane Jacobs, *The Death and Life of Great American Cities* (New York, 1961); Peter Calthorpe, *The Next American Metropolis: Ecology, Community, and the American Dream* (New York, 1993); Peter Katz, *The New Urbanism: Toward an Architectural Community* (New York, 1994); James Howard Kunstler, *Home from Nowhere: Remaking Our Everyday World for the Twenty-First Century* (New York, 1996); John O. Norquist, *The Wealth of Cities: Revitalizing the Centers of American Life* (Reading, MA, 1998); Andres Duany, Elizabeth Plater-Zyberk, and Jeff Speck, *Suburban Nation: The Rise of Sprawl and the Decline of the American Dream* (New York, 2000); Emily Talen, *New Urbanism and American Planning: The Conflict of Cultures* (New York, 2005); Andrew Ross, *The Celebration Chronicles: Life, Liberty, and the Pursuit of Property Value in Disney's New Town* (New York, 1999); Douglas Frantz and Catherine Collins, *Celebration, U.S.A.: Living in Disney's Brave New Town* (New York, 1999).

101. Anthony Sutcliffe, *Towards the Planned City: Germany, Britain, the United States, and France, 1780–1914* (Oxford, UK, 1981): 88–125; Peter Marcuse, "Housing in Early City Planning," *Journal of Urban History* 6 (February 1980): 153–76.

102. Gary Nash, *The Urban Crucible: Social Change, Political Consciousness, and the Origins of the American Revolution* (Cambridge, MA, 1979); Billy G. Smith, *The "Lower Sort": Philadelphia's Laboring People, 1750–1800* (Ithaca, NY, 1990).

103. Bernard L. Herman, *Town House: Architecture and Material Life in the Early American City, 1780–1830* (Chapel Hill, NC, 2005); Donna J. Rilling, *Making Houses, Crafting Capitalism: Builders in Philadelphia, 1790–1850* (Philadelphia, 2001); Elizabeth Backmar, *Manhattan for Rent, 1750–1850* (Ithaca, NY, 1989).

104. Elizabeth Hawes, *New York, New York: How the Apartment House Transformed the Life of the City* (New York, 1993); Elizabeth C. Cromley, *Alone Together: A History of New York's Early Apartments* (Ithaca, NY, 1990); Sam Bass Warner Jr., *Streetcar Suburbs: The Process of Growth in Boston, 1870–1900* (Cambridge, MA, 1962); Douglas Shand-Tucci, *Built in Boston: City and Suburb, 1800–1950* (Boston, 1978); Charles Lockwood, *Bricks and Brownstones: The New York Row House, 1783–1929* (New York, 1972); Mary Ellen Hayward and Charles Belfoure, *The Baltimore Rowhouse* (New York, 1999); Andrew S. Dolkart, *The Rowhouse Reborn: Architecture and Neighborhoods in New York City, 1908–1929* (Baltimore, 2009).

105. Jacob Riis, *How the Other Half Lives: Studies among the Tenements of New York* (New York, 1890; new ed., 2010); Robert H. Bremner, *From the Depths: The Discovery of Poverty in the United States* (New York, 1956); Tyler Anbinder, *Five Points* (New York, 2001).

106. Roy Lubove, *The Progressives and the Slums: Tenement House Reform in New York City, 1890–1917* (Pittsburgh, PA, 1962); Thomas L. Philpott, *The Slum and the Ghetto: Neighborhood Deterioration and Middle-Class Reform in Chicago, 1880–1930* (Chicago, 1978); Robert B. Fairbanks, *Making Better Citizens: Housing Reform and the Community Development Strategy in Cincinnati* (Urbana, IL, 1988); Ronald Lawson, ed., *The Tenant Movement in New York City, 1904–1984* (New Brunswick, NJ, 1986); Jared N. Day, *Urban Castles: Tenement Housing and Landlord Activism in New York City, 1890–1943* (New York, 1999). See also Andrew Dolkart, *Biography of a Tenement House in New York City: An Architectural History of 97 Orchard Street* (Charlottesville, VA, 2008).

107. Gwendolyn Wright, *Building the Dream: A Social History of Housing in America* (New York, 1981); Peter G. Rowe, *Modernity and Housing* (Cambridge, MA, 1993). Also see Margaret Garb, *City of American Dreams: A History of Homeownership and Housing in Chicago* (Chicago, 2005); Joseph Bigott, *From Cottage to Bungalow: Houses and the Working Class in Metropolitan Chicago, 1869–1929* (Chicago, 2001); and Richard Longstreth, ed., *Housing Washington: Two Centuries of Residential Development and Planning in the National Capital Area* (Chicago, 2010).

108. John F. Bauman, Roger Biles, and Kristin M. Szylvian, *From Tenements to the Taylor Homes: In Search of an Urban Housing Policy in Twentieth-Century America* (University Park, PA, 2000).

109. Gail Radford, *Modern Housing for America: Policy Struggles in the New Deal Era* (Chicago, 1996). On the key federal housing legislation, see Kenneth T. Jackson, "Race, Ethnicity, and Real Estate Appraisal: The Home Owners Loan Corporation and the Federal Housing Administration," *Journal of Urban History* 6 (August 1980): 419–52; Timothy L. McDonnell, *The Wagner Housing Act: A Case Study in the Legislative Process* (Chicago: 1957); and J. Joseph Huthmacher, *Senator Robert F. Wagner and the Rise of Urban Liberalism* (New York, 1971). The best discussion of federal housing programs during World War II is Phillip J. Funigiello, *The Challenge to Urban Liberalism: Federal-City Relations during World War II* (Knoxville, TN, 1978). For the immediate postwar years, see Richard O. Davies, *Housing Reform during the Truman Administration* (Columbia, MO, 1966).

110. John F. Bauman, *Public Housing, Race, and Renewal: Urban Planning in Philadelphia, 1920–1974* (Philadelphia, 1987); D. Bradford Hunt, *Blueprint for Disaster: The Unravel-

ing of Chicago Public Housing (Chicago, 2009); Don Parson, *Making a Better World: Public Housing, the Red Scare, and the Direction of Modern Los Angeles* (Minneapolis, 2005); A. Scott Henderson, *Housing and the Democratic Ideal: The Life and Thought of Charles Abrams* (New York, 2000). Also see Richard Plunz, *A History of Housing in New York City: Dwelling Type and Social Change in the American Metropolis* (New York, 1990); Devereaux Bowly Jr., *The Poorhouse: Subsidized Housing in Chicago, 1895–1976* (Carbondale, IL, 1978); Dominic J. Capeci Jr., *Race and Inequality in Postwar Detroit: The Sojourner Truth Housing Controversy of 1942* (Philadelphia, 1984); Lee Rainwater, *Behind Ghetto Walls: Black Family Life in a Federal Slum* (Chicago, 1970); Lawrence Vale, *From the Puritans to the Project: Public Housing and Public Neighbors* (Cambridge, MA, 2000).

111. Nicholas Dagen Bloom, *Public Housing That Worked: New York in the Twentieth Century* (Philadelphia, 2008); William Moore Jr., *The Vertical Ghetto: Everyday Life in a Housing Project* (New York, 1969); Sudhir Venkatesh, *American Project: The Rise and Fall of a Modern Ghetto* (Cambridge, MA, 2000); Alex Kotlowitz, *There Are No Children Here* (New York, 1991); Susan J. Popkin et al., *The Hidden War: Crime and the Tragedy of Public Housing in Chicago* (New Brunswick, NJ, 2000); and Rhonda Y. Williams, *The Politics of Public Housing: Black Women's Struggles against Urban Inequality* (New York, 2004).

112. Kevin Boyle, *Arc of Justice: A Saga of Race, Civil Rights, and Murder in the Jazz Age* (New York, 2005); David M. P. Freund, *Colored Property: State Policy and White Racial Politics in Suburban America* (Chicago, 2007); Arnold R. Hirsch, *Making the Second Ghetto: Race and Housing in Chicago, 1940–1960* (Cambridge, UK, 1983); Amanda I. Seligman, *Block by Block: Neighborhoods and Public Policy on Chicago's West Side* (Chicago, 2005); Beryl Satter, *Family Properties: Race, Real Estate, and the Exploitation of Black Urban America* (New York, 2009).

113. Thomas J. Sugrue, *The Origins of the Urban Crisis: Race and Inequality in Postwar Detroit* (Princeton, NJ, 1996); Robert O. Self, *American Babylon: Race and the Struggle for Postwar Oakland* (Princeton, NJ, 2003); W. Edward Orser, *Blockbusting in Baltimore: The Edmondson Village Story* (Lexington, KY, 1994); Stephen Grant Meyer, *As Long As They Don't Move Next Door: Segregation and Racial Conflict in American Neighborhoods* (Lanham, MD, 2000); Gerald Gamm, *Urban Exodus: Why the Jews Left Boston and the Catholics Stayed* (Cambridge, MA, 1999); Hillel Levine and Lawrence Harmon, *The Death of an American Jewish Community: A Tragedy of Good Intentions* (New York, 1992); Antero Pietila, *Not in My Neighborhood: How Bigotry Shaped a Great American City* (New York, 2010); Wendell Pritchett, *Brownsville, Brooklyn: Blacks, Jews, and the Changing Face of the Ghetto* (Chicago, 2002); Walter Thabit, *How East New York Became a Ghetto* (New York, 2003).

114. Patricia Mooney Melvin, *The Organic City: Urban Definition and Community Organization, 1880–1920* (Lexington, KY, 1987); Alexander von Hoffman, *Local Attachments: The Making of an American Urban Neighborhood, 1850 to 1920* (Baltimore, 1994); von Hoffman, *House by House, Block by Block: The Rebirth of America's Urban Neighborhoods* (New York, 2004). See also von Hoffman's overview article, "Housing and Planning: A Century of Social Reform and Local Power," *Journal of the American Planning Association* 75 (Spring 2009): 231–44.

115. Mark I. Gelfand, *A Nation of Cities: The Federal Government and Urban America, 1933–1965* (New York, 1975); Philip J. Funigiello, *The Challenge to Urban Liberalism: Federal–City Relations during World War II* (Knoxville, TN, 1978).

116. Roger W. Lotchin, *The Martial Metropolis: U.S. Cities in War and Peace* (New York, 1984); Lotchin, *Fortress California, 1910–1961: From Warfare to Welfare* (New York, 1992); Ann Markusen et al., *The Rise of the Gunbelt: The Military Remapping of Industrial America* (New York, 1991). See also Lotchin's *The Bad City in the Good War: San Francisco, Los An-*

geles, Oakland, and San Diego (Bloomington, IN, 2003); and Marilynn S. Johnson, *The Second Gold Rush: Oakland and the East Bay in World War II* (Berkeley, CA, 1993).

117. John Mollenkopf, *The Contested City* (Princeton, NJ, 1983); Kenneth Fox, *Metropolitan America: Urban Life and Urban Policy in the United States, 1940–1980* (Jackson, MS, 1986); Roger Biles, *The Fate of Cities: Urban America and the Federal Government, 1945–2000* (Lawrence, KS, 2011). Also see Peter Dreier, John Mollenkopf, and Todd Swanstrom, *Place Matters: Metropolitics for the Twenty-first Century* (2nd ed., Lawrence, KS, 2004); and Alice O'Connor, "Swimming against the Tide: A Brief History of Federal Policy in Poor Communities," in *Urban Problems and Community Development*, ed. Ronald Ferguson and William Dickens (Washington, DC, 1999), 77–137.

118. Arnold R. Hirsch and Raymond A. Mohl, eds., *Urban Policy in Twentieth-Century America* (New Brunswick, NJ, 1993); Jon C. Teaford, *The Metropolitan Revolution: The Rise of Post-Urban America* (New York, 2006); R. Allen Hays, *The Federal Government and Urban Housing: Ideology and Change in Public Policy* (Albany, NY, 1985; 2nd ed., 1995); Robert Halpern, *Rebuilding the Inner City: A History of Neighborhood Initiatives to Address Poverty in the United States* (New York, 1995); Robert A. Beauregard, *Voices of Decline: The Postwar Fate of U.S. Cities* (2nd ed., New York, 2003). Also see Martin V. Melosi, ed., *Urban Public Policy: Historical Modes and Methods* (University Park, PA, 1994); and Peter K. Eisinger, "The Search for a National Urban Policy, 1968–1980," *Journal of Urban History* 12 (November 1985): 3–23.

119. Martin Anderson, *The Federal Bulldozer: A Critical Analysis of Urban Renewal, 1949–1962* (Cambridge, MA, 1964); Jon C. Teaford, *The Rough Road to Renaissance: Urban Revitalization in America, 1940–1985* (Baltimore, 1990); Samuel Zipp, *Manhattan Projects: The Rise and Fall of Urban Renewal in Cold War New York* (New York, 2010). See also Scott Greer, *Urban Renewal and American Cities* (Indianapolis, IN, 1965); and Marc A Weiss, "The Origins and Legacy of Urban Renewal," in *Urban Planning in an Age of Austerity*, ed. Pierre Clavel, John Forester, and William W. Goldsmith (New York, 1980), 53–80.

120. Sidney Fine, *Violence in the Model* City (Ann Arbor, MI, 1989); Charles M. Haar, *Between the Idea and the Reality: A Study in the Origin, Fate, and Legacy of the Model Cities Program* (Boston, 1975); Mandi Isaacs Jackson, *Model City Blues: Urban Space and Organized Resistance in New Haven* (Philadelphia, 2008).

121. Charles H. Trout, *Boston, the Great Depression, and the New Deal* (New York, 1977); Roger Biles, *Big City Boss in Depression and War: Mayor Edward J. Kelly of Chicago* (DeKalb, IL, 1984); Thomas Kessner, *Fiorello H. La Guardia and the Making of Modern New York* (New York, 1989); Jo Ann E. Argersinger, *Toward a New Deal in Baltimore* (Chapel Hill, NC, 1988); William H. Mullins, *The Depression and the Urban West Coast, 1929–1933: Los Angeles, San Francisco, Seattle, and Portland* (Bloomington, IN, 1991).

122. Robert M. Fogelson, *Downtown: Its Rise and Fall, 1880–1950* (New Haven, CT, 2001).

123. Joel Schwartz, *The New York Approach: Robert Moses, Urban Liberals, and the Redevelopment of the Inner City* (Columbus, OH, 1993); Robert A. Caro, *The Power Broker: Robert Moses and the Fall of New York* (New York, 1974); Hilary Ballon and Kenneth T. Jackson, eds., *Robert Moses and the Modern City* (New York, 2007); Robert Fitch, *The Assassination of New York* (London, 1993); John H. Mollenkopf, *A Phoenix in the Ashes: The Rise and Fall of the Koch Coalition in New York City Politics* (Princeton, NJ, 1994); Vincent Cannato, *The Ungovernable City: John Lindsay and the Struggle to Save New York* (New York, 2002). Also see Evelyn Gonzalez, *The Bronx* (New York, 2004); and Max Page, *The Creative Destruction of Manhattan, 1900–1940* (Chicago, 1999).

124. Howard Gillette Jr., *Between Justice and Beauty: Race, Planning, and the Failure of Public Policy in Washington, D.C.* (Baltimore, 1995); Gregory J. Crowley, *The Politics of*

Place: Contentious Urban Redevelopment in Pittsburgh (Pittsburgh, PA, 2005). For similar policy conflicts and contradictions in other cities, see Lawrence W. Kennedy, *Planning the City upon a Hill: Boston since 1630* (Amherst, MA, 1992); Thomas O'Connor, *Building a New Boston: Politics and Urban Renewal, 1950 to 1970* (Boston, 1993); and Janet R. Daley-Bednarek, *The Changing Image of the City: Planning for Downtown Omaha, 1945–1973* (Lincoln, NE, 1992). For Chicago, see Joel Rast, *Remaking Chicago: The Political Origins of Urban Industrial Change* (DeKalb, IL, 1999); and George Rosen, *Decision-Making Chicago-Style: The Genesis of a University of Illinois Campus* (Urbana, IL, 1980). For a comparison of fiscal management in Chicago and New York, see Ester R. Fuchs, *Mayors and Money: Fiscal Policy in New York and Chicago* (Chicago, 1992). For additional local studies, see Robert Kerstein, *Politics and Growth in Twentieth-Century Tampa* (Gainesville, FL, 2001); and James B. Crooks, *Jacksonville: The Consolidation Story, from Civil Rights to the Jaguars* (Gainesville, FL, 2004).

125. Ronald H. Bayor, *Race and the Shaping of Twentieth-Century Atlanta* (Chapel Hill, NC, 1996). On race and urban policy, see also Henry Louis Taylor Jr., *Race and the City: Work, Community, and Protest in Cincinnati, 1820–1970* (Urbana, IL, 1993); Christopher Silver and John V. Moeser, *The Separate City: Black Communities in the Urban South, 1940–1968* (Lexington, KY, 1995); Larry Keating, *Atlanta: Race, Class, and Urban Expansion* (Philadelphia, 2001); and David Schuyler, *A City Transformed: Redevelopment, Race, and Suburbanization in Lancaster, Pennsylvania, 1940–1980* (University Park, PA, 2002).

126. Kent B. Germany, *New Orleans after the Promises: Poverty, Citizenship, and the Search for the Great Society* (Athens, GA, 2007).

127. Douglas C. Rae, *City: Urbanism and Its End* (New Haven, CT, 2003). For good contemporary accounts, see Allan R. Talbot, *The Mayor's Game: Richard Lee of New Haven and the Politics of Change* (New York, 1970); and Fred Powledge, *Model City* (New York, 1970).

128. Thomas J. Sugrue, *The Origins of the Urban Crisis: Race and Inequality in Postwar Detroit* (Princeton, NJ, 1996); Roy Lubove, *Twentieth-Century Pittsburgh: The Post-Steel Era* (Pittsburgh, PA, 1996); Howard Gillette, *Camden after the Fall: Decline and Renewal in a Post-Industrial City* (Philadelphia, 2005); Guian McKee, *The Problem of Jobs: Liberalism, Race, and Deindustrialization in Philadelphia* (Chicago, 2008); Jefferson Cowie and Joseph Heathcott, eds., *Beyond the Ruins: The Meanings of Deindustrialization* (Ithaca, NY, 2003); Dennis Keating, Norman Krumholz, and Philip Star, *Revitalizing Urban Neighborhoods* (Lawrence, KS, 1996). The key early work on this subject is Barry Bluestone and Bennett Harrison, *The Deindustrialization of America: Plant Closings, Community Abandonment, and the Dismantling of Basic Industry* (New York, 1982).

129. Daniel T. Rodgers, *Atlantic Crossings: Social Politics in a Progressive Age* (Cambridge, MA, 1998). For an earlier book with a similar wide-ranging trans-Atlantic perspective, see James T. Kloppenberg, *Uncertain Victory: Social Democracy and Progressivism in European and American Thought, 1870–1920* (New York, 1986).

130. Jane Jacobs, *The Death and Life of Great American Cities* (New York, 1961); Alice Sparberg Alexiou, *Jane Jacobs: Urban Visionary* (New Brunswick, NJ, 2006). For Jacobs's battles with New York's public works czar Robert Moses, see Anthony Flint, *Wrestling with Moses: How Jane Jacobs Took on New York's Master Builder and Transformed the American City* (New York, 2009); and Roberta Brandes Gratz, *The Battle for Gotham: New York in the Shadow of Robert Moses and Jane Jacobs* (New York, 2010).

131. Daniel P. Moynihan, "New Roads and Urban Chaos," *The Reporter* (April 14, 1960): 13–20; Moynihan, ed., *On Understanding Poverty* (New York, 1969); Moynihan, ed., *Toward a National Urban Policy* (New York, 1970); Moynihan, *The Politics of a Guaranteed Income: The Nixon Administration and the Family Assistance Plan* (New York, 1973); Robert

A. Katzman, ed., *Daniel Patrick Moynihan: The Intellectual in Public Life* (Washington, DC, 1998); James T. Patterson, *Freedom Is Not Enough: The Moynihan Report and America's Struggle over Black Family Life* (New York, 2010).

132. Lewis Mumford, *The Highway and the City* (New York, 1963); Mumford, *The Urban Prospect* (New York, 1968); Mark Luccarelli, *Lewis Mumford and the Ecological Region: The Politics of Planning* (New York, 1995); Donald L. Miller, *Lewis Mumford: A Life* (New York, 1989).

133. Alice O'Connor, *Poverty Knowledge: Social Science, Social Policy, and the Poor in Twentieth-Century U.S. History* (Princeton, NJ, 2001). Nicholas Lemann discussed the social science thinking that shaped the 1960s War on Poverty in his book *The Promised Land: The Great Black Migration and How It Changed America* (New York, 1991), 111–221.

134. Jennifer S. Light, *From Warfare to Welfare: Defense Intellectuals and Urban Problems in Cold War America* (Baltimore, 2003); Light, *The Nature of Cities: Ecological Visions and the American Urban Professions, 1920–1960* (Baltimore, 2009).

135. Margaret Pugh O'Mara, *Cities of Knowledge: Cold War Science and the Search for the Next Silicon Valley* (Princeton, NJ, 2005).

136. Zane L. Miller, *Boss Cox's Cincinnati: Urban Politics in the Progressive Era* (New York, 1968), 94. The reinterpretation of the urban political machine began with Robert K. Merton, *Social Theory and Social Structure* (New York, 1957). Other revisionist studies include Seymour J. Mandelbaum, *Boss Tweed's New York* (New York, 1965); and John M. Allswang, *Bosses, Machines, and Urban Voters: An American Symbiosis* (Port Washington, NY, 1977). Two useful collections of readings are Alexander B. Callow Jr., ed., *The City Boss in America: An Interpretive Reader* (New York, 1976); and Bruce M. Stave and Sondra Astor Stave, eds., *Urban Bosses, Machines, and Progressive Reformers* (Malabar, FL, 1984).

137. Leo Hershkowitz, *Tweed's New York: Another Look* (Garden City, NY, 1977), 348. For an earlier contradictory view, see Alexander B. Callow, *The Tweed Ring* (New York, 1965), which emphasized Tammany's graft and corruption. Kenneth D. Ackerman's *Boss Tweed: The Rise and Fall of the Corrupt Pol Who Conceived the Soul of Modern New York* (New York, 2005) provided a more balanced account.

138. For an instructive overview, see Bruce M. Stave et al., "A Reassessment of the Urban Political Boss: An Exchange of Views," *The History Teacher* 21 (May 1988): 293–312. For post-1980 studies of the machine, see Edward K. Spann, *The New Metropolis: New York City, 1840–1857* (New York, 1981); Scott Greer, ed., *Ethnics, Machines, and the American Urban Future* (Cambridge, MA, 1981); Paul Kleppner, *Chicago Divided: The Making of a Black Mayor* (DeKalb, IL, 1985); Steven P. Erie, *Rainbow's End: Irish-Americans and the Dilemmas of Urban Machine Politics, 1840–1985* (Berkeley, CA, 1988); William J. Grimshaw, *Bitter Fruit: Black Politics and the Chicago Machine, 1931–1991* (Chicago, 1992); Chris McNickle, *To Be Mayor of New York: Ethnic Politics in the City* (New York, 1993); Peter McCaffery, *When Bosses Ruled Philadelphia: The Emergence of the Republican Machine, 1867–1933* (University Park, PA, 1993); James D. Bolin, *Bossism and Reform in a Southern City: Lexington, Kentucky, 1880–1940* (Lexington, KY, 2000); and Alan Lessoff, *The Nation and Its City: Politics, "Corruption," and Progress in Washington, D.C., 1861–1902* (Baltimore, 1994).

139. Important urban political biographies include Jerome Mushkat, *Fernando Wood: A Political Biography* (Kent, OH, 1990); Thomas Kessner, *Fiorello H. La Guardia and the Making of Modern New York* (New York, 1989); Jack Beatty, *The Rascal King: The Life and Times of James Michael Curley* (Reading, MA, 1992); Roger Biles, *Big City Boss in Depression and War: Mayor Edward J. Kelly of Chicago* (DeKalb, IL, 1984); Joel A. Tarr, *A Study in Boss Politics: William Lorimer of Chicago* (Urbana, IL, 1971); Douglas Bukowski, *Big Bill Thompson, Chicago, and the Politics of Image* (Urbana, IL, 1998); Lawrence Larsen and Nancy J. Hulston,

Pendergast! (Columbia, MO, 1997); Edward F. Haas, *DeLesseps S. Morrison and the Image of Reform: New Orleans Politics, 1946–1961* (Baton Rouge, LA, 1974); William A. Bullough, *The Blind Boss and His City: Christopher Augustine Buckley and Nineteenth-Century San Francisco* (Berkeley, CA, 1979); and Walton Bean, *Boss Ruef's San Francisco: The Story of the Union Labor Party, Big Business, and the Graft Prosecution* (Berkeley, CA, 1952). Roger Biles's *Memphis in the Great Depression* (Knoxville, TN, 1986) and David M. Tucker's *Memphis since Crump: Bossism, Blacks, and Civic Reformers, 1948–1968* (Knoxville, TN, 1980) considered Boss Ed Crump's immediate and lasting impact on Memphis.

140. John D. Buenker, *Urban Liberalism and Progressive Reform* (New York, 1973); Michael H. Ebner and Eugene M. Tobin, eds., *The Age of Urban Reform: New Perspectives on the Progressive Era* (Port Washington, NY, 1977); Paul S. Boyer, *Urban Masses and Moral Order in America, 1880–1920* (Cambridge, MA, 1978); Morton Keller, *Regulating a New Society: Public Policy and Social Change in America, 1900–1933* (Cambridge, MA, 1994); Michael McGerr, *A Fierce Discontent: The Rise and Fall of the Progressive Movement in America, 1870–1920* (New York, 2003); Maureen A. Flanagan, *America Reformed: Progressives and Progressivism, 1890s–1920s* (New York, 2007).

141. Samuel P. Hays, "The Social Analysis of American Political History, 1880–1920," *Political Science Quarterly* 80 (September 1965): 373–94; Hays, "The Changing Political Structure of the City in Industrial America," *Journal of Urban History* 1 (November 1974): 6–38; Hays, *American Political History as Social Analysis* (Knoxville, TN, 1980). See also Bradley R. Rice, *Progressive Cities: The Commission Government Movement in America, 1901–1920* (Austin, TX, 1977); Martin J. Schiesl, *The Politics of Efficiency: Municipal Administration and Reform in America, 1880–1920* (Berkeley, CA, 1977); Kenneth Fox, *Better City Government: Innovation in American Urban Politics, 1850–1937* (Philadelphia, 1977); Lynette B. Wrenn, *Crisis and Commission Government in Memphis* (Knoxville, TN, 1998).

142. Jon C. Teaford, "Finis for Tweed and Steffens: Rewriting the History of Urban Rule," *Reviews in American History* 10 (December 1982): 136; Teaford, *The Unheralded Triumph: City Government in America, 1870–1900* (Baltimore, 1984). See also Roger W. Lotchin, "Reclaiming the Reputation of the City in the Gilded Age and Progressive Era," *Continuity: A Journal of History* 20 (Spring 1996): 13–38.

143. Kenneth Finegold, *Experts and Politicians: Reform Challenges to Machine Politics in New York, Cleveland, and Chicago* (Princeton, NJ, 1995); Keith D. Revell, *Building Gotham: Civic Culture and Public Policy in New York City, 1898–1938* (Baltimore, 2003).

144. Terrence J. McDonald, *The Parameters of Urban Fiscal Policy: Socioeconomic Change and Political Culture in San Francisco, 1860–1906* (Berkeley, CA, 1986); McDonald, "The Problem of the Political in Recent American Urban History," *Social History* 19 (October 1985): 323–45; McDonald and Sally K. Ward, eds., *The Politics of Urban Fiscal Policy* (Beverly Hills, CA, 1984); Eric H. Monkkonen, *America Becomes Urban: The Development of U.S. Cities and Towns, 1780–1980* (Berkeley, CA, 1988); Monkkonen, *The Local State: Public Money and American Cities* (Stanford, CA, 1996); Robin L. Einhorn, *Property Rules: Political Economy in Chicago, 1833–1872* (Chicago, 1991); Alan D. Anderson, *The Origin and Resolution of an Urban Crisis: Baltimore, 1890–1930* (Baltimore, 1977).

145. Carl V. Harris, *Political Power in Birmingham, 1871–1921* (Knoxville, TN, 1977). For an alternative approach to studying urban political power and office holding through the use of "social filter" analysis, see Eugene J. Watts, *The Social Bases of City Politics: Atlanta, 1865–1903* (Westport, CT, 1978).

146. David C. Hammack, *Power and Society: Greater New York at the Turn of the Century* (New York, 1982), 180. For a different approach to the question of political power, see William

Issel and Robert W. Cherny, *San Francisco, 1865–1932: Politics, Power, and Urban Development* (Berkeley, CA, 1986).

147. Amy Bridges, *A City in the Republic: Antebellum New York and the Origins of Machine Politics* (Cambridge, UK, 1984); Martin Shefter, *Political Parties and the State: The American Historical Experience* (Princeton, NJ, 1994); Shefter, "The Electoral Foundations of the Political Machine: New York City, 1884–1897," in *The History of American Electoral Behavior*, ed. Joel Silbey et al. (Princeton, 1978), 263–98; Shefter, "The Emergence of the Political Machine: An Alternative View," in *Theoretical Perspectives on Urban Politics*, ed. Willis D. Hawley et al., (Englewood Cliffs, NJ, 1976), 14–44; Ira Katznelson, *Urban Trenches: Urban Politics and the Patterning of Class in the United States* (New York, 1981).

148. Philip J. Ethington, *The Public City: The Political Construction of Urban Life in San Francisco, 1850–1900* (Cambridge, UK, 1994).

149. David Quigley, *Second Founding: New York City, Reconstruction, and the Making of American Democracy* (New York, 2004); James J. Connolly, *The Triumph of Ethnic Progressivism: Urban Political Culture in Boston, 1900–1925* (Cambridge, MA, 1998); Connolly, *An Elusive Unity: Urban Democracy and Machine Politics in Industrializing America* (Ithaca, NY, 2010). See also Evelyn Savidge Sterne, "Beyond the Boss: Immigration and American Political Culture, 1880–1940," in *E Pluribus Unum? Contemporary and Historical Perspectives on Immigrant Political Incorporation*, ed. Gary Gerstle and John Mollenkopf (New York, 2001), 33–66.

150. Eric L. Hirsch, *Urban Revolt: Ethnic Politics in the Nineteenth-Century Chicago Labor Movement* (Berkeley, CA, 1990); Leon Fink, *Workingmen's Democracy: The Knights of Labor and American Politics* (Urbana, IL, 1983); Shelton Stromquist, *Re-inventing "The People": The Progressive Movement, the Class Problem, and the Origins of Modern Liberalism* (Urbana, IL, 2006).

151. Amy Bridges, *Morning Glories: Municipal Reform in the Southwest* (Princeton, NJ, 1997); Robert B. Fairbanks, *For the City as a Whole: Planning, Politics, and the Public Interest in Dallas, Texas, 1900–1965* (Columbus, OH, 1998); David R. Johnson, John A. Booth, and Richard J. Harris, *The Politics of San Antonio: Community, Progress, and Power* (Lincoln, NE, 1983); Bradford Luckingham, *Phoenix: The History of a Southwest Metropolis* (Tucson, AZ, 1989); Leonard E. Goodall, ed., *Urban Politics in the Southwest* (Tempe, AZ, 1967); Nancy A. Hewitt, *Southern Discomfort: Women's Activism in Tampa, Florida, 1880s–1920s* (Urbana, IL, 2001); Raphael Sonenshein, *The City at Stake: Secession, Reform, and the Battle for Los Angeles* (Princeton, NJ, 2006).

152. E. P. Thompson, *The Making of the English Working Class* (New York, 1963); Herbert G. Gutman, *Work, Culture, and Society in Industrializing America* (New York, 1976); Gutman, *Power and Culture: Essays on the American Working Class* (New York, 1987).

153. Gary B. Nash, *The Urban Crucible: Social Change, Political Consciousness, and the Origins of the American Revolution* (Cambridge, MA, 1979). See also Dirk Hoerder, *Crowd Action in Revolutionary Massachusetts, 1765–1780* (New York, 1977); Charles G. Steffen, *The Mechanics of Baltimore: Workers and Politics in the Age of Revolution, 1763–1812* (Urbana, IL, 1984); Paul A. Gilje, *Liberty on the Waterfront: American Maritime Culture in the Age of Revolution* (Philadelphia, 2007).

154. Sean Wilentz, *Chants Democratic: New York City and the Rise of the American Working Class, 1788–1850* (New York, 1984); Graham R. Hodges, *New York City Cartmen, 1667–1850* (New York, 1986); Howard B. Rock, *Artisans of the New Republic: Tradesmen of New York City in the Age of Jefferson* (New York, 1979); Ronald Schultz, *The Republic of Labor: Philadelphia Artisans and the Politics of Class, 1720–1830* (New York, 1993); David A. Zonderman, *Aspirations and Anxieties: New England Workers and the Mechanized Factory System, 1815–1850* (New York, 1992).

428   *Raymond A. Mohl and Roger Biles*

155. David R. Roediger, *The Wages of Whiteness: Race and the Making of the American Working Class* (London, 1991); Eric Lott, *Love and Theft: Blackface Minstrelsy and the American Working Class* (New York, 1995); Peter Way, *Common Labour: Workers and the Digging of North American Canals, 1780–1860* (Cambridge, UK, 1993).

156. Daniel J. Walkowitz, *Worker City, Company Town: Iron and Cotton-Worker Protest in Troy and Cohoes, New York, 1855–84* (Urbana, IL, 1978); Alan Dawley, *Class and Community: The Industrial Revolution in Lynn* (Cambridge, MA, 1976); Paul G. Faler, *Mechanics and Manufacturers in the Early Industrial Revolution: Lynn, Massachusetts, 1780–1860* (Albany, NY, 1981); Susan E. Hirsch, *Roots of the American Working Class: The Industrialization of Crafts in Newark, 1800–1860* (Philadelphia, 1978); Bruce Laurie, *Working People of Philadelphia, 1800–1850* (Philadelphia, 1980); Frances G. Couvares, *The Remaking of Pittsburgh: Class and Culture in an Industrializing City, 1877–1919* (Albany, NY, 1984); Stephen J. Ross, *Workers on the Edge: Work, Leisure, and Politics in Industrializing Cincinnati, 1788–1890* (New York, 1985); Jeffrey Haydu, *Citizen Employers: Business Communities and Labor in Cincinnati and San Francisco* (Ithaca, NY, 2008); Richard Oestreicher, *Solidarity and Fragmentation: Working People and Class Consciousness in Detroit, 1875–1900* (Urbana, IL, 1986); Brian Greenberg, *Worker and Community: Response to Industrialization in a Nineteenth-Century American City, Albany, New York, 1850–1884* (Albany, NY, 1985); Hartmut Keil and John B. Jentz, eds., *German Workers in Industrial Chicago, 1850–1910: A Comparative Perspective* (DeKalb, IL, 1983); David Brundage, *The Making of Western Labor Radicalism: Denver's Organized Workers, 1878–1905* (Urbana, IL, 1994); Gary Gerstle, *Working-Class Americanism: The Politics of Labor in a Textile City, 1914–1960* (Cambridge, UK, 1989). For an excellent collection of essays, see Michael H. Frisch and Daniel J. Walkowitz, eds., *Working-Class America: Essays on Labor, Community, and American Society* (Urbana, IL, 1983).

157. Dominic A. Pacyga, *Polish Immigrants and Industrial Chicago: Workers on the South Side, 1880–1922* (Chicago, 2003); James R. Barrett, *Work and Community in the Jungle: Chicago's Packinghouse Workers, 1894–1922* (Urbana, IL, 1987); Louise C. Wade, *Chicago's Pride: The Stockyards, Packingtown, and Environs in the Nineteenth Century* (Urbana, IL, 1987); Rick Halpern, *Down on the Killing Floor: Black and White Workers in Chicago's Packinghouses, 1904–54* (Urbana, IL, 1997).

158. Daniel T. Rodgers, *The Work Ethic in Industrial America, 1850–1920* (Chicago, 1978), quotation on p. 155; David Montgomery, *Workers' Control in America* (Cambridge, UK, 1979); Montgomery, *The Fall of the House of Labor* (Cambridge, UK, 1987); and Montgomery, *Citizen Worker* (Cambridge, UK, 1993).

159. Peter Cole, *Wobblies on the Waterfront: Interracial Unionism in Progressive Era Philadelphia* (Urbana, IL, 2007); Anne Huber Tripp, *The IWW and the Paterson Silk Strike of 1913* (Urbana, IL, 1987); Leon Fink, *Workingmen's Democracy: The Knights of Labor and American Politics* (Urbana, IL, 1983); Kim Voss, *The Making of American Exceptionalism: Knights of Labor and Class Formation in the Nineteenth Century* (Ithaca, NY, 1994); David J. Goldberg, *A Tale of Three Cities: Labor Organization and Protest in Paterson, Passaic, and Lawrence, 1916–1921* (New Brunswick, NJ, 1989); Jennifer Guglielmo, *Living the Revolution: Italian Women's Resistance and Radicalism in New York City, 1880–1945* (Chapel Hill, NC, 2010).

160. Richard Schneirov, *Labor and Urban Politics: Class Conflict and the Origins of Modern Liberalism in Chicago, 1864–1897* (Urbana, IL, 1998); David O. Stowell, *Streets, Railroads, and the Great Strike of 1877* (Chicago, 1999); Paul Avrich, *The Haymarket Tragedy* (Princeton, NJ, 1984); Carl Smith, *Urban Disorder and the Shape of Belief: The Great Chicago Fire, the Haymarket Bomb, and the Model Town of Pullman* (Chicago, 1995); James Green, *Death in the Haymarket: A Story of Chicago, the First Labor Movement, and the Bombing That*

Divided Gilded Age America (New York, 2006); Eric Arneson, *Waterfront Workers of New Orleans: Race, Class, and Politics, 1863–1923* (New York, 1991); Daniel Rosenberg, *New Orleans Dockworkers: Race, Labor, and Unionism, 1892–1923* (Albany, NY, 1988).

161. Tom Goyens, *Beer and Revolution: The German Anarchist Movement in New York City, 1880–1914* (Urbana, IL, 2007); Tony Michels, *A Fire in Their Hearts: Yiddish Socialists in New York* (Cambridge, MA, 2005); Bruce M. Stave, ed., *Socialism and the Cities* (Port Washington, NY, 1975); Donald T. Critchlow, ed., *Socialism in the Heartland: The Midwestern Experience, 1900–1925* (Notre Dame, IN, 1986); Randi Storch, *Red Chicago: American Communism at Its Grassroots, 1928–35* (Urbana, IL, 2007); Paul Lyons, *Philadelphia Communists, 1936–1956* (Philadelphia, 1982); Mark Naison, *Communists in Harlem during the Depression* (New York, 1983); Joshua B. Freeman, *Working-Class New York: Life and Labor since World War II* (New York, 2000).

162. Alice Kessler-Harris, *Out to Work: A History of Wage-Earning Women in America* (New York, 2003); Lisa M. Fine, *The Souls of the Skyscraper: Female Clerical Workers in Chicago, 1870–1930* (Philadelphia, 1990); Sharon H. Strom, *Beyond the Typewriter: Gender, Class, and the Origins of Modern American Office Work, 1900–1930* (Urbana, IL, 1992); Margery W. Davies, *Women's Place Is at the Typewriter: Office Work and Office Workers, 1870–1930* (Philadelphia, 1982); Stephen H. Norwood, *Labor's Flaming Youth: Telephone Operators and Worker Militancy, 1878–1923* (Urbana, IL, 1990); Venus Green, *Race on the Line: Gender, Labor, and Technology in the Bell System, 1880–1980* (Durham, NC, 2001); Susan P. Benson, *Counter Cultures: Saleswomen, Managers, and Customers in American Department Stores, 1890–1940* (Urbana, IL, 1986); See also Leslie Woodcock Tentler, *Wage-Earning Women: Industrial Work and Family Life in the United States, 1900–1930* (New York, 1979).

163. Eileen Boris, *Home to Work: Motherhood and the Politics of Industrial Homework in the United States* (Cambridge, UK, 1994); David M. Katzman, *Seven Days a Week: Women and Domestic Service in Industrializing America* (New York, 1978); Tera W. Hunter, *To 'Joy My Freedom: Southern Black Women's Lives and Labors after the Civil War* (Cambridge, MA, 1997).

164. Joanne J. Meyerowitz, *Women Adrift: Independent Wage Earners in Chicago, 1880–1930* (Chicago, 1988); Miriam Cohen, *Workshop to Office: Two Generations of Italian Women in New York City, 1900–1950* (Ithaca, NY, 1993); S. J. Kleinberg, *The Shadow of the Mills: Working-Class Families in Pittsburgh, 1870–1907* (Pittsburgh, PA, 1989). Women also found wide-ranging types of work in the industrial sector. See Thomas Dublin, *Transforming Women's Work: New England Lives in the Industrial Revolution* (Ithaca, NY, 1994); Carole Turbin, *Working Women of Collar City: Gender, Class, and Community in Troy, New York, 1864–86* (Urbana, IL, 1992); Patricia A. Cooper, *Once a Cigar Maker: Men, Women, and Work Culture in American Cigar Factories, 1900–1919* (Urbana, IL, 1987); Mary H. Blewett, *Men, Women, and Work: Class, Gender, and Protest in the New England Shoe Industry, 1780–1910* (Urbana, IL, 1988); and Ardis Cameron, *Radicals of the Worst Sort: Laboring Women in Lawrence, Massachusetts, 1860–1912* (Urbana, IL, 1993).

165. Dana Frank, *Purchasing Power: Consumer Organizing, Gender, and the Seattle Labor Movement, 1919–1929* (Cambridge, UK, 1994); Nancy F. Gabin, *Feminism in the Labor Movement: Women and the United Auto Workers, 1935–1975* (Ithaca, NY, 1990); Amy Kesselman, *Fleeting Opportunities: Women Shipyard Workers in Portland and Vancouver during World War II and Reconversion* (Albany, NY, 1990), Elizabeth Faue, *Community of Suffering and Struggle: Women, Men, and the Labor Movement in Minneapolis, 1915–1945* (Chapel Hill, NC, 1991.

166. Richard L. Bushman, *The Refinement of America: Persons, Houses, Cities* (New York, 1992); E. Digby Baltzell, *The Protestant Establishment: Aristocracy and Caste in America*

(New York, 1964); Baltzell, *Puritan Boston and Quaker Philadelphia* (Boston, 1979); Frederic C. Jaher, *The Urban Establishment: Upper Strata in Boston, New York, Charleston, Chicago, and Los Angeles* (Urbana, IL, 1982).

167. Edward Pessen, *Riches, Class, and Power before the Civil War* (Lexington, MA, 1973); Sven Beckert, *The Monied Metropolis: New York City and the Consolidation of the American Bourgeoisie, 1850–1896* (Cambridge, UK, 1993); Thomas Kessner, *Capital City: New York City and the Men behind America's Rise to Economic Dominance, 1860–1900* (New York, 2003); Eric Homberger, *Mrs. Astor's New York: Money and Social Power in a Gilded Age* (New Haven, CT, 2002).

168. Stuart M. Blumin, *The Emergence of the Middle Class: Social Experience in the American City, 1760–1900* (Cambridge, UK, 1989); Mary P. Ryan, *The Cradle of the Middle Class: The Family in Oneida County, New York, 1790–1865* (Cambridge, UK, 1981); John S. Gilkeson Jr., *Middle-Class Providence, 1820–1940* (Princeton, NJ, 1986); Cindy Sondik Aron, *Ladies and Gentlemen of the Civil Service: Middle-Class Workers in Victorian America* (New York, 1987); William H. Pease and Jane H. Pease, *The Web of Progress: Private Values and Public Styles in Boston and Charleston, 1828–1843* (New York, 1985).

169. Thomas Bender, *New York Intellect: A History of Intellectual Life in New York City, from 1750 to the Beginnings of Our Own Time* (New York, 1987); Bender, *The Unfinished City: New York and the Metropolitan Idea* (New York, 2002).

170. Oscar Handlin, *The Uprooted: The Epic Story of the Great Migrations That Made the American People* (Boston, 1951); David J. Rothman, "*The Uprooted*: Thirty Years Later," *Reviews in American History* 10 (September 1982): 311–19; Peter Kvisto, "The Transplanted Then and Now: The Reorientation of Immigration Studies from the Chicago School to the New Social History," *Ethnic and Racial Studies* 13 (October 1990): 455–81; Rudolph J. Vecoli, "From *The Uprooted* to *The Transplanted*: The Writing of American Immigration History, 1951–1989," in *From "Melting Pot" to Multiculturalism*, ed. Valeria Gennaro Lerda (Rome, 1990), 25–53. See also Handlin's earlier book, *Boston's Immigrants: A Study in Acculturation* (Cambridge, MA, 1941).

171. A key source on the geography of immigration is David Ward, *Cities and Immigrants: A Geography of Change in Nineteenth-Century America* (New York, 1971). On chain migration, see Josef J. Barton, *Peasants and Strangers: Italians, Rumanians, and Slovaks in an American City, 1890–1950* (Cambridge, MA, 1975); John W. Briggs, *An Italian Passage: Immigrants to Three American Cities, 1890–1930* (New Haven, CT, 1978); Dino Cinel, *From Italy to San Francisco: The Immigrant Experience* (Stanford, CA, 1982); Walter Kamphoefner, *The Westphalians: From Germany to Missouri* (Princeton, NJ, 1987); Donna R. Gabaccia, *Militants and Migrants: Rural Sicilians Become American Workers* (New Brunswick, NJ, 1988); Robert C. Ostergren, *A Community Transplanted: The Trans-Atlantic Experience of a Swedish Immigrant Settlement in the Upper Middle West, 1835–1915* (Madison, WI, 1988); Walter Nugent, *Crossings: The Great Transatlantic Migrations, 1870–1914* (Bloomington, IN, 1992). On new forms of transnationalism, see Hector R. Cordero-Guzman, Robert C. Smith, and Ramon Grosfoguel, eds., *Migration, Transnationalization, and Race in a Changing New York* (Philadelphia, 2001); and David Gerber, "Internationalization and Transnationalization," in *A Companion to American Immigration*, ed. Reed Ueda (Malden, MA, 2006), 225–54.

172. Virginia Yans-McLaughlin, *Family and Community: Italian Immigrants in Buffalo, 1880–1930* (Ithaca, NY, 1977); Tamara K. Hareven, *Family Time and Industrial Time: The Relationship between the Family and Work in a New England Industrial Community* (Cambridge, UK, 1982); John Bodnar, Roger Simon, and Michael P. Weber, *Lives of Their Own: Blacks, Italians, and Poles in Pittsburgh, 1900–1960* (Urbana, IL, 1982); Olivier Zunz, *The*

Changing Face of Inequality: Urbanization, Industrial Development, and Immigrants in Detroit, 1880–1920 (Chicago, 1982); Judith E. Smith, *Family Connections: A History of Italian and Jewish Immigrant Lives in Providence, Rhode Island, 1900–1940* (Albany, NY, 1985); Gary R. Mormino, *Immigrants on the Hill: Italian-Americans in St. Louis, 1882–1982* (Urbana, IL, 1986); Gary R. Mormino and George E. Pozzetta, *The Immigrant World of Ybor City: Italians and Their Latin Neighbors in Tampa, 1885–1985* (Urbana, IL, 1987); Hartmut Keil, ed., *German Workers' Culture in the United States, 1850 to 1920* (Washington, DC, 1988); David G. Gutierrez, *Walls and Mirrors: Mexican Americans, Mexican Immigrants, and the Politics of Ethnicity* (Berkeley, CA, 1995). Immigrants who rejected American urban life and returned to Europe are discussed in Mark Wyman, *Round-Trip to America: The Immigrants Return to Europe, 1880–1930* (Ithaca, NY, 1993).

173. Moses Rischin, *The Promised City: New York's Jews, 1870–1914* (Cambridge, MA, 1962); Jay Dolan, *The Immigrant Church: New York's Irish and German Catholics, 1815–1865* (Baltimore, 1975); Victor Greene, *For God and Country: The Rise of Polish and Lithuanian Ethnic Consciousness in America, 1860–1910* (Madison, WI, 1975); Randall M. Miller and Thomas D. Marzik, eds., *Immigrants and Religion in Urban America* (Philadelphia, 1977); Robert Anthony Orsi, *The Madonna of 115th Street: Faith and Community in Italian Harlem, 1880–1950* (New Haven, CT, 1985); June G. Alexander, *The Immigrant Church and Community: Pittsburgh's Slovak Catholics and Lutherans, 1880–1915* (Pittsburgh, PA, 1987); April R. Schultz, *Ethnicity on Parade. Inventing the Norwegian American Tradition through Celebration* (Amherst, MA, 1994); James W. Sanders, *The Education of an Urban Minority: Catholics in Chicago, 1833–1965* (New York, 1977); Raymond A. Mohl and Neil Betten, *Steel City: Urban and Ethnic Patterns in Gary, Indiana, 1906–1950* (New York, 1986); Scott Cummings, ed., *Self-Help in Urban America: Patterns of Minority Economic Development* (Port Washington, NY, 1979); Frederick M. Binder and David M. Reimers, *All the Nations under Heaven: An Ethnic and Racial History of New York City* (New York, 1995).

174. Rudolph J. Vecoli, "*Contadini* in Chicago: A Critique of *The Uprooted*," *Journal of American History* 51 (December 1964): 404–16; Vecoli, "The Formation of Chicago's 'Little Italies,'" *Journal of American Ethnic History* 2 (Spring 1983): 5–20; William DeMarco, *Ethnics and Enclaves: Boston's Italian North End* (Ann Arbor, MI, 1981); Caroline Golab, *Immigrant Destinations* (Philadelphia, 1977). See also John Bodnar, *The Transplanted: A History of Immigrants in Urban America* (Bloomington, IN, 1985); Nora Faires et al., "John Bodnar's *The Transplanted*: A Roundtable," *Social Science History* 12 (Fall 1988): 217–68; and Bodnar's now classic microhistory, *Immigration and Industrialization: Ethnicity in an American Mill Town, 1900–1940* (Pittsburgh, PA, 1977).

175. Ulf Beijbom, *Swedes in Chicago: A Demographic and Social Study of the 1846–1889 Immigration* (Stockholm, 1971); Dennis Clark, *The Irish in Philadelphia: Ten Generations of Urban Experience* (Philadelphia, 1973); JoEllen M. Vinyard, *The Irish on the Urban Frontier: Detroit, 1850–1880* (New York, 1976); R. A. Burchell, *The San Francisco Irish, 1848–1880* (Berkeley, CA, 1980); Stanley Nadel, *Little Germany: Ethnicity, Religion, and Class in New York City, 1845–89* (Urbana, IL, 1990); Humbert S. Nelli, *The Italians in Chicago, 1880–1930: A Study in Ethnic Mobility* (New York, 1970); Thomas Kessner, *The Golden Door. Italian and Jewish Immigrant Mobility in New York City, 1880–1915* (New York, 1977); Kathleen Neils Conzen, *Immigrant Milwaukee: Accommodation and Community in a Frontier City* (Cambridge, MA, 1976); Deborah Dash Moore, *At Home in America: Second Generation New York Jews* (New York, 1981); Jenna Weisman Joselit, *Our Gang: Jewish Crime and the New York Jewish Community, 1900–1940* (Bloomington, IN, 1983); Ewa Morawska, *For Bread with Butter: Life-Worlds of East Central Europeans in Johnstown, Pennsylvania, 1890–1940*

(Cambridge, UK, 1985); Robert A. Rockaway, *The Jews of Detroit: From the Beginning, 1762–1914* (Detroit, MI, 1986); Ronald H. Bayor and Timothy J. Meagher, eds., *The New York Irish* (Baltimore, 1996); Richard N. Juliani, *Building Little Italy: Philadelphia's Italians before Mass Migration* (University Park, PA, 1998).

176. Gary B. Nash, *The Urban Crucible: Social Change, Political Consciousness, and the Origins of the American Revolution* (Cambridge, MA, 1979); Joyce D. Goodfriend, *Before the Melting Pot: Society and Culture in Colonial New York City, 1664–1730* (Princeton, NJ, 1992).

177. Victor Greene, *The Slavic Community on Strike: Immigrant Labor in Pennsylvania* (Notre Dame, IN, 1968); Hartmut Keil and John B. Jentz, eds., *German Workers in Industrial Chicago, 1850–1910: A Comparative Perspective* (DeKalb, IL, 1983); David J. Goldberg, *A Tale of Three Cities: Labor Organization and Protest in Paterson, Passaic, and Lawrence, 1916–1921* (New Brunswick, NJ, 1989); Dominic A. Pacyga, *Polish Immigrants and Industrial Chicago: Workers on the South Side, 1880–1922* (Columbus, OH, 1991); Bruce C. Levine, *The Spirit of 1848: German Immigrants, Labor Conflict, and the Coming of the Civil War* (Urbana, IL, 1992); Gilbert G. Gonzalez, *Labor and Community: Mexican Citrus Workers Villages in a Southern California County, 1900–1950* (Urbana, IL, 1994); David M. Emmons, *The Butte Irish: Class and Ethnicity in an American Mining Town, 1875–1925* (Urbana, IL, 1989).

178. Hasia Diner, *Erin's Daughters in America: Irish Immigrant Women in the Nineteenth Century* (Baltimore, 1983); Elizabeth Ewen, *Immigrant Women in the Land of Dollars: Life and Culture on the Lower East Side, 1890–1925* (New York, 1985); Louise Lamphere, *From Working Daughters to Working Mothers: Immigrant Women in a New England Industrial Community* (Ithaca, NY, 1987); Susan A. Glenn, *Daughters of the Shtetl: Life and Labor in the Immigrant Generation* (Ithaca, NY, 1990); Donna Gabaccia, *From the Other Side: Women, Gender, and Immigrant Life in the U.S., 1820–1990* (Bloomington, IN, 1994); Christiane Harzig, ed., *Peasant Maids—City Women: From the European Countryside to Urban America* (Ithaca, NY, 1997).

179. David R. Roediger, *The Wages of Whiteness: Race and the Making of the American Working Class* (London, 1991); Noel Ignatiev, *How the Irish Became White* (New York, 1995); Stefano Luconi, *From Paesani to White Ethnics: The Italian Experience in Philadelphia* (Albany, NY, 2001); Thomas A. Guglielmo, *White on Arrival: Italians, Race, Color, and Power in Chicago, 1890–1945* (New York, 2004).

180. Nathan Glazer and Daniel P. Moynihan, *Beyond the Melting Pot: The Negroes, Puerto Ricans, Jews, Italians, and Irish of New York City* (Cambridge, MA, 1963); Ronald H. Bayor, *Neighbors in Conflict: The Irish, Germans, Jews, and Italians of New York City, 1929–1941* (Baltimore, 1978); David A. Gerber, *The Making of an American Pluralism: Buffalo, New York, 1825–60* (Urbana, IL, 1989). On the role of American politics, see John M. Allswang, *A House for All Peoples: Ethnic Politics in Chicago, 1890–1936* (Lexington, KY, 1971); Edward R. Kantowicz, *Polish-American Politics in Chicago, 1888–1940* (Chicago, 1975); Richard Schneirov, *Labor and Urban Politics: Class Conflict and the Origins of Modern Liberalism in Chicago, 1864–97* (Urbana, IL, 1998); James J. Connolly, *The Triumph of Ethnic Progressivism: Urban Political Culture in Boston, 1900–1925* (Cambridge, MA, 1998); Leland T. Saito, *Race and Politics: Asian Americans, Latinos, and Whites in a Los Angeles Suburb* (Urbana, IL, 1998); Melvin G. Holli and Peter D'A. Jones, eds., *Ethnic Chicago: A Multicultural Portrait* (4th ed.; Grand Rapids, MI, 1995).

181. Irma Watkins-Owens, *Blood Relations: Caribbean Immigrants and the Harlem Community, 1900–1930* (Bloomington, IN, 1996); Marilyn Halter, *Between Race and Ethnicity: Cape Verdean American Immigrants, 1860–1965* (Urbana, IL, 1993); Philip Kasinitz, *Caribbean New York: Black Immigrants and the Politics of Race* (Ithaca, NY, 1992); Nancy Foner, ed., *Islands in the City: West Indian Migration to New York* (Berkeley, CA, 2001);

Foner, *From Ellis Island to JFK: New York's Two Great Waves of Immigration* (New Haven, CT, 2000); Foner, ed., *New Immigrants in New York* (2nd ed., New York, 2001); Michel S. Laguerre, *American Odyssey: Haitians in New York City* (Ithaca, NY, 1984); Susan D. Greenbaum, *More Than Black: Afro-Cubans in Tampa* (Gainesville, FL, 2002); Sherri Grasmuck and Patricia R. Pessar, *Between Two Islands: Dominican International Migration* (Berkeley, CA, 1991); Jesse Hoffnung-Garskof, *A Tale of Two Cities: Santo Domingo and New York after 1950* (Princeton, NJ, 2010).

182. Ricardo Romo, *East Los Angeles: History of a Barrio* (Austin, TX, 1983); Alberto Camarillo, *Chicanos in a Changing Society: From Mexican Pueblos to American Barrios in Santa Barbara and Southern California, 1848–1930* (Cambridge, MA, 1979); George J. Sanchez, *Becoming Mexican American: Ethnicity, Culture, and Identity in Chicano Los Angeles, 1900–1945* (New York, 1993); Edward J. Escobar, *Race, Police, and the Making of a Political Identity: Mexican Americans and the Los Angeles Police Department, 1900–1944* (Berkeley, CA, 1999); Douglas Monroy, *Rebirth: Mexican Los Angeles from the Great Migration to the Great Depression* (Berkeley, CA, 1999); Matt Garcia, *A World of Its Own: Race, Labor, and Citrus in the Making of Greater Los Angeles, 1900–1970* (Chapel Hill, NC, 2001); Stephanie Lewthwaite, *Race, Place, and Reform in Mexican Los Angeles: A Transnational Perspective, 1890–1940* (Tucson, AZ, 2009).

183. Mario Garcia, *Desert Immigrants: The Mexicans of El Paso, 1880–1920* (New Haven, CT, 1981); Zaragosa Vargas, *Proletarians of the North: A History of Mexican Industrial Workers in Detroit and the Midwest, 1917–1933* (Berkeley, CA, 1993); Robert C. Smith, *Mexican New York: Transnational Lives of New Immigrants* (Berkeley, CA, 2005); Roberto R. Trevino, *The Church in the Barrio: Mexican American Ethno-Catholicism in Houston* (Chapel Hill, NC, 2006); Gabriella F. Arredondo, *Mexican Chicago: Race, Identity and Nation, 1981–36* (Urbana, IL, 2008); Raul A. Romos, *Beyond the Alamo: Forging Mexican Ethnicity in San Antonio, 1821–1861* (Chapel Hill, NC, 2008); Daniel D. Arreola, ed., *Hispanic Spaces, Latino Places: Community and Cultural Diversity in Contemporary America* (Austin, TX, 2004).

184. Virginia E. Sanchez Korrol, *From Colonia to Community: The History of Puerto Ricans in New York City* (Berkeley, CA, 1994); Carmen Teresa Whalen, *From Puerto Rico to Philadelphia: Puerto Rican Workers and Postwar Economies* (Philadelphia, 2001); Felix M. Padilla, *Latino Ethnic Consciousness: The Case of Mexican Americans and Puerto Ricans in Chicago* (South Bend, IN, 1985).

185. Maria Christina Garcia, *Havana, USA: Cuban Exiles and Cuban Americans in South Florida, 1959–1994* (Berkeley, CA, 1996); Maria de los Angeles Torres, *In the Land of Mirrors: Cuban Exile Politics in the United States* (Ann Arbor, MI, 1999); Alejandro Portes and Alex Stepick, *City on the Edge: The Transformation of Miami* (Berkeley, CA, 1993).

186. Yong Chen, *Chinese San Francisco, 1850–1943: A Trans-Pacific Community* (Stanford, CA, 2000); Judy Yung, *Unbound Feet: A Social History of Chinese Women in San Francisco* (Berkeley, CA, 1995); John Kuo Wei Tchen, *New York before Chinatown: Orientalism and the Shaping of American Culture, 1776–1882* (Baltimore, 1999); Peter Kwong, *Chinatown, N.Y.: Labor and Politics, 1930–1950* (New York, 1979); Adam McKeown, *Chinese Migrant Networks and Cultural Change: Peru, Chicago, Hawaii, 1900–1936* (Chicago, 2001); Timothy Fong, *The First Suburban Chinatown: The Remaking of Monterey Park, California* (Philadelphia, 1994).

187. Illsoo Kim, *New Urban Immigrants: The Korean Community in New York* (Princeton, NJ, 1981); Nancy Abelmann and John Lie, *Blue Dreams: Korean Americans and the Los Angeles Riots* (Cambridge, MA, 1995). See also Pyong Gap Min, *Caught in the Middle: Korean Communities in New York and Los Angeles* (Berkeley, CA, 1996); Kyeyoung Park, *The Korean American Dream: Immigrants and Small Business in New York City* (Ithaca, NY, 1997); Pat-

rick D. Joyce, *No Fire Next Time: Black-Korean Conflicts and the Future of America's Cities* (Ithaca, NY, 2003).

188. Mitzika Sawada, *Tokyo Life, New York Dreams: Urban Japanese Visions of America, 1890–1924* (Berkeley, CA , 1996); Lon Kurashige, *Japanese American Celebration and Conflict: A History of Ethnic Identity and Festival in Los Angeles, 1934–1990* (Berkeley, CA, 2002); Jacalyn D. Harden, *Double Cross: Japanese Americans in Black and White Chicago* (Minneapolis, 2003).

189. Padma Rangaswamy, *Namaste America: Indian Immigrants in an American Metropolis* (University Park, PA, 2000). For additional bibliography on these and other Asian immigrants, see Sucheng Chan, "Asian American Historiography," *Pacific Historical Review* 65 (August 1996): 363–99; Sucheng Chan, "The Changing Contours of Asian-American Historiography," *Rethinking History* 11 (March 2007): 125–47.

190. Gilbert Osofsky, *Harlem: The Making of a Ghetto; Negro New York, 1890–1930* (New York, 1963); Allan H. Spear, *Black Chicago: The Making of a Negro Ghetto* (Chicago, 1967); Thomas Lee Philpott, *The Slum and the Ghetto: Neighborhood Deterioration and Middle-Class Reform, Chicago, 1880–1930* (New York, 1978); David M. Katzman, *Before the Ghetto: Black Detroit in the Nineteenth Century* (Urbana, IL, 1973); Kenneth L. Kusmer, *A Ghetto Takes Shape: Black Cleveland, 1870–1930* (Urbana, IL, 1976). See also Seth Scheiner, *Negro Mecca: A History of the Negro in New York City, 1865–1920* (New York, 1965); and Leonard P. Curry, *The Free Black in Urban America, 1800–1850: The Shadow of a Dream* (Chicago, 1981).

191. Herbert G. Gutman, *The Black Family in Slavery and Freedom, 1750–1925* (New York, 1976); Elizabeth Pleck, *Black Migration and Poverty: Boston, 1865–1900* (New York, 1979); James Borchert, *Alley Life in Washington: Family, Community, Religion, and Folklife in the City, 1850–1970* (Urbana, IL, 1980); Howard Rabinowitz, *Race Relations in the Urban South, 1865–1890* (New York, 1978); Douglas H. Daniels, *Pioneer Urbanites: A Social and Cultural History of Black San Francisco* (Philadelphia, 1980). For an early historiographical analysis, see Kenneth L. Kusmer, "The Black Urban Experience in American History," in *The State of Afro-American History: Past, Present, and Future*, ed. Darlene Clark Hine (Baton Rouge, LA, 1986), 91–122.

192. Joe William Trotter Jr., *Black Milwaukee: The Making of an Industrial Proletariat, 1915–45* (Urbana, IL, 1985); Trotter, "African Americans in the City: The Industrial Era, 1900–1950," *Journal of Urban History* 21 (May 1995): 438–57. See also the special section on Trotter's book in the *Journal of Urban History* 33 (May 2007); and Trotter's *River Jordan: African American Urban Life in the Ohio Valley* (Lexington, KY, 1998). For studies pursuing key elements of the Trotter model, see George C. Wright, *Life behind a Veil: Blacks in Louisville, Kentucky, 1865–1930* (Baton Rouge, LA, 1985); Albert S. Brousard, *Black San Francisco: The Struggle for Racial Equality in the West* (Lawrence, KS, 1993); Quintard Taylor, *The Forging of a Black Community: Seattle's Central District from 1870 through the Civil Rights Era* (Seattle, WA, 1994); and Earl Lewis, *In Their Own Interests: Race, Class, and Power in Twentieth-Century Norfolk, Virginia* (Berkeley, CA, 1991); Henry Louis Taylor Jr., ed., *Race and the City: Work, Community, and Protest in Cincinnati, 1820–1970* (Urbana, IL, 1993).

193. Gary B. Nash, *Forging Freedom: The Formation of Philadelphia's Black Community, 1720–1840* (Cambridge, MA, 1988); Thelma W. Foote, *Black and White Manhattan: The History of Racial Formation in Colonial New York City* (New York, 2004); Shane White, *Somewhat More Independent: The End of Slavery in New York City, 1770–1810* (Athens, GA, 1991); White, *Stories of Freedom in Black New York* (Cambridge, MA, 2002); Leslie M. Harris, *In the Shadow of Slavery: African Americans in New York City, 1626–1863* (Chicago, 2003); Leslie M. Alexander, *African or American? Black Identity and Political Activism in New York City,*

1784–1861 (Urbana, IL, 2008); Graham Russell Hodges, *Root and Branch: African Americans in New York and East Jersey, 1613–1863* (Chapel Hill, NC, 1999); Seth Rockman, *Scraping By: Wage Labor, Slavery, and Survival in Early Baltimore* (Baltimore, 2008).

194. Robin D. G. Kelley, *Race Rebels: Culture, Politics, and the Black Working Class* (New York, 1994); Kenneth W. Goings and Gerald L. Smith, "'Unhidden' Transcripts: Memphis and African American Agency, 1862–1920," *Journal of Urban History* 21 (March 1995): 372–94; Kate Masur, *An Example for All the Land: Emancipation and the Struggle over Equality in Washington, D.C.* (Chapel Hill, NC, 2010); Michael W. Fitzgerald, *Urban Emancipation: Popular Politics in Reconstruction Mobile, 1860–1890* (Baton Rouge, LA, 2002); Blair L. M. Kelley, *Right to Ride: Streetcar Boycotts and African American Citizenship in the Era of Plessy v. Ferguson* (Chapel Hill, NC, 2010). On the streetcar boycotts, see also August Meier and Elliott Rudwick, "The Boycott Movement against Jim Crow Streetcars in the South, 1900–1906," *Journal of American History* 55 (March 1969): 756–75; Robert Cassanello, "Avoiding 'Jim Crow': Negotiating Separate and Equal on Florida's Railroads and Streetcars and the Progressive Era Origins of the Modern Civil Rights Movement," *Journal of Urban History* 34 (March 2008): 435–57. On retail job boycotts, see Andor Skotnes, "'Buy Where You Can Work': Boycotting for Jobs in African-American Baltimore, 1933–1934," *Journal of Social History* 27 (Summer 1994): 735–61; Cheryl Lynn Greenberg, *Or Does It Explode? Black Harlem in the Great Depression* (New York, 1991), 114–39.

195. William Cohen, *At Freedom's Edge: Black Mobility and the Southern White Quest for Racial Control, 1861–1915* (Baton Rouge, LA, 1991); Marcy S. Sacks, *Before Harlem: The Black Experience in New York City before World War I* (Philadelphia, 2006); Peter Gottlieb, *Making Their Own Way: Southern Blacks' Migration to Pittsburgh, 1916–30* (Urbana, IL, 1987); James R. Grossman, *Land of Hope: Chicago, Black Southerners, and the Great Migration* (Chicago, 1989); Kimberley L. Phillips, *Alabama North: African-American Migrants, Community, and Working-Class Activism in Cleveland, 1915–45* (Urbana, IL, 1999); Gretchen Lemke-Santangelo, *Abiding Courage: African-American Migrant Women and the East Bay Community* (Chapel Hill, NC, 1996); Victoria W. Wolcott, *Remaking Respectability: African American Women in Interwar Detroit* (Chapel Hill, NC, 2001).

196. Nicolas Lemann, *The Promised Land: The Great Black Migration and How It Changed America* (New York, 1991); Isabel Wilkerson, *The Warmth of Other Suns: The Epic Story of America's Great Migration* (New York, 2010); James M. Gregory, *The Southern Diaspora: How the Great Migrations of Black and White Southerners Transformed America* (Chapel Hill, NC, 2005). See also Joe William Trotter Jr., ed., *The Great Migration in Historical Perspective: New Dimensions of Race, Class, and Gender* (Bloomington, IN, 1991); and Steven A. Reich, ed., *Encyclopedia of the Great Black Migration* (3 vols.; Westport, CT, 2006).

197. Richard W. Thomas, *Life for Us Is What We Make It: Building Black Community in Detroit, 1915–1945* (Bloomington, IN, 1992); Roger Lane, *William Dorsey's Philadelphia and Ours: On the Past and Future of the Black City in America* (New York, 1991); Christopher Silver and John V. Moeser, *The Separate City: Black Communities in the Urban South, 1940–1968* (Lexington, KY, 1995); Lillian S. Williams, *Strangers in the Land of Paradise: The Creation of an African American Community, Buffalo, New York, 1900–1940* (Bloomington, IN, 1999); Shirley Ann Wilson Moore, *To Place Our Deeds: The African American Community in Richmond, California, 1910–1963* (Berkeley, CA, 2000); Allison Dorsey, *To Build Our Lives Together: Community Formation in Black Atlanta, 1875–1906* (Athens, GA, 2004).

198. Davarian Baldwin, *Chicago's New Negroes: Modernity, the Great Migration, and Black Urban Life* (Chapel Hill, NC, 2007); Adam Green, *Selling the Race: Culture, Community, and Black Chicago, 1940–1955* (Chicago, 2007); Josh Sides, *L.A. City Limits: African American Los Angeles from the Great Depression to the Present* (Berkeley, CA, 2003);

Douglas Flamming, *Bound for Freedom: Black Los Angeles in Jim Crow America* (Berkeley, CA, 2005); Marvin Dunn, *Black Miami in the Twentieth Century* (Gainesville, FL, 1997); Tera W. Hunter, *To 'Joy My Freedom: Southern Black Women's Lives and Labors after the Civil War* (Cambridge, MA, 1997); Elizabeth Clark-Lewis, *Living In, Living Out: African American Domestics in Washington, D.C., 1910–1940* (Washington, DC, 1994); Jacqueline Jones, *Labor of Love, Labor of Sorrow: Black Women, Work, and the Family, from Slavery to the Present* (New York, 1985); Joe W. Trotter and Jared N. Day, *Race and Residence: African Americans in Pittsburgh since World War II* (Pittsburgh, PA, 2010); Luther Adams, *Way Up North in Louisville: African American Migration in the Urban South, 1930–1970* (Chapel Hill, NC, 2010).

199. William H. Chafe, *Civilities and Civil Rights; Greensboro, North Carolina, and the Black Struggle for Freedom* (New York, 1980); David R. Colburn, *Racial Change and Community Crisis: St. Augustine, Florida, 1877–1980* (New York, 1985); Robert J. Norrell, *Reaping the Whirlwind: The Civil Rights Movement in Tuskegee* (New York, 1985); Alan B. Anderson and George W. Pickering, *Confronting the Color Line: The Broken Promise of the Civil Rights Movement in Chicago* (Athens, GA, 1987); Michael K. Honey, *Southern Labor and Black Civil Rights: Organizing Memphis Workers* (Urbana, IL, 1993); James R. Ralph Jr., *Northern Protest: Martin Luther King, Jr., Chicago, and the Civil Rights Movement* (Cambridge, MA, 1993); Kim Lacy Rogers, *Righteous Lives: Narratives of the New Orleans Civil Rights Movement* (New York, 1993); Glenn T. Eskew, *But for Birmingham: The Local and National Movements in the Civil Rights Struggle* (Chapel Hill, NC, 1997); Diane McWhorter, *Carry Me Home: Birmingham, Alabama; The Climactic Battle of the Civil Rights Revolution* (New York, 2002); Glenda A. Rabby, *The Pain and the Promise: The Struggle for Civil Rights in Tallahassee, Florida* (Athens, GA, 1999); John A. Kirk, *Redefining the Color Line: Black Activism in Little Rock, Arkansas, 1940–1970* (Gainesville, FL, 2002); Martha Biondi, *To Stand and Fight: The Struggle for Civil Rights in Postwar New York City* (Cambridge, MA, 2003); Raymond A. Mohl, *South of the South: Jewish Activists and the Civil Rights Movement in Miami, 1945–1960* (Gainesville, FL, 2004); Matthew C. Whitaker, *Race Work: The Rise of Civil Rights in the Urban West* (Lincoln, NE, 2005); Matthew J. Countryman, *Up South: Civil Rights and Black Power in Philadelphia* (Philadelphia, 2007); Laurie B. Green, *Battling the Plantation Mentality: Memphis and the Black Freedom Struggle* (Chapel Hill, NC, 2007); Clarence Lang, *Grassroots at the Gateway: Class Politics and Black Freedom Struggle in St. Louis, 1936–75* (Ann Arbor, MI, 2009); Patrick D. Jones, *The Selma of the North: Civil Rights Insurgency in Milwaukee* (Cambridge, MA, 2010); Shana Bernstein, *Bridges of Reform: Interracial Civil Rights Activism in Twentieth-Century Los Angeles* (New York, 2011); Tomiko Brown-Nagin, *Courage to Dissent: Atlanta and the Long History of the Civil Rights Movement* (New York, 2011).

200. J. Mills Thornton, *Dividing Lines: Municipal Politics and the Struggle for Civil Rights in Montgomery, Birmingham, and Selma* (Tuscaloosa, AL, 2005); Thomas J. Sugrue, *Sweet Land of Liberty: The Forgotten Struggle for Civil Rights in the North* (New York, 2008); Jeanne Theoharis and Komozi Woodard, eds., *Freedom North: Black Freedom Struggles outside the South, 1940–1980* (New York, 2003); Theoharis and Woodard, eds., *Groundwork: Local Black Freedom Movements in America* (New York, 2005); Samuel C. Hyde Jr., *Sunbelt Revolution: The Historical Progression of the Civil Rights Struggle in the Gulf South* (Gainesville, FL, 2003).

201. Arvarh E. Strickland, *History of the Chicago Urban League* (Urbana, IL, 1966); Christopher Robert Reed, *The Chicago NAACP and the Rise of Black Professional Leadership, 1910–1966* (Bloomington, IN, 1997); Kevin Boyle, *Arc of Justice: A Saga of Race, Civil Rights, and Murder in the Jazz Age* (New York, 2004); August Meier and Elliott Rudwick, *CORE: A Study in the Civil Rights Movement* (New York, 1973); Gerald Horne, *Communist*

Front? The Civil Rights Congress, 1946–1956 (Rutherford, NJ, 1988); Claudrena N. Harold, *The Rise and Fall of the Garvey Movement in the Urban South, 1918–1942* (New York, 2007).

202. Adrian Cook, *Armies of the Streets: The New York City Draft Riots of 1863* (Lexington, KY, 1974); Iver Bernstein, *The New York City Draft Riots: Their Significance for American Society and Politics in the Age of the Civil War* (New York, 1990).

203. Elliott Rudwick, *Race Riot at East St. Louis, July 2, 1917* (Carbondale, IL, 1964); William M. Tuttle Jr., *Race Riot: Chicago in the Red Summer of 1919* (New York, 1970). See also Dominic J. Capeci Jr., "Race Riot Redux: William Tuttle Jr. and the Study of Racial Violence," *Reviews in American History* 29 (March 2001): 165–81.

204. William Ivy Hair, *Robert Charles and the New Orleans Race Riot of 1900* (Baton Rouge, LA, 1976); Mark Bauerlein, *Negrophobia: A Race Riot in Atlanta, 1906* (San Francisco, 2001); Gregory Mixon, *The Atlanta Riot: Race, Class, and Violence in a New South City* (Gainesville, FL, 2004); David Fort Godshalk, *Veiled Visions: The 1906 Atlanta Race Riot and the Reshaping of American Race Relations* (Chapel Hill, NC, 2009); Roberta Senechal, *The Sociogenesis of a Race Riot: Springfield, Illinois, in 1908* (Urbana, IL, 1990); Robert V. Haynes, *A Night of Violence: The Houston Riot of 1917* (Baton Rouge, LA, 1976); Scott Ellsworth, *Death in a Promised Land: The Tulsa Riot of 1921* (Baton Rouge, LA, 1982); James S. Hirsch, *Riot and Remembrance: The Tulsa Race War and Its Legacy* (New York, 2002). See also David S. Cecelski and Timothy B. Tyson, eds., *Democracy Betrayed: The Wilmington Race Riot of 1898 and Its Legacy* (Chapel Hill, NC, 1998).

205. Dominic J. Capeci, *The Harlem Riot of 1943* (Philadelphia, 1977); Dominic J. Capeci and Martha Wilkerson, *Layered Violence: The Detroit Rioters of 1943* (Jackson, MS, 1991); Eduardo Obregon Pagan, *Murder at the Sleepy Lagoon: Zoot Suits, Race, and Riot in Wartime L.A.* (Chapel Hill, NC, 2003); Kevin Allen Leonard, *The Battle for Los Angeles: Racial Ideology and World War II* (Albuquerque, NM, 2006).

206. Gerald Horne, *Fire This Time: The Watts Uprising and the 1960s* (Charlottesville, VA, 1995); Sidney Fine, *Violence in the Model City: The Cavanaugh Administration, Race Relations, and the Detroit Riot of 1967* (Ann Arbor, MI, 1989); Kevin Mumford, *Newark: A History of Race, Rights, and Riots in America* (New York, 2007). See also David Boesel and Peter H. Rossi, eds., *Cities under Siege: An Anatomy of the Ghetto Riots, 1964–1968* (New York, 1971); Joe R. Feagin and Harlan Hahn, eds., *Ghetto Revolts: The Politics of Violence in American Cities* (New York, 1973); and Heather Ann Thompson, "Urban Uprisings: Riots or Rebellions?" in *The Columbia Guide to America in the 1960s*, ed. David Farber and Beth Bailey (New York, 2001), 109–17.

207. Bruce Porter and Marvin Dunn, *The Miami Riot of 1980: Crossing the Bounds* (Lexington, MA, 1984); Raphael Sonenshein, *Politics in Black and White: Race and Power in Los Angeles* (Princeton, NJ, 1993); Nancy Abelmann and John Lie, *Blue Dreams: Korean Americans and the Los Angeles Riots* (Cambridge, MA, 1995).

208. Herbert Shapiro, *White Violence and Black Response: From Reconstruction to Montgomery* (Amherst, MA, 1988); Janet Abu-Lughod, *Race, Space, and Riots in Chicago, New York, and Los Angeles* (New York, 2007).

209. Ronald H. Bayor, *Race and the Shaping of Twentieth-Century Atlanta* (Chapel Hill, NC, 1996); John T. McGreevy, *Parish Boundaries: The Catholic Encounter with Race in the Twentieth-Century Urban North* (Chicago, 1996); Elisabeth Lasch-Quinn, *Black Neighbors: Race and the Limits of Reform in the American Settlement House Movement, 1890–1945* (Chapel Hill, NC, 1993); and, more generally, Gary Gerstle, *American Crucible: Race and Nation in the Twentieth Century* (Princeton, NJ, 2001).

210. Representative works include August Meier and Elliott Rudwick, *Black Detroit and the Rise of the UAW* (New York, 1979); Peter Rachleff, *Black Labor in Richmond, 1865–1890*

(Philadelphia, 1984); Daniel Rosenberg, *New Orleans Dockworkers: Race, Labor, and Union-ism, 1892–1923* (Albany, NY, 1988); Eric Arnesen, *Waterfront Workers of New Orleans: Race, Class, and Politics, 1863–1922* (New York, 1991); Heather Ann Thompson, *Whose Detroit? Politics, Labor, and Race in a Modern American City* (Ithaca, NY, 2002); Mark Naison, *Communists in Harlem during the Depression* (Urbana, IL, 1983); Robin D. G. Kelley, *Hammer and Hoe: Alabama Communists during the Great Depression* (Chapel Hill, NC, 1990); Bill V. Mullen, *Popular Fronts: Chicago and African-American Cultural Politics, 1935–46* (Urbana, IL, 1999).

211. On the black church, see Robert Gregg, *Sparks from the Anvil of Oppression: Phila-delphia's African Methodist and Southern Migrants, 1890–1940* (Philadelphia, 1993); Milton C. Sernett, *Bound for the Promised Land: African American Religion and the Great Migration* (Durham, NC, 1997); Evelyn Brooks Higginbotham, *Righteous Discontent: The Women's Movement in the Black Baptist Church, 1880–1920* (Cambridge, MA, 1993). On black sports, see Jules Tygiel, *Baseball's Great Experiment: Jackie Robinson and His Legacy* (New York, 1983); Rob Ruck, *Sandlot Seasons: Sport in Black Pittsburgh* (Urbana, IL, 1987); Neil Lanc-tot, *Negro League Baseball: The Rise and Ruin of a Black Institution* (Philadelphia, 2004); and Bob Kuska, *Hot Potato: How Washington and New York Gave Birth to Black Basketball and Changed America's Game Forever* (Charlottesville, VA, 2004). On black women in civil rights, see Vickie L. Crawford et al., eds., *Women in the Civil Rights Movement: Trailblazers and Torchbearers, 1941–1965* (Bloomington, IN, 1990); Belinda Robnett, *How Long? How Long? African-American Women in the Struggle for Civil Rights* (New York, 1997); and Bettye Collier-Thomas and V. P. Franklin, eds., *Sisters in the Struggle: African-American Women in the Civil Rights–Black Power Movement* (New York, 2001).

212. For representative works, see William J. Grimshaw, *Bitter Fruit: Black Politics and the Chicago Machine, 1931–1991* (Chicago, 1992); Karen Ferguson, *Black Politics in New Deal Atlanta* (Chapel Hill, NC, 2002); Chris Rhomberg, *No There There: Race, Class, and Political Community in Oakland* (Berkeley, CA, 2007); James Wolfinger, *Philadelphia Divided: Race and Politics in the City of Brotherly Love* (Chapel Hill, NC, 2007); David R. Colburn and Jef-frey S. Adler, eds., *African-American Mayors: Race, Politics, and the American City* (Urbana, IL, 2001); Edward Greer, *Big Steel: Black Politics and Corporate Power in Gary, Indiana* (New York, 1979).

213. David R. Roediger, *The Wages of Whiteness: Race and the Making of the American Working Class* (New York, 1991); Roediger, *Working toward Whiteness: How America's Immigrants Became White* (New York, 2005); Noel Ignatiev, *How the Irish Became White* (New York, 1995); Anthony Gronowicz, *Race and Class Politics in New York City before the Civil War* (Boston, 1998); Thomas A. Guglielmo, *White on Arrival: Italians, Race, Color, and Power in Chicago, 1890–1945* (New York, 2003); Nancy Foner and George M. Frederickson, eds., *Not Just Black and White: Historical and Contemporary Perspectives on Immigration, Race, and Ethnicity in the United States* (New York, 2004). For historiographical perspectives on whiteness scholarship, see Eric Arnesen, "Whiteness and the Historians' Imagination," *International Labor and Working-Class History* 60 (Fall 2001): 3–32; Peter Kolchin, "White-ness Studies: The New History of Race in America," *Journal of American History* 89 (June 2002): 154–73.

214. James W. Loewen, *Sundown Towns: A Hidden Dimension of American Racism* (New York, 2005).

215. William Julius Wilson, *The Truly Disadvantaged: The Inner City, The Underclass, and Public Policy* (Chicago, 1987); Wilson, *When Work Disappears: The World of the New Urban Poor* (New York, 1996); Wilson, ed., *The Ghetto Underclass: Social Science Perspectives* (Newbury Park, CA, 1993); Douglas S. Massey and Nancy A. Denton, *American Apartheid:*

Segregation and the Making of the Underclass (Cambridge, MA, 1993); Thomas J. Sugrue, *The Origins of the Urban Crisis: Race and Inequality in Postwar Detroit* (Princeton, NJ, 1996); Michael B. Katz, ed., *The "Underclass" Debate: Views from History* (Princeton, NJ, 1993). See also Joe W. Trotter, Earl Lewis, and Tera W. Hunter, "Connecting African American Urban History, Social Science Research, and Policy Debates," in *The African American Urban Experience: Perspectives from the Colonial Period to the Present*, ed. Trotter, Lewis, and Hunter (New York, 2004), 1–20. Additional historiographical perspective on blacks in the cities can be found in Kenneth W. Goings and Raymond A. Mohl, eds., *The New African American Urban History* (Thousand Oaks, CA, 1996); and Kenneth L. Kusmer and Joe W. Trotter, eds., *African American Urban History since World War II* (Chicago, 2009).

216. Laurel Thatcher Ulrich, *Good Wives: Images and Reality in the Lives of Women in Northern New England, 1650–1750* (New York, 1982); Karin Wulf, *Not All Wives: Women of Colonial Philadelphia* (Philadelphia, 2000); Kathleen Brown, *Good Wives, Nasty Wenches, and Anxious Patriarchs: Gender, Race, and Power in Colonial Virginia* (Chapel Hill, NC, 1996); Mary Beth Norton, *Founding Mothers and Fathers: Gendered Power and the Forming of American Society* (New York, 1996); Norton, *Liberty's Daughters: The Revolutionary Experience of American Women, 1750–1800* (Ithaca, NY, 1980). See also Elaine Forman Crane, *Ebb Tide in New England: Women, Seaports, and Social Change, 1630–1800* (Boston, 1998); and Cynthia M. Kennedy, *Braided Relations, Entwined Lives: The Women of Charleston's Urban Slave Society* (Bloomington, IN, 2005).

217. Christine Stansell, *City of Women: Sex and Class in New York, 1789–1860* (New York, 1987); Susan Strasser, *Never Done: A History of American Housework* (New York, 1982); Jeanne Boydston, *Home and Work: Housework, Wages, and the Ideology of Labor in the Early Republic* (New York, 1994); Suzanne Lebsock, *The Free Women of Petersburg: Status and Culture in a Southern Town, 1784–1860* (New York, 1984); Mary P. Ryan, *Women in Public: Between Banners and Ballots, 1825–1880* (Baltimore, 1990).

218. Barbara Berg, *The Remembered Gate: Origins of American Feminism: Women and the City, 1800–1860* (New York, 1978); Nancy A. Hewitt, *Women's Activism and Social Change: Rochester, New York, 1822–1872* (Lexington, MA, 1984); Teresa Anne Murphy, *Ten Hours' Labor: Religion, Reform, and Gender in Early New England* (Ithaca, NY, 1992); Anne M. Boylan, *The Origins of Women's Activism: New York and Boston, 1797–1840* (Chapel Hill, NC, 2002).

219. Maureen A. Flanagan, *Seeing with Their Hearts: Chicago Women and the Vision of the Good City, 1871–1933* (Princeton, NJ, 2002); Flanagan, "Women in the City, Women of the City: Where Do Women Fit in Urban History?" *Journal of Urban History* 23 (March 1997): 251–59.

220. Robyn Muncy, *Creating a Female Dominion in American Reform, 1890–1935* (New York, 1991); Lori D. Ginzberg, *Women and the Work of Benevolence: Morality, Politics, and Class in the Nineteenth-Century United States* (New Haven, CT, 1990); Ruth Bordin, *Women and Temperance: The Quest for Power and Liberty, 1871–1900* (New Brunswick, NJ, 1981); Nancy A. Hewitt, *Southern Discomfort: Women's Activism in Tampa, Florida, 1880s–1920s* (Urbana, IL, 2001); Suellen Hoy, *Chasing Dirt: The American Pursuit of Cleanliness* (New York, 1995); Sarah Deutsch, *Women and the City: Gender, Space, and Power in Boston, 1870–1940* (New York, 2000).

221. Kathryn Kish Sklar, *Florence Kelley and the Nation's Work* (New Haven, CT, 1995); Elizabeth Israels Perry, *Belle Moskowitz: Feminine Politics and the Exercise of Power in the Age of Alfred E. Smith* (New York, 1987); Eleanor J. Stebner, *The Women of Hull House: A Study of Spirituality, Vocation, and Friendship* (Albany, NY, 1997). For overviews of the settlement house movement, see Allen F. Davis, *Spearheads for Reform: The Social Settle-*

ments and the Progressive Movement, 1890–1914 (New York, 1967); and Mina Carson, *Settlement Folk: Social Thought and the American Settlement Movement, 1885–1930* (Chicago,
1990). The literature on Jane Addams and Hull House is extensive. See Daniel Levine, *Jane
Addams and the Liberal Tradition* (Madison, WI, 1971); Allen F. Davis, *American Heroine:
The Life and Legend of Jane Addams* (New York, 1973); Mary Jo Deegan, *Jane Addams
and the Men of the Chicago School, 1892–1918* (New Brunswick, NJ, 1986); Rivka Shpak
Lissak, *Pluralism and Progressives: Hull House and the New Immigrants, 1890–1919* (Chi-
cago, 1989); Jean Bethke Elshtain, *Jane Addams and the Dream of American Democracy*
(New York, 2002); Louise W. Knight, *Citizen: Jane Addams and the Struggle for Democracy*
(Chicago, 2005); Knight, *Jane Addams: Spirit in Action* (New York, 2010); and Marilyn
Fischer, Carol Nacjennoff, and Wendy Chemielewsky, eds., *Jane Addams and the Practice
of Democracy* (Urbana, IL, 2009).

222. Daphne Spain, *How Women Saved the City* (Minneapolis, 2001); Susan Lynn, *Progressive Women in Conservative Times: Racial Justice, Peace, and Feminism, 1945 to the 1960s*
(New Brunswick, NJ, 1992).

223. Suellen Hoy, *Good Hearts: Catholic Sisters in Chicago's Past* (Urbana, IL, 2006);
Maureen Fitzgerald, *Habits of Compassion: Irish Catholic Nuns and the Origins of New York's
Welfare System, 1830–1920* (Urbana, IL, 2006).

224. Mari Jo Buhle, *Women and American Socialism, 1870–1920* (Urbana, IL, 1981).

225. Anne Firor Scott, *Natural Allies: Women's Voluntary Associations in America* (Urbana, IL, 1991); Mary P. Ryan, *Civic Wars: Democracy and Public Life in the American City
during the Nineteenth Century* (Berkeley, CA, 1997); Priscilla Murolo, *The Common Ground
of Womanhood: Class, Gender, and Working Girls' Clubs, 1884–1928* (Urbana, IL, 1997);
Anne Meis Knupfer, *Toward a Tenderer Humanity and a Nobler Womanhood: African-
American Women's Clubs in Turn-of-the-Century Chicago* (New York, 1996); Dorothy Salem,
To Better Our World: Black Women in Organized Reform, 1890–1920 (Brooklyn, NY, 1990);
Glenda E. Gilmore, *Gender and Jim Crow: Women and the Politics of White Supremacy in
North Carolina, 1896–1920* (Chapel Hill, NC, 1996); and several essays in Noralee Frankel
and Nancy S. Dye, eds., *Gender, Class, Race, and Reform in the Progressive Era* (Lexington,
KY, 1991).

226. Donna R. Gabaccia, *From the Other Side: Women, Gender, and Immigrant Life in
the United States, 1820–1990* (Bloomington, IN, 1994); Martha Gardner, *The Qualities of a
Citizen: Women, Immigration, and Citizenship, 1870–1965* (Princeton, NJ, 2009); Susan A.
Glenn, *Daughters of the Shtetl: Life and Labor in the Immigrant Generation* (Ithaca, NY,
1990); Elizabeth Ewen, *Immigrant Women in the Land of Dollars: Life and Culture in the
Lower East Side, 1890–1925* (New York, 1985); Paula Hyman, *Gender and Assimilation in
Modern Jewish History: The Roles and Representation of Women* (Seattle, WA, 1995); Diane
C. Vecchio, *Merchants, Midwives, and Laboring Women: Italian Migrants in Urban America*
(Urbana, IL, 2006); Judith E. Smith, *Family Connections: A History of Italian and Jewish
Immigrant Lives in Providence, Rhode Island, 1900–1940* (Albany, NY, 1985); Hasia Diner,
Lower East Side Memories: A Jewish Place in America (Princeton, NJ, 2002); Diner, *Erin's
Daughters in America: Irish Immigrant Women in the Nineteenth Century* (Baltimore, 1983);
Diner, *Hungering for America: Italian, Irish, and Jewish Foodways in the Age of Migration*
(Cambridge, MA, 2003); Judy Yung, *Unbound Feet: A Social History of Chinese Women in
San Francisco* (Berkeley, CA, 1995).

227. Thomas J. Schlereth, *Victorian America: Transformations in Everyday Life* (New
York, 1997); Glenna Matthews, *"Just a Housewife": The Rise and Fall of Domesticity in
America* (New York, 1987); Ruth Schwartz Cowan, *More Work for Mother: The Ironies of
Household Technology from the Open Hearth to the Microwave* (New York, 1985); Dolores

Hayden, *The Grand Domestic Revolution: A History of Feminist Designs for American Homes, Neighborhoods, and Cities* (Cambridge, MA, 1982); Tracey Deutsch, *Building a Housewife's Paradise: Gender, Politics, and American Grocery Stores in the Twentieth Century* (Chapel Hill, NC, 2010); Sylvie Murray, *The Progressive Housewife: Community Activism in Suburban Queens, 1945–1965* (Philadelphia, 2003).

228. Clare A. Lyons, *Sex among the Rabble: An Intimate History of Gender and Power in the Age of Revolution, Philadelphia, 1730–1830* (Chapel Hill, NC, 2006); Patricia Cline Cohen, Timothy J. Gilfoyle, and Helen Lefkowitz, *The Flash Press: Sporting Male Weeklies in 1840's New York* (Chicago, 2008); Donna Dennis, *Licentious Gotham: Erotic Publishing and Its Persecution in Nineteenth-Century New York* (Cambridge, MA, 2009); Chad C. Heap, *Slumming: Sexual and Racial Encounters in American Nightlife, 1885–1940* (Chicago, 2010).

229. Timothy Gilfoyle, *City of Eros: New York City, Prostitution, and the Commercialization of Sex, 1790–1920* (New York, 1994); Ruth Rosen, *The Lost Sisterhood: Prostitution in America, 1900–1918* (Baltimore, 1982); Jacqueline B. Barnhart, *The Fair but Frail: Prostitution in San Francisco, 1849–1900* (Reno, NV, 1986); Mark Thomas Connelly, *The Response to Prostitution in the Progressive Era* (Chapel Hill, NC, 1980); Barbara M. Hobson, *Uneasy Virtue: The Politics of Prostitution and the American Reform Tradition* (Chicago, 1997); Thomas C. Mackey, *Red Lights Out: A Legal History of Prostitution, Disorderly Houses, and Vice Districts, 1870–1917* (New York, 1987); David Langum, *Crossing the Lines: Legislating Morality and the Mann Act* (Chicago, 1994); Brian Donovan, *White Slave Crusades: Race, Gender, and Anti-Vice Activism, 1887–1917* (Urbana, IL, 2006); Karen Abbott, *Sin in the Second City: Madams, Ministers, Playboys, and the Battle for America's Soul* (New York, 2007). Also see Elizabeth Clement, *Love for Sale: Courting, Treating, and Prostitution in New York City, 1900–1945* (Chapel Hill, NC, 2006); Marilynn Wood Hill, *Their Sisters' Keepers: Prostitution in New York City, 1830–1870* (Berkeley, CA, 1993); Anne M. Butler, *Daughters of Joy, Sisters of Misery: Prostitutes in the American West* (Urbana, IL, 1987); and Jan MacKell, *Brothels, Bordellos, and Bad Girls: Prostitution in Colorado, 1860–1930* (Albuquerque, NM, 2007).

230. John D'Emilio, *Sexual Politics, Sexual Communities: The Making of a Homosexual Minority in the United States, 1940–1970* (Chicago, 1983); Martin Duberman, *Stonewall: The Riots That Sparked the Gay Revolution* (New York, 1993); George Chauncey, *Gay New York: Gender, Urban Culture, and the Making of the Gay Male World, 1890–1940* (New York, 1994); Allan Bérubé, *Coming Out under Fire: The History of Gay Men and Women in World War II* (New York, 1990); Charles Kaiser, *The Gay Metropolis: The Landmark History of Gay Life in America* (New York, 2007).

231. Lillian Faderman, *Odd Girls and Twilight Lovers: A History of Lesbian Life in Twentieth-Century America* (New York, 1991); Elizabeth L. Kennedy and Madeline Davis, *Boots of Leather, Slippers of Gold: The History of a Lesbian Community* (New York, 1993); John Howard, *Carryin' on in the Lesbian and Gay South* (New York, 1997); James T. Sears, *Lonely Hunters: An Oral History of Lesbian and Gay Southern Life, 1948–1968* (New York, 1997); Sears, *Rebels, Rubyfruit, and Rhinestones: Queering Space in the Stonewall South* (New Brunswick, NJ, 2001).

232. Christine Stansell, *American Moderns: Bohemian New York and the Creation of a New Century* (New York, 2000); Judith Schwarz, *Radical Feminists of Heterodoxy: Greenwich Village, 1912–1940* (Lebanon, NH, 1982); June Sochen, *The New Woman: Feminism in Greenwich Village, 1910–1920* (New York, 1972); Ross Wetzsteon, *Republic of Dreams: Greenwich Village, the American Bohemia, 1910–1960* (New York, 2002); Kevin J. Mumford, *Interzones: Black/White Sex Districts in Chicago and New York in the Early Twentieth Century* (New York, 1997); Beth Bailey and David Farber, *The First Strange Place: Race and Sex in World War II Hawaii* (Baltimore, 1994).

233. Esther Newton, *Cherry Grove, Fire Island: Sixty Years in America's First Gay and Lesbian Town* (Boston, 1995).

234. Nan Boyd, *Wide-Open Town: A History of Queer San Francisco to 1865* (Berkeley, 2003); Josh Sides, *Erotic City: Sexual Revolutions and the Making of Modern San Francisco* (New York, 2009); Martin Meeker, *Contacts Desired: Gay and Lesbian Communications and Community, 1940s–1970s* (Chicago, 2008).

235. Daniel Hurewitz, *Bohemian Los Angeles and the Making of Modern Politics* (Berkeley, CA, 2007); Moira Kenney, *Mapping Gay L.A.: The Intersection of Place and Politics* (Philadelphia, 2001); Lillian Faderman and Stuart Timmons, *Gay L.A.: A History of Sexual Outlaws, Power Politics, and Lipstick Lesbians* (Berkeley, CA, 2009).

236. Alicia P. Long, *The Great Southern Babylon: Sex, Race, and Respectability in New Orleans, 1865–1920* (Baton Rouge, LA, 2004); Jennifer M. Spear, *Race, Sex, and Social Order in Early New Orleans* (Baltimore, 2009); Judith Kelleher Schafer, *Brothels, Depravity, and Abandoned Women: Illegal Sex in Antebellum New Orleans* (Baton Rouge, LA, 2009).

237. See Beth Bailey, *Sex in the Heartland* (Cambridge, MA, 2002). Other studies of sexuality and the cities include Julie Abraham, *Metropolitan Lovers: The Homosexuality of Cities* (Minneapolis, 2009); Marc Stein, *City of Sisterly and Brotherly Loves: Lesbian and Gay Philadelphia, 1945–1972* (Philadelphia, 2004); Peter Boag, *Same-Sex Affairs: Constructing and Controlling Homosexuality in the Pacific Northwest* (Berkeley, CA, 2003); and Brett Beemyn, ed., *Creating a Place for Ourselves: Lesbian, Gay, and Bisexual Community Histories* (New York, 1997), which contains essays on New York City, Chicago, Detroit, Philadelphia, Washington, D.C., San Francisco, Buffalo, and Flint, Michigan.

238. Howard P. Chudacoff, *The Age of the Bachelor: Creating an Urban Subculture* (Princeton, NJ, 1999). For the Minneapolis-St. Paul community, see the Twin Cities GLBT Oral History Project, *Queer Twin Cities* (Minneapolis, 2010).

239. Lizabeth Cohen, *A Consumer's Republic: The Politics of Mass Consumption in Postwar America* (New York, 2003); Cohen, "Is There an Urban History of Consumption?" *Journal of Urban History* 29 (December 2003): 87–106; Cohen, "From Town Center to Shopping Center: The Reconfiguration of Community Marketplaces in Postwar America," *American Historical Review* 101 (October 1996): 1050–81.

240. Sharon Zukin, *Point of Purchase: How Shopping Changed America* (New York, 2004); Gary Cross, *An All-Consuming Century: Why Commercialism Won in Modern America* (New York, 2000); Cross, *Time and Money: The Making of Consumer Culture* (New York, 1993); Ann Satterthwaite, *Going Shopping: Consumer Choices and Community Consequences* (New Haven, CT, 2001).

241. Timothy H. Breen, "'Baubles of Britain': The American and Consumer Revolutions of the Eighteenth Century," *Past and Present* 119 (May 1988): 73–104; Breen, *The Marketplace of Revolution: How Consumer Politics Shaped American Independence* (New York, 2004).

242. David E. Meyer, *The Roots of American Industrialization* (Baltimore, 2003); Helen Tangires, *Public Markets and Civic Culture in Nineteenth-Century America* (Baltimore, 2003).

243. Glenn Porter and Harold C. Livesay, *Merchants and Manufacturers: Studies in the Changing Structure of Nineteenth-Century Marketing* (Baltimore, 1971); Jennifer Scanlon, *Inarticulate Longings: The* Ladies' Home Journal, *Gender, and the Promise of Consumer Culture* (New York, 1995); Matthew Schneirov, *The Dream of a New Social Order: Popular Magazines in America, 1893–1914* (New York, 1994); Richard Ohmann, *Selling Culture: Magazines, Markets, and Class at the Turn of the Century* (New York, 1996).

244. T. J. Jackson Lears, *Fables of Abundance: A Cultural History of Advertising in America* (New York, 1994). Considerable discussion on consumption can be found throughout Lears's *Rebirth of a Nation: The Making of Modern America, 1877–1920* (New York, 2009).

245. Susan Strasser, *Satisfaction Guaranteed: The Making of the American Mass Market* (New York, 1989); Thomas Hine, *The Total Package: The Evolution and Secret Meanings of Boxes, Bottles, Cans, and Tubes* (Boston, 1995); Roland Marchand, *Advertising and the American Dream: Making Way for Modernity, 1920–1940* (Berkeley, CA, 1985); Stuart Ewen, *Captains of Consciousness: Advertising and the Social Roots of the Consumer Culture* (New York, 1976). On the relationship between mass images and consumer culture, see also Stuart Ewen and Elizabeth Ewen, *Channels of Desire: Mass Images and the Shaping of American Consciousness* (New York, 1982); and Stuart Ewen, *All Consuming Images: The Politics of Style in Contemporary Culture* (New York, 1988).

246. Kathy Peiss, "American Women and the Making of Modern Consumer Culture," *Journal for MultiMedia History* 1 (Fall 1998), Peiss, *Hope in a Jar: The Making of America's Beauty Culture* (New York, 1998); Lisa Jacobson, *Raising Consumers: Children and the American Mass Market in the Twentieth Century* (New York, 2004); Andrew R. Heinze, *Adapting to Abundance: Jewish Immigrants, Mass Consumption, and the Search for American Identity* (New York, 1990); Jenna Weissman Joselit, *The Wonders of America: Reinventing Jewish Culture, 1880–1950* (New York, 1994). See also Daniel Delis Hill, *Advertising to the American Woman, 1900–1999* (Columbus, OH, 2002).

247. T. J. Jackson Lears, *No Place of Grace: Antimodernism and the Transformation of American Culture, 1880–1920* (Chicago, 1983). See also Lears's "From Salvation to Self-Realization: Advertising and the Therapeutic Roots of the Consumer Culture, 1880–1930," in *The Culture of Consumption: Critical Essays in American History, 1880–1980,* ed. Richard Wightman and T. J. Jackson Lears (New York, 1983), 1–38, 213–18.

248. Lizabeth Cohen, *Making a New Deal: Industrial Workers in Chicago, 1919–1939* (Cambridge, UK, 1990; new ed., 2008); Cohen, "The Class Experience of Mass Consumption: Workers as Consumers in Interwar America," in *The Power of Culture: Critical Essays in American History,* ed. Richard Wightman Fox and T. J. Jackson Lears (Chicago, 1993), 135–60.

249. Meg Jacobs, *Pocketbook Politics: Economic Citizenship in Twentieth-Century America* (Princeton, NJ, 2005); Charles F. McGovern, *Sold American: Consumption and Citizenship, 1890–1945* (Chapel Hill, NC, 2006); Dana Frank, *Purchasing Power: Consumer Organizing, Gender, and the Seattle Labor Movement, 1919–1929* (New York, 1994); Robert E. Weems Jr., *Desegregating the Dollar: African American Consumerism in the Twentieth Century* (New York, 1998).

250. William R. Leach, *Land of Desire: Merchants, Power, and the Rise of a New American Dream* (New York, 1993); Leach, "Transformations in a Culture of Consumption: Women and Department Stores, 1890–1925,"*Journal of American History* 71 (September 1984): 319–42. On department stores, see also Mona Domosh, *Invented Cities: The Creation of Landscape in Nineteenth Century New York and Boston* (New Haven, CT, 1996), 35–64; Jan Whitaker, *Service and Style: How the American Department Store Fashioned the Middle Class* (New York, 2006); Gunther Barth, *City People: The Rise of Modern City Culture in Nineteenth-Century America* (New York, 1980), 110–47; Neil Harris, *Cultural Excursions: Marketing Appetites and Cultural Tastes in Modern America* (Chicago, 1990), 174–97. There are few recent histories of individual department store magnates, but see Herbert Ershkowitz, *John Wanamaker: Philadelphia Merchant* (Conshohocken, PA, 1999).

251. Susan Porter Benson, *Counter Cultures: Saleswomen, Managers, and Customers in American Department Stores, 1890–1940* (Urbana, IL, 1986); Kathy Peiss, *Cheap Amusements: Working Women and Leisure in Turn-of-the-Century New York* (Philadelphia, 1986); Elaine S. Abelson, *When Ladies Go A-Thieving: Middle-Class Shoplifters in the Victorian Department Store* (New York, 1989).

252. Richard Longstreth, *City Center to Regional Mall: Architecture, the Automobile, and Retailing in Los Angeles, 1920–1950* (Cambridge, MA, 1998); Longstreth, *The Drive-in, the Supermarket, and the Transformation of Commercial Space in Los Angeles, 1914–1941* (Cambridge, MA, 2000); Catherine Gudis, *Buyways: Billboards, Automobiles, and the American Landscape* (New York, 2004).

253. M. Jeffrey Hardwick, *Mall Maker: Victor Gruen, Architect of an American Dream* (Philadelphia, 2004); Nicholas Dagen Bloom, *Merchant of Illusion: James Rouse, America's Salesman of the Businessman's Utopia* (Columbus, OH, 2004); Joshua Olsen, *Better Places, Better Lives: A Life of James Rouse* (Washington, DC, 2004); William Severini Kowlinski, *The Malling of America: An Inside Look at the Great American Consumer Paradise* (New York, 1985). See also Thomas W. Hanchett, "U.S. Tax Policy and the Shopping Center Boom of the 1950s and 1960s," *American Historical Review* 101 (October 1996): 1082–1110, which discusses accelerated depreciation tax benefits granted to shopping-center developers.

254. Bernard J. Frieden and Lynne B. Sagalyn, *Downtown, Inc.: How America Rebuilds Cities* (Cambridge, MA, 1989); Alison Isenberg, *Downtown America: A History of the Place and the People Who Made It* (Chicago, 2004); Lizabeth Cohen, "Buying into Downtown Revival: The Centrality of Retail to Postwar Urban Renewal in American Cities," *Annals of the American Academy of Political and Social Science* 611 (May 2007): 82–95.

255. Susan Smulyan, *Selling Radio: The Commercialization of American Broadcasting, 1920–1934* (Washington, DC, 1994); Lynn Spigel and Denise Mann, *Private Screenings: Television and the Female Consumer* (Minneapolis, 1992). For additional historiographical insight, see Frank Trentman, "Beyond Consumption: New Historical Perspectives on Consumption," *Journal of Contemporary History* 39 (July 2004): 373–401.

256. Steven A. Riess, *City Games: The Evolution of American Urban Society and the Rise of Sports* (Urbana, IL, 1989); Riess, *The Sport of Kings and the Kings of Crime: Horse Racing, Politics, and Organized Crime in New York, 1865–1913* (Syracuse, NY, 2011); Riess, *Sport in Industrial America, 1850–1920* (Wheeling, IL, 1995).

257. Stephen Hardy, *How Boston Played: Sport, Recreation, and Community, 1865–1915* (Boston, 1982); Dale Somers, *The Rise of Sports in New Orleans, 1850–1900* (Baton Rouge, LA, 1972); Steven A. Riess, *Touching Base: Professional Baseball and American Culture in the Progressive Era* (Westport, CT, 1980); Melvin A. Adelman, *A Sporting Time: New York City and the Rise of Modern Athletics, 1820–1870* (Urbana, IL, 1986); Bruce Kuklick, *To Every Thing a Season: Shibe Park and Urban Philadelphia, 1909–1976* (Princeton, NJ, 1991); Elliott J. Gorn, *The Manly Art: Bare-Knuckle Prizefighting in America* (Ithaca, NY, 1986); Jeffrey T. Sammons, *Beyond the Ring: The Role of Boxing in American Society* (Urbana, IL, 1988); Kathryn Grover, ed., *Hard at Play: Leisure in America, 1840–1940* (Amherst, MA, 1992).

258. Dominick Cavallo, *Muscles and Morals: Organized Playgrounds and Urban Reform, 1880–1920* (Philadelphia, 1981); Peter Levine, *Ellis Island to Ebbets Field: Sport and the American Jewish Experience* (New York, 1992); Neil Lanctot, *Negro League Baseball: The Rise and Decline of a Black Institution* (Philadelphia, 2004); Rob Ruck, *Sandlot Seasons: Sport in Black Pittsburgh* (Urbana, IL, 1987), quotation on p. 3.

259. David W. Conroy, *In Public Houses: Drink and the Revolution of Authority in Colonial Massachusetts* (Chapel Hill, NC, 1995); Peter Thompson, *Rum Punch and Revolution: Taverngoing and Public Life in Eighteenth-Century Philadelphia* (Philadelphia, 1999); Sharon V. Salinger, *Taverns and Drinking in Early America* (Baltimore, 2002); Benjamin L. Carp, *Rebels Rising: Cities and the American Revolution* (New York, 2007), 62–98, quotation on p. 63.

260. Roy Rosenzweig, *Eight Hours for What We Will: Workers and Leisure in an Industrial City, 1870–1920* (Cambridge, UK, 1983); Perry R. Duis, *The Saloon: Public Drinking in Chicago and Boston, 1880–1920* (Urbana, IL, 1983); Thomas J. Noel, *The City and the*

Saloon: Denver, 1858–1916 (Lincoln, NE, 1982); Madelon Powers, *Faces along the Bar: Lore and Order in the Workingmen's Saloon, 1870–1920* (Chicago, 1998); Mary Murphy, *Mining Cultures: Men, Women, and Leisure in Butte, 1914–41* (Urbana, IL, 1997); Michael A. Lerner, *Dry Manhattan: Prohibition in New York City* (Cambridge, MA, 2007); Burton W. Peretti, *Nightclub City: Politics and Amusement in Manhattan* (Philadelphia, 2007), quotation on p. xii.

261. David Nasaw, *Going Out: The Rise and Fall of Public Amusements* (Cambridge, MA, 1993); Gunther Barth, *City People: The Rise of Modern City Culture in Nineteenth-Century America* (New York, 1980); Patricia C. Click, *The Spirit of the Times: Amusements in Nineteenth-Century Baltimore, Norfolk, and Richmond* (Charlottesville, VA, 1989); Scott C. Martin, *Killing Time: Leisure and Culture in Southwestern Pennsylvania, 1800–1850* (Pittsburgh, PA, 1995); Barbara Berglund, *Making San Francisco American: Cultural Frontiers in the Urban West, 1846–1906* (Lawrence, KS, 2007); John Kasson, *Amusing the Million: Coney Island at the Turn of the Century* (New York, 1978); Woody Register, *The Kid of Coney Island: Fred Thompson and the Rise of American Amusements* (New York, 2001); Robert W. Snyder, *The Voice of the City: Vaudeville and Popular Culture in New York* (Chicago, 1989); Robert C. Allen, *Horrible Prettiness: Burlesque and American Culture* (Chapel Hill, NC, 1991).

262. Lewis A. Ehrenberg, *Steppin' Out: New York Nightlife and the Transformation of American Culture* (Chicago, 1981); Ehrenberg, *Swingin' the Dream: Big Band Jazz and the Rebirth of American Culture* (Chicago, 1998); Burton W. Peretti, *The Creation of Jazz: Music, Race, and Culture in Urban America* (Urbana, IL, 1992).

263. Kathy Peiss, *Cheap Amusements: Working Girls and Leisure in Turn-of-the-Century New York* (Philadelphia, 1986); Lauren Rabinovitz, *For the Love of Pleasure: Women, Movies, and Culture in Turn-of-the-Century Chicago* (New Brunswick, NJ, 1998); Gregory A. Waller, *Main Street Amusements: Movies and Commercial Entertainment in a Southern City* (Washington, DC, 1995); Richard Butsch, *For Fun and Profit: The Transformation of Leisure into Consumption* (Philadelphia, 1990).

264. John Hope Franklin, *A Southern Odyssey: Travelers in the Antebellum North* (Baton Rouge, LA, 1976); Catherine Cocks, *Doing the Town: The Rise of Urban Tourism in the United States, 1859–1914* (Berkeley, CA, 2001); Angela M. Blake, *How New York Became American, 1890–1924* (Baltimore, 2006); Harvey K. Newman, *Southern Hospitality: Tourism and the Growth of Atlanta* (Tuscaloosa, AL, 1999); Mark S. Foster, *Castles in the Sand: The Life and Times of Carl Graham Fisher* (Gainesville, FL, 2000); Susan R. Braden, *The Architecture of Leisure: The Florida Resort Hotels of Henry Flagler and Henry Plant* (Gainesville, FL, 2002).

265. J. Mark Souther, *New Orleans on Parade: Tourism and the Transformation of the Crescent City* (Baton Rouge, LA, 2006); Anthony J. Stanonis, *Creating the Big Easy: New Orleans and the Emergence of Modern Tourism, 1918–1945* (Athens, GA, 2006); Kevin Fox Gotham, *Authentic New Orleans: Tourism, Culture, and Race in the Big Easy* (New York, 2007); Samuel Kinser, *Carnival, American Style: Mardi Gras at New Orleans and Mobile* (Chicago, 1990); Reid Mitchell, *All on a Mardi Gras Day: Episodes in the History of New Orleans Carnival* (Cambridge, MA, 1995).

266. Hal K. Rothman, *Devil's Bargains: Tourism in the Twentieth-Century American West* (Lawrence, KS, 1998); John M. Findlay, *Magic Lands: Western Cityscapes and American Culture after 1940* (Berkeley, CA, 1992); Richard E. Fogelsong, *Married to the Mouse: Walt Disney World and Orlando* (New Haven, CT, 2001).

267. Robert W. Rydell, *All the World's a Fair: Visions of Empire at American International Expositions, 1876–1916* (Chicago, 1987); Rydell, *World of Fairs: The Century-of-Progress Expositions* (Chicago, 1993); Robert W. Rydell, John E. Findling, and Kimberly D. Pelle, *Fair America: World's Fairs in the United States* (Washington, DC, 2000); James Gilbert, *Whose Fair? Experience, Memory, and the History of the Great St. Louis Exposition* (Chicago, 2009);

Cheryl R. Ganz, *The 1933 Chicago World's Fair: A Century of Progress* (Urbana, IL, 2008); James Gilbert, *Perfect Cities: Chicago's Utopias of 1893* (Chicago, 1991); David F. Burg, *Chicago's White City of 1893* (Lexington, KY, 1976); R. Reid Badger, *The Great American Fair: The World's Columbian Exposition and American Culture* (Chicago, 1979). Neil Harris's *Cultural Excursions: Marketing Appetites and Cultural Tastes in Modern America* (Chicago, 1990) considers world's fairs along with other elements of popular culture that promoted social cohesion during times of rapid urban change. See also James Mauro's *Twilight at the World of Tomorrow: Genius, Madness, Murder, and the 1939 World's Fair on the Brink of War* (New York, 2010).

268. John Hannigan, *Fantasy City: Pleasure and Profit in the Postwar Metropolis* (New York, 1998); Dennis R. Judd and Susan S. Fainstein, eds., *The Tourist City* (New Haven, CT, 1999); Dennis R. Judd, ed., *The Infrastructure of Play: Building the Tourist City* (Armonk, NY, 2003); Michael N. Danielson, *Home Team: Professional Sports and the American Metropolis* (Princeton, NJ, 1997); John M. Findlay, *People of Chance: Gambling in American Society from Jamestown to Las Vegas* (New York, 1986); Eugene P. Moehring, *Resort City in the Sunbelt: Las Vegas, 1930–1970* (Reno, NV, 1989); Hal K. Rothman, *Neon Metropolis: How Las Vegas Started the Twenty-First Century* (New York, 2003); Charles E. Funnell, *By the Beautiful Sea: The Rise and High Times of That Great American Resort, Atlantic City* (New York, 1975); Bryant Simon, *Boardwalk of Dreams: Atlantic City and the Fate of Urban America* (New York, 2004).

269. Shane White, Stephen Garton, Stephen Robertson, and Graham White, *Playing the Numbers: Gambling in Harlem between the Wars* (Cambridge, MA, 2010); Victoria W. Wolcott, "The Culture of the Informal Economy: Numbers Runners in Inter-War Black Detroit," *Radical History Review* 69 (Fall 1997): 69–75.

270. Eric H. Monkkonen and Eric A. Johnson, eds., *The Civilization of Crime: Violence in Town and Country since the Middle Ages* (Urbana, IL, 1996).

271. James F. Richardson, *The New York Police: Colonial Times to 1901* (New York, 1970); Roger Lane, *Murder in America: A History* (Columbus, OH, 1997).

272. Paul A. Gilje, *The Road to Mobocracy: Popular Disorder in New York City, 1763–1834* (Chapel Hill, NC, 1987); Gilje, *Rioting in America* (Bloomington, IN, 1996); David Grimsted, *American Mobbing, 1828–1861: Toward the Civil War* (New York, 1998); Paul O. Weinbaum, *Mobs and Demagogues: The New York Response to Collective Violence in the Early Nineteenth Century* (Ann Arbor, MI, 1979); Michael Feldberg, *The Philadelphia Riots of 1844: A Study in Ethnic Conflict* (New York, 1975); Feldberg, *The Turbulent Era: Riot and Disorder in Jacksonian America* (New York, 1980); Nigel Cliff, *The Shakespeare Riots: Revenge, Drama, and Death in Nineteenth-Century America* (New York, 2007); Robert A. Gordon, *The Orange Riots: Irish Political Violence in New York City, 1870 and 1871* (Ithaca, NY, 1993); Robert M. Fogelson, *America's Armories: Architecture, Society, and Public Order* (Cambridge, MA, 1989); Patricia Cline Cohen, *The Murder of Helen Jewett* (New York, 1998). See also Jack Tager, *Boston Riots: Three Centuries of Social Violence* (Boston, 2001). For a discussion of race riots, see the section of this essay on African American urban history.

273. Roger Lane, *Violent Death in the City: Suicide, Accident, and Murder in Nineteenth-Century Philadelphia* (Columbus, OH, 1979); Lane, *Roots of Violence in Black Philadelphia, 1860–1900* (Cambridge, MA, 1989); Jeffrey S. Adler, *First in Violence, Deepest in Dirt: Homicide in Chicago, 1875–1920* (Cambridge, MA, 2006); Eric H. Monkkonen, *Murder in New York City* (Berkeley, CA, 2000).

274. David Courtwright, *Violent Land: Single Men and Social Disorder from the Frontier to the Inner City* (Cambridge, MA, 1996); Kevin J. Mullen, *Let Justice Be Done: Crime and Politics in Early San Francisco* (Reno, NV, 1980); Mullen, *Dangerous Strangers: Minority*

Newcomers and Criminal Violence in the Urban West, 1850–2000 (New York, 2005); Kali N. Gross, *Colored Amazons: Crime, Violence, and Black Women in the City of Brotherly Love* (Durham, NC, 2006); Cheryl D. Hicks, *Talk with You Like a Woman: African American Women, Justice, and Reform in New York, 1890–1935* (Chapel Hill, NC, 2010); Timothy Gilfoyle, *A Pickpocket's Tale: The Underworld of Nineteenth-Century New York* (New York, 2007); John C. Schneider, *Detroit and the Problem of Order, 1830–1880: A Geography of Crime, Riot, and Policing* (Lincoln, NE, 1980); Allen Steinberg, *The Transformation of Criminal Justice: Philadelphia, 1800–1880* (Chapel Hill, NC, 1989); Michael Willrich, *City of Courts: Socializing Justice in Progressive Era Chicago* (Cambridge, UK, 2003); Eric Monkkonen, *The Dangerous Class: Crime and Poverty in Columbus, Ohio* (Cambridge, MA, 1975). See also Jennifer Fronc, *New York Undercover: Private Surveillance in the Progressive Era* (Chicago, 2009).

275. David R. Johnson, *Policing the Urban Underworld: The Impact of Crime on the Development of the American Police, 1800–1887* (Philadelphia, 1979); Roger Lane, *Policing the City: Boston, 1822–1885* (New York, 1971); James F. Richardson, *A History of Urban Police in the United States* (Port Washington, NY, 1974); Eric H. Monkkonen, *Police in Urban America, 1860–1920* (Cambridge, UK, 2004); Robert M. Fogelson, *Big-City Police* (Cambridge, MA, 1979). On police in a southern city, see Dennis Rousey, *Policing the Southern City: New Orleans, 1805–1889* (Baton Rouge, LA, 1997). For a comparison of developing police forces in New York City and London, see William R. Miller Jr., *Cops and Bobbies: Police Authority in New York and London, 1830–1870* (Chicago, 1977)

276. Marilynn Johnson, *Street Justice: A History of Police Violence in New York City* (New York, 2003); Richard C. Lindberg, *To Serve and Collect: Chicago Politics and Police Corruption from the Lager Beer Riot to the Summerdale Scandal* (New York, 1991); Leonard N. Moore, *Black Rage in New Orleans: Police Brutality and African American Activism from World War II to Hurricane Katrina* (Baton Rouge, LA, 2010).

277. Humbert S. Nelli, *The Business of Crime: Italians and Syndicate Crime in the United States* (Chicago, 1976); David Critchley, *The Origin of Organized Crime in America: The New York City Mafia, 1891–1931* (New York, 2008); Rufus Schatzberg, *Black Organized Crime in Harlem, 1920–1930* (New York, 1993); Schatzberg and Robert J. Kelly, *African American Organized Crime: A Social History* (New Brunswick, NJ, 1996).

278. Eric C. Schneider, *Vampires, Dragons, and Egyptian Kings: Youth Gangs in Postwar New York* (Princeton, NJ, 1999); James Diego Vigil, *Barrio Gangs: Street Life and Identity in Southern California* (Austin, TX, 1988); Malcolm W. Klein, *The American Street Gang: Its Nature, Prevalence, and Control* (New York, 1995); Martin Sanchez Jankowski, *Islands in the Street: Gangs and American Urban Society* (Berkeley, CA, 1991); Andrew J. Diamond, *Mean Streets: Chicago Youths and the Everyday Struggle for Empowerment in the Multiracial City, 1908–1969* (Berkeley, CA, 2009); Elijah Anderson, *Code of the Street: Decency, Violence, and the Moral Life of the Inner City* (New York, 2000); Eric C. Schneider, *Smack: Heroin and the American City* (Philadelphia, 2008).

279. Kenneth T. Jackson, *The Ku Klux Klan in the City, 1915–1930* (New York, 1967); William D. Jenkins, *Steel Valley Klan: The Ku Klux Klan in Ohio's Mahoning Valley* (Kent, OH, 1990); Shawn Lay, *Invisible Empire in the West: Toward a New Historical Appraisal of the Ku Klux Klan of the 1920s* (Urbana, IL, 1992); Lay, *Hooded Knights on the Niagara: The Ku Klux Klan in Buffalo, New York* (New York, 1995).

280. Nicholas Christopher, *Somewhere in the Night: Film Noir and the American City* (New York, 1997); Steve Macek, *Urban Nightmares: The Media, the Right, and the Moral Panic over the City* (Minneapolis, 2006).

281. Charles N. Glaab and A. Theodore Brown, *A History of Urban America* (3rd ed., New York, 1983); Howard Chudacoff and Judith E. Smith, *The Evolution of American Urban*

Society (7th ed., Englewood Cliffs, NJ, 2009); Zane L. Miller and Patricia M. Melvin, *The Urbanization of Modern America: A Brief History* (2nd ed., San Diego, 1987); David R. Goldfield and Blaine A. Brownell, *Urban America: A History* (2nd ed., Boston, 1990).

282. Blake McKelvey, *The Urbanization of America, 1860–1915* (New Brunswick, NJ, 1963); McKelvey, *The Emergence of Metropolitan America, 1915–1966* (New Brunswick, NJ, 1968); Maury Klein and Harvey A. Kantor, *Prisoners of Progress: American Industrial Cities, 1850–1920* (New York, 1976); Raymond A. Mohl, *The New City: Urban America in the Industrial Age, 1860–1920* (Arlington Heights, IL, 1985); Kenneth Fox, *Metropolitan America: Urban Life and Urban Policy in the United States, 1940–1980* (Jackson, MS, 1986); Carl Abbott, *Urban America in the Modern Age, 1920 to the Present* (2nd ed., Wheeling, IL, 2007); Jon C. Teaford, *The Twentieth-Century American City* (2nd ed., Baltimore, 1993); Teaford, *The Metropolitan Revolution: The Rise of Post-Modern America* (New York, 2006); Robert A. Beauregard, *Voices of Decline: The Postwar Fate of U.S. Cities* (2nd ed., New York, 2003).

Index

About the Editors

Raymond A. Mohl is distinguished professor of history at the University of Alabama at Birmingham. He is a native of Tarrytown, New York, and a graduate of Hamilton College. He earned a masters degree at Yale University and a Ph.D. in history at New York University. He is the author, editor, coauthor, or coeditor of eleven books, including *Poverty in New York, 1783–1825* (1971), *The Paradox of Progressive Education* (1979), *The New City: Urban America in the Industrial Age* (1985), *Steel City: Urban and Ethnic Patterns in Gary, Indiana* (1986), *Searching for the Sunbelt* (1990), *Urban Policy in Twentieth-Century America* (1993), *The New African American Urban History* (1996), and *South of the South: Jewish Activists and the Civil Rights Movement in Miami, 1945–1960* (2004). His research articles have appeared as book chapters and in such publications as *Journal of American History*, *Journal of Urban History*, *Journal of Planning History*, *Journal of Policy History*, *Journal of American Ethnic History*, *Social Science Quarterly*, *Labor History*, *International Migration Review*, *Peace and Change*, and many other journals. He has held Fulbright Professorships at Tel Aviv University, the University of Western Australia, and the University of Gottingen, as well as major research fellowships from the National Endowment for the Humanities, the American Council of Learned Societies, and the Poverty and Race Research Action Council. He is currently completing a history of race and ethnic relations in twentieth-century Miami, Florida.

Roger Biles is professor of history at Illinois State University. He received his Ph.D. in history from the University of Illinois at Chicago in 1981. He is the author, coauthor, or editor of twelve books, including *The Fate of Cities: Urban America and the Federal Government, 1945–2000* (2011), *The Human Tradition in Urban America* (2002), *From Tenements to the Taylor Homes: In Search of an Urban Housing Policy in Twentieth Century America* (2000), *Richard J. Daley: Politics, Race, and the Governing of Chicago* (1995), *Memphis in the Great Depression* (1986), and *Big City Boss in Depression and War: Mayor Edward J. Kelly of Chicago* (1984). His articles have appeared in such journals as *Journal of Urban History*, *Journal of Planning*

History, *Planning Perspectives*, *Chicago History*, *Journal of Negro History*, *Labor History*, *Journal of Southern History*, and *Southwestern Historical Quarterly*. He is currently completing a book with John F. Bauman and Kristin M. Szylvian on the history of post–World War II American cities.